The Illustrated Practical
HOME
Encyclopedia

The Illustrated Practical
HOME
Encyclopedia

1001 step-by-step hints, tips and household skills

Consultant editor Margaret Malone

HERMES
HOUSE

This edition is published by Hermes House

Hermes House is an imprint of
Anness Publishing Limited
Hermes House
88–89 Blackfriars Road
London SE1 8HA
tel. 020 7401 2077; fax 020 7633 9499; info@anness.com

A CIP catalogue record for this book is available from the British Library

Publisher: Joanna Lorenz
Editor: Margaret Malone
Designer: Bill Mason
Jacket designer: Mark Stevens
Copy editors: Jackie Matthews and Emma Callery
Typesetter: Jonathan Harley
Editorial reader: Richard McGinlay
Production controller: Ben Worley

Printed and bound in China

1 3 5 7 9 10 8 6 4 2

Both imperial and metric measurements have been given in the text. Where conversions produce an awkward number,
these have been rounded for convenience, but will produce an accurate result if one system is used throughout.

CONTENTS

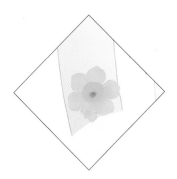

GETTING STARTED

Unless you are lucky enough to be able to design and build your own home, you will be faced with the alternative of adapting an existing building to suit your needs… and your dreams. It may be an older property, but even if brand new it will still reflect someone else's taste in layout, design and function. Your goal in either case is to turn the house into your home, and then to make the most of living in it.

How your home improvement strategy evolves will depend on two critical factors: time and money. These are inextricably linked, in the sense that time is money. You can either use your own time, or use your money to buy time by hiring someone else. Only you can decide what is best for your needs, but the information in this section will help you to make up your mind.

Whatever home improvements you decide to attempt, the effort you expend on the preliminary stages of assessment and planning will be repaid further down the line. You will know you have made the right decisions at the beginning, and you will gain the breadth of vision to know what your ultimate target is.

ASSESSING YOUR HOME

The best way to get an objective view of your home's interior condition is to imagine that it is up for sale and to view it in the role of a prospective purchaser. The aim of the exercise is not to give rise to a severe bout of depression on your part, but to determine what exists in the home and what could be done to change or improve it.

Start at the front door, and step into the hallway. Is it bright and well-lit, or gloomy and unwelcoming? A lighter colour scheme could make a narrow area appear more spacious, and better lighting would make it seem more inviting. Decorating the wall opposite the front door would make a long hall appear shorter, while changing the way the staircase is decorated could make it a less – or more – dominant feature. Is the staircase well-lit, for safety's sake as well as for looks? Opening up the space beneath the stairs could get rid of what is typically an untidy gloryhole (storage room), taking up space without saving

ABOVE **Choose an integrated decorating scheme for the hallway, stairs and landing area. Bring down the apparent ceiling height using a dado (chair) rail or decorative border.**

BELOW **The living room has to be light and airy during the day, yet cosy and comfortable in the evening. The fireplace and a central table provide the main focal points here.**

any. Lastly, are the wall and floor coverings practical? The hall floor is bound to be well-trodden, and needs to be durable and easy to clean as well as looking attractive.

Now move into the main living room. This is always the most difficult room in the house to decorate and furnish successfully because of its dual purpose. It is used both for daily life and to entertain visitors. It must be fresh and lively by day, yet cosy and peaceful in the evening. One of the chief keys to success is flexible lighting that can be altered to suit the room's different uses, but the decorations and furnishings all have their part to play too.

Look at the colour scheme. How well does it blend in with the furnishings, the curtains and drapes, and the floor covering? Are there any interesting features such as a fireplace, an alcove, an archway into another room – even an ornate cornice (crown molding) around the ceiling? Some of these features might benefit from being highlighted – with special lighting, for instance – while other less-attractive ones would be better disguised.

Next, examine how the room works. Are 'traffic routes' congested? Are the seating arrangements flexible? Are there surfaces on which things can easily be put down? Does any storage or display provision look good and work well? Can everyone who is seated see the television? Does everyone want to? Assessing the room in this way reveals its successes and failures, and shows how to eliminate the latter.

Continue the guided tour with the dining room – or dining area, if it is part of a through room. This is often the least-used room in the house, so its design tends to be neglected. As it is generally used for just one purpose – eating – it needs to be decorated in a way that avoids visual indigestion. Warm, welcoming colour schemes and flexible lighting work best in this

LEFT Bedrooms are the most private of rooms, and their colour schemes and furnishings should reflect the personal tastes of their occupants.

BELOW The kitchen is the engine room of the house. It must be well-planned with plenty of work and storage space, and be pleasant to work in and easy to clean.

location; strident patterns and harsh colours are to be avoided.

Now turn to the kitchen. Whatever type of room this is, the most important consideration is that it should be hygienic, for obvious reasons. Are the various surfaces in the room easy to keep clean, and to re-decorate when necessary? Are there dust and grease traps? Is the lighting over the hob (burners) and counter tops adequate? Is the floor covering a practical choice? As the kitchen is often the hub of family life, it needs to be functional but adaptable, and also pleasant to be in so that the cook does not mind the time spent slaving over a hot stove.

Bathrooms have their own special requirements, mainly revolving around combining comfort with a degree of waterproofing, especially if there are young children in the family. Are the decorations and floor covering suitable? How well do they complement the bathroom suite? What about the space available within the room? Could congestion be relieved by moving things around, or by moving them out altogether? Having a shower instead of a bath, for example, could create lots of

extra space. Could a second bathroom be created elsewhere in the house? Otherwise, putting washbasins in some of the bedrooms could take the pressure off the family bathroom during the morning rush hour.

Lastly, bedrooms. In most, the bed is the focal point of the room, so the way it is dressed will be the main influence on the room's appearance. The colour scheme also has its part to play in making a bedroom look comfortable and relaxing; remember that the room's occupant will see it from 2 viewpoints – on entering, and from the bed – so take this into account when making your assessment. What about the ceiling? In the one room where people actually spend some time staring at it, does it deserve something a little more adventurous than white paint? Is the floor covering warm to the touch of bare feet? In a child's room, is it also capable of withstanding the occasional rough and tumble or a disaster with the finger paints? Lastly, is the lighting adequate for all requirements? Most bedrooms need a combination of subdued general lighting and brighter local task lighting for occupations such

as reading in bed, putting on make-up or tackling school homework. Some changes here may make the room function much more satisfactorily.

Once your tour around the house is complete, you should have a clear picture of its condition and how well it works, and some ideas as to how it might be improved. Above all, you will have viewed it as a whole, not just as a series of individual rooms. That is the first step towards creating an attractive, stylish and, above all, practical home.

ABOVE The bathroom needs tailoring to family requirements. A double vanity unit such as this one would provide valuable extra washing facilities for a busy couple or a growing family.

TIME AND BUDGET MANAGEMENT

Now that you have a realistic idea of what needs doing to your home, the next step is to plan what the various improvement options will involve in terms of time, logistics and, of course, money. The most common projects can be divided up into a number of groups; here is a brief summary of what each one might involve.

Changing the room usage

Just because a particular room in the house currently has a particular function, it does not have to maintain that function. For example, if you have the traditional arrangement of two rooms, one used for sitting and one for dining, you could consider swapping their functions. Similarly, a bedroom swap could involve parents giving up their large bedroom to a teenage child for use as a study and recreation room. Other possible options include turning a spare bedroom into a home office, switching the kitchen and dining rooms to make better use of space and access, or fitting out a small spare room as a second bathroom.

Altering the existing room layout

Sometimes the way your house is laid out no longer suits the way you want to live. Rearranging the room layout is a bigger job than changing the room usage, since it usually involves removing or building internal walls. It will not give you any extra floor space, but it will let you use the existing floor space more efficiently and creatively. Options that involve knocking down walls include creating a joined living and dining room, a combined kitchen-diner, or a master bedroom with en-suite bathroom from two smaller adjacent rooms.

You can build partition walls in large spaces to create extra rooms, and you can also change the size of adjacent rooms by repositioning dividing walls. Repositioning doors to alter traffic routes can make a difference, and you could even consider altering the way the staircase runs.

Converting uninhabited areas

Unless your house has a flat roof, you will have a loft (attic), and this could offer the perfect opportunity for conversion to valuable extra living space. The conversion is a complex job to carry out, since its feasibility depends on the way the roof was built, how access to the loft (attic) can be created and how safety requirements can be met. It is definitely a job to be left to an architect and builder or to a specialty loft-conversion company.

Older houses with basements offer another conversion option. Here the feasibility depends on the size of the basement (many are just small storage cellars), how damp-proof it is and how easy it will be to provide ventilation and some degree of natural light – all essential if the basement is to be used as a habitable room.

RIGHT Installing tall glass doors leading on to an outdoor area is a simple alteration to a room that makes a dramatic difference.

The third uninhabited area you may have available for conversion into extra living space is an integral or attached garage. If you intend to create habitable rooms, you will have to upgrade the damp-proofing (water-proofing) and insulation. Garages can provide the opportunity for some creative converting, and it is worth taking the time to consider what is possible. The garage-door opening, for example, can be filled in as a large window. A doorway into the house will be needed unless one exists already.

Building an extension

If rearranging existing space or carrying out internal conversions cannot give you the extra living space you need, then building an extension is the only solution (apart, of course, from moving house). Its feasibility depends mainly on whether you have the space to extend and whether the work counts as permitted development under the local building codes. Depending on where you have the space and what you want the extension to provide, you could build a one-storey or two-storey building at the side or rear of the property; front extensions seldom get planning permission. The design and construction of a home extension is definitely a job to leave to the professionals unless you are a highly skilled and motivated person with enormous organizational skills.

If all you want is some extra room downstairs, adding a conservatory (porch) to the side or rear of the house could be the answer. Modern conservatories are modular buildings, so they are quick and simple to erect – even on a do-it-yourself basis, although most people leave their construction to a specialist supplier. Adding one is also relatively non-disruptive, since all the construction work occurs outside the house. Conservatories count as home extensions for planning purposes.

Getting better services

Older houses are likely to benefit from some upgrading of their services – the plumbing, the wiring and the central heating system. Plumbing improvements could include washbasins (sinks) in bedrooms, a second lavatory, plumbing in a utility room and so on. Wiring work can provide extra socket outlets and up-to-date lighting. Heating improvements can bring more efficient water and room heating. The kitchen and the bathroom seem to need upgrading every ten years or so to keep them looking up-to-date and working efficiently.

Improving the site

Not all home improvements involve the house. Improvements to the site could include building a garage or carport, providing extra car-parking space in front of the house, creating walls, paths and steps and adding outbuildings such as a garden shed, a greenhouse, a children's play house or an aviary. All can add significantly to the way in which you live in and enjoy your home.

ABOVE Converting a loft or attic could be the perfect solution as children grow up and desire more space. This can be quite complicated however, so do seek specialist advice.

COMMISSIONING PROFESSIONALS

It is likely that you will want to have some professional help for many home-improvement projects. The experts can help you solve design problems, make sure you satisfy the requirements of the building regulations and stop you falling foul of your local government planning committee. They can also organize and manage large-scale projects in a way that no home-owner with a full-time job could hope to do. Which experts you call in and what you get them to do for you depends on the project concerned.

Architects and surveyors

You are most likely to call on the services of an architect or a building surveyor if you are building a home extension, converting a loft (attic) or carrying out major internal alterations to your house. Apart from their skill in

LEFT Many jobs around the home, such as replacing tiles on the roof, can be done safely and thoroughly by the home-owner. If major repair or renovation work is needed, however, it is always worth obtaining a quote from a contractor before starting the project yourself.

solving design problems, each of these professionals will help ensure that your project runs smoothly. He or she will prepare drawings, obtain local government approval, get tenders (bids) for the work from contractors, prepare contracts, devise work schedules and supervise work on site. Architects and surveyors will usually charge a percentage of the project cost as their fee.

Specialist companies

If you are planning a loft (attic) conversion, a conservatory, replacement windows, or a kitchen or bathroom refit, you can call in firms who specialize in each of these areas. Since each may offer a complete package, from computer-aided design to completion, they may be very tempting to employ. However, this area is very much one of 'buyer beware'. If you decide to use this route, try to find a firm that either comes with a personal recommendation or is prepared to put you in touch with several satisfied customers. Read the contract offered by the firm in detail, querying any unclear terms and, above all, do not part with any money in advance.

LEFT Calling in professional help with your home improvements raises a few questions, since you are effectively handing over the work to a third party. You need to keep control over the job to ensure you get the results you want.

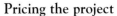

LEFT If embarking on a home-renovation project, visit local stores and suppliers before you spend valuable time and money – they can often be a source of good information.

Finding contractors

If you need contractors to carry out the work for you, decide first of all whether you want a main contractor to run the entire project and bring in his or her own specialist subcontractors – roofers, plasterers, plumbers, electricians and so on – for individual parts of the job.

The alternative is to employ those sub-contractors yourself for the parts of the job that are beyond your abilities. As always, the best way of finding contractors and subcontractors is by personal recommendation. If you are employing an architect on your project, he or she may be able to recommend firms in your area.

Other ways of finding contractors include local newspaper advertisements, telephone directories and trade associations, which will send lists of their members working in your area. One last method involves looking round your area for houses where projects similar to yours are being carried out. Knock at the door and ask the owner how the work is going; people cannot resist discussing things if they are going well.

Pricing the project

What a home-improvement project will cost is of prime importance to every householder. If you are doing the job yourself, make contact with all the relevant local trade suppliers – builders and other specialist merchants, plus second-hand outlets such as salvage yards – and explain to them what you are doing and what your requirements are. Some projects will be easier to price than others, but suppliers will generally be eager to help you estimate costs if there is an order in it for them.

Don't forget about hire (rental) shops for the equipment not included in your do-it-yourself toolkit. It is also worth hiring (or even better, buying) heavy-duty versions of your existing power tools, which are likely to be burnt out by the sort of use they will get on a major improvement project.

If you are employing an architect, he or she will be responsible for obtaining costs for the job. If you are putting the entire job in the hands of builders, they will be responsible for pricing the job and for buying all the materials.

Drawing up contracts

Never employ any contractors on a home-improvement project without a contract, however simple. This will give both parties a clear description of what the job involves and who is responsible for what. Above all, it will give each party the protection of the law if the other breaks its terms.

A simple job probably needs no more than a letter of agreement. This should include a description of the work to be done, the price, the agreed starting and finishing dates and details of how payments will be made. On more complex jobs, a contractor's detailed quotation plus your signature will constitute a valid contract.

LEFT A builder will save you the trouble of hiring specialist equipment unlikely to be found in many a home-owner's toolkit.

HOME BASICS

When redecorating the home, choosing colour schemes and a style to suit your taste and way of life should be fun. This chapter helps you make the right choices about the way you want your home to look, and to gain the satisfaction of completing all the work yourself. In addition to helpful information on reorganizing spaces, using colour and lighting, you will find instructive information on painting and decorating as well as tiling, covering floors, adding decorative features to rooms, and storage.

DECORATING DECISIONS

The hardest part of any do-it-yourself project is deciding precisely what is wanted and planning how to achieve it. The decision may simply involve a choice of colour or pattern, or may be more complex, perhaps involving major changes to the style, layout, features and fittings of a room or rooms.

For example, it may seem likely that better use can be made of the interior space that is available. An easy way of doing this is to rearrange or change some of the furniture, whether it is free-standing or built-in – but a more radical approach may bring even more dramatic gains. Partitioning some rooms, linking others, even changing the use to which individual rooms have previously been put, can revolutionize the way a home works. This approach is particularly relevant as the occupants' needs alter over the years, since a house that worked well with young children will not suit a family with teenagers, and once the children have flown the nest their parents will want to use the house in a different way again.

On a smaller scale, even the way in which individual rooms are decorated and furnished can have a major effect on the way the home looks and feels. Many people find that achieving the style they want is often a process of evolution rather than revolution; few people can get everything right first time. The secret of success lies in understanding the basic rules of colour scheming and in learning how to make the best use of the wide range of materials and techniques available to the interior designer today.

Finally, it is also a good idea to take a close look at what lighting contributes to the scheme. Few homes make use of the possibilities explored so imaginatively in many public buildings, yet some minor changes to lighting could bring a home alive. Some interior designers even dream of the day when they can create and change interior colour schemes with the flick of a switch. However, until that day the big decorating decisions are still the same as they always were; the following pages should render them somewhat easier to make.

OPPOSITE The art of successful decoration lies in marrying materials that protect and enhance the various surfaces around the home with a touch of decorative flair and originality that will give every room a style all of its own and reflect the owner's personal taste and lifestyle.

CHOOSING THEMES

Faced with giving a room or the whole house a new look involves the home decorator in some crucial decision making. The first thing to decide is what 'look' to go for, and to consider if this fits in with the original style of the room or house.

There are many styles to choose from, and a good way to help decide on the look you want is to read as many style books and magazines as you can to see what you like and dislike. Once you know what you like, you can introduce into the room the relevant features and colours that will contribute to the overall look.

Giving your home a particular look requires attention to the basics – the walls and floors. Get these right and the rest is easy. For example, a bare room with powdery wall paint, stencilling and a stripped, limed floor has a real country feeling, whereas no number of folk artefacts and rustic furniture can transform to 'country' a tastefully wallpapered, corniced and thick-pile carpeted living room.

Whatever you choose for your walls and floor, it is important to see them in terms of a backdrop for your own tastes and possessions. Paintings, mirrors, lamps, plants, shelves, rugs and furniture will all add to the final effect. Whether you go for a total look for your home, or just a few details, try to decorate in a way that is sympathetic to the character and age of your house. What follows are a few ideas for themed looks that can be adopted for a room or house, or can form the basis for your own personal style.

Country style

As the pressures of modern living increase, many people living in urban environments want to put some of the tranquility of the countryside back into our lives. One of the easiest ways of doing this is to recreate some elements of country style in the home, providing a restful and welcoming environment to return to. Fortunately, you don't have to live in a cottage to create a country look.

Country style may vary according to nationality and local climate, but there is a core of recognizable elements. It is a home-made, functional, comfortable style. There is often a big kitchen area, with a large scrubbed pine table and an assortment of comfortable chairs. Country kitchens can be a riot of pattern and colour, where the dresser (hutch) is stacked with displays of china and the beams are hung with baskets full of drying flowers and herbs. Floors need to be practical, tough and easy to keep clean, so floorboards, flagstones, cork tiles or linoleum are the favourite choices, and they can all be softened with cotton durries or rugs.

To give a room a country feel, choose natural colours that make you happy, selecting your palette from nature's harmonies and avoiding artificially brilliant shades. Colours can be as rich as autumn, with touches of brilliance, or as warm as a summer meadow filled with buttercups or a field of ripe corn. Remember, too, that country-style decorating is not about everything matching. You don't need co-ordinating curtains, carpets and lampshades. On the contrary, the more eclectic the choice, the more stunning the effect can often be. Country style is more about relaxation, comfort and harmony than precision.

Folk style

Folk interiors and furniture have an enduring appeal. The soft harmonies of the wall colours and stencil patterns are complemented by sturdy, practical pieces of furniture – massive armchairs with simple turned front legs and solid backs, long benches, open cupboards and painted chests. Often decorated with brilliant colours, folk furniture displays the folk artist's inherent love

LEFT Introduce the colours and textures of nature through the simple addition of flowers, dried herbs and spices.

for pattern and colour as much as other smaller objects in the home. Colour is often applied to all surfaces of a room as well as the decorated furniture, patchwork throws and painted tinware.

The 'busy' decorative folk style originally sprang from a combination of the improved circumstances and the desire to show the family's social status along with a natural love of colour and decoration. As the burden of poverty eased for most of Europe's peasants after the sixteenth century, rural craftsmen began making furniture out of local woods which were carved or painted in imitation of the furniture of the wealthy classes. In addition, great pride was attached to owning furniture, pottery and tin or silver plate.

When decorating a home in this style, it is important not to be too 'precious'; imperfect plasterwork and sloping floors only add to the charm. If your home is perfectly sound and symmetrical, colourwashing will soften hard edges, particularly if you choose

ABOVE Folk patterns can be highly varied. Mix and match colours and fabrics to add your own personal feel to a room.

the colour scheme to harmonize with one featured folk art piece such as a patchwork quilt or a painted chest.

Traditional colours trace back to the original materials used. A beige plaster made from crushed oyster shells mixed with sand was overpainted with a whitewash made from quicklime, or strained stale (sour) butter-milk mixed with sifted river sand and vegetable pigment. When new paints were developed new techniques were invented, such as graining (painting common woods such as pine to look like more expensive mahogany or walnut), marbling, stippling, ragging and glazing, which involved applying two coats of paint, the first a flat colour which was left to dry before being glazed with a different colour top coat. Many of these old painting techniques have been revived and are now extremely popular.

Modern style

At some point, every home needs decoration or updating to keep it looking fresh and stylish. The beauty of 'modern' looks is that they encompass an enormous range of styles, materials and approaches. If you are short of

ABOVE Often the greatest impact comes from doing less rather than more. Modern looks rely on a prudent use of colour and furniture.

time, have a limited budget, and more imagination than skill, simple but original adaptations of everyday materials could be the most practical and versatile option, rather than trying to follow an established theme, such as folk. What links modern styles is the feeling of experimentation and freedom of approach; window treatments, paint effects, soft furnishings and lighting ideas all deal with familiar materials but treat them in new, highly personal ways. Transparent glass beads sparkle like jewels when used as a curtain, tartan (plaid) wool rugs become lovely heavy curtains and versatile, cheap polypropylene mats (linoleum tiles) can be used to create a dramatic chequerboard effect.

Trawl through junk shops and market stalls, experiment with different paints and dyes, objects from nature and adapt everyday materials (such as matting, fake fur, metals, beads) – the list is endless, as are the possible uses they can be put to. Furthermore, it is very easy to start all over again without spending a lot of money or effort.

REORGANIZING SPACE

If a home does not function well, there are three choices. Two of these are thoroughly defeatist and may also be impractical: learn to live with it, or move to a more suitable house. The third is much more positive; alter it so that it gives the extra living space and the additional features needed.

The average home is basically a box, within which internal partitions create individual rooms, doors allow movement and windows let in light and air. Various services are included within the structure – heating, plumbing, wiring and so on. All these features can be altered, within reason, to make them work better.

When planning alterations, there are two considerations which should constantly be borne in mind: are the changes feasible and are they legal? It is essential to check with the local planning (zoning) and building control bodies to find out whether the work requires official approval.

Where to improve

Alterations to the use of space in the home are of two kinds. The first is intended to create an entirely new living space. The second is to alter the present layout of the interior and to change or improve the services. Here are some of the possibilities.

In the attic, unused space beneath a pitched roof could well become valuable extra living space. Remember, though, that providing access to the new rooms will mean losing some space on the floor below.

In the existing upstairs rooms, re-arranging internal walls could create an extra bedroom or bathroom, while providing plumbing facilities in bedrooms could ease the pressure on the existing bathrooms.

ABOVE Subdividing large rooms can help to create a more effective use of space, by redefining traffic zones and providing more wall space for planning furniture.

LEFT Bathing facilities are often overstretched, especially in large family homes. Finding space for an extra shower cubicle can greatly relieve the traffic jams.

Downstairs, removing dividing walls to create large through rooms or partitioning large rooms to create two smaller ones, moving doorways to improve traffic flow, or altering the kitchen layout could all be considered. It might even be possible to turn an integral garage into extra living space.

Look at the possibility of changing the use to which individual rooms are put, especially if the size of the family is changing. Reorganization can bring dramatic improvements to the way the house works.

Creating a through room

Creating a through room means removing an existing dividing wall, and may also require the repositioning of existing doorways and the formation of new windows. If the existing wall is loadbearing, a steel beam will have to be installed to carry the load, and lintels will also be needed over new windows and over new doors in other loadbearing walls. It may be necessary to re-route existing plumbing and electrical services that cross the wall that is to be removed. Once the new opening has been formed, there will be extensive replastering to be done, and the floors in the two rooms will have to be linked smoothly. The original colour schemes of the two rooms will also probably be different, which may entail complete redecoration.

Partitioning an existing room

Subdividing an existing room into two smaller ones means building a new wall, possibly adding a door or window to one of the new rooms, and perhaps altering or extending existing plumbing, heating and electrical services to serve the separate rooms.

The new dividing wall will generally be built as a timber-framed partition wall faced with plasterboard (gypsum board), but a solid blockwork wall could be built on suitable foundations, which may well need to be inserted.

Creating a new door opening

If the new opening is to be made in a loadbearing wall, a lintel must be used to bridge the opening. However, if the wall is a non-loadbearing partition, simple alterations to the wall framing are all that will be needed. The job will also involve some replastering work, making alterations to skirtings (baseboards) and floor surfaces, the fitting of architraves (trims) around the opening, and possibly alterations to existing plumbing, heating and electrical services if pipes or cables cross the area where the new door will be installed.

Altering the kitchen layout

The amount of work depends on how extensive the rearrangement will be. At the very least there will be new base and wall units (cabinets) and counter tops, and these will probably involve some work on wall and floor surfaces. If repositioning sinks, cookers (stoves), dishwashers and the like, there will have to be alterations to plumbing and electrical services.

CONVERTING AN ATTIC

A full-scale conversion into one or more habitable rooms – that is, bedrooms and the like rather than just play or hobby space – is one of the biggest and most complex indoor home improvement projects. It involves altering the roof structure to make space for the rooms, strengthening the existing attic floor, providing access from the floor below, installing roof or dormer windows and extending existing services into the new rooms. Professional advice is needed here, and it is advisable to hand over the main structural alterations to a builder or specialist conversion firm. This still leaves plenty of scope for do-it-yourself finishing and fitting of the new rooms.

In many older homes, the space beneath a pitched (sloping) roof can be used to provide valuable extra living space, often with spectacular results.

USING COLOUR, PATTERN AND TEXTURE

After redesigning the house layout and reorganizing each room, the next task is to start planning the colour schemes. To do this successfully, it helps to understand the basics of colour and how to use pattern and texture to good effect. When putting a colour scheme together, a device called the colour wheel can be used to help plan the various decorative effects.

All colours are made by mixing together varying proportions of the three primary colours – red, yellow and blue. Mixing them in pairs creates three new secondary colours, with red and yellow making orange, yellow and blue making green, and blue and red making violet. Imagine these six colours making up segments of a circle in the order red, orange, yellow, green, blue and violet. Mix adjacent pairs together again, and you create six tertiary colours – red/orange, orange/yellow, yellow/green, green/blue, blue/violet and violet/red. Adding these to the circle gives the basic colour wheel of twelve segments.

There is one more ingredient to add to these colours: colour intensity or tone. By adding different amounts of white or black, you can produce lighter or darker shades of the original colours in almost infinite variety. And you can also, of course, use white, black and varying shades of grey as colours in their own right.

On the wheel, the 12 colours split into two groups. The colours from violet/red round to yellow are known as advancing colours because they appear to make wall and ceiling surfaces look nearer to the viewer than they really are. They make a room seem warm and welcoming, but also smaller. The remaining colours are known as receding colours because they have the

THE COLOUR WHEEL

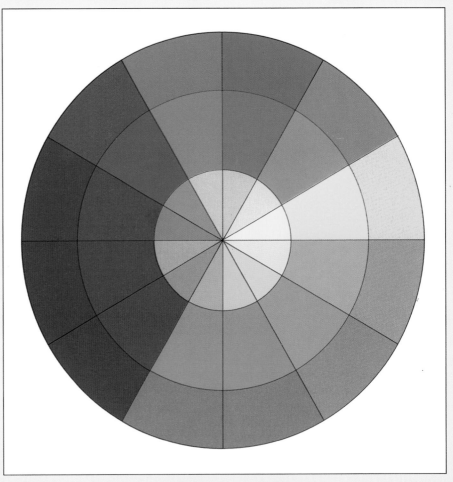

An understanding of colour and colour mixing will be invaluable when choosing a new colour scheme. The colour wheel is divided into 12 segments, and the intermediate ring shows the primary, secondary and tertiary colours described in the text. The outer ring shows darker tones of these colours and the inner ring lighter ones.

LEFT Blues, greys and plenty of white space create a cool, airy colour scheme that is the perfect complement for wooden fixtures and furnishings in a light shade of pine.

LEFT Blues and greens are naturally cool, receding colours, ideal for well-lit south-facing rooms, but they can be warmed by splashes of contrast in orange and yellow.

opposite visual effect, making a room look cool, and also larger than in reality. Which group is chosen as the basis for a colour scheme depends on the overall effect that is desired in that particular room.

The colour wheel also helps to create colour harmony or contrast. Colours next to or near each other are said to be in colour harmony, giving a restful effect. However, too much colour harmony can become visually rather dull; it needs livening up with some elements of colour contrast, which come from using colours at opposite sides of the wheel. Colours exactly opposite each other, such as red and green, are called complementary.

Colour intensity (tone) can also play tricks on the eye, which can be used to good effect in colour scheming. Deep colours tend to bring walls inwards, and light colours give the illusion of pushing them away from you. A light colour will make a small area seem larger, while a deep colour will do the opposite. You should also bear in mind the proportions of your room.

BELOW Nothing succeeds in creating a feeling of cosiness so well as the red/pink section of the colour wheel. Surface texture plays its part too, as does warm, natural wood fittings.

ABOVE Neutral tones – beiges, creams and browns – create an overall colour scheme that is restful on the eye and can be teamed with accessories in almost any shade.

BELOW Wall coverings with a vertical pattern can help to make rooms appear taller, but work well only when the walls are perfectly square.

If you have, for example, a room with a high ceiling, you can create the effect of more harmonious proportions by dividing the walls in half horizontally, and painting the top half and the ceiling in a darker colour. This will make the ceiling appear lower. Following the same principle, a low ceiling can be made to appear higher by painting the top half of the walls in a light colour, which is advantageous in a small room.

Using pattern

Patterns on walls, ceilings and floors add visual interest to a colour scheme either in harmony with the overall effect or to provide contrast – for example, by having a patterned covering on one wall, and the rest painted. Pattern as well as colour can cheat the eye and alter the apparent dimensions of a room. Wall coverings with a distinct horizontal pattern make walls seem wider and ceilings lower; strong vertical designs such as stripes have the opposite effect. The same applies to patterns on floor coverings, which can make a room look wider or narrower depending on which way the pattern element runs.

Pattern size has its own contribution to make. Wall and floor coverings with large pattern motifs make the surface seem to advance and so make the room appear smaller, while tiny motifs have the opposite effect of making the surface appear to recede from the eye. Choosing patterned fabrics for cushions, curtains and drapes or bed linen is an ideal way of enlivening a decor with plain walls and woodwork.

ABOVE Small patterns are a better choice than larger motifs for small rooms, and are ideal for decorating areas where perfect pattern matching can be difficult.

LEFT Luxurious fabrics used for curtains, cushions and upholstery are often the ideal medium for adding patterned and textured elements to a decor.

Using texture

Surface texture – in other words, a surface that is not completely smooth – helps to add variety and visual interest to your colour schemes. Wall coverings with a textured or embossed surface generally have a comparatively low relief which helps to soften the decorative effect of the material, while texture paints can be used to create effects that have quite a high relief and consequently look particularly striking when lit from the side. Textured finishes also have another benefit, of helping to disguise slightly irregular wall and ceiling surfaces.

RIGHT Sometimes richly textured upholstery and floor coverings benefit from the simplest of settings. Here textured walls and painted floorboards in pure white are the perfect backdrop.

LIGHTING FOR THE LIVING ROOM, DINING ROOM AND BEDROOMS

The key to success with any lighting scheme is to ensure that it meets two criteria: it must give light where it is needed, and the effect it produces should enhance the room's appearance by creating a balanced mixture of light and shadow. The type of light fittings chosen has a major part to play, and so does the positioning of the fittings. The illustration on the opposite page (bottom) shows how both the type and positioning of ceiling lights can create different lighting effects on room walls.

The living room is one of the most difficult areas to light successfully, because of the many different uses to which the room is put. The aim should be to provide background lighting that can be bright or dim according to the mood of the moment, and then to add separately controllable feature lighting to highlight the room's focal points, and local task lighting where required. The accent is on flexibility. Choosing fittings in keeping with the style of the room will help to ensure that its lighting looks good by day or night.

The dining room has slightly different needs. The main requirement is a table that is well-lit without glare, which you can achieve with a rise-and-fall fitting or carefully targeted downlighters. The background lighting should be subdued, preferably under dimmer control – note that fluorescent lights cannot be easily dimmed. Additional lighting from wall lights or wall washers can be used to illuminate the serving and carving area, and uplighters for dramatic effect.

Bedroom lighting requires a combination of restful background lighting and easily controllable local lighting to cover separate activities including dressing and undressing, applying make-up, reading in bed, or perhaps watching television.

Background lighting can be provided by wall lights, by table lamps on bedside tables, by recessed downlighters or, very appropriately for bedrooms, by the wall- or ceiling-mounted fittings known as uplighters, which throw light on to the ceiling and completely conceal the lamp when viewed from below. The general light level can be lower than for the living room, as long as the task lighting does its job. Bright, glare-free lighting is needed at a dressing table, and light from above to check clothes.

ABOVE Recessed downlighters are the ideal light source for a child's room, providing good illumination of play and storage areas yet remaining safely out of harm's way.

ABOVE A rise-and-fall fitting provides glare-free light over the dining table, while a free-standing uplighter casts a gentle glow across the ceiling.

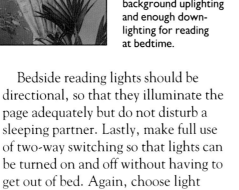

RIGHT An opaque shade on a bedside light prevents glare while providing gentle background uplighting and enough down-lighting for reading at bedtime.

ABOVE For lighting with minimal glare, team an opaque central fitting with strip lights behind pelmets (valances) to light up a cornice (crown molding) and the ceiling surface above.

OPPOSITE Pastel-shaded lamps in opaque lampshades help to create soft background lighting effects that complement the room's colour scheme.

Bedside reading lights should be directional, so that they illuminate the page adequately but do not disturb a sleeping partner. Lastly, make full use of two-way switching so that lights can be turned on and off without having to get out of bed. Again, choose light fittings to complement the room's décor and colour scheme.

Children's bedrooms, especially nurseries, have some slightly different requirements. Good task lighting is essential for jobs such as changing or dressing a baby, and young children will want a higher overall lighting level than that in an adult's room when playing. They may also need a low-wattage night light for comfort and safety. Finally, older children will want portable task lighting for activities such as hobbies and homework.

WASHING WALLS WITH LIGHT

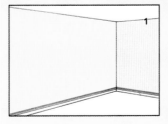

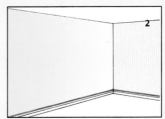

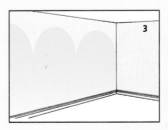

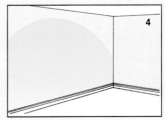

A row of wall washers of the same wattage creates a perfect wash (1), while decreasing wattages along the row give a graded wash (2). A row of downlighters can create a scalloped effect (3), while a single downlighter casts a parabola (4).

LIGHTING FOR THE KITCHEN, BATHROOM AND HALLWAY

The kitchen poses special lighting problems, mainly owing to the wide use of the fitted kitchen. In the old days most food preparation was done on a central table, so a central light was generally adequate. Now almost every task is carried out close to the perimeter of the room, making a central light – still the standard fitting in many homes – useless, and condemning the cook to working in his or her own shadow. What a modern kitchen really needs is lighting tailored to provide good illumination at each of the main work stations – the cooker (stove), the sink and the food-preparation area. There should also be a reasonable level of general background lighting, plus lighting to illuminate the insides of cupboards (closets). All of these requirements can only be achieved by separate, flexible and independently controllable light sources.

If the cooker has an extractor hood over it, containing a downlighter, this will illuminate the hob (burners) satisfactorily. Otherwise the aim should be to provide ceiling-mounted lights, positioned so that they shine directly on the hob without casting a shadow. The same is needed over the sink. Ideally each of these lights or sets of lights should have its own switch so that it can be turned on and off as required. For counter tops below wall-storage units, lighting is best provided by strip lights fixed beneath the wall units and shielded by baffles to prevent glare. Walk-in cupboards and open display units can be lit by recessed downlighters, and base units by small interior lights with automatic switches worked by opening the doors. If the kitchen is also used for eating, it is a good idea to provide a rise-and-fall fitting or recessed downlighters over the table so that the rest of the kitchen lighting can be turned off – not least to hide cooking debris during the meal.

The bathroom is much less demanding. The basic requirement is for a modest level of background lighting, provided by a close-mounted central light or some recessed fittings. If the washbasin area is used for shaving, add a wall strip (fluorescent) light over the basin to provide good, glare-free illumination there. Do not install a fluorescent light if this area is to be used for applying make-up, however, as even the best types of this lighting give a slightly inaccurate rendering of some colours. There may also be a need for a splashproof recessed light fitting in a shower cubicle.

LEFT The kitchen is difficult to light because most tasks take place around the perimeter of the room. Lights positioned above the counter tops are the perfect solution.

LEFT In the bathroom, enclosed fittings are a must for safety reasons. A central fitting with an opaque diffuser will cast a soft overall light.

ABOVE The hallway and stairwell need good illumination for safety reasons. Here, recessed downlighters illuminate every tread of the staircase and highlight the hall's features.

When you are thinking about the lighting in the different areas of your home, the landing, hallway and stairwell should not be forgotten. The latter is one area of the home in which good, bright lighting is essential; the safety aspect is more important than mood here, ensuring that all parts of the staircase are clearly lit without glare. For the best effect, fittings should be positioned so that the treads of the stairs are well-lit but the risers are in shadow. Make sure that any suspended fittings do not impede passage up and down the staircase, and check that any recessed fittings are readily accessible – it is irritating to have to get a ladder out to reach a high-level fitting whenever a lightbulb happens to fail.

LEFT Wall-mounted downlighters can also be used to light a staircase, casting the risers into shadow and making the treads clearly visible.

LIGHTING FOR DISPLAY AND SECURITY

Most of the lighting schemes mentioned so far have concentrated on illuminating individual rooms and providing good task lighting for the various activities carried out in them. However, lighting can also be used as a means of decorating rooms and highlighting their best features.

Spotlights offer great flexibility here. They are available as single, double and triple spot units for wall or ceiling mounting, as individual spotlights designed to fit on a lighting track, or as recessed 'eyeball' ceiling fittings. The beam direction can be adjusted to 'wash' walls, curtains (drapes) or ceilings with light, which may be coloured instead of white; or to illuminate an individual area of the room such as a fireplace, an arch, an alcove, a display unit (cabinet) or some other feature.

Small spotlights, especially the recessed eyeball types, can be used to illuminate individual pictures or picture groups. Alternatively, a traditional picture light – a small strip light in a wall-mounted holder – may be set above or below the picture.

Shelves or closed cabinets displaying china, glass or other *objets d'art* can be lit in several ways. Spotlighting is one, but this can look harsh. What often works better is either backlighting via small tungsten filament strip lights fitted beneath the shelves or, where glass shelves are used, a lamp behind a frosted glass panel at the top or bottom of the unit.

The last area of lighting that needs to be considered is indoor security lighting. It is well known that intruders are deterred by good lighting outside the house and this also applies indoors. If a would-be intruder sees an indoor light, he or she can never be sure

whether the house is occupied or not, especially if the curtains are drawn. Even if the owners are out, an intruder will be less keen to break in and risk being seen from outside.

There are several types of programmable controls which can be used to switch on both fixed lighting and plug-in lights, either at preset times or at sunset. Some can then mimic human behaviour by turning lights on and off at random during the night, and will switch off at dawn. Others turn lights on – and can also trigger a burglar alarm – if they detect the body heat of an intruder, much like the sensors used out of doors. All give extra protection, especially if combined with electrically controlled curtain closers.

ABOVE Coloured lamps can help to accentuate a room's colour scheme, while concealed lighting in alcoves makes the most of china and other treasures.

ABOVE Pictures can be brought to life if highlighted by an individual spotlight or a linear picture light.

OPPOSITE Low-voltage tungsten halogen lighting sheds a crisp white light that is perfect for highlighting a collection of ornamental glass.

LEFT You can use a combination of small clip-on spotlights and free-standing fittings to cast individual pools of light on special objects within an alcove.

PAINTING AND PAPERHANGING

Modern paints and improvements in the design and manufacture of decorating tools have certainly made the task of painting less arduous than it was in the days of traditional oil-based paints and distemper, and have also made it easier for the amateur decorator to get professional-looking results.

One major shift in paint technology is the trend away from using solvent-based varnishes and paints for wood, and towards water-based products which do not give off harmful vapours as they dry. Water-based (latex) finishes are not as durable as solvent-based (oil) ones, but are no longer as far behind them in performance terms as they once were, and they have other advantages such as faster drying times, virtually no smell and easier cleaning of brushes, rollers and pads.

The term 'wall coverings' is used to describe the whole range of decorative materials sold in roll form and designed to be stuck to wall and ceiling surfaces with a strippable adhesive. The range includes an enormous variety of designs, patterns and colourways. Most are made entirely from paper, or have a plastic or cloth layer bonded to a paper backing so that they can be hung in the same way as all-paper types. The following section describes the various types of paint, varnish and stain on the market; how to prepare surfaces for redecoration; how to apply the new paint finish – especially to the more awkward surfaces such as windows and panelled doors – and how to create a range of special paint effects as dramatic alternatives to wall coverings.

This section also gives information on the various types of wall covering available and on the tools, materials and other equipment needed to hang or strip them. There is advice on how to go about removing existing wall decorations – other wall coverings, materials such as texture paints, wall panelling and tiles of various types – and on preparing the surface. This is followed by detailed step-by-step instructions on how to hang a new wall covering on walls and ceilings, and on how to cope with awkward areas such as door and window openings, arches and stairwells.

OPPOSITE Paint offers a huge palette of colours, and complementary and contrasting shades can create the subtlest and most restful of colour schemes. It is the easiest finish to change, too, when a room needs a new look.

CHOOSING PAINTS, VARNISHES AND STAINS

Paint works by forming a film on the surface to which it is applied. This film has to do three things: it must hide the surface underneath; it must protect it; and it must stay put. All paint has three main ingredients: pigment, binder and carrier. The pigment gives the film its colour and hiding power. The binder binds the pigment particles together into a continuous film as the paint dries, and also bonds the film to the surface beneath. The third ingredient, the carrier, makes the paint flow smoothly as it is applied to the surface, and evaporates as the paint dries.

By adjusting the ratio of pigment to binder, paint manufacturers can produce paints that dry to a flat matt finish; to a silky sheen (eggshell); or to a high gloss. The choice depends on personal preference, tempered by the condition of the surface: high-gloss finishes highlight any imperfections, while matt finishes disguise them.

Paint types

Water-based paint has the pigment and binder suspended in water as tiny droplets. It is usually called emulsion (latex) paint. Solvent-based alkyd (oil or oil-based) paint has pigment and binder dissolved in a petroleum-based solvent, and takes longer to dry than water-based paint. Because of growing awareness of the risks of inhaling solvents, the use of this paint is declining in popularity and is already legally restricted in some countries.

Paint also contains a range of other additives to improve its performance. The most notable is one that makes the paint thixotropic or non-drip, allowing more paint to be loaded on to the brush and a thicker paint film to be applied; one coat of this is often sufficient.

Paint systems

A single coat of paint is too thin to form a durable paint film. To provide adequate cover and performance there must be a paint system consisting of several coats. What these are depends on the type of paint used, and on the surface being painted.

The first coat is a sealer, which is used where necessary to seal the natural resin in wood, or to prevent the paint from soaking into a porous surface. The second coat is a primer; this provides a good key to which the paint film can stick. On metal surfaces, this also stops the metal corroding or oxidizing. A primer can, in addition, act as a sealer. The third coat is the undercoat, which builds up the film to form a flexible, non-absorbent base of uniform colour close to that of the fourth and final layer, the top coat, which gives the actual finish and colour.

On walls, the system consists simply of two or three coats of the same paint, unless there is a need for a sealer or primer to cure a fault such as high alkalinity or excessive porosity. The first coat is a mist coat of thinned paint.

ABOVE Blues and greys are cool, fresh colours that particularly suit a well-lit children's room. The brightly painted ladder provides the perfect contrast. Painted surfaces need to withstand some rough treatment in a location such as this.

BELOW The yellow water-based paint chosen for the walls of this kitchen creates a basically warm colour scheme that is off-set by the gloss paint in cool colours selected for the woodwork. Solvent-based (oil) paint is ideal for surfaces which need washing down regularly.

A primer is also used if walls are being painted with solvent-based paints.

On woodwork, the first step is to apply a liquid called knotting (shellac) to any knots to prevent resin from bleeding through the paint film. Then comes a wood primer, followed by an undercoat and then the top coat. To speed up the painting process, paint manufacturers have now perfected combined primer/undercoats, and self-undercoating gloss paint which just needs a primer.

On metal, a primer is generally needed. A zinc-phosphate primer is used for iron or steel, and there are special primers for aluminium. This is then followed by an undercoat and top coat, as for wood. Copper, brass and lead can be painted directly, as long as they are thoroughly de-greased with white spirit (paint thinner).

Varnishes and wood stains

Varnish is basically paint without the pigment. Most types of varnish contain polyurethane resins and are solvent-based (like oil paint), although water-based acrylic varnishes are becoming more popular. Varnishes are available with a satin/silk or a high-gloss finish, either clear or with the addition of small amounts of colour.

Varnish is its own primer and undercoat, although it is best to thin the first coat with about 10 per cent white spirit (paint thinner) for solvent-based types, or water for acrylic types, and to apply it with a lint-free cloth rather than a brush so that you can rub it well into the wood grain. When this first coat has dried, 'key' or roughen it by rubbing very lightly with fine-grade sandpaper, dust it off, and then apply a second, full-strength coat. For surfaces likely to receive a lot of wear, it is advisable to key the second coat as before and apply an additional coat.

Wood stain, unlike both paint and varnish, is designed to soak into wood.

LEFT Coloured varnishes help to enhance the colour of the wood grain without obliterating it completely, as paint will do.

BELOW Varnish can be used to enhance the beauty of wood throughout the home, from floors and fire surrounds to storage units and other items of furniture.

It may subsequently be sealed with clear varnish to improve the finish and make the surface more durable. Wood stain is available in water-based or solvent-based types in a wide range of colours and wood shades. Different colours can also be blended to obtain intermediate shades, and the stain can be thinned with water or white spirit as appropriate to give a paler effect.

Wood stain can be applied with a brush, a paint pad or a lint-free cloth. Quick work is needed to blend wet edges together, and to avoid overlaps which will leave darker patches as the stain dries. A water-based stain will raise fibres on the surface of the wood, which will spoil the evenness of the colour. The solution is to sand the surface perfectly smooth first and then to dampen it with a wet cloth. This will raise the surface fibres. When the wood is dry, sand off the fibres with fine-grade sandpaper, ready to receive the stain.

CLEANING PAINTING EQUIPMENT

Wash tools and equipment in soapy water if using a water-based paint, and with white spirit (paint thinner) or a proprietary brush cleaner for solvent-based (oil) paint. Soak hardened paint in paint remover overnight, then wash out with hot, soapy water.

PAINTING TOOLS AND EQUIPMENT

Two groups of tools are needed for painting, one for preparing the surface and one for actually applying the paint. For a masonry wall, the minimum preparation is to wash down any previously painted surface. This calls for a bucket, sponges and cloths, strong household detergent or sugar soap (all-purpose cleaner), and rubber gloves to protect the hands.

If the washed-down surface has a high-gloss finish, or feels rough to the touch, use fine-grade sandpaper and a sanding block to smooth it down. Wet-and-dry (silicon carbide) paper, used wet, is best for sanding down existing paintwork; remember to thoroughly rinse off the resulting fine slurry of paint with water afterwards. Use ordinary sandpaper for bare wood.

Defects in the surface need filling. Use a traditional cellulose filler (spackle) for small cracks, chips and other surface blemishes, and an expanding filler foam which can be shaped and sanded when hard for larger defects. To apply filler paste use a filling knife (putty knife).

To strip existing paintwork, use either a heat gun – easier to control and much safer to use than a blowtorch – or a chemical paint remover, plus scrapers of various shapes to remove the softened paint. For removing wall coverings in order to apply a painted wall or ceiling finish, a steam wallpaper stripper will be worth the investment. The small all-in-one strippers which resemble a large steam iron are the easiest type to use.

Painting tools

The paintbrush is still the favourite tool for applying paint to walls, ceilings, woodwork and metalwork around the house. Most are made with natural bristle, held in a metal ferrule which is attached to a wooden or plastic handle, but there are also brushes with synthetic fibre bristles which are sometimes recommended for applying water-based (latex) paints.

Brushes come in widths from 12 mm/½ in up to 15 cm/6 in. The smallest sizes are used for fiddly jobs such as painting glazing bars (muntins), while the widest are ideal for flat uninterrupted wall and ceiling surfaces. However, a wide brush can be tiring to use, especially with solvent-based (oil) paints. There are also long-handled

PREPARATION EQUIPMENT

The following tools and equipment are the general items needed to prepare for re-painting: steam wallpaper stripper (1), liquid paint remover (2), paste paint remover (3), cellulose filler (spackle) (4), expanding filler foam (5), rubber gloves (6), bucket (7), sugar soap (all-purpose cleaner) (8), sponge (9), cloth (10), spray gun (11), sandpaper (12), sanding block (13), shavehooks (triangular scrapers) (14), scrapers (15), heat gun and attachments (a directional nozzle and two integral scrapers) (16).

brushes with angled heads for painting behind radiators, and narrow brushes called cutting-in (sash) brushes, which have the bristle tips cut off at an angle for painting into internal angles. For the best results, buy good-quality brushes and look after them, rather than buy cheap ones and throw them away after finishing each job.

Paint rollers are used mainly for painting walls and ceilings with water-based paints, although they can be used with solvent-based types too. They consist of a metal roller cage mounted on a handle, plus a hollow sleeve that fits onto the cage and actually applies the paint. Some can be fitted with an extension pole, which is useful if there are high ceilings or stairwells to paint. Most rollers are 18 cm/7 in wide; larger

sizes are available, but can be harder to 'drive'. There are also slim mini-rollers for painting awkward-to-reach areas such as walls behind radiators. For any type, a roller tray is used to load paint on to the sleeve. Solid water-based paint is sold in its own tray.

The sleeves are waterproof tubes with a layer of foam plastic or cloth stuck to the outside – another type may be made from natural or synthetic fibre, and have a short, medium or long pile, to suit different types of surface. Choose the pile length to match the surface being painted: short for flat surfaces, medium for those with a slight texture and long for embossed surfaces.

Paint pads are squares or rectangles of short-pile cloth stuck to a foam backing and mounted on a plastic or

metal handle. The pad is dipped in a shallow container, or loaded from a special paint container with a roller feed, and then drawn across the surface. Pads come in a range of sizes.

Paint and varnish are also sold in aerosol form. This is ideal for small areas or fiddly materials such as wickerwork, but too expensive to use on large areas.

Lastly, do not forget the decorating sundries. A paint kettle is needed for decanting the paint and straining out any foreign bodies. Hand-held paint masks or masking tape are invaluable aids to getting straight edges and keeping paint off adjacent surfaces. Above all, remember to provide dust sheets (drop cloths), which perform better than plastic sheets.

PAINTING EQUIPMENT

This selection of equipment includes: brushes in various sizes (1), aerosol paint (2), long-handled brush for use behind radiators (3), handheld skirting (baseboard) masks (4), slimline mini-roller (5), roller extension pole (6), a full-sized roller with short-pile sleeve and roller tray (7), dust sheet (drop cloth) (8), white spirit (paint thinner) (9), long pile and textured roller sleeves (10), paint shield (11), masking tape (12), paint kettle (13), paint pads in various sizes and shapes (14), paint-loading containers for paint pads (15).

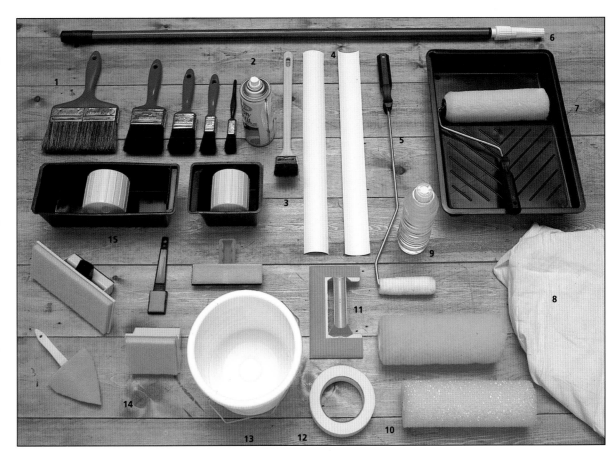

USING BRUSHES, ROLLERS AND PAINT PADS

The paintbrush is the most versatile and widely used tool for applying paint. Choose the brush size to match the surface that you are painting. For example, for painting glazing bars (muntins) on windows or narrow mouldings on a door, use a slim brush – or perhaps a cutting-in (sash) brush if you are painting up to an unpainted surface, such as glass, where a neat edge is needed. For expansive, flat areas, select a larger brush for quick coverage.

Get rid of any loose bristles in a new brush by flicking it vigorously across the palm of your hand before using it. Wash previously used brushes that have been stored unwrapped to remove any dust or other debris from the bristles, and leave them to dry out before using them to apply a solvent-based paint.

Paint rollers are generally used to apply water-based (latex) paints to large, flat areas such as walls and ceilings. Choose a sleeve with a short pile for painting plaster, a medium pile for painting embossed or textured wall coverings, or a long pile for sculpted surfaces such as those created with textured finishes (texture paints). Rollers can also be used to apply solvent-based (oil) paint to flat surfaces such as flush doors, but tend to leave a distinctive 'orange-peel' texture rather than the smooth finish left by a brush.

There are some drawbacks with paint rollers: they cannot paint right up to internal corners or wall/ceiling angles, so these need to be painted first with a brush or pad. They can also splash if 'driven' too fast, and the sleeves take a good deal of time and effort to clean thoroughly, especially if they have been used for a long period and there is dried paint in the pile.

Paint pads tend to apply less paint per coat than either a brush or a roller, so an additional coat may be needed in some circumstances, but they make it easy to apply paint smoothly and evenly with no risk of brushmarks.

PREPARING THE PAINT

1 Wipe the lid to remove any dust, then prise it off with a wide lever such as the back of a table knife to avoid damage to the lip. Decant some paint into a paint kettle or small bucket. This will be easier to handle than a full container.

2 Remove any paint skin from partly used containers. Strain the paint into the paint kettle through a piece of old stocking or tights (pantyhose), or a piece of muslin (cheesecloth), to filter out any dirt.

USING A BRUSH

1 Tie a length of string or wire across the mouth of the paint kettle. To load the brush, dip it into the paint, but only to about one-third of the bristle depth. An overloaded brush will cause drips, and paint will run down the handle. Use the string or wire to scrape excess paint from the bristles.

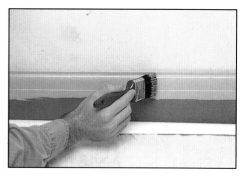

2 Apply the paint to the wood in long, sweeping strokes, along the grain, until the brush begins to run dry. Load up the brush with more paint and apply it to the next area. Blend the paint using short, light strokes, again along the grain direction, so that no join is visible.

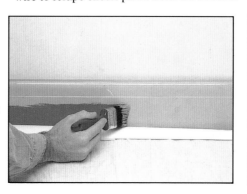

3 Repeat this process while working your way across the whole area to be painted, always blending the edges of adjacent areas together using light brushstrokes.

4 At edges and external corners, let the brush run off the edge to avoid a build-up of paint on the corner. Repeat the process for the opposite edge.

USING A ROLLER

1 Decant some paint (previously strained if from an old can) into the roller tray until the paint level just laps up to the sloping section. Slide a sleeve on to the roller.

2 Brush a band of paint about 5 cm/2 in wide into internal corners and wall/ceiling angles, around doors and windows, and above skirtings (baseboards).

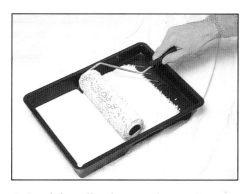

3 Load the roller sleeve with paint by running it down the sloping section into the paint, then roll it up and down the slope to remove the excess.

4 Start applying the paint in a series of overlapping diagonal strokes to ensure complete coverage of the surface. Continue until the sleeve runs dry.

5 Re-load the sleeve and tackle the next section in the same way. Finish off by blending the areas together, working parallel to corners and edges.

USING AEROSOL PAINT

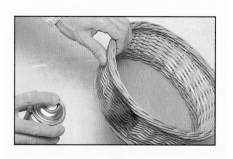

Aerosol paints and varnishes are ideal for hard-to-decorate surfaces such as wickerwork. Always follow the maker's instructions when using them.

USING A PAINT PAD

1 Pour some paint into the special applicator tray. Load the pad by running it backwards and forwards over the ridged loading roller.

2 On walls, apply the paint in a series of overlapping parallel bands. Use a small pad or a special edging pad (see step 4) to paint right up to corners or angles.

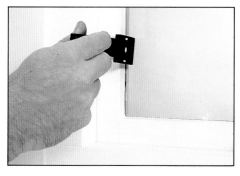

3 Use smaller pads for painting narrow areas such as mouldings on doors or glazing bars (muntins) on windows, brushing out the paint along the direction of the grain.

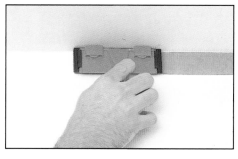

4 Special edging pads are designed for painting right up to internal angles, and have small wheels which guide the pad along the adjacent surface as you work.

5 Some larger pads can be fitted to an extension pole to make it easier to paint ceilings and high walls. Make sure that the pad is attached securely.

PREPARING SURFACES FOR PAINTING

Modern paints have excellent adhesion and covering power, but to get the best performance from them you must prepare the surface thoroughly. To prepare painted woodwork, use fine-grade sandpaper wrapped around a sanding block to remove 'nibs' from the paint surface and to key the paint film ready for re-painting. Wash the surface using a solution of strong household detergent or sugar soap (all-purpose cleaner). Rinse very thoroughly and allow the surface to dry completely.

Remove areas of flaking paint using a scraper or filling knife (putty knife), and then either touch in the bare area with more paint or fill it flush with the surrounding paint film by using fine filler (spackle). Sand this smooth when it has hardened. Use a clean cloth moistened with white spirit (paint thinner) to remove dust from recessed mouldings and other awkward corners.

If knots are showing through on painted woodwork, sand back to bare wood and apply knotting (shellac) to the knot, then prime and undercoat to bring the new paint film level with the surrounding paintwork. Sand between coats. Resinous knots may produce stains which can only be prevented by drying out the knots with a blowtorch.

Stripping paint

Every time a surface is re-painted, a little more thickness is added to the paint layer. This does not matter much on wall or ceiling surfaces, but on woodwork (and, to a lesser extent, on metalwork) this build-up of successive layers of paint can eventually lead to the clogging of detail on mouldings.

More importantly, moving parts such as doors and windows start to bind and catch against their frames. If this happens, it is time to strip back to bare wood and build up a new paint system.

There are 2 methods of removing paint from wood and metal surfaces. The first is using heat, traditionally from a blowtorch but nowadays more often from an electric heat gun. The second is to use a chemical paint remover, which contains either dimethylene chloride or caustic soda. Heat works well on wood (although it can scorch the surface), but it is less successful on metal because the material conducts heat away as it is applied. Chemicals work well on all surfaces, but need handling with care; always follow the manufacturer's instructions to the letter.

USING A HEAT GUN

1 Play the air stream from the heat gun over the surface to soften the paint film. Scrape it off with a flat scraper as it bubbles up, and deposit the hot scrapings in an old metal container.

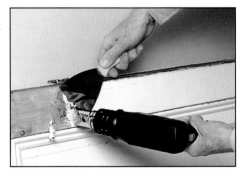

2 Use a shavehook (triangular scraper) instead of a flat scraper to remove the paint from mouldings. Take care not to scorch the wood if you intend to varnish it afterwards.

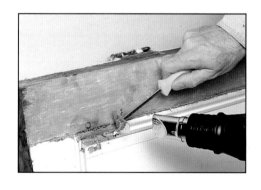

3 Remove any remnants of paint using wire wool soaked in white spirit (paint thinner), working along the grain. Use a hand vacuum cleaner to remove any remaining loose particles of paint.

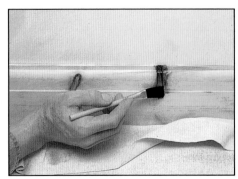

4 Sand the wood to remove any raised fibres, then wipe it over with a cloth moistened with white spirit. Seal the resin in any exposed knots by brushing on liquid knotting (shellac). Leave to dry.

5 Apply a coat of either wood primer or a combined primer/undercoat to the stripped wood surface. This will provide optimum adhesion for the subsequent top coats, ensuring a really good finish.

FILLING DEFECTS IN WOOD

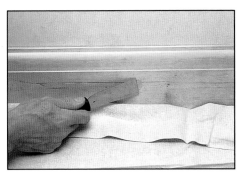

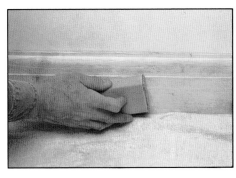

1 Fill splits and dents in wood using filler (spackle) on surfaces that are already painted, and tinted wood stopper (patcher) on new or stripped wood that you intend to finish with a coat of varnish.

2 Use the corner of a filling knife (putty knife), or a finger, to work the filler into recesses and other awkward-to-reach places. Smooth off the excess filler before it dries and hardens.

3 When the filler or wood stopper has hardened completely, use a piece of fine-grade sandpaper wrapped around a sanding block to sand down the repair until it is flush with the rest of the wood.

USING LIQUID REMOVER

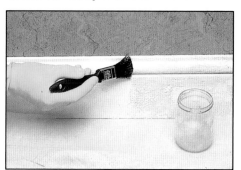

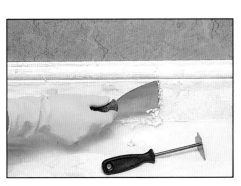

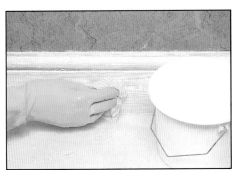

1 Wear rubber gloves and old clothing. Decant the liquid into a polythene (polyethylene) container or an old can, then brush it on to the surface to be stripped. Leave it until the paint bubbles.

2 Use a flat scraper or shavehook (triangular scraper) as appropriate to remove the softened paint. Deposit the scrapings safely in an old container.

3 Neutralize the stripper by washing down the surface with water or white spirit (paint thinner), as recommended by the manufacturer. Leave it to dry.

USING PASTE REMOVER

1 Paste remover is especially good for removing paint from intricate mouldings because it dries very slowly. Apply the paste liberally to the surface.

2 Give the paste plenty of time to work, especially on thick paint layers, then scrape it off. Wash down the surface with plenty of water to neutralize the chemical.

HOME-MADE PASTE REMOVER

Add caustic soda to water until no more will dissolve. Thicken to a paste with oatmeal and use as for proprietary paste remover. Be particularly careful when using this corrosive solution. If it splashes on the skin, rinse at once with plenty of cold water.

PAINTING WALLS AND CEILINGS

Paint is a popular decorative finish for walls and ceilings because it is quick and easy to apply, offers a huge range of colours and is relatively inexpensive compared with rival products such as wall coverings. It can be used over plain plaster, or can be applied over embossed relief wall coverings and textured finishes.

Before starting to paint, clear the room and prepare the surfaces. Start by taking down curtains and blinds (drapes and shades). Remove furniture to another room if possible, or else group it in the middle of the room and cover it with clear plastic sheeting. Take down lampshades and pendant light fittings (after turning off the power supply). Unscrew wall-mounted fittings and remove the hardware from doors and windows if they are being repainted at the same time.

Protect surfaces not being repainted, such as wall switches and socket outlets (receptacles), with masking tape. Finally, cover the floor with dust sheets (drop cloths), which will absorb paint splashes; vacuum-clean surfaces such as windowsills, picture rails and skirtings (baseboards) where dust can settle, and turn off forced-air heating so that dust is not recirculated into the room.

Access equipment

Normally most of the surfaces to be painted can be reached from a standing or a kneeling position, but some access equipment is needed for ceilings, the tops of room walls and the upper reaches of stairwells. A simple stepladder, ideally with a top platform big enough to support a paint kettle or roller tray, will be adequate for painting walls and ceilings.

PAINTING WALLS AND CEILINGS

Paint walls and ceilings in a series of overlapping bands. Start painting the ceiling next to the window wall so that reflected light on the wet paint shows if coverage is even. On walls, right-handed people should work from right to left, and vice-versa.

For stairwells, use steps or ladder sections plus secured scaffold boards or the components of a slot-together access tower to set up a work platform that allows you to get to all the surfaces without over-reaching.

Texture paints

Texture paints are water-based (latex) paints thickened with added fillers. Once the paint has been applied to the decorating surface, a range of three-dimensional effects can be created byusing various patterning or texturing techniques. These paints are ideal for covering up surfaces in poor condition. Most are white, but they can be overpainted with ordinary water-based paint for a coloured effect, if desired. Avoid using them in kitchens – the textured surface will trap dirt and grease making it difficult to clean.

PAINT COVERAGE

Paint coverage depends on several factors, including the roughness and porosity of the surface to which it is being applied and the thickness of the coating. For example, the first coat of paint will soak into new plaster, so the coverage will be less than is achieved with subsequent coats. Similarly, a textured surface will hold more paint than a smooth one, again reducing the paint coverage. The figures given here are intended as a rough guide only.

Estimating quantities

Paint type	sq m per litre	sq ft per gallon
Liquid gloss (oil) paint	16	650
Non-drip gloss paint	13	530
Eggshell	12	490
Matt (flat) water-based (latex) paint	15	610
Silk (satin) water-based paint	14	570
Non-drip water-based paint	12	490
Undercoat	11	450
Wood primer	12	490
Metal primer	10	410
Varnish	15-20	610-820

USING TEXTURE PAINT

1 Start by gradually applying the paint to the wall or ceiling in a series of overlapping random strokes, recharging the roller or brush at intervals.

2 When an area of about 1 sq m/11 sq ft is covered, go over the whole area with a series of parallel strokes for an even surface texture.

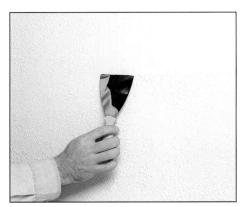

3 Give the textured finish the look of tree bark by drawing a flat-bladed scraper over the surface to flatten off high spots.

4 Use a texturing comb to create overlapping swirls, working across the area. Practise on cardboard first.

5 Twist a sponge before pulling it away from the wall surface to create small, overlapping swirls. Rinse the sponge regularly.

6 You can buy patterning roller sleeves in a range of different designs for use with texture paints. This one creates a regular diamond pattern.

7 This patterning sleeve gives a random streaked effect when rolled down the wall. Apply the texture paint to the roller with a brush first if using a patterning sleeve.

PAINTING DOORS AND WINDOWS

The main problem with painting doors – or indeed any woodwork with a large surface area – involves keeping what professional decorators call a 'wet edge'. Obviously the door has to be painted bit by bit, and, if the edge of one area begins to dry before this is joined up to the next area, the join will show when the paint dries completely.

The secret of success is to work in an ordered sequence, as shown in these illustrations of flush and panelled doors, and to complete the painting job in one continuous operation, working as fast as is reasonably possible.

Windows are more difficult to paint than doors because they contain so many different surfaces, especially small-paned types criss-crossed with slim glazing bars (muntins). There is also the additional problem of paint straying on to the glass. The ideal is a neat paint line that covers the bedding putty and extends on to the glass surface by about 3 mm/⅛ in to seal the joint and prevent condensation from running down between putty and glass.

Remove the window hardware before you start painting. On casement windows, tap a nail into the bottom edge of the casement and into the lower frame rebate and then link them with stiff wire to stop the casement from swinging about.

For the best results, remove sash windows from their frames before painting. Modern spring-mounted windows are easy to release from their frames. With older cord-operated types, remove the staff beads (window stops) first to free the sashes. Although quite a major task, take the opportunity to renew the sash cords (pulley ropes). This makes it possible to cut the cords to free the window.

PAINTING A PANELLED DOOR

1 Tackle a panelled door by painting the mouldings (**1**) around the recessed panels first. Take care not to let paint build up in the corners or to stray on to the faces of the cross-rails at this stage. Next, paint the recessed panels (**2**).

2 Paint the horizontal cross-rails (**3**), brushing lightly inwards towards the painted panel mouldings to leave a sharp paint edge. Feather out the paint thinly where it runs on to the vertical stiles at each end of the rails.

3 Finish the door by painting the vertical centre rail (**4**) and the outer stiles (**5**), again brushing inwards towards the panel mouldings. Where the rail abuts the cross-rails, finish with light brushstrokes parallel to the cross-rails.

VARNISHING WOOD

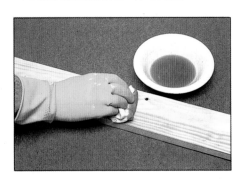

1 On bare wood, use a clean lint-free cloth to wipe the first coat on to the wood, working along the grain direction. This coat acts as a primer/sealer. When it is dry, sand it lightly and then wipe off the dust.

2 Brush on the second and subsequent coats of varnish, applying them along the grain and linking up adjacent areas using light brushstrokes.

USING STAIN

Test the stain on an offcut of the same wood, or in an inconspicuous area. If necessary, dilute it. Use a clean lint-free cloth to apply stain to bare wood. If the result is too pale, apply further coats when the first is dry. Avoid overlapping parallel bands of stain; the overlap will show up as a darker area when the stain dries.

PAINTING A FLUSH DOOR

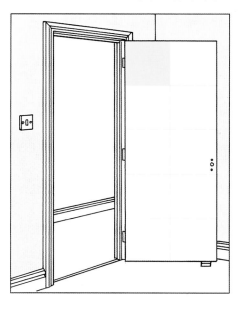

1 Remove the door furniture and wedge open the door. Divide it up into 8 or 10 imaginary squares, and start at the top by filling in the first square. Brush the paint out towards the door edges so that it does not build up on external angles. Paint the next block at the top of the door. Blend the 2 areas with horizontal brushstrokes, then with light, vertical laying-off strokes.

2 Continue to work down the door surface block by block, blending the wet edges of adjacent blocks together as you paint them. Always aim to complete a flush door in 1 session to prevent the joints between blocks showing up as hard lines. Replace the door furniture when the paint is touch-dry.

PAINTING A CASEMENT WINDOW

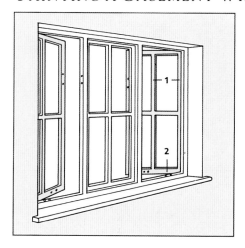

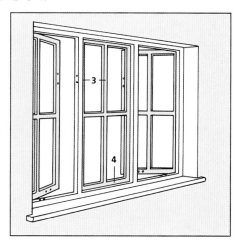

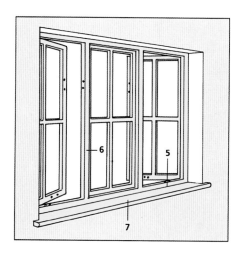

1 Remove the window furniture from the opening casement and wedge the window open while you work. Tackle the glazing bars (muntins) and edge mouldings first (**1**), then the face of the surrounding casement frame (**2**), and finally the hinged edge of the casement. Paint the other edges from outside the house.

2 Move on to paint the glazing bars and edge mouldings (**3**) of the fixed casement. Use masking tape or a paint shield to ensure neat, straight edges here and on the opening casement; the paint should overlap the glass by about 3 mm (⅛ in). Paint the face of the surrounding casement frame (**4**).

3 Paint the outer frame (**5**), then the centre-frame member between the opening and fixed casements (**6**). Complete the job by painting the window sill (**7**), followed by the rebate into which the opening casement closes.

PAINTING AROUND GLASS

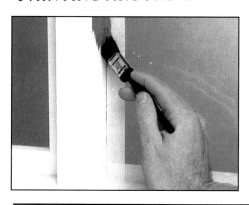

1 Stick masking tape to the glass with its edge 3 mm/ ⅛ in from the wood. Paint the surrounding wood, removing the tape when the paint is touch-dry.

2 Alternatively, hold a small paint shield against the edge of the glazing bar (muntin) or the surrounding moulding while you paint. Wipe the shield regularly to prevent smears.

CHOOSING WALL COVERINGS

Wall coverings fall into 2 basic groups: those with a printed design or a surface material that is decorative in its own right, and those with a surface texture or embossing that is designed to be painted over once the coverings have been hung on the wall.

Printed wallpaper is exactly what its name implies – paper with a coloured design printed on it. It may also be embossed or have a distinctive surface texture. Cheaper types may be awkward to hang, tearing easily or stretching so as to make accurate pattern-matching difficult. The strongest printed wallpapers are called duplex papers, and are made by bonding 2 layers of paper together during the manufacturing process. Most printed papers can be wiped with a damp cloth if they become stained. All are easy to strip, making them a good choice if you like to re-decorate regularly.

Washable wallpaper is a printed wallpaper which has a thin, clear, plastic coating applied over the design during manufacture to render it water- and stain-resistant. As with printed types, the surface may be embossed or textured. Washable wallpapers are also widely available in ready-pasted form. The plastic surface will withstand gentle washing and sponging with a mild detergent, but not prolonged scrubbing. Choose washable wallpapers for rooms in which they will be subject to moderate wear, or for hot, steamy conditions such as those found in the kitchen and bathroom. The main drawback of these papers is that they are difficult to remove.

Vinyl wall coverings consist of a plastic film on to which the design is printed, laminated to a paper backing. Again, the surface may also be textured or embossed, or may have a metallic appearance – the so-called vinyl foils. The result is a wall covering that is much tougher than a washable type; it can be scrubbed to remove stains and

ABOVE Contrasting wall coverings can help to change the proportions of a room. Here a border at picture-rail level provides a natural break, and the darker wall covering above it helps to lower the ceiling, emphasizing the country-style décor.

LEFT In a bathroom, a vinyl wall covering resists steam and splashes well and is easy to wipe clean. Foamed types offer excellent imitations of materials such as ceramic tiles.

marks, although care must be taken not to lift the seams by oversoaking the surface. Vinyl wall coverings are widely available in ready-pasted form, and are extremely easy to strip as the plastic layer can be peeled off dry, leaving the paper backing behind on the wall. This backing can then be wetted and removed easily.

Tougher still are the foamed-vinyl wall coverings, which have a surface layer aerated with tiny bubbles to produce a slightly cushioned feel. The surface may be heavily textured or embossed to imitate materials such as ceramic tiles and wood grains, and is warm to the touch, making it a good choice for any rooms that are prone to mild condensation.

Flock wall coverings are either printed papers or vinyls on which parts of the design have a raised pile – of fine wool or silk fibres on paper types and of synthetic fibres on vinyls – that closely resembles velvet. The paper types are quite delicate and must be hung with care, but vinyl flocks are extremely tough and hardwearing.

Yet another printed wall covering is made from foamed polythene (polyethylene) with no paper backing. This is hung by pasting the wall and then brushing the covering into position direct from the roll. The surface can be washed, but is relatively fragile and will not withstand repeated scuffing or knocks. The material can be simply dry-stripped from walls and ceilings, like the plastic surface layer of a vinyl wall covering.

An alternative to a printed surface design is a texture. This can be achieved with a paper-backed fabric wall covering. The most common of these is hessian (burlap), but other materials include silk, tweed, wool strands, grasscloth and linen, offering a range of softly tinted or boldly coloured wall finishes. With the exception of hessian, these types of wall coverings

are comparatively expensive to buy. They can also be fairly difficult to hang and to remove for re-decorating, and so are really best used for decorating or highlighting small and relatively well-protected areas such as alcoves.

The other kind of textured wall covering is intended for overpainting. These materials are generally known as relief wall coverings or 'whites'. The cheapest is woodchip paper, also known as oatmeal or ingrain, which has small chips of wood sandwiched at random between a heavy backing paper and a thinner surface layer.

ABOVE A frieze with a 3-dimensional design is an unusual way of filling in above a picture rail. The embossed panels are butt-joined to form a continuous strip.

LEFT A low-relief wall covering is the ideal cover-up for a less-than-perfect wall surface, and is available in a wide range of random and regular designs.

Vinyls are also made as relief wall coverings, with a plain white aerated plastic surface layer that is moulded during manufacture into a range of random or repeating patterns.

Other relief wall coverings are embossed to produce a random or regular surface pattern. Those with a relatively low-relief design are generally two-layer duplex papers; those with more pronounced embossing are made from stronger paper containing cotton fibres rather than wood.

All the different types of relief wall coverings can be painted with either water-based (latex) or solvent-based

(oil) paints after hanging. You will need the help of a steam wallpaper stripper to remove them.

There is an additional type of wall covering: lining (liner) paper. As its name suggests, this is a plain paper used for lining wall surfaces that are in poor condition, or that have uneven or zero porosity, before a decorative wall covering is hung. It comes in weights from 55 g per sq m/360 lb per sq yd up to 90 g per sq m/600 lb per sq yd, and in 2 grades, white and extra-white. The latter can also be used as an economy wall covering, and is hung in the usual way and then overpainted.

PAPERHANGING TOOLS AND EQUIPMENT

As for painting, there are 2 distinct groups of tools, equipment and materials to deal with wall coverings.

Stripping tools

The basic technique for removing an old wall covering is to soften the paste used to stick it to the wall so that it can be scraped off and discarded. To strip porous materials such as ordinary printed paper and the backing paper left behind after dry-stripping vinyl wall covering, use a bucket of water and a sponge or a garden spray gun to apply the water, dust sheets (drop cloths) to protect floor coverings, and a broad-bladed scraping knife to remove the softened paper.

To remove wall coverings with a water-resistant plastic or painted surface, it is necessary to pierce the surface film and so allow the water to penetrate. This can be done with a serrated wallpaper scraper or preferably a toothed roller or wheel, which is rolled backwards and forwards over the surface to create hundreds of little perforations. The water will take longer to penetrate this type of wall covering.

Stripping can be speeded up dramatically on coated wall coverings (and also on paper-backed fabrics and texture paints) by using a steam stripper. This consists of a perforated steaming plate and a water reservoir heated by electricity or bottled gas. Steam penetrates the surface far more quickly than water does, enabling the covering to be stripped more quickly and effectively.

Paperhanging tools

There are 4 separate operations involved in hanging a new wall covering: cutting to length, pasting, hanging and trimming.

For cutting, the tools are a retractable steel tape measure, a pencil and a pair of scissors (or a sharp utility knife and a steel straightedge).

For pasting the wall covering, there should be a bucket in which to mix the paste (unless using ready-mixed tub paste), plus a stirrer and a brush with which to apply the paste. A standard 10 cm/4 in wide paintbrush is usually satisfactory, but special pasting brushes can be bought.

When choosing the paste, follow the instructions for the wall covering concerned. In particular, remember that a paste containing a fungicide should be used for washable and vinyl coverings, to prevent mould from growing in the paste as it slowly dries under the impervious covering.

A special overlap adhesive is needed for lap joints in internal and external corners when using washables or vinyls.

All that is needed when hanging a ready-pasted wall covering is a large plastic soaking trough in which you can immerse the rolled-up lengths of wall covering.

Before starting hanging, a plumb bob and line are needed to mark a true vertical line on the wall against which to hang the first length.

Most wall coverings are applied with a special soft-bristled paperhanging brush. These are generally between 19 cm/7½ in and 25 cm/10 in wide, and have a slim handle. The soft

bristles help to make the wall covering follow the contours of the wall surface beneath, and also eliminate undue hand contact with the face of the covering, which might mark it.

A sponge can be used instead of a brush for hanging washables or vinyls, especially if they are ready-pasted, since here the sponge helps to mop water from the surface of the wall covering as well as smoothing it into place.

The final stage is trimming, and the best tool for this is a special pair of paperhangers' scissors. These have blades up to 30 cm/12 in long for making long, straight cuts.

For papering walls, a stepladder is needed which should be tall enough to enable the ceiling to be easily touched. For papering ceilings, set up a proper platform across the width of the room at a comfortable height, using scaffold boards or staging on trestles or other low supports to ensure complete stability. Do not step from chair to chair or set up similar dangerous makeshift arrangements.

PASTING TABLES

A flat surface is needed to lay the paper on while it is being pasted. It is best to use a proper pasting table. This is a lightweight folding table covered in hardboard or plywood on a softwood frame, and is usually about 1.8 m/6 ft long and just wider than a standard roll of wall covering. If you cannot buy, borrow or hire a pasting table, one can he improvised by cutting a standard sheet of plywood or chipboard (particle board) down to the same width and supporting it on trestles or sawhorses.

SEAM ROLLERS

For smooth wall coverings, a tool called a seam roller can be used to make sure that the seams are well bonded to the wall. Do not use a seam roller on textured or embossed wall coverings, though, as it will flatten the embossing.

OPPOSITE Displayed on a fold-up pasting table are a soaking trough (1), rubber gloves (2), sponge (3), pencil (4), sharp utility knife (5), paperhangers' scissors (6), plumb bob and line (7), retractable steel tape measure (8), steel straightedge (9), paste bucket (10), pasting brush (11), packet of ready-mixed paste (12), seam roller (13) and paperhanging brush (14). A spirit level (15) can do double duty in checking verticals and as a straightedge.

PREPARING FOR PAPERHANGING

Unrestricted access is a must for paperhanging. If working on just the walls, move all the furniture to the centre of the room and cover it with dust sheets (drop cloths). When tackling the ceiling too, it is best to remove all the furniture completely if there is space to store it elsewhere in the house; otherwise group it at one end of the room so that most of the ceiling can be done, and then move it to the other end to complete the job.

Next, take down curtains and blinds (drapes and shades) and remove wall- or ceiling-mounted tracks. Turn off the electricity supply at the mains, then disconnect and remove wall or ceiling light fittings as necessary, covering the bare wire ends thoroughly with insulating tape before restoring the power supply to the rest of the house. In the USA, ceiling roses, wall switch plates and socket outlets can be unscrewed and removed without

disconnecting the wall receptacles or switches. Isolate, drain, disconnect and remove radiators, and unscrew their wall brackets. Call in a professional electrician or plumber for these jobs if you are unsure of how to do them safely.

Take down pictures, and remove other wall-mounted fittings such as shelves and display units. To make it easy to locate the screw holes afterwards, push a matchstick (wooden match) into each one (*see Tip*).

CHOOSING THE STARTING POINT

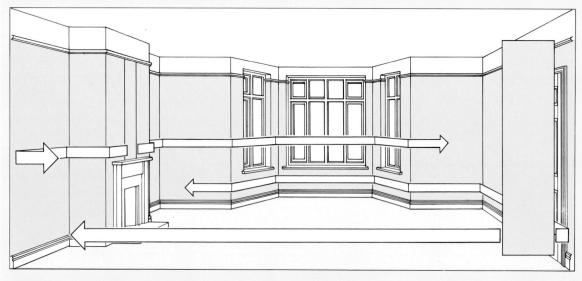

ABOVE Start paperhanging at the centre of a chimney breast (fireplace projection) if the wall covering has a large, dominant pattern. Otherwise start next to the door so the inevitable pattern break can be disguised above it.

RIGHT Work outwards from the centre of a dormer window so the design is centred on the window recess.

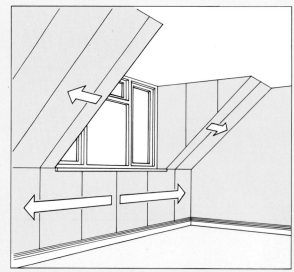

ESTIMATING WALL COVERINGS

Height	Distance around room																	
	9 m 30 ft	10 m 33 ft	12 m 40 ft	13 m 42 ft	14 m 46 ft	15 m 50 ft	16 m 52 ft	17 m 56 ft	19 m 62 ft	20 m 66 ft	21 m 69 ft	22 m 72 ft	23 m 75 ft	25 m 82 ft	26 m 85 ft	27 m 88 ft	28 m 92 ft	30 m 98 ft
2.15–2.30 m/7–7½ ft	4	5	5	6	6	7	7	8	8	9	9	10	10	11	12	12	13	13
2.30–2.45 m/7½–8 ft	5	5	6	6	7	7	8	8	9	9	10	10	11	11	12	13	13	14
2.45–2.60 m/8–8½ ft	5	5	6	7	7	8	9	9	10	10	11	12	12	13	14	14	15	15
2.60–2.75 m/8½–9 ft	5	5	6	7	7	8	9	9	10	10	11	12	12	13	14	14	15	15
2.75–2.90 m/9–9½ ft	6	6	7	7	8	9	9	10	10	11	12	12	13	14	14	15	15	16
2.90–3.05 m/9½–10 ft	6	6	7	8	8	9	10	10	11	12	12	13	14	14	15	16	16	17
3.05–3.20 m/10–10½ ft	6	7	8	8	9	10	10	11	12	13	13	14	15	16	16	17	18	19

Numbers are based on a standard roll size of 10.05 m/33 ft long and 50 cm/20½ in wide. Room measurement includes all windows and doorway.

If the walls and ceiling are at present painted, they need washing down to remove dirt, grease, smoke stains and the like. If they are decorated with another wall covering, this will have to be removed and any defects in the surface put right. Finally, they need sizing – treating with a diluted coat of wallpaper adhesive to even out the porosity of the surface and to help to improve the 'slip' of the pasted wall covering during hanging.

Measuring up

The next job is to estimate how many rolls of wall covering will be needed to decorate the room. If using a material that comes in standard-sized rolls, simply measure the room dimensions and refer to the charts given here for the number of rolls needed to cover the walls and ceiling. They allow for a typical door and window area; fewer rolls are needed for a room with large picture windows or wide door openings. If using a paper-backed cloth covering which comes in a non-standard width, measure up each wall, and ask the supplier to estimate what length of material you will need; such materials

are too expensive to waste. Wall coverings in the USA vary in width and length but are usually available in rolls sized to cover a specified area, allowing for trimming.

Buying wall coverings

Wall coverings are made in batches, with a number printed on the label, and it is important to check that there

are sufficient rolls with the same batch number; colours may not match exactly between batches.

When hanging a wall covering with a particularly large pattern repeat, wastage is often unusually high and it may be wise to purchase one or two extra rolls, over and above the numbers given in the charts. Most suppliers will take back unopened rolls.

ESTIMATING CEILING COVERINGS

Distance around room		No of
m	ft	rolls
12	40	2
13	42	3
14	46	3
15	50	4
16	52	4
17	56	4
18	59	5
19	62	5
20	66	5
21	69	6
22	72	7
23	75	7

TIP

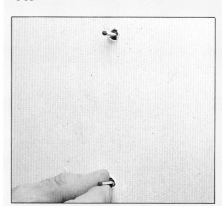

Insert a matchstick (wooden match) in each hole left when unscrewing wall-mounted fixtures and fittings that will be replaced afterwards. The match will burst through the wall covering as this is applied and will make it easy to find the screw holes.

STRIPPING OLD WALL COVERINGS

Formerly when ordinary printed wall coverings were all that were readily available, it was common practice to paper over existing wallpaper, often to the point where four or five successive layers would accumulate. This is no longer considered acceptable (and will not work at all over today's washable and vinyl wall coverings), and it is always best to strip all old coverings before hanging new ones. Even if the old material looks sound, hanging a newly pasted wall covering over it may cause it to lift from the wall, creating ugly bubbles that are impossible to disguise. This also applies to the backing paper that is left on the wall after dry-stripping a vinyl wall covering; there is no guarantee that it is perfectly bonded to the wall, and so hanging another wall covering over it could give very poor results.

Once the room is cleared and dust sheets (drop cloths) are spread over the floor and any remaining furniture, the next step is to identify what type of wall covering is to be removed. An ordinary printed paper will absorb water splashed on it immediately; other types will not. To tell washables from vinyls, pick and lift a corner and try to strip the dry wall covering. The printed plastic layer of a vinyl wall covering will peel off dry, but the surface of a washable paper will not come off in the same way unless it is a duplex paper made in two layers. With paper-backed fabric wall coverings, it is often possible to peel the fabric away from its paper backing; try this before turning to more complicated methods of removal.

1 To strip printed wallpapers, wet the surface with a sponge or a garden spray gun. Wait for the water to penetrate, and repeat if necessary.

2 Using a stiff wallpaper scraper – not a filling (putty) knife – start scraping the old paper from the wall at a seam. If necessary, wet the surface again while you are working.

3 Turn off the power before stripping around switches and other fittings, then loosen the faceplate screws to strip the wallpaper behind the fitting.

4 After removing the bulk of the old wallpaper, go back over the wall surface and remove any remaining 'nibs' of paper with a sponge or spray gun and a scraper.

5 To strip a washable wallpaper, start by scoring the plastic coating with a serrated scraper or toothed roller, then soak and scrape the wallpaper as before.

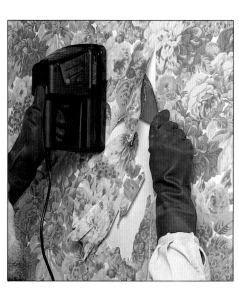

6 For quicker results, use a steam stripper to remove washable papers. Press the steaming plate to the next area of the wall while stripping the area just steamed.

STRIPPING VINYLS

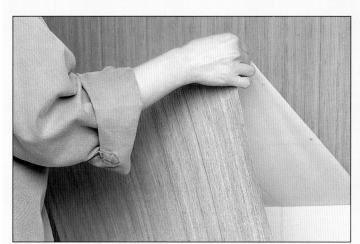

1 Strip vinyl wall coverings by lifting a corner to separate the vinyl layer from the paper backing. Strip it off by pulling it away from the wall surface.

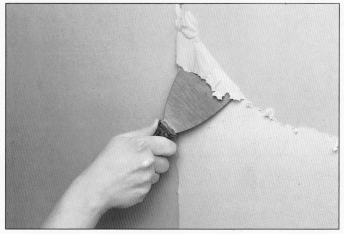

2 Always soak and remove the plain backing paper left on the wall after stripping away the vinyl. It may well not be a sound lining for a new wall covering.

REMOVING OTHER OLD FINISHES

If the wall or ceiling to be given a new covering is painted or wallpapered, preparing the surface for its new finish is quite straightforward. However, if it was previously covered with materials such as texture paint, ceramic or polystyrene (plastic foam) tiles or wall panelling, more work will be needed to remove the old finishes and return the surface to its original condition.

Textured finishes are tackled in different ways, depending on their type. Texture paints are basically thick water-based (latex) paints, normally used to create relatively low-relief effects, and can be removed with specially formulated paint removers. Some textured effects formed with a powder or ready-mixed compound are best removed with a steam wallpaper stripper, which softens the compound so that it can be easily scraped away from the wall.

Never attempt to sand off a textured finish. There are two reasons. The first is that it will create huge quantities of very fine dust; the second is that older versions of this product contained asbestos fibres as a filler, and any action that might release these into the atmosphere as inhalable dust must be avoided at all costs.

For tiles and wall panelling, complete removal or a cover-up with plasterboard (gypsum board) are the two options available. The former will leave a surface in need of considerable renovation, while the latter will cause a slight loss of space within the room, as well as some complications at door and window openings.

REMOVING TEXTURED FINISHES

1 Strip texture paint by brushing on a generous coat of a proprietary texture paint remover. Stipple it well into the paint and leave it to penetrate.

2 When the paint has softened, scrape it off with a broad-bladed scraper. Wear gloves, and also safety goggles if working on a ceiling.

3 Once the bulk of the coating has been removed, use wire wool dipped in the paint remover to strip off any remaining flecks of paint.

4 Remove powder-based or ready-mixed types using a steam stripper, which will soften the finish. Never try to sand off this type of finish.

REMOVING CERAMIC TILES

1 On a completely tiled wall, use a hammer to crack a tile and create a starting point for the stripping. On partly tiled walls, always start at the tile edge.

2 Use a broad bolster (stonecutter's) chisel and a club (spalling) hammer to chip the old tiles off the wall. Have the wall replastered afterwards rather than trying to patch the surface.

REMOVING POLYSTYRENE (PLASTIC FOAM) TILES

1 Lever the tiles away from the ceiling with a scraper. If they were fixed with a continuous coat of adhesive, consider temporarily covering the tiles with heavy lining paper. For the best finish, fit a new plasterboard (gypsum board) ceiling, nailing through to the ceiling joists.

2 If the tiles were fixed in place with blobs of adhesive, use a heat gun to soften the old adhesive so it can be removed with a broad-bladed scraper.

REMOVING WALL PANELLING

1 The last board to be fixed will have been nailed to the fixing grounds through its face. Use a nail punch to drive the nails in and free the board.

2 The other boards will have been secret-nailed through their tongues. Use a crowbar (wrecking bar) to prise them away from their grounds.

3 Finally, prise the grounds off the wall, and use a claw hammer or crowbar with some protective packing to lever the fixing nails out of the wall.

PREPARING SURFACES FOR COVERING

Once the previous wall and ceiling decorations have been removed the next task is to restore any defects in the surfaces to be covered, and then to prepare them so that they present the perfect substrate for successful paperhanging.

The first step is to put down some heavy-duty plastic sheeting on the floor to catch splashes, and then to wash down the bare wall and ceiling surfaces thoroughly with strong household detergent or sugar soap (all-purpose cleaner), working from the bottom up on walls, and then to rinse them off with clean water, working this time from top to bottom on walls. Turn off the electricity supply first in case water gets into light switches and socket outlets (receptacles). Leave the surfaces to dry out thoroughly.

Next, repair defects such as cracks, holes and other surface damage which may have been concealed by the previous decorations, or even caused by their removal.

Finally, treat the wall and ceiling surfaces with a coat of size or diluted wallpaper paste, and leave this to dry before starting paperhanging. Size seals porous plaster, providing a surface with even absorption, and also makes it easier to slide the pasted lengths of wall covering into position on the wall.

PREPARING WALLS AND CEILINGS

1 Wash wall surfaces with sugar soap (all-purpose cleaner) or detergent, working from the bottom up, then rinse them with clean water, working from the top down.

2 Wash ceilings with a floor mop or squeegee, after disconnecting and removing light fittings. Again, rinse off with clean water.

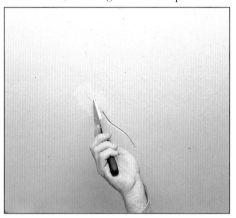

3 Fill cracks, holes and other defects in the wall and ceiling surfaces as appropriate, leave the filler to harden and then sand the repair down flush.

4 Apply a coat of size or diluted wallpaper paste to wall and ceiling surfaces that are to be papered, and leave them to dry before starting paperhanging.

CROSS-LINING

If the wall surface is in poor condition, has been previously decorated with gloss paint or is being decorated with a thin fabric wall covering, it is best to hang lining (liner) paper first. This is usually hung horizontally rather than vertically, with butt joints between lengths and with ends and edges trimmed just short of adjacent ceiling and wall surfaces. Use the same type of paste for the lining paper as for the subsequent wall covering.

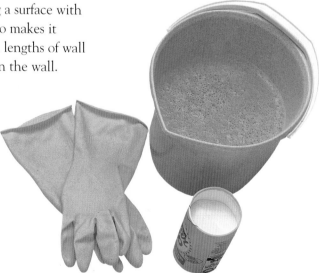

MEASURING AND CUTTING TO LENGTH

1 For quick and easy calculations, mark the length of the pasting table at 30 cm/12 in intervals using a pencil and metal straightedge.

2 Measure the length of wall covering needed for the drop, including trim allowances, and mark this on the paper. Cut the first piece to length.

PASTING WALL COVERINGS

1 Face the light to make it easy to spot any unpasted areas – they look dull, not shiny. Apply a generous band of paste down the centre of the length.

2 Align one edge of the wall covering with the edge of the pasting table, then brush the paste out towards that edge from the centre band.

3 Draw the length across to the other edge of the table, and apply paste out to that edge too. Check that there are no dry or thinly pasted areas.

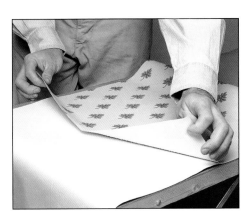

4 Continue pasting until the end of the table is reached. Then lift the pasted end of the wall covering and fold it over on itself, pasted side to pasted side.

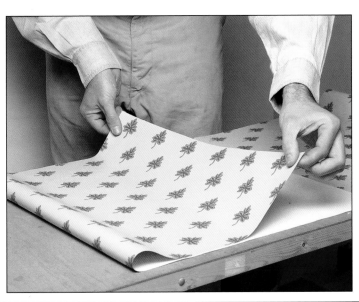

5 Slide the paper along the table so the folded section hangs down. Paste the rest of the length and fold the opposite end over on itself.

HANGING THE FIRST LENGTH

The first length of wall covering must be hung correctly if the decoration of the rest of the room is to go according to plan. The first thing to do, therefore, is to decide on exactly where to hang this. The usual starting point is close to the door, just less than the wall-covering's width away from the frame, so that the inevitable pattern discontinuity that will occur on returning to the starting point can be concealed on the short join above the door. If you are using a wall covering with a large design motif in a room which has a chimney breast (fireplace projection), it is preferable to start paperhanging on the chimney breast itself so that the design can be centred on it. When papering only part of a room, the starting point should be just less than the width of the wall covering from one corner of the room, to allow the edge of the covering to be trimmed accurately into the corner angle.

Next, use a roll of wall covering as a yardstick and mark off successive widths around the room walls with a pencil to check that there will not be any joins on external corners such as the sides of window reveals. If these occur, move the starting point along by about 5 cm/ 2 in and then re-check the positions of the joins all round.

Finally, mark a true vertical line on the wall at the chosen starting point, using a pencil and a plumb bob and line. Failure to do this could result in the pattern starting to run seriously out of alignment as you hang successive lengths, with disastrous results.

Other paperhanging techniques

As well as the traditional method of pasting the wall covering on a pasting table and then hanging it, you may sometimes also need to use 2 other techniques. The first is hanging ready-pasted wall coverings, which are growing in popularity, and the second is hanging speciality wall coverings.

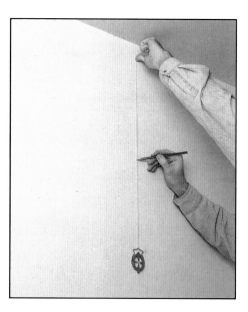

1 At your chosen starting point, use a plumb bob and line to mark a vertical line on the wall surface. Join up the pencil marks using a straightedge.

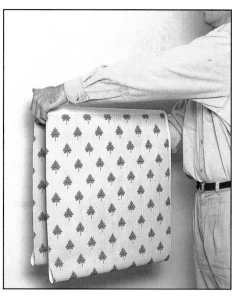

2 Fetch the first length of pasted wall covering, having left it to soak for the time recommended on the label. Carry it draped over your arm.

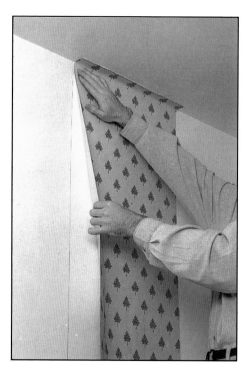

3 Unfold the upper flap and press the top edge of the length against the wall. Slide it across the wall until the edge lines up with your marked line. Use a paperhanging brush (or a sponge for washables and vinyls) to smooth the covering into place, working from the middle outwards.

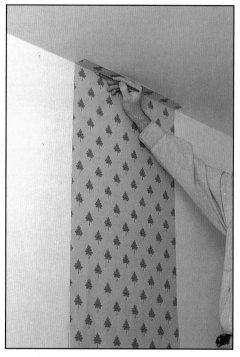

4 Use a pencil or the curved back of paperhanging-scissors blades to mark the trimming line at ceiling level. Do the same at floor level.

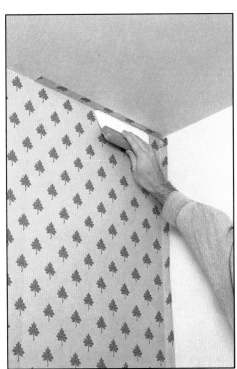

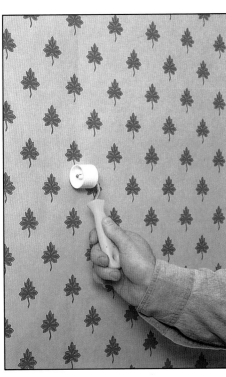

5 Peel the end of the length away from the wall so that you can trim the excess using scissors. Brush the end back into place. Repeat at the bottom.

6 Hang the next drop with the lengths exactly edge to edge. Brush the wall covering into the wall/ceiling angle and into the internal angle.

7 On flat wall coverings, run a seam roller down the joins to ensure that they stick securely. Never use a seam roller on embossed or relief wall coverings, as this will ruin the pattern.

Hanging ready-pasted wall coverings could not be easier. The back of the wall covering – usually a washable or vinyl type – is coated during manufacture with an even layer of dried paste. To activate this, simply cut the length that you need, roll it up with the top of the length on the outside of the roll, and immerse it in water. Special soaking troughs are sold by most wall-covering suppliers, and are intended to be placed next to the skirting (baseboard) beneath the point at which the length is to be hung. Fill the trough with cold (not hot) water, immerse the length and then draw it upwards on to the wall so that all the excess water drains back into the soaking trough. Hang and trim the covering in the usual way.

Many speciality wall coverings are designed to be hung by pasting the wall itself, rather than the covering, which some people find easier. Some types of coverings also have untrimmed edges, which need to be cut after overlapping adjoining lengths, but this is simple to do.

HANGING A READY-PASTED WALL COVERING

1 Place the trough next to the wall, fill it with cold water and immerse the rolled-up length in it, with the top end outermost, for the recommended time.

2 At the end of the soaking time, grasp the top end of the length and draw it upwards so that the excess water runs off and back into the trough.

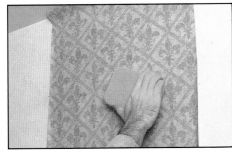

3 Slide the top of the length into position on the wall, aligning it with a marked line or butting it up against its neighbour. Take care not to step in the trough.

4 Use a sponge rather than a paperhanging brush to smooth the length into place on the wall – this will help to absorb excess water from the surface.

PAPERHANGING AROUND CORNERS

In a perfect world, rooms would have corners that were truly square and truly vertical, and it would be possible to hang a wall covering all around the room in a continuous operation, simply turning the lengths that ran into the room corners straight on to the adjoining walls. In reality, corners are seldom square or true, and, if the covering were hung in this way, lengths would be vertical on the first wall but could be running well off the vertical by the time they returned to the starting point. This would be visually disastrous, with vertical pattern elements out of alignment at corners, and sloping horizontal pattern features.

The way to avoid these problems is to complete each wall with a cut-down strip that only just turns on to the next wall. Then hang the remainder of the strip with its machine-cut edge against a newly drawn vertical line on the second wall, so that you can trim its other edge to follow the internal angle precisely. Any slight discontinuity of pattern will not be noticeable except to the very closest scrutiny, and the remaining lengths on the second wall will be hung truly vertically. The same applies to paperhanging around external corners.

PAPERING AN INTERNAL CORNER

1 Hang the last full length before the corner of the room, then measure the distance to the corner from the edge of the length and add about 12 mm/½ in.

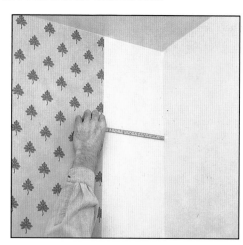

2 Use a pencil and straightedge to mark a strip of the required width, measured from the relevant edge (here, the left one), and cut it from the length.

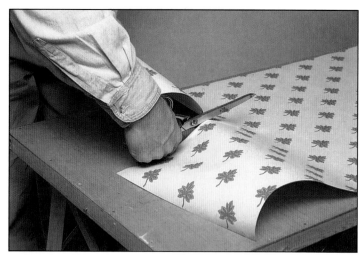

PAPERING TIP

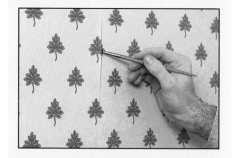

If a seam refuses to lie flat because it was inadequately pasted and has begun to dry out, brush a little paste underneath it and roll with a seam roller.

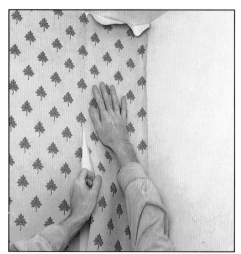

3 Paste the strip and hang it in the usual way, allowing the hand-cut edge to lap on to the adjoining wall. Trim the top and bottom edges as usual.

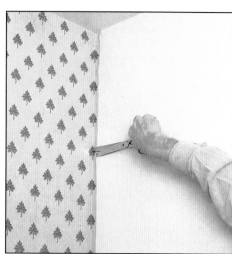

4 Brush the tongue into the internal angle. If it will not lie flat because the corner is out of true, make small release cuts in the edge and brush it flat.

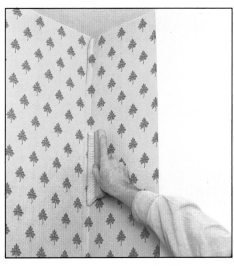

5 Measure the width of the remaining strip, subtract 12 mm/½ in and mark a fresh vertical line on the adjoining wall at this distance from the corner.

6 Hang the strip to the marked line, brushing the wall covering into the angle so that it just turns on to the surface of the first wall.

7 Use the back of the scissors blades to mark the line of the corner on the wall covering, then cut along the line and smooth the cut edge back into the angle. Use special overlap adhesive when using washables and vinyls on all lap joints.

PAPERING AN EXTERNAL CORNER

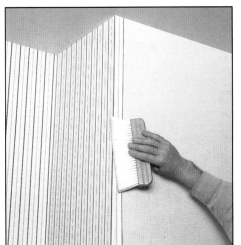

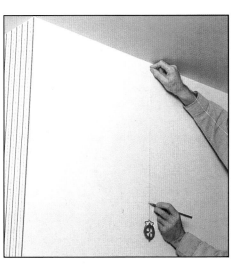

1 Plan the starting point so that lengths turn external corners by about 2.5 cm/1 in. Brush the paper on to the next wall, making small cuts so that it lies flat.

2 Carefully tear off a narrow strip of the wall covering along the turned edge to leave a 'feathered' edge that will not show through the next length.

3 Mark a vertical line on the next wall surface, at a distance from the corner equal to the width of the wall covering plus about 6 mm/¼ in.

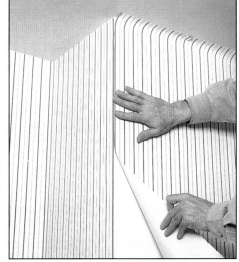

4 Hang the next full length to the marked line, with its other edge overlapping the feathered edge of the strip turned from the previous wall.

5 Brush this length into position, trim it at the top and bottom as before, and run a seam roller down the overlap (do not do this on embossed or textured wall coverings). Again, use a special overlap adhesive with washable and vinyl coverings.

PAPERHANGING AROUND DOORS AND WINDOWS

Paperhanging on flat, uninterrupted walls is quite straightforward, calling only for the basic positioning and trimming techniques. Turning corners is only slightly more difficult. The trouble is that rooms also contain doors and windows, as well as wall-mounted fittings and fixtures such as light switches and socket outlets (receptacles). Paperhanging around these obstacles can be fairly tricky, but there are procedures for dealing with them successfully.

Doors and window frames fitted flush with the internal wall surface present few problems; all that is necessary here is to trim the wall covering so that it finishes flush with the edge of the architrave (trim) or casing. Where the window or door is recessed, however, you will need to do some careful patching-in of extra pieces in order to cover all the surfaces of the reveal. It is also important in this case to select the correct starting point, to avoid joins between lengths falling on the external corners of such reveals; always check this point before beginning paper-hanging, and adjust the starting point by about 5 cm/2 in if it will occur.

Paperhanging around electrical fittings (fixtures) is fairly easy. Always turn off the power supply to the accessory first. The idea is to make diagonal cuts over the faceplate, cut away most of the resulting triangular tongues and tuck what remains behind the loosened faceplate. Do not do this with vinyl foils, which can conduct electricity; instead, simply trim the covering flush with the edges of the accessory faceplate. In the USA, it is possible to remove wall plates and socket outlets separately without disconnect-ing the wall receptacles or switches, which makes the task of paperhanging around them much simpler.

PAPERING AROUND A FLUSH DOOR OR WINDOW

1 On reaching a flush door or a window frame, hang the previous length as normal. Then hang the next length to overlap the door or window frame.

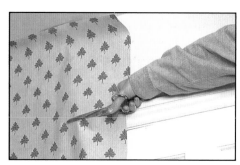

2 Cut away the unwanted wall covering to within about 2.5 cm/1 in of the edge of the architrave (trim) or window casing, and discard the waste strip.

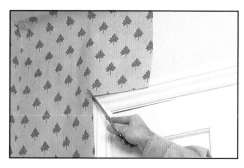

3 Press the covering against the frame so that its corner is visible, and make a diagonal cut from the waste edge of the paper to the mark.

4 Use a paperhanging brush to press the tongues of paper well into the angles between the wall and the door architrave or window casing.

5 Carefully peel back the tongues and cut along the marked lines with paperhanging scissors. Brush the trimmed edges back into position.

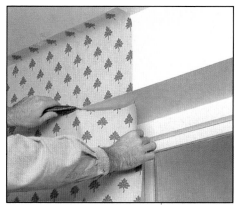

1 On reaching a recessed door or window frame, hang the previous length as normal. Then hang the next length, allowing it to overlap the recess.

2 Carefully make a horizontal cut into the overlapping edge, level with the underside of the reveal, to allow the central portion of the length to cover the side wall.

PAPERING AROUND AN ELECTRICAL FITTING (FIXTURE)

Always turn off the power supply before you begin. Make diagonal cuts in the paper towards the corners, trim off the triangles and tuck the edges behind the loosened faceplate.

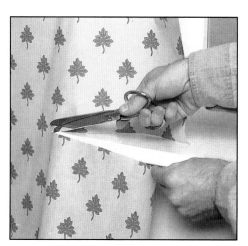

3 On a recessed window, make a similar cut lower down the length, level with the top surface of the window sill. Trim it to fit round the end of the sill.

4 Cut a patch to fit on the underside of the reveal, big enough to turn on to the adjoining wall and frame surfaces. Press it well into the internal angles.

5 Tear along the edges of the patch that will be covered when you brush the piece above the reveal and the tongue covering its side wall into place.

6 Trim the edges of the patch and tongue to meet the frame neatly. Hang full widths when you reach the other side of the reveal, and repeat steps 1–6.

PAINTING AND PAPERHANGING

PAPERING STAIRWELLS

Paperhanging in stairwells is no different in principle from work in any other room. However, the job is made more difficult by the need to handle longer lengths of wall covering, and also because access to the higher reaches of the stairwell walls can be awkward. It is a job that requires careful planning, and is best tackled with the assistance of a second person.

First of all, work out the starting point. It is best to hang the longest drop – the one that reaches from landing ceiling to hall floor – first of all. Mark its position and check that other joins will not fall awkwardly round the rest of the stairwell, especially if it has a window opening onto it. Adjust if necessary.

The next thing to do is to work out how to gain access to the various wall surfaces involved without obstructing passage up and down the stairwell or blocking off the walls themselves. On a straight flight it may be possible to use components from a hired slot-together scaffold tower to make a suitable working platform. On flights with quarter or half-landings it will probably be necessary to tailor-make an assembly of ladder sections, stepladders, homemade supports and scaffold boards; two typical arrangements are shown below. Nail scrap wood to stair treads to locate ladder feet securely, and lock scaffold boards together by drilling holes through them where they overlap and dropping a bolt through the holes (no need for a nut). Note that ladders or steps shown resting against wall surfaces will have to be repositioned as the work progresses.

ACCESS EQUIPMENT FOR STAIRWELLS

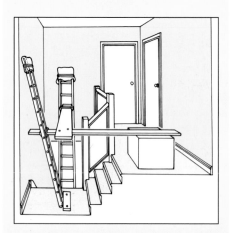

Use a selection of ladders, steps, scaffold boards and homemade supports to construct a platform that allows access to all the wall surfaces being decorated without obstructing the stairs themselves.

THE STARTING POINT

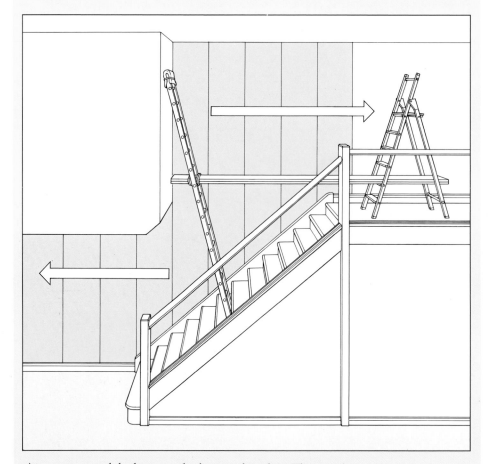

Aim to start work by hanging the longest drop first. Then work along the stairwell walls in sequence, turning corners and tackling obstacles as for other rooms.

1 Fold up long lengths of wall covering concertina-fashion with the top end of the length uppermost, and carry them to the stairs supported over the arm.

2 Get a helper to support the folds of wall covering while positioning the top end of the length on the stairwell wall against a vertical line.

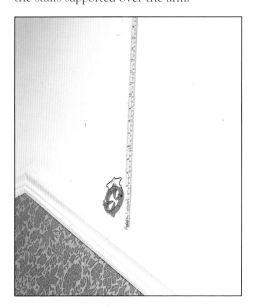

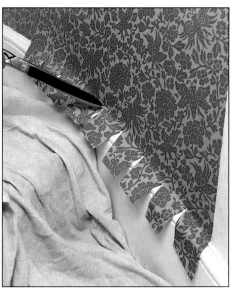

3 When measuring lengths that will meet a dado (chair) rail or skirting (baseboard) at an angle, remember to measure the longer edge of the length.

4 Where the bottom edge of the length meets a shaped skirting, make small release cuts in the edge and trim it to follow the curve.

PAPERING AROUND OBSTACLES

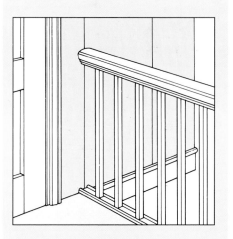

Where the end of a handrail fits flush with the wall, cut the lower part of the length into two strips so their edges can be trimmed around the rail and joined edge-to-edge beneath it. Use a similar technique to fit the wall covering around a flush newel post.

PAPERING CEILINGS

Many people regard the papering of ceilings with horror. In reality they are easier to deal with than walls because they are flat, do not have any awkward angles (except in rooms with sloping ceilings and dormer windows), and have few obstacles attached to them apart from the occasional light fitting (fixture), which can in any case usually be removed quite easily.

The only thing that takes getting used to when papering ceilings is working on an upside-down surface, but the basic technique is no different from working on walls. The wall covering is simply positioned, brushed into place and then trimmed where it meets adjoining surfaces.

The most important thing to plan carefully is access equipment that will safely allow a complete length to be hung across the room. Nothing is more dangerous than attempting to step from chair to chair; proper access is a must. The best solution is to use scaffold boards or lengths of staging, supported by stepladders, trestles or home-made supports to create a flat, level walkway spanning the room from wall to wall at a height that allows the ceiling to be reached comfortably. It will take only a few seconds to reposition after hanging each length, ready for the next.

This is also a job where an additional pair of hands will be a big help, at least before gaining the knack of supporting a concertina of pasted wall covering with one hand while brushing it into position with the other – this can be done only with practice.

The first length should be hung to a guideline on the ceiling. The best way of marking this is with a chalked line, held against the ceiling at both ends and snapped against it. Use red chalk for a white ceiling.

1 Paste the wall covering in the usual way, but fold it up concertina-fashion with the starting end of the length folded over on itself. Lining (liner) paper has been used here.

ACCESS EQUIPMENT FOR CEILINGS

Set up an access platform across the room, using scaffold boards supported on staging or stepladders, to create a walkway at a height that allows the ceiling to be comfortably reached.

2 Hang the first length to a chalked line just less than the width of the wall covering from the side wall. Support the folds on a spare roll of wall covering.

The shape of an arch makes it impossible to get a pattern match along the curved join. It is best to choose a wall covering with a small design motif and a random pattern, to use different but complementary designs for the face walls and the arch surface, or to use lining (liner) paper inside the arch and paint it a plain colour.

To paper an arched recess, cover the face and back walls first turning cut tongues of wall covering onto the arched surface. Then cover the arch surface as described below.

3 Trim the overlaps at the ends and along the side wall. Then hang the second length in the same way, butted up against the edge of the first length.

4 On meeting a pendant light fitting (fixture) pierce the wall covering over its centre and make a series of radial cuts outwards from the pierced point.

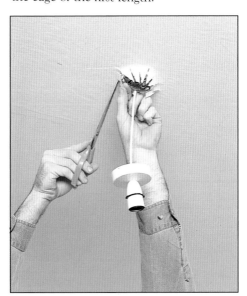

5 With the power turned off at the mains, unscrew the cover and trim the tongues off, flush with the base of the fitting. Replace the cover.

6 Where the ceiling runs into an alcove, cut the wall covering in line with the side wall of the recess and brush it into place. Trim off the waste section.

To paper a through archway, hang the wall covering on the two face walls and trim out the waste to leave an overlap of about 25 mm/1 in all around. Make cuts in the edge so that the tongues can be turned on to the arch surface. Then cut a strip of wall covering a fraction narrower than the width of the arch surface and long enough to cover it in one piece, and brush this into place. Work from the bottom of one side upwards to the top of the arch, and then down the other side. Always use special overlap adhesive with washables and vinyls.

PUTTING UP FRIEZES AND BORDERS

Friezes and borders are narrow strips of printed paper or vinyl wall covering sold in rolls, and often come in colours and designs that complement wall coverings and fabrics manufactured by the same firm. A frieze is usually applied as a horizontal band running around the room, and can be positioned at ceiling level or next to a picture rail or dado (chair) rail. Borders, on the other hand, are used either to frame features of the room such as a door or window opening, or to create decorative panels on wall or ceiling surfaces – perhaps to frame a group of pictures, for example. They come in a range of widths.

Friezes and borders are available in plain and self-adhesive versions. The former is pasted in the same way as an ordinary wall covering, so this type is ideal for use on walls that have been painted or decorated with a plain printed wallpaper. If a border or frieze is to go over a washable or vinyl wall covering, use a special overlap adhesive or choose a self-adhesive type since ordinary wallpaper paste will not stick to the surface of the covering. Simply cut these to length, then peel off the backing paper bit by bit while positioning the length on the wall.

APPLYING A FRIEZE

1 Decide on the precise position of the frieze or border, then measure the distance from a nearby feature, such as a ceiling.

2 Use a spirit level and pencil to draw true horizontal and vertical guidelines on the wall or ceiling at the marked position.

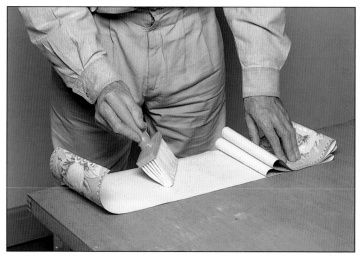

3 Cut the frieze or border to length and carefully apply paste to the length. Fold it up concertina-fashion while working along it.

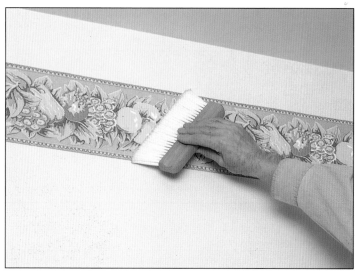

4 Offer the free end of the concertina up to the marked line and brush it into place. It will help to have a second person for hanging long lengths.

TIP

To gauge the effect a frieze or border will have, and to decide on the best position for it, stick lengths to the wall surface with masking tape before fixing them up permanently.

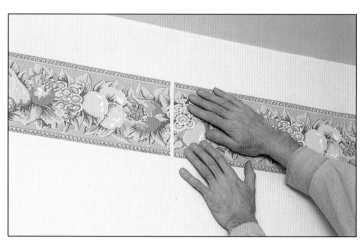

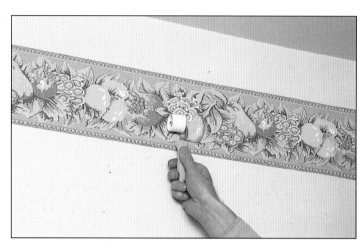

5 Join successive lengths end-to-end when starting a new roll. If the pattern does not match, overlap the ends so that it does and cut through both layers.

6 Finally, check that all horizontal edges and vertical joints are well bonded to the wall by running over them with a seam roller. Remove excess paste.

APPLYING A BORDER

1 Put up the individual lengths of a border in the same way as a frieze. To form corners, overlap the lengths at right angles and cut through both layers at 45°.

2 Peel away the two waste sections and press the neatly mitred ends back into place. Adjust their positions if necessary to get a perfect joint.

3 The finished corner joint, pictured above, shows how accurate alignment and careful cutting result in a neat joint with the pattern meeting evenly along the mitred cuts.

TILING

Tiles have a long pedigree in the interior decoration business. Faience (glazed earthenware) plaques have been found in Cretan buildings dating from around 1800 BC, and a tradition of ceramic wall and floor decoration was established soon after this farther east in Syria and Persia (now Iran). Mosaic wall and floor decorations, incorporating stone (usually marble), glass and ceramic tesserae, were also a major feature of Roman interiors. The technique spread to North Africa and thence to Spain, and the Renaissance soon led to widespread use of decorative tiling all over Europe.

Probably the most important centre of ceramic tile making in Europe was Holland, where the creation of individually hand-painted tiles in a unique blue-grey colour soon made Delft famous in the early seventeenth century. From there, the use of tiles spread rapidly, and it was not long before mass production was introduced. The end product is the familiar ceramic tile we use today. The manufacturing and printing technology may have changed, and the adhesives and grouts used may have improved, but the result would be familiar to a seventeenth-century Dutchman.

The twentieth century has brought new kinds of tile, notably vinyl, linoleum and cork tiles which owe their existence to advances in plastics and resins technology. They offer a combination of properties that make them useful alternatives to traditional ceramics in a wide range of situations, and are generally much less expensive.

The following chapter explains how to work with ceramic wall tiles, since they are the most popular of the types available. A wide range of situations is dealt with, from splashbacks to whole walls, and includes information on working around obstacles such as door and window openings and on creating special effects with tiled borders and feature panels. There are also sections on using other types of wall tiles. Different types of floor tiles are also discussed, as well as how they are laid.

OPPOSITE Wall tiles have never before been available in such a profusion of styles and designs, ranging from highly glazed plain types to more rustic versions with matt or textured surfaces and patterns that look as though they have been hand-painted.

CHOOSING WALL AND FLOOR TILES

Ceramic tiles provide the most durable of all finishes in the home, whether they are used for walls, floors or work tops, and there has never been a bigger choice of colours, designs, shapes and sizes. Vinyl, lino and cork tiles offer alternative floor finishes to ceramics. They have the same advantages of ease of laying small units, combined with a surface finish that is warmer to the touch and also less noisy underfoot than their ceramic counterparts.

Ceramic tiles for walls

In today's homes, the surfaces that are tiled more often than any others are walls, especially in rooms such as the kitchen and bathroom where a hard-wearing, water-resistant and easy-clean decorative finish is required. Tile designs tend to change with fashions in interior design. Plain tiles, often with a simple border frame, are always popular, as are tiles which create a frieze effect when laid alongside one another. Some sets of tiles build up into larger designs (known as feature panels), which can look quite striking when surrounded by plain tiling.

The surface of ceramic wall tiles is no longer always highly glazed, as was traditionally the case. There are now semi-matt finishes available, too, often with a slight surface texture that softens the somewhat harsh glare of a high-gloss surface.

Tile edges have also changed over the years. Once special round-edged tiles were used for the exposed edges of tiled areas, and plain ones with unglazed square edges (known as field tiles) were used elsewhere. Nowadays tiles are either the universal type or the standard square-edged variety. The former have angled edges so that, when butted together, they leave a gap for the grouting, which fills the spaces between them. The latter, as their name suggests, have square edges and so must be positioned with the aid of spacers.

Tiles for floors and work tops

Ceramic floor tiles are a popular choice for 'heavy traffic' areas such as porches and hallways. They are generally thicker and harder-fired than wall tiles, to enable them to stand up to heavy wear. Again, a wide range of plain colours, simple textures and more elaborate designs is available. The most common shapes are squares and rectangles; hexagons are also sold in plain colours, and a popular variation is a plain octagonal tile laid with small square coloured or decorated inserts at the intersections.

Quarry tiles are unglazed ceramic floor tiles with a brown, buff or reddish colour, and are a practical choice for hallways, conservatories and country-style kitchens. They are usually laid in a mortar bed, and, once the joints have been grouted, the tiles must be sealed with boiled linseed oil or a recommended proprietary sealer. Special shaped tiles are also available for forming upstands at floor edges. Terracotta tiles look similar to quarry tiles but are larger, and are fired at lower temperatures and so are more porous. They need to be sealed in the same way as quarry tiles.

LEFT Many tile ranges include a variety of plain and patterned field tiles, teamed up with a complementary border tile, allowing the home decorator complete freedom to decide on the finished design.

BELOW Ceramic tiles provide a durable and waterproof floor surface for bathrooms. Here, coloured corner insets are used to set off the dazzling white octagonal tiles.

Mosaics

Mosaics are just tiny tiles – usually plain in colour, sometimes with a pattern – which are sold made up in sheets on an open-weave cloth backing. These sheets are laid like larger tiles in a bed of adhesive, and all the gaps, including those on the surface of the sheet, are grouted afterwards. Square mosaics are the most common, but roundels, hexagons and other interlocking shapes are also available. Mosaics intended for laying on walls and floors are made in different thicknesses, as with ordinary ceramic tiles.

Cork, vinyl and lino tiles

Cork tiles come in a small range of colours and textures. They feel warm and relatively soft underfoot, and also give some worthwhile heat and sound insulation. The cheapest types have to be sealed to protect the surface, but the more expensive vinyl-coated floor types

ABOVE Lino tiles offer a warm, attractive and durable alternative to cork or vinyl floor coverings in rooms such as kitchens and hallways. Borders can be used to frame individual tiles.

LEFT Cork is the warmest of tiled floor coverings underfoot, and when sealed is also good-looking, hardwearing and durable.

can be walked on as soon as they have been stuck down, and need little more than an occasional wash and polish to keep them in good condition.

Vinyl tiles come in a very wide range of plain and patterned types. They are generally more resilient than cork and so can be used on floors subject to fairly heavy wear, but they are a little less gentle on the feet. Some of the more expensive types give very passable

imitations of luxury floor coverings such as marble and terrazzo. Most are made in self-adhesive form and need very little maintenance.

Modern lino tiles, made from natural materials rather than the plastic resins used in vinyl tiles, offer far better performance than traditional linoleum. They come in a range of bright and subtle colours and interesting patterns, often with pre-cut borders.

TILING

TILING TOOLS AND EQUIPMENT

Tools for ceramic tiles

For almost any ceramic tiling job, large or small, the following are needed: tile adhesive; a notched adhesive spreader; some tile spacers; lengths of tile edge trim (optional); grout plus a flexible spreader; a steel tape measure; some lengths of 38 x 12 mm/1½ x ½ in softwood battening (furring strips), plus masonry pins and a hammer for supporting the tiles on large wall areas; a spirit level; a tile cutter; a tile saw; a tile file; a piece of dowel for shaping the grout lines; a pencil and felt-tip pen; some sponges and cloths for wiping and polishing. Silicone sealant or mastic (caulking) is also useful for waterproofing joints where tiling abuts baths, basins and shower trays.

Tile cutters range from the basic – an angled cutting tip attached to a handle – to elaborate cutting jigs that guarantee perfectly accurate cuts every time. A tile saw is useful for making shaped cut-outs to fit around obstacles such as pipework, and a tile file helps to smooth cut edges.

Both adhesive and grout for wall tiling are now usually sold ready-mixed in plastic tubs complete with a notched plastic spreader. For areas that will get the occasional splash or may suffer from condensation, a water-resistant adhesive and grout is perfectly adequate, but for surfaces such as shower cubicles which will have to withstand prolonged wetting it is essential to use both waterproof adhesive and waterproof grout. Always use waterproof grout on tiled worktops; ordinary grout will harbour germs.

Grout is generally white, but coloured grout is on sale and will make a feature of the grout lines (an effect that looks best with plain or fairly neutral patterned tiles).

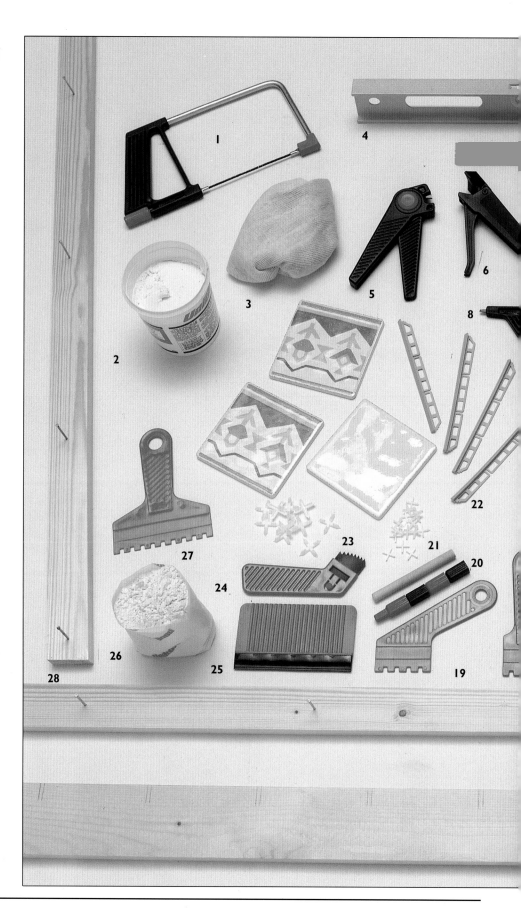

TILING TOOLS, MATERIALS AND EQUIPMENT

These include a tile saw (1), adhesive (2), a polishing cloth (3), a spirit level (4), tile edge nippers (5), a tile cutter/snapper (6) or a tiling jig (7), a tile scriber (8), a tile cutter with width and angle jig (9), a heavy duty tile cutter (10), tile files (11) or a tile edge sander with abrasive strips (12), masking tape (13), masonry nails (14), a hammer (15), a home-made tile gauge (16), a retractable steel measure (17), a pencil (18), adhesive spreaders (19 and 27), a grout finisher (20) or dowel (21), tile edging trim (22), small and large tile spacers (23), a grout remover (24), a grout spreader (25), grout (26) and battens (furring strips) (28).

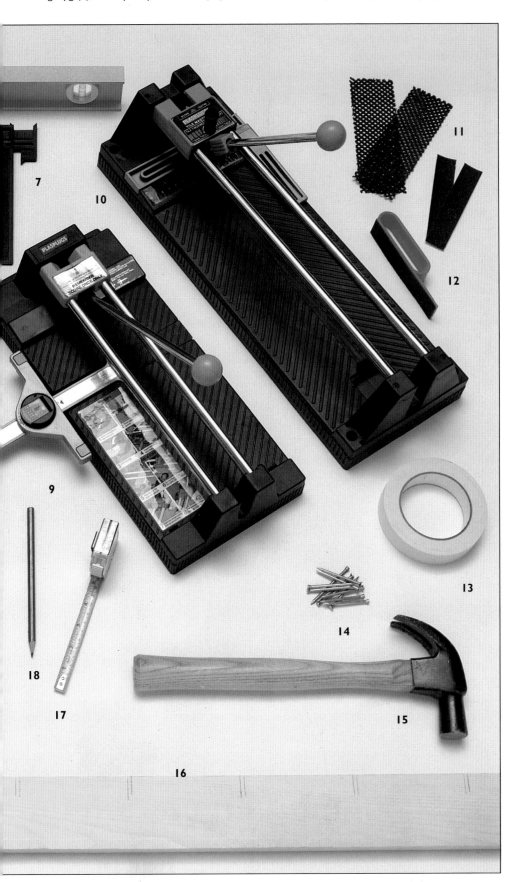

Ceramic floor tile adhesive is widely available in powder form as well as ready-mixed. It is best always to use a waterproof type (plus waterproof grout), even in theoretically dry areas.

Adhesive and grout are both sold in a range of quantities, sometimes labelled by weight, sometimes by volume; always check the coverage specified by the manufacturer on the packaging when buying, so as not to overbuy or run out during the job.

Tools for cork, vinyl and lino tiles

Only a few simple tools are needed to lay cork and vinyl tiles, but, except for the self-adhesive type, special tile adhesive is required. This is sold ready-mixed in tubs, and usually comes complete with a notched spreader.

Special water-based adhesive is the type to choose for both cork and linoleum tiles; solvent-based contact adhesives were formerly the first choice, but their fumes are extremely unpleasant and also dangerously flammable, and they are no longer recommended. For vinyl-coated cork tiles a special vinyl acrylic adhesive is needed. For vinyl tiles, an emulsion-type latex flooring adhesive is best.

For unsealed cork tiles a sealer is required. Ordinary polyurethane varnish, as used for furniture, will do; there are also special floor sealers. Three coats will be needed.

Tools are simply a tape measure, a sharp utility knife and a steel straightedge for marking and cutting border tiles. A proprietary profile gauge with sliding steel or plastic needles makes it easy to cut tiles to fit round awkward obstacles such as architraves (trims) and pipework. But it is just as effective, and less costly, to cut a template from card or paper.

PREPARING A WALL FOR TILING

The wall surface should be clean and dry. It is possible to tile over painted plaster or plasterboard (gypsum board), but old wall coverings should be removed and brick walls must be rendered. Note that modern tile adhesives allow tiling over existing tiles, so there is no need to remove these if they are securely bonded to the wall surface. There is also no need to fill minor cracks or holes; the tile adhesive will bridge these as it is applied to the wall surface.

When estimating quantities, first select the tile size. Then set out the area to be tiled on the wall using a device called a tiling gauge – a batten (furring strip) marked out in tile widths. Use the setting-out marks to count how many tiles will be needed in each horizontal row and each vertical column. Count cut tiles as whole tiles, and then multiply the two figures together to reach the total required. Always add a further 5 per cent to the total to allow for possible breakages and miscalculations.

MAKING AND USING A TILING GAUGE

1 Use a pencil and one of the chosen tiles to mark up a straight piece of timber about 1.2 m/4 ft long, for use as a tiling gauge. Allow for the width of tile spacers if using them.

2 Hold the tiling gauge horizontally against the wall to see how many tiles each row will take, and also to centre the tiling on a wall or window opening.

3 Similarly, hold the gauge vertically to assess how many tiles will fill each column, and where best to position any cut tiles that may be needed.

MARKING OUT A SPLASHBACK

1 When tiling a small area with rows of whole tiles, use a tiling gauge to mark the extent of the tiled area on the wall. Here each row will have five tiles.

2 Next, use a spirit level to mark a true horizontal base line above which the first row of whole tiles will be fixed. Cut tiles will fit below it.

3 Then use the spirit level again to complete a grid of horizontal and vertical guidelines on the wall surface, ready for a tile support to be fixed.

FITTING TILE SUPPORTS

1 Use masonry pins (tacks) to fix support battens (furring strips) to the wall, aligned with the guide line. Drive the pins in only part of the way so that they can be removed later.

ABOVE Be adventurous when choosing tiles. Search through second-hand shops and market stalls for old and unusual tiles. Once assembled, the final effect can be wonderful.

POSITIONING CUT TILES FOR PANELS

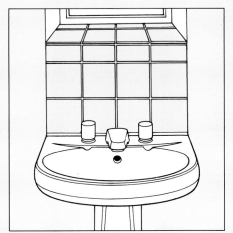

ABOVE If the height of a tiled splashback is determined by a feature such as a mirror or window, position a row of cut tiles along the top of the panel.

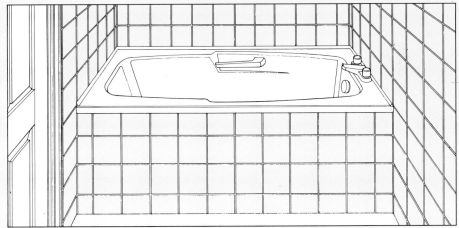

ABOVE If the width of the tiling is defined, as with a bath panel, always position cut tiles of equal size at either side.

ESTIMATING QUANTITIES

Tile size	No/sq m	No/sq yd
106 × 106 mm (4¼ × 4¼ in)	86	71
200 × 100 mm (8 × 4 in)	48	41
150 × 150 mm (6 × 6 in)	43	36

TILING A WALL

For any large area of tiling – a whole wall, or perhaps even a complete room such as a utility area or bathroom – the preliminary setting-out is by far the most important part of the whole project; any errors will spoil the overall effect of the tiling.

You must first plan precisely where the whole tiles will fall. It is best to use a device called a tiling gauge to work this out (see making and using a tiling gauge, on the previous page). Use the gauge to ensure that the tiles will be centred accurately on major features such as window reveals, with a border of cut tiles of equal width at the end of each row or column of tiles.

With a large area of tiling, 2 main factors are vital. First, the tile rows must be exactly horizontal; if they are not, errors will accumulate as the tiles extend across the wall, throwing the verticals out of alignment. Second, the tiles need some means of support while the adhesive sets; without it, they may slump down the wall.

The solution is to fix a line of battens across the wall just above the level of the skirtings (baseboards), securing them with partly driven masonry nails so that you can remove them later. The precise level will be dictated by setting out with the tiling gauge, but will usually be about three-quarters of a tile width above the skirtings. Do not rely on this being level; it may not be. Draw out the line in pencil first, using a spirit level, and then pin the battens up and check the level again. Use vertical battens as necessary – next to a door architrave (trim) that is not truly straight, for example – to ensure vertical alignment.

Once all the necessary setting-out work has been done, the actual technique of fixing tiles to walls is quite simple: spread the adhesive evenly and press the tiles into place. Apply enough adhesive to fix 10 or 12 tiles at a time. When all the whole tiles are in place,

FIXING WHOLE TILES

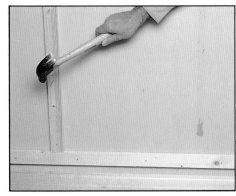

1 When tiling a large area, pin vertical and horizontal guide battens (furring strips) to the wall to help keep the tile columns truly square and aligned.

2 Use a notched spreader to scoop some adhesive from the tub and spread it on the wall. Press the teeth against the wall to leave ridges of even height.

3 Place the first tile on the tile support, with its side edge against the pencilled guideline or vertical guide batten (furring strip) as appropriate.

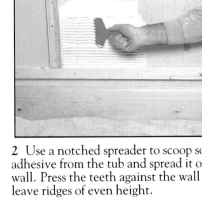

4 Add a tile spacer against the tile corner and position the second tile. Add more tiles to complete the row, then build up succeeding rows in the same way.

CUTTING TILES

1 Use a pencil-type tile cutter and a straightedge to make a straight cut. Measure and mark the tile width needed and score a line across the glaze.

2 Place a nail or matchstick (wooden match) under the scored line at each side of the tile, and break it with downward hand pressure on each half of the tile.

you will need to tackle any cut tiles required at the ends of rows, and along the base of the tiled area beneath the horizontal tile support. Remove this, and the tile spacers, only when the adhesive has set; allow 24 hours. The final stage is to fill in the joint lines with grout. This can be bought in powder form or ready-mixed. Use a flexible spreader (usually supplied with the grout) to apply it.

Most ceramic wall tiles have 2 glazed edges, making it possible to finish off an area of tiling or an external corner with a glazed edge exposed. Alternatively, finish off tiling by edging it with wooden mouldings or plastic trims bedded into the adhesive.

COMPLETING THE WALL

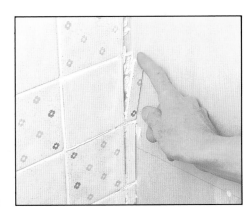 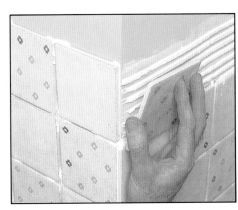

1 Measure, mark and cut the sections of tile needed to complete each row. Spread adhesive on them and press into place. When tiling adjacent walls, place all the cut pieces on the first wall. Repeat on the second wall, overlapping the cut pieces.

2 When tiling external corners, always set out the tiles so that whole tiles meet on the corner. Overlap the tiles as shown.

GROUTING THE TILES

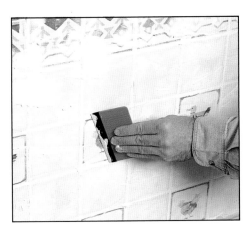 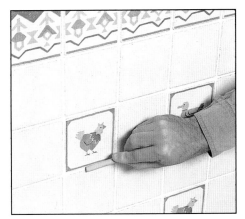

1 Apply the grout to the tile joins by drawing the loaded spreader across them at right-angles to the join lines. Scrape off any excess grout and re-use it. Use a damp sponge or cloth to wipe the surface of the tiles before the grout dries out.

2 Use a short length of wooden dowel or a similar implement to smooth the grout lines to a gently concave cross-section. Allow the grout to harden completely, then polish the tiles with a dry cloth to remove any slight remaining bloom and to leave them clean and shiny.

3 Use a cutting guide, or a tile-cutting jig if you prefer, especially for cutting narrow strips. This type holds the tile securely and also guides the tile cutter accurately.

4 The traditional way of making a cut-out in a tile is to score its outline and then gradually to nibble away the waste material with pincers.

5 An alternative is to use a special abrasive-coated tile saw. This is indispensable for making internal cutouts – to fit around pipes, for example.

ALTERNATIVE EDGING TECHNIQUES

Edges and external corners of tiling can be finished off with wooden mouldings or plastic trim strips.

Wooden mouldings can be bedded into the tile adhesive on walls; to edge worktops they can be pinned (tacked) or screwed to the worktop edge.

Plastic edge and corner mouldings (nosings) have a perforated flange which is bedded in the tile adhesive before the tiles are placed. These mouldings come in a range of pastel and bright primary colours to complement or contrast with the tiling.

1 Bed the plastic edge or corner trim into the adhesive, then position the tiles so that they fit flush against the curved edge of the trim strip.

2 As an alternative to plastic, use wooden mouldings bedded in the tile adhesive. Here an L-shaped moulding forms a neat external corner trim.

3 When tiling over existing tiles, a quadrant (quarter-round) moulding will be helpful in disguising the double thickness along exposed edges.

4 Wood can be used to edge a tiled counter top. Start by attaching the moulding to the edge of the counter so it will fit flush with the tiled surface.

5 Spread the tile adhesive and bed the tiles in place, checking that they lie level with the top edge of the moulding and flush with each other.

6 Plug the counterbored screw holes by gluing in short lengths of dowel and chiselling them off flush with the moulding. Finally, grout the tile joints.

DECORATIVE TECHNIQUES

The preceding pages have dealt with tiling walls in the technical sense of planning the layout and fixing the tiles. However, tiles are more than just wall covering units; they come in a range of sizes and designs which can also be used creatively in a variety of ways.

The first involves finishing off a part-tiled wall with a band of narrow tiles in a colour or design that complements or contrasts with the main tiled area, to form a decorative border. These tiles are available in lengths that match standard tile widths, and are usually 50–75 mm/ 2–3 in wide. They are cut and fixed just like any other tile.

The second method is to incorporate a group of patterned tiles as a feature panel within a larger area of plain tiling. The group may simply be contrasting patterned tiles, or may be a multi-tile motif – a group of four, six or more tiles that fit together to form one large design when they are fixed in position. Tile manufacturers offer a range of mass-produced designs you can choose from, or a motif panel can be commissioned from a specialist tile supplier. Plan the motif's position on the wall carefully, and build it in the usual way as tiling progresses.

1 Use a tiling gauge to mark the position of the first row of tiles on the wall surface. Put up a support batten (furring strip) if necessary, then spread some tile adhesive on the wall, and place any plain tiles that will be below the decorative panel. Start placing the first tiles that will form the decorative panel. Here the tiles are being laid at an angle of 45°, so half-tiles are placed first.

2 Continue adding whole and half-tiles to build up the pattern, checking as you work that the edges of the panel are truly horizontal and vertical.

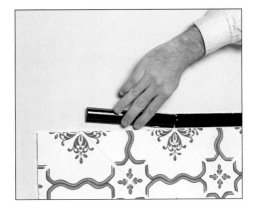

3 Here the panel is being surrounded by slim border tiles. Add whole border tiles to the top of the panel first, working from the centre line outwards.

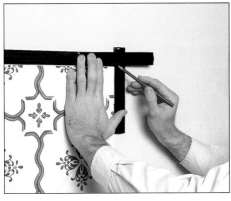

4 At the corners of the panel, fit an over-long horizontal border tile and hold another vertically over it so you can mark a 45° cutting line on each tile.

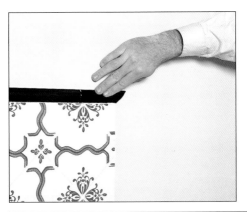

5 Make the 45° cuts on the end of each corner tile, then bed the horizontal tile in place. Check that the cut end is precisely aligned with the panel corner. Repeat the process at the other end of the horizontal section of the border. Both end pieces should be the same length, as the border is centred.

6 Fit the border tiles up each side of the decorative panel, then mark the position of the mitre cut on the final tiles, cut them and fit them in place.

LAYING FLOOR TILES

Both glazed ceramic and quarry tiles can be laid directly over a concrete floor, as long as it is both sound and dry. They can also be laid on to a suspended timber floor, but only if it is strong enough to support the not-inconsiderable extra weight (it is advisable to check this with a building surveyor). In this case, cover the floorboards with exterior-grade plywood, screwed down or secured with annular nails (spiral flooring nails) to prevent it from lifting; this will provide a stable and level base for the tiles.

You will need specially formulated adhesive for laying glazed ceramic floor tiles – this should be a waterproof type in bathrooms and a flexible type if you are tiling on a suspended floor. Lay quarry and terracotta tiles on mortar over a solid concrete floor, or in thick-bed tile adhesive over plywood.

You should lift old floor coverings before laying ceramic or quarry tiles, but, if a solid floor is covered with well-bonded vinyl or cork tiles, you can leave these in place. Remove any wax polish used on them, then tile over them using tile adhesive.

Setting out a tiled floor
Like a tiled wall, a tiled floor needs careful setting-out if the end result is to look neat and professional. This is especially important with glazed ceramic and quarry tiles, and patterned vinyl and lino tiles, but matters rather less with plain vinyl or cork tiles where the finished effect is of uniform colour and the joins between the tiles are virtually invisible.

The necessary setting-out is, fortunately, much easier with floor tiles than it is with wall tiles, as you can dry-lay the tiles on the floor surface and move them around until you find a starting point that gives the best arrangement, with cut border tiles of approximately equal size used all around the perimeter of the room.

LAYING CERAMIC FLOOR TILES

1 Pin (tack) tiling guides to the floor in the corner of the room at right-angles to each other, then spread some adhesive on the floor using a notched-edge trowel.

2 Place the first tile in the angle between the tiling guides, butting it tightly against them and pressing it down firmly into the adhesive bed.

3 As you lay the tiles, use tile spacers to ensure even gaps between them. Use a straightedge to check that all the tiles are horizontal and level.

4 To cut border tiles, lay a whole tile over the last whole tile laid, butt another against the skirting (baseboard) and mark its edge on the tile beneath.

Start by finding the centre point of the floor, by linking the mid-points of opposite pairs of walls with string lines. Dry-lay rows of tiles out towards the walls in each direction, remembering to allow for the joint thickness if appropriate, to see how many whole tiles will fit in and to check whether this starting point results in over-narrow border tiles or awkward cuts against obstacles. Move the rows slightly to improve the fit if necessary,

then mark the string lines using a pencil. Begin tiling in the corner of the room furthest from the door.

TILING TIP

Remember to take off and shorten room doors before laying floor tiles, and to remove sufficient depth to allow the door to clear both the plywood underlay (if used) and the new tiles.

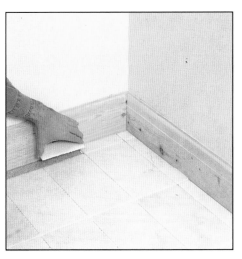

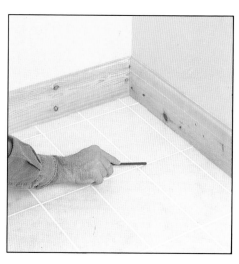

5 Cut the tile and use the exposed part of the sandwiched tile in step 4 to fill the border gap. Use the offcut to fill the next border gap if it is wider than the gap.

6 Use a squeegee to spread grout over the tiles and fill all the join lines. Wipe excess adhesive from the surface of the tiles with a damp cloth.

7 Use a piece of wooden dowel or a similar rounded implement to smooth the grout lines. Finally, polish the tile surface with a clean, dry cloth.

LAYING QUARRY TILES

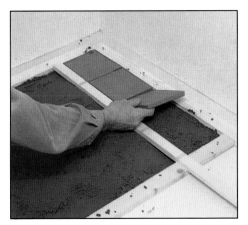

1 Add a third tiling guide to form a bay that is 4 tiles wide. Put down a thin mortar bed and place the first row of tiles, using a tiling gauge to space them.

2 Complete 4 rows of 4 tiles, then check that they are completely level. Tamp down any that are proud, and lift and re-bed any that are lying lower than the other tiles.

3 Complete the first bay, then remove the third tiling guide and re-position it another 4 tile widths away. Fill the second bay with mortar and tamp it down.

4 Complete the second bay in the same way as the first. Continue in this fashion across the room until you have laid all the whole tiles.

5 If you are installing a tiled upstand, place this next, aligning individual units with the floor tiling, then cut and fit the border tiles.

6 Mix up a fairly dry mortar mix and use a stiff-bristled brush to work it well into the joins between the tiles. Brush away excess mortar as you work.

LAYING VINYL, LINO AND CORK FLOOR TILES

Vinyl, linoleum and cork floor tiles are available in both plain and self-adhesive types. Cork tiles may be unsealed or vinyl-coated. For plain vinyl tiles an emulsion-type latex flooring adhesive is used, while plain cork tiles and lino tiles are best stuck with a water-based contact adhesive; solvent-based types give off fumes that are most unpleasant and are also dangerously flammable. For vinyl-coated cork tiles, use a special vinyl acrylic adhesive.

Since these tiles are comparatively thin, any unevenness in the subfloor will show through the tiles. Cover timber floors with a hardboard underlay first. Concrete floors may need localized repairs or treatment with a self-smoothing compound to give them a smooth finish.

If laying patterned tiles, set the floor out carefully. With plain tiles, setting-out may not appear to be so important, but nevertheless the floor should still be set out carefully to ensure that the tile rows run out at right angles from the room door.

1 If using self-adhesive tiles, simply peel the backing paper off and place the tile in position on the subfloor against the marked guidelines.

2 Align self-adhesive tiles carefully with their neighbours before sticking them down; the adhesive grabs positively and repositioning may be difficult.

3 If using non-adhesive tiles, spread the appropriate type of adhesive on the subfloor, using a notched spreader to ensure an even thickness.

4 After placing an area of tiles, use a smooth block of wood to work along the joints. This will ensure that they are all well bedded in the adhesive.

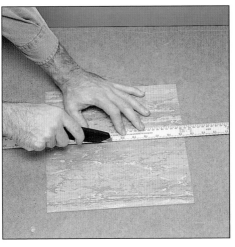

5 To cut border tiles, lay a whole tile over the last whole tile laid, butt another against the skirting (baseboard) and mark its edge on the tile underneath.

6 Place the marked tile on a board and cut it with a sharp utility knife. The exposed part of the sandwiched tile in step 5 will fit the border gap perfectly.

7 Fit the cut piece of border tile in place. Trim its edge slightly if it is a tight fit. Mark, cut and fit the other border tiles in exactly the same way.

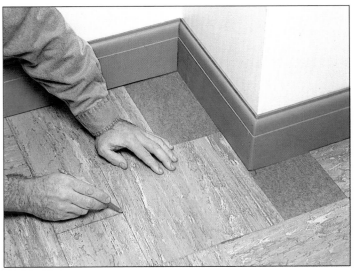

8 To cut a tile at an external corner, lay a whole tile over the last whole tile in one adjacent row, butt another against the wall and draw along its edge.

9 Move the sandwiched tile to the other side of the corner, again butt the second whole tile against the wall and mark its edge on the sandwiched tile.

10 Use the utility knife to cut out the square waste section along the marked lines, and offer up the L-shaped border tile to check its fit before fixing it.

SEALING CORK TILES

When laying unsealed cork tiles, take care not to get adhesive on the faces of the tiles, and seal the surface with three coats of polyurethane varnish or a proprietary cork sealer to protect the surface from dirt and moisture. If access to the room is necessary while the floor is being sealed, do half of the floor one day and the other half the next day.

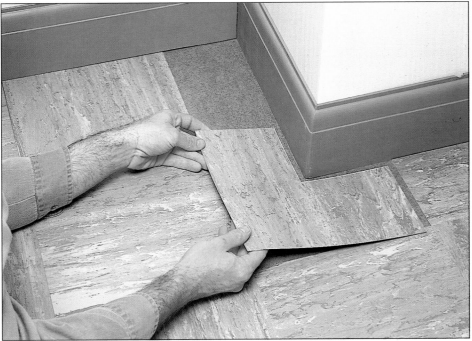

COVERING FLOORS

Floors are the very base of your living space and their coverings are often the first thing you have to replace or renew when moving into a home. In previous years, people wanted floors to last a lifetime. The major consideration was durability and home-owners spent as much as they could afford on it. Now we are much more mobile and many homes are often seen as short- or medium-term accommodation, because of work or the planned growth of the family. We also change our furnishings more frequently, so often instant design impact and cost are just as important as durability. Thankfully, there is a wide range of floor coverings including carpets, sheet vinyl, and decorative wood panels and strips, to satisfy all requirements.

Carpets laid loose have been used on floors for millennia, but it is only a few decades ago that wall-to-wall fitted carpeting became popular. Traditional woven carpets made from natural fibres have been challenged by carpets made from synthetic fibres and by alternative methods of manufacture. There is now a huge choice of colours and patterns in types to suit all locations and wear conditions, available in various widths.

Sheet vinyl floor coverings come in a huge range of colours and patterns, and may also have a surface embossed along the lines of the design to give plausible imitations of other floor coverings such as tiles, marble, wood and cork. Some more expensive types have a cushioned underside formed by incorporating small air bubbles during manufacture, which makes them warmer and softer underfoot than their solid counterparts.

There are two main types of wooden floor covering: wood-block, sometimes called wood mosaic, and wood-strip. The former consists of small slivers of wood (usually a hardwood) laid in groups and stuck to strong cloth to form wooden 'tiles', while the latter is just what its name implies: narrow hardwood planks laid over an existing floor.

Practicality is important when embarking on floor work but take time also to decide on a project that you will enjoy creating and living with.

OPPOSITE Fitted carpet is still the most popular choice for living rooms. The combination of hardwearing fibres and stunning designs now available makes it possible to complement and enhance any style of interior.

CHOOSING FLOOR COVERINGS

In principle it is possible to lay any floor covering in any room of a home, but custom and the practicalities of life generally tend to divide up the home into 3 broad areas.

Access areas such as the hallway, landing and stairs need a floor covering that is able to cope with heavy 'traffic' and muddy shoes. Ideal choices for a hallway are materials with a water-repellent and easy-to-clean surface – for example, sheet vinyl, vinyl tiles, a wood-strip or wood-block floor, sanded and sealed floorboards, or glazed ceramic or quarry tiles. For stairs, where safety is paramount, the best material to choose is a heavy-duty carpet with a short pile, which can also be used on the landing.

Work areas such as the kitchen and bathroom also need durable floor coverings that are easy to clean and, especially in the case of the bathroom, water-resistant as well. Sheet vinyl is a popular choice for both rooms, but tiles of various types can also provide an excellent surface – sealed cork, with its warm feel underfoot, is particularly suitable for a bathroom. However, if you prefer carpet for these rooms, there are extremely hardwearing kitchen carpets available, with a specially treated short nylon pile that is easy to keep clean, and also water-resistant bathroom carpets that give a touch of luxury underfoot without turning into a swamp at bathtime.

Leisure areas – the living room, dining room and bedrooms – are commonly carpeted wall-to-wall. Do not be tempted to skimp on quality in the living room, which gets the most wear and tends to develop distinct 'traffic' routes. It is reasonable, however, to choose light-duty types for carpeting bedrooms.

Alternatives to carpets depend simply on taste in home décor. Options include sanded and sealed floorboards teamed with scatter rugs, or a parquet

ABOVE Plain – or almost plain – carpets are the key to simple yet sophisticated colour schemes. Neutral tones, here softly textured with a twist pile, can be offset with the subtlest of colour contrasts.

LEFT Natural mattings in coir or sisal provide a hardwearing floor covering. Available in a wide range of neutral shades and textures, as well as striped and check designs, they are at home in traditional or modern interiors.

perimeter to a fine specimen carpet. Sheet vinyl or cork tiles may also be worth considering for children's rooms.

Carpets

Carpets consist of fibre tufts or loops woven or stuck to a durable backing. Woven carpets are generally the most expensive. Tufted carpets are made by stitching tufts of fibre into a woven backing, where they are secured by attaching a second backing under the first with adhesive. Some of the less-expensive types have a foam underlay bonded directly to the backing; others require a separate underlay.

A wide range of fibre types is used in carpet construction today, including wool, nylon, acrylic, polypropylene and viscose rayon. Fibre blends can improve carpet performance; a mixture of 80 per cent wool and 20 per cent nylon is particularly popular for providing a combination of warmth, resilience, wear, low flammability and resistance to soiling.

Pile length and density affect a carpet's performance as well as its looks, and most are classified to indicate the sort of wear they can be expected to withstand. The pile can be cut, often to different lengths, giving a sculptured effect; looped (shag), that is, uncut and left long; corded, which means uncut and pulled tight to the backing; or twisted, which gives a tufty effect. A dense pile wears better than a loosely woven one that can be parted to reveal the backing. Carpet widths are described as broadloom, when more than 1.8 m/6 ft wide; or body (stair carpet), which is usually up to 90 cm/ 3 ft wide.

Carpet tiles are small squares of carpet of various types, designed to be loose-laid. Cheaper tiles resemble cord and felt carpets, while more expensive ones may have a short- or long-cut pile. The most common sizes are 30, 45, 50 and 60 cm/12, 18, 20 and 24 in square.

Sheet-vinyl flooring

This is a relatively thin material which provides a smooth, hygienic and easy-to-clean floor covering that is widely used in rooms such as kitchens, bathrooms and hallways. It is made from layers of plastic resins, with a clear wear layer protecting the printed design and frequently with an air cushion layer between this and the backing for extra comfort and warmth underfoot. It is fairly flexible and easy to cut for an exact fit; it is generally loose-laid, with double-sided adhesive tape used only at seams and edges.

Vinyl flooring is available in a wide range of designs, including realistic imitations of ceramic tiles, wood, cork and stone. It is sold by the linear metre (or yard) from rolls 2, 3 or 4 m/6 ft 6 in, 10 ft or 13 ft wide.

Wood floor coverings

These come in two main forms: as square wood-block panels made up of individual fingers of wood stuck to a cloth or felt backing for ease of handling and laying; or as wood-strip flooring – interlocking planks, often of veneer on a plywood backing. They are laid over the existing floor surface. Most types are tongued-and-grooved, so only occasional nailing or clipping is required to hold them in place. Wood-block panels are usually 30 or

ABOVE Modern sheet linoleum has taken on a new lease of life, offering a range of sophisticated colourways teamed with stylish borders that are perfect for kitchens, utility rooms and hallways.

BELOW Sanded floorboards can be further enhanced with a delicate stencilled border design. Always seal floorboards with several coats of good-quality varnish for a hardwearing finish.

45 cm/12 or 18 in square, while planks are generally 7.5 or 10 cm/3 or 4 in wide and come in a range of lengths to allow the end joins to be staggered from one row to the next.

FLOORING TOOLS AND EQUIPMENT

For laying carpet the basic essentials are a tape measure and a sharp utility knife with a good supply of extra blades for cutting and trimming the carpet to fit. As an alternative, special carpet shears can be used.

For a woven carpet a carpet stretcher is invaluable. This is a device with a horizontal pad of metal spikes at one end which is locked into the carpet, and a cushioned pad at the other end which is nudged with the knee to stretch the carpet into place. It is probably best to hire this relatively expensive tool, which will not be needed very often.

Also needed for woven carpet are carpet gripper strips to hold the carpet in position around the perimeter of the room. Gripper strips are thin strips of plywood fitted with angled nails that grip the underside of the carpet. The strips are nailed to the floor about 10 mm/⅜ in from the skirting (baseboard) all around the room. The edge of the carpet is then tucked down into the gap, usually with a carpet fitter's bolster. A wide brick bolster (stonecutter's chisel) may be used instead, as long as it is clean.

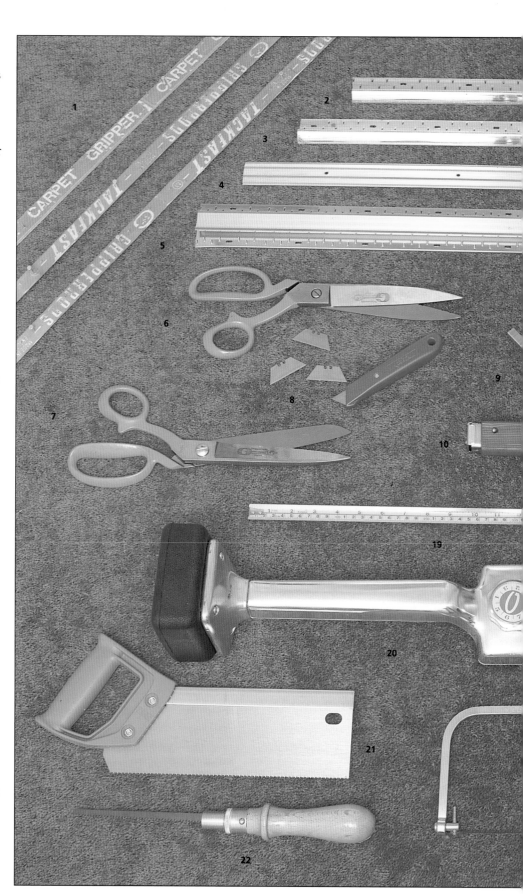

FLOORING TOOLS AND EQUIPMENT

A range of tools for laying carpet, vinyl and wooden floorings include: gripper rods (1), a single-sided brass threshold (saddle) strip (2), an aluminium carpet-to-vinyl strip (3), a threshold cover strip (4), a carpet-to-carpet strip (5), right-handed (6) or left-handed (7) carpet shears, a carpet knife with spare blades (8), staples (9) and a staple hammer (10), a recess scriber (11), a tack hammer (12), a carpet fitter's bolster (13), dividers (14), an adjustable straightedge (15), hessian (burlap) carpet tape (16), liquid adhesive (17), double-sided tape (18), a retractable steel tape measure (19), a carpet stretcher (20), a tenon saw (21), a pad saw (22), a coping saw (23) and an electric jigsaw (saber saw) (24).

Foam-backed carpet does not need gripper strips. It may be stapled to the floor with a staple gun, or stuck down with double-sided adhesive tape. For both woven and foam-backed types, adhesive seaming tape may also be needed to join sections of carpet together and threshold (saddle) strips to neatly finish the carpeted edge off at door openings.

For laying sheet vinyl, again a tape measure and a sharp utility knife are needed. A long steel straightedge will also be invaluable. For bonding the lengths to the floor along edges and seams, use either double-sided tape or bands of liquid adhesive, spread with a toothed spreader. Lastly, a pair of compasses or a scribing block and pencil, plus a shape tracer, are needed to transfer onto the sheet the outlines of the various floor-level obstacles around the edge of the room.

For laying wood-block and wood-strip floor coverings, the requirements are general woodworking tools, some adhesive and a spreader for wood-block floors, and pins (tacks) or fixing clips for wood-strip floors, plus varnish or sealer if laying an unsealed type.

UNDERLAYS

Lining paper or cloth underlay is recommended for foam-backed carpets as it prevents the foam from sticking to the floor surface. For woven carpets use either a foam or felt underlay: they are available in various grades and should be matched to the carpet being laid.

Heavy-duty underlays are recommended for heavy wear areas such as hallways, or where extra insulation is required.

PREPARING WOOD FLOORS

Securing loose boards

For suspended wood floors – boards laid over floor joists – start by lifting the old floor covering and checking that all the boards are securely fixed to their joists, and that they are reasonably flat and level. Loose boards will creak annoyingly when walked on, and raised edges or pronounced warping may show as lines through the covering.

Use either cut nails or large oval-headed nails to secure loose boards, and then recess their heads slightly using a nail punch. If nails will not hold the floorboard flat against the joist, drill pilot and clearance.

Laying hardboard

Covering the existing boards with a hardboard underlay is an alternative to floor sanding as a way of ensuring a smooth, flat surface ideal for thin sheet coverings. Lay the boards in rows with the joints staggered from row to row, and pin them down with hardboard pins driven in at 15 cm/6 in spacings. Lay separate strips above pipe runs.

If preparing to lay glazed ceramic or quarry tiles on a suspended wood floor, put down exterior-grade plywood.

Sanding floors

Where old floorboards are very uneven, or it is planned to leave them exposed but they are badly stained and marked, hire a floor sanding machine. This resembles a cylinder (reel) lawnmower, with a drum to which sheets of abrasive paper are fitted. A bag at the rear collects the sawdust; however, always wear a face mask when sanding floors. Also hire a smaller disc or belt sander for finishing off the room edges.

If necessary, drive any visible nail heads below the surface before using the sander. When sanding floorboards, always raise the drum at the end of each pass to prevent the abrasives from damaging the boards while the machine is stationary.

LAYING A HARDWOOD FLOOR

1 If hardboard sheets are used as an underlay for a new floor covering, start by punching in any raised nail heads all over the floor.

2 Nail the hardboard sheets to the floorboards at 15 cm/6 in intervals along the edges and also 30 cm/12 in apart across the face of each sheet.

SANDING FLOORBOARDS

1 Use a floor sander to smooth and strip old floorboards. Drape the flex (cord) over one shoulder and raise the drum before starting the machine up.

2 Using coarse abrasive paper, run the machine at an angle of 45° to the board direction to begin with, first in one direction and then at right angles to the original passes.

3 Then switch to a medium-grade abrasive and run the sander back and forth parallel with the board direction. Finish off with fine-grade abrasive.

4 Use a smaller disc or belt sander to strip areas close to the skirtings (baseboards) and door thresholds, where the larger drum sander cannot reach.

PREPARING SOLID FLOORS

Ground floors of solid concrete are prone to two main problems: cracking or potholing of the surface, and rising damp caused by a failure in the damp-proof membrane within the floor structure. Cracks and depressions may show through new floor coverings, especially thinner types such as sheet vinyl, while dampness will encourage mould growth beneath the covering.

Relatively narrow cracks can be patched with a repair mortar of 1 part cement to 3 parts sand, or an exterior-quality masonry filler. If the floor surface is uneven or pitted, it can be covered with a thin layer of self-smoothing compound. The mixture is made up in a bucket, poured on to the floor surface, and trowelled out to a thickness of about 3 mm/⅛ in. The liquid finds its own level and dries to give a hard, smooth surface which can be walked on in about 1 hour. For best results, leave it to dry for at least 24 hours before laying your floor covering over it.

An alternative approach is to cover the concrete with a floating floor of chipboard (particle board), if raising the floor level will not cause problems at door thresholds. The boards can be laid directly on the concrete over heavy-duty polythene (plastic) sheeting, which acts as a vapour barrier. If additional insulation is required, put down polystyrene (plastic foam) boards first and lay the new flooring over them.

Treat damp floors with two coats of a proprietary damp-proofing liquid.

LAYING A SELF-SMOOTHING COMPOUND

1 Sweep the concrete floor clear of dust and debris. Then scrub away any patches of grease with strong detergent solution. If the surface is very dusty or appears unduly porous, seal it by brushing on a generous coat of diluted PVA building adhesive (white general-purpose adhesive).

2 Mix up the self-smoothing compound in a bucket, following the manufacturer's instructions carefully to ensure that the mix is the right consistency and is free from lumps. Starting in the corner farthest from the room door, pour the compound out on to the floor surface to cover an area of about 1 sq m/11 sq ft.

3 Use a plasterer's trowel to smooth the compound out to a thickness of about 3 mm/⅛ in. Mix, pour and level further batches as required.

LAYING A CHIPBOARD FLOOR

1 You can level and insulate a concrete floor by laying a floating floor of chipboard (particle board) over it. Put down heavy-duty polythene (plastic) sheeting first.

2 Tape the sheet to the walls; this will be hidden behind the new skirting (baseboard) later. Then carefully butt-joint 25 mm/ 1 in polystyrene (plastic foam) insulation boards.

3 Cover the insulation with tongued-and-grooved flooring-grade chipboard. Use cut pieces to fit as necessary, and add a tapered threshold (saddle) strip at the door.

LAYING A FOAM-BACKED CARPET

Laying a traditional woven carpet can be a difficult task for the amateur to undertake, because the carpet must be correctly tensioned across the room by using gripper strips and a carpet stretcher if it is to wear well. Because of the cost of such carpet, it may be considered best to leave the job to professionals. However, there is no reason why you should not get some practice by laying less-expensive foam-backed carpet in, for example, a spare bedroom. It is possible to disguise any slight inaccuracies that creep into the cutting and fitting process more easily here than when using smooth sheet floor coverings such as vinyl, so a job such as this would be an excellent introduction to the general technique of laying roll floor coverings.

Start by putting down a paper or cloth underlay on the floor, taping the joins and stapling down the underlay so that it cannot creep as you lay down the carpet. Unroll the carpet right across the room, with the excess lapping up the walls. Using a sharp utility knife, roughly trim the excess all around the room, leaving approximately 5 cm/2 in for final trimming. Carefully make small cuts at any external corners such as around a chimney breast (fireplace projection), and let the tongues fall back into the alcoves, then trim off the waste carpet neatly across the face of the chimney breast.

Next, press the carpet into internal corners and mark the corner point with a finger. Make cuts to remove the triangle of carpet from the internal angle. Finally, trim the perimeter by drawing a knife along the angle between the skirtings (baseboards) and wall, and secure the edges with double-sided adhesive tape. Fit a threshold (saddle) strip across the door opening to give a neat finish.

1 Before laying a foam-backed carpet, put down a paper or cloth underlay to keep the foam from sticking to the floor. Tape any joins and staple the underlay in place.

2 Stick double-sided adhesive tape all around the perimeter of the room, leaving the top backing paper on the tape. Unroll the carpet and position it so that it laps up the room walls.

3 Butt the edge of the carpet up against the longest straight wall in the room. Peel the backing paper off the tape and bed the edge into place.

4 Work the carpet across the floor to the opposite wall to ensure that it is lying flat. Trim this edge against the skirting (baseboard) and then tape it down as before.

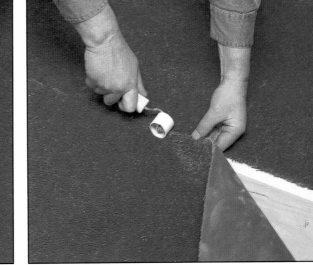

5 Make cuts at internal and external corners in order to bed the carpet on to the tape. Trim excess carpet by drawing a knife along the angle, taking care not to trim away too much.

6 Use adhesive seaming tape to join pieces of carpet together where necessary in particularly large rooms. Applied pressure from a wallpaper seam roller will ensure a good, lasting bond.

LAYING CARPET TILES

Carpet tiles are among the simplest floor coverings to lay, because they are highly tolerant of any slight inaccuracy in cutting to fit. The cheapest types are usually plain in colour and have a very short pile or a corded appearance, while more expensive tiles may have a longer pile and are available in patterns as well as plain colours. Most are designed to be loose-laid, with just the edges and door thresholds (saddles) secured with bands of adhesive or double-sided tape. This makes it easy to lift individual tiles for cleaning or to even out wear.

Most carpet tiles are marked on the back with an arrow to indicate the pile direction. Align these for a plain effect, or lay them at right-angles to create a chequerboard effect. When you are satisfied with the layout, lift the perimeter tiles and put down double-sided tape all around the room. Peel the backing paper off the top of the tape and press the tiles into place. Finish off the doorway with a threshold (saddle) strip.

CUTTING CARPET TILES

1 Measure the size of the cut tile required and mark the back accordingly. Cut the tile from the back on a cutting board, using a sharp utility knife and a metal straightedge.

2 After cutting cleanly through the backing, separate the 2 halves and trim away any frayed pile with scissors. Lay the cut tile in place.

LAYING A WOVEN CARPET

The laying and trimming technique used for woven carpets is broadly similar to that described for foam-backed carpets on the previous page, with two important exceptions: the edges of the woven carpet are secured on toothed gripper strips, and the carpet must be tensioned across the room to ensure that it wears evenly and cannot ruck up in use.

Start by nailing the gripper strips to the floor all around the room, using a hardboard or cardboard spacer to set them about 10 mm/³⁄₈ in away from the skirtings (baseboards). Then put down a good-quality foam underlay, paper side up, cutting it to fit just inside the gripper strips.

Unroll the carpet, trim it roughly and make small diagonal cuts at internal and external corners. Use a carpet fitter's bolster or a clean brick bolster (stonecutter's chisel) to press one edge of the carpet down on to the gripper strips, then trim off excess carpet and use the bolster to tuck the edge into the gap between the strips and the wall.

Use a carpet stretcher to tension the carpet along the adjacent walls and across the room, hooking it on to the gripper strips as each section is stretched. Trim the carpet along the other walls too, and finally fit the carpet neatly into the doorway, securing it with a threshold (saddle) strip.

1 Nail gripper strips all around the perimeter of the room, using a spacer to set them slightly away from the skirting (baseboard). Lay underlay, trimmed to butt up to the gripper strips. Tape pieces together as necessary, then staple the underlay to a wood floor at intervals.

2 Unroll the carpet and trim it roughly all around. Then make cuts at external corners so that tongues of carpet will fit around them. Press one edge of the carpet onto the gripper strips with a carpet fitter's bolster to ensure that the angled teeth grip the carpet backing securely.

3 Cut off the excess carpet along this edge by running a sharp utility knife along the angle between the gripper strip and the skirting, as shown.

4 Use the blade of the bolster to tuck the trimmed edge of the carpet into the angle between strip and the skirting. Then tension the carpet along adjacent walls.

5 Make release cuts at internal corners too, then trim the waste along the other walls of the room as before and tuck the cut edges into the perimeter gap.

6 At door frames and similar obstacles, trim the carpet to follow the contours of the obstacle as closely as possible, and press it on to the gripper strip. Complete the installation by fitting a door threshold (saddle) strip. Different types are available for linking carpet to carpet and carpet to smooth floor coverings.

LAYING STAIR CARPET

The technique of carpeting a flight of stairs is similar in principle to that used for carpeting a room, with gripper strips being used to hold the carpet to the treads. The job is easiest on a straight flight, but it is not too difficult to cope with winding flights or projecting bullnose steps because cuts can be made across the carpet at any point on the flight and the joins hidden neatly.

Start by nailing on the gripper strips. Next, cut pieces of underlay to cover each tread and the face of the riser below, and fix them in position with a staple gun or carpet tacks.

Start laying the carpet at the top of the flight. If the same carpet is being used on the landing, this should be brought over the edge of the top step and down the face of the first riser. Therefore the top edge of the stair carpet should be tucked into the gripper strips at the bottom of the first riser. Trim the edges of the carpet on the first tread, then on the next riser, and tuck them in before locking the fold of carpet into the gripper strips at the back of the next tread with a carpet fitter's bolster. Continue in this way to the bottom of the flight, where the stair carpet finishes at the base of the first riser whether or not the floor below uses the same carpet.

Alternative fixings

Special one-piece L-section metal grippers can be used in the tread/riser angle instead of wood gripper strips. If you are using foam-backed carpet on your stairs, fit special gripper strips for foam-backed carpet into the angles between treads and risers. When fitting a stair runner rather than a full-width carpet, paint or stain the stair treads and anchor the carpet with stair rods.

1 Nail gripper strips across the width of the flight at the foot of each riser and at the back of each tread, the thickness of a single fold of carpet apart. Fit a length of gripper strip to the sides of each tread, just less than the carpet thickness away from the sides of the flight. Staple to fit over the nose of the front of the tread.

2 Start fitting the carpet at the top of the flight, trimming each tread and riser in turn and then forcing a fold of carpet into the angled gripper strips.

3 On an open-string staircase, either trim the carpet to fit around each baluster or fold over the edge and tack it to fit against the baluster as shown here.

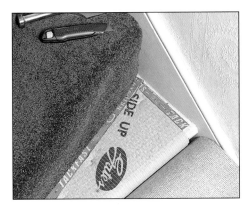

4 On winder (curved) stairs, cut a piece of carpet to cover each tread and the riser beneath it. Align it so that the weave is at right angles to the riser.

5 Secure each piece of carpet to the gripper strip at the rear of the tread first, then stretch it over the tread and down to the next gripper strip. Trim off the waste from the bottom edge of the riser.

6 If the flight finishes with a projecting bullnose step, trim and tack the carpet to the riser as shown and cover the riser with a separate strip.

LAYING SHEET VINYL

Sheet-vinyl flooring can be difficult to lay because it is wide and comparatively stiff to handle, and edge-cutting must be done accurately if gaps are not to be noticeable against skirtings (baseboards). Lengths of quadrant beading (a base shoe) can be pinned (tacked) around the perimeter of the room to disguise any serious mistakes.

Most rooms contain at least one long straight wall, and it is often easiest to butt one edge of the vinyl up against this first of all. Use a block of wood and a pencil to scribe the wall profile on to the vinyl and cut along this line for a perfect fit. Alternatively, simply press the vinyl into the angle between wall and floor, and cut along it using a sharp utility knife held at a 45° angle. Press the ends of the length neatly against the walls at right-angles to the first wall, make small diagonal cuts at internal and external angles, and trim the edges to fit there. Finally, stick down the edges and any seams with double-sided adhesive tape. Finish off the doorway with a proprietary threshold (saddle) strip.

The best way of achieving an accurate fit when laying sheet-vinyl flooring around unusual-shaped obstacles, such as washbasin pedestals and piping, is to make a template of the obstacle so that you can transfer its shape on to the vinyl. Use taped-together sheets of paper cut or torn to roughly the outline of the room and the obstacle. Tape the template to the floor, and use a block of wood and a pencil (or a pair of compasses) to draw a line on the template parallel with the outline of the obstacle.

Next, transfer the template to the vinyl, and use the same block of wood or compass setting to scribe lines back on to the vinyl itself. These lines will accurately represent the shape of the room and the obstacle. Cut along them and remove the waste, then stick down edges and seams as before.

1 Unless the wall is perfectly straight, carefully make a cut at the corner and then trim the adjacent edges of the sheet using a sharp utility knife along the angle of wall and floor.

2 At the door architraves (trims), make cuts into the edge of the sheet so that it will lie flat, and trim off the tongues. Use a similar technique for trimming around larger obstacles such as washbasin pedestals.

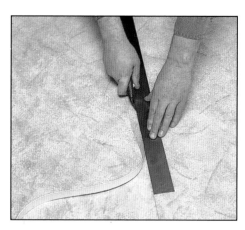

3 To join sheet vinyl edge to edge, overlap the 2 sheets so that the pattern matches, then cut through both layers against a metal straightedge. Discard the waste strips.

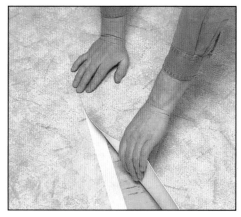

4 Place a strip of double-sided tape underneath the join line, peel off the backing paper and press the 2 cut edges firmly down on to the tape.

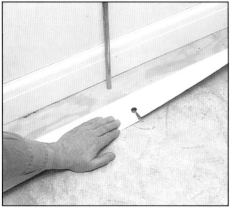

5 To fit the sheet around plumbing pipework, make a cut into it at the pipe position and then trim out a circle of the material to fit around it.

6 At the door opening, fit a threshold (saddle) strip to anchor the edge of the sheet. Here, an existing strip has been prised up and is being hammered down again.

MAKING TEMPLATES FOR SHEET VINYL

PREPARING A TEMPLATE TO FIT AROUND OBSTACLES

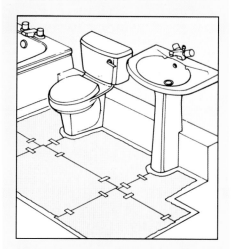

To make a cutting template for a room full of obstacles, such as a bathroom, tape sheets of paper together with their edges about 5 cm/2 in from the room walls all around. Tear in from the edges to fit the template around the obstacles as shown, ready for the outline of the room and the obstacles to be scribed on to the template.

1 Use a block and pencil to scribe the wall outline on to the paper.

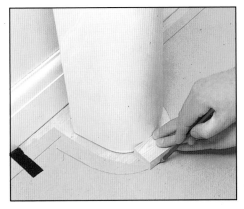

3 Use the same scribing technique as in step 1 to draw the outline of obstacles such as washbasin pedestals on to the paper template. Fix the pencil to the block with tape or a rubber band if you find that this makes it easier to use.

2 Tape the template over the sheet vinyl and use the same block with a pencil to scribe a copy of the room outline back on to the vinyl.

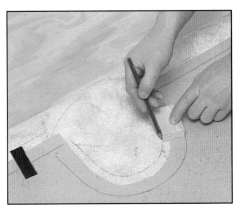

4 Repeat step 2 to scribe the outline of the obstacle on to the vinyl. Using a sharp utility knife, cut carefully around the outline of the obstacle. Make a cut into the waste area, test the cut-out for fit, and trim it slightly if necessary.

5 To make a cut-out around a pipe, use a slim block and a pencil to scribe the pipe position on to the template as four lines at right-angles to each other.

6 Place the template over the vinyl at the pipe position, and use the same block and pencil to mark the cut-out on the vinyl as a small square.

7 Use a pair of compasses or a pipe offcut to draw a circle inside the square. Cut carefully around the circle and cut into the waste area from the edge.

LAYING WOOD-STRIP FLOORING

All the hard work involved in putting down wood-strip flooring lies in the preparation; the actual laying, like so many decorating jobs, is simple and proceeds gratifyingly quickly.

The flooring is available in 2 main types: as solid planks, and as laminated strips with a decorative surface veneer. Lengths range from as little as 40 cm/ 16 in up to 1.8 m/6 ft, and widths from 7 cm/2¾ in up to 20 cm/8 in. Solid planks are usually 15 mm/⅝ in thick; laminated strips are a little thinner.

Both types are generally tongued-and-grooved on their long edges for easy fitting. Some are designed to be fixed to a wooden sub-floor by secret nailing; others are loose-laid, using ingenious metal clips to hold adjacent strips together. A wide range of wood varieties is available in each type. Laminated strips are generally pre-finished, as are some solid types, but others may need sealing once they have been laid down.

Always unpack the strips and leave them in the room where they will be laid for about a week to acclimatize to the temperature and humidity levels in the home. This will prevent buckling due to expansion, or shrinkage due to contraction, when the flooring is laid.

If the manufacturer recommends the use of a special underlay – which may be polythene (polyethylene) sheeting, glass-fibre matting or foam – put this down next, and tape or staple the joins together so that they do not ruck up while you lay the floor.

REMOVING OLD FLOOR COVERINGS

Generally speaking, old floor coverings should always be lifted before you lay new ones. This also provides an opportunity to inspect the floor itself and to carry out any repairs that may be necessary.

1 Make sure that the sub-floor is clean, dry and level, and remove the skirtings (baseboards) if necessary. Unroll the special underlay (if using) across the floor, taping 1 end to keep it in place.

2 Prepare all the lengths of board by hammering the special metal joint clips into the grooves on the undersides of the boards, next to the tongued edges.

3 Lay the first length, clips outwards, against the wall, using spacers to create an expansion gap next to the wall. Glue the ends of butt-jointed lengths.

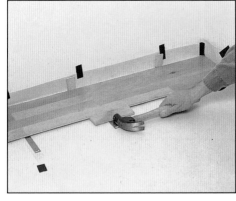

4 Position the second row of boards, tapping them together with a hammer and an offcut so that the clips on the first row engage in the groove of the second.

5 The last board is fitted without clips. Cut it to width, allowing for the spacers as in step 3, and apply adhesive along its grooved edge.

6 Insert some protective packing against the wall before levering the strip into place. Tamp it down level with a hammer and protect the floor with a board offcut.

8 To fit a board around a pipe, mark its position and drill a suitable-sized hole. Cut out a tapered wedge, fit the board and then replace the wedge.

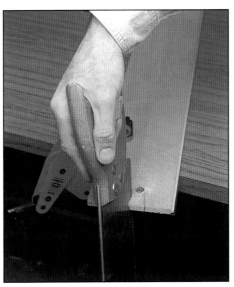

ABOVE Hardwearing and elegant, wood-strip flooring is a practical choice for a living room, especially if teamed with a colourful rug.

7 Replace skirtings or pin (tack) on lengths of quadrant beading (a base shoe) to hide any gap. Weight down the board so that it fits tightly against the floor.

FEATURES AND FITTINGS

A bare room with its areas of flat and featureless plasterwork is a blank canvas which can be embellished in many different ways. Paint and wall coverings obviously play their part, but there is also a wide range of other features which can be added to the room to give it its own personality. Some are purely decorative, but the majority are practical as well.

In the purely decorative department come features such as cornices (crown moldings) which run around the angle between wall and ceiling, friezes and panel mouldings used to frame door and window openings or groups of pictures, and even such things as recessed ornamental niches for displaying treasures.

In the more practical group come wooden mouldings fitted to protect the fragile plaster surfaces. These include skirtings (baseboards) fitted around the walls at floor level, architraves (trims) around flush door and window openings, and dado (chair) rails to prevent furniture – especially chairs – from damaging the walls. Picture rails belong in this group too, allowing pictures and mirrors to be hung anywhere without having to make new fixings.

On a larger scale are add-on features such as wall panelling, which can be fixed to wall and ceiling surfaces as an alternative to more usual wall coverings, and replacement doors and ornamental fire surrounds. These can set off a chimney breast (fireplace projection) to excellent effect even if the fireplace is not in use.

The scheme is completed with the right choice of fittings – handles, catches and so on – for the doors and windows, and also with the selection of hardware to support curtains and drapes, whether this is a simple unobtrusive track or a more decorative pole. There is a huge range of products to choose from in all of these categories.

Once everything else is in place, walls can be brought to life by carefully chosen paintings, photographs or prints. How they are framed makes all the difference to their impact.

OPPOSITE The decoration of wall, ceiling and floor surfaces sets the tone for any colour scheme, but it is the fixtures and fittings – the extra touches such as decorative mouldings, door and window furniture, even pictures and mirrors – that give a room its individual look.

FEATURES AND FITTINGS

PUTTING UP DECORATIVE FEATURES

You can enhance the walls and ceilings of your rooms in many ways: for example, with decorative wood or plaster mouldings, fire surrounds, wall panelling, replacement doors, new door and window furniture, and curtain (drapery) tracks and poles. Pictures and mirrors provide the finishing touches.

Plaster mouldings

Perhaps the simplest type of ornamental plasterwork is panel moulding. This is a decorative strip used to outline areas on walls or a ceiling that will be treated in a different way to the rest of the room, especially as a way of highlighting pictures, mirrors or alcoves.

Panel mouldings are made in a wide range of profiles to suit every taste, from plain fluted and reeded effects to more elaborate versions such as egg-and-dart, flower-and-husk, Roman vine and Greek key. Corners can be mitred, or formed with matching corner blocks or special re-entrant curves.

Cornices (crown moldings)

These decorative plaster features were originally used externally in classical architecture at the edges of roofs, but were soon also used inside on the perimeter of ceilings. As with panel mouldings, a huge range of profiles is available, from authentic Greek and Roman forms through 18th- and 19th-century styles, and featuring such classic motifs as acanthus, dentil, swag-and-drop and egg-and-dart. Plain concave mouldings – known as coving – are also available, made either as a paper-faced moulding with a plaster core, or machined from wood.

ABOVE Ornamental plasterwork, such as cornices (crown moldings) and corbels supporting delicate arches, add a flourish to any décor, especially in period homes.

LEFT Decorative mouldings are very much in vogue as a means of breaking up large expanses of wall and displaying picture groups. The choice of paint colours is important in balancing the different, defined areas of wall.

RIGHT Wood panelling below dado- (chair-) rail level is a durable alternative to wall coverings. The natural divide can be highlighted with an attractive stencil border.

RIGHT Panelled doors can be made part of an overall colour scheme by highlighting the panel surrounds to match the other decorative mouldings in the room and to complement the soft-furnishing fabrics.

BELOW Window dressing adds the finishing touch to any room. Here, a festoon blind is suspended from a decorative wooden pole.

Wooden mouldings
Most wooden mouldings are machined either from softwood or from a cheap hardwood, in a wide range of cross-sections. The larger mouldings – architraves (door and window trims), skirtings (baseboards) and the like – are cut from softwood, while mouldings with smaller and more intricate profiles are made from hardwood. Mouldings can be given a coloured finish, or stained and varnished.

Skirtings (baseboards)
These boards are fitted to plastered walls at ground level to protect the plaster surface from damage by careless feet or furniture, and also allow floor-cleaning implements to be used right up to the floor edge without wetting or marking the walls. Until recently, the fashion was for low, plain skirtings, but in many homes there is now a switch back to more ornate types, often stained and varnished.

Dado (chair) and picture rails
These are horizontal mouldings fixed to wall surfaces, the former about 90 cm/ 3 ft from the floor and the latter a short way below ceiling level. The dado rail was designed to protect the plaster from damage by chair backs, and also provided a break in the walls' colour scheme. Traditionally, the area below the rail was panelled or finished in a relief wall covering, while that above it was papered or painted. The picture rail allowed pictures to be hung and moved about, and also provided a visual break in rooms with high ceilings.

Doors and windows
Replacing room doors is one way of giving a room a dramatic facelift, especially if the existing doors are out of keeping with the look of the room. New doors deserve new fittings, and again there is a wide range of handles, knobs and latches from which to choose, including various metallic finishes, wood, plastic and even glass and ceramics. The same applies to windows. Changing these is a bigger job than replacing a door, but simply fitting new stays and catches can give an old window frame a new lease of life.

Curtain (drapery) tracks and poles
One last fixture that deserves some attention is the hardware that supports the curtains (drapes). Curtain tracks and poles may be wall- or ceiling-mounted, and can be made of metal, wood or plastic in a range of styles and finishes. The simplest types of tracks are unobtrusive; more complex versions include cords or motor drives to move the curtains. Ornamental poles make a feature in their own right.

PUTTING UP A CORNICE (CROWN MOLDING)

There are 3 types of decorative cornice commonly used in today's homes. The first type is coving, a relative of sheet plasterboard (gypsum board), which consists of a concave hollow-backed plaster core sheathed in a strong paper envelope. It is fixed in place with adhesive. The second is moulded cornice; this is made either from traditional fibrous plaster or from modern foamed plastics to imitate the ornate decorative cornices often found in older buildings, and comes in a range of profiles. Plaster types must generally be secured in place with screws because of their weight, but plastic types can simply be stuck in position with adhesive. The third type is a machined wooden trim with a similar profile to plasterboard cornice, and is either nailed direct to the wall framing or to a nailing strip or batten (furring strip) in the angle of the wall and ceiling.

Apart from its decorative appearance in framing the ceiling, a cornice can also help to conceal unsightly cracks. These often open up around the ceiling perimeter as the ceiling expands and contracts with changes in temperature and humidity, or as the building settles.

FITTING A CORNICE (CROWN MOLDING)

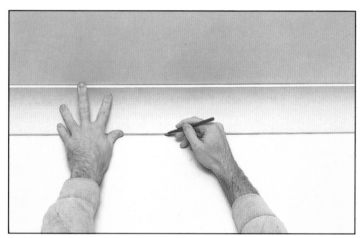

1 Hold a length of cornice squarely in the wall/ceiling angle and draw 2 guidelines on the wall and ceiling surfaces. Cut any mitred edges (see opposite page, below).

2 Remove any old wall coverings from between the guidelines by dry-scraping them. Cross-hatch painted or bare plaster to key the surface.

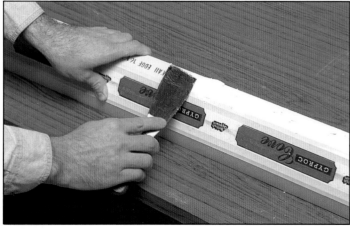

3 Either mix up powder adhesive or use a ready-mixed type. Using a flat scraper, 'butter' the adhesive on to both edges of the rear of the cornice.

4 Press the length into place between the guidelines, supporting it if necessary with partly driven masonry nails. Remove the nails (if used) once the adhesive has set.

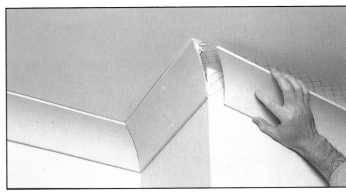

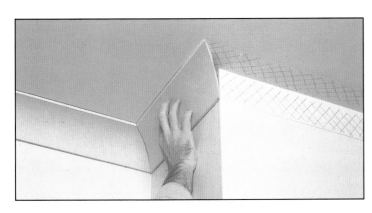

5 Fit the adjacent corner piece next. Here, the next section also incorporates an external mitre; measure and cut this carefully before fitting the length.

6 Complete the external corner with a further length of cornice, butting the cut ends closely together and ensuring that the length fits between the lines.

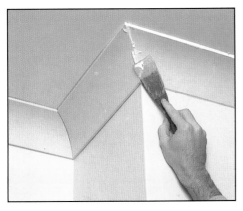

7 Fill any slight gaps at external and internal angles with a little cellulose filler (spackle), applied with a filling knife (putty knife) to leave a crisp, clean joint. Sand the filler smooth once it has hardened.

8 Before the adhesive sets hard, use a damp sponge to remove any excess from wall and ceiling surfaces and also to smooth over the filled joints.

CUTTING A CORNICE (CROWN MOLDING)

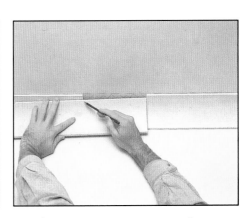

1 Make up a large mitre block big enough to hold the cornice, and use this and a tenon saw to make accurate 45° cuts for internal and external corners.

2 Some cornice manufacturers supply a paper template that enables cutting lines to be marked accurately for internal and external corners.

3 When using cut pieces to complete a wall, mark off the length required directly, square a line across the cornice with a pencil and cut it to length.

PUTTING UP A DADO (CHAIR) OR PICTURE RAIL

A dado (chair) rail is a flat-backed wooden moulding that runs around the room about one-third of the way up from the floor. Its primary purpose is to protect the wall surfaces from damage caused by furniture – especially chair backs – knocking against them. Once fitted, it can be painted, varnished or stained to complement or contrast with the room's colour scheme. It also serves as a visual break in the surface of the wall, as different treatments can be used above and below the rail – wallpaper above, for example, and wood panelling below.

The area below the rail, which is known as the dado (wainscot) was traditionally panelled or decorated with a relief wall covering and painted, while the surface above the rail was generally papered or painted in a plain colour. The wide range of decorative techniques in use today, however – including special paint effects such as sponging, rag-rolling, stippling and marbling – offer great potential for quick and interesting results.

A dado rail can be nailed to wood-framed walls after using a stud finder to locate the vertical members of the frame. On masonry walls, do not use masonry nails, as the rail may need to be removed in the future; use screws and wall plugs instead.

A picture rail is, as its name implies, used to support pictures. It is fixed to the wall a short distance below the ceiling, and has a curved upper edge designed to accept S-shaped picture hooks, from which the pictures can hang on wire, cord or chain. As large pictures (and also large mirrors) can be heavy, the rail must be securely fixed – with screws rather than nails. As with a dado rail, a picture rail can be decorated to complement or contrast with the wall covering. Its presence also allows the ceiling decoration to be carried down to rail level, a useful trick for making a high ceiling appear lower.

1 Start by deciding on the precise height at which to fix the rail, and use a pencil and spirit level to draw a horizontal line around the room.

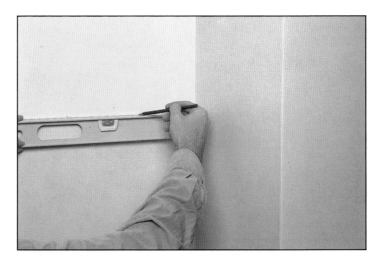

2 Alternatively, use a chalked string line pinned to the wall to mark the horizontal guideline on each wall of the room in turn.

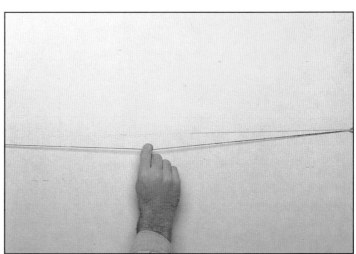

3 Drill clearance and countersink holes in the moulding at roughly 60 cm/2 ft intervals. Alternatively, counter-bore holes for wooden plugs instead.

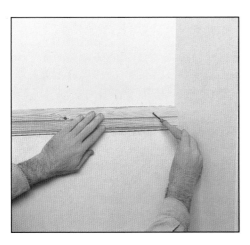

4 Hold the first length of rail up to the guideline and use a bradawl or similar tool to mark the fixing positions on the wall through the screw holes.

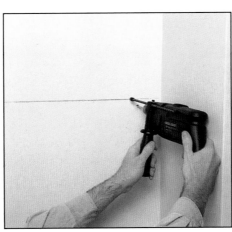

5 On masonry walls, drill holes for wall plugs. On wood-framed walls, use cavity fixings or locate the studs so that nails can go directly into them.

6 Drive in the first screw at one end of the length, then the next at the other end before driving in intermediate screws. This will keep the rail exactly on line.

MAKING ANGLED JOINS

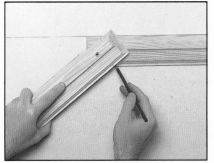

1 If you wish to fit a dado (chair) rail down a staircase, draw guidelines parallel with the flight on the staircase wall and mark the 2 meeting rails.

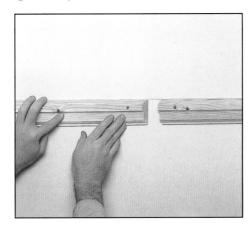

7 If lengths need joining along the length of a wall, make 45° mitre cuts on the meeting ends so that any shrinkage which occurs will not open up a visible gap.

8 Always use butt joins at internal angles. Scribe the rail profile on to the rear face of the length that will go on the second wall.

2 Cut the ends of the 2 rail sections so that they will form a neat join line; this should exactly bisect the angle between the 2 sections.

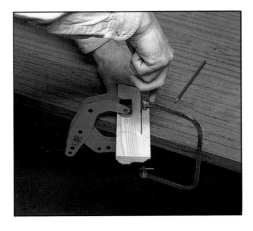

9 Cut carefully along the marked line with a coping saw, then fit the cut end so that it butts tightly against the face of the rail on the first wall.

10 Use mitred joints at external corners, cutting at just under 45° so that there is no chance of an ugly gap at the corner.

HANGING A NEW DOOR

Fitting new internal doors can go a long way towards giving the home a completely new look. A new door may be fitted for purely cosmetic reasons – because the existing one is out of style with the room's décor – or because the old one is warped or damaged. Whatever the reason, there is a huge selection of replacement doors available, made from hardwood or softwood in styles ranging from plain flush doors to highly ornate ones with solid or glazed panels. Glazed doors are ideal for admitting extra light to dark rooms or passageways, but national building regulations or local building code requirements must be followed in the choice of glass – reinforced (safety) glass may be required if there is any danger of an accident.

When replacing a door, it is generally advisable to fit new hardware – hinges and latches especially. Door handles and knobs can be removed and replaced if they must match others in the room. In countries where wood-frame construction is the norm, pre-hung doors complete with frame and architrave (trim) are widely available. These are very convenient, as to fit them, all that is necessary is to set the unit in the opening, using wood shims to get it plumb, and then nail it into position ready for the trim mouldings to be attached. The door is even pre-bored to accept the new lock or latch.

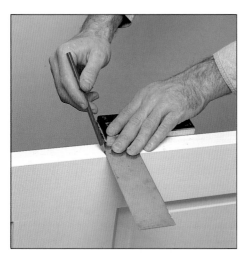

1 Remove the old door and use it as a guide to marking the hinge positions on the edge of the new door. Square the lines across it with a T-square.

2 Set a marking gauge to match the width of the hinge, and scribe a line parallel to the door edge between those made in step 1.

3 Use a chisel and mallet to cut into the door along the marked lines and then to chop out a shallow recess to match the thickness of the hinge leaf.

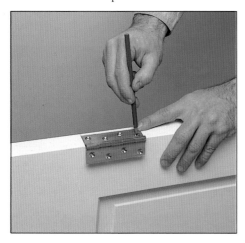

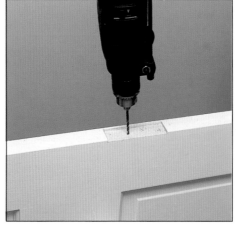

4 Hold the hinge in position in the recess, and mark the positions of all the screw holes on the door edge with a pencil or bradawl.

5 Drill pilot holes into the door edge at each of the marks. Check that they are at right angles to the door edge. If not, the screws will be crooked.

6 Screw the hinge to the door with matching screws. Drive them fully home and check that the screw heads sit square and flush in the countersinks.

DOOR SIZES

Doors are made in a range of standard sizes. If the old door is a standard size, buying the correct replacement is simple; but if it is not, a door in the next largest size will need to be sawn or planed down as required. Bear this in mind when deciding on the style of door. Panelled doors can be reduced in size more easily (and by more) than flush ones. However, doors cannot be cut down excessively or they come apart: do not cut away the tenon joints in the corners, nor remove too much of the edge wood on a flush door.

7 If re-using the old hinge recesses, screw the door to the frame using screws one size up from the originals. If cutting new recesses, prop the door in the opening and, with a pencil, mark the hinge positions. Remember to lift it a little clear of the floor to allow for easy opening and shutting.

8 Square lines across the frame at the marks, then measure the width of the hinge leaf and mark the width of the recess required on the frame.

9 Cut along the marked lines with a sharp chisel, then carefully cut out the recess to the required depth. Take care not to let the chisel slip.

10 Prop the door back in position and mark the hinge screw positions. Drill pilot holes, then drive in the screws to secure the hinges to the door frame.

TIP

If the door binds on the hinge side and will not close properly, the hinge recesses are too deep. Unscrew the hinges and insert cardboard packing pieces.

FEATURES AND FITTINGS

FITTING DOOR AND WINDOW HARDWARE

Door and window fittings can be ornamental as well as practical and secure. The simplest type of door catch is a spring-loaded ball which is recessed into the door edge. The ball engages in a recess in the door frame as the door is pushed closed, and retracts as the door is pulled open. This type of catch is inexpensive to buy and easy to fit.

A more positive action is provided by a mortise latch; this is also recessed into the door edge and has a projecting bolt that is flat on one face and curved on the other. As the door is pushed shut, the curved face hits the striking plate on the door frame and pushes the bolt back into the latch body. When the door is fully closed the bolt springs out into the recess in the striking plate, with its flat face providing a positive latching movement. The action of turning the handle rotates a spindle, withdrawing the bolt from the striking plate and allowing the door to open again. A mortise lock combines the same type of latch mechanism with a lockable bolt.

The most common items of hardware used on hinged windows are a rotating cockspur handle that is used simply to fasten the window, and a casement stay that props it open in one of several different positions. On sliding sash windows, the basic hardware consists of a catch screwed to the 'back' window that swings across to lock the 2 sashes together when they are closed.

SAFETY TIP

If you are fitting lockable window catches and stays, do not leave the keys in the locks in case they fall out as you open and close the window. Instead, hang them on a pin driven into the window frame. This will also ensure that they are readily available should the window have to be opened quickly in an emergency.

FITTING A MORTISE LATCH

1 To fit a mortise latch to a new door, use the latch body to mark the mortise position on the door edge, in line with the centre rail or lock block.

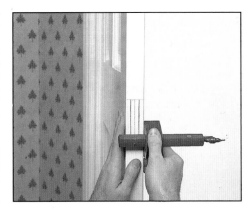

2 Set a mortise gauge to a setting just wider than the thickness of the latch body, and scribe the outline of the mortise centred on the door edge.

3 Use a flat wood bit in a power drill to make a series of holes between the guidelines, a little deeper than the length of the latch body.

4 Chop out the waste using a chisel and mallet, then pare down the sides of the mortise and clean out the recess. Try the latch for fit in the mortise.

5 Draw around the latch faceplate on the edge of the door, then cut around the lines with a chisel and make a series of parallel cuts across the grain.

6 Carefully chisel out the waste wood between the marked guidelines, taking care not to let the chisel slip and cut beyond the ends of the recess.

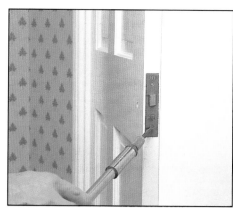

7 Hold the latch body against the face of the door, in line with the mortise and with its faceplate flush with the door edge. Mark the spindle position.

8 Clamp a piece of scrap wood to the other side of the door. Drill a hole large enough to accept the spindle through the door into the scrap wood.

9 Slide the latch into place in its mortise, and make pilot holes through the faceplate with a bradawl. Drive in the faceplate fixing screws.

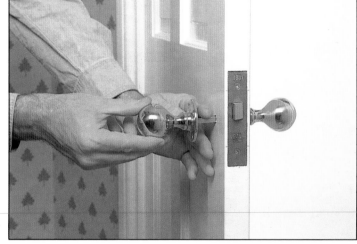

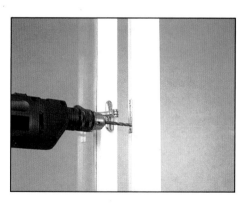

10 Insert the spindle and fit a handle on to each end. Check that the spindle rotates freely, then screw both handles to the door.

11 Close the door in order to mark where the latch bolt meets the frame. Chisel out the recesses for the bolt and striking plate, and screw on the plate.

FITTING A WINDOW HANDLE AND STAY

1 Decide where the cockspur handle should sit on the casement and make pilot holes through it with a bradawl. Screw the handle to the casement.

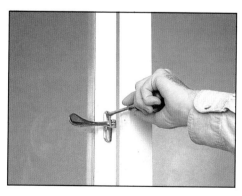

2 Fit the striking plate to the frame so that the cockspur will engage in it. Drill out the frame to a depth of about 20 mm/¾ in through the slot in the plate.

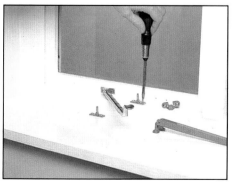

3 Fit the casement stay by screwing its baseplate to the bottom rail of the casement, about one-third of the way along from the hinged edge.

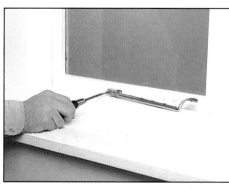

4 Open the window to find the correct position for the pins to sit on the frame. Attach the pins, then fit the stay rest on the casement rail.

FITTING CURTAIN (DRAPERY) POLES AND TRACKS

There are many different methods of hanging curtains and drapes, ranging from simple rings on a wooden pole to complex tracks that are often cord-operated and may even be motor-driven. Poles may be wooden or metal, while tracks are either metal or plastic. Some are designed to be unobtrusive, others to be a definite design feature. The choice depends on the style of décor, and also to some extent on the curtains themselves, as some heading styles work better with one type than another. Check with the supplier to see which track style will work best.

Fixing curtain tracks can be tricky on a masonry wall. The top of the window opening may be bridged by a reinforced concrete or galvanized-steel beam, concealed behind the plaster. The problem lies in making firm fixings into this beam, as drilling concrete at a precise spot to take a wall plug and screw can be difficult, and you will need a cavity fixing such as a spring toggle for a steel beam. It is often easier either to fit the track above the beam, or to put up a wooden support strip first and then attach the track to that. If the worst comes to the worst, you could use a ceiling-mounted track. Fixing tracks to wood-framed walls, by contrast, could not be easier. You can fix the brackets anywhere on the wooden beam over the window opening.

TIP

Before you buy your curtain (drapery) pole or track, measure the width of the window carefully, and add extra width at the sides. The amount you add will depend on the bulk of the curtains, and how much space they will take up when they are open. With a narrow window, it is important to allow enough width for the pole or track so that the curtains do not obscure the window at all.

PUTTING UP A CURTAIN (DRAPERY) POLE

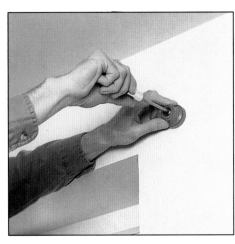

1 Draw a pencil guideline on the wall, and mark the bracket positions along it. Attach the bracket bases after drilling and/or plugging the holes.

2 Slot in the bracket extensions and tighten the locking screws. Slide in the pole, fit the rings and finial, and screw through the brackets into the pole.

PUTTING UP A ROLLER BLIND (SHADE)

A roller blind, as its name implies, consists of a length of material – usually fabric – wound on to a roller that is mounted in brackets close to the window. It can be used instead of curtains and drapes for a simple, uncluttered effect, or in conjunction with them – for example if extra shade is required in a sunny window.

1 Screw the roller brackets to the frame close to the top corners, with the fixing flanges facing inwards so that you have room to use a screwdriver.

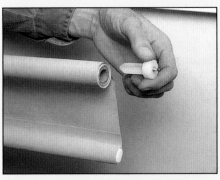

2 Cut the roller and fabric to the required width, and insert the pin caps at each end to match the brackets – one is round, the other rectangular.

3 Hang the roller on its brackets, then pull it down to check the tension. If it will not retract, lift off the ratchet end, roll up the blind and replace it.

PUTTING UP A CURTAIN (DRAPERY) TRACK

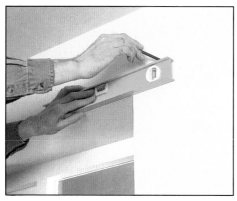

1 Decide at what level to fit the track, and use a pencil and spirit level to draw a guideline on the wall surface. Extend the line at the sides.

2 Drill holes for wall plugs in a masonry wall, or make pilot holes in a wood-framed one, at the spacings recommended in the instructions. Fit the brackets.

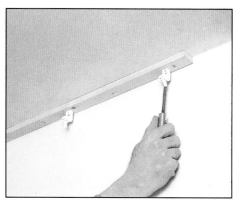

3 If you need to use a ceiling-mounted track, locate the joist or joists and screw a support strip into place. Attach the track brackets to the support strip.

4 If you have to fit lengths of track together to cope with wide windows, you must use special connectors that do not interfere with the runners.

5 Mount the track on the brackets. Here, this is done by rotating a locking cam via a small lever; on other types there is a locking screw.

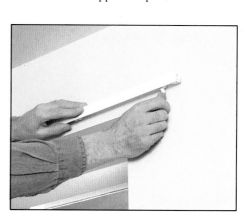

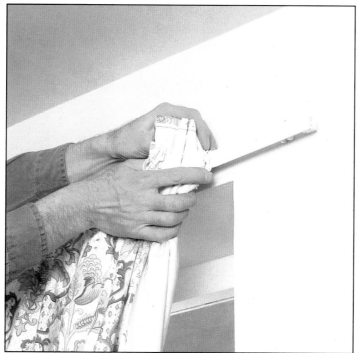

6 Fit the curtain hooks to the heading tape, then clip the hooks to the track. Some types have hooks on the track already, in which case you can simply hook on the curtains.

MAKING AN OVERLAP

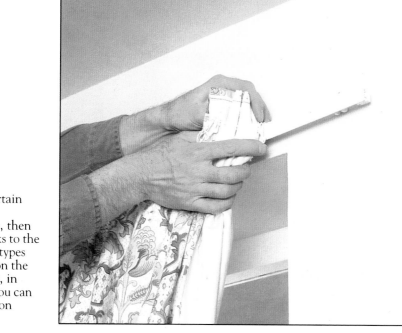

If you require a curtain overlap, form an S-bend on a length of track so that it overlaps the track behind. Clip the extension bracket to the tracks and screw the bracket to the wall.

HANGING PICTURES AND MIRRORS

However beautifully walls are decorated, they will still look rather featureless unless they are brightened up by hanging some pictures, and perhaps a mirror or too as well. Apart from their obvious function, mirrors can make a room seem brighter by reflecting light from the window.

For hanging pictures there is a choice of using individual supports for each picture, or hanging them from a picture rail. Individual supports range from small plastic or metal picture hooks, which are simply nailed to the wall, to heavy-duty fixings attached with screws – and wall plugs on masonry walls. The choice depends solely on the weight of the picture. Use single-pin picture hooks for pictures with a slimline frame up to around 60 cm/2 ft in either dimension, and a two-pin hook for anything of similar size in a heavy frame. Use two hooks, one at each side of the frame, for pictures up to about 90 cm/3 ft across, and switch to a screw-in hook for anything larger. With picture rails, the standard S-shaped hooks will support reasonable weights.

Mirrors can be hung like pictures as long as the fixing is strong enough to take the weight. Otherwise they can be secured directly to the wall with special mirror clips. If they have pre-drilled holes at the corners they can be fixed with screws – ideally, mirror screws with special domes or clip-on covers (rosette fastenings).

MIRROR FIXINGS

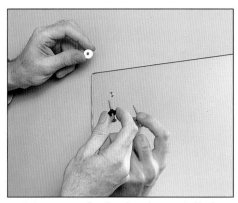

1 Mirrors can be fixed with pre-drilled holes, using screws plus special washers and spacers that cushion the mirror and allow air circulation.

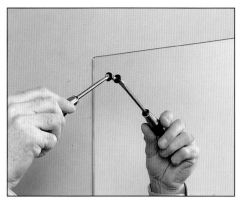

2 Mark and drill the fixing holes, then thread the screw through the washer, the mirror and the rear spacer before driving the screw. Do not overtighten it.

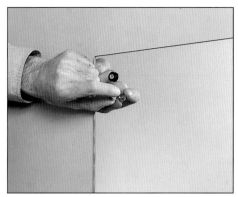

3 The screw head should just start to compress the washer. Cover it with a screw-on dome (rosette fastening) if using mirror screws, or with a plastic cover otherwise.

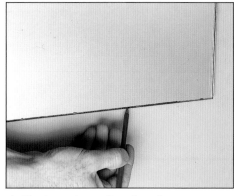

4 If using mirror clips, first draw a guideline on the wall where the bottom of the mirror will go, and fit the fixed bottom clips at each end.

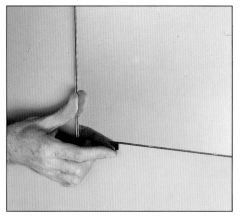

5 Set the bottom edge of the mirror in the bottom clips, checking that it is truly level, and mark the wall to indicate where its top edge will be.

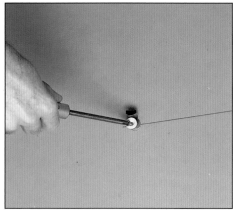

6 Screw the slotted top clips to the wall so their top edges are just above the line. Raise them, set the mirror in place, and press the top clips down.

BELOW For a more attractive finish, choose special screws with screw-on domes (rosette fastenings) for fixing mirrors.

PICTURE FIXINGS

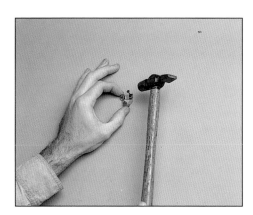

1 Traditional brass picture hooks come in one-pin and two-pin versions. The holes in the hook guide the pin in at an angle to the wall for a firmer fixing.

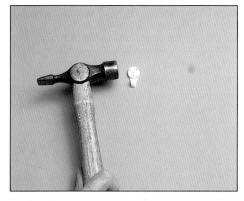

2 Small plastic picture hooks have three or four short pins to help locate the hook, and are secured by a longer pin driven through the centre hole.

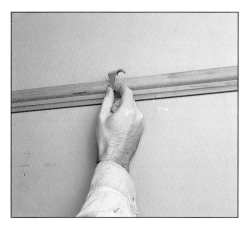

3 A picture rail allows pictures to be hung in any position and at any height. Simply place the hook over the rail and hang the picture wire over it.

PICTURE FRAMES

Well-chosen pictures can make all the difference to any room, but how they are framed and mounted are as important as the choice of subject matter and style. The moulding must suit the subject, as well as your décor. It may be big and bold or small and delicate, modern or traditional, and you can choose from a vast range of profiles. The finish of the moulding and the type of mount is also important, and you can buy ready-decorated mouldings in almost any type of finish. Alternatively, you can add your own paint effect or finish.

The techniques for framing can vary according to the type of frame and the style of decoration, and you may decide to ask a professional to frame a special painting for you. However, the technique shown here for making a standard frame is straightforward. The most important things to get right are accuracy when cutting, and neatness, as these affect how the finished frame will look. A mitre block and tenon saw are essential for cutting perfect 45° angles and two corner clamps are needed for holding the frame together while the wood glue dries. In addition, a 45° mat cutter will give a good clean angle and a professional look to the mount. Corrugated fasteners are used to strengthen the corners.

Once you have joined the pieces of moulding, you can assemble the other frame components. Ask a glazier to cut 3 mm/¼ in picture glass, to fit inside the rebate of the frame. The hardboard backing is secured in place with panel pins (tacks), and the join covered with brown paper tape.

Pictures can be hung from a hook, in which case brass picture wire or string needs to be attached to the frame using ring screws. Larger pictures can be mounted on to a wall with brass mirror plates. These are a strong and secure way of hanging, and can be painted the same colour as the wall.

MAKING A PICTURE FRAME

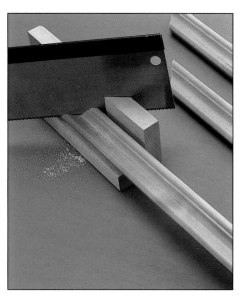

1 Cut the picture moulding to length, using a mitre block and a tenon saw. This allows you to achieve accurate 45° angles. Measure the frame from the inside edge and allow for the extra wood needed to take the 45° mitre cut.

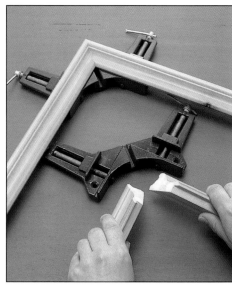

2 Glue two pairs of corners at a time with wood glue and place in corner clamps so that you have a good strong seam that will need no filling later. Allow the glue to dry completely.

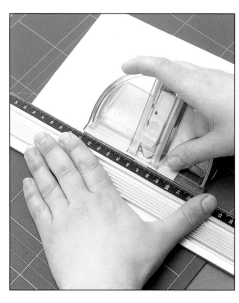

4 Cut the mount cardboard with a 45° mat cutter. Working on the back of the mount, score the line first with a blade using a metal ruler as a guide. Gradually lower the blade and slice through the cardboard. To achieve good, crisp corners, slightly over-cut each side so that the middle of the cardboard just drops out. Tape the picture to the mount with masking tape.

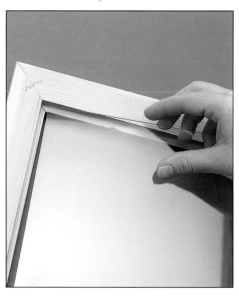

5 With the frame face down, lower in the 3 mm/¼ in picture glass so that it sits in the rebate of the frame. Then drop in the mount and picture.

3 To add strength to the frame, hammer in a corrugated fastener at each corner. Make sure that the fasteners are hammered straight down.

ABOVE This sitting room has made a real focal point of the walls by using a variety of different sized and shaped frames. The slightly random effect adds a note of fun to the arrangement.

6 Use a junior hacksaw to cut a piece of hardboard to fit inside the rebate. Secure the hardboard in place with panel pins (tacks). To seal the frame and prevent any dust from getting in, cover the seam between the frame and the hardboard with brown paper tape. Let dry thoroughly.

MAKING A PICTURE STAND   HANGING PICTURES

1 Make a hardboard stand and paint it to match the picture frame. Glue it to the back of the frame with a hinge so that it can also lie flat. Alternatively, drill two holes into the back of the picture frame at its base, and insert a short length of wooden dowel into each, to act as stands.

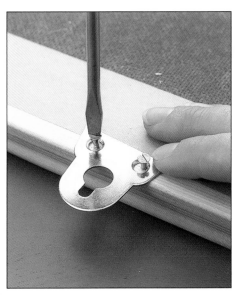

1 To hang a picture, screw a ring screw into either side of the frame and securely tie on brass picture wire. To hold the frame flush against a wall, use mirror plates. Screw them into the back of the frame and then slot them over screws in the wall.

STORAGE

Finding suitable storage space around the house for all the personal and household belongings every family accumulates can be quite a challenge. One difficulty is making a sensible compromise between tidiness and accessibility; it is no good having a place for everything if that means spending hours each day laboriously taking things out and putting them back again.

The solution is to tailor-make storage to suit its purpose. Some things need a temporary resting place where they remain readily accessible. Others need long-term storage, perhaps being retrieved and used only occasionally. And there is a third storage category, that of display – simply to show things off.

In a typical home, possessions are stored in one of three main ways: on shelves, in cupboards (closets) or in drawers. These may be combined in a variety of storage or display units, and the amount of each type of space that is required will vary from house to house. For example, the avid bookworm will have miles of shelves lining the walls, while the clothes horse will need more wardrobe space.

The storage that is needed can be provided in one of two ways. One is to buy or make pieces of free-standing furniture that match the required storage function. The other is to use raw materials such as wood and manufactured boards plus the appropriate hardware to create built-in storage space – arrays of shelving, cupboards in alcoves and so on. The former is the best solution for those who value furniture more than function, since the pieces can be moved from one house to another. However, built-in storage is generally more effective in providing the most space for the least money, since the house walls can often be used as part of the structure. The following pages look at some of the storage options available.

OPPOSITE Shelving is an indispensable requirement when it comes to providing storage and display space around the house. It can be free-standing, wall-hung or built in to corners and alcoves, and can be tailor-made to suit a specific task or adjustable for maximum flexibility.

STORAGE

INCREASING STORAGE SPACE

Apart from obvious places such as kitchen units (cabinets) and bedroom wardrobes (closets), there are many places in the house in which you can store items without spoiling the look of the room. Properly planned storage space can be not only practical and capacious, but positively elegant.

In the kitchen, storage is a serious business, and what you need and how you provide it will depend on what kind of kitchen it is and how you use it. The fully fitted kitchen is popular because it packs the most storage into the least space, whereas the farmhouse-style kitchen, with free-standing furniture, reduces the amount of storage space. There is, however, one big advantage with free-standing furniture: you can take it along when you move house.

In deciding what you want, analyse your storage needs thoroughly. Think about food, cooking utensils and small appliances for a start; all need a place close to cooking and food-preparation areas. Move on to items such as china, cutlery and glassware; do they need to be in the kitchen at all, or would the dining room be a better place to keep them? Then consider non-culinary items – cleaning materials, table linen and so on – and make sure that there is enough space for them.

Always make the best possible use of cupboard (closet) space. Fit extra shelves where necessary, use wire baskets for ventilated storage, hang small racks on the backs of doors and use swing-out carousels to gain access to corner cupboards.

In the living room, storage needs are likely to be leisure-oriented. There has to be enough room for books, cassettes, compact discs and videotapes, not to mention display space for ornaments. The choice is again between free-standing and built-in furniture, and is much freer than in the kitchen because in this room looks are just as important as performance.

Built-in furniture can make optimum use of alcoves and other recesses. A more radical option is a complete wall of storage units, which could include space for home-entertainment equipment as well as features such as a drinks cupboard (cabinet). While planning living-room storage, pay particular attention to working requirements for power points (receptacles), especially if you have a lot of hi-fi (stereo) equipment, and for any concealed lighting in the unit.

Storage needs in the dining room relate mainly to providing places for china, glassware and cutlery (flatware)

ABOVE Wall-mounted shelving in this hallway provides an unobtrusive home for the telephone.

LEFT Fitted kitchen units (cabinets) offer much more than a home for provisions and pots and pans. Tailor-made units can now store and display everything from wine bottles to the family china.

Simple hooks and an umbrella stand are the bare minimum, but consider having an enclosed cupboard (closet) that is built-in rather than free-standing. It is simple to 'borrow' some porch- or hall-floor space to create a suitable enclosure. If you fit the cupboard with a door to match others leading to the rest of the house, it will blend in perfectly. Make sure that the cupboard is ventilated so that any damp clothes will be able to dry.

LEFT An alcove is the perfect site for built-in shelving for books, or for display and storage cupboards (cabinets) for music cassettes and discs, videos, hi-fi (stereo) equipment and so on.

BELOW A beautifully tiled bathroom is further enhanced with an attractive vanity unit, which can offer valuable storage space for toiletries.

– especially any that is kept for special occasions. Think too about storage for table mats, cloths and other table accessories. Once again, the choice is between built-in storage units and free-standing furniture.

Now take a look at your storage requirements upstairs, starting with the bedrooms. Here the main need is for space to store clothes, and this is one area in which built-in (and ideally, walk-in) storage is the perfect solution. Space can often be 'poached' between

USING THE ROOF SPACE

Except in older houses, the roof space is usually cluttered with all the woodwork that makes up a modern trussed-rafter roof and is of little use for storage. However, it is still worth boarding over the area immediately around the access hatch so that you can put luggage, boxes and the like there. If the roof construction permits, however, there is a chance to create an almost unlimited storage capacity. Fit a proper fixed ladder to allow both safe and easy access.

bedrooms by forming a deep partition wall, accessible from one or both rooms; this can actually save money, as there will be no furniture to buy. An alternative if overall space permits is to create a separate dressing room, at least for the master bedroom.

Bedrooms built under the roof slope offer an unparalleled opportunity to make use of the space behind the room walls by creating fully lined eaves cupboards (closets). These are ideal for long-term storage of items such as luggage which may be needed only occasionally, as well as providing a home for toys in children's rooms.

Finally, look at the bathroom. Here requirements are likely to be relatively low-key – somewhere to keep toiletries and cleaning materials, for example. The choice is likely to be between a floor-standing vanity unit and some wall-hung cupboards (cabinets), although if space permits you might give some thought to the growing number of fully fitted bathroom-furniture ranges. Where space is very limited, make use of the 'hidden' space behind a removable bath panel to store small items such as children's bath toys.

ABOVE Pull-out baskets are often more accessible than traditional shelving in kitchen base units (cabinets).

FITTING FIXED AND ADJUSTABLE SHELVING

Wall-mounted shelving is either fixed or adjustable. With fixed shelving, each shelf is supported independently using 2 or more shelf brackets, which are fixed both to the wall and to the underside of the shelf. With adjustable shelving, the shelves are carried on brackets, studs or tongues which are slotted or clipped into vertical support strips screwed to the wall.

Shelves can be made of natural wood or manufactured boards. Ready-made shelves are usually made of veneered or plastic-coated chipboard (particle board). The latter traditionally have either a white or imitation wood-grain finish, but pastel shades and bold colours are now more widely available. Otherwise, you can cut shelves from full-sized boards: chipboard, plywood, MDF (medium-density fibreboard) and blockboard are all suitable.

There are many types of adjustable shelving on the market, with uprights and brackets usually made of metal but occasionally of wood. All operate on broadly the same principle. Start by deciding on the position and spacing of the uprights; this will depend on what sort of shelf material you are using and what load it will carry. Hang the uprights on the wall, making sure that they are perfectly vertical and level with each other. Finally, clip in the brackets and fit the shelves.

You may also want adjustable shelves inside a storage unit. There are 2 options. The first involves drilling a series of aligned holes in each side of the unit, then inserting small shelf-support studs. The second uses book-case strip – a metal moulding with slots into which small pegs or tongues are fitted to support the shelves. You will need 2 strips at each side of the unit.

USING SHELF BRACKETS

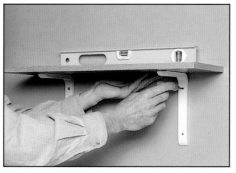

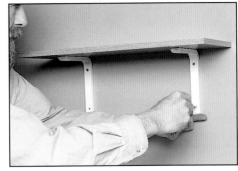

1 Select the correct bracket spacing, then attach the shorter arm of each bracket to the underside of the shelf, so that it is flush with the rear edge.

2 Fix the shelf to the wall with a screw driven through one bracket, check that it is horizontal and mark the remaining screw positions. Let the shelf swing downwards on the first screw, then drill the other holes.

3 Insert plugs for masonry wall fixings if needed. Swing the shelf back up and drive in the remaining fixing screws. Tighten them fully so that the screw heads pull the brackets against the wall.

PUTTING UP ADJUSTABLE SHELVES

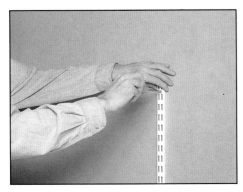

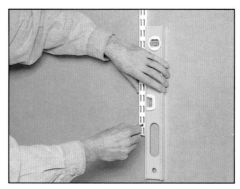

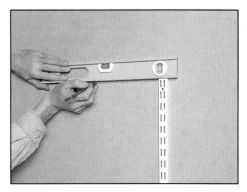

1 Decide where to position the shelves, then fix the first upright to the wall by driving a screw through the topmost hole. Do not tighten it fully.

2 Pivot the upright until it is vertical. Mark the position of all the other fixing holes. Swing the upright aside, drill the rest of the holes and drive in the screws.

3 Use a spirit level to make a mark on the wall, level with the top of the first upright and at the required distance from it. Fix the second upright there.

4 Mark the upright positions on the rear edge of each shelf. Align the back of each bracket with the edge of the shelf and with the mark, and screw it on.

5 If the shelves are to fit flush against the wall, cut notches at the upright positions to fit around them and then attach the brackets as shown.

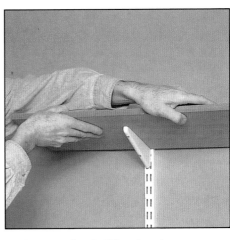

6 Position the shelf brackets by inserting their tongues into the slots in the uprights. The weight of the shelf will lock them in place. Adjust the shelf spacings as wished.

PLANNING SHELVES

Think of how to make best use of your new storage area. It is a good idea to make a rough sketch initially, in order to take account of factors such as the height of books or record sleeves, or the clearance that ornaments or photographs will require. Aim to keep everyday items within easy reach – in practice, between about 75 cm/2 ft 6 in and 1.5 m/5 ft above the floor. Position deep shelves near the bottom so that it is easy to see and reach the back. Allow 2.5–5 cm/1–2 in of clearance on top of the height of objects to be stored, so that they are easy to take down and put back.

Think about weight, too. If the shelves will store heavy objects, you must choose the shelving material with care – thin shelves will sag if heavily laden unless they are well-supported. With 12 mm/½ in chipboard (particle board) and ready-made veneered or melamine-faced shelves, space brackets at 45 cm/18 in for heavy loads or 60 cm/2 ft for light loads. With 20 mm/¾ in chipboard or 12 mm/ ½ in plywood, increase the spacing to 60 cm/2 ft and 75 cm/2 ft 6 in respectively. For 20 mm/¾ in plywood, blockboard, MDF (medium-density fibreboard) or natural wood, the bracket spacing can be 75 cm/2 ft 6 in for heavy loads, or 90 cm/3 ft for light ones.

USING BOOKCASE STRIP

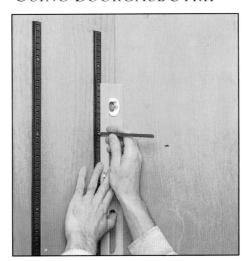

1 Mark the positions of the top ends of the strips to ensure that they are level, then mark the screw positions to a true vertical and screw on the strips.

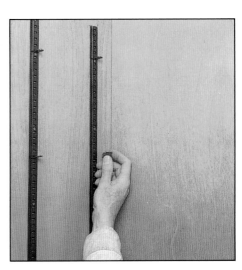

2 Insert pairs of pegs into the strips at each shelf position, checking that their lugs are properly engaged in the slots. Lift the shelf into place.

USING SHELF SUPPORTS

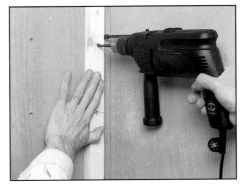

1 Use a simple pre-drilled jig to make the holes for the shelf supports in the sides of the unit. A depth stop will prevent you from drilling too deep.

2 Drill 2 sets of holes in each side of the unit, with the top of the jig held against the top of the unit to guarantee alignment. Insert the supports.

FREE-STANDING SHELVING

Free-standing shelf units have several advantages over wall-mounted or built-in ones. They can easily be moved if the room layout is changed. They can be moved away from the wall to allow painting or papering. They can even be taken along when moving house. However, they have drawbacks too. Some manufactured shelving and display units are rather flimsy, and may twist out of square or sag if they are heavily loaded. In general, better results come from building units from stronger materials such as natural wood and plywood. The other problem is getting them to stand upright against the wall; skirtings (baseboards) prevent

standard units from being pushed back flush with the wall surface, and carpet gripper strips make them lean forwards slightly. The answer is to design the side supports on the cantilever principle with just one point of contact with the floor, as far as possible from the wall, so that the unit presses more firmly against the wall as the load on the shelves is increased.

Since a shelf unit is basically a box with internal dividers, it can be constructed in several different ways, using simple butt joints or more complicated housings. Perhaps the best compromise between strength and ease of construction is to use glued butt

joints reinforced with hardwood dowels, which give the joints the extra rigidity they need in a unit of this sort.

Start by deciding on the dimensions of the unit, then select materials to suit the likely loading the shelves will have to support. Mark up and cut matching groups of components to length in batches to ensure that they are all precisely the same size. Pre-drill all the dowel holes, using a drill stand and depth stop for holes in the board faces and a dowelling jig for those in the board ends. Insert the dowels and make up the joints. A thin plywood or hardboard backing panel can be pinned (tacked) on to give the unit extra rigidity.

CONSTRUCTING A FREE-STANDING SHELF UNIT

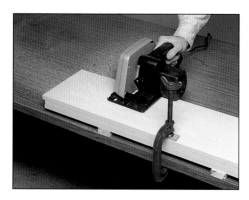

1 Clamp groups of identical components together. Mark them to length and cut them in one operation to ensure that they are all the same length.

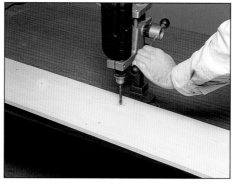

2 Mark the positions of the shelf dowel holes on the unit sides, ensuring that they match. Drill them all to the required depth, using a drill stand if possible.

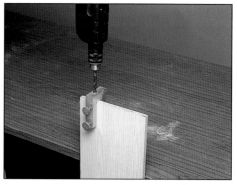

3 Use a dowelling jig to drill the dowel holes in the shelf ends. This ensures that the holes are correctly positioned and centred, and are drilled straight.

4 Glue the dowels and tap them into the holes in the shelf ends. Check that they all project by the same amount, and cut down any that are overlong.

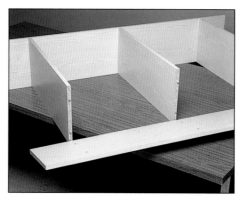

5 Assemble the unit by gluing one end of each of the three shelves and joining them to a side panels. Then glue the other ends and add the second side panel.

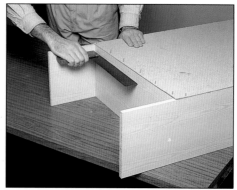

6 Cut a hardboard or plywood backing panel. Check that it is perfectly square, then pin (tack) it to the back of the unit.

BELOW Free-standing shelves combined with cupboards (cabinets) and an office area offer valuable storage potential. The natural wood finish harmonizes with the décor and handsome beech wood-strip flooring.

FITTING SHELVES IN AN ALCOVE

An alcove beside a chimney breast (fireplace projection) or similar protrusion makes a perfect site for shelves, as the back and side walls can be used as supports. Although it is easy to use fixed shelf brackets or an adjustable-shelving system to support shelves, it is cheaper to fix wood or metal support strips to the alcove walls and to rest the shelves on these.

If you are using wooden supports, cut their front ends at an angle so that they are less noticeable when the shelves are fitted. Paint them the same colour as the walls (or to tone with the wall covering) to make them even less obtrusive. If you use L-shaped metal strips for the supports, choose a size that matches the shelf thickness so that they will be almost invisible once you have fitted the shelves.

The actual job is quite simple. Mark the shelf level on the alcove walls, cut the supports to the required lengths and screw them to the walls. Then cut your shelf to size and slip it into place, so that it rests on the supports. You can nail, screw or glue it in place for extra stability. The only difficult part lies in making the shelf a good fit, as the alcove walls may not be truly square. Accurate measuring of the alcove width at front and back, plus some careful scribing of the rear edge of the shelf, will ensure good results.

WORKSHOP STORAGE

An area where some storage space is certainly needed is the workshop, whether this is a spare room, an area at the back of the garage or a separate building. The basic need is for shelf space, to take everything from cans of paint to garden products, and also some form of tool storage to keep everything in order. Freestanding utility shelving is the ideal way of providing sturdy and compact garage or workshop storage.

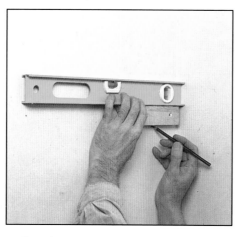

1 Decide on the shelf positions, then use a spirit level to mark the position of the first shelf support on one alcove wall.

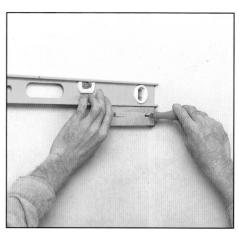

2 Drill clearance and countersink holes in the supports, and use the first one to mark the fixing hole positions on the wall. Drill the holes and fix this support.

3 Rest a shelf on the first support, adjust it until it is level and mark the shelf position on the opposite wall of the alcove. Prepare the second shelf support.

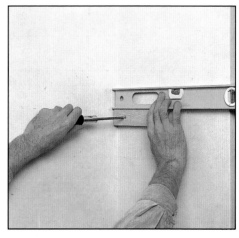

4 Screw the second support in place after using it to mark the positions of the fixing holes on the wall, as in step 2. Check again that it is level.

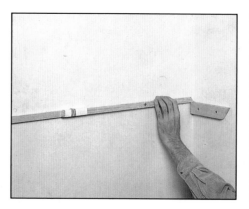

5 Make up a set of pinch rods from scrap wood, held together as shown with a rubber band. Extend the rods to span the rear wall of the alcove.

6 Lift out the rods carefully without disturbing their positions. Lay them on the rear edge of the shelf and mark on it the width of the alcove.

RIGHT Alcove shelving can be put to practical or decorative use. Here, painted shelves form a focal point in the room for the display of boxes and wicker baskets.

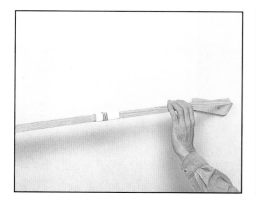

7 Repeat the operation in step 5 to measure the width at the point where the front edge of the shelf will be, then transfer the measurement to the shelf.

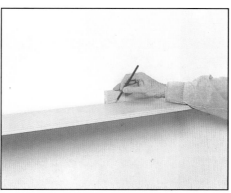

8 Cut the shelf to width and lay it on the supports. If the fit is poor against the back wall, use a block and pencil to scribe the wall outline on the shelf.

9 Saw carefully along the scribed line with a power jigsaw (saber saw). Sand the cut edge until it is smooth and then fit the shelf back in position.

MAKING CABINETS

Free-standing storage units (cabinets) consist simply of a basic box, fitted out internally as required. For example, these can include one or more shelves, vertical dividers, hanging rails, drawers and doors. All this applies to units as diverse in scale as a small hi-fi (stereo) cabinet and a large double wardrobe (closet). A pair of boxes can be placed under a counter top to create a desk or dressing table.

Units will probably be made from manufactured boards. It is difficult to get natural wood wider than about 22.5 cm/9 in, which rather restricts its scope; it is also more expensive. The most popular material for making box furniture is chipboard (particle board), especially the veneered and melamine-faced varieties which are sold in planks and boards of various sizes with the long edges (and sometimes the ends) already veneered or faced. Its main

disadvantage as a constructional board is its weakness – it will sag under its own weight across spans of more than about 90 cm/3 ft.

Stronger alternatives are plywood, MDF (medium-density fibreboard) and blockboard. Blockboard is the strongest – a 19 mm/¼ in) thick board can be used unsupported over spans twice as great as for chipboard. Sheets of blockboard sold as door blanks usually have the long edges faced.

Plywood offers the best of both worlds – it is almost as strong as blockboard, and has edges that can be neatly finished. It also has the added advantage of being available in thicknesses from 4 mm/⅛ in up to 19 mm/¾ in, so there should be a perfect match for any application.

MDF is a popular choice for box furniture as well as shelves as it cuts beautifully without the need for

finishing sawn edges. It is a medium-strength material and its very smooth surface finish can be painted, varnished or stained, as wished. Available in 244 x 120 cm/8 x 4 ft sheets and in thicknesses ranging from 6 to 25 mm/¼ to 1 in, MDF falls into the medium price range.

Those who are inexperienced in using power tools to make rebates and housing joints will probably prefer to make up boxes using glued butt joints, nailed or screwed for extra strength. These are adequate for small items, but will need reinforcing on larger pieces. The ideal way of doing this is with hardwood dowels. It is advisable to use dowels for chipboard, in which nails and even screws will not hold well. Alternatives, for light loads only however, are special chipboard screws, or ordinary screws set in glued-in fibre wall plugs.

MAKING BUTT JOINTS

1 To make a box, take measurements and start by cutting the components to size. Use a circular saw or a jigsaw (saber saw) to ensure clean, square edges.

2 While cutting the various components, label each piece in pencil and mark both halves of each joint with matching letters to avoid mix-ups during assembly.

3 To make a straightforward glued butt joint, spread woodworking adhesive along the edge of one component. Assemble the joint and clamp it to keep it square.

4 Reinforce a glued joint with pins (tacks) driven in so they pass into the centre of the panel underneath. Use a damp cloth to remove any excess adhesive.

5 Screwed joints are stronger than nailed ones. Place the edge component against the face component and mark its position on the latter.

6 Mark the screw positions carefully, especially if the joint is a T-joint rather than a corner. Double-check all measurements from nearby edges.

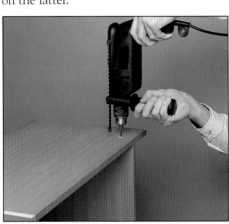

7 Drill clearance holes through the face component, then pilot holes in the edge piece. Countersink the clearance holes and carefully drive in chipboard (particle board) screws.

Using Dowels

1 Draw a pencil line along the centre of the joint position, then align the two components and carefully mark corresponding dowel hole positions on both pieces.

2 Drill the dowel holes in the face component, using a depth stop to avoid drilling too deep. Use a dowelling jig to drill holes in board edges.

3 Insert glued dowels in the holes in the edge component, then glue this to the face component. Add glue along the joint line too for extra strength.

4 A back panel will give any box extra strength, and also helps to resist skewing. Cut the panel fractionally under size and then pin (tack) in place.

FIXING DOORS AND DRAWERS

Adding doors and drawers to a basic storage box will turn it into a cupboard (cabinet) or a chest. Doors can be hung on any one of the many types of hinge available, but two of the most versatile are the flush hinge and the concealed hinge. The former has one leaf fitting into a cut-out in the other, and so can be surface-mounted to the door edge and the frame, without the need to cut recesses.

The concealed hinge is a little more complex to fit – the hinge body sits in a round hole bored in the rear face of the door, while the hinge arm is attached to a surface-mounted baseplate fitted to the side of the cabinet carcass – but it can be adjusted after fitting to ensure perfect alignment on multi-door installations, as in kitchens.

When it comes to adding drawers to cabinets, the simplest solution is to use plastic drawer kits. These consist of moulded sections that interlock to form the sides and back of the drawer, special corner blocks to allow a drawer front of any chosen material to be attached, and a base (usually of a piece of enamelled hardboard). The drawer sides are grooved to fit over runners that are screwed to the cabinet sides. The sides, back and base can be cut down to size if necessary.

FITTING FLUSH HINGES

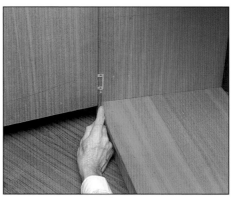

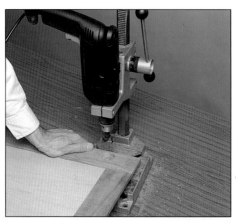

1 Mark the hinge position on the door edge, then make pilot holes and screw the smaller flap to the door. Check that the hinge knuckle faces the right way.

2 Hold the door in position against the cabinet carcass, and mark the hinge position on it. Mark the screw holes too, and drill pilot holes for the screws.

3 Reposition the door and attach the larger hinge leaf to the carcass. Check the door alignment carefully, then attach the other hinge in the same way.

FITTING A CONCEALED HINGE

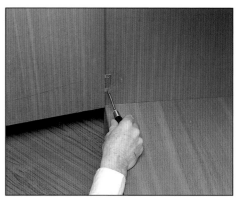

1 Mark the centre line of the hinge baseplate on the side wall of the cabinet, then lay the door flat against the carcass and extend the line on to it.

2 Use a power drill with an end mill, held in a drill stand, to cut the recess for the hinge body to the required depth in the rear face of the door.

3 Press the hinge body into the recess, check that the arm is at right angles to the door edge, and make pilot holes for the fixing screws. Drive these in.

MAKING UP A DRAWER KIT

1 Cut the sides and back to size if necessary, then stick the side and back sections together, using the clips and adhesive provided in the kit.

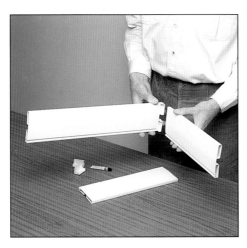

2 Cut the base down in size too if the drawer size was altered. Then slide the panel into place in the grooves in the side and back sections.

3 Screw the two corner joint blocks to the inner face of the drawer front, stick on the drawer base support channel, and then glue the front to the sides.

4 Hold the drawer within the cabinet to mark the position of its side grooves on the side walls. Then attach the plastic drawer runners.

4 Next, attach the baseplates to the side wall of the cabinet, centred on the guidelines drawn earlier. Check that they are fitted the right way around.

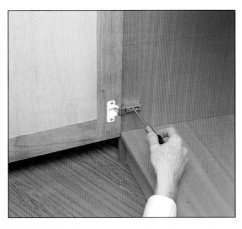

5 Hold the door against the cabinet, slot the hinge arm over the screw on the baseplate, and tighten it to lock the hinge arm in place.

TIPS

Make in-out adjustments to the door by loosening the mounting screw and repositioning the door.

Make neat side-to-side adjustments by using the smaller screw.

FITTING A BUILT-IN WARDROBE (CLOSET)

The walls of a room can be used to create larger storage spaces. These can range from filling in an alcove, through a unit in the corner of a room, to one running right across the room to the opposite wall. If the room has a central chimney breast (fireplace projection) with an alcove at either side, both alcoves can be used for storage and the chimney breast can be concealed with a dummy door.

In each case, the most important part is a frame to support the doors; these can be conventionally hinged or suspended from ceiling-mounted track. Remember that hinged doors allow unlimited access but need floor space in front of them so they can be opened easily. Sliding doors do not need this floor space, but they do have the minor disadvantage that access to the interior is sometimes restricted – when one door is open, it blocks access to the next section. Sliding doors can also catch on things such as suitcases inside the unit.

Such a flexible structure affords an opportunity to plan storage needs precisely. Start by selecting the depth needed to allow clothes to hang freely on hanging rails without dragging, then work out what width should be given to hanging space and what to shelving, drawers or basket space for storing other items of clothing. The space at the top level is suitable for storing seldom-used items, such as suitcases and hat and shoe boxes. Shoe racks can be added at floor level.

Doors can either be made into a feature of the room, or else painted or covered to blend unobtrusively with the room's colour scheme. Large flat-surfaced doors become almost invisible if decorated with a wall covering.

FITTING SLIDING DOORS TO STORAGE UNITS

1 Decide on the unit depth required, then locate the positions of the ceiling joists and screw a track support strip to them. Use packing to level it.

2 Next, screw the top track to the support strip, making sure that it is fitted parallel with the strip. Leave a gap next to the wall for the side upright.

6 Realign the side upright with the positioning marks made earlier, and screw it to the wall. Repeat the process at the other side of the opening.

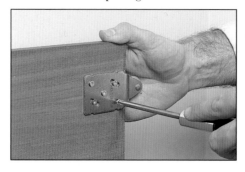

7 Cut the doors to size if necessary, allowing for clearances or overlaps as required in the door gear instructions, and then fit the door hangers.

8 Hang the doors by engaging the hanger wheels on the track as shown and then lowering the door to the vertical position. Finally, fit the floor guides.

3 Hold the length of wood that will form the side frame upright against the wall, and mark the profile of the skirting (baseboard) on it.

4 Use a coping saw or power jigsaw (saber saw) to cut away the waste wood from the foot of the upright, then test it for fit against the wall.

5 Use a spirit level to check that the side upright is vertical, then mark its position on the wall and drill the necessary clearance and fixing holes.

9 Conceal the track and door hangers by pinning (tacking) a decorative moulding to the track support batten. Some tracks come complete with a metal pelmet strip.

10 Finish off the installation by pinning slim wooden mouldings to the front edges of the side uprights. These will hide any slight gaps when the doors are closed.

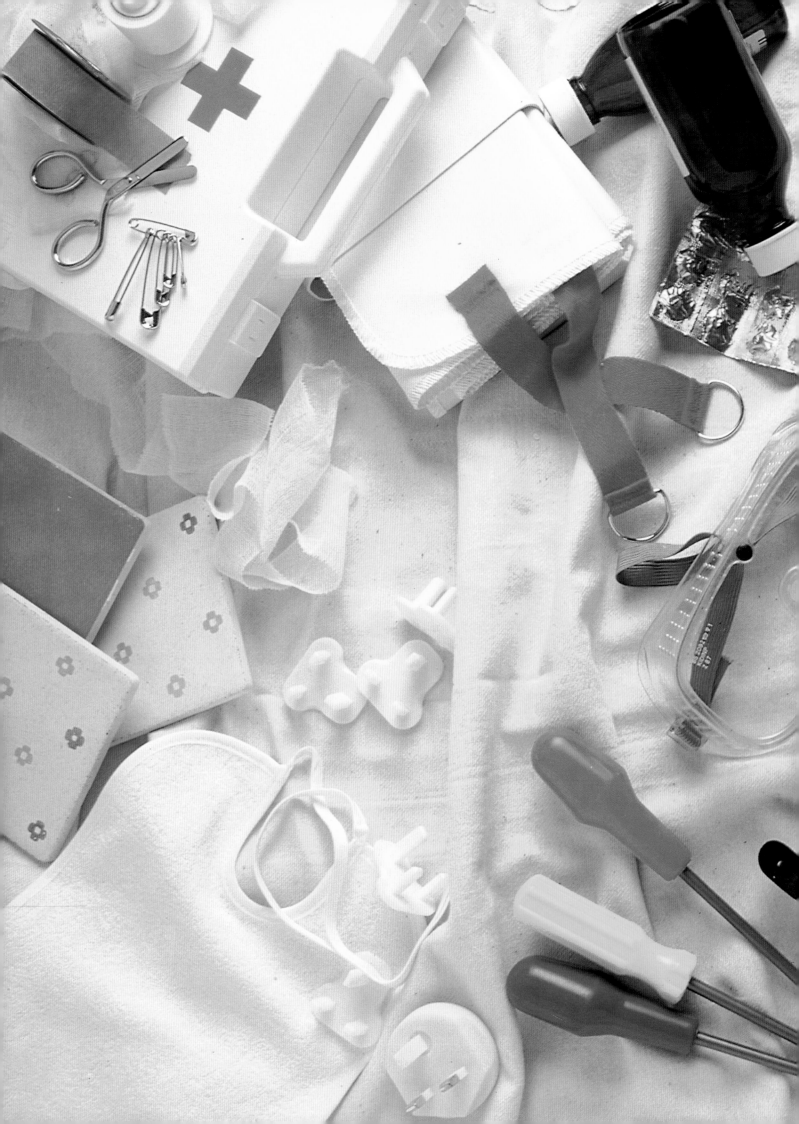

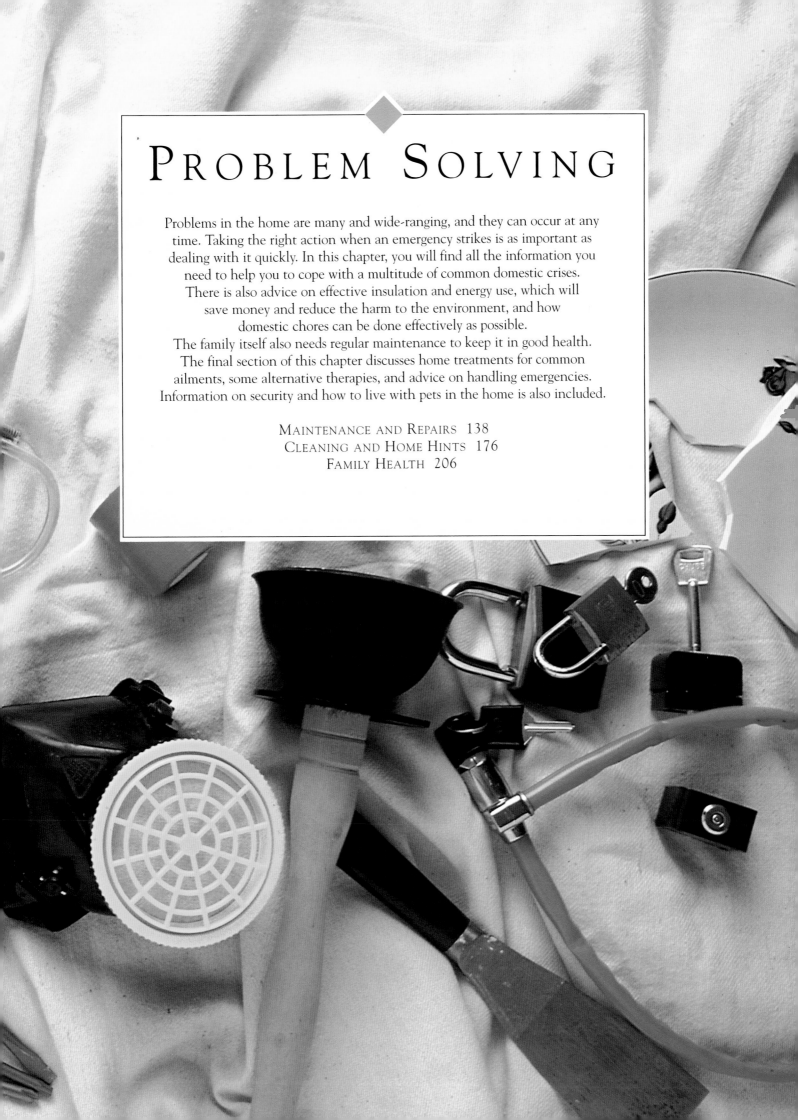

PROBLEM SOLVING

Problems in the home are many and wide-ranging, and they can occur at any time. Taking the right action when an emergency strikes is as important as dealing with it quickly. In this chapter, you will find all the information you need to help you to cope with a multitude of common domestic crises. There is also advice on effective insulation and energy use, which will save money and reduce the harm to the environment, and how domestic chores can be done effectively as possible. The family itself also needs regular maintenance to keep it in good health. The final section of this chapter discusses home treatments for common ailments, some alternative therapies, and advice on handling emergencies. Information on security and how to live with pets in the home is also included.

Maintenance and Repairs

Creating a well-appointed home is a thoroughly satisfying leisure activity pursued by millions of householders. Unfortunately, being creative is not the whole story; houses, their contents and even their occupants, like anything else, develop faults from time to time and need some attention to keep them in good working order. The good news is, however, that many repairs and regular maintenance work can be carried out by the occupants of the house, with a minimum of fuss and expense.

The first section of this problem-solving chapter looks at some of the everyday maintenance and repair situations which may occur in the home, ranging from walls, ceilings and floors, to doors and windows, mouldings, furniture and even household appliances, and also explains how to use the right products – adhesives, mastics, fillers, repair tapes and fixing devices – to get good results.

It also deals with a subject that is of increasing importance to householders everywhere: energy conservation and the efficient use of resources. Many homes, especially older ones, are very inefficient in terms of energy conservation; they cost a lot to heat, and leak warm air like sieves so that much of the heat supplied is completely wasted. However, creating a well-insulated and draughtproofed house is not the complete answer.

Activities such as cooking, bathing and washing clothes create large amounts of water vapour, and if this accumulates in a poorly ventilated building, condensation will result. This can be more than just a nuisance; it can actually damage the house structure and can also be bad for the health of the building's occupants. Getting the right balance of heat input, insulation and controlled ventilation is the solution and is well worth the effort.

OPPOSITE Keeping track of running repairs and updating insulation and ventilation needs are necessary tasks for the home owner. Shown here, from left to right and top to bottom: applying flashing tape; fixing insulation tape around doorways; removing window beads; repairing wallpaper blisters; sealing cracks with mastic; laying roof insulation; insulating sash windows; insulating pipework; and repairing stairs.

ADHESIVES, MASTICS AND REPAIR TAPES

There is a huge range of adhesives available nowadays. Their labelling, is now generally much clearer than it was a few years ago, so finding the right product is considerably easier than it used to be. Here is a guide to the types that are likely to be needed for most repair jobs in the home.

General-purpose adhesives

These are clear solvent-based adhesives which will stick paper and cardboard, wood, leather and a few types of plastic, such as solid polystyrene (plastic foam) and ABS. They are used straight from the tube. Check the instructions carefully; some recommend applying the adhesive to both surfaces, others to just one. Whichever method is used, hold or clamp the repair for a while; the adhesive takes some time after assembly to gain full strength. The joint is generally not heat-resistant and may not be water-resistant either. Adhesive can be removed from fingers, or anywhere else it gets by mistake, with cellulose thinner, acetone or nail varnish remover – but the last will attack gloss paint, french polish, some varnishes, and any plastic that the adhesive will stick.

Adhesives for wood

The most widely used type of adhesive for general woodwork is PVA woodworking adhesive, often referred to as 'white glue'. It will bond softwood, hardwood and all manufactured boards, and is colourless when dry; spills can be wiped away with a damp cloth before the adhesive sets. The joint must be clamped until the adhesive hardens – for a couple of hours at least – to get the best results. Exposure to damp will weaken the adhesive and cause failure. If such exposure is likely, be sure to use one of the cross-linking versions which give a high degree of water resistance.

Adhesives for laminates

Plastic laminates, flexible sheet materials such as foam and leather, and vinyl or cork floor tiles are stuck in place with a contact adhesive. This is spread on both surfaces and is allowed to become touch-dry before the two are pressed together. The resulting bond is instant, and cannot normally be repositioned; but some kinds offer a degree of slip – they are often called thixotropic adhesives. Contact adhesive is also moderately heatproof and water-resistant.

Most contact adhesives are solvent-based, and the fumes are both inflammable and noxious to inhale, so work with good ventilation and no naked lights. Clean up spills with the manufacturer's own solvent, cellulose thinner, acetone or nail varnish remover. Water-based contact adhesives are also available, and these are much safer and more pleasant to use; spills can be removed while still wet with a damp cloth.

Adhesives for plastics

Some plastics are very difficult to stick with adhesives. Two which cannot be stuck by any means are polythene (polyethylene) and polypropylene, the bendy plastics used for such things as washing-up bowls (wash-bowls) and buckets; they must be fused by heat.

Flexible PVC – used for seat covers, sunbeds and beach balls, for example – can be stuck with special vinyl repair adhesive. Polystyrene cement or general-purpose adhesive will mend rigid polystyrene – used for some kitchen and bathroom accessories – and the similar but tougher ABS. Do not use it for expanded polystyrene ceiling tiles or coving (crown molding),

ABOVE Use silicone mastic to seal around bathroom fittings. Carefully push the nozzle along the gap so it leaves a neat concave finish to the mastic bead.

ABOVE Use acrylic mastic indoors and frame sealant outdoors to seal gaps between wood and masonry where a rigid filler would tend to crack and fall out.

ABOVE Use repair tapes to make temporary repairs to cracked glass, or to waterproof glazing bars on glass roofs. Simply press the tape into place.

though, as the adhesive will eat these away. Always use a special adhesive paste made for the purpose.

For other plastics, experiment with epoxy resin adhesives, two-part acrylics or cyanoacrylates (see below).

Mastics and repair tapes

Mastic is a permanently flexible adhesive filler that is used to seal joints indoors and outdoors. The material comes in cartridges, and is usually extruded by using a hand-held gun. The resulting bead of mastic is simply piped into place, and may be smoothed out with a wet finger or a filling knife (putty knife) if necessary. Various types are available: acrylic types are used as a general-purpose decorating filler indoors; silicone types are best for such jobs as waterproofing joints around bathroom and kitchen fittings; and frame sealants are designed for filling and sealing gaps around window and door frames.

Repair tapes of various types are used to make temporary repairs to things such as cracked glass, leaky glazing bars and porous flashings. As with mastics, choose the type appropriate to the task in hand.

Adhesives for glass, china and metal

Three types of adhesive can be used for repairing these materials. Each has advantages and disadvantages.

Epoxy resin adhesives are two-part products, prepared by mixing equal quantities of resin and hardener, and generally applied to both surfaces. Quick-setting types set hard in a few minutes, others take about half an hour, with full bond strength developing more slowly. Once set, the bond is heat- and waterproof, and the adhesive will fill gaps; however, it does leave a noticeable glue line, and this may darken with time. Clean up spills with white spirit (paint thinner) or methylated spirit (wood alcohol) and trim off dried adhesive with a sharp utility knife.

Cyanoacrylate adhesives, also known as superglues, are liquids applied sparingly to just one surface. The resulting glue line is very thin, so they are ideal for repairing china and glass, but apart from the newer gel types the adhesive has negligible gap-filling properties so the parts must be a good fit. With most brands, the joint is not waterproof, but some are specially formulated for repairing items that will

have to be washed or must hold liquids. Avoid skin contact when using this type of adhesive; if fingers, or anything else, get stuck together, instantly immerse them in hot soapy water and gently peel the stuck areas apart. Some manufacturers supply a special release agent with the adhesive. Always keep glues away from children, but especially this type.

Two-part acrylic adhesives are not mixed directly; instead adhesive is applied to one surface and hardener to the other, and the two brought together to form the bond. This sticks immediately, and reaches full strength in a few hours. The adhesive has good heat resistance and is fairly waterproof, but does not fill gaps very well. Wipe up spills with a dry cloth or a little methylated spirits. Alternatively, trim off dried adhesive with a sharp knife.

Speciality adhesives

The shelves of a do-it-yourself (hardware) store will also contain all kinds of special-purpose adhesives, clearly labelled as to their use. These include wallpaper paste, ceramic tile and coving (crown molding) adhesive.

1 Use flashing tape to seal porous felt or metal flashings. Start by brushing on a coat of special primer; use an old paintbrush and wear protective gloves.

2 Unroll the flashing tape, peel off the release paper and press the strip into position over the band of primer, bedding it well into the roof/wall angle.

3 To ensure that the tape bonds well to the wall and roof surfaces, run a wallpaper seam roller firmly along both edges of the tape strip.

MAINTENANCE AND REPAIRS

PATCHING WALL AND CEILING DAMAGE

Plasterboard (gypsum board) is an immensely versatile material for lining walls and ceilings, as it provides a smooth surface for any finish and also has useful sound-deadening and fireproofing properties. The one thing it does not do very well is to resist impacts, and resulting holes cannot simply be patched with filler (spackle) because the board's strength will have been lost at the point of damage. The solution is either to strengthen the board or to replace a section altogether.

Very small holes can be disguised with self-adhesive scrim tape and cellulose filler, but holes more than about 5 cm/2 in across need a more substantial repair. Use an offcut of plasterboard and cut a piece slightly narrower than the hole width and twice as long as its height to use as a patch. Pierce a hole in it, thread through a piece of string, tie one end to a nail and pull this against the face of the patch. Then butter some plaster or filler on to the other face of the patch and push it into the hole, keeping hold of the string with the other hand. Position the patch against the inner face of the plasterboard, pulling on the string to help the filler stick it in place. When it has stuck fast, fill the hole and cut off the string.

For larger holes – a foot through the ceiling, for example – in plasterboard and (in older properties) lath-and-plaster surfaces, the only solution is to cut out the damaged piece and nail on a new section in its place. You will need to fix supports around the edges of the opening where you have cut out the damaged section. Fill the cut edges, apply joint tape to hide them and then skim over the patch with a little plaster to complete the repair.

PATCHING A SMALL HOLE IN PLASTERBOARD (GYPSUM BOARD)

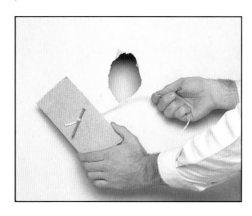

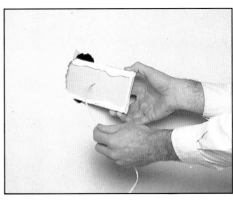

1 Cut a plasterboard patch slightly longer and narrower than the hole, and thread a length of string with a nail tied on through a hole in its centre.

2 Butter some plaster or filler (spackle) on to the edges of the patch and feed it end-on into the hole, keeping hold of the string with the other hand.

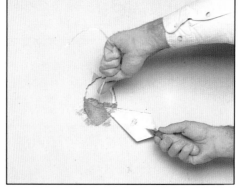

3 Pull the string to hold the patch against the rear face of the board, then fill the recess with either plaster or filler and cut off the string.

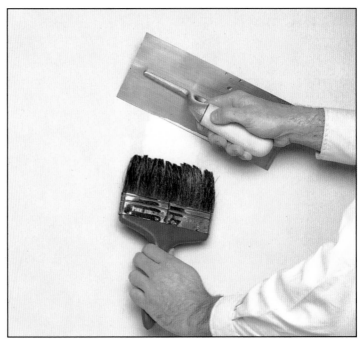

4 Complete the repair by applying a skim coat of plaster over the patch. Flick water on to the plaster with a brush and polish it smooth with a steel float.

PATCHING A LARGER HOLE IN PLASTERBOARD (GYPSUM BOARD)

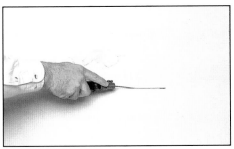

1 If the plasterboard surface is more extensively damaged, cut through it with a sharp knife back to the adjacent wall studs or ceiling joists.

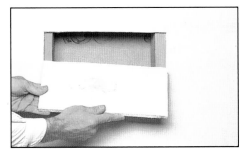

2 Cut across to the stud or joist centres, then make 2 vertical cuts down the centre of the stud or joist to free the damaged panel and remove it.

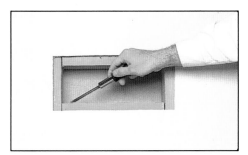

3 Cut 2 strips of wood to fit between the studs/joists, and screw or nail them into place so that they will support the edges of the main board and the patch.

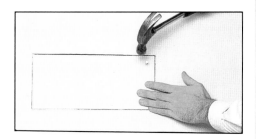

4 Cut a plasterboard patch to match the section removed, and nail it into place. Fill and tape the joints and skim plaster over the repair, then polish with a steel float.

REPAIRING A LATH-AND-PLASTER SURFACE

1 If the wood laths are split or broken, pull them away from the surface. Remove any loose sections of plaster from around the site of the damage.

2 Continue cutting back the old plaster and the laths behind it to expose the studs or ceiling joists at each side of the hole. Square off the edges.

3 Cut a plasterboard patch to fit the hole, and nail it in place. Add two support strips as described for patching plasterboard if the panel is large.

4 Complete the repair by plastering over the patch after filling and taping the cut edges all around. Then polish the repair with a steel float.

REPAIRING A FLOOR

Floorboards suffer more from being lifted for access to pipes and cables beneath them than they do from everyday wear and tear. If the floor has nothing worse than the occasional creak, the trouble can generally be cured by lifting floor coverings and then nailing – or better still, screwing – the offending board down again. With a chipboard (particle board) floor, make sure that the boards are nailed to every joist they cross, not just at the edges; if they are not, the boards can bow upwards and will then bang against the joists when walked on.

Before lifting a section of floor to gain access to services below it, look first of all to see whether someone has already cut an access panel. If they have not, it will be necessary to create one. Locate the joist position closest to where access is needed – the positions of the flooring nail will reveal its whereabouts. Then drill a starter hole and use a power jigsaw (saber saw) to make a 45° cut next to the joist. Prise up the cut end and wedge a strip of wood underneath it, then saw through the board over the centre of the next joist to free the section. To replace it,

nail one end to the joist and either skew nail (toe nail) the other angled end to its neighbour or nail a support block to the side of the joist and nail or screw the board end to that.

With a concrete floor, the only repair that is likely to be needed is the filling of cracks or small potholes that may be revealed when an old floor covering is lifted. Cut back any loose edges, brush away loose material and fill the cracks with a fine mortar mix. If the floor surface is sound but uneven or out of level, lay a self-smoothing compound over it.

CREATING AN ACCESS PANEL

1 Start by locating an adjacent joist. Drill a starter hole for the saw blade. Cut through the board at 45° next to the joist with a power jigsaw (saber saw).

2 Use a bolster (stonecutter's chisel) or a similar broad-bladed levering tool to prise up the cut end of the board and release its fixing nails.

3 Slide a length of scrap wood under the raised end of the board to hold it clear of the floor, and saw through the board above the centre of the next joist.

4 To replace the panel, simply lay it back in position. Nail the square-cut end to its joist and skew nail (toe nail) the angled end to the neighbouring board.

5 An alternative way of supporting the cut ends of an access panel is to nail small wood blocks to each side of the adjacent joists.

6 You can also screw down the panel on to the wooden blocks. This will allow easy access without damaging the panel.

REPAIRING A CONCRETE FLOOR

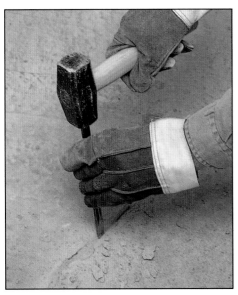

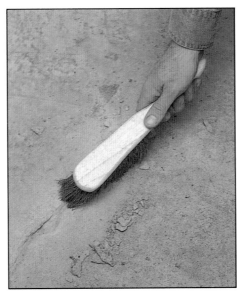

1 If you discover cracks in a concrete floor after lifting old floor coverings, use a cold (box) chisel and club (spalling) hammer to undercut the edges of the crack.

2 Brush away all loose material from the crack and use a vacuum cleaner to pick up the dust.

3 Dilute some PVA building (white general-purpose) adhesive, and brush it along the surface of the crack to help the repair mortar to bond to it securely.

5 If the floor has noticeable potholes in its surface, pack the hole with some small pieces of stone or other non-compressible filler.

4 Mix up some quick-setting repair mortar and trowel it into the crack, levelling it flush with the surrounding concrete. Leave it to harden.

6 Patch the pothole with quick-setting mortar, using the edge of a steel float to remove excess mortar so that the patch is flush with its surroundings.

REPAIRING WALLPAPER AND CARPETS

It is a simple matter to repair minor damage to painted walls and ceilings and then to cover it up with a fresh coat of paint. With wall coverings, patching damage or curing paperhanging defects requires a different approach.

The most common form of damage to a wall covering is an impact that leaves a jagged tear. If the torn part is still attached, brush some paste on to its rear face and press it back into place. Use a seam roller to apply pressure to the flap and roll it flat.

If the torn part is missing it will be necessary to patch the damage. If there are some offcuts from the original papering job, cut a patch from them. If not, cut and dry-strip a patch from an out-of-sight area behind a piece of furniture to use for the repair. Tear around the edges of the patch, holding it face-down, to create a thin 'feathered' edge, then paste it, place it over the damaged area and flatten it with a seam roller. If the paper is a thick 2-layer duplex type, try to peel away the backing paper to reduce the thickness of the patch and make it less noticeable once it is in position. Feather the edge and paste in position.

Another common problem, blistering, is the result of inadequate pasting during paperhanging. It is a relatively simple task to slit blisters open and lift dry seams to apply a little fresh paste and stick the covering firmly back to the wall. With fragile printed or flocked wall coverings, take care not to get paste on the surface.

If a carpet becomes damaged in one area – perhaps as a result of a cigarette burn, for example – and you cannot remove the mark, trim back the pile of the carpet with a razor blade. If this does not work, the answer is to patch the mark with a new piece of carpet. Use a spare offcut if you have one available, or cut the patch from an area in the room that will not be visible, such as under a sofa.

PATCHING DAMAGED WALLPAPER

1 Cut a repair patch from an offcut of the original wall covering, or strip one from behind a piece of furniture. Check that the patch will cover the damage and match the pattern.

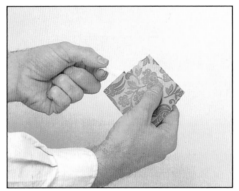

2 Carefully tear along the edges of the patch to reduce its thickness and create a thin feathered edge. Check that no backing paper is visible.

3 Some 2-layer duplex papers are too thick to use as a patch. Try to separate the backing paper at a corner of the patch and peel it off.

4 Paste the back of the patch and place it over the damaged area, aligning the pattern carefully. 'Iron' it into place with the aid of a seam roller.

CURING A DRY BLISTER

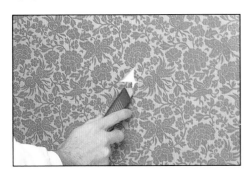

1 If a dry blister appears after wallpapering, use a sharp utility knife to make 2 cuts through the blister at right-angles.

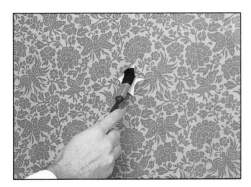

2 Peel back the triangular tongues formed and apply a little paste to the wall surface and to the back of the tongues. Leave to soak for a few minutes.

3 Press the triangles back into place and run a seam roller along the cuts to bond the paper firmly to the wall and leave an almost invisible repair.

STICKING DRY SEAMS

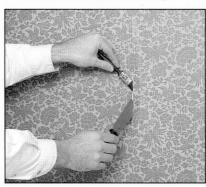

If a seam has failed to stick flat, lift it with a filling knife (putty knife) and use a slip of abrasive paper to sand off the dried paste behind it. Use the filling knife to hold the edge of the wall covering away from the wall, and brush a little paste on to the back of the paper and also on to the wall surface. Leave to soak. Press the seam down flat with a seam·roller, then use a sponge or damp cloth to remove any paste that has oozed on to the face of the wall covering before it dries.

PATCHING A CARPET

1 First remove as much of the dirt as you can by vacuuming, placing the nozzle down over the dirt rather than sweeping it back and forth to avoid rubbing in the mark.

2 If the mark is only fairly light, try carefully trimming back the carpet pile, using a razor blade.

3 If the mark is ingrained, lift the carpet and place a piece of hardboard on top of the underlay, beneath the damage. Cut a matching piece of carpet, slightly larger than the damaged area, and place over the damaged area with the pile running the same way. Cut right through both carpets, then replace the old patch with the new.

DARNING AND PATCHING

Clothes and soft furnishings such as linen, cushions and the fabric on chairs will need some repair work when an area becomes worn or gives way due to constant wear or an accidental tear. Preventive strengthening measures can be taken in certain instances, such as decorative patches on seat cushions or the arms of padded chairs, and elbows and knees on clothes. Other embellished items, such as cushions and table cloths, can also be reinforced with interfacing on the wrong side before sewing on decorative elements, such as buttons and tassels, to further strengthen the fabric.

Once an area of fabric, whether clothing or soft furnishing, has become worn or frayed, the techniques for darning and repairing are not difficult to learn and are well worth the effort if it saves you from having to replace a much-loved family item.

DARNING BY HAND

Choose a thread for darning that matches the fabric colour as closely as possible. Use one that is slightly thinner than the fabric threads, otherwise the darning will be too thick, and work with a long length.

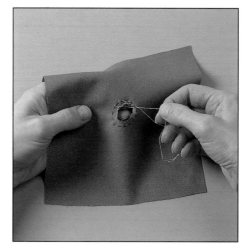

1 Work small running stitches back and forth across the fabric within the marked area. Leave a slight loop at the end of each row so that the darn doesn't become too tight. At the worn area, leave the thread lying parallel across the hole and work running stitches on each side.

2 Turn the work so that the laid threads are horizontal. Begin to weave over and under the stitches and threads until the entire area is covered with a woven patch. Avoid pulling the threads tight.

RIGHT-ANGLED TEAR

1 Bring the edges of the tear together by loosely oversewing them. Beginning and ending 6 mm/¼ in beyond each end of the tear, work tiny stitches across the tear.

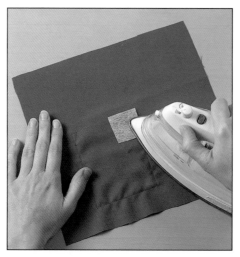

2 On a worn garment or pocket tear, iron a square of iron-on interfacing to the wrong side before working the stitches. Pin the pocket back in position and restitch over the repair.

3 A button can be replaced over a right-angled tear once it has been repaired with interfacing and machine stitching.

HAND PATCH

This type of patch is normally used to repair garments but will come in handy with bed linen, curtains and cushions. To make the patch less obvious, cut the fabric to match the colour and pattern of the worn area as closely as possible.

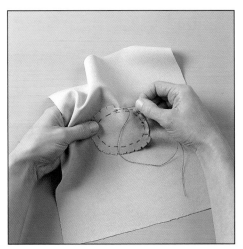

1 Cut a patch about 3–4 cm/1¼–1½ in larger than the worn area. Baste the patch 6 mm/¼ in from the raw edge and notch any curves. Turn under and baste the raw edge. Work small, neat hemming stitches to secure.

2 On the wrong side, trim away the worn fabric to leave a 5 mm/¼ in allowance. Work overcasting or buttonhole stitches over the raw edges without stitching into the front side of the patch.

MACHINE PATCH

This quick and easy patch is a hard-wearing way of repairing most utility items around the home. Use fabric from another similar item, if possible, or pre-wash a new piece of fabric to soften it. Stitch with a matching thread.

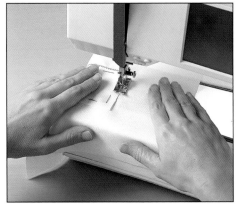

1 Cut a square or rectangular patch about 2–3 cm/¾–1¼ in larger than the worn area and baste in position on the right side, matching the grain of the fabric. Machine zigzag over the edge to secure.

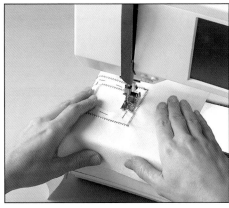

2 Turn the garment over and trim the worn areas of the patch to 1 cm/⅜ in. Machine zigzag over the raw edge. The finished patch will have two rows of zigzag showing on the right side.

DARNING BY MACHINE

Machine darning is suitable for strengthening worn areas such as the knees of trousers, but can be rather solid if used to fill a hole on a piece of furniture or fabric. Use a darning foot on the machine and stitch with finer fibre such as machine embroidery thread, in a colour to match the fabric.

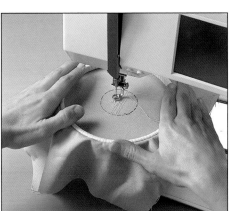

1 Baste a circle of running stitches around the outside of the worn area. If possible, fit the fabric into an embroidery hoop so that it lies flat against the needle plate. Lower the darning foot and work parallel rows of stitching fairly close together back and forth across the marked area.

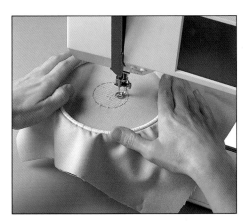

2 Stop with the needle in the fabric and turn the hoop until the stitches lie across the other way. Stitch more parallel rows slightly further apart to form a stitched grid over the marked area. If filling a hole, turn the hoop back round and work a third set of parallel rows across the hole.

MAKING FIRM FIXINGS

Before making fixings into solid masonry, make a couple of test drillings to find out whether the wall is built of brick or lightweight blocks. If brick is identified from red or yellow bore dust, use ordinary plastic wall plugs; but if grey dust suggests lightweight blocks it is better to use a proprietary block plug which is fatter and has larger 'wings' to grip the softer material. In either case the screw must be long enough to penetrate at least 38 mm/1½ in into the masonry behind plaster, so use screws at least 62 mm/2½ in long for a plastered wall. Increase this to 75 mm/3 in for fixings that will carry heavy loads. Screw gauge 8 will be adequate for normal loads; increase this to gauge 10 for 75 mm/3 in screws. Make sure, too, that the screw and wall plug sizes are compatible, and take care to drill the holes at right angles to the wall surface, deep enough to accept the screw length.

Making fixings to stud (dry) walls poses different fixing problems. Cavity fixing devices such as spring or gravity toggles and cavity anchors can be used only for fixings that will carry the lightest loads. For any other use, the fixing must be made either to a horizontal nogging (cross bridging) fixed between adjacent studs – difficult to fit except during construction of the wall framework – or directly to the vertical studs themselves. These will have to be located with an electronic stud finder or, less satisfactorily, by tapping and test drilling – they are usually at 400 mm/16 in or 600 mm/24 in centres. Make sure that pilot holes are drilled into the centre of the stud, not near its edge, since this could result in a weak fixing. Use screws 50 mm/2 in long for medium loads, 75 mm/3 in long for heavy ones.

MAKING FIXINGS IN MASONRY

1 Mark where the fixing is to go and use a masonry drill, sized to match the wall plug. Wind some tape around the drill bit to act as a depth guide.

2 If the drill has an adjustable depth stop attachment, use it instead of the tape flag to set the drilling depth. Drill until the stop touches the wall surface.

MAKING FIXINGS IN PLASTERBOARD (GYPSUM BOARD)

1 If the fixing must be between joists or studs rather than into them, drill a clearance hole for the fixing device through the plasterboard.

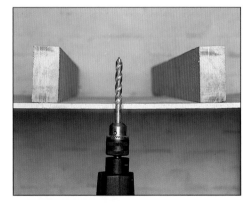

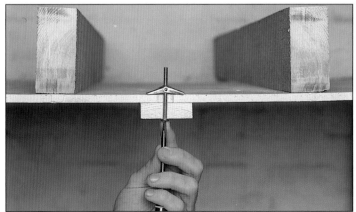

2 Push a cavity anchor into the hole so it can expand against the back of the board, and drive in the screw. Using toggles, thread the screw through the object first.

3 Choose a wall plug sized to match the screw being used, and push it into the hole until its rim is flush with the wall. Tap it with a hammer if necessary.

4 Thread the screw through a clearance hole drilled in the object being fixed, insert it in the mouth of the wall plug and drive it home.

5 Alternatively, use long-sleeved frame plugs. Drill holes through the wood and into the wall, insert the plug and tighten the screw to make the fixing.

MAKING FIXINGS INTO STUDS

1 Use an electronic stud finder to locate the stud or ceiling joist positions. It works by detecting the nails which secure the plasterboard (gypsum board).

2 When the stud or joist positions are marked, drill clearance holes in the object to be fixed at matching centres. Check these for accuracy.

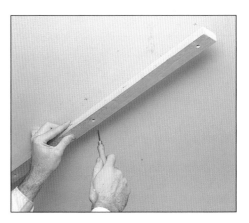

3 Drill pilot holes through the board surface and into the stud or joist. Make sure that the drill bit is at right angles to the surface of the wall.

4 Insert screws in all the clearance holes, then offer up the object to be fixed, align it with the pre-drilled pilot holes and drive the screws home.

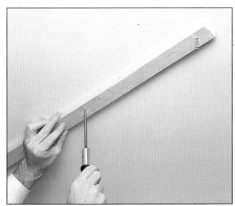

REPLACING TRIM MOULDINGS

Trim mouldings are both practical and decorative. They are used as skirtings (baseboards) to protect wall surfaces at floor level from accidental damage, and around door and window openings as architraves (trims) to frame the opening and disguise the joint between the frame and the wall surface. Both can be plain or ornate, and can be painted, stained or varnished. They may need replacing if they are damaged or simply look unfashionable.

Skirtings are often fixed directly to masonry walls with large cut nails in older homes, or with masonry nails in more recent ones. Alternatively, they may be nailed to rough timber fixing blocks or grounds (furrings) which are themselves nailed to the masonry. Boards fixed to blocks are much easier to remove than those nailed directly to the wall, as both cut and masonry nails can have a ferocious grip. In the latter situation it is often easier to punch the

nails through the boards and into the walls than to try to prise them out. Boards on wood-framed walls are simply nailed to the frame, and so are easy and quick to remove.

Architraves are pinned (tacked) in place to the edges of the door or window frame. It is an easy job to prise the trims away using a bolster (stonecutter's) chisel, without causing undue damage to the frame or the surrounding wall surface.

REPLACING ARCHITRAVES (TRIMS)

1 Prise off the old mouldings. They should come away easily. If necessary, lever against a small wooden block to avoid damaging the surface of the wall.

2 Hold an upright against the frame so that you can mark the inside of the mitre joint on it. Repeat for the other upright.

3 Cut the end of the moulding, using a mitre block or box. Alternatively, mark the line across the moulding with a protractor or combination square.

4 Fix the uprights to the frame by driving in nails at 30 cm/12 in intervals. Recess the heads with a nail punch and fill the holes later.

5 Hold the top piece above the uprights to mark the position for the mitre cut at each end. Make the cuts as before and test the piece for fit.

6 Nail the top piece to the frame, checking that the mitre joints are accurately aligned. Finally, drive a nail through each corner to secure the joint.

REPLACING SKIRTINGS (BASEBOARDS)

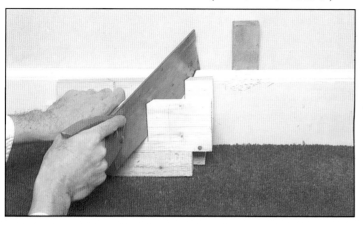

1 To replace a small area of damaged board, prise it away from the wall slightly, wedge it and use a tenon saw and mitre box to cut out a section.

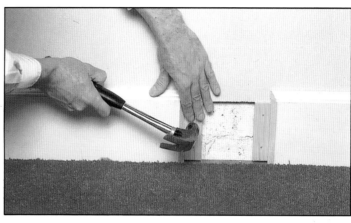

2 Nail small support blocks behind the cut ends of the board, using masonry nails on solid walls, and then nail the cut ends to the support blocks.

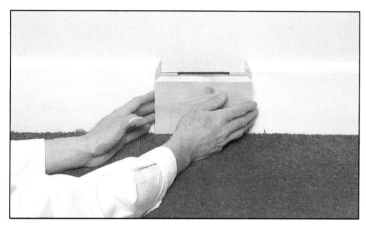

3 Cut a piece of replacement board to fit, with its ends mitred to match the cut-out section. Use plain wood if you are unable to match the skirting profile.

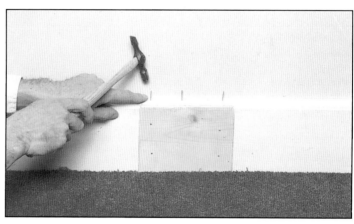

4 Nail the replacement board to the support blocks. If you are using plain wood, pin (tack) on decorative mouldings to build up a close match to the existing board.

5 When replacing whole lengths, use mitre joints at external corners. Fix the first length, then mark the inside of the mitre on the back of the next board.

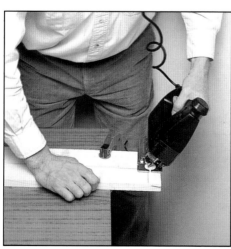

6 Cut the mitre joints with a power jigsaw (saber saw) with an adjustable sole plate. Set the cutting angle to just under 45° to ensure that the joint will fit well.

7 At internal corners, fit the first length right into the corner. Scribe its profile on to the second board, cut this with a coping saw and then fit it.

CURING DOOR PROBLEMS

A well-fitted door should have a long and trouble-free life. If it does start to misbehave, the problem is likely to be the door binding against its frame and, in extreme cases, failing to shut properly. There are 3 possible causes: a build-up of paint on the door and frame surfaces after years of re-painting, expansion due to atmospheric conditions – the door sticks in damp weather as moisture causes it to swell slightly, but shrinks and closes freely in dry weather; and hinge faults caused either by wear and tear or bad fitting.

Where a paint build-up is to blame, the remedy is quite simple: strip off the old paint from the door edge back to bare wood, and re-paint from scratch.

If atmospheric conditions are to blame, the solution is to plane down the door edges slightly to increase the clearance between door and frame. You will have to take the door off its hinges to do this unless it is only the leading edge that is binding.

Hinge faults that can cause binding include hinge screws standing proud or working loose, and hinge recesses being cut too deep or too shallow. In each case the cure is relatively simple; the biggest problem is often trying to undo the old hinge screws, especially if they have become encrusted with paint over the years. Clean out the slots in the screw heads thoroughly before trying to remove the screws; paint remover is useful for this. Then position the screwdriver in the slot and give the handle a sharp blow with a hammer in order to help free the grip of the threads in the wood.

1 If the hinge screws show signs of pulling out, remove them, drill out the screw holes and hammer in glued dowels. Then drill new pilot holes.

2 If the door is striking the frame because it has expanded over time, close it and mark a pencil line on the door face against the edge of the frame.

5 If the door binds on the hinge side of the frame, the hinge recesses may be too deep. Remove the hinge and pin some packing into the recess.

6 Drill fresh pilot holes for the screws through the packing piece, and drive the fixing screws back into place. Make sure that their heads fit in the countersinks.

3 Take the door off its hinges, remove the handles and the latch mechanism, and plane down the leading edge of the door until the pencil line has disappeared.

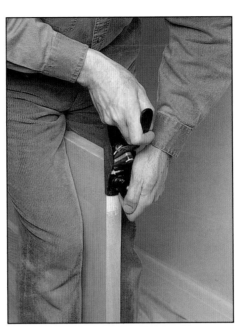

4 If the door is binding either at the top or bottom, take this opportunity to plane off a little wood there too. Plane inwards from the corners to avoid causing splits.

7 Alternatively, re-locate the hinges in a new position. Chisel out the new recesses and re-fit the hinges.

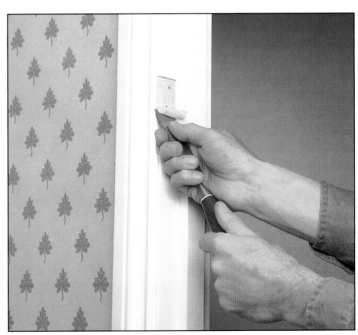

8 If the hinge recesses are too shallow, the hinge leaves will bind and prevent the door from closing. Remove the hinges and chisel out the recesses slightly.

CURING WINDOW PROBLEMS

By far the most common window problem is a cracked or broken pane, caused by a flying object or by the window being allowed to slam. Make a temporary repair to cracked glass with a clear waterproof repair tape – not household adhesive tape – but aim to replace the pane at the earliest opportunity. If the glass is broken, lift out all the loose pieces for safety's sake and make a temporary repair by fixing heavy-duty polythene (polyethylene) sheeting or a piece of board over the opening to keep out the cold.

When measuring up for the replacement glass, measure all four sides in case the rebate in the frame is not perfectly square, and use the smaller of each pair of figures. Subtract 3 mm/ ⅛ in from each one to allow for clearance all around, and note which way the pattern ran if the glass was obscured rather than clear. Take a piece of patterned glass with you when buying a replacement, so as to be sure of getting the correct type.

The other problems that windows suffer from are similar to those affecting doors – paint build-up, expansion and warping. They may also pull out of square if the frame corner joints start to open up, causing the casement to bind in its frame and possibly also cracking the glass. The trouble can be cured by strengthening the frame corners with small L-shaped metal repair plates; cut shallow recesses for them and disguise their presence with filler (spackle) and a coat of paint.

REPLACING BROKEN GLASS

1 When a window breaks, remove all the loose glass immediately for safety's sake. Wear stout gloves to protect your hands and dispose of the glass safely.

TIP

Always dispose of broken glass safely, by wrapping it in newspaper and then packing it in a box so that it cannot injure anyone.

2 Use an old chisel or a glazier's knife to remove all the old putty from the rebate in the frame. Take care not to cut into the wood while doing this.

3 Use a pair of pincers or pliers to pull out the old glazing sprigs all around the frame. Metal frames have glazing clips; save these and re-use them.

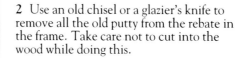

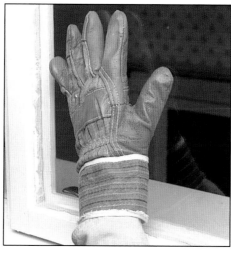

4 Knead some putty with your hands to warm and soften it, then press it into the rebate by extruding it between your thumb and forefinger.

5 Set the replacement pane in position against the bedding putty with equal clearance all around, and press it into place around the edges to compress the putty.

6 Secure the pane in the rebate by tapping in glazing sprigs at roughly 30 cm/12 in intervals. Replace clips in their locating holes in metal frames.

7 Repeat step 4 to extrude a bead of facing putty all around the pane, then neaten it to a 45° bevel by drawing the blade of a putty knife along it.

8 Trim off excess putty from the outside and inside of the pane and leave it to harden for about 14 days before painting over it to disguise and seal the joints.

CURING A BINDING CASEMENT

1 If a build-up of paint is causing the edge of the casement to bind against the frame, strip it back. Use chemical strippers for this, as heat may crack the glass.

2 If the frame has swollen because of moisture penetration, plane a little wood off the leading edge. Prime and paint it immediately to keep the wood dry.

3 If the corner joints of a casement show signs of opening up and the frame is pulling out of square, screw on small L-shaped metal repair plates.

REPAIRING AND RESTORING FURNITURE

You can give a new lease of life to old wooden furniture by stripping the existing finish to bare wood and then applying a new finish. How you tackle this job depends on what finish the piece already has, and how you intend to refinish it once you have stripped it.

The most common finishes on everyday furniture are paint, varnish and lacquer and the most satisfactory way of removing these is to use a liquid chemical paint and various removers. Several different formulations are available, but the safest to use is a non-caustic (toxic) and solvent-free remover. It may take longer than other types to remove the paint, but it is much more environmentally friendly than other types. If left on for long enough, it will also remove numerous coats of paint in one application, and the stripped surface can then be varnished or stained as an alternative to repainting.

You should also use a chemical remover on old furniture that may have been painted more than 30 years ago with primers and paints containing lead pigments. If possible, wrap the scrapings from such pieces in cooking foil (tin foil), then dispose of them according to local regulations.

Always follow the manufacturer's instructions carefully when using a paint remover, especially as far as neutralizing the product before applying any new finish.

You can also strip old finishes using a hot-air gun instead of a chemical remover. This method is quicker and, in the long term, cheaper once the tool has repaid its original purchase price. However, there is a slight risk of charring the wood, especially on mouldings and external corners, so it is best used if you definitely intend to repaint the piece.

STRIPPING OLD FINISHES

1 Select an old paintbrush for the job, and wear rubber or PVC (vinyl) gloves and safety glasses to protect you from any splashes of the paint remover. Following the manufacturer's instructions, apply a thick coat and leave it to soften the paint.

2 Test the softened paint with a flat-bladed scraper to see whether the remover has penetrated to the bare wood. Then scrape it off, working along the grain, and deposit the scrapings in a tin or other non-plastic container.

3 Use the appropriate blade of a combination shavehook to scrape the paint from concave or convex mouldings and other curved surfaces.

4 Use an old toothbrush to work the remover into corners and the hard-to-reach recesses of mouldings. Scrape out any paint that conventional tools cannot reach by improvizing with household implements such as toothpicks.

5 Use a pad of fine wire (steel) wool to scrub the last of the remover from the wood grain, and strip any stubborn paint or varnish from hard-to-reach corners.

6 Use a hot-air gun to soften paint on large, flat areas where you are able to use a broad scraper to work quickly and on surfaces you will be repainting.

SIMPLE REPAIRS FOR WOODEN CHAIRS

If you need extra seats around the kitchen table, look out for inexpensive second-hand wooden chairs which can be renovated easily and then refinished to look as good as new. Typical utility chairs like these often suffer from loose joints, especially where the rails meet the legs, and from split rails. Both problems are caused mainly by people rocking on the chair's back legs, straining the components and often twisting the chair out of shape.

However, all these defects are relatively easy to put right. All you need are some simple woodworking tools, a portable workbench to hold your patient still while you operate, and a couple of hours of spare time.

1 Turn the chair upside down on your workbench and inspect all the joints. If you detect any movement, carefully knock the joint apart with a soft-faced (rubber) mallet. Number mating components first if dismantling several joints.

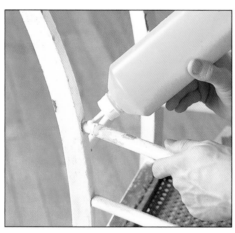

2 Use fine abrasive paper (sandpaper) to remove all traces of old adhesive from the ends of the dismantled rails, and clean up the holes or mortises into which they fit. Then apply PVA (white) woodworking adhesive (wood glue) to each rail end.

3 Reassemble the joint by hand, tapping it with the mallet if necessary to coax reluctant members (pieces) back together again. Then use a web cramp (bar clamp or strap clamp) to hold the joint securely while the adhesive sets.

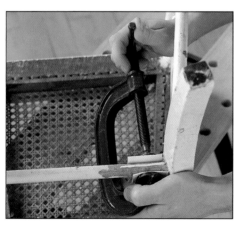

4 Repair splits in chair rails by prising (prying) them open and squirting in some woodworking adhesive (wood glue). Then use a G-cramp (C-clamp) and a piece of card (cardboard) as packing to cramp (clamp) the split tightly shut. Wipe off excess adhesive (glue) before it sets.

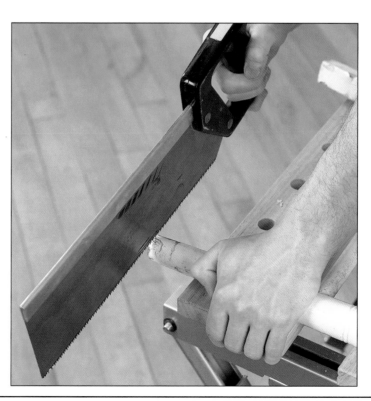

5 If the chair does not stand square after you have remade any loose joints, stand it squarely on three legs and carefully measure by how much the fourth leg is off the ground. Saw this amount from the ends of the other three legs.

REPAIRING AND RESTORING DROP-IN SEATS

You can restore chairs with drop-in seats by removing the seat from the chair frame, stripping off the old material and re-covering it with a new wadding pad (seat pad), some lining fabric and your choice of finish fabric. You can obtain the materials from craft stores, and buy yourself an invaluable staple gun from do-it-yourself (hardware) stores.

1 Remove all the old, stained or damaged material from the seat. Then use the existing seat pad to cut a piece of lining fabric just large enough to cover the underside of the pad. It will be used later on in step 5.

2 If the existing seat pad is sagging, help it by adding more wadding (batting). To give the pad a smooth, rounded shape, cover the whole surface with a thin layer of wadding (batting). Turn this to the underside of the pad and staple it in place.

3 Cut out a piece of lining fabric big enough to cover the top and sides of the pad, plus a generous allowance for folding to the underside.

4 Place the pad face down squarely on the fabric, pull each edge of the fabric over to the underside and secure it initially with a staple at each corner.

5 Hold the fabric taut along each edge of the seat in turn and staple it at intervals of about 25 mm/1 in. Turn the fabric edges in and press them flat with an iron. Then staple or slip-stitch the underneath piece of fabric in place.

REPLACING DAMAGED WEBBING

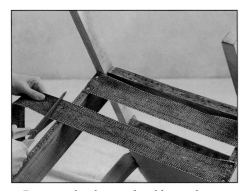

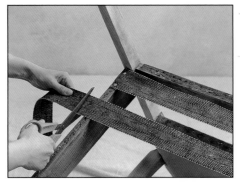

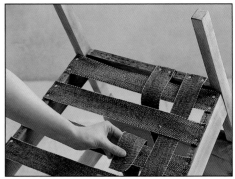

1 Remove the damaged webbing after prising out all the old tacks with a tack lifter. Count up how many strips run in each direction and measure their length so that you can estimate how much webbing you will need to buy.

2 Fit the cross strips first. Fold over one end of each new strip of webbing and tack it to the frame. Then pull it across, cut it 20 mm/¾ in overlong and fold the end over as before. Hold the strip taut and tack the other end to the frame.

3 Tack the rear end of each front-to-back strip to the frame, then weave it over and under the cross strips to the front of the seat. Pull it taut, turn the end over and tack it down to complete the repair.

STAINING AND VARNISHING WOOD

Once you have stripped your furniture back to bare wood, you can finish it in one of several ways to enhance the colour and grain of the wood – or you can simply repaint it. The choice is yours, and which you select will probably depend most of all on the quality of the wood your stripping activities have revealed. If you decide on a 'clear' finish, the next decision is whether merely to varnish the wood or to add some colour to it as well.

Adding colour can be done in several ways; by applying wood stain followed by varnish, by using tinted varnish or by rubbing in one of the coloured wax finishes available for a subtle (though not so durable) effect.

1 Once you have neutralized the effects of the paint remover according to the manufacturer's instructions, rub down the surface of the wood and flatten the grain with fine glass paper or fine sandpaper wrapped around a sanding block.

2 Wipe the surface of the wood over using a cloth pad moistened with white spirit (paint thinner) or a tack cloth to lift off any sanding dust and to remove any greasy finger marks. Allow to dry.

3 If you have chosen to use a wood stain, apply the first coat with a cloth pad, moving it quickly and with even pressure along the grain to avoid overlaps that would spoil the finish. Repeat the procedure for a deeper colour.

4 If you want a quick-drying finish – on bare wood or over a wood stain – apply a clear water-based acrylic varnish. Tinted versions are also available if you want to add a little colour to bare wood.

5 Coloured rubbing waxes are quick and easy to apply with a cloth pad, and give a softer-looking finish than varnish. However, the finish will need further, regular applications of clear wax to keep it looking good and wearing well.

ABOVE Apply a simple wood stain or varnish to a wooden table for a contrasting effect against a stripped wooden floor.

REPAIRING HOUSEHOLD ITEMS

Being able to deal confidently with simple household repairs is an important part of running a home with the minimum of fuss and expense. Many common problems – blocked drains, overflowing cisterns or even noisy pipes – are often very easy to remedy if you are prepared to spend a little time and effort on them. More importantly, you will save a great deal of unnecessary expense by tackling the job yourself rather than calling out an expert to deal with it.

Renovating a bath

Acrylic: use a hard paint such as radiator enamel to paint out marks on this type of bath. Small chips in the surface can also be repaired using a 2-part car-repair filler (spackle). Mix the filler following the instructions on the packet and mix a little paint colour into the paste to blend with the bath. When the filler is hard, rub it down with wet-and-dry sandpaper, keeping this wet as you work.

Enamel: heavy limescale deposits can etch into the surface of a bath. Remove these using a chemical limescale remover applied with a brush. Chips in the enamel coating of a bath can lead to the metal rusting. Use limescale remover to shift any rust stains around the chips, and, when dry, sand with an emery cloth to remove loose particles. Re-paint with an enamel paint, blending colours if necessary to achieve a perfect match.

Repairing china

Clean new breaks thoroughly using methylated spirits and a lint-free cloth before gluing the pieces together with a cyanoacrylate (super glue). Badly repaired breaks will show in time. Start by removing the old glue in hot, soapy water, using an old toothbrush. Apply neat bleach to stains along the crack, using cotton buds (swabs). Rinse and repeat until the stain disappears.

REPAIRING A CLEAN BREAK IN CHINA

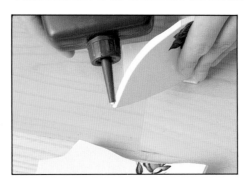

1 Having cleaned the broken edges thoroughly, apply a cyanoacrylate (super glue), following the manufacturer's instructions carefully.

2 Press the broken edges together for a few seconds, then apply strips of masking tape to hold the pieces securely. Leave to dry, and repeat with the other broken pieces.

Bond simple breaks in pottery with a 2-part epoxy resin or PVA (white) glue. Use cyanoacrylate adhesives for fine breaks and porcelain. Multiple breaks should only be glued piece by piece and allowed to dry between stages. Using acrylic paints, it is possible to 'hide' cracks and even to replace parts of a missing pattern if you fill the area with Plaster of Paris and carefully paint over it. Repaired china and pottery will never be as strong as it was formerly, so do not use it in an oven, or to carry hot foods or drinks.

An overflowing cistern

If the ball-float allows too much water into the cistern, the water could start to run out of the overflow pipe. Older-style Portsmouth-type valves can be adjusted by bending the metal float arm down. When full, the cistern's water level should be about 2.5 cm/1 in below the overflow. If the problem is caused by corrosion or scale, the Portsmouth valves may have failed and the washer may have worn away too.

Newer cisterns have plastic diaphragm valves. The float arm can be adjusted by the screw that is secured with a locknut. Release the locknut, then turn the screw towards the valve to reduce the amount of water. Re-tighten the locknut afterwards.

Radiator 'cold spots'

These are usually caused by air becoming locked inside the top of the radiator and preventing the water from reaching the whole of the inside. Hold a rag under the square valve and, using the radiator key gently release it until the air starts to hiss out. When the hissing stops and water starts to dribble out, close it up again. If the air released from the radiator smells of gas, it could be due to corrosion in the system. If this is the case, ask a central-heating engineer for advice.

ABOVE Hold a cloth underneath a radiator valve to catch any drips as the air is released.

REPAIRING A DIAPHRAGM VALVE

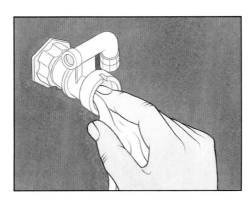

1 If the rubber diaphragm has worn or its action been disrupted by debris in the water, turn off the water supply. Dismantle the valve and lay out the parts in the order they come off, to make re-assembly easier.

2 Clean the diaphragm in warm, soapy water or, if it is damaged, replace it with a new one. Turn on the water to flush out any debris and then replace the diaphragm, ensuring that the rim faces inwards. Re-assemble the valve.

REPAIRING A PORTSMOUTH VALVE

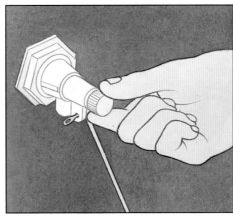

1 Turn off the water supply and unscrew the cap at the end of the valve. If the cap is tight or rusted, use pliers to loosen before taking it off.

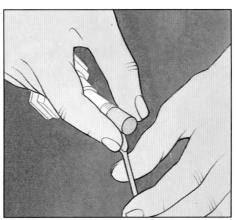

3 Push the valve plug out with a screwdriver and clean it thoroughly, inside and out, using wire wool.

2 Dismantle the valve by removing the split pin securing the float arm. If this is rusty it may snap, so have a spare split pin to hand.

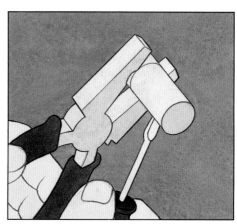

4 Unscrew the valve cap by turning a screwdriver in the slot of the valve plug and remove the washer. Replace the washer with a new one if necessary and re-assemble the plug and valve.

UNBLOCKING A SINK

1 LEFT If the water will not run out of the sink, place a sink plunger over the plughole and cover the overflow with a damp cloth. Pump the plunger hard up and down a few times to release the blockage.

   If the blockage still remains, hold a large dish or other container beneath the U-bend under the sink. Keep the plug in the sink, then unscrew the U-bend, remove it for cleaning and then replace it.

2 RIGHT If the obstruction is not in the U-bend, probe a piece of thick wire or an unravelled wire coat hanger into the waste pipe to hook out the blockage.

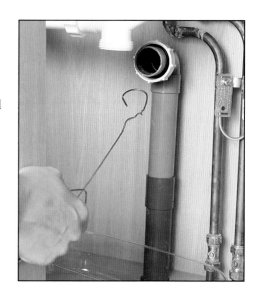

APPLIANCE BREAKDOWN

Before calling in a specialist to deal with an appliance that has stopped working, there are certain basic checks that you can carry out yourself to remedy the most commonly occurring problems. Always unplug an appliance while fault finding until you are ready to test it. With all appliances, first check the instruction manual under 'Fault Finding' and follow the recommendations for your particular make of appliance. Ensure that the plug or plugs are pushed in firmly and that the socket (receptacle) switch is on. This may seem an obvious point, but can easily be overlooked if the switch is hidden behind the appliance. Look to see whether the flex is loose or split – if so, switch off the power and replace the flex as soon as possible.

If all these things are in order, refer to the following list of simple checks and repairs that you can carry out yourself. If these are not successful you will have to call in an engineer.

A portable air conditioner

If an air conditioner is not cooling properly, or is operating erratically, it may be the incorrect size for the room. (If too small, it will operate continually and may ice up, making the room feel cold and damp.) Check to see whether the filter needs cleaning, or whether the seal or panels are out of position. Also check the internal evaporator and exterior condenser coils, and clean them as necessary.

If an air conditioner is not working at all, the thermostat control may be incorrectly set. Alternatively, if the machine has a water reservoir, this may need emptying.

A dishwasher

If the hose is leaking, it may be due to a loose clip, or the hose may be damaged. Ensure that clips are tight and secure, and either tape up the hose or replace it as necessary.

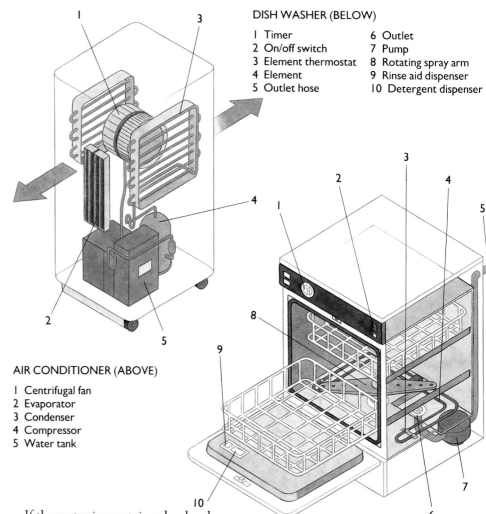

DISH WASHER (BELOW)

1 Timer	6 Outlet
2 On/off switch	7 Pump
3 Element thermostat	8 Rotating spray arm
4 Element	9 Rinse aid dispenser
5 Outlet hose	10 Detergent dispenser

AIR CONDITIONER (ABOVE)

1 Centrifugal fan
2 Evaporator
3 Condenser
4 Compressor
5 Water tank

If the water is emptying slowly, there may be a blockage in the pump or outlet filter. Disconnect the outlet hose and remove any debris. Prise out the filter and clean.

If the dishwasher is simply not cleaning the dishes properly, you may be using the wrong programme, or there may be a blockage in the spray arms. If the programme is correct, unscrew the central hub cap on the spray arm and wash it out if necessary.

A food processor

If a food processor only produces intermittent bursts of power, or the speed is erratic, the causes could be a worn drive belt, or food clogged inside the casing or commutator. Undo the machine casing screws and check the belt for nicks or signs of perishing.

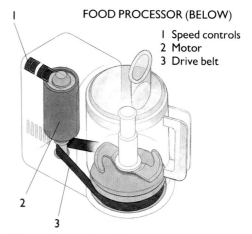

FOOD PROCESSOR (BELOW)

1 Speed controls
2 Motor
3 Drive belt

Clean the inside of the machine thoroughly using a soft, dry brush. The commutator contains lots of copper strips and is situated between the brushes in the motor. Clean gently with methylated spirits (denatured alcohol).

A kettle

If there is no power, and the kettle will not heat up, check for any loose wiring or poor connections in the lead and plug and re-wire as necessary. If this does not solve the problem, the cut-out device may have been triggered. Try re-setting the cut-out but, if it continues to trip, you will need to replace it. Another possibility is that the element is damaged, so check for hairline cracks. If the repair is likely to be costly, however, it may be easier simply to replace the kettle.

A refrigerator

If the problem is poor cooling, causing the ice box to melt, the causes are likely to be a faulty door seal or a faulty condenser, or it could be that the fridge simply needs de-frosting. Check the door seal for perished or damaged areas, and replace it if necessary. Check the condenser by turning the temperature control to the lowest setting. Leave the door open for 5 minutes, then see whether the motor comes on when you shut the door. If nothing happens, the condenser is probably faulty and you will need to call in an engineer. You should de-frost the refrigerator approximately every month.

If the refrigerator temperature is too cold, causing some foods to freeze, the problem may simply be an incorrect thermostat setting, or the thermostat may be faulty.

A tumble drier

If a drier is particularly noisy when in use, the drum bearings may be worn or the fan could be loose. Check the condition of the front and rear bearings, and that the large fan on the main motor is secure and not rotating independently. Check the fan for damage and replace it if necessary.

If loads of washing are not drying properly, the cause may be a blocked filter, or it could be that you are simply overloading the machine. Remove the filter and clean away any fluff. Place a smaller quantity of laundry in the drum before re-starting the drier.

A washing machine

If the problem is leaking water, the causes could be a faulty hose or hose connection, a perished door seal, a blocked outlet or a faulty pump. Switch off the machine and remove any washing from inside. Check that the filter is not blocked, check the outlet hose for any blockage, and check the pump by switching to the rinse cycle. Check the hose and connections for any leaks, and make a temporary repair with adhesive tape if possible to prevent further leakage. Examine the door seal and replace it if damaged, or see whether garments or an object have been caught in the door gasket.

WASHING MACHINE (RIGHT)

1	Door seal	6	Motor
2	Timer	7	Pump
3	Drive belt	8	Sump hose
4	Outlet hose	9	Drum
5	Heater		

If the problem is that the machine is not emptying, the causes could be a faulty pump, or a blocked filter or outlet hose. Switch off the machine, and drain down the system following the instruction manual. Open the filter and remove any debris or objects using an old toothbrush. Also check the pump chamber and remove any blockage.

If the drum of the machine will not turn, the reason may be a slack or broken drive belt.

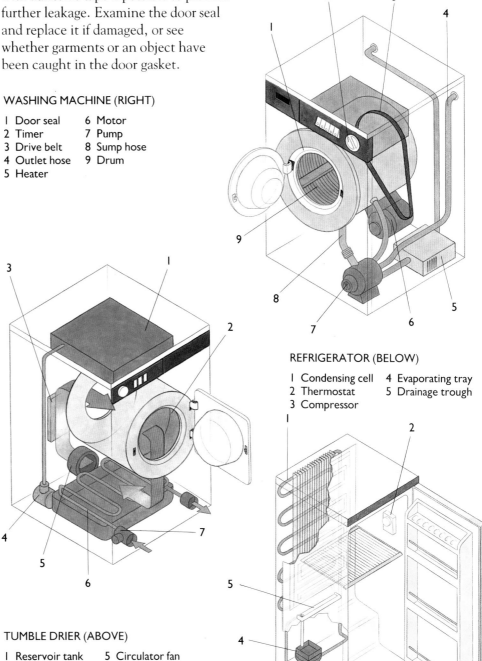

REFRIGERATOR (BELOW)

1	Condensing cell	4	Evaporating tray
2	Thermostat	5	Drainage trough
3	Compressor		

TUMBLE DRIER (ABOVE)

1	Reservoir tank	5	Circulator fan
2	Circulating drum	6	Cool metal ducting
3	Heater unit	7	Air vent
4	Pump		

SAVING ENERGY IN THE HOME

Insulation means saving energy, and that is becoming more and more essential on every level, from the personal to the global. People are increasingly conscious of the importance of environmental issues. One of the greatest contributions that any one household can make is to cut down on the unnecessary wastage of fossil fuels, and so to reduce the amount of carbon dioxide released into the atmosphere by burning them. This means making more efficient use of energy, and insulation has a big part to play in this. It saves money, too.

Insulation is a means of reducing heat transfer from a warm area to a cold one, and substantially reduces heat loss. In temperate countries, the external air temperature is below what most people regard as a comfortable level for much of the year, so heating is needed for fairly long periods and heat is constantly lost to the outside.

All materials conduct heat to a greater or lesser extent. Wood is a good insulator, brick an average one and glass is downright poor, as anyone who has sat next to a window on a cold winter's day will testify.

Except in countries which have very cold winters, proper insulation of homes has until recently been a very low priority, both for housebuilders – who will not pay for something that provides only a hidden benefit unless they have to – and for the legislators

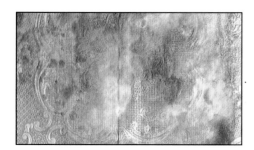

ABOVE Poor insulation, inadequate ventilation and poor heating levels can, in extreme cases, lead to patches of mould occurring around windows and inside fitted cupboards (closets).

SOURCES OF MOISTURE

People themselves are a major source of the moisture in the air inside a building. Breath is moist and sweat evaporates; one person gives off 250 ml/½ pint of water during 8 hours of sleep: 3 times that during the day.

Domestic activities create even more moisture. Cooking, washing up, a hot bath or shower, washing and drying clothes and so on can create as much as a further 10 to 12 litres/3 gallons of water a day, and every litre of fuel burnt in a flueless oil or paraffin heater gives off roughly another litre of water vapour. The air in the house is expected to soak up all this extra moisture invisibly, but it may not be able to manage unaided. However, a combination of improved insulation and controlled ventilation will go a long way towards eliminating the problem of condensation.

who frame the regulations and codes with which builders must comply. At last, however, the tide is turning, and current building rules call for much higher standards of insulation than ever before. They have also recognized that over-insulation can cause condensation, both inside the rooms and within the building's structure.

This will not help people living in older properties, many of which were built with no thought to their insulation performance at all. Over the years, various attempts will have been made to insulate houses like these, but what was deemed adequate 20 years ago will be well below par for today.

Condensation

Condensation is a big problem in many homes. It can lead to serious health problems and can also cause damage to the structure of the home.

The air always contains a certain amount of moisture – a lot on a humid

summer's day, less on a clear winter one. When the air at a particular temperature cannot hold any more moisture, it is said to have reached saturation point, described as a relative humidity of 100 per cent.

Air at saturation point is the key to the problem. If that saturated air is cooled – for example, by coming into contact with a surface such as a window pane on a chilly day – it can no longer hold so much vapour. The excess moisture vapour in the air condenses into droplets of water, and these are deposited on the cold surface – first as a fine film that mists up the glass but then, as more moisture is deposited, the droplets combine to form rivulets that run down the surface to create pools of water on the window sill. This can ruin decorations and cause window sills and frames to rot and rust; it can also cause 2 further problems, both of which are potentially more serious.

ABOVE Constant condensation ruins paintwork and will eventually cause wooden window frames and sills to rot.

ABOVE Fit an extractor fan (exhaust fan) to control ventilation in a steamy room such as a kitchen or bathroom. The type linked to a humidity detector activates automatically.

ABOVE Fit a special brush draught excluder over a letter-box opening, and also to the bottoms of doors to minimize heat loss.

ABOVE If the roof of your house is pitched (sloping), lay blanket insulation over the loft (attic) floor to prevent heat loss.

ABOVE Glass is an extremely poor insulator. Secondary glazing, known as double glazing, can cut down on heat loss, provided that the inner panes are well-sealed to their tracks.

ABOVE With a suspended floor, you can lift the floorboards and suspend blanket insulation on netting stapled to the joists. Lay a vapour barrier, such as heavy plastic sheeting, on top.

The first is mould. Apart from moisture vapour, the air also contains millions of tiny spores which float around looking for somewhere to live and multiply. The one thing they need is a damp surface. The result is the patches of black, brown or dark green mould seen especially around windows, in fitted cupboards (closets) and in the upper corners of those rooms that have poor insulation and ventilation and inadequate heating.

The second problem is interstitial condensation. If the materials used to build walls, roofs and other parts of a building allow water vapour to penetrate, condensation can actually occur inside the structure. If moisture cannot evaporate to the outside the affected part of the structure remains damp; this can then encourage rot to grow on wood, and may also result in frost damage to masonry in cold weather, caused by the water expanding as it freezes. What is more, a damp wall has a lower resistance to the passage of heat than a dry one, and therefore becomes colder and encourages yet more condensation.

Ventilation

Always be aware that, no matter how well the home has been insulated, it is vital to ensure that it is well-ventilated too and that air can circulate freely to prevent the problems of condensation. When insulating your home it is essential to make allowances for air circulation by installing, for example, an extra air-brick, an extractor fan (exhaust fan) or window vents in a bathroom or kitchen, and even a cooker hood. Simply opening a window while cooking to allow steam out can make a difference. Fuel-burning appliances such as paraffin heaters, gas cookers, central-heating boilers and fires also require ventilation to work efficiently and to dispel potentially dangerous fumes.

QUICK WAYS TO INSULATE

Once icy winds begin to whistle around your home in the winter, you will soon find out where the chill gusts blow in and where all the expensive heat escapes. The following steps will all contribute to keeping your home warmer and energy-efficient.

• Sash windows are notorious for draughts, and their sliding action calls for special weatherproofing. A brush seal (with soft bristles) against inside sliding faces and a V-strip seal where sashes close against the top and bottom of the frame are best.

• An outside door is prone to swelling in cold, wet conditions. Seal it with a flexible PVC (vinyl) or brush strip pinned to the outer face.

• Keyholes can let in cold air, so fit coverplates on the outside.

• Fill gaps around overflow and waste pipes that pass through holes in exterior walls with an exterior-grade filler (spackle), mortar or an expanding foam filler.

• Fill any gaps in windows that remain closed throughout the winter with a flexible, clear sealant. Apply it with a mastic gun and, when you wish to open the windows again, simply peel off the sealant and discard.

• A porch built over a front or back door acts as an insulating barrier by preventing cold air from entering the house and keeping warm air in. It will also keep wet boots and coats from dripping over floors.

• In addition to traditional sausage-shaped door draught excluders, door curtains are a very effective way of reducing heat loss, and can also add a decorative finish to rooms.

• Insulate the wall immediately behind a radiator by simply placing tin foil behind it to reflect the heat back into the room again.

• Fix temporary 'double glazing' by sticking clear cellophane to the window frame with double-sided tape.

• Cling film (plastic wrap) can also serve as temporary double glazing. Stretch it over the window and make it taut with gentle heat blown from a hairdryer.

INSULATING A ROOF, FLOOR AND PIPEWORK

In a building with a pitched (sloping) roof, where the loft (attic) space is used only for storage, it is usual to insulate the loft floor, using either blankets of glass fibre or mineral wool (this is sold by the roll and is fireproof and resistant to damp or vermin attack); or else loose-fill material (vermiculite, a lightweight expanded mineral, is the most widely used).

Blanket materials are generally easier to handle than loose-fill types. The rolls are generally 450 mm/18 in wide to match standard joist spacing, and common thicknesses are 100 mm/4 in and 150 mm/6 in. Choose the latter unless there is already some thin loft insulation, and ensure that it is laid with eaves baffles to allow adequate ventilation of the loft. It is essential to wear protective clothing when handling glass-fibre insulation.

Loose-fill materials need laying to a greater depth – usually at least an extra 2.5 cm/1 in. With few ceiling joists being deeper than about 15 cm/6 in, there is nothing to contain the insulation and allow for maintenance access unless strips of wood are fixed along the top edge of every joist.

When the loft floor is completely insulated, remember to insulate any water tanks and pipework within the loft, as they will now be at the risk of freezing. For this reason, do not lay insulation under water tanks.

WALL INSULATION

Up to one-quarter of a home's heat loss can occur through the walls. The space between cavity walls can be filled with a variety of insulating materials, including polystyrene (styrofoam) pellets and expanding foam. These have to be pumped through holes drilled in the external wall, so you will need to call in a professional to undertake this job.

LAYING ROOF INSULATION

1 Clear all stored items from the loft (attic) area, then put down a sturdy kneeling board and vacuum up the dust and debris. Always put on gloves and a face-mask and wear long sleeves to handle the insulation. Unroll it between the joists, leaving the eaves clear for ventilation.

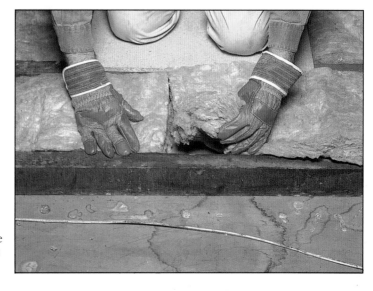

2 Butt-join the ends of successive lengths of blanket. To cut the material to length, either use long-bladed scissors or simply tear it.

3 While working across the loft, make sure that any electrical cables are lifted clear of the insulation so they cannot overheat.

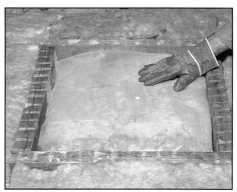

4 Insulate the upper surface of the loft hatch by wrapping a piece of blanket in plastic sheeting and then stapling this to the hatch door.

INSULATING A WOODEN FLOOR

1 To insulate beneath a wooden floor, lift all the floorboards. Drape lengths of garden netting loosely over the joists and staple them in place.

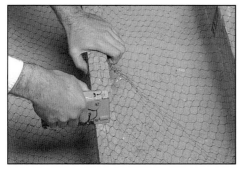

2 Lay loft-insulation blanket or wall-insulation batts in the 'hammocks' between the joists. If the netting sags, pull it up a little and staple it again.

3 To prevent moisture from the house condensing within the insulation, cover it with a vapour barrier of heavy-duty polythene (polyethylene) sheeting.

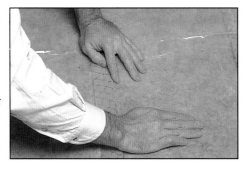

4 Re-lay the floorboards by nailing them to the joists. Take this opportunity to close up any gaps in the joints between the boards for a neat finish.

INSULATING PIPEWORK

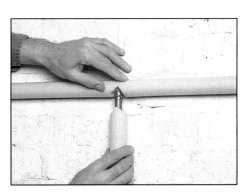

1 The quickest way of insulating pipework is to slip on lengths of foam pipe insulation, slit lengthwise. Use PVC (vinyl) tape to secure the sections together.

2 To make neat joins in the insulation at corners, cut the ends at 45°, using a mitre box and a carving knife or hacksaw blade. Tape the corner joint.

3 Make a V-shaped cut-out in the insulation at tee joints, then cut an arrow shape on the end of the insulation that will cover the branch pipe.

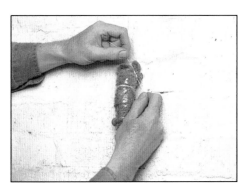

4 As with butt and corner joints, use PVC (vinyl) tape to secure the sections of insulation together and to prevent them from slipping out of position.

5 Pipe bandage can be used instead of foam insulation. Wrap it around the pipe in a spiral, with the turns just overlapping.

6 Tie the insulation bandage in place at the end of each length, or where the pipe passes through a wall. Simply tear the material to length as necessary.

DOUBLE GLAZING

The glass in windows is the least efficiently insulated aspect of the house, and the only way of cutting the heat loss while still being able to see out is to add another layer of glass. Double glazing can be done in two ways: existing panes of glass can be replaced with special double-glazed panes called sealed units, or a second pane can be installed inside the existing one – so-called secondary glazing.

Secondary glazing is the only practical course of action unless the existing windows are being completely replaced. There are dozens of types available for do-it-yourself installation, providing hinged and sliding inner

panes that blend in well with most types of window; similar systems are also available from professional installers. The panes are either fixed to the window frame itself, or else fit within the window reveal on special track. An effective but flimsy alternative is clear acetate or PVC (vinyl) film fixed to the inside of the frame with double-sided tape.

Apart from reducing heat losses through the windows, double glazing eliminates 'cold spots' in the room next to the windows. It also helps to reduce noise penetration from outside as long as the inner panes are kept closed. It will reduce condensation too, but only

if the inner panes are well sealed to their track to stop warm moist air getting into the air gap between them and the window itself. Lastly, lockable types will give a measure of additional security; burglars may tackle one pane of glass, but many will flinch at two.

As far as external doors are concerned, solid doors offer better insulation than glazed ones, so go for this type if planning a replacement. If a glazed panel is a must, choose one with a sealed double glazing unit using safety glass. Heat loss through any external door can be reduced by building a porch outside it, to create an airlock between the house and the outdoors.

FITTING SLIDING UNITS

1 Measure the height and width of the window reveal at each side. If the figures differ, work from the smaller measurements for height and width.

2 Cut the track sections to length with a fine-toothed saw and sand the cut ends smooth. Make cut-outs following the kit instructions to form corners.

3 Offer up the side track sections and screw them in place. Use thin packing to get them truly vertical if the walls are out of square.

4 Next, secure the top track section in place. Screw it directly to a wooden lintel or pre-drill holes in concrete ones and insert wall plugs first.

FITTING THIN-FILM DOUBLE GLAZING

1 Start by sticking lengths of double-sided adhesive tape to the window frame, about 12 mm/½ in in from the surrounding masonry.

2 Press the film on to the tape, pulling it as taut as possible. Then play hot air from a hair-drier over it to tighten it up and pull out any wrinkles.

3 When you are sure the film is even and wrinkle-free, trim off the excess film all the way around the window using a sharp utility knife.

5 When positioning the bottom track on the windowsill, use a straightedge and a spirit level to check that it is perfectly aligned with the top track.

6 Measure up for the glass as directed in the kit manufacturer's instructions, and order the glass. Fit cut lengths of glazing gasket to the edges of each pane.

7 Fit the first pane into the track by inserting its top edge in the top channel, and then lowering its bottom edge. Repeat the procedure for any remaining panes.

DRAUGHTPROOFING

Ill-fitting windows and doors are a major source of heat loss, as well as causing cold draughts. Fitting efficient draught stripping around them will reduce the losses and cut down the draughts, and is a simple job to carry out. Modern self-adhesive foams are much more efficient and longer-lasting than older types, and are ideal for windows, while doors and sash windows are best draughtproofed with pin-on (tack-on) plastic or sprung metal strips or types containing a compressible rubber seal. Special draught excluders are available for door thresholds (saddles), and can be fitted to the door bottom or across the threshold. There are even excluders designed to fit over letter-box openings.

Remember that draughtproofing a home will close off many 'unofficial' sources of ventilation, turning it into a well sealed box. Fuel-burning appliances such as boilers and room heaters must have an adequate source of fresh air to burn safely, so it is wise to ask a fuel supplier to check that there is adequate ventilation in rooms containing such appliances. Often a ventilator in a window pane will solve the problem. Efficient draughtproofing may also increase condensation, especially in kitchens and bathrooms. This can be prevented by providing controlled ventilation in these rooms with an extractor fan.

DRAUGHTPROOFING DOORS

1 The simplest type of door-bottom draught excluder is a brush seal mounted in a wood or plastic strip. Cut it to length and screw it on to the foot of the door.

2 Alternatively, fit a threshold (saddle) strip. Cut the metal bar to length and screw it to the sill, then fit the compressible sealing strip in the channel.

3 Draughtproof a letter-box opening by screwing on a special brush seal. Check that it does not foul the letter plate flap if this opens inwards.

4 Draughtproof the sides and top of the door frame by pinning (tacking) on plastic or sprung metal sealing strips. Pin the edge farthest from the doorstop bead.

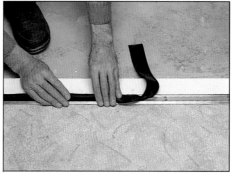

5 Alternatively, stick lengths of self-adhesive foam excluder to the stop bead against which the door closes. At the hinge side, stick it to the frame.

6 A third option is to use lengths of self-adhesive brush strip excluder. These three types can also be used for draughtproofing hinged casement windows.

DRAUGHTPROOFING SASH WINDOWS

1 To fit sprung metal strip excluder to a sliding sash window first prise off the staff beads (window stops) that hold the inner sash in position, and swing it out.

2 Measure the lengths of strip needed to fit the height of the window, and cut to length with scissors. Beware the sharp edges of the metal.

3 Pin (tack) a strip to each side of the frame so it will press against the edge of the sliding sash. Pin it through the edge facing towards the room.

4 Use the special wheeled springing tool provided with the excluder to make a small groove in each strip, causing it to spring outwards.

5 Pin a strip along the inner face of the top sash meeting rail (mullion), and 'spring' it so that it presses against the outer face of the bottom sash rail. Swing the sash back into position.

6 Draughtproof the bottom edge of the lower sash and the top edge of the upper one by sticking on lengths of self-adhesive foam excluder.

PROVIDING CONTROLLABLE VENTILATION

In every house stale, moist air must be removed and replaced with fresh air from outside. This happens not only in an obvious way when a window is opened or an extractor fan switched on, but all the time. For example, air passes up chimney flues, or finds a way out through the inevitable small gaps in the house structure.

Unless power ventilated, most modern houses have very little chance of such natural ventilation because improved standards of insulation and draughtproofing have made them much more airtight than formerly. Of course this is advantageous as it reduces

heating bills and keeps the house's occupants warm and comfortable. The danger, however, is to prevent the occupants creating too much moisture for the air to hold. If this happens, condensation will be the inevitable result, and extra ventilation will then be needed.

This reduction in natural ventilation not only causes trouble within the house, it can also affect its structure. Two particular problem areas are roof spaces and under-floor voids. To prevent it, more ventilation must be provided via ridge and eaves-level vents in roofs, and airbricks in walls.

For ventilating rooms, what is needed is some controllable means of getting rid of excess moist air without wasting too much valuable heat. In habitually steamy rooms such as kitchens and bathrooms, an extractor fan is the best solution. It will extract the moist air quickly, and will also help to get rid of unwanted smells.

In other rooms, it is worth considering fitting small 'trickle' ventilators at the top of window frames and putting in extra airbricks, as these will often supply enough ventilation to allow the moist air to disperse before condensation becomes a problem.

FITTING AN EXTRACTOR FAN

1 Decide on the fan position, then mark the outline of the ducting on the wall outside. Drill holes right through the wall to mark it on the inside as well.

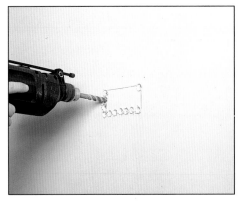

2 Drill a series of closely spaced holes through the wall from inside, working within the guide holes drilled from outside. Repeat on the wall outside.

3 Chop out the brickwork with a wide bolster (stonecutter's chisel) and club (spalling) hammer, again working from inside and outside the house.

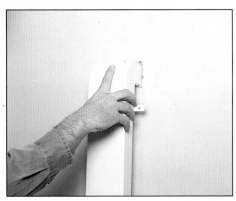

4 Use ducting for a cooker (stove) hood. Line the hole with a short length of pipe, then use connectors as required to connect the hood to the outlet.

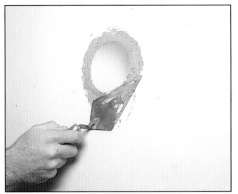

5 Wall-mounted fans usually need a round hole. Cut it out, line it with a short length of sleeving and make good around it inside and outside using plaster.

6 Fit the fan into the sleeving, ready for its electrical supply to be connected. Fit a cover grille to the outside end of the fan ducting.

SAFE VENTILATION

There are two very important points to remember concerning ventilation. Firstly, many fuel-burning appliances need an adequate supply of fresh air to work efficiently and safely, so rooms where they are sited must contain provision for this if they are well sealed against natural draughts. Secondly, disused flues must be ventilated at top and bottom; if they are not, condensation can occur within the flue, which may show up as damp patches on the internal chimney walls.

FITTING EXTRA AIRBRICKS

1 Airbricks are available the same size as one, two or three bricks. To fit one, start by drilling a series of closely spaced holes through the wall.

2 Use a club (spalling) hammer and a bolster (stonecutter's chisel) to cut out the brickwork. With solid walls, drill holes right through and also work from inside.

3 Fit a cavity liner if the wall is of cavity construction, then carefully trowel a bed of fairly wet mortar on to the bottom of the opening.

4 'Butter' mortar on to the top of the airbrick and slide it into the opening. Push mortar into the gaps at the sides and pack it down well.

5 Use drier mortar to point neatly all around the airbrick. Inside, make good the wall with plaster and cover the opening with a ventilator grille.

6 As an alternative to a terracotta airbrick, fit a two-part plastic type. The sleeves interlock to line the hole as the two parts are pushed together.

7 Slide the outer section into place, and point around it. Then slide the inner section into place from inside the house, and fit its cover grille.

CLEANING AND HOME HINTS

Most of us can only relax once the house looks spotless and the chores are all finished, but this can be a never-ending task if not organized properly and carried out efficiently. Regular, sometimes daily, attention to many aspects of home care will ensure that the house is always well maintained and presentable without the need for a great input of time and effort.

Many items in the home are often best cleaned using different types of cleaners, and then not always using proprietary products. The following section begins with a directory of domestic objects, each entry containing information on how to clean and preserve them easily. Most domestic items are covered, including baths and cookers, fireplaces, ceilings, floors, drains, carpets, curtains (drapes), telephones, computers, china and glassware, furniture and even valuable antiques. A further directory is devoted to stains, which are best removed individually with a special treatment according to the nature of each blemish. There are also invaluable hints on eliminating unpleasant household odours.

A successful routine of regular dusting and polishing will ensure that unsightly (and, to many, unhealthy) dust is kept at bay while ensuring that paintwork and furniture always look good. The information given on this subject includes advice on cleaning different types of metal and how to avoid ruining a finish on woodwork.

When the wrong washing machine programme or detergent is used, it can result in disaster, with precious clothes inadvertently being shrunk, or coloured a delicate pink or dingy blue. By following the advice given in these pages on washing and drying you can avoid such problems. Advice is also offered on ironing different types of fabric correctly.

Suggestions are made for fitting everyday chores, such as bed making and bathroom cleaning, easily into the day's routine and for getting the whole family involved in a regime of daily maintenance. There are also useful tips on conservation and waste recycling, plus preparing the house and yourself for going on holiday or moving house.

OPPOSITE Armed with just a few essential items and a sensible, organized approach to cleaning, most domestic chores need take up only a small part of the day.

CLEANING THE HOME

With so many objects around the home and numerous cleaning products from which to choose, it can be difficult to match object with product. Simple solutions are often the best, and, if you are unsure of how to tackle the cleaning of a specific item or the removal of a difficult stain without causing more damage, the following reference pages could save you a great deal of time, effort and money.

Antiques

Cleaning antiques must be done with the greatest of care – even damaging the patina can drastically reduce the value of an antique object.

Furniture: a damp, soft cloth with a little liquid soap should be sufficient to remove grubby marks from furniture. Wipe with a clean, damp cloth and use natural beeswax to polish, then buff softly to a shine.

Pictures: dust the frames of pictures with a feather duster, or use a soft make-up brush on elaborate gilded frames. You can clean old, but not particularly valuable, paintings with a special picture cleaner (available from artists' suppliers) – always follow the manufacturer's instructions. If you do not wish to clean a painting yourself, take it to a qualified restorer.

Appliances

Wipe the door fronts and sides of appliances with a cloth dipped in hot water and detergent, and wrung out until it is just damp. Move appliances easily to clean underneath and behind them by rubbing a little liquid soap in front of their feet before pulling.

Baths

Acrylic: never use scourers on acrylic or glass-fibre baths – a sponge and a gentle spray cleaner should be all that are required. Rinse thoroughly.

Enamelled: avoid using acid-based cleaners on enamelled baths as they will gradually etch into the surface. Use a cellulose sponge and liquid detergent to clean off tidemarks. Turpentine or white spirit (paint thinner) rubbed on with a soft cloth will remove stubborn marks. Use a limescale remover around the bases of the taps (faucets) to break down hard-water deposits.

Blinds and shades

Remove roller-type blinds and shades from their fixings and unroll them before washing with hot water and detergent. Use a soft brush on stubborn marks, if necessary. Rinse well with clean water, and leave to dry thoroughly before replacing.

Clean slatted blinds with a special U-shaped duster brush, or wear cotton gloves to grip and wipe along each slat. Always work from the top to the bottom to avoid dust settling on the cleaned slats beneath.

ABOVE **A lemon dipped in salt is an effective brass cleaner, but rinse thoroughly after use.**

Brass and copper

Wash lacquered brass in warm, soapy water, then rinse it and buff dry. Unlacquered brass should be cleaned with a proprietary brand of brass and copper polish – use an old toothbrush to reach fine detailing. A cut lemon dipped in salt is effective on very dirty areas – always wash the brass afterwards in hot, soapy water. Try a silicone car wax (marble-polishing powder) to maintain the shiny finish on brass.

Bronze

The characteristic patina on bronze should not be cleaned and scrubbed away. Remove surface marks with pure turpentine applied with a soft cloth. Alternatively, wash in warm, soapy water and buff up with a soft cloth.

Cane furniture

Most cane and wicker furniture has a lacquered finish, and only requires occasional buffing with a soft cloth and furniture polish. Clean ground-in dirt on cane furniture with fine steel wool dipped in a washing-soda solution (a handful of soda to a bucket of warm water), or use a soft brush and warm, soapy water. Place old newspapers under the piece to be cleaned to catch drips. Wipe over with a clean, damp cloth and allow the cane to dry away from direct heat.

Carpets

Before shampooing a carpet, vacuum it thoroughly to remove grit, dust and crumbs. Move the furniture out of the room or stack it at one end. Choose a day when you can open the windows to let the carpets dry naturally. Use a special carpet shampoo and follow the manufacturer's instructions. If you do not have an electrical carpet cleaner of your own, you will be able to hire (rent) one fairly cheaply from DIY stores and some electrical suppliers.

Always check first that the colour will not run by rubbing an unobtrusive area with shampoo solution.

Start at the corner of the room furthest from the door and work back across the room to avoid treading on the damp areas. Cover an area of approximately 1 sq m/1 sq yd at a time, drawing the brush head of the cleaner towards you in strips across the area until no more water is drawn back into the head. Allow the carpet to dry thoroughly before replacing furniture.

Ceilings

Cigarette smoke and cooking can make ceilings dirty over time. Cover the furniture and carpet with old sheets or decorator's cloths (drop cloths) and brush away any loose cobwebs or dust first. Dip a clean floor mop (preferably one with a foam head) in warm water mixed with a little detergent. Squeeze out as much excess water as possible before working your way across the ceiling in a back-and-forth movement. Change the water as soon as it begins to look murky. Finish with clean water and leave to dry. Never allow water near light fittings (fixtures) or switches – use a damp cloth instead.

ABOVE Use a make-up brush and soapy water to clean delicate china ornaments.

Chimneys

It is usually best to call in a professional to clean the flue and chimney, but you can hire (rent) or buy chimney rods if you prefer to do the job yourself. Before starting, ensure that all the furniture and carpets are covered and that the windows and doors in the room are shut. Have a vacuum cleaner ready and old newspapers laid around the fireplace. Wear old clothes, shoes, rubber gloves and a protective face-mask. Follow the directions given with the rods, and, as the soot starts to drop, be ready to vacuum it up quickly. When leaving the room, remove your shoes to avoid the risk of treading soot into other rooms. Remove and wash the brush head on the vacuum cleaner.

China

Immerse china ornaments in warm, soapy water, and use an old shaving or make-up brush to work into awkward crevices. Rinse well and dry with a soft cloth. Clean china candlesticks that are covered in wax by immersing them in hot water to melt the wax, then clean them in soapy water.

To clean china plant pots with water marks, place them in a bowl and apply neat limescale remover to the marks. Leave for half an hour or until the limescale dissolves, then rinse and dry.

Chopping boards

After use, place chopping boards in the sink and carefully pour boiling water over them. Use a scrubbing brush, disinfectant and soapy water to clean it thoroughly. Rinse and allow to dry naturally. Do not soak wooden boards as they may warp. You should replace a chopping board that is heavily worn, as cuts and cracks can allow harmful bacteria to multiply.

Computers

Always unplug a computer before cleaning it. Vacuum regularly using the soft-brush attachment, and turn the keyboard over and tap it lightly to dislodge any crumbs or dust. Use a cotton bud (swab) dipped in neat methylated spirits (denatured alcohol) to clean individual keys. Finally, wiping a little dilute fabric conditioner over the computer with a damp cloth will help to reduce the static.

Cookers

Before cleaning, always switch off the power supply to an electric cooker. A self-cleaning oven can use up a lot of power when burning off food residues; it helps to line the bottom of the oven with heavy-duty tin foil which you can throw away once dirty. A watery paste of bicarbonate of soda and water,

ABOVE Allow hob (burner) covers to soak before cleaning.

CLEANING THE HOME (continued)

allowed to dry on the oven floor, will absorb grease spatters and is easy to wipe out after cooking.

You can deal with a heavily soiled oven easily with proprietary brands of oven cleaners. Many contain sodium hydroxide which can cause serious burns, so follow the manufacturer's instructions carefully, wear protective gloves and goggles, and ensure that the kitchen is well-ventilated.

Always give the hob (burners) a quick wipe over after every use, in order to prevent foods from solidifying on the surfaces. Remove burned-on foods with an abrasive cream cleaner, or with a scourer and hot water with a few drops of ammonia added. Remove the ring trims and wipe underneath them. Do not wipe over a ceramic glass hob with a dishcloth, as food particles will cause staining once the heat is switched on. Instead, use the manufacturer's recommended cleaner. Be sure to clean up any acidic spillages such as fruit, vinegar, or sauces and sugar from the hob immediately, as they will pit the surface, otherwise leave the cleaning until the cooker has cooled.

Cooking pans
Aluminium: clean using a paste made from equal parts of baking powder, cream of tartar, washing powder and vinegar. Use a cellulose scourer to bring the surface to a shine, then rinse thoroughly. Leave the juice of a lemon diluted in 0.75 l/1 pint of water in pans overnight to remove water marks.
Enamelled: do not use scourers on vitreous-enamelled pans. Remove stains by soaking in a weak solution of bleach, and scrub dirt around handles with an old toothbrush and detergent.

Crystal stemware
High temperatures in a dishwasher will gradually weaken lead crystal, so wash this carefully in hand-hot water using a mild liquid detergent. Use a soft

ABOVE **A handful of rice and a warm detergent solution will clean marks from inside decanters or narrow-necked vases.**

dishcloth to wipe rims, but do not try to force it into narrow-necked vases or decanters. Crevices in cut crystal can be cleaned with an old toothbrush and soapy water. Rinse thoroughly and allow to dry before polishing with a glass cloth. Clean the inside of a decanter by swishing around a handful of rice grains mixed with some detergent and warm water. Dilute limescale remover will also tackle the white film found in vases.

Curtains and drapes
Close the curtains or drapes to spread out the gathers, then vacuum from the top down to the bottom. Gathered valances and pelmets should also be vacuumed regularly. When removing curtains and valances for cleaning, make sure that you know which side each should hang from by marking the linings with a small letter 'L' in waterproof ink at the top left and 'R' at the top right. Remove the hooks and keep them in a safe place. Flatten out the heading tapes for even cleaning.

Curtain tracks and poles
Dust and grime can settle on tracks and poles, preventing the smooth opening of curtains, so dust regularly with a soft cloth and wipe clean with a damp cloth and a few drops of liquid detergent. Wipe with clean water and allow to dry. Rub silicone wipes along the surfaces of tracks and poles for smooth, gliding curtains.

Cutlery (Flatware)
Wash, rinse and dry cutlery (flatware) as soon as possible after using it in order to prevent food from becoming dried on, or salt and acidic foods from staining the finish. Only place dishwasher-proof cutlery in the dishwasher; silver, bronze and bone-handled cutlery should always be washed by hand. Never leave bone-handled cutlery to soak, as this will cause the handles to work loose over time. Buff cutlery with a soft, clean cloth before putting away.

If you have several items of silver or silver-plated cutlery to clean, line the bottom of a plastic bowl with tin foil and place the cutlery on top. Add a handful of washing soda and cover with boiling water. The electrochemical reaction will remove the tarnish. Rinse and dry the cutlery before storing away.

Double glazing
Wear stout gloves before removing secondary double glazing for cleaning. Chamois leathers give professional results, but avoid using them with detergents. Use a solution of methylated spirits (denatured alcohol) or white-wine vinegar in tepid water. Particularly dirty windows can be cleaned using a solution of 120 ml/4 fl oz/$\frac{1}{2}$ cup each of ammonia and white-wine vinegar mixed into a bucket of water. Scrunched-up newspapers are also excellent for adding a gleam to windows – dip them in the solution and use instead of a chamois leather.

ABOVE Water and vinegar rubbed on to window panes with an old newspaper will really make them sparkle.

and surrounds with a wire brush. Use neat malt vinegar to scrub the bricks and rinse with clean water.

Cast-iron: when cool, dampen the ashes and vacuum away dust and soot from the hearth and surround. Use a grate blackener or high-temperature stove paint to burnish and protect the metal. Do not wipe a tiled surround while it is hot, as water can cause the surface of the tiles to craze.

Stone: scrub a stone fireplace with a solution of 1 part bleach to 8 parts tepid water. Rinse with clean water and pat dry with absorbent cloths. Once dry, apply a clear brick and stone sealant for protection from further staining.

Floors

Brick and stone: sweep and wash with warm water and a mild detergent. Red brick can be brightened and polished with 'Cardinal Red' brick polish (all-purpose powdered cleanser).

Floorboards: vacuum out dirt from the gaps between floorboards before cleaning or polishing. Wipe over unvarnished boards with a damp cloth and leave them to dry before polishing with a wax floor polish. Buff varnished boards with a non-slip polish.

Linoleum: start by removing obvious marks by scrubbing with a gentle cellulose scourer and soap. An abrasive cream cleaner applied with a cloth will also work well. Use a damp mop and soapy water to clean the linoleum thoroughly, then rinse.

Marble: avoid using any abrasive cleaner or applicator on marble. Mop the floor with warm water and a mild detergent, using a blunt knife to lift any stuck-on dirt. The surface can be polished with a silicone wax.

Slate: wash regularly with soap and detergent and rinse thoroughly. Restore the shine of slate by wiping a little milk over the surface.

Vinyl: grimy vinyl will clean up more easily if you mop a proprietary brand of floor cleaner over the floor and allow it to soak for 10 minutes before cleaning.

Drains

Fish out any debris caught in the cover of a drain and place it in a plastic bag before throwing away. Regularly rinse down drains with a household bleach or disinfectant. If fat has solidified around the drain, pour some neat ammonia on to it and leave for a couple of minutes, then carefully pour boiling water down it to flush.

Extractor fans

Switch off an electric extractor fan before removing the cover to clean the vents. Wipe the plastic cover with a cloth dipped in warm, soapy water.

Unscrew a non-electric, plastic window fan from its mountings and soak in warm, soapy water to remove dust and grit. Rinse and allow to dry.

Fireplaces

Brick: cleaning out a fire grate can create a lot of dust, so damp down the ashes first using either a plant spray gun or some used, damp coffee grounds. Rub soot deposits on brick fire backs

ABOVE Dirt and grit can soon make a window extractor work less efficiently.

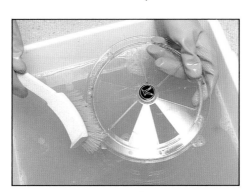

ABOVE Remove the extractor and allow to soak in a detergent solution to release the dirt gently then use a soft brush to clean the grooves.

FLOOR-CLEANING TIPS

- Remove a build-up of solvent-based polish by using medium-grade wire wool and white spirit (paint thinner). Use an ordinary floor cleaner with a little ammonia added to remove emulsion polish, then mop over.
- Always sweep or vacuum the floor before cleaning.
- Remove thick grime under a cooker by first softening the patch using a sponge dipped in hot water. Leave for 5 minutes, then use an old wallpaper-stripping blade wrapped in a cloth to prise off the grime.

CLEANING THE HOME (continued)

Freezers

A freezer needs to be de-frosted regularly. Start by removing all the food, packing it tightly in cold boxes or cardboard boxes lined with a thick layer of newspaper. Turn off the freezer and take out all the trays to be washed. Use a plastic spatula to prise off loose pieces of ice in the freezer, but do not hack at them as you may damage the freezer lining irreparably. Use a toothbrush dipped in warm, soapy water to reach into the seals, then rinse and wipe dry. If the ice is thick, direct the warm heat from a hairdryer on to it to speed the melting, keeping a plastic bowl to hand to catch the water. Wipe the inside of the freezer with a clean cloth, replace the shelves and re-pack the food.

Furniture

For home-made furniture cleaner, mix 2 parts white-wine vinegar, 2 parts turpentine and 2 parts paraffin with 1 part methylated spirits (paint thinner) in an old jar. Apply the solution to furniture with an old cloth and polish off straight away.

ABOVE Carefully lift all the items from a display cabinet so that you can give it a thorough clean before replacing the ornaments.

Some polishes clean and shine at the same time, and are most suited to varnished finishes. With old or valuable items, it is best to wipe them over with a barely damp cloth dipped in lukewarm water and a mild detergent to remove sticky marks, before polishing with a proprietary wax polish.

French polish: wipe off greasy and sticky marks with a damp cloth and wipe dry immediately.

Oiled wood: clean with a cloth moistened with turpentine.

Painted finishes: clean painted pieces of furniture with a soft cloth wrung out in warm, soapy water. Use clean water to wipe off any residue and leave to dry away from direct heat.

Varnished and sealed woods: treat as for painted finishes.

Waxed wood: wipe with a cloth wrung out in warm, soapy water. Wash down any heavily marked pieces and rub particularly bad patches with a cellulose sponge scourer. Remember always to follow the wood grain. Rinse and wipe with clean, absorbent cloths to remove all traces of water.

Glass

Add a water softener when washing everyday glass in a dishwasher. Clean delicate and cut glass by hand.

Grout

Revive the grouting between tiles using a little bicarbonate of soda (baking soda) mixed to a paste with bleach. Apply the paste with a toothbrush and

---

REMOVING DENTS

Remove dents in wood furniture by placing a thick, damp cloth over the area, then placing the tip of a hot iron immediately over the dent. The steam will penetrate and swell the compacted wood, which can then be re-polished afterwards.

---

leave for a few minutes. Rinse well and dry with a soft cloth. Scrape out heavy soap deposits with a blunt knife to aid the action of the paste.

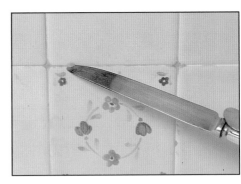

ABOVE Kitchen grease builds up quickly. Scrape it from the grouting around tiles using a blunt knife.

ABOVE Once washed and buffed, the tiles are as good as new.

Headboards

Iron: wipe over the bars and finials using a cloth wrung out in warm water and detergent. Wipe over with clean water and polish with a soft cloth.

Upholstered: use a proprietary brand of dry-clean foam, following the manufacturer's instructions.

Wood: wipe in the direction of the grain with warm water and detergent, or use a combined cleaner/polish spray.

Irons

Clean the casing when the iron is cool. The sole plate is best cleaned while hot. Use a proprietary brand of iron cleaner or bicarbonate of soda (baking soda), rubbed over with a damp cloth. Or rub the iron over a damp towel.

Jewellery

Wrap delicate filigree jewellery in fine cotton muslin (cheesecloth) and dip it into a proprietary brand of jewellery-cleaning solution. Otherwise, warm water with a few drops of ammonia, applied with a soft make-up brush, will remove dirt.

Most gemstones are fairly resilient but their settings may be delicate, so treat these with care. Use an old toothbrush and a liquid jewellery cleaner to reach behind the settings, or dip them in the solution. Rinse and dry with a soft cloth.

Lampshades

Brush or vacuum off dust, then 'spot clean' using dry-clean foam. Use the soft-brush attachment of the vacuum cleaner for pleated shades.

ABOVE Use a duster with an extending handle to reach high lampshades and cobwebs.

Lightbulbs

First switch off the electricity. If the light has been turned on, allow the bulb to cool before removing it. Wear cotton gloves to remove. A cotton bud (swab) dipped in methylated spirits (denatured alcohol) will remove fly marks. Remove a fluorescent tube from its fixing and wipe along the length using a cloth wrung out in soapy water and detergent. A cloth dipped in white spirit (paint thinner) will remove a greasy film on the tube. Dry thoroughly.

Marble

Avoid scratching the surface of marble with abrasive scourers, as this can lead to ingrained staining. Remove stains by dabbing neat lemon juice or white-wine vinegar on the mark. This will also etch the surface, so be sure to wash off the lemon juice or vinegar after a couple of minutes. 15 ml/1 tbsp of Borax mixed with 0.75 l/1 pt of water will also clean a marble surface, but always rinse before buffing dry with a soft cloth.

Mats and rugs

Clean bath mats in the washing machine and hang them up to dry. Vacuum other mats and rugs regularly to remove grit and dirt that can damage the pile. Take them outside occasionally, throw over the washing line or a garden seat and beat with a broom. Turn the rug every fortnight to ensure that all areas receive even wear. Valuable rugs should be cleaned professionally, otherwise clean as described for carpets.

Mattresses

Clean marks on mattresses using a special 'dry-clean' foam (available from department stores and supermarkets). Follow the manufacturer's instructions on the aerosol. Do not use water and detergent to clean a mattress, as it will only spread the mark.

Microwave ovens

Keep cleaning to a minimum by covering foods to prevent spatters from baking hard on the walls of the oven. Turn off the power at the wall before cleaning a microwave oven. Wipe it over with a damp cloth wrung out in warm, soapy water and detergent. A bowl of water brought to the boil inside the microwave will soften any tough pieces. Wipe the inside of the oven occasionally with a special disinfectant that will not taint foods. Leave the door ajar so that the oven can dry naturally.

Mirrors and mirror tiles

A soft cloth moistened with methylated spirits (denatured alcohol) will remove most marks from a mirror – even hairspray. Prevent a mirror from misting over in a steamy bathroom by rubbing a little washing-up liquid over it and polishing with a clean cloth.

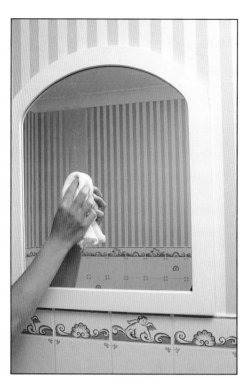

ABOVE Wipe a little washing-up liquid over a bathroom mirror to prevent misting.

Patio furniture

At the end of the summer, clean and cover all patio furniture before the icy weather sets in.

Wrought-iron furniture: wash this down with a solution of warm water and detergent to remove tree sap and bird droppings. Allow to dry and either polish with a silicone wax or touch up chipped paintwork with a rust-inhibiting paint to prevent it from deteriorating over the winter.

Wood: wipe over wooden furniture and apply a good wax to unsealed wood, or varnish any areas that look worn.

Plastic and plastic-coated wire furniture: clean this with a window and conservatory cleaner, or wash it down with a solution of warm water and detergent. Rinse and dry. Do not use abrasives on the furniture – remove any scuffs using a cloth moistened with methylated spirits (denatured alcohol).

Pewter

Clean old or valuable pewter gently in a solution of warm water and washing-up liquid, then rinse and buff with a soft cloth. Clean new pewter with a non-abrasive metal polish.

CLEANING AND HOME HINTS

CLEANING THE HOME (continued)

Refrigerators

You should sort out the fridge regularly and throw away any old and out-of-date foods. Pack all other items in a cold box. Switch off the power and remove all shelves and trays. Wash these in warm water and detergent, rinse and leave to dry. Wipe the inside of the refrigerator with a damp cloth wrung out in a solution of warm water and detergent, then rinse and dry. Use a nailbrush dipped in warm, soapy water to reach into the grooves of the seal, then rinse and dry. Replace the shelves and food only when the refrigerator is completely dry.

ABOVE A nail- or washing brush is excellent for cleaning out the seals on a refrigerator.

REFRIGERATOR SEALS

Rubber refrigerator seals need to be in good condition. Check that the seals on your fridge are in good working order by closing the door on a sheet of paper. If you can pull it out easily, either the seal needs replacing or the hinges need adjusting.

Shower curtain

Put a nylon shower curtain in with the normal wash when putting a load through the machine – the biological action of the detergent will remove soap build-up and mould spots. For other finishes, wash by hand in a solution of warm water and detergent, then rinse and allow to drip dry.

Shower head

Remove the shower head and immerse it in a dish of limescale remover or white-wine vinegar to clear deposits. An old toothbrush will clear blocked holes and debris from behind the plate.

Silver

Use a soft cloth and a non-abrasive cleaner – silver is a soft metal and easily damaged, and silver plate can be worn away to expose the base metal by constant cleaning. Embossed, engraved or raised decoration can accumulate dirt and polish. A badger-bristle shaving brush or soft artist's paintbrush dipped in polish is useful for reaching difficult areas. See cutlery (flatware) for cleaning silver cutlery.

Sinks

Tip a little neat disinfectant down the outlet and overflow once a week and leave overnight to work.
Vitreous-enamel: remove discolouration sing a weak solution of beach. Clean regularly with a liquid detergent to remove grease.
Stainless-steel: wipe a damp cloth dipped in a little limescale remover to clean white patches from a sink, drainer and taps (faucets). Rub with bicarbonate of soda (baking soda) mixed with a little water to make the sink gleam. Tough marks can be removed with a cellulose scourer and cleaning cream. Rinse and wipe dry.

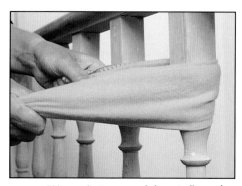

ABOVE Wrap a duster around the spindles and bannisters on a staircase to dust and polish.

SILVER TIPS

● Check with an expert before attempting to clean a valuable silver antique in case you damage it.
● Store silver in a dry place, wrapped in sheets of black or acid-free tissue to prevent tarnishing.
● Silver-cleaning fluids will stain a stainless-steel sink or cutlery. If contact occurs, wash immediately with water.

Taps (Faucets)

Wash taps (faucets) using a bathroom cream cleaner, then rinse and buff with a soft cloth. Remove dirt at the bases and behind the taps by brushing with an old toothbrush dipped in cleaner, and break down limescale deposits around the spouts of taps by filling a small plastic bag with dissolved water softener. Tie the bag around the spout so that it sits in the water solution. Leave overnight, then remove the bag and brush away any remaining scale.

ABOVE An old toothbrush is excellent for cleaning behind taps (faucets).

Telephones

Wipe over telephones regularly using a damp cloth and soapy water. Do not allow any water near the dialling keys or handset. Wipe the handset using some cotton wool (absorbent cotton) dipped in a dilute solution of disinfectant. A cotton bud (swab) dipped in methylated spirits (paint thinner) will clean the dialling pad.

Televisions

Switch off the power at the wall and pull the television forward slightly to vacuum all the surfaces. Wipe over the screen with a few drops of glass cleaner on a soft cloth and polish off immediately. Anti-static wipes are useful for reducing a build-up of dust.

Tiles

Ceramic floor tiles: sweep the floor thoroughly, then wash the tiles with a mop and warm, soapy water. Rinse but do not polish. Clean the grout between the tiles with a scrubbing brush dipped in soapy water.

Ceramic wall tiles: remove soap deposits with a liquid bathroom cleaner and a cellulose scourer. Dirty grout around the tiles is usually more of a problem when soap and limescale build up in the ridges. In this case, use a blunt knife to work your way gently along the grout to remove the worst of the grime. Finish with a nailbrush dipped in an abrasive cream cleaner, rinse well and wipe with a soft cloth.

Toilets

A quick 'flush and brush' in the morning and a little bleach or disinfectant at night should keep most toilets sparkling. Use a limescale remover on water marks and leave it to work for a little while before flushing it away. Wipe the seat regularly with disinfectant and use an old toothbrush to clean around the seat hinges.

Vases

Cracks in china vases can discolour after a time. Apply a little dilute bleach on a cotton bud (swab) to the crack and leave it to work for 10–15 minutes before rinsing and drying. Remove water marks with limescale remover. Clean the inside of a narrow-necked glass vase by swishing a mixture of rice, warm water and detergent around.

Upholstery

Remove pet hairs and fluff with a length of sticky tape wrapped around your hand.

Fabric: vacuum fabric-covered upholstery thoroughly, then clean off spots and marks before cleaning the whole piece of furniture. Use a foam upholstery shampoo and follow the manufacturer's instructions very carefully. Always test a small patch on a hidden area first to see if the dyes are fast. If not, call in professional cleaners.

ABOVE Regularly vacuum upholstery to keep it looking fresh.

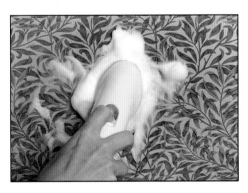

ABOVE 'Spot-clean' dirty marks on a sofa and chairs with a dry-foam cleaner.

To clean loose covers, remove them and follow the directions on the care-guide label inside. If there are no instructions, clean the covers on a low-temperature programme and dry them away from any direct source of heat.

Leather: before cleaning, check whether the leather is washable by putting a small drop of water on an unobtrusive area. If it remains on the surface you can clean it, if it sinks in and darkens the leather you must only dust and give it an occasional wipe with a damp cloth. Soap flakes dissolved in warm water will clean washable leather. Do not overwet the upholstery. Keep leather supple by 'feeding' it regularly with a leather cream.

Wall coverings

Read the care label supplied with a roll of wallpaper and follow its cleaning instructions. If the label is lost, try a small test patch (behind the door is a good place) and sponge the wallpaper with a little warm water and liquid detergent. If the colour does not smudge and the surface does not blister, continue around the room, working from the bottom of the walls to the top. Rinse with clean water by starting from the top of the walls and working to the bottom to prevent streaks appearing.

Remove grease splashes by covering the patch with a paper towel and then a warm iron. The warmth will draw the grease into the paper.

Walls

On painted walls, clean obvious marks first by gently rubbing with a damp cloth and a cream cleaner. Use warm, soapy water and work from the bottom of the walls to the top. Change the water regularly in order to prevent streaks from appearing. Use a long-handled sponge-head mop to reach and clean the tops of walls. Rinse from the top to the bottom, and finish by cleaning the skirtings (baseboards).

Window frames

Use a fungicidal wash to deal with mildew and follow the manufacturer's instructions for cleaning.

Painted and varnished: these should only require an occasional wipe over with a damp cloth wrung out in soapy water. Use a combined cleaner/polish spray to bring them to a shine.

Aluminium: Rub with a paste of Borax and water. Rinse and buff dry.

CLEANING LEATHER UPHOLSTERY

Try a suede-and-leather shoe cleaner for small areas. A water-repellent suede-and-leather shoe spray can protect the leather – always test a small area first in a hidden place.

CURING HOUSEHOLD SMELLS

Household smells can usually be remedied by removing the source, by cleaning the offending item or by disguising the unpalatable smell with a more pleasant one.

The kitchen
Old or rotting vegetables can be surprisingly pungent. To avoid this, keep vegetables in a cool, dark place and preferably in a paper bag.

A refrigerator can harbour a variety of smells which can emanate from strong cheese, spicy food or mouldy left-overs. Check the contents regularly and throw out any that have passed their 'best-before' date. Clean the fridge, including the shelves and seals, at least once a month.

To minimize cooking smells, close the doors to other rooms in the house when cooking and open the kitchen windows to allow steam and smells to escape. Buy an extractor fan or switch on the cooker hood, and leave them running for a time after you have finished cooking. Wipe over surfaces with a cloth wrung out in hot water to which lemon juice and detergent have been added. Wipe over chopping boards with half a cut lemon to leave them fresh. Lemon juice and water

ABOVE A halved lemon rubbed over a wooden chopping board will remove unpleasant odours.

boiled in a microwave oven will also help to deodorize the interior.

To counteract odorous kitchen sinks, pour a little neat bleach down the plughole and outlet every few days, leave overnight and then rinse thoroughly.

ABOVE Keep drains fresh by pouring disinfectant down the sink outlet every day, followed by plenty of hot water.

The bathroom
Regular cleaning should keep the bathroom smelling fresh, but, on the odd occasion when this is not the case, light a scented candle or simply a match to clear the air. Protect the carpet around the toilet with a mat, and wash this regularly. Keep a disinfectant block looped inside the rim of the toilet.

Water trapped behind bath seals or tiles can smell, and condensation will eventually make the room damp and musty. Ensure the bathroom is well-ventilated, and, if necessary, add air vents or an extractor fan as well.

Pour disinfectant down the waste outlets in baths, bidets and basins to keep them fresh. If they do smell, they may be blocked and should be dealt with promptly.

The living room
Cigarette smoke can be neutralized by waving a dish towel dampened in water and vinegar around the room.

Try to prevent pets from lying on furniture, as their hair and body oils can leave an unpleasant odour. If they do, cover chairs and sofas with throw-over cloths that you can wash regularly. Place dishes of pot pourri in the room to disguise stale smells.

The bedrooms
Remove stale odours in a bedroom by opening the windows and spraying the room with an air freshener. Sprinkle the mattress with Borax and leave it for a few hours before vacuuming. Always air the bed, before making, and keep the room well-ventilated.

Outdoors
Cats who love to spray near doorways can be discouraged by rubbing the doorsteps with either menthol oil or orange peel.

POT-POURRI INGREDIENTS

Many fragrant ingredients can be used for making pot pourri. These include: dried rosemary, lavender and bay leaves, dried ground orris-root powder, dried rosemary leaves, a selection of essential oils, ground cinnamon, dried chillies and cinnamon sticks, whole cloves, a blend of dried flowers, and limes and lemons. The finely grated dried peel of citrus fruit can be added. Fresh flower petals smell sweet for a few days (shown here).

VACUUMING

The vacuum cleaner that you use is purely a matter of personal choice, but there are 5 main types from which to select, as described below. If you are buying a new cleaner, the layout of your home, the number of stairs, accessibility and so on, will probably determine your choice.

Cylinder
This type of vacuum cleaner is useful for cleaning curtains, drapes, rugs and floor coverings. Look for a compact but powerful suction rating (usually around 1000 watts). The flexible hose is useful for vacuuming stairs and narrow, awkward-to-reach areas such as under beds and pieces of furniture. The only disadvantage is that a cylinder cleaner has a tendency to tip over on uneven surfaces, or to knock into furniture when dragged behind you.

Upright
Look for beater bars that are good on fitted carpets and for removing embedded dirt and pet hairs. An upright cleaner is difficult to use on stairs and, unless it is used with attachments, may not lie flat enough to reach under furniture.

Wet-and-dry
This tends to be heavier and bulkier than a cylinder model, as it is designed to roll along – even when filled with water. It will also require more storage space. Most models vacuum, shampoo and suck up water. The hoses tend to be wider than average, which means that they can cope with bulky debris.

Cordless
This is best used for lightweight cleaning jobs, as its suction is not very strong. It can reach awkward areas and is useful for areas in which there are no sockets (receptacles), but it will only work for up to 15 minutes before it needs re-charging.

ABOVE **For textured wall coverings or decorative finishes use a brush attachment.**

ABOVE **Use a crevice nozzle for fine gathers on curtains (drapes) and valances.**

Built-in central system
With this cleaning system, outlets in each room enable a light hose to be attached. When switched on, the dirt is carried to the outlet and then carried through hidden suction pipes to a central bin. The system is quiet to use and easy to operate but is also expensive to install, so it is not recommended if you move house regularly.

VACUUMING TIPS

- If you drop a fine screw or even a contact lens, locate it with a vacuum nozzle covered with a piece cut from stockings (pantyhose) secured with an elastic band. Anything that the vacuum sucks up will be held against the stocking until you remove it.
- Use the flat, rectangular floor and carpet nozzle of a vacuum cleaner for cleaning carpets and hard floors.
- The narrow, angled crevice nozzle also works well on stairs, curtains and drapes, and will remove dust from around the buttoning on mattresses and along skirtings (baseboards). Use it to clean refrigerator grilles.
- The more powerful 'wet-and-dry' cleaners can unblock a drain by sucking up the blockage. You can also use them to suck out leaves from drain covers.
- Check the bag and empty it if necessary, and clean the filter before you put the vacuum cleaner away so that it works efficiently every time.
- If you run out of disposable dust bags, cut neatly along the base of the old one and shake out the contents. Fold the cut end over twice and staple securely before re-using.
- If you vacuum hard floors regularly, you will find that dirt is easier to remove, as it will not have time to build up into a sticky layer of grime.
- Fine ash from fires tends to blow about very easily. Wait until it is cold before vacuuming away, and clean the nozzle afterwards.
- Never attempt to suck up water or spills with an ordinary vacuum cleaner – the results of doing so could literally be electrifying.

CLEANING AND HOME HINTS

DUSTING AND POLISHING

No matter how frequently you clean your home, dust will form and re-form continually, settling on every surface. Dust consists of many elements including tiny particles of fabric, dead skin cells, pollen and microscopic dust mites which can cause allergic reaction. Keeping a home well-dusted not only helps to reduce this risk but can also help appliances to work much more efficiently. A coating of dust on freezer and refrigerator coils prevents heat from being expelled, resulting in the appliance working harder to keep the temperature low.

Polishing is also an important part of keeping a home looking its best. The polishing of any surface – whether French-polished furniture or brass door knobs – needs to be done carefully, or the results can ruin its finish. The polishing of everyday items is less specialized and time-consuming, but needs to be done on a regular basis. Keeping all surfaces smooth and shiny will help to make the removal of dust and dirt easier, and will prevent stains from penetrating.

ABOVE Remove dust from artificial or dried-flower arrangements by blowing it away with a hairdryer.

ABOVE Dust lightbulbs wearing a pair of cotton gloves.

Dusting equipment

A traditional feather duster is very gentle and can be used to flick the dust off every item in the house, as it is unlikely to damage even the most delicate piece. It will collect very little dust, however, so most of it tends to fall on the surfaces beneath, which in turn will need to be dusted or vacuumed. Replace feather dusters every couple of years, as they tend to shed their feathers.

A 'static wand' (static duster) is also very useful. Look for the nylon-fluff type with the extendable handle – this will reach into the corners of ceilings and on to light shades.

The most effective types of dusting cloths are the traditional soft-cotton ones, or home-made ones made from old T-shirts. Keep a pile of these to hand, and wash them after each use. A tiny amount of water sprayed on before use will prevent the dust from floating off the surface of the duster.

Frequent vacuuming is particularly recommended for homes in which dust mites cause allergic reaction, but remember to replace the dust bags regularly and to use them in conjunction with an insecticidal spray specifically designed to eradicate dust mites. Vacuuming is also a particularly effective way of removing dust that has settled on the mesh or grilles on electrical equipment.

ABOVE Clean Venetian blinds (shades) by wiping along the slats wearing cotton gloves.

EFFECTIVE DUSTING

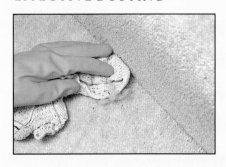

- Wipe hard-to-reach crevices on stair carpets with a damp cloth.
- As dust will float downwards to settle on the surfaces beneath, always dust from the top of a room down.
- Reduce the amount of dust attracted to the surface of a television, hi-fi (stereo) system, or glass-topped tables that are prone to static electricity by wiping them with a cloth wrung out in a solution mixed with 15 ml/1 tbsp liquid fabric conditioner and 150 ml/1/4 pt/2/3 cup warm water.
- Shake duvets, pillows, small rugs and loose cushions outdoors to freshen them and remove dust where it can blow away in the breeze.
- Do not forget to dust the panels and mouldings on traditional doors, or the top edges, as dust will dull the paintwork over time.
- A baby's bottle-brush works wonders on louvre doors and between and behind radiators.

Polishing wood

Polishing wood will help to nourish it, but do not use liquid or spray polishes containing silicone or acrylic resin on antique wood, as they will seal the surface. Genuine beeswax is the best type of polish to use, and will have been responsible for helping old furniture to maintain its sheen over the years. Most wooden furniture tends to be varnished, lacquered or waxed. Oiled wood has a soft, low sheen and should not be polished. Instead, use a proprietary wood oil applied sparingly with a soft cloth. Rub this in the direction of the grain and gently buff to a lustre using a clean, soft cloth.

If you wish, save money by making your own furniture polish. Combine 30 ml/2 tbsp each of water and turpentine with 450 ml/3/4 pt/2 cups of boiled linseed oil and mix together thoroughly. This polish requires a lot of buffing but will give a rich, deep shine to wood.

ABOVE Apply polish to furniture and buff in the direction of the wood grain using a clean, soft cloth or duster.

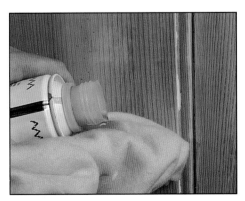

ABOVE Oiled wood only requires re-oiling once or twice a year to maintain its looks.

WOOD-POLISHING TIPS

- Always wipe a wood surface with a damp, lint-free cloth first to remove dust and grime, or the polishing action will simply grind them in.
- Select a polish that is recommended for the type of wood or finish required.
- Colours added to some waxes will help to disguise fine scratches and blemishes at the same time as polishing the surface.
- Heat and damp will damage polish. If it has done so, remove the flaking layer using the finest-grade of steel wool dipped in a little turpentine. Wipe it off immediately and re-polish to blend in.
- Apply floor polish sparingly, as too much will be difficult to shine and will cause dust to stick as it settles. Use only one type of floor polish, as different makes can react with one another resulting in a patchy, tacky finish.

Polishing metal

Aluminium: place lemon rind, apple peelings, rhubarb or any other acidic food in aluminium cooking pans, then top up with water and simmer for 5 minutes. Rinse in clean water and buff to a shine. Alternatively, rub on a paste of Borax and water, rinse and buff with a soft cloth.

Brass and copper: wash lacquered items before polishing, and then buff using a soft cloth. Polish unlacquered pieces with a tarnish-inhibiting brass-and-copper polish. To clean a heavily tarnished item, rub a wedge of lemon that has been dipped in salt over it. Rinse thoroughly, dry and polish.

Soak items that have a build-up of verdigris in a strong washing-soda solution, and brush the affected areas with an old toothbrush. Rinse and buff with a soft cloth.

Chrome: this can be polished by applying bicarbonate of soda (baking soda) on a damp cloth and rubbing to a bright shine.

Make your own chrome polish by mixing together 2 parts paraffin with 1 part methylated spirits (denatured alcohol). Apply to the item using a damp cloth, then buff with a soft cloth. A piece of scrunched-up tin foil rubbed on chrome will also polish it to a shine. *Bronze:* apply a little brown shoe polish or a coloured-wax polish to bronze, then buff with a soft cloth.

Pewter: avoid abrasive cleaners on pewter – use all-purpose metal-polish wadding instead. An application of clear-wax polish will inhibit tarnishing. *Silver:* use impregnated polishing mitts for large items, and dip smaller items in a dish of silver dip. Rinse silver in warm water containing a little washing-up liquid, then rinse again in clear water before buffing to a shine.

ABOVE Polish silver with soft wadding impregnated with a non-abrasive polish.

Polishing lead crystal and glass

Polish lead crystal and glass by hand using a soft, lint-free cloth. Hold the cloth in one hand and rotate the item against it until it sparkles. A little methylated spirits (denatured alcohol) or white-wine vinegar added to the final rinsing water will make lead crystal or glass ornaments gleam.

Polish glass window panes to a shine using a mixture of equal parts of paraffin, water and methylated spirits.

Polishing ceramic tiles

Do not use polish on ceramic floor or wall tiles. Simply clean them with a damp cloth and cream cleaner, rinse and leave to dry. Use a soft cloth to buff the tiles to a shine. Multi-purpose bathroom spray foams are quick to use and will also leave tiles sparkling.

WASHING AND DRYING

Start by finding the international textile-care label, which is usually sewn to an inside seam of a garment. Check the symbols against the chart shown opposite and follow them closely. If the garment does not have detailed instructions, establish what type of fabric it is made from and then follow the directions given below.

Fabric-cleaning guide
Acetate: dry clean unless the label says 'hand-washable'. In this case, pre-treat stains with a pre-wash stain remover, and wash using a mild liquid detergent and warm water. Rinse and dry away from direct heat.

Acrylic: acrylic garments are best cleaned inside-out. Pre-treat stains, then either hand wash in a mild liquid detergent and warm water or in a machine on the low-temperature 'synthetics' cycle. Dry flat.

Cotton: this is strong and can be washed at higher temperatures than synthetics. Iron when still slightly damp, using a hot iron on a 'steam' setting or spray starch for the best results. White cotton can be brightened by soaking in a mild bleach solution, but you must rinse it thoroughly.

Linen: linen can be dry cleaned, machine washed or hand-laundered. Iron on a hot setting while still damp. White linen can be bleached by soaking

briefly in a mild bleach solution, then rinsing thoroughly.

Lycra/Spandex: use warm water and a mild detergent for hand washing or set the machine to the low-temperature 'synthetics' cycle. Avoid washing white Lycra with coloured garments and never use bleach, as this will perish the fibres. Drip dry or place in a tumble drier on a low setting. Iron while damp on a low setting.

Nylon: delicates are best washed by hand or in a protective mesh bag in a washing machine. In a machine, use the 'synthetics' cycle and a biological detergent. Let the garments drip dry, or tumble dry on a low setting. Brighten nylon net curtains by washing in a proprietary nylon-whitener. For best results, rinse the nets first to remove loose dirt and dust, then wash following the manufacturer's instructions.

Polyester: hand or machine wash polyester garments in warm water or on a warm setting, and tumble dry on a low setting. Iron on a moderate setting with a water-spray mist.

Silk: dyes used to colour silk can run, so dry clean if in doubt. Otherwise, hand wash items separately in warm, soapy water. Gently squeeze out excess moisture but do not wring. Dry away from direct heat and iron while damp.

Wool: this must never be washed in hot water as it will shrink, so either dry clean or wash carefully by hand.

Washing awkward or delicate items
You can wash large, bulky items such as curtains, drapes, blankets and quilts by hand in a bath or a large sink if the label says that they are washable.

Lingerie is best washed by hand, but you can wash several pairs of tights or stockings (pantyhose) in the washing machine by placing them in a pillow case tied at the open end.

Trainers and soft toys made with synthetic fabrics can be machine washed if the label recommends it.

ABOVE **Apply a neat biological detergent to marks on garments before placing them in a washing machine.**

WASHING GUIDELINES

- Follow the cleaning guidelines on the international care-guide label inside the garment (see symbol chart).
- Sort washing into 'Whites' and 'Coloureds', and wash each bundle separately to avoid problems with colours running.
- Always check that pockets of garments are empty before putting the garments in a washing machine.
- Treat heavy soiling with neat liquid detergent before washing.
- Select the correct machine programme for the type of wash required.
- Only use the recommended dose of detergent for each wash.
- Rinse garments thoroughly after hand washing.
- Regularly remove fluff and debris from both washing-machine and tumble-drier filters.
- Secure zips (zippers) and fastenings before washing to prevent them from snagging other garments.

Drying garments
There are 3 basic methods to use for removing the moisture from washed clothes. The first is spin drying, which is usually combined with the wash cycle on washing machines. 'Spin-only' programmes are useful for items that have been hand washed.

Tumble drying uses a lot of electricity, so remove as much water as possible from the items first. It is vital to choose the correct setting on a tumble drier for the type of fabric, as excessive heat can damage fibres causing them to shrink, crease or melt. If in doubt, always refer to the instruction manual.

Line drying is the most natural and economic way of drying clothes. You can stretch an indoor clothes' line across the laundry room or, if space is limited, across the bath.

Drying different items

Sweaters: a synthetic or wool sweater can be dried successfully from a clothes' line by threading a pair of old tights (pantyhose) through the armholes and pegging them at the wrist and neck holes to support the garment. Dry delicate sweaters or shawls flat over a rack suspended over a bath or sink.

T-shirts: the cotton knit of T-shirts will tend to pull in different directions, so either peg from the bottom or place on a hanger to dry.

Trousers: hang trousers from the turn-ups or hems on the inside legs, or drape over trouser hangers before hanging on the line.

Pleated skirts: clip pleats together with clothes pegs (pins).

LEFT Prevent clothes-peg (-pin) marks from spoiling a sweater by running a pair of tights (pantyhose) through the cuffs and neck to hang the sweater from a washing line to dry.

Shirts: hang shirts from 2 hangers with the hooks facing so that they will not be blown off a washing line.

ABOVE Dry delicate sweaters or other wool garments flat on a rack suspended over a bath to catch the drips.

INTERNATIONAL WASHING, DRYING AND IRONING SYMBOLS

COTTON WASHES

Items will withstand a normal, full wash cycle at the temperature advised

SYNTHETIC WASHES

Items, such as blends and synthetics, will withstand a medium wash cycle at advised temperature

WOOL WASH

Items, wool blends and machine-washable wools, will withstand a minimum wash cycle at this temperature

HAND WASH ONLY

Items must not be machine-washed

TUMBLE DRYING

Items can be tumble-dried

Items can be tumble-dried using a high heat setting

Items can only be tumble-dried using a low heat setting

BLEACHING

Items can be treated with chlorine bleach

IRONING

Items, such as cotton and linen, can be ironed on a hot setting

Items, such as polyester mixtures and wool, can be ironed on a warm setting

Items, such as acrylic, nylon and polyester, can be ironed on a cool setting

DRY CLEANING

Items can be dry cleaned

DRYING TIPS

• Do not leave damp garments in a washing machine or drier as they will soon start to smell musty and will have to be rinsed again to freshen them up.

• Do not leave a tumble drier running for longer than required, as this wastes electricity, as well as 'setting' creases.

• Overloading a tumble drier will lead to patchy drying. Leave a gap at the top of the drum to allow the clothes to move about freely.

• The action of tumble drying can cause static to build up, so use a fabric conditioner with each wash.

• Remove fluff from the tumble-drier filter after each use, or it will reduce the amount of water vapour that can escape in subsequent cycles.

IRONING

Freshly ironed shirts, blouses and bed linen look good and feel even better. The difference between pressing and ironing is that, to press fabrics, the iron is lifted and lowered lightly on to the fabric, whereas to iron fabrics, the iron should be glided smoothly up and down. Delicate fabrics, jersey, wool and pleated fabrics should be pressed, and bed linens, cotton, polyester and silk can be ironed.

Before ironing any fabric, check the care-label guide and then set the iron temperature accordingly.

Avoiding shiny patches

Iron acrylic or fabrics with a slightly raised nap on the reverse side, or press them using a pressing cloth – a clean dish towel placed over the fabric is ideal. Avoid shine appearing on bulky patches such as thick seams or zip (zipper) fastenings by pressing over a cloth. If it is too late and the fabric is already shiny, wring out the pressing cloth in clean water, place it over the area and steam press it. Use a soft brush to raise a flattened nap.

Ironing bulky fabrics

Always iron bulky fabrics, such as denim and canvas, inside-out, particularly if the fabric is dark, in order to avoid fabric shine on thick seams.

Large items

Fold sheets, duvet covers and table cloths first and then place them on the ironing board before ironing each folded section – rather like ironing the pages of a book. Obtain crease-free curtains and drapes by ironing them from top to bottom with a chair placed behind the ironing board to prevent the fabric from dropping on to the floor.

Silk

Ensure that the fabric is damp, then iron the reverse of the garment using a pressing cloth to prevent the iron

ABOVE Keep ironing to a minimum by hanging up or folding clothes as soon as they come out of the tumble drier.

from making shiny patches. Place embroidered silk face-down on to a white towel, then press it on the reverse side. This will make the embroidery stand out attractively.

Pleats

Lay out very fine pleats in sections no more than 15 cm/6 in wide and press them carefully to secure. Allow to cool before repeating with the next section. Press wide pleats individually.

ABOVE Fold a sheet into manageable sections, and then iron them flat one by one.

IRONING TIPS

● Cover metal, mother-of-pearl or plastic buttons with a spoon to prevent heat from the iron damaging them.
● Clean an iron while it is still hot. Rub it on an old piece of towel to remove stickiness, then dip a damp rag in bicarbonate of soda (baking soda) or a proprietary sole-plate cleaner. Wipe with a clean, damp cloth.
● If you are away on business or holiday and cannot borrow an iron, hang creased clothes in a steamy bathroom or sprinkle water over them and blow air from a hairdryer to help the creases to drop out.
● Padded hangers will prevent 'shoulder marks' from appearing on delicate fabrics.

GOOD HOUSEKEEPING

With an average of 2 out of every 3 women working outside the home, research shows that, despite the advent of the 'new man', most housework is still done by women. How you tackle the household chores will depend a great deal on your lifestyle. If you have children, keeping the house in order can sometimes seem an impossible task, so perhaps now is the time to become organized and make sure that everyone helps to get the chores done.

Begin by organizing a rota, so that everyone knows what they are expected to do, and make sure that they stick to it by putting up a star every time a job is completed. Try using incentives to get the jobs done rather than punishment if they are not – extra pocket money or a treat means that everyone ends up happy. Encourage young children to tidy up their toys and pull their quilts down to air the beds in the morning, or ask them to help you make your bed so that they learn how it is done properly at the same time. Laying the table and wiping down low cupboard doors are also easy tasks for them to do. Older children can help with dusting, cleaning or washing up. Do not differentiate between boys' and girls' jobs, as everyone needs to know how to clean, tidy and wash up.

Keep the mop and cleaning materials together so that no one will have an excuse to say that they could not find the right things. A plastic bucket with dusters, rags and polish is useful – check it regularly and replace contents as containers become empty.

Ask the family to fill in a 'Weekly Planner' or to tell you what they are doing, where and when. Keep the planner pinned to the wall where you can see it easily – you will find it invaluable when you need to check that children are safe or whether you will be free to take them to and collect them from an after-school activity. Keep a note of the telephone numbers of their friends to check that children are safe if they do not get home on time.

A year planner takes up wall space, but is useful for jotting down important dates for the family such as birthdays, anniversaries and holidays. A wipeable planner is useful where dates are regularly changed.

When you sit down together in the evening, ask the members of the family whether there are any items of shopping that need to be bought the following day, or appointments for the dentist or doctor to be made. Put letters to be posted near the door so that they will not be forgotten when you leave the

ORGANIZED FILING

Keep a general file with receipts for goods that are under guarantee, and instruction manuals for all electrical appliances in case you need to refer to them. Keep another file containing all important documents such as birth certificates, driving licences, passports, insurance documents and even your Will in a safe place so that you can find it quickly if necessary.

house. Keep a working list of jobs that need doing and cross them out as soon as you have dealt with them.

Prevent panics in the morning when clothes cannot be found or homework has not been finished by checking the night before. Even if there is a good programme on the television, the ironing can still be done, shoes polished and clothes mended while it is on. An extra washbasin or shower installed in a bedroom can also help to relieve the morning rush and inevitable queues for the bathroom.

Keep a small notebook and pencil with you at all times so that a job you have overlooked, or a telephone call you must remember to make, is noted down and not forgotten again. If you wake in the night and remember a string of things that you have forgotten to do during the day, a piece of paper and a pencil next to the bed will get them written down for the morning.

Put telephone messages or reminders in one place where everyone is likely to look. Papers with a tacky strip on one side are ideal for sticking on doors at eye-level where they will not be overlooked, or next to the item that needs dealing with.

LEFT Even young children can help with the housework: ask them to tidy up their toys and to pull their quilts down to air their own beds in the morning.

EVERYDAY CHORES

Busy lifestyles can leave little time for all the essential household chores. Fortunately, however, there are plenty of shortcuts that still give good results.

The kitchen

Do not waste time scrubbing out the burned-on mess in saucepans. Fill non-stick and enamelled pans with water, add a handful of washing soda and leave it to soak overnight. Use a biological detergent and water in aluminium pans, as washing soda reacts with the aluminium to create toxic fumes.

Clean a very dirty kitchen floor by swishing it first with a solution of hot water and detergent. Leave for 10 minutes before washing and rinsing.

If you do not own a self-cleaning oven, wipe a fairly strong solution of bicarbonate of soda (baking soda) and water over the walls, door and shelves. Set the oven to a low heat for 30 minutes, then leave it to cool. Clean with hot water and detergent, and then give the oven a final wipe over with a weak solution of bicarbonate of soda and water – this will make it much easier to clean the next time.

Wash plates and cutlery (flatware) quickly after using them to prevent food from drying on and becoming difficult to shift. Rinse off suds with hot water so that the heat will dry the cutlery and plates as they drain.

Rinse the sink with a little liquid fabric detergent after washing up to remove stains and grease.

Strips of paper placed on the tops of cupboards (closets) will absorb the grease and dust that inevitably accumulate in the kitchen. Simply throw the paper away when it becomes dirty and replace with more paper to save time on cleaning.

The bathroom

The following tips take no time at all to carry out every day, and will cut down the time and effort needed for an 'all-over' bathroom clean.

At night, squirt a little toilet cleaner around the bowl so that a quick brush in the morning keeps it sparkling. As the bath water is emptying, add a few drops of liquid detergent to the water – this will remove any scum from the water as it drains away.

LEFT Use hot water to rinse suds from plates, glasses and cutlery (flatware) to help them to dry quickly by themselves.

BELOW A quick rub with a clean cloth will keep taps (faucets) gleaming and mirrors bright, and make the bathroom look fresh.

Keep a clean cloth under the washbasin to wipe over the taps (faucets) and mirror as they become dirty. Wipe the washbasin, too, after the morning rush ready for the evening.

ABOVE Add a little liquid detergent to the bath water as it drains away to remove any scum. A dash of disinfectant down the plughole every now and then will keep it fresh.

The living room

Wipe a little white spirit (paint thinner) mixed with water over furniture to give it an instant gleam. Open windows to freshen the room, and shake cushions or rugs out of the windows in order to minimize the amount of dust in the house. A quick vacuum will pick up stray crumbs, ash from ashtrays and dust from every nook and cranny. Just 5 minutes a day should keep the cleaning well in hand.

Try sprinkling the carpet with herbs or lavender and leaving for an hour before vacuuming if the room smells stale. A vacuum cleaner can be used to remove dust from a multitude of surfaces, but empty the bag straight into the dustbin (trash can) to prevent dust from blowing back into the house.

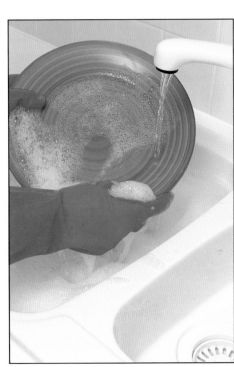

The bedrooms

When you get up, roll back the bedding and allow the beds to air while you have breakfast. Air pillows, too, and check them regularly to pull out any protruding feathers or to even out lumps and bumps. If a pillow is limp and saggy and flops when placed over

ABOVE After getting up in the morning, turn down the bedding for a while to allow the bed to air before re-making it.

your arm, you need to replace it. Once beds have aired, you can make them.

There is nothing quite like the feel of a bed newly made up in the traditional way with sheets and blankets, and the technique actually becomes very quick and easy with practice. Many people now prefer duvets, however.

Getting a duvet into its cover can be done simply by pushing a corner of the duvet into place. Use 1 or 2 clothes pegs (pins) to hold it in position. Do the same with the other corner, then just shake the duvet down into the clean cover before removing the pegs.

Finally, having made the bed, quickly flick a duster over the furniture, curtains or drapes and shelves, then leave for the dust to settle before vacuuming it all up.

TRADITIONAL BED-MAKING

1 Start with the bottom sheet. Tuck in the sheet along the edges and just at the base of the mattress, starting at the head end and working towards the base.

2 Pull the bottom of the sheet taut and fold it in an 'envelope' over the tucked-in corners to make a neat fold.

3 Centre the top sheet on the bed with the wide or embroidered hem at the top so that it almost touches the headboard. Lay the blankets on top of the sheet, and tuck both blankets and sheet under the mattress in one go. Make an 'envelope' at the corners as with the bottom sheet, ensuring that the corners are pulled taut.

4 Place the bed cover over the bed, turn the top sheet and blanket over it and replace the pillows.

CLEANING AND HOME HINTS

REMOVING STAINS

Stains that are not treated at an early stage run the risk of 'setting' and becoming permanent. Take immediate action to stop a stain from spreading or sinking deeper into the fibres by blotting up the excess with a clean cloth, absorbent tissues or salt.

Stains generally fall into 4 simple categories:
• Stains that can be removed with normal washing, such as water-based paints and milk.
• Those that can be removed by bleaching or a combination of a hot wash and detergent – for example, tea, fruit juice or non-permanent ink.
• Those requiring a pre-wash treatment and/or soak before washing, such as grass stains or blood.
• Those requiring special treatments before cleaning, such as gloss paint.

Sometimes a combination of these treatments will be necessary to remove a stain completely, but remember never to mix more than one chemical at a time, as toxic fumes can be given off. Always bear in mind the key factor of speed, as stains that have been left too long or have become set by heat can be virtually impossible to remove, and none of the treatments will be likely to succeed without damaging the item they are on.

On garments, even if a care label says that the fabric is colourfast, always check this by carrying out a 'test run' on a hidden part such as a seam, hem or inside the waistband. Hold a clean, white cloth behind the fabric and dab on the cleaning fluid (whether water, detergent or solvent). If colour seeps on to the cloth, the garment should be professionally cleaned.

Carpets and upholstery can be more of a problem, so a sample test is important. Specific carpet and upholstery foams and dry-cleaning fluids are available, but, unless you are confident that you can deal with a stain successfully yourself, it is advisable to call in professional cleaners.

If you are in the middle of a party and someone spills a drink over the carpet, there is no need to panic. Act quickly by blotting up the liquid, then tackle it more thoroughly once the guests have left – or, easier still, remove the carpets before they arrive.

STAIN REMOVAL KIT

Keep a stock of as many of the following items as possible, so that you will be prepared to deal with any stain or spillage as soon as it occurs. Refer to the following pages as to which product to use for each type of stain.

Talcum powder: use this to blot up grease or oil as soon as it is spilled.

A blunt knife: this is useful for scraping off matter such as jam or egg.

Clean white cloths: keep these at hand to soak up spills or to apply cleaner. A small, natural sea sponge, cotton wool (absorbent cotton) and white paper towels will also be very useful.

Detergents: spray pre-wash liquid, a detergent soap bar and liquid biological detergent are all good stain removers.

Methylated spirits (denatured alcohol): helpful for removing grass stains on colourfast fabrics.

Glycerine: this should be diluted with an equal amount of water to soften dried-in stains. Leave it for up to an hour before washing the garment.

Acetone or nail-polish remover: good for dealing with nail-varnish stains, but do not use on acetate fabrics.

Hydrogen peroxide: test fabrics for colourfastness before using. Buy the 20-volume strength and mix 1 part to 9 parts water for soaking dried-in stains before washing.

Dry-cleaning fluid or white spirit (paint thinner): pre-test fabrics for colourfastness and use neat, dabbed on grease or fresh paint stains (not to be used on acetates).

White-wine vinegar: vinegar helps to neutralize odours as well as removing pet stains and perspiration marks on garments.

Borax: this is a mild alkali and will work to neutralize acid stains such as wine, fruit juice and coffee.

LEFT The key factor to removing stains is speed: quickly blot up the excess with a clean cloth or tissues. Soaking or a pre-wash treatment before washing will dissolve many stains, but some need special treatment.

Bleaches

There are 2 types of bleach – chlorine bleach and oxygen bleach. Chlorine bleach deodorizes, accelerates the action of detergents, kills germs and generally cleans. It is not suitable for coloured clothes, silk, wool, mohair, leather or Lycra, and should never be poured directly on to clothes. Oxygen bleach is 'colour-safe' and, although it brightens colours and keeps whites white, it is unlikely to make greying nylon whiter. It can be used on coloured fabrics and unbleachable whites (such as silk and wool).

Specific stain removal

When a stain only covers a small area on a garment, you should apply the cleaning solution only to that area, and prevent it from spreading to other areas of the fabric. Place an absorbent cloth or towel underneath the area that is to be cleaned. If the stain is on a trouser leg or sleeve, slide the cloth or towel down the middle to prevent the cleaning solution and stain from working through to the other side.

When a small stain requires saturating in cleaning solution, hold the cloth by the stained area, then twist the unstained area before dipping in the fabric. This will prevent the solution from spreading. If the stain requires soaking for a long period, wrap the unstained parts of the garment in a plastic bag and lie them slightly higher than the stained area, or the solution will spread along the fibres.

Check on the following list to find the stain closest to the one that you need to treat, then follow the instructions given. Once the stain has been removed, wash the item as usual.

Adhesives

Cyanoacrylate or 'super glues' should be treated immediately with a little lighter fuel dabbed on before they set. Very hot or boiling water can be effective, but is only recommended for use on cotton or linen. Other glues can be removed with amyl acetate, which is available from chemists (drugstores).

Ballpoint pen

Use a proprietary cleaner or dab with nail-polish remover or surgical spirit (rubbing alcohol).

ABOVE Surgical spirit (rubbing alcohol) or nail-polish remover will lift ballpoint-pen and ink stains.

Beer or lager

Apply a little dilute glycerine, then follow by treating with a pre-wash laundry aid. Alternatively, a brief soak in a mild white-wine vinegar/water solution should be sufficient.

BELOW Pick off cold candle wax using your fingers or a blunt knife, depending on the surface. Place blotting paper or paper towels over the top of the wax (or on either side if it is a garment) before ironing with a warm iron.

Blood

Rinse off under cold running water, then soak the garment in a solution of biological washing liquid and tepid water. Soak white garments in a mild ammonia/water solution, then wash.

Burns

Scorch marks can sometimes be rubbed off with a blunt knife. Treat fine fabrics with a little dilute glycerine and wash as usual. Treat more stubborn marks with a hydrogen-peroxide solution of 1 part to 9 parts water.

Butter and margarine

Scrape off as much of the grease as possible, then apply a biological liquid to the patch. Wash in as high a temperature as the fabric will stand.

Candle wax

Gently pick or scrape off the cooled wax using a blunt knife. Place blotting paper or paper towels above and beneath the mark, then iron over the top paper, replacing it as soon as it becomes saturated with wax. Repeat until no more wax comes off. Coloured wax may leave a deeper mark: treat with methylated spirits (denatured alcohol) before washing.

Car oil

Dab the mark with a proprietary grease solvent, or treat with a pre-wash aid.

CLEANING AND HOME HINTS

REMOVING STAINS (Continued)

Chewing gum
Chill the garment in the refrigerator, then pick off the solid matter. Dab with methylated spirits (denatured alcohol) or dry-cleaning fluid.

Chocolate
Apply neat biological washing liquid to the stain. Sponge the area with warm water, then wash as usual.

Coffee
Wash immediately under cold running water, then soak in a strong detergent solution. Treat stubborn marks with a dilute hydrogen-peroxide solution (1 part hydrogen peroxide to 9 parts water) before washing.

Crayon
Dab the affected area with white spirit (paint thinner). Use a heavy-duty detergent containing oxygen bleach for the remainder.

Discoloration and dyes
Use a glycerine solution to soak the area, or a dilute solution of household bleach and water on white fabrics only. Alternatively, wash in a heavy-duty detergent containing oxygen bleach.

Egg
Scrape off the excess using a blunt knife, then apply a neat biological washing liquid to the stain. Old stains can be removed by soaking in a solution of 1 part hydrogen peroxide to 9 parts water before washing as usual.

Fats, grease and cooking oils
Dampen the fabric with water and apply a heavy-duty liquid detergent to the stain. Wash immediately in the hottest water the fabric will stand.

Fruit and fruit juice
Sprinkle Borax over the stain to absorb the moisture and neutralize the acid. Rinse in cold water, then wash in a solution of hot water and detergent. Treat stubborn marks with a solution of dilute household bleach and water (1 part bleach to 4 parts water).

Grass stains
Dab these with methylated spirits (denatured alcohol) (not to be used on acetate or tri-acetate fabrics), then rinse and wash.

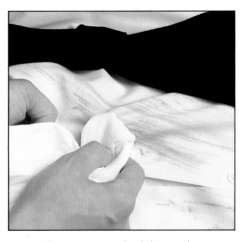

ABOVE **Grass stains on school shirts and gym clothes can be removed with methylated spirits (denatured alcohol) before washing.**

Heat rings
Rub along the grain of the wood with a soft cloth dipped in turpentine. Alternatively, metal polish rubbed over the marks should remove them. Wipe over with a clean, damp cloth before re-polishing.

Inks
Dab unknown inks with nail-varnish remover. Cover blue and black fountain-pen inks with salt and lemon juice, and leave them overnight. Finally, rinse and wash with a biological liquid detergent.

Jam
Scrape off the excess using a blunt knife, and dab with a pre-wash laundry aid. Wash as usual.

Tomato ketchup (catsup)
Scrape off the excess, then hold the garment under cold running water. Dab the area with a little neat biological washing liquid or a detergent soap bar, then wash as usual. Treat deep stains with a solution of 1 part hydrogen peroxide to 9 parts water.

Lipstick
Dab first with white spirit (paint thinner), then apply a liquid detergent straight on to the mark and work it into the fibres. Wash in water as hot as the fabric will stand.

ABOVE **Remove heat rings on furniture with a little metal polish rubbed over the affected area before re-polishing.**

ABOVE **With a lipstick stain, scrape off as much of the excess as possible. Apply a strong detergent solution, and work from the outside in.**

Milk

Rinse under cold running water, then wash using a biological detergent.

Mud

Scrape off the excess using a blunt knife, then apply neat biological washing liquid or soap before washing as usual.

Nail varnish

Dab with nail-varnish remover or acetone before washing as usual. Non-colourfast fabrics should be dry cleaned professionally.

Perfume

Rinse in cold water before washing, or, if the perfume stains, dab the area with white spirit (paint thinner) and wash using a biological detergent.

Perspiration

Dab with a solution of 1 part white-wine vinegar to 10 parts water, or treat the affected area with a biological pre-wash detergent, then wash as usual. White cotton and linen can be treated with a dilute household-bleach solution, and silk, wool and synthetics with a hydrogen-peroxide solution (see **Tomato ketchup** for proportions).

Plasticine and moulding paste

Scrape off the excess matter using a blunt knife, then dab the area with white spirit (paint thinner) or lighter fuel. Wash using a heavy-duty detergent containing oxygen bleach.

Shoe polish

Scrape off any surface polish, then dab the area either with a grease solvent or methylated spirits (denatured alcohol). Soak in a strong detergent solution, then wash.

Tar and beach oil

Scrape off the excess using a blunt knife, and soften the remaining deposit with butter, turpentine or lighter fuel. Wipe away with a clean cloth, then rub the spot with neat liquid detergent before washing.

ABOVE Tar and beach oil can be softened prior to washing by applying butter or turpentine.

Urine

Soak in a gentle solution of cold water and ammonia. Alternatively, soak for a short time with biological washing liquid before washing in the hottest water that the fabric will stand.

ABOVE Urine stains can be soaked in a mild solution of cold water and ammonia. Or soak in biological washing powder before a hot wash.

Vomit

Scrape off the excess or blot it with old cloths. Scrub with a solution of tepid water and a biological detergent to which a little white-wine vinegar and disinfectant have been added. Rinse and repeat if necessary before washing.

Wine

For red wine, cover the stain with salt, then scrape up the saturated salt/wine mixture before blotting with clean, absorbent cloths. Apply cold water to the affected area. Always work from the outside in, to prevent the stain from spreading. Blot again and clean in the usual manner. For white wine, blot up as much as possible with a dry cloth. Treat with cold water before washing.

ABOVE Tip salt over red wine to soak it up as soon as it has been spilled.

STAIN-REMOVAL TIPS

- Always follow the manufacturer's directions before using any stain-removing product.
- Never mix chemicals – if you do, the resulting fumes could be lethal. Never smoke or have an exposed flame near cleaning fluids, as many are highly flammable. Keep the room well-ventilated while working with them in order to avoid inhaling fumes. Wear household gloves when using solvent and bleach cleaners.
- Expensive carpets and upholstery should always be treated with a water and stain repellent. This will help accidental spills to bead up on the surface and not penetrate the fibres.

SEWING AND MENDING

Even if you have little or no needlework knowledge, the following guidelines will help you to deal quickly with minor repair jobs and simple alterations. Always keep a basic sewing kit in the house, containing the following items: a packet of assorted needles; a needle threader; a tape measure; a box of dressmaking pins; a pair of small, sharp scissors; white polyester thread; black polyester thread; invisible thread (transparent nylon monofilament to match all colours); assorted white and black buttons; iron-on invisible mending tape (for hems and turn-ups); and iron-on patches for lightweight fabrics. A kit consisting of these basic items should be sufficient for most minor repairs and sewing tasks.

Sewing on buttons

Buttons need to be sewn to fabric with small lengths of thread remaining underneath the buttons, making them flexible but strong. If they are too tightly sewn, the buttons will not have sufficient space to lie flat against the buttonholes, resulting in the fabric being pulled.

Remove an old or broken button by sliding the teeth of a comb around the base threads, then cutting through with a razor blade. To sew on a replacement button, cut a length of thread approximately 50 cm/20 in long. Thread a needle and pull half the thread through, let the other piece hang down, then grip both ends together and tie a knot about 20 mm/¾ in from the cut ends. This will give you a strong doubled thread of a manageable length for sewing. If you try to work with a longer thread, in an attempt to avoid re-threading for sewing on several buttons, you may find it a false economy, as the thread will twist and tangle very easily, forcing you to cut the thread and begin again.

Starting on the underside of the fabric, push the needle up and through

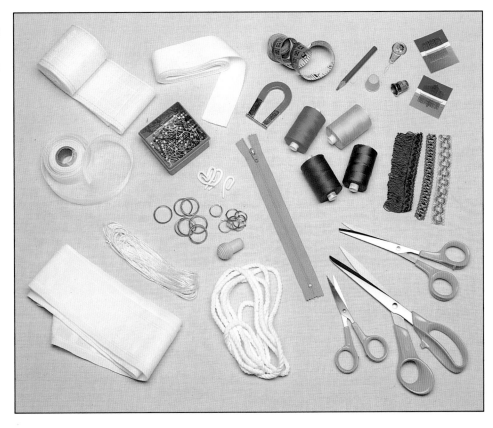

ABOVE A basic sewing and mending kit should contain scissors, various coloured threads, spare zips (zippers), pins and needles, a tape measure, a thimble and iron-on invisible mending tape.

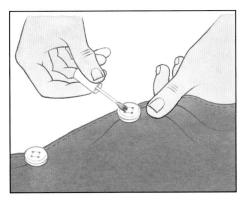

LEFT A little clear nail varnish dabbed on the threads after sewing on a button will help it stay on securely.

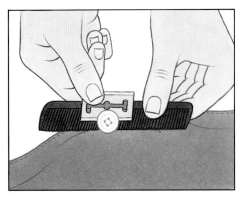

ABOVE Protect garments when removing buttons by sliding a comb under the button.

one hole in the button, and back through the opposite hole. A matchstick (wooden match) placed between the button and fabric will ensure that you leave enough thread to give flexibility. After going in and out of the hole 6 to 8 times, remove the matchstick and wind the thread around the stitches a few times. Push the needle through to the underside of the fabric and secure with a few more stitches before cutting off the thread end close to the fabric.

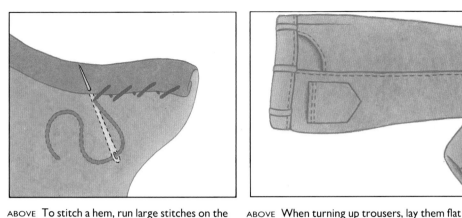

ABOVE To stitch a hem, run large stitches on the inside of the garment, catching a single thread on the outside of the garment each time.

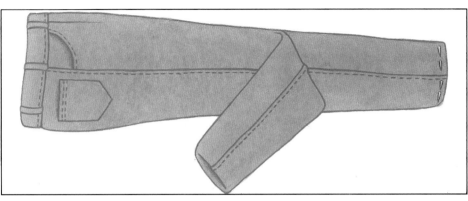

ABOVE When turning up trousers, lay them flat on a table to check that both hems are even and the same length. But first check that the length is right by asking the person who is going to wear the trousers to try them on.

Turning up hems and trousers

Ask the person who is going to wear the garment to put it on to make accurate alterations. If it is your own garment, use a tape measure or use existing hemlines or trouser lengths as a guide.

If the existing hem is straight, cut the fabric to a point approximately 5 cm/ 2 in below the length at which you wish the hem to be. Turn the garment inside-out, turn up the raw edge by about 20 mm/¾ in, pinning it all round as you go, and press it with an iron. Remove the pins and turn up the remaining 3 cm/1¼ in, then pin and press again. Stitch the hem securely by running large stitches on the inside of the garment and catching just a single strand of fibre each time on the outside of the garment.

Mending a zip (zipper)

A zip (zipper) that has become stuck can be loosened with a little liquid soap rubbed on to the teeth. Fabric that has been caught needs to be gently wriggled and prised free. If the zip head comes right off the top or bottom, cut off the lowest few teeth and push it back on. Oversew the patch where you have cut off the teeth in order to prevent the zip from coming off again.

Mending a tear

Rips in bed linen or garments can be invisibly mended by 'patching' the reverse with an iron-on adhesive patch – follow the manufacturer's instructions for use. Prevent further stress from pulling the area by running stitches around the edge of the tear.

MENDING TIPS

- When a hem drops and cannot be mended immediately, use a length of sticky tape to make a temporary invisible mend.
- Stop runs in stockings and tights (pantyhose) by dabbing on a little clear nail varnish at the top and bottom of the run.
- Dab a little nail varnish on to the threads holding metal buttons in place to prevent them from wearing away.
- If you find it difficult to pass a piece of thread through the eye of a needle, wipe a little soap on it to keep the ends from splitting.
- As soon as you notice that a button is coming loose, tie a knot in the unravelling thread until you find time to mend it properly.
- A quick alternative to sewing a hem is iron-on invisible mending tape, which creates a long-lasting and invisible repair.

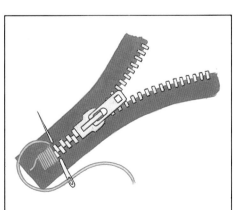

ABOVE Use strong cotton to stitch over the base of a weak zip (zipper).

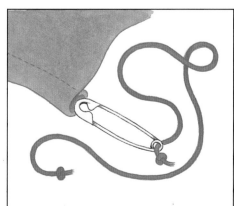

ABOVE Attach a safety pin to the end of a drawstring to make threading easier.

GOING ON HOLIDAY AND MOVING HOME

Taking a holiday is all about relaxing, not about worrying that you have left the oven on, the door open or have forgotten to take out insurance cover.

Moving home, on the other hand, is considered to be one of the most stressful and exhausting experiences that we have to face. You can, however, make it less of an ordeal by ensuring that you are well-prepared before the day itself, to minimize the risk of anything going wrong.

Holiday preparations

Whether you will be travelling by air, sea or car, choose the best luggage that you can afford, as cheap suitcases will soon weaken. Tie round a coloured tape or buy straps with your name woven on them to help you to identify your luggage quickly at an airport. Never write your name and home address on luggage labels where they can easily be seen – anyone dishonest will instantly know where their next 'job' is to be.

Several weeks before you are due to travel, check that all passports are up to date and will not expire while you are away. You will also need to find out well in advance whether you need visas for the countries to which you will be travelling, and, if so, to organize them with the relevant authorities, which can take some time.

Take out holiday insurance and make sure that, in the event of having to cancel at the last moment, you will be given a refund. Holidays in which sports are involved may require additional cover. Always check that, in the case of an accident, you will be flown back home for long or specialist treatment. Check with your doctor whether any vaccinations or a course of tablets are required for the country or countries that you will be visiting.

Order some currency and arrange traveller's cheques for the remainder of the money – this is both safer in case of loss or theft, and more convenient.

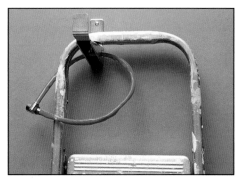

ABOVE Lock ladders to a garage or shed wall so that would-be burglars cannot use them to gain entry to your home.

ABOVE Mark all your valuables with an engraver and stencil or ultra-violet pen so that, in the event of a burglary while you are on holiday, the items can be identified should they be recovered. Many stolen items such as hi-fi (stereo) equipment are found by the police, but cannot be returned because of lack of identification.

Home security

Giving a little thought to security before you go on holiday will greatly reduce the chances of a burglary while you are away. Some of these suggestions may seem obvious, but it is surprising how often they are forgotten.

Ask a neighbour to call in every day to remove flyers and letters from the mat, as a pile of these is a good indication that you are away. Cancel milk and paper deliveries, as these can alert any passer by to the fact that no one is at home, if they are stacked up on the doorstep. Keeping houseplants watered is also a good way of ensuring that the house looks occupied.

Fit door and window locks if you have not already done so (this may be a

requirement of your insurance policy in any case, so you must do this or your policy could be invalidated in the event of a burglary). Padlock ladders to a wall and lock up the garden shed if you have one so that tools cannot be used by burglars to gain entry. Buy timeswitches to operate the television and some lights to give the impression that people are in the house.

Leaving washing up on the drainer and a couple of magazines scattered around will also make it look as if the house is occupied.

Travelling with children

Stop boredom from setting in by taking a selection of games and toys with you. Guessing games and stories also help to pass the time enjoyably. Acupressure wristbands and travel-sickness tablets are useful for long journeys. Another remedy is to eat crystallized (preserved) ginger, which prevents nausea.

TRAVEL KIT

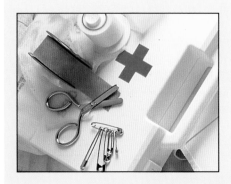

This should include the following:
- Sun-screen lotion.
- After-sun lotion.
- Insect repellent.
- Antiseptic wipes.
- Sticking plasters and bandages.
- Upset-stomach tablets or medicine.
- Tweezers.
- Thermometer.
- Paracetamol or other pain-relief tablets for adults and children.
- Rehydration packs for diarrhoea.

BEFORE MOVING

- Buy a pack of change-of-address cards, or fill one out and photocopy it to save time writing out dozens. Ensure that your insurance company, bank, credit card issuer, pension company, and all the other businesses you deal with know of your move.
- Arrange building and contents insurance at the new house to start from the day you move in.
- Cancel regular deliveries of groceries or newspapers.
- Arrange by telephone, and confirm in writing, transfers of the electricity, gas, water and telephone accounts. Before leaving, read the meters.
- Make arrangements for the gas, electricity and water to be switched on at the new house.

House-moving preparations

If you intend to use a professional removal company, contact 2 or 3 different removal companies as soon as you know that the move is on and ask them to visit and quote for the job. Ask neighbours or friends for their recommendations, too, as they may be able to offer useful advice on local companies. Firms which are reluctant to visit may be best avoided, as a guessed estimate may cause problems on the day if they do not know, for instance, that there will be a spiral staircase, low doors or an attic or loft stashed with boxes to cope with.

When the removal men arrive, point out anything that may make parking near the house a problem, and remember to tell them if they are likely to encounter difficulties at the new address. Show items requiring careful handling such as antiques, computer or hi-fi (stereo) equipment, as well as anything that has to be dismantled before it can be moved such as large wardrobes (closets). Giving all this information at the start will make the removal company's quotation as accurate as possible and prevent a nasty surprise when the bill arrives.

Removal insurance

Always read the small print on the documentation and check that the house contents will be insured for the duration of the move. Many removal firms' contracts state that you must let them know within 10 days of the move if anything is damaged or missing. Be sure to open every box and inspect the contents thoroughly as soon as you arrive, even if they remain otherwise untouched for weeks afterwards. Most firms will pack and unpack the contents themselves, but may give a discount if you do it yourself. This could affect the insurance cover, however, so check this before you decide.

Check your own house-contents insurance, as it is likely that the insurance will not cover items lost or damaged during a move. If necessary, ask the company to extend the cover.

Hiring (renting) a van

Doing the move yourself is cheaper, but driving a large van packed with furniture can be an alarming experience if you are unused to it. Unless you are fit and reasonably strong and can spare the time, it can in fact end up being a false economy. Hiring (renting) a van

BELOW Wrap plates individually and pack them vertically to minimize the risk of breakages.

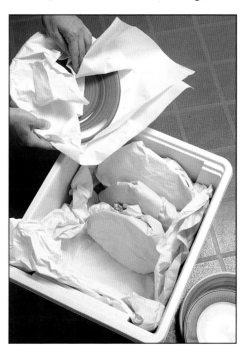

and driver could be a happy medium – check whether you will be charged extra for mileage, or whether the price quoted is inclusive.

Packing

Begin packing a few weeks ahead of the move. Start with items in the attic or loft that you rarely use – this is also a good time to throw out items that you no longer need. Additional, purely decorative items and ornaments can also be wrapped up at this early stage.

Collect boxes from the supermarket and save newspapers for packing items. Buy bubble wrap (padded plastic wrapping, available from stationers) to protect delicate or easily marked items. Use large but manageable boxes, and mark each lid with a bold pen to show which room it belongs in at the new house. Alternatively, place a colour-coded label on the box, for example blue for the bathroom, yellow for the kitchen, green for the living room, and so on. When you arrive at the new house, stick matching labels on the relevant door to each room so that the removal company knows exactly where everything needs to go. When labelling boxes, give details of the contents (e.g., kitchen pans and crockery; food processor and attachments) so that you do not spend frustrating time trying to find one item.

Line boxes containing china with a thick layer of bubble wrap or with scrunched-up paper to protect the contents. Wrap plates in paper or bubble wrap and stack them vertically in the boxes. In the event of the box being knocked or dropped, the plates will be less likely to crack if the weight is not resting on those at the bottom.

Leave soap, toilet paper, hand towels and tea- and coffee-making items (including cups and the kettle) until last, then pack them in a brightly coloured plastic box so that you can see it easily the instant you arrive. Pack tools, lightbulbs, extension cables, spare fuses and screws in another brightly coloured box so that rooms can be lit and quick repairs undertaken.

CONSERVATION AND RECYCLING

We all know of the need to reduce the level of environmental pollution. No matter how insignificant a small action may seem – such as placing a jar in a recycling bin, switching off a light when it is not needed or mending a dripping tap (faucet) – if everyone made an effort, the waste of vital resources could be drastically reduced.

Everyday recycling

Buy re-fill containers to fill up bottles and minimize the number of unwanted plastic containers ending up on landfill sites. Separate your household waste into groups: vegetable waste which can be composted in the garden; items that you can take to a local recycling centre such as paper, card (cardboard) and newspaper, metal drinks and food cans and tin foil, glass jars and bottles; and finally any waste which cannot be recycled and needs to go in the dustbin (trash can).

Re-use old envelopes and cut up old letters and scrap paper for writing lists and messages. Keep old margarine tubs to store nails, screws and small fittings, and use jars or bottles to keep scraps of ribbon, string and elastic together – the latter containers are especially convenient as they enable you to see at a glance the contents inside.

ABOVE Keep a large bag in which to place recyclable waste such as cans, jars and bottles until you can take them to the recycling centre.

Home ideas

It takes the energy of 1 gallon/4.5 litres of petrol (gasoline) to make just 30 house bricks. Use reclaimed bricks when building to help save the earth's resources and to give a traditional weathered look to houses, gardens and patios at the same time. The use of reclaimed architectural materials such as floorboards, baths and windows looks good and rarely costs more than the modern equivalent.

ABOVE Using architectural salvage not only recycles unwanted items, but also adds character to a home.

When buying woods, choose only those that you are satisfied come from sustainable sources. Avoid hardwoods cut from tropical rainforests, including teak and mahogany – the de-forestation caused by the removal of such woods results in rare species being forced into extinction, and massive forest fires which contribute to global warming. There are plenty of sustainable alternatives, with pine, beech and rubberwood being among the best. These woods can be stained, waxed or varnished to darken them or even painted to achieve a range of attractive effects. To save on new paper, buy toilet paper and kitchen paper (paper towels) that contains a high percentage of recycled material, and look for 'non-chlorine-bleached' labels as the use of bleach increases pollution.

Avoid buying aerosols that contain CFCs (chlorofluorocarbons). These destroy the ozone layer, resulting in dangerous ultra-violet radiation from the sun penetrating to the earth. Foam-blown plastics (used for food cartons), air conditioners and some refrigerators also release CFCs into the atmosphere, so bear this in mind when buying. There are so many excellent alternatives to all these products that there is no excuse for buying them.

You can also greatly reduce your consumption of fuel by insulating your home properly. Good insulation saves money on heating bills as well as reducing the amount of pollution, so it is a good idea for both reasons. The burning of fossil fuels also creates 'acid rain' which kills forests and eats away at buildings that form our architectural heritage, and should be reduced as much as possible.

Electrical appliances

When replacing an appliance such as a refrigerator, freezer, cooker or washing machine, look for the models that are energy-efficient and have 'economy' programmes. Take your old fridge or freezer for recycling, and to a place where harmful CFCs can be recycled or disposed of safely. For economic running, place the refrigerator and freezer on an outside wall and well away from the cooker or a hot dishwasher. De-frosting the freezer regularly will prevent thick layers of ice from building up, which in turn prevent the freezer from functioning correctly and cause it to use more electricity to maintain a low temperature.

Try to cook in batches when using the oven, by making several dishes at one time and using all the oven-shelf space. A microwave oven cooks quickly and consumes far less energy than a conventional oven. It is ideal for re-heating foods which tend to dry up under a grill (broiler) or in an oven.

If you plan to install a gas central-heating system, choose one of the latest energy-efficient condensing boilers, as it will save both on fuel bills and on unwanted carbon-dioxide emissions.

Only operate a dishwasher when you have a full load, and use the 'economy' setting for normal soiling.

Heat and light

Avoid wasting heat by fitting thermostatic radiator valves to each radiator, so that you can control the temperature of each room to suit your needs. Shelves above radiators help to deflect heat back into the room, as well as creating valuable storage space. Turning down the central-heating thermostat by just a degree or so and reducing the length of time that your central heating is switched on makes little difference to comfort levels, but saves a considerable amount of energy during the course of a year.

Line curtains or drapes with special insulating fabric to help keep the heat in a room. Blinds (shades) also act as simple heat barriers, so close them at night for additional insulation. Block gaps under doors and prevent draughts by using 'sausage' draught excluders.

To save on the cost of lighting, switch to low-energy lightbulbs. Although these are more expensive than ordinary bulbs, they last up to 6 times longer and use approximately 75 per cent less energy. Try also to get into the habit of switching off lights as you leave a room. Fitting 2-way switches in the hallway and on the landing will ensure that you have good lighting while going up and down stairs, but can also switch off the lights when they are not required.

ENERGY-SAVING TIPS

● Taking a shower instead of a bath uses up to 60 per cent less water and the energy required to heat it.

● Use stacking saucepans rather than individual ones, so that you can cook several different items over a single ring (burner).

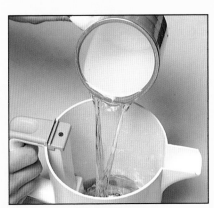

● When boiling a kettle for just one mug of tea, fill the mug with water and then tip this into the kettle so that you do not heat up unwanted water.

ABOVE Fit thermostatic radiator valves to each radiator to avoid wasting heat. They mean that you can control the temperature of each room separately.

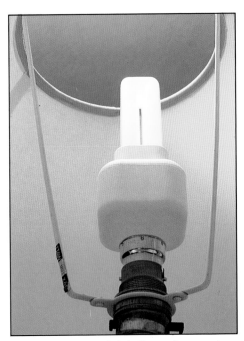

ABOVE Low-energy lightbulbs cut down on the amount of electricity required to use them, ultimately reducing the carbon dioxide released into the atmosphere from power stations.

FAMILY HEALTH

Maintaining a home in good decorative order and repair as well as keeping it clean and tidy require an organized and knowledgeable approach which has been the subject of this chapter so far. But what about the occupants of that home, namely the family itself?

There are many areas where a little effort and planning can go a long way in improving the security and safety of the family in their environment. This can extend from identifying potential danger areas in the house and making them safer to improving basic security measures.

Halls and landings, living rooms, kitchens and bathrooms, and even the areas around the house, all have their own particular inherent dangers, which often go unnoticed until too late. By assessing the potential risks and acting upon them in good time to install simple safety measures, accidents can often be avoided. Even active adults can benefit

from some of these, especially where fire and electricity are concerned.

No householder can ignore the threat of burglary, which can often be deterred by the installation of some simple devices. It is usually a simple matter to assess the efficacy of your current window and door locks and upgrade them. Introducing some passive infra-red devices to detect intruders and some motion-sensitive lighting inside and outside will deter most opportunist burglars.

In addition to ensuring the safety and security of the occupants of your home, you will also want to safeguard their health and to look after them should they succumb to everyday ailments or be involved in a domestic accident. You also need to know how to deal with serious injury and life-threatening emergencies.

The following pages provide valuable information on all the above topics as well as hints for living safely with pets.

OPPOSITE All over the world, in all cultures and throughout time, people have used plants not only as food but also for medicinal purposes. Herbalism, just one alternative approach to treating illness, is a gentle, accessible therapy.

HOME SECURITY

Statistics show that domestic burglaries are on the increase, but many of these break-ins need not have occurred if just a few basic security measures had been taken. It is easy to prevent opportunist thieves from being tempted by the sight of open windows and doors by always being sure to close them both at night and even when you go out for a short time during the day. Even the most determined burglar who sets out with a crowbar to force an entry can be thwarted by sturdy locks, bolts and security floodlights. As well as giving peace of mind, a well-secured home can save money on insurance premiums and, more importantly, the anguish of losing your valued possessions.

Outside the house

Check that garden gates at the rear of the house close firmly, and can be secured if you go away for long periods. A garden fence with gaping holes can provide a discreet entry for a burglar, so be sure to keep this in good repair. Another frequent entry point is a garage – if attached to a house, this can allow a thief to force a door into the house unseen. Always fit secure locks to garage doors to minimize the risk of this happening. Padlock a garden shed if you have one in order to prevent tools from being stolen or used to gain entry to your home.

Remember that high shrubs and hedges at the front of your house may give privacy but can also screen a burglar from the street or neighbours. Large trees situated very close to a flat roof or window can also give an easy access route.

Fit a passive infra-red (PIR) floodlight to the front and back of the house. This will automatically switch on if activated by a passer by, making a pleasant welcome for a visitor but a strong deterrent for intruders. Choose one that has a variable light duration and an adjustable sensor for covering large or small areas. A bell box is another good deterrent – even a false one can deter an opportunist thief.

A spy-hole fitted in the front door discreetly lets people outside know that you can observe their movements while you are still secure behind the door. Always use the spy-hole before opening the door, and never open it unless you are sure of the identity of the person.

Door security

On a front door, replace a standard 'nightlatch' with a 5-lever mortise lock that cannot be opened without the key, even if the burglar can reach it via a broken pane of glass in the door. Remember, however, that good door

ABOVE Fit a strong mortise lock that can be locked from the inside to prevent a burglar from opening it through an adjacent broken pane.

locks are only as strong as the door that they are on, so choose a solid door and hinges so that both the opening and the hinged side will withstand an attempted forced entry. If you are in doubt, insert hinge bolts on the hinge side of the door. These fit into corresponding holes in the door frame, providing extra strength and preventing the door from being forced off its hinges. Even if the door does eventually give way, there is a good chance that the noise created by the burglar will have attracted someone's attention.

Fit a door chain or bar restraint to the front door. These both work in the same way by restricting the amount by which a door can be opened, giving you valuable time to assess the validity of a caller. A bar restraint is stronger than a chain, as it consists of a solid metal bar. Both require the door to be closed for the bar or chain to be released before the door can be opened to its full extent.

ABOVE A door chain or bar restraint will allow you to see who is calling at the door without the risk of the door being burst open.

Fit French windows and casement doors with additional rack bolts at the top and bottom, which slide into the frame. Keep the key out of sight of intruders, but where it can be found by you and all the other members of the family in an emergency. Special patio-door locks, which are fitted to the top, bottom or side of the door, prevent these doors from being slid open or lifted out of the frame. Look for the new 3-figure combination locks that do not need a key.

Window security

Most insurance companies now demand that key-operated window locks are fitted to all the windows in a house, and these do contribute greatly to security. Before buying window locks, however, check that they are suitable for the windows to which you intend to fit them. Measure the window frames before you go to buy, and check that they will accommodate the type of locks that you have in mind. In the case of very narrow frames, use a surface-fitted lock.

Sash windows can be fitted with dual screws, where a bolt passes through the inner frame into the outer frame to hold the 2 sections together; or with surface-fitted bolts that fit on the upper sashes and allow a small gap for ventilation. Replace existing handles with lockable ones that, once locked, cannot be re-opened without the key.

EMERGENCY ACTION

- A length of wooden dowel cut to the exact length to fit inside the bottom track of a patio door can wedge it closed. Similarly, if a dowel is placed vertically in the side runner of a sash window, it cannot be opened.
- Sink a screw into the wood frame beside a handle to prevent it from being opened.
- Stay-bars on casement windows can be secured by sinking a screw through a hole into the wooden frame.

When you are out

Light-sensitive fittings on interior and exterior lights sense when it is growing dark and turn on automatically. Time switches are also an excellent idea. These can be used to operate a number of appliances, making it appear as if the house is inhabited – televisions and radios create enough noise to be convincing. Electronic curtain controllers are also available, to close curtains automatically at a pre-set time. This will give the impression that the house is occupied.

Marking property

Ultra-violet pens are easy to use, and leave an invisible mark that will only show when placed under an ultra-violet lamp. Engraving scribers, ranging from simple carbide or diamond-tipped pens to electric engraving tools can be used to scratch a postcode, telephone

ABOVE Engraving scribers are an effective and easy method for marking hi-fi equipment.

number or other identifiable code. Use stencils with an engraver to give a neat, legible result. Another option is an etching kit, which is ideal for marking glass objects. Stencil transfers mask off the security code, and acid brushed over the surface etches the code.

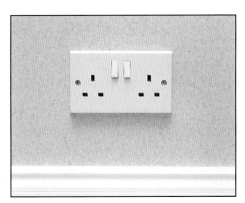

ABOVE A socket (receptacle) safe looks just like an ordinary socket, but is large enough to hold cash and jewellery in the box behind it.

SECURITY MEASURES

- If you return home to find signs of a break-in, do not enter but go straight to a neighbour's house to telephone the police.
- If you hear an intruder in the house or trying to break in, put on the lights and make a noise to alert them to the fact that you are there. If you are upstairs, do not go downstairs to investigate but telephone the police from your bedroom if possible.

ABOVE Lockable window handles are useful for keeping children in and burglars out.

ABOVE A time switch set to operate while you are out will give the impression that the house is still occupied.

HOME SAFETY

Unfortunately, accidents do happen, and often in what is usually considered to be the safest of places – the home. There are simple preventive measures that you can take to reduce the risks of serious injury, however, most of which are simply a question of common sense. Every member of the family should be fully aware of the dangers present in all areas of the home.

Just a little thought and planning as to the potential dangers can give peace of mind and, more importantly, reduce the risks of a serious accident occurring. The elderly are especially vulnerable to accidents in the home, as are children – particularly those under 4 years of age. If you have young children, or even grandchildren, who visit, look around your home to count the hazards lurking there; it is surprising how many there are. It is impossible to watch children every minute of the day, so it is vital that you make every effort to eliminate potential hazards, most of which can quickly be removed.

Different areas of the home present different safety issues – refer to the information given below and take the necessary action. Any safety products that you need to buy are relatively inexpensive, and will be a small price to pay for the creation of a safer home environment for all the family.

The hallway, staircase and landing
The first priority if you do not already have one is to install a smoke detector – or 2 if your home is on different levels – so that every member of the household can be quickly alerted in the event of a fire. Smoke alarms are inexpensive and widely available, and can save lives. Regularly check that the alarms are functioning properly by vacuuming the vents to remove dust and letting the smoke from a snuffed candle drift into them as a test. Alternatively, some alarms have a special button for testing on a weekly basis. Always follow the

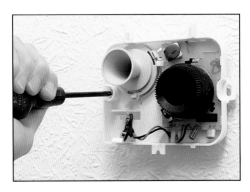

ABOVE A smoke detector can be installed easily by screwing the base to the ceiling, fitting the battery and clipping on the cover.

ABOVE Test the detector regularly and vacuum dust away from the sensor to ensure that it works efficiently at all times.

fixing and siting instructions supplied by the manufacturer, and replace batteries as soon as they run down – keep spares in the house so that you can fit them straight away.

Sufficient lighting is vital on the staircase and in the hallway to avoid misleading shadows being cast on steps and stair treads. Rugs on polished floors can easily slip when trodden on, so attach special non-slip backing strips to prevent them from sliding. Make sure, too, that the carpet is securely fitted with no tears or gaping seams, as these can cause a serious fall.

The living room
Ensure that any glass-topped tables, patio doors and interior glass doors are fitted with toughened or laminated safety glass. You can buy a special safety

film (available from DIY stores) that is invisible once fitted, but will prevent shards of glass from causing injuries should the glass shatter.

Never overload a socket outlet (receptacle) – ideally, there should only be one plug to one socket. If numerous electrical appliances are in use, be sure to use the correct adapter – ask your retailer for the one most suited to your needs. Avoid trailing flexes which can easily be tripped over.

If anyone smokes in the household, insist that cigarette butts are placed in an ashtray that is washed out before going to bed. This will ensure that any smouldering ashes are extinguished and will leave the room fresher too. Ensure that an open fire is always covered with a fire guard whenever the room is unoccupied – even for 5 minutes.

The kitchen
Buy a kettle guard to hold a kettle safely in place so that it cannot be tipped or pulled. Alternatively, a 'curly' cord will prevent the hazard of a trailing flex but will still allow the kettle to be lifted.

ABOVE Fit a curly cord to prevent the risk of a trailing flex from a kettle.

ABOVE Buy a fire extinguisher to keep in the kitchen or garage.

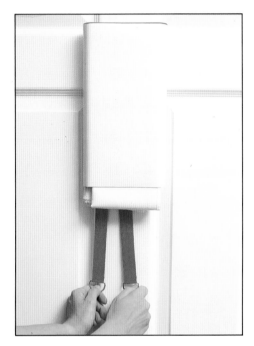

ABOVE Keep a fire blanket on the wall or back of a door so that you can reach it easily in the event of a kitchen fire.

Keep a domestic fire extinguisher in the kitchen, but do not position it too close to or above the cooker as a pan fire would make it inaccessible. Check that everyone knows how the extinguisher works and if possible choose one that is suitable for electrical fires. A compact fire blanket, hung on the wall, will suffocate flames from deep-fat fryers, which are a major cause of household fires. You should never throw water on this type of fire.

Take care not to stretch your arm over a gas cooker if you are wearing clothing with loose sleeves, such as a dressing-gown or baggy sweater – especially with synthetic fabrics. The gas could catch on to the fabric and

ABOVE Turn pan handles inwards to avoid them being caught in loose clothing.

cause a severe burn. Always turn saucepan handles inwards so that you do not inadvertently knock them, and so that loose clothing cannot catch them as you pass by.

The bathroom
Prevent a slippery floor, bath or shower from causing falls by installing 'grab' rails at a height that can be easily reached. Modern baths often have an integral safety rail. If yours does not, fit a rail to the nearest wall. Mop up splashes of water and even body lotion on vinyl or tiled floors quickly, and always have a bath or shower mat on the floor so that wet feet do not slip. Non-slip rubber safety mats and stickers will prevent slipping while getting in or out of the bath.

Keep all electrical appliances away from sources of water where they are likely to get splashed or saturated with steam. Remember that even cordless gadgets can deliver a powerful shock if dropped into water. Replace flick switches with pull-cord light switches.

ABOVE Avoid slipping in a wet shower or bath by placing a safety mat or stickers on the surface.

Outside
Keep a check on the state of paving stones and paths, as a loose stone can easily trip an unwary visitor.

Never use petrol (gasoline) or any other household chemical to light a fire or barbecue. These can ignite with an explosion, causing burning debris to land on people, pets and possessions. Keep a bucket of water handy to douse a fire that gets out of hand.

When using outdoor electrical equipment, plug the appliance into a residual circuit breaker (RCD), which will cut off the power should the cable be accidentally cut or a fault occur. After finishing with any tools, make sure that you put them away in order to prevent children or pets from cutting themselves on sharp blades.

Wear safety goggles and a face-mask when clearing guttering situated above you, when drilling into masonry, or when applying paint or creosote, in order to prevent dust or specks from falling into your eyes, nose or mouth.

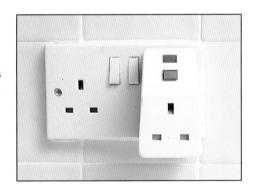

ABOVE Use an RCD (Residual Current Device) when using power tools – this will break the circuit should an electrical fault occur.

ABOVE Wear a pair of stout gloves and protective goggles when doing potentially dangerous jobs.

HOME SAFETY (continued)

IN THE EVENT OF A FIRE

● Immediately you discover a house fire, get everyone out safely – then telephone the fire services.

● With a pan fire, switch off the heat and cover the pan with a lid, plate, damp towel or fire blanket. Wait until the flames are extinguished and the pan is cool before touching it.

With an electrical fire, before dealing with a burning electrical appliance or socket outlet (receptacle), switch off the electricity at the consumer unit. Put out the fire with a fire extinguisher or water.

If a television or computer is on fire, switch off the electricity at the consumer unit or at the socket if you can reach it safely. Do not use water, as residual electricity may still be present. Always smother the flames with a rug or blanket to extinguish them.

● If a fire is too big to deal with without danger, leave the room immediately, closing the door firmly behind you. Ensure that everyone leaves the house, closing doors behind them to slow down the spread of smoke and flames. Telephone the fire services from a telephone box or from a neighbour's house.

● Smoke kills more people than flames do. It is vital to get out of a smoke-filled house as soon as you can.

● Smoke and heat rise, so if the smoke is very dense, crawl on your hands and knees and you should be able to see and feel your way to safety.

● A damp towel or cloth tied over your nose and mouth can help to reduce smoke inhalation.

● If you are trapped on an upstairs floor, open the window to call for help. A wet towel placed at the gap under the door will help to prevent smoke from penetrating. Double-glazed windows that are sealed create a barrier of astonishing strength. Do not attempt to smash them with your hands – instead, try to find a chair or other heavy object.

Child safety

In the kitchen: only buy detergent and cleaning chemicals with child-proof tops, as not all dangerous products have these. As many such products are often stored conveniently under the sink where youngsters can reach, fit cupboard (closet) locks as well. Ideally, store the cleaning materials in a high cupboard or on a shelf out of their reach. Never decant household cleaning agents or chemicals into other containers.

Never leave out knives and scissors once you have finished with them. Keep them safe and beyond reach in a wooden knife tidy, on a magnetic rack or in a lockable drawer.

Even if you make sure that pan handles are kept pointing inwards so that children cannot reach them, hob and cooker guards that clip to the edges are an additional safety measure for the one time they can.

A hot oven front can give a nasty burn to an unsuspecting child. Look for the cool-touch oven fronts that are available on many new ovens, or buy an oven guard which forms a neat but effective barrier between the heat and the child. If you are using a frying pan, avoid spots of hot fat landing on the floor where a child could easily slip – or even worse falling on a child standing nearby – by placing a spatter guard over the pan while you are cooking.

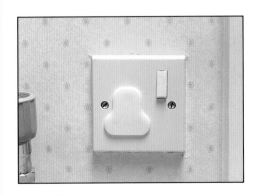

ABOVE Cover sockets (receptacles) with special covers to prevent young children from poking their fingers or pencils into them.

In the bathroom: when running a bath, even if you have mixer taps (faucets), run the cold water first, then top it up with hot water to bring the bath temperature to the correct degree. Always test the water first by dipping your elbow (which is as sensitive as a child's delicate skin) into it. Similarly, never turn on a shower while you are standing underneath it – switch it on first, check that the temperature is not too hot, and then step in.

Unfortunately, children can find the toilet a wonderful place for dropping in your toiletries and their toys. Keep them safe by fitting special lid locks which are easy and quick to open.

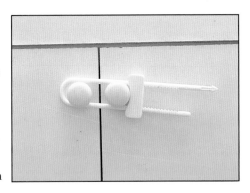

ABOVE Cupboard (closet) locks on bathroom cabinets keep small hands away from cleaning chemicals and medicines.

Always keep medicines locked away in a safe, dry place. Wall-mounted bathroom cabinets are ideal, and can be situated where children are unable to reach them. Flush old and out-of-date medicines down the toilet, or take them to your chemist (drugstore) for safe disposal.

On the staircase: discourage children from leaving toys or clothing on the stairs, as they can be a hazard.

Fit a safety gate at the bottom *and* the top of the stairs, so that babies cannot crawl up only to try going back once they find their way blocked.

Windows and doorways: fit safety locks to upstairs windows to prevent them from being opened by children.

Make sure that older members of the family know how to work them in the event of an emergency. In very hot weather, look for an extending safety gate that can also be used as a static barrier across both open windows and doorways.

In the bedroom: jumping on beds can be great fun but the consequences lethal if a child should crash into a pane of glass. Cover any potentially dangerous windows with special self-adhesive safety film, which will stop the glass from breaking into sharp, jagged pieces. Jumping on sofas can be equally hazardous if you have glass-fronted units or glass-topped tables, so ensure that these too are covered with sheets of safety film.

RIGHT A socket nightlight will provide children with a reassuring glow and help them to see their way out of the room at night.

ABOVE Fit safety film to window panes, glass doors or tables to prevent shards of glass from causing injury if they break.

BELOW Choose children's toys carefully, checking for any loose parts or sharp edges.

BELOW RIGHT Always place a fire guard in front of the fire – even if the fire is electric.

Provide a nursery light or a simple night light that plugs directly into a socket outlet (receptacle) to give a soft, reassuring glow and to enable a child to find his or her way if they happen to wake at night.

Choose children's toys carefully, checking for any loose parts, sharp points and edges or rough joins, all of which can cause injury. Pulling any suspect parts is worth doing before you buy, to find out whether the toy comes apart and could hurt a child.

When re-painting a child's bedroom, remember that old paint may contain lead. If unsure, remove paint with a chemical stripper, not a sander or a scraper. The stripper will form a paste which will prevent any lead from entering the atmosphere.

When young children are unwell, a portable baby monitor will alert you to all the sounds from the nursery, leaving you to move about freely while the children sleep.

In the living room: always place a fire guard in front of a fire – even an electric one, as children may be fascinated by the glow that it emits. If possible, choose a guard with a sloping top so that toys or drinks cannot sit on it.

Outside: swimming pools and ponds should be covered when not in use, or

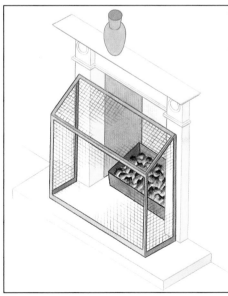

surrounded by a child-proof fence that cannot be climbed or crawled under. An unobtrusive wire cover can be placed over ponds and left in place throughout the year.

FOOD SAFETY

In addition to improving general safety within the home and making the boundaries more secure, perhaps the main area where you can safeguard your family is by making sure that the food they eat is always safe. How you shop for, store and handle food can have far-reaching effects. An understanding of how germs breed and travel underpins the safe kitchen and strict hygiene is essential to safeguard you and your family from the risk of food poisoning.

Shopping for chilled food

The colder you keep chilled and frozen food between buying it and storing it at home, the safer it is. This is because if the food warms up while you are taking it home, bacteria could grow and multiply. To avoid this, keep chilled foods together in the shopping trolley (cart), then pack them together, preferably in a cool bag, making sure that you wrap separately anything that is likely to drip. At home, transfer chilled or frozen food to the refrigerator or freezer immediately. Leaving chilled food in a shopping bag or car for any length of time can raise the temperature sufficiently to allow bacteria to thrive.

CHECKING FOOD LABELS

It is becoming increasingly difficult to guarantee that the food we eat really is what we think it is. With so many additives, genetically-modified and substitute foods, it is now wise to carefully read ingredient labels to check what is in any packaged food. For those wishing to control their intake of certain ingredients such as salt, sugar or fat, this is the only way to be sure. It is also essential if anyone in the family suffers from an allergic reaction to any food.

HYGIENE

Keep your hands and all equipment scrupulously clean. Never use a knife with which you have cut raw meat or fish to cut anything else without first washing it thoroughly. Get into the habit of scrubbing chopping boards and worktops (counters) between uses; keep separate boards for chopping raw meat and vegetables or cooked meat. Always store cooked food or any salad items separately from raw food such as meat or fish. Disinfect all work surfaces and the sink regularly, and especially all cloths used for washing up and/or wiping down surfaces, as these can transfer germs readily. Never wipe your hands on towels used for drying utensils.

Refrigerator safety

You need to keep your refrigerator running at the right temperature, because if it is not cold enough, harmful bacteria can grow and may cause food poisoning – anything from a stomach upset to serious illness.

Store the most perishable food in the coldest part of the refrigerator; these are pre-cooked chilled foods, soft cheeses, cooked meats, prepared salads (including pre-washed greens as well as potato salads etc.), desserts, cream or custard-filled cakes, home-prepared food and leftovers. Foods that are best kept cool to help them stay fresher longer can be stored in the cool zones (which often include special compartments); milk, yogurt, fruit juices, hard cheeses, opened jars and bottles, fats such as butter, margarine, lard and low-fat spreads, and eggs fall into this category. The salad crisper is the warmest part of the refrigerator; it is designed for storing whole vegetables, fruit and fresh salad items such as unwashed whole lettuce, tomatoes, radishes etc. Try to keep raw meat, poultry and fish on the bottom shelf in case they drip. Prevent them from touching other foods by storing them in containers for added safety.

BELOW When shopping, make a list of fresh foods needed and frequently used foods whose stocks are running low. Check food labels for nutritional information and 'use by' dates.

Do not keep food for too long and always observe 'use by' dates. Once opened, canned food can be kept in the refrigerator for up to 48 hours.

To get the coldest part of the refrigerator to run between 0–5°C/32–41°F, put a thermometer in the coldest part (refer to the manufacturer's instructions to locate this) where you

REFRIGERATOR CHECKLIST

- Keep the coldest part of the refrigerator around 0–5°C/32–41°F.
- Keep a thermometer in the coldest part and check the temperature regularly.
- Keep the most perishable foods, such as meat, in the coldest part of the refrigerator.

- Wrap and cover all raw and uncooked foods, to prevent them from touching other foods.
- Return perishable foods, such as butter, to the refrigerator as soon as possible after use.
- Don't overload the refrigerator; this can block the circulation of the cooling air.
- Don't put hot food into the refrigerator; let it cool first, because hot food could heat up other foods and bacteria breed in warm temperatures.
- Don't keep food beyond its 'use by' or 'best before' date.

can read it as soon as you open the door. Don't use a mercury thermometer as this could break and contaminate food. Close the door and leave for several hours, preferably overnight. Open the door and read the thermometer without touching it. If it is not between 0–5°C/32–41°F, adjust the thermostat dial and leave as before. If the temperature is still not right after several hours, try again.

Avoiding cross-contamination

Bacteria will readily cross from one food to another, especially from raw meat to cooked or processed foods, so the prevention of cross-contamination is paramount for anyone in charge of preparing food for others.

Cooking food

High temperatures kill most bacteria, so always make sure that raw food, especially meat, is cooked right through; the temperature at the centre should reach 70°C/158°F for at least two minutes. Large meat joints need care to make sure that the centre is well cooked; a meat thermometer can help. Microwave cookers do not always heat food to the high temperatures that kill food-poisoning bacteria, so when using them make sure that the food is piping hot at the centre before serving. If frozen meat, poultry or fish is not completely thawed, the centre may not be properly cooked. The best way to thaw food is either in a microwave or refrigerator.

Raw eggs sometimes contain bacteria which is destroyed by cooking. Current advice is that you should avoid recipes using uncooked eggs.

When re-heating food, always heat until it is piping hot all the way through. Never re-heat food more than once. When using a microwave for re-heating check the instructions regarding standing times, to allow the heat to reach all parts of the food.

Insects

Insects, especially flies and cockroaches can transfer germs on to food so it is essential to keep them out of the kitchen. Insect repellents may contain poisons that are also harmful to you, so try to use herbal repellents. Metal gauze screens across open windows will provide a physical barrier, or you may prefer to try a crayon type of repellent that is applied around all openings. Always cover food that is left out for any length of time, with a purpose-made cover of fabric mesh or a sieve, or use greaseproof (waxed) paper or foil.

HYGIENE AROUND THE KITCHEN

- Wash your hands in warm water with soap:
  – before touching food.
  – after touching raw food and before touching ready-to-eat food.
  – after touching pets, dirty washing (laundry), the dustbin (trash can).
  – after going to the lavatory.
- Cover cuts and grazes.
- Wipe hands on a separate kitchen towel, not the tea towel (dish towel).
- Bleach, disinfect or change kitchen cloths or sponges often, especially after raw meat, poultry or fish has been prepared.
- Wipe the tops of all cans before opening them.
- Wash dishes, worktops (counters) and cutlery with hot water and detergent. Rinse washing up and let it drip dry if possible.
- Keep pets away from food, dishes and worktops.
- Keep food covered. Open packets or spilt food can attract flies, ants and mice, which spread bacteria. Clear up spilt food straight away.
- Avoid using the same knife or chopping board for raw meat, cooked food and fresh vegetables. If you have to use the same knife or board, always wash them thoroughly between uses.

THE HEALTHY FAMILY

ABOVE Diet, exercise and relaxation are all important in maintaining the health of the family.

While a healthy diet and plenty of exercise will keep the family's health at optimum level, illness and injuries can strike at any time, especially where there are children or older people concerned. Being able to recognize symptoms and knowing what to do will help you when the time comes for action. The information contained in the following few pages will help you to cope with most eventualities.

Minor injury and illness can often be easily treated at home, but deciding if the problem is serious enough for a doctor's attention can often be difficult; if you are not sure, always err on the side of caution.

There are numerous medicines and preparations that can be bought over the counter of a chemist (drugstore) which can help to alleviate the symptoms of everyday minor ailments (see following). In addition to the more conventional treatments, there are many so-called alternative therapies that can also be used at home.

Herbs are almost certainly the most popular alternative method of self-help for minor complaints. The easiest method of taking herbs internally is to make a tea, but for stronger, more medicinal brews, you need to make either an infusion or a decoction. Infusions and decoctions can also be used to make a compress or poultice, which is applied externally.

The beneficial use of pure essential oils extracted from plants is another time-honoured traditional practice, known as aromatherapy. A common way of using aromas for self-treatment is in the bath. A few drops create a thin film on the surface of the water which coats the skin as the patient steps into the bath, and is partially absorbed by it. When essential oils are diluted into a base vegetable oil, they can be applied to the skin for soothing and healing massage.

Serious injuries should always be treated by a doctor at a health centre or the emergency department of a hospital. However, minor ones can often be treated at home. In real emergencies, such as heart attack or drowning, quick, on-the-spot action can save a life before an ambulance or doctor can be called out.

- Make sure that only the recommended dose is taken.
- Always ask the pharmacist for help and advice, and tell him or her if you are taking any other medication.
- Always read the directions on the packet and label.
- If you are pregnant, always consult your doctor before taking medicines.
- Keep all medicines locked away and out of the sight of children.
- Never tell children that the medicine you are giving is like a sweet or tastes nice – they may try to take more when you are not looking.
- Take out-of-date medicines to your pharmacist for safe disposal; or ask how to dispose of them.

CALLING THE DOCTOR

Simple home remedies will usually relieve a patient's symptoms, but should these persist for more than a few days consult a doctor. If you have any concerns at all about a child, even if there are no obvious symptoms, do not hesitate about telephoning your doctor. You must contact the doctor if a child experiences any of the following:

- Any sign of illness for more than three days, especially a high temperature.
- A high temperature that abates then returns.
- A low temperature with cold skin and drowsiness.
- Vomiting or diarrhoea for several hours.
- Severe pain on the right side of the abdomen.
- Fit or convulsion.
- Turns blue or very pale.
- A headache with blurred vision or dizziness.
- Dizziness after bumping the head.
- Quick or difficult breathing.
- Loss of interest in food, especially if aged under six months.

Given time, the human body will heal itself from most minor infections and illnesses. Colds, coughs, stomach upsets and sore throats will all eventually clear up by themselves, but keeping the body rested, the temperature down and pain to a minimum all help to make the sufferer comfortable while giving the body's own defences time to work.

When using traditional over-the-counter medicines, always check the dosage and follow the instructions carefully, especially when treating children. Herbal teas are one of the most suitable alternative treatments for children. With stronger infusions and decoctions, it is sensible to work on reaching an adult dose at age 16, so a child of 8 will be given half the dose and one of four, a quarter of the dose; achieve this either by reducing the amount of herb in the preparation per given amount of water, or by reducing the amount of the preparation given. Herbs which stimulate the circulation should be avoided for children because they have a higher metabolic rate than adults. When treating children with essential oils, always dilute them: dilute in a base oil before adding it to a bath and reduce the dosage to a maximum of 4 drops per bath; for massage use lower dilutions – maximum 1 per cent for 12–16 years, ½ per cent for 8–12, ¼ per cent for 4–8 years.

COMMON ILLNESSES

Abdominal pain

This can be caused by indigestion, colic or wind, and antacids or charcoal tablets will help to relieve the symptoms quickly. Anyone suffering from abdominal pain accompanied by diarrhoea, vomiting or fever should be seen by a doctor.

LEFT **It is common to feel concerned about treating very young children, with either alternative or traditional Western medicine. Seek out local clinics for advice on what medicines and treatments are suitable.**

Bad breath

Bad breath may simply be the result of smoking or eating spicy foods, but can also be caused by gum disease. Cleaning teeth regularly and using dental floss will ensure the health of gums and, with the use of antiseptic mouth washes, the problem should disappear. If gums are not the problem, there may be a digestive disorder and you should seek the advice of a doctor.

Chickenpox

In the first few days a slight fever may occur, which can be treated with paracetamol. Try to prevent a child from scratching the spots, as this may lead to infection. A daily bath or shower will prevent the spots from becoming infected, and calamine lotion applied afterwards will help to reduce and relieve the itching.

Colds

Resting as much as possible and taking plenty of fluids will help to clear up a cold quickly. Aspirin or paracetamol will help to reduce the discomfort and lower fever, and medicines containing decongestants will ease congestion.

The herbalists' traditional standby is an infusion of equal amounts of peppermint (*Mentha piperita*), elderflower (*Sambucus nigra*) and yarrow (*Achillea millefolium*). Taken hot just before going to bed, this will induce a sweat, and if the cold is caught early enough, may stop it altogether.

Cold sores

After the initial infection, the virus that causes cold sores lies dormant in nerve cells until, under the right conditions, it re-activates and causes the familiar blistering. The blisters are highly contagious, so avoid touching them as the virus can easily be transferred. Cold-sore creams are available from chemists (drugstores). They should be applied when the symptoms of 'prickling' start, but before blisters appear.

Constipation

Lack of dietary fibre and exercise, and an insufficient fluid intake can cause constipation. Eat plenty of foods containing bran, wholemeal (whole grain) bread, vegetables, pulses and fruits. If the problem persists, it would be advisable to see a doctor.

ALTERNATIVE MEDICINE

The main branches of alternative medicine are: acupuncture, the ancient Chinese practice of inserting needles into the body to restore the balance of 'vital energy', which can be used for a wide range of conditions, including headaches, sprains and even strokes; osteopathy and chiropractic, which involve the manipulation of bones and joints; and homeopathy, which takes into account the patient as a whole rather than just the physical symptom and treats them accordingly. You may wish to try some of the homeopathic remedies, available at many chemists (drugstores) and health food shops, for treating simple complaints at home, but for a full diagnosis of a serious complaint, it is essential to see a qualified homeopathic doctor.

If you do try alternative medicine for treating more serious conditions, let both your orthodox doctor and the alternative practitioner know about each other. Tell each of them what the other has prescribed and about any medicines or treatments you are already having. Make sure you see a fully qualified practitioner before embarking on any new treatments.

F A M I L Y   H E A L T H

Convulsions

Convulsions usually affect small children and are often the result of a high fever. These are known as febrile convulsions, and will only last for a few minutes at a time. Reduce the child's temperature by sponging with tepid water. Once the convulsion has passed, paracetamol elixir will help to reduce the fever. Always call a doctor even when the convulsion has stopped.

Coughs

Numerous cough remedies are available, depending on the type of cough – ask your pharmacist for advice. Whichever treatment you use, if a cough does not improve within a few days, seek professional help, especially for children. Breathing in steamy air can help to loosen phlegm, and inhaling a few drops of eucalyptus oil in a bowl of hot water can have a cleansing effect.

This is an area where herbs are of special benefit; if in doubt get qualified treatment. Choose from one or a mixture of the following, taken as warm infusions. Coltsfoot (*Tussilago farfara*), one of the best cough remedies, particularly for irritating, spasmodic coughs, will soothe, loosen mucus and reduce the spasm. Hyssop (*Hyssopus officinalis*) is a calming and relaxing expectorant for a cough that is associated with restlessness and irritation. For a harsh, dry and painful cough always include marshmallow (*Althea officinalis*) in a mixture, to ease the soreness. Thyme (*Thymus vulgaris*) is powerfully antiseptic and relieves a dry cough linked with a respiratory infection. As an expectorant, white horehound (*Marrubium vulgare*) frees up thick, sticky mucus.

Aromatherapy oils used in a steam inhalation can help a cough do its job more effectively; they can be chosen to soothe the lining of the air passages, fight infection if needed, and loosen

ABOVE Essential oils have an ancient link with water and have been used since classical times.

mucus to make it easier to be removed. Soothing oils include benzoin and lavender; thyme and eucalyptus are antiseptic; and frankincense or marjoram increase expectoration. Choose a blend that you like the smell of.

Diarrhoea

Loose, frequent bowel movements can happen as a short-term reaction to infection, inflammation or food poisoning, and as such are quite a positive, cleansing action. A common experience is holiday diarrhoea, and this is usually a response to exposure to unfamiliar bacteria.

As a herbal treatment if mild food poisoning or infection has upset the bowels, try eating garlic as a natural gut disinfectant. Agrimony (*Agrimonia eupatoria*), astringent and healing to the inflamed and swollen membrane lining the gut, is helpful in mild gastro-enteritis. Chamomile (*Chamomilla recutita*), one of the first herbs for many digestive disorders, is calming and anti-inflammatory, so reduces the impact of tension on the digestive tract. Meadowsweet (*Filipendula ulmaria*) will help to settle an acidic stomach. Ribwort (*Plantago lanceolata*) has excellent toning, soothing and healing properties for use in diarrhoea from many causes where there is

inflammation. Thyme (*Thymus vulgaris*) will fight infections and improve digestion generally, settling churning, loose bowels and killing harmful bacteria.

Massage of the abdomen with antiseptic and relaxing oils like chamomile, lavender and neroli can ease diarrhoea caused by minor upsets and also by anxiety and nervousness. Eucalyptus can be used in the same way if an infection is definitely suspected as the cause. Add fennel or ginger if there are griping pains with the diarrhoea. For all these oils, dilute to 3 per cent in a base oil.

Causes of diarrhoea: Some foods have a laxative effect naturally, for instance prunes or figs, so over-indulgence will give temporary diarrhoea. Stress and anxiety often increase peristalsis and hurry bowel contents through. Repeated diarrhoea may indicate more complex digestive problems and should be treated professionally. Prolonged diarrhoea, especially in young children, can be quite serious as it causes dehydration; ensure adequate fluid intake and seek professional advice. A simple yet dramatically effective rehydration drink can be made by dissolving 5 ml/1 tsp salt and 15 ml/ 1 tbsp sugar in 600 ml/1 pt/2½ cups of boiled water. Keep in the refrigerator in a screw-topped bottle and give small amounts frequently. Use for a short time only.

Earache

This can be the result of a heavy cold, or of an infection of the inner or outer ear causing pain and deafness. Aspirin or paracetamol will help the pain. See a doctor if fluid builds up behind the ear drum, causing it to rupture and the fluid to seep out.

Hot compresses over the ear are the most effective home herbal treatment; chamomile (*Chamomilla recutita*) may be used as an infusion for this purpose.

Taking garlic internally will help to reduce any catarrh and fight infection. If on professional examination the eardrum is not perforated, then crush some garlic into 5 ml/1 tsp of olive oil; this is warmed to blood temperature and a few drops gently inserted into the ear for a local antibiotic.

Two very good essential oils to draw the inflammation outwards as hot compresses are chamomile and lavender; or try a combination of both.

ABOVE The pungency of garlic and other bulbs and fruits, speeds up the metabolism and acts as an antiseptic.

Earache in children
Earaches, especially in children, need to be treated quickly as an infection within the middle ear can be both painful and damaging. Speedy home help can be very useful to avoid these problems, but get medical help if earache worsens or persists.

Eye infections
Conjunctivitis is a common eye infection that results in sticky eyelids and sore, bloodshot eyes. Make up a dilute solution of 1 part bicarbonate of soda (baking soda) to 20 parts of boiled and then cooled water, and use cotton-wool (absorbent cotton) swabs to gently ease the sticky 'glue' from the eyelids. Always use a fresh swab on each eye.

Food poisoning
The sufferer should have plenty of rest and only be given fluids for 24 hours. With an adult, call a doctor if the condition does not improve within this period. Food poisoning can be more serious with children and the elderly, so they should be watched carefully. Call a doctor straight away if a baby or young child is suffering from sickness and diarrhoea.

Hayfever
Hayfever symptoms can be similar to those of a common cold. Antihistamine medicines can be prescribed by your doctor, and air purifiers in the house can help to reduce airborne irritants.

Headaches
A doctor should be seen for long-lasting, acute and recurring headaches, as they could be caused by another ailment. However, a rest in a quiet, and possibly darkened, room, a cold compress on the forehead and an analgesic will be sufficient to deal with most headaches.

Indigestion
This can be caused by eating too large a meal or rich and spicy foods, or by eating in a hurry or just before going to bed. For immediate relief take antacids. Alternatively, 2.5 ml/½ tsp of bicarbonate of soda (baking soda) dissolved in a glass of water will relieve indigestion.

Herbal teas may well sort out indigestion. Choose from the following. Chamomile (*Chamomilla recutita*) relieves the effects of over-eating, and being in a stressed state. Lemon balm (*Melissa officinalis*) settles a churning stomach due to nervous indigestion, whether related to meals or not. Meadowsweet (*Filipendula ulmaria*) is good for acid indigestion, especially if accompanied by some looseness in the bowels. Peppermint (*Mentha piperita*) is good for indigestion coupled with flatulence and bloated abdomen, or even nausea. Also think of taking slippery elm (*Ulmus fulva*) if indigestion pains are persistent, either 5 ml/1 tsp of the powder thoroughly blended in a cupful of water, or the pure tablets, with one or more meals, to soothe the stomach.

A warm compress of some essential oils, including chamomile or lavender, may give some relief. For mild indigestion, try gently massaging a 2 per cent dilution of either of these into the abdomen.

Influenza
The symptoms of influenza often include fever, aching muscles, nausea, headaches, a cough, a sore throat and a running nose. A doctor may prescribe antibiotics to prevent a secondary infection from causing additional problems. Otherwise, rest in bed, plenty of fluids and an analgesic taken every 4 hours should help.

Note: the first symptoms of meningitis can be similar to those of influenza. If the symptoms shown are accompanied by vomiting, a stiff and sore neck and joints, a skin rash, bruising or some patchiness of the skin and an aversion to bright lights, call a doctor at once.

Insomnia
Irregular working hours, depression, stress or being in an unfamiliar room can lead to sleeplessness. A doctor can prescribe drugs to help, but try to restrict their use as it is easy to become dependent on them.

A milky drink before going to bed can be relaxing – avoid alcohol and stimulants, such as coffee and tea, as these will all only exacerbate the problem. A walk during the day in fresh air and a warm bath before going to bed may also help.

Measles

All children should be immunized against measles, but can suffer from the disease before then if they come into contact with an infected person. A blocked nose, fever and conjunctivitis are the first symptoms, followed a few days later by a red, blotchy rash spreading from the head downwards. Call your doctor to see whether the child should be examined. Otherwise, give plenty of fluids and paracetamol elixir to reduce the fever.

Mumps

This is a viral infection of the parotid glands, which are situated just in front of and below the ear. Discomfort and fever can be reduced by giving either paracetamol or aspirin, or paracetamol elixir to young children. The virus is usually infectious for up to 6 days before the swelling appears, and for 10 days after the onset of the swelling. Adult men can suffer from swollen testes and should visit a doctor.

Nausea and vomiting

The remedy of first choice is probably ginger (*Zingiber officinalis*); either take frequent sips of a weak tea, or 10 drops of tincture in a little water, or chew a small piece of fresh ginger. Another possibility, say, for travel sickness, is to chew a little crystallized ginger, or drink flat ginger ale. Other potentially useful herbs to settle the stomach are chamomile (*Chamomilla recutita*), lemon balm (*Melissa officinalis*) and peppermint (*Mentha piperita*); try weakish herb teas. All these herbs aid digestion, so can help to sort out the causes of nausea as well as the symptoms themselves.

Causes of nausea: Nausea or vomiting can usually be linked to a specific situation – eating too much rich food, or drinking too much alcohol, anxiety or travel are common triggers. Continual feelings of nausea indicate a greater disturbance; again this may be obvious as in morning sickness of pregnancy. Where the cause is not obvious, and if symptoms are not quickly cleared up with self-help, get medical advice as soon as possible. Children in particular can easily become dehydrated.

Occupational hazards

Many occupations involve excessive use of the voice, e.g. teaching, and sore throats are commonplace. The regular use of herbal gargles can ease this discomfort, and help to prevent loss of voice or an actual infection. Keep the throat moist by drinking liquids.

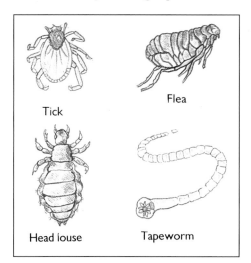

Tick

Flea

Head louse

Tapeworm

Parasites

At one time or another, most children and some adults suffer from parasites.

Fleas: these are usually passed on to their host by cats, birds or other pets, or in infected bedding, carpets or upholstery. Treat animals with a veterinary insecticide. Where flea bites have occurred on your skin, use an antiseptic wash to prevent infection. Spray throughout the house with a flea killer and vacuum thoroughly.

Head lice: these are tiny brown insects with 6 legs. They feed on blood and lay eggs (known as nits) which are attached to the base of the hair shaft. They are usually found behind the ears and cause irritation. If head lice are detected, the whole family should be treated with insecticidal shampoo.

Tapeworm: eggs can be seen in faeces. Consult your doctor, who will prescribe a suitable medicine.

Threadworms: live in the lower bowel and lay eggs around the anus, causing itchiness. The eggs are minute, but occasionally a fine, thread-like worm may be seen around the anus or on bedding. A doctor will prescribe a suitable medicine to eradicate them.

Ticks: these live in long grass and will latch on to humans and animals to suck blood. Remove with tweezers, using a rocking motion to release them then wipe the area with an antiseptic.

Sore throats

With increased airborne pollution, smoky, dry atmospheres in air-conditioned buildings and so on, sore throats are more and more common. The irritation can range from an annoying tickle to a rasping soreness, and may be linked to other infections. Where the throat inflammation, or pharyngitis, also extends down to the larynx, the voice may be affected.

If possible, use the following herbs as tinctures for gargling; if unavailable then use cooled infusions: agrimony (*Agrimonia eupatoria*), sage (*Salvia officinalis*) and thyme (*Thymus vulgaris*) are all astringent, toning up the membranes, the latter two also being quite antiseptic. For a more powerful effect try using a tincture of myrrh (*Commiphora molmol*), together with one or more of the others. If making infusions, add two liquorice sticks to give a more soothing effect, or else use marshmallow (*Althea officinalis*) leaf in equal amounts with the other herb(s).

With essential oils such as benzoin or thyme, use steam inhalations. One drop only of essential oil of lemon on 2.5 ml/½ tsp of honey acts as a local antiseptic, as well as being soothing.

USING HERBS AND OILS

Making a tincture

A tincture is an extract of a herb in a mixture of alcohol and water, normally 25 per cent alcohol. The alcohol used commercially is ethyl alcohol, but a spirit such as brandy or vodka can be used for home tinctures. As tinctures are concentrated extracts, use them only as recommended and for a short time; do not give tinctures to children. Standard quantities are 200 g/7 oz dried herbs or 40 g /1½ oz fresh herb to 1 litre/1¾ pint/4 cups 25 per cent alcohol/water mixture. The standard dose is up to 5 ml/1 tsp, to be taken three times a day.

Making an infusion

An infusion, or herbal tea, is made by pouring boiling water over the herb to extract the properties. It is suitable for leaves and flowers, whose parts are easily extracted. Standard quantities are 25 g/1 oz dried herb or 50 g/2 oz fresh herb to 500 ml/16 fl oz/2 cups. The standard dose is 100–150 ml/ 4–5 fl oz/½–⅔ cup three times a day.

Compresses

A compress is a way of applying herbal extracts directly to the skin, to reduce the inflammation or promote healing. Usually, an infusion of a herb is prepared for use in the compress, or simply hot or cold water can be used.

Mixing essential oils for massage

When preparing essential oils for aromatherapy massage, different oils, such as sweet almond, grapeseed, sunflower or safflower, are combined to increase their therapeutic effect. For home use the general dilution rate should be 1 per cent (i.e. a maximum of 20 drops per 100 ml/4 fl oz/½ cup of base oil). Use only utensils that are clean and dry. Leave the lids on the bottles of the essential oils until required. Keep the mixed oils in a cool, dark place.

PREPARING A TINCTURE

1 Put the herb into a large jar and pour on the alcohol/water mixture. Seal the jar and store in a cool place for two weeks. Shake the jar occasionally.

2 Pour the mixture through a jelly (cheesecloth) bag into a clean jug (pitcher). Squeeze out the tincture from the bag. Pour the strained liquid into clean, dark bottles. Seal and store. Label and keep in a cool dry place.

PREPARING INFUSIONS

1 Place the herb in a teapot with a close-fitting lid. Pour in boiling water and leave to infuse for up to 10 minutes.

2 Strain the liquid through a sieve or strainer into a cup. Store the remainder in the refrigerator, in a tightly stoppered container, for up to three days.

USING A COMPRESS

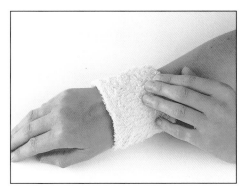

1 Soak a clean cloth or flannel in a hot infusion or hot water then lightly wring it out. Place the cloth on the affected area and hold it firmly in place.

USING ESSENTIAL OILS

2 Put 10 ml/2 tsp of your chosen vegetable base oil in a blending bowl. Add the essential oil, one drop at a time. Use a clean, dry toothpick to blend the oils.

EMERGENCIES AND FIRST AID

Increasing knowledge and advances in medicine constantly update first-aid techniques in the event of an emergency, but the emphasis remains on the prompt and proper care of the casualty by helping to alleviate pain and suffering. Whether first aid involves being able to deal with a suspected broken leg or stopping a nose bleed, it is vital to know the right steps to take in order to prevent further complications and to reassure the casualty that they are in good hands.

Learning basic first-aid techniques is straightforward and is something that everyone should do. Knowing how to act in some emergency situations may well make the difference between life and death.

Animal bites and scratches

All animals carry germs in their mouths and on their claws. When these penetrate the skin, the germs will be left in the muscle tissues and may cause infection if not cleaned thoroughly.

Hold the wound under warm running water and wash the affected area with soap for at least 5 minutes to remove any saliva or dirt particles. Gently pat the area dry, then wipe the wound with a mild antiseptic solution before covering it with a sticking plaster or sterile dressing. A serious wound should always be referred to hospital.

Broken bones

Always treat any doubtful cases of injured bones as if they were broken in order to prevent additional internal injuries. Do not attempt to move the casualty until the injured part is secured and supported, unless he is in danger. If the broken limb is an arm, it may then be reasonable to take the casualty to hospital by car, otherwise call for an ambulance immediately. Do not give the casualty anything to eat or drink, as surgery may be required if bones are badly broken.

TREATING A BROKEN LEG

1 Ensure that the casualty remains still, and support the leg above and below the injury with your hands. Move the uninjured leg against it and place padding between the knees, ankles and hollows.

2 Using a scarf, tie or cloth, tie the feet together in a figure-of-8 to secure them, and tie on the outer edge of the foot on the uninjured leg.

3 Immobilize the joints by tying both knees and ankles together. Tie additional bandages above and below the injured area.

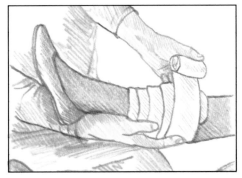

4 Should the bone protrude through the skin, cover the wound with a sterile dressing or clean pad, and apply pressure to control the bleeding. Use a bandage to secure the pad and immobilize the limb.

TREATING A BROKEN ARM

1 Sit the casualty in a chair and carefully place the injured arm across his chest in the position that is most comfortable. Ask him to support the arm or place a cushion underneath it to take the weight.

2 Use a shawl or piece of sheeting (approximately 1 sq m/1 sq yd in size) and fold it diagonally into a triangle. Slide this under the injured arm and secure by tying the ends by the collarbone on the injured side. Strap the arm to the body using a wide piece of fabric and tie as shown.

Burns and scalds

Immediately douse the burned or scalded area in cold running water. Gently try to remove any jewellery or constricting clothing from near the burn before it starts to swell. Keep the affected part in cold water for at least 10 minutes, then place a clean dressing over the burn and gently bandage it. Any injury larger than 2.5 cm/1 in will require treatment at hospital.

TREATING BURNS

- Never break blisters.
- Never use a sticking plaster.
- Never apply butter, lotions or ointment to the affected area.

Choking

Remove any food or false teeth from the mouth, but never attempt to locate the obstruction by putting your fingers down the casualty's throat, as this can push the obstruction further in.

If the casualty becomes unconscious this may relieve muscle spasm, so check to see whether he has begun to breathe. If not, turn him on his side and give 4 blows between the shoulder blades. Should this fail, place one hand above the other just below the ribcage and perform abdominal thrusts. If the casualty still does not start to breathe, call immediately for an ambulance and give the kiss of life (see next page).

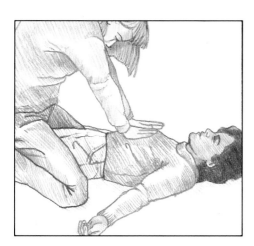

ABOVE **If a choking casualty becomes unconscious, kneel astride him and, placing one hand above the other, perform abdominal thrusts.**

DEALING WITH A CHOKING PERSON

1 Bend the casualty forward so that the head is lower than the chest, and encourage him to cough. If this does not dislodge the object, sharply slap him up to 5 times between the shoulder blades using the flat of your hand.

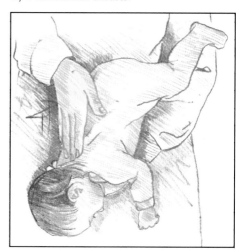

2 If this fails, stand behind him and grip your hands together just below the rib cage. Pull sharply inwards and upwards from your elbows to deliver up to 5 abdominal thrusts. This action causes the diaphragm to compress the chest and should force out the obstruction. If the blockage still remains, repeat the process of 5 back slaps followed by 5 abdominal thrusts.

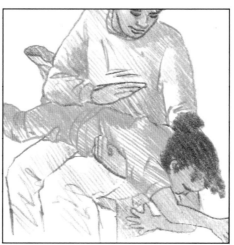

3 If a child is choking, place him across your knees with the head down. Holding him securely, slap smartly between the shoulder blades (using less force than that required for an adult) to dislodge the object. If the child continues to choke, sit him on your knees and, using just one clenched hand, perform gentle abdominal thrusts to avoid causing injury.

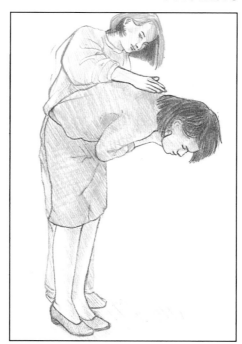

4 If a baby or toddler is choking, lay him along your forearm with the head down, using your hand to support the head. Use your fingers to slap the baby smartly between the shoulder blades, but remember to use less force than you would for an older child.

If the baby fails to start breathing, turn him over on to his back so that the head is tilted down. Using only 2 fingers, apply up to 4 abdominal thrusts just above the navel by pressing quickly forwards towards the area of the chest.

FAMILY HEALTH

EMERGENCIES AND FIRST AID (continued)

Drowning

When carrying a drowning casualty, the head should be lower than the rest of the body to avoid inhalation of swallowed water. Lie him down on a blanket or towel. Turn the head to one side to allow water to drain from the mouth. If the casualty stops breathing, brain damage can occur in less than 5 minutes. It is vital to ensure that oxygen reaches the brain, and the kiss of life puts air into the lungs until they are able to breathe again by themselves.

Electric shocks

It is vital not to put yourself at the risk of an electric shock as well when dealing with a casualty. Immediately switch off the source of power at the mains. If you are unable to do so, stand on any good insulating material such as a thick book, a rubber mat or a pile of newspapers before attempting to help the casualty.

Use a wooden broom handle, walking stick or chair to push the casualty away from the source of electricity. Otherwise, without touching the casualty, a scarf or rope looped around their arms or feet can drag them clear. Once the victim is free from the electric current, place him in the recovery position or, if unconscious be prepared to resuscitate (see right). Treat any burns.

DEALING WITH ELECTRIC SHOCKS

- Do not touch the casualty until you are sure that the electric current has been switched off.
- Never use a damp or wet towel or a metal object to free the casualty, even when the power has been turned off.

GIVING THE KISS OF LIFE

1 First turn the head sideways and remove any obstruction from the mouth.

2 Placing 1 hand on the forehead and the other under the chin, tilt the head back to open the airway.

3 Close the nose by pinching the nostrils together. Take a full breath and, placing your lips over the casualty's mouth, blow firmly into the mouth until you see the chest rising. (With a small child or baby, cover both the mouth and nose with your mouth.) Remove your lips to allow the air to be exhaled and the chest to fall fully. Repeat the sequence at the rate of 15–16 breaths per minute (for a small child or baby, take quicker and more shallow breaths to avoid injuring the lungs).

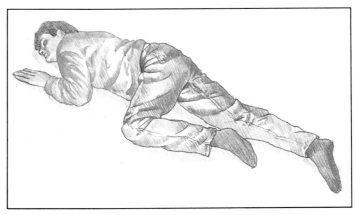

4 When breathing begins, place the casualty in the 'recovery' position. Tilt the head back to open the airway, adjust the uppermost arm so that the hand supports the head and bend the uppermost knee so that it is at right-angles to the hip.

Eye injuries

Do not attempt to remove any foreign body that is sticking to or into the eyeball. Cover the eye with a sterile pad, bandage both eyes to prevent them from moving and seek hospital treatment immediately.

Wash out any grit, dust or other small particles. Ask the casualty to tilt his head to the injured side, and rest a towel on his shoulder. Using your finger and thumb, hold the eyelid open and gently wash out the particles using a glass of clean, warm water.

Heart massage

When the heart stops beating, artificial circulation is vital in order to maintain a supply of oxygen to the brain. To enable this, heart massage needs to be administered intermittently with the kiss of life (see left) so that oxygen in the lungs can pass into the blood.

Insect stings

Remove a sting that is left in the skin by carefully pulling it out, using a pair of tweezers. Rinse the area under cold running water. Wine or vinegar can reduce the swelling caused by a sting from a jellyfish or sea anemone, but seek medical advice if the pain does not subside after a few hours.

Nose bleeds

Help the casualty to sit down so that his head is well forward. Ask him to pinch his nose just below the bridge and to breathe through his mouth. After 10 minutes the pressure can be released

FIRST-AID BOX

Always keep the following items of first-aid equipment in a clean container where you can find them in a hurry.
● Sticking plasters – either a box of assorted sizes or a strip that can be cut to the correct size.
● Crêpe bandages for bandaging wounds in awkward places, such as elbows, and to bind sprains.
● Sterile dressings in various sizes.
● Blunt-ended scissors for cutting bandages and dressings to size.
● Sterile cotton wool (absorbent cotton) for cleaning cuts and grazes.
● Antiseptic wipes and cream for cuts and grazes.
● Pain killers – keep paracetamol and aspirin that are suitable for both children and adults.
● Tweezers for removing insect stings or splinters.
● Antihistamine cream for treating insect bites and stings.
● Triangular bandage to make a sling.
● Safety pins to hold bandages or a sling in place.

GIVING HEART MASSAGE

Lie the casualty flat on his back and kneel at his side. Find his lowest rib and follow it up until it meets the base of the breastbone. Approximately 2–3 cm/ ¾–1¼ in above this point is where the pressure must be applied.
● Interlocking your fingers, place the heel of your lower hand just above the base of the breastbone. Keeping your elbows straight, press down on the heels of your hands to depress the breastbone by 4–5 cm/1½–2 in. Release the pressure without removing your hands.
● Repeat at around 80 compressions per minute.

but, if the nose is still bleeding, re-apply the pressure for a further 10 minutes. Once the bleeding has subsided, gently swab around the nose and mouth with warm water.

Puncture wounds

Any object that pierces the skin, such as a nail or a metal spoke, may not create a large entry wound but will cause damage deep in the tissues where infection can start. Occasionally, an unseen piece of an object may remain embedded, so ensure that the casualty is taken to hospital.

Start by stemming the flow of blood by applying pressure around the wound. If the bleeding is severe, raise the injured part above the level of the heart to slow the rate of flow, then cover with a sterile dressing and bandage.

Severe open wounds and cuts

The first priority with a wound of this kind is to control the bleeding, and also to prevent shock and infection before the casualty is taken to hospital. Ask someone to call for an ambulance immediately. Ideally, wear disposable gloves or protect yourself by ensuring that any sores or cuts are covered with a waterproof dressing.

Hold a sterile dressing or clean pad over the wound and apply direct pressure to the wound with your fingers. If there is an object such as glass or metal protruding, squeeze the edges of the wound around the object. Keep the injured part raised, as this will help to

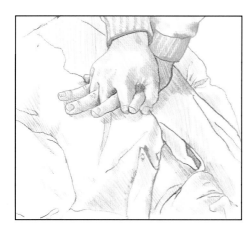

reduce the blood flow and minimize shock. Continue to apply pressure to the wound for at least 10 minutes to allow time for the blood to clot. If the dressing or pad becomes soaked with blood, place a fresh one over it – never remove the original dressing, as this will re-open the wound.

Sprain, strain and bruise injuries

A sprain or strain will cause swelling of the injured area, but raising the part and applying cold compresses or a bag of ice wrapped in a cloth will ease it. Wrap the area in thick padding, then bandage it firmly before resting it in a slightly raised position.

Bruising may take time to develop and often requires little more than a cold compress to relieve the pain. Severe bruising that develops quickly may indicate a deeper injury such as a fracture, in which case the casualty should seek medical advice.

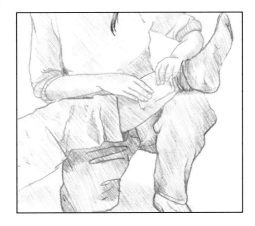

ABOVE Treat a puncture wound by raising the injured part above the level of the heart.

FAMILY HEALTH

PET SAFETY

Pets can give a lot of pleasure. They make good companions for all ages and are an excellent way for children to learn about responsibility and caring for others. Being a deterrent to burglars and an intruder alarm, a family dog also helps to safeguard the home.

Keeping pets involves a lot of responsibility, however, and they can cause accidents and spread disease if not properly looked after. Make sure you know how to care for any animal you own and that whichever member of the family takes on the routine tasks will have enough time and commitment to do the job properly. Bear these points in mind when deciding what sort of pet to bring into the home.

Living with dogs

Dogs interact with humans so well that they soon become a member of the household, demanding their equal share of company and attention to keep them happy and well behaved. As dogs can live for ten to 15 years or even more, owning one is a long-term commitment. Feeds need to be regular, as does exercise. Grooming is necessary to keep the dog's skin and coat in good condition, and to minimize the amount of hair shed in the house, and with long-haired varieties, this can over time become more of a chore than a pleasure. Dogs bring dirt and dust into the house, so increasing the amount of housework around them.

Choose the breed carefully to suit your family situation; dogs are bred for certain characteristics and different types can require much more exercise and feeding than others. Most dogs do not like to be left alone for long periods, and some can become destructive in the home. Check on the dog's likely temperament and if you are buying a puppy try to see both parents.

Training is another important aspect in a dog's life. Dogs must always be kept under control and well behaved, especially in public. An uncontrollable dog is a potential danger in the home and on the street. If you have any difficulty with training your dog, seek out a training group, where your dog can learn to socialize with other canines and learn to respond to your commands.

Keeping cats

Cats are much more independent than dogs, and require less care and attention. They groom themselves, unless they are long-haired, and often spend a lot of their time on their own. However, when they do want attention, or a nice warm lap to snuggle into, they can be very affectionate and rewarding as pets. They will even play with you, but on their terms and only when they feel like it.

It is wise to get a male cat neutered and a female cat spayed. Males grow into rangy beasts which take to fighting and spraying your property as they mark out their own territory. Females can, and most probably will, start to reproduce at six months of age and can produce two litters a year. Finding good homes for the kittens can become a regular headache. Talk to your local vet about the best time to spay and neuter your pet, if unsure.

Small rodents

Mice, hamsters, guinea pigs and rabbits all have their particular charms. They are generally relatively short-lived, although some rabbits do go on for many years. Although they are much cheaper to keep than either dogs or cats, they all need to be contained in cages, preferably with areas or runs large enough for them to exercise in. Hamsters particularly like toys and wheels to play with and guinea pigs and rabbits benefit from being allowed to run out of doors. Cages should be cleaned weekly.

BELOW **Many children are wonderfully at ease with pets, but it is a good idea to show them how to hold and handle animals safely.**

Cats need access to outdoors or a litter tray in the home. This needs to be kept well away from any food-preparation areas and cleaned on a daily basis. Women who are pregnant, or who could be pregnant, should not handle the contents of a soiled cat litter tray as there is a slight risk of their contracting toxoplasmosis, which is caused by a organism found in cat faeces and can be harmful to the foetus.

House pets may also introduce fleas and the occasional tick, which need to be got rid of as soon as they are discovered. Cats and dogs can be dusted with flea powder, but make sure you attend to bedding as well, as this is where the larvae are likely lurk. Alternatively, fleas can be controlled by fitting a collar impregnated with insecticide. These are safe to use and last for several months.

ABOVE Some rabbits can live for years if looked after properly, with a clean cage and enough room to exercise in. They make charming pets for young children.

Birds

Different sizes of bird, from canaries to parrots, can be kept as pets. They need to be kept in cages or aviaries large enough for the bird to move around and exercise its wings in. Birds need fresh water and seed daily, as well as cuttlefish for trimming their beaks and claws. Keep cages fresh through regular cleaning.

Hygiene

With any animal living in the home or garden, hygiene is all important, both for the animal and human members of the family. Animal food and drinking bowls must be kept clean. Bedding, too must be changed regularly to keep it clean. With cats and dogs, this will involve washing beds.

Human hands always need to be washed after handling animals, especially before preparing or eating food. Children should be discouraged from putting their hands in their mouths when playing with pets or allowing dogs and cats to lick their faces. Dogs and cats should not be allowed to sleep with their owners.

Regular worming programmes are essential for both cats and dogs, as they can regularly pick up roundworms and tapeworms. Tapeworms can be passed on to humans and, rarely, the larval form of the roundworm most common in puppies (Toxocara) can invade humans, especially children, and cause blindness. But where common sense and good hygiene are practised the danger is negligible. Your vet will advise you on good worming practice.

With increased awareness about dog-fouling of public areas, be prepared to 'poop-scoop' after your dog. If you encourage your pet to relieve itself in your garden (yard), train it to use one particular area which you can easily clear up on a daily basis. Consider installing a cheap sanitary disposal unit designed for this purpose; ask your pet shop or garden centre.

CHILDREN AND ANIMALS

Teach children to respect animals and to avoid annoying them. Stroking fur the wrong way or blowing on it, for example, can hurt and cause an animal to snap or bite. Pulling ears or tails is also dangerous. Nor should children interfere with an animal that is eating, chewing a bone or asleep, especially a dog or cat. Children also need to be taught that while their own pet may be very friendly, strange animals in the street may be less so, and even aggressive.

PERFECT HOME SKILLS

Creating the right ambience at home is a question of adding a personal touch. Home-made curtains and drapes, cushion covers and bed linen can have dramatic impacts. Hints on how to set the mood when you're entertaining, whether it's an intimate dinner party or a huge birthday celebration, are accompanied by innovative tips on decorating tables and arranging flowers. Houseplant and floral displays provide the finishing touches.

SOFT FURNISHINGS

Most items of soft furnishing are expensive to buy ready-made but they can be made just as successfully at home and much more cheaply. Curtains and drapes, cushion covers, bed linen and table linen require the minimum of sewing skills and little equipment beyond a sewing machine and an iron.

The choice of fabric plays a major part in setting the style of a room, creating accents of colour to enliven a neutral décor or providing a means of co-ordinating different elements effectively in a room. Colour is an important consideration when furnishing a room – light shades tend to open it out, while dark and vivid shades tend to enclose it. Many people tend to play safe by choosing neutral or pastel shades which, although easy to live with, can look rather boring and impersonal.

Making soft furnishings at home is the perfect way to experiment with colour and make a visual statement. Most items require a few metres (yards) of fabric at the most. A good point to bear in mind when selecting fabric is that there are no hard-and-fast rules, apart from trying not to mix too many different colours and patterns in one setting. Most good stores will supply swatches of furnishing fabrics without charge for colour matching at home.

Another consideration is that the chosen fabric should be suitable for the intended purpose – for example, heavyweight cloths will make up into good curtains and cushion covers but will be too stiff to make a successful tablecloth or bed valance. Many of these details are primarily common sense but, when in doubt, be guided by the sales assistant's specialist knowledge.

This section contains information about the types of fabric and curtain-heading tapes, tools and equipment required as well as comprehensive step-by-step instructions showing how to make a variety of soft furnishings from lined curtains to tablemats. When making any of the projects in this section, read through the instructions carefully before starting, especially those which refer to calculating the amount of fabric required. Finally, make sure that each stage is clearly understood before starting to cut out the fabric.

OPPOSITE Soft furnishings in stunning fabric designs can transform a room. Curtains and drapes, tie-backs, piped and frilled scatter cushions and stylish box cushions for benches and window seats are just some of the projects featured in this section.

SOFT-FURNISHING FABRICS

Most ready-made items of soft furnishing are expensive, but you can make them just as well at home and much more cheaply. Curtains and drapes, blinds and shades, cushion covers and bed linen require the minimum of sewing skills and little in the way of equipment beyond a sewing machine and an iron.

The choice of fabric plays a major part in setting the style of a room, creating accents of colour to enliven a neutral décor or co-ordinating different elements. Colour is an important consideration when furnishing a room – light shades will tend to open it out, while dark and vivid shades will generally close it up. Many people play safe by choosing neutral shades which, although easy to live with, can look rather dull and impersonal.

The ideal colour scheme is usually a basically harmonious one, with interest added by the judicious use of contrasting or complementary colours for some elements of the design. Soft furnishings, such as cushions or blinds and shades, chosen in fabrics to contrast with the overall colour scheme, can add just the right amount of colour to brighten up a room.

Making soft furnishings at home is the perfect way to experiment with colour and make a visual statement. Most items require a few metres (yards) of fabric at the most. A good point to bear in mind when selecting fabric is that there are no hard-and-fast rules, apart from trying not to mix too many different colours and patterns in one setting. Most good stores will supply swatches of furnishing fabrics without charge for colour matching at home.

Another consideration is that the chosen fabric should be suitable for the intended purpose – for example, heavyweight cloths will make up into good curtains and cushion covers, but will be too stiff and unyielding to make a successful bed valance.

Cotton is the fabric most commonly used for soft furnishings, often with small amounts of synthetic fibres added for strength and to improve crease resistance. Linen is extremely strong, although expensive and inclined to crease badly; the addition of both cotton for economy and synthetics to help prevent creasing is usual. Both cotton and linen shrink when laundered, and you should take this into account when estimating the amounts that you require. Some furnishing fabrics are pre-shrunk during manufacture, and you should also always check this when purchasing.

Man-made fibres have different properties, depending on their composition, but the majority resist creases and shrinking. Their most common use for soft furnishings, apart from being added to cotton and linen blends, is for making easy-care nets and sheer curtains (drapes) which are lightweight and launder well.

ABOVE Neutral tones – beiges, creams and browns – used both for the soft furnishings and for the wall and ceiling decoration create a colour scheme that is attractive and restful on the eye in this living room.

BELOW Nothing succeeds in creating a feeling of cosiness as well as a red/pink colour scheme for soft furnishings – here complemented by the warm red wall covering.

Fabrics suitable for making soft furnishings are as follows:

Brocade: cotton, cotton/synthetic blend or acetate with a woven self-pattern created by areas of different weaves. Used for making formal curtains and drapes and cushion covers.

Calico: inexpensive, medium-weight woven cotton, either dyed or printed, or sold unbleached. Used for curtains and blinds (shades), in particular.

Chintz: glazed, medium-weight furnishing cotton, traditionally printed with patterns of roses and other flowers, birds and animals.

Gingham: inexpensive checked fabric woven from cotton or cotton/polyester blends. Often used for making soft furnishings for kitchens.

Hand-woven fabric: heavyweight or medium-weight cotton with an irregular, rather rough weave. Used for curtains and drapes, cushion covers and bedspreads.

Linen union: hardwearing, heavyweight fabric made from linen with some added cotton, often printed with floral designs. Suitable for curtains and covering upholstery.

Madras: hand-woven pure cotton originating from Madras in India. Usually dyed in brilliant colours, often with a woven pattern of checks, plaids and stripes.

Poplin: a lightweight or medium-weight cotton, either plain or printed.

Sateen: cotton or cotton/synthetic fabric with a slight sheen. Curtain lining is usually made of lightweight cotton sateen.

Sheeting: extra-wide fabric for making bed linen. Usually woven from a mixture of 50 per cent cotton and 50 per cent polyester or other man-made fibre, making it easy-care.

Ticking: heavy woven cloth with narrow stripes. Originally used for covering pillows, mattresses and bolsters, but today used as a decorative fabric in its own right.

Velvet: heavy fabric made from cotton or cotton/synthetic blends with a cut pile, used for formal curtains and cushion covers. Corduroy (needlecord) is similar, but here the cut pile forms regular ridges down the cloth.

Voile: light, semi-transparent cotton or synthetic fabric. Used for sheer curtains and bed drapes.

ABOVE Luxurious fabrics used for curtains or drapes, cushions and upholstery are often the ideal medium for adding patterned elements to a room's décor.

BELOW Blues and greens are naturally cool, receding colours, ideal for well-lit south-facing rooms, but can be warmed by splashes of contrast in orange and yellow.

ABOVE Bright, cheerful soft-furnishing fabrics make an excellent foil to a plain floor covering.

TOOLS AND EQUIPMENT FOR SOFT FURNISHINGS

The most expensive piece of equipment needed for making soft furnishings is a sewing machine. Although a modern swing-needle machine is preferable because of its zigzag stitching, an ordinary straight stitch machine, either hand or electric, is perfectly adequate. Always work a small piece of practice stitching on a fabric sample before starting a project, adjusting the stitch length and tension as necessary. Fit a new needle whenever necessary;

machine needles become blunt very quickly, especially when sewing on synthetic blends, and a blunt needle can cause uneven stitches and puckering. Have the machine serviced by a professional repairer at regular intervals and put it away after each sewing session to prevent it from becoming covered with dust.

A steam iron is also essential. Choose a fairly heavyweight one and keep the sole plate spotlessly clean at

all times. Fill the iron with distilled water (available from a pharmacy or motor accessory shop) when using the steam facility to avoid limescale forming inside the water reservoir and clogging the steam jets. A sturdy ironing board with a well-padded surface or slip-on cover is also needed.

Sewing needles come in various shapes and sizes; choose a type of needle which feels comfortable when stitching. As a general guide, *betweens*

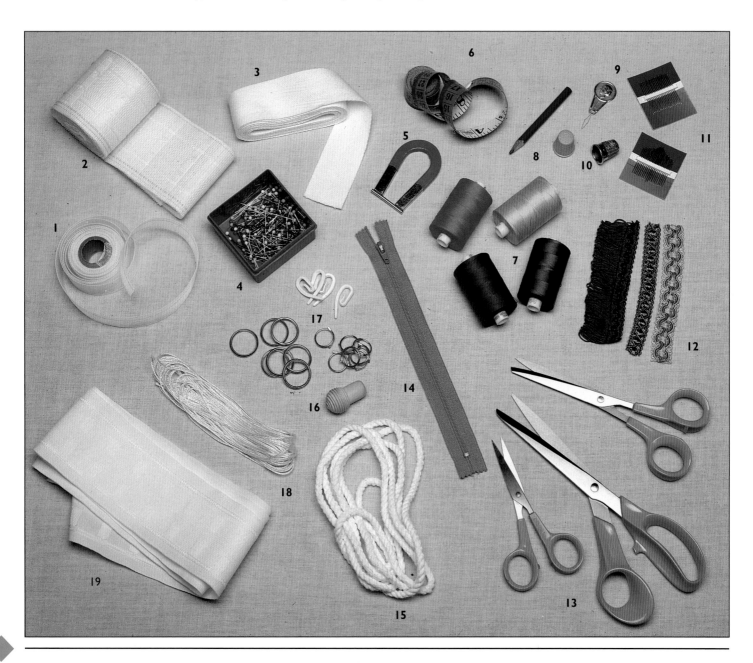

RIGHT Choose fabrics from a wide range of plain, woven and printed patterns, accessorizing with ribbons, cords and braid in complementary or contrasting colours.

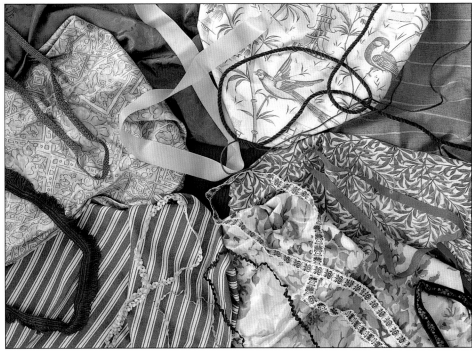

are short needles, *sharps* are slightly longer and used when tacking (basting) or gathering, *straws* or *milliner's needles* are very long and useful when sewing through several layers of fabric.

STORING EQUIPMENT

Try to keep the necessary equipment in good order, clean and tidily stored so it is always easy to find immediately. A plastic tool box with divided trays is useful for this purpose.

Fabric, threads and trimmings should be stored in a cool, dust-free place. Keep offcuts of fabric in self-seal plastic bags with the appropriate threads and label the bags with the date and the name of the project. This is useful in case the stitching needs to be repaired or a patch needs to be added to conceal a damaged area.

TOOLS AND EQUIPMENT

OPPOSITE This selection of useful sewing aids includes: looped vertical tape for Austrian and Roman blinds (shades) (1), curtain (drapery) heading tape (2 & 19), woven curtain tape (3), pins (4), magnet (5), tape measure (6), sewing threads (7), dressmaker's pencil (8), needle threader (9), thimbles (10), sewing needles (11), furnishing braid and fringe (12), three sizes of scissors (13), zip fastener (14), piping cord (15), toggle for blind or curtain pull cords (16), curtain rings and hooks (17) and blind cord (18).

There are different types of needle threader available and these can be helpful when using fine, hard-to-thread needles. Whether or not a thimble is used when hand sewing is largely a matter of personal preference, but using one will protect the fingers.

Glass-headed pins are easy to see and handle. If the ordinary type of pin is preferred, choose a brand which is stainless and rustproof to avoid marking the fabric. Store pins in a dry place. A small horseshoe magnet is useful to retrieve pins and needles from the floor after a sewing session.

There are several types of sewing threads for both hand and machine use. Use mercerized cotton thread when sewing pure cotton and linen; core-spun thread (thread with a coating of cotton around a polyester core) for general purpose stitching; spun polyester thread on synthetic fabrics. Use tacking thread for tacking in preference to sewing thread as it breaks easily and tacking can be removed without damaging the fabric.

Good quality scissors are a real investment as they will cut accurately and stay sharp longer than cheaper ones. Drop-forged scissors are heavy, but the blades can be sharpened repeatedly over many years while the

lightweight type with plastic handles are very comfortable to use. Buy a large pair with 28 cm/11 in blades for cutting out fabric, a medium-sized pair with 10 to 12.5 cm/4 to 5 in blades for trimming seams and cutting small pieces of fabric and a small pair of needlework scissors for unpicking or snipping thread ends.

Choose a fibreglass tape measure as fabric and plastic tape measures will eventually stretch and become inaccurate. A wooden metre ruler or yard stick is also useful. A dressmaker's pencil is more convenient for marking fabric than tailor's chalk as it can be sharpened to a fine point. Choose white or yellow for marking dark fabrics and blue for light ones.

NOTE

The metric and imperial measurements quoted in the following projects are not exact equivalents. Always follow just one set of measures, either centimetres or inches, to ensure perfect results. Note also that contrasting thread has been used for the stitching for clarity only; it is normal to match the colour of the thread with the dominant shade of the furnishing fabric.

SEWING BY HAND

In the days before sewing machines, every garment, curtain or soft furnishing item was sewn by hand. It seems miraculous now that so much was achieved, often in poor light. Sewing machines have, without doubt, taken the drudgery out of sewing, but they cannot entirely replace hand sewing. This process should not be hurried as the quality of your stitches will affect the finished appearance.

GETTING STARTED

Hand-sewing stitches are normally worked using thread that closely matches the fabric. Work in good light either close to a window or with an angled lamp. Use a short length of thread, and a short, fine needle to suit the fabric you are using. Use a length of thread no longer than the distance between your elbow and wrist. Cut the thread at an angle to make it easier to feed through the eye of the needle. Pull the cut end through to about three-quarters of its length.

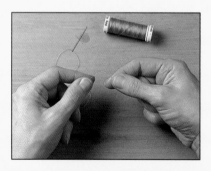

Wind the end of the thread around your forefinger about 13 mm/½ in from the tip and hold it in place with your thumb. Rub your finger down your thumb until the threads form a twisted loop. Slide your finger and thumb down the thread to tighten the loop and form a small knot. Take the first stitch on the wrong side of the fabric. Use a small double backstitch on fine or see-through fabric where a knot would show.

TYPES OF STITCHES

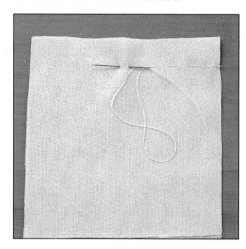

1 Running stitch: This basic stitch is used for gathering, smocking and quilting. Make several small even stitches at a time, weaving the needle in and out of the fabric at regular intervals. The spaces should be the same size as the stitches. Use longer stitches for gathering and leave the thread end loose for pulling up.

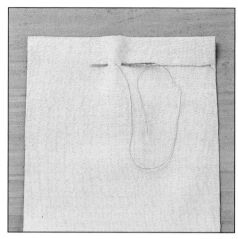

2 Backstitch: Use this strong stitch for repairing or sewing lengths of seam that are difficult to reach by machine. Bring the needle up through the fabric on the seam line. Take a small stitch back along the seam line and bring the needle out an equal distance in front of where the thread last emerged. Continue along the seam line, inserting the needle in front of the last stitch and bringing it out one stitch length ahead.

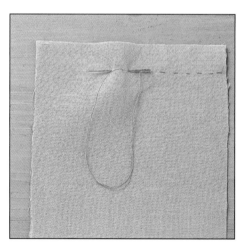

3 Half backstitch: Suitable for stitching seams or inserting sleeves by hand. The small stitches are more attractive and stronger than ordinary backstitch. The stitch is also used on facings to prevent the edge from showing on the right side of the garment. Work this stitch in the same way as backstitch but take only a half stitch back and a whole stitch forward. This forms small even stitches on the top side and long overlapping stitches on the under side.

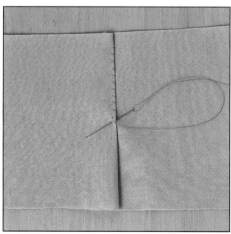

4 Hem stitch: This is a diagonal stitch worked to hold down a fold of fabric such as a binding. Despite its name, it is not suitable for hemming a garment or curtains because it shows on the right side. Hem stitch can be worked into a row of machine stitching to finish cuffs or waistbands on the inside. Take a tiny stitch through the fabric and diagonally up through the edge of the fold at the same time. Continue in this way, keeping the stitches 3–6 mm/ ⅛–¼ in apart depending on the thickness of the fabric.

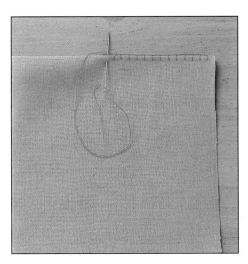

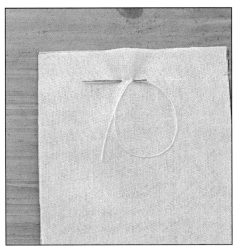

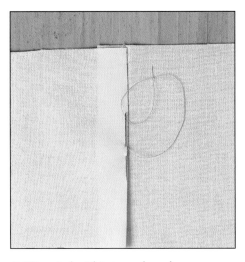

5 Blanket stitch: Traditionally used to neaten the raw edges of wool blankets, this stitch is quick to work and ideal for preventing fabric from fraying while working embroidery. It can be used as a decorative stitch and also for appliqué.

Secure your first stitch at the edge of the fabric and then work from left to right with the edge towards you. Insert the needle through the right side about 6 mm/¼ in from the edge. Bring the needle back out over the thread loop and pull taut. Continue working evenly-spaced stitches in this way, adding a neat finishing edge to the fabric.

6 Prick stitch: This is an almost invisible stitch. It is used to insert zips in fine or sheer fabrics and to sew layers of fabrics together from the right side where a row of machine stitching would be too stiff or unsightly. Work in the same way as for half backstitch but take the needle back over only one or two threads each time to form a row of tiny surface stitches with longer reinforcing stitches on the wrong side.

7 Slip stitch: This is used to close gaps, attach pockets and insert linings. A variation of it, known as slip hemming, is used to sew hems. When worked neatly, it is an almost invisible stitch.

Take a small stitch through the fold and then another through the fabric underneath. Make the stitches the same length and keep the threads straight. Pull the thread taut without causing the fabric to pucker. Slip hemming is worked in the same way but only a tiny stitch is taken through the fabric underneath.

FINISHING OFF

Finish hand sewing with a knot or several backstitches, one on top of the other, on the wrong side, ideally hidden in a seam or fold. The finishing knot is flatter than a beginning knot.

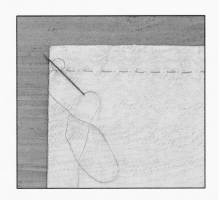

Make a loop by taking a tiny backstitch on the wrong side of the fabric. Take the needle through the loop and pull through until a second loop forms. Finally take the needle back through the second loop and pull the thread tight.

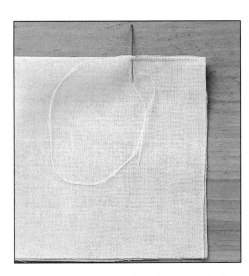

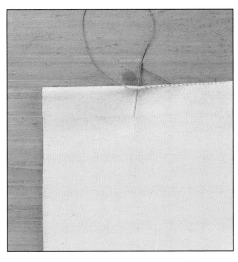

8 Closed blanket stitch: This is worked in the same way as blanket stitch but with the stitches close together. It is often confused with buttonhole stitch which has a knot at the top of each stitch.

Closed blanket stitch is used to neaten raw edges in drawn thread, cut work and for hand-embroidered scallop edges. It is also worked over a group of threads to make thread bars for belt carriers (loops), hooks or buttons. Work this stitch in the same way as blanket stitch but sew the stitches side-by-side.

9 Oversewing: This is used to hold two folded edges together. It is more visible, but also much stronger, than slip stitching. Work with the two folds held together in your hand. Take a tiny stitch straight through both folds, if possible catching only one thread. Continue along the folds, making a row of very small slanting stitches on the right side. In traditional patchwork the oversewing which holds patches together is worked from the wrong side.

SEWING BY MACHINE

Few people would even think of beginning a sewing project without a sewing machine. Sewing by machine is quick and, if the tension has been set correctly, extremely neat. Machine stitching is indispensable when sewing long straight seams in soft furnishings and also produces strong seams in dressmaking. Use machine stitching in conjunction with hand sewing for the most professional-looking result.

SEWING A SEAM

One of the first tasks in any sewing project is sewing a seam. Most soft furnishing and dressmaking patterns use a 15 mm/⅝ in seam allowance unless otherwise stated.

Begin by basting or pinning the seam across the seam line with the right sides of the fabric together. Place the fabric under the presser foot so that the edge of the seam is next to the 15 mm/⅝ in line on the needle plate and the fabric is 5 mm/¼ in behind the needle. Use the hand wheel to take the needle down into the fabric and begin to sew. Work at a speed that is comfortable for you, guiding, but not forcing, the fabric along the line on the needle plate.

TURNING CORNERS

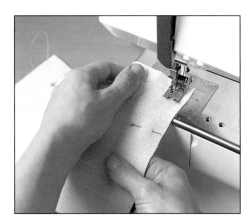

1 Slow down as you approach the corner and work the last few stitches by turning the hand wheel. Stop 15 mm/⅝ in from the edge with the needle in the fabric. Lift the presser foot and swing the fabric round until the next seam is lined up with the guideline on the needle plate. Lower the foot and continue. You may have to turn the fabric back a little and take another stitch or two until the edge is exactly on the 15 mm/⅝ in line on the needle plate.

REMOVING STITCHES

Unless the fabric is fine or delicate, the easiest way to remove stitches is with an unpicker. Slip the point underneath a stitch and cut it against the sharp, curved edge of the tool. Cut every two or three stitches and then turn the fabric over and pull the reverse-side thread out. Brush the loose threads from the right side and steam press to close the holes. On fine or delicate fabrics, lift and cut the stitches one at a time.

SEWING CURVES

1 Sew slowly round soft curves, keeping the edge of the fabric opposite the presser foot on the guideline of the needle plate. On tighter curves stop and turn the fabric slightly into the curve before beginning. Keep stopping every few stitches to adjust the line of the fabric until the curve is complete. To ensure that two curves are exactly the same, for example on a collar, make a template and mark the curve along the seam line before sewing.

ABOVE This beautiful wall hanging is made with a combination of hand and machine sewing. Experiment with complementing colours until you are happy with your final design.

MACHINE STITCHES

The type of machine you have will determine the range of stitches at your disposal. The stitches listed here are the most common ones used in general sewing. Look in your handbook for the complete range of stitches possible on your machine. Try out a stitch on a double scrap of the fabric you will be using before you start.

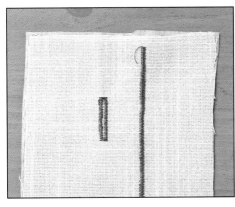

1 Satin stitch: A zigzag with the stitch length set almost at zero. It is used for buttonholes and machine appliqué. Use a clear-view foot to allow enough room for the bulky stitch underneath. Satin stitch can make the fabric gather if the stitches are too wide, so check the stitch width is right for the fabric before you start. Buttonholes consist of two parallel rows of narrow satin stitches with a few double-width stitches at each end to finish.

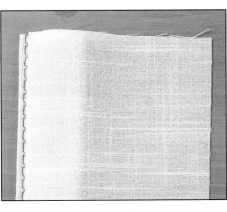

2 Blind hemming (blind stitch hem): Use in conjunction with a blind-hemming foot. This stitch is suitable for heavy or bulky fabrics where the stitch won't show on the right side. The hem is tacked (basted) and then fed under the foot and is sewn with a series of straight stitches followed by a zigzag stitch which picks up the main fabric. Adjust the zigzag length to make the stitch into the fold as small as possible.

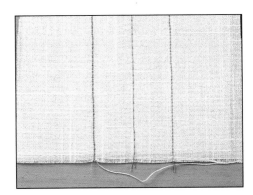

3 Straight stitch: This is the stitch most widely used to join two pieces of fabric together. For ordinary fabric set the stitch length dial between 2 and 3. If the fabric is very fine or heavy, alter the stitch length to suit: use a shorter stitch for fine fabrics and a longer one for heavy fabrics. If you have an automatic sewing machine you can work a stretch straight stitch – useful for sewing fabrics such as jersey. Quick basting stitches can be worked by machine. Use the longest straight stitch possible for this to make it easy to pull out the thread.

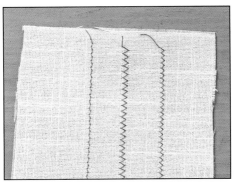

4 Zigzag: These stitches are used for finishing edges, for machine appliqué and as decoration. Try different lengths and widths of stitch to find which one suits the fabric best. In general, the stitch should be as small, narrow and as straight as possible.

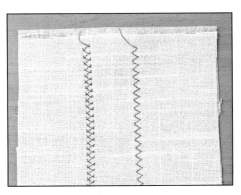

5 Multi-zigzag: Wider versions of zigzag such as triple zigzag and herringbone stitch are useful for sewing elastic on to fabric. Triple zigzag can be used for finishing seams on soft or fine fabrics. Both stitches can be used to prevent the edges of towelling or knitted fabrics from curling before sewing.

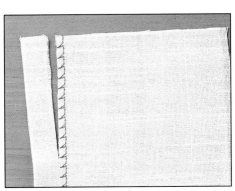

6 Overlocking: This is worked directly over the edge of the fabric, stitching and finishing the seam in one. Alternately, stitch along the seam line and trim.

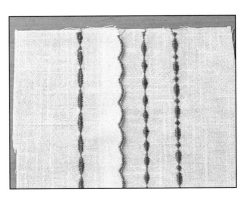

7 Decorative stitches: Automatic machines contain a device called a pattern cam which allows a range of stitches to be formed. Suitable for machine embroidery or to finish hems.

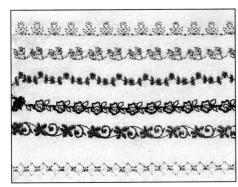

8 Computer-generated stitches: The most advanced machines have a silicone chip to create many decorative stitches. These stitches take time to complete as the fabric moves in a circular direction to create the pattern, but the results are very effective.

WINDOW DRESSING

When planning a window treatment, think of the scheme as an integral part of the whole room. Consider the proportions of the window with respect to the rest of the room, the contents and the dominant colours. Successful window dressing should be part of the ensemble rather than influenced by the whim of fashion.

If you are starting from scratch, with bare walls and no furniture, then you almost have free range. For some, total freedom can be daunting, so if you have an existing carpet or soft furnishing fabric, take this as a starting point when making your fabric colour choice. The best way to choose colour is to do it on site, with the windows and the rest of your belongings around you. Look through glossy magazines, books about art, travel, style, food, gardens – anything where you see combinations of colours that appeal to you. This should be fun and not a chore, so feel free to draw inspiration from whatever appeals to you. It's easy to become bewildered by choice when looking through fabrics in a store, so allow yourself time to consider the other options available.

Bear in mind, however, that your personal preference is the most important of all, so go with your instincts. There are so many reasons why we like or dislike a colour, so even if purple is the most fashionable colour of the moment but you find it depressing, avoid it. Beauty is in the eye of the beholder, and one person's boring beige is another's delicious oatmeal. If you like the natural look, consider earthy reds, oranges and browns that have been dyed with natural pigments. They are warm and restful and look good with ethnic trimmings and accessories.

Practically speaking, you should consider two main elements when deciding on which treatment to use – the weight of the fabric and the state of

the wall. A heavy fabric needs the security of strong brackets supporting the pole. You will need brackets at both ends and possibly in the middle as well. It should stay level, not bow in the middle. Check the walls before you invest in the coveted iron pole. Old plaster does not always conceal sound masonry, and it will need to be rock solid. Check both sides of the windows.

If the fabric is light, it may need no more than a wooden dowel and two cup hooks. Sew a channel along the top of the curtain (drape), and feed the fabric on to the dowel to cover it. Then paint the small exposed ends. With this method, the hooks screw into the wooden window frame, so no drilling is needed. Curtain clips are another option for lightweight fabrics. You can adjust their spacing at will to change the way they drape and, with ring attachments, draw the curtains.

The very simplest no-sew way to drape a window is to use a pair of sheets over a pole. Simply throw them over and pull the back and front to the same length. The two sheets should meet in the middle of the pole and be

ABOVE A selection of materials suitable for hanging, attaching and decorating curtains. Most materials are easily bought and are not difficult to use. It is worth going to a good fabric or furnishing store to ensure the widest selection of materials, such as rings, hooks, brackets, cord and wire.

EQUIPMENT FOR ATTACHING POLES, TRACKS AND FABRICS

Creative window dressers have a few key tools in their tool box. The first is the staple gun. These come in a range of sizes and take staples of varying lengths. The smallest is not suitable for holding heavy fabric, and the largest is for the building trade. So buy one somewhere in the middle.

You also need a hammer, pliers, tape measure, spirit (carpenter's) level and electric drill. A screwdriver, awl and various pairs of scissors should complete the kit. Hardware stores have interesting materials, such as garage hooks, plumbing pipe holders and balls of string of every thickness. Wire, in various thicknesses and coatings, will also come in handy.

pulled back to each side of the window. The idea can be adjusted to fit most windows. Any extra fabric could be arranged on the floor below for a touch of opulence. Fabrics like suit lining, mattress ticking and calico are ideal for draping this way. Allow about three times the drop of your window, and start in the middle at the top. Arrange folds and swags, pleating as you staple. Be creative, and don't feel as if you have to copy any 'correct' way of draping the fabric. There are no set rules, just ideas and inspiration.

In addition to the basic equipment needed for soft furnishings there are some specific items required for curtain and blind (shade) making:

Cord: fine nylon cord used to draw up Roman blinds into pleats.

Curtain hooks and rings: available in a variety of different sizes, weights and designs to suit all fabrics.

Curtain rods and wire: tension rods and screw-in net rods used for small or recessed windows. Plastic-covered wire is used for fine curtains.

Dowel: narrow wooden rods used when making Roman blinds. They pass through horizontal channels.

Fabric stiffener: spray-on fabric stiffener adds body to fine fabric when making roller blinds or window panels.

Lath: thin stripwood inserted in a casing at the bottom of a blind to keep it straight and to add weight.

Screw-in hooks and eyes: hooks screwed at the top of the window frame can support a lightweight blind. Screw-in eyes are used in the end of curtain wires and under battens to take the cords for raising blinds.

Touch-and-close fasteners: used to fix blinds or pelmets to battens, touch-and-close strips and patches may be self-adhesive or sewing quality or a combination of both.

RIGHT Creating highly individual and personal curtains need not require expensive materials – often a little flair makes the greatest difference.

SOFT FURNISHINGS

BASIC TECHNIQUES FOR WINDOW DRESSINGS

When cutting out fabric, always lay it out on a large flat table or the floor before opening to cut. Begin with a straight edge: to do this draw out a weft (horizontal) thread from the width of the fabric, then use this line as a guide to cutting. Measure the first fabric piece from this edge.

If the fabric is patterned, you must take care to match the pattern repeats on each piece cut. It is usually easiest to cut the first piece, then lay it on the rest of the fabric and use it as a guide for subsequent pieces.

PLEATING WITH A STAPLE GUN

1 Use a length of wooden batten (furring strip) for the pleating, attached to the wall with a couple of strong screws. Start by putting the first staple into the corner of the fabric. Use the staple gun on its side so the staples are vertical, not horizontal, which would cause more stress on the fabric and possible tearing.

2 Allowing an equal distance between pleats, pinch the same amount each time between your finger and thumb, lifting it clear of the batten. Place a staple on each side of the pinched pleat. When you reach the end of the length, go back to the beginning and staple all the pinched pleats down flat in the same direction. If your pelmet (valance) is deep, you may prefer to leave out this stage.

HANGING A CURTAIN ROD

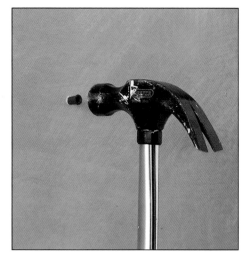

1 To insert a wall plug, match the drill bit number to the size of the wall plug. They are coded, so check the numbers. Hold the wall plug next to the bit, then use a strip of tape to mark its length on the bit. Don't drill deeper than this or the wall plug will be lost in the wall. Use a masonry bit for drilling walls, recognized by their light colour and squared-off tips. Wood drill bits are made of darker metal.

2 Tap the wall plug into the hole with a hammer. The plug should fit snugly right up to the collar. If it is too loose, fill the hole and re-locate at least 5 cm/2 in from it. If the hole is too tight, the wall plug will not fit securely. Check the drill bit, and go up one size if necessary.

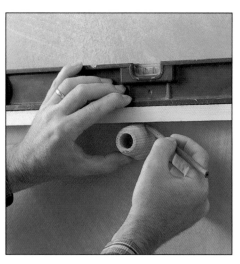

3 A standard wooden curtain rod fitting comes in two parts. The first is a cup shape with a hole drilled through the middle for a screw. The second has a peg that fits into the hole and a ring at the other end to hold the pole. Measure above the window to get the position for the first support attachment. Drill and plug a hole. Then screw the wooden cup in place. Peg the second half of the fitting into it, and firmly put in the securing screw through the hole provided.

4 To position the second support attachment, rest a length of plank on the first attachment, and place a spirit (carpenter's) level on top of it. Hold the wooden cup in your spare hand and, when you find the level, mark through the hole with a pencil. You can then dispense with the plank and the level. Drill, plug and screw in the attachment as before. Thread the rod through the rings or rest it in the grooves. Then push the finials on to the ends to finish off the curtain rod.

HEADING TAPE STYLES

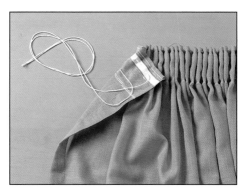

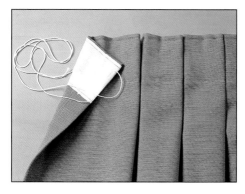

1 Standard tape: A simple gathered effect which works most successfully on lightweight or unlined curtains. Fabric fullness required: 1½ times track/pole measurement.

2 Pencil pleat: A popular heading resulting in tall regular pleats across the curtain, available in various depths and also in a lightweight version. Fabric fullness required: 2–2½ times track/pole measurement.

3 Box pleat: By drawing up the cords, the curtain forms flat box pleats at regular intervals across the width. Fabric fullness required: 2 times track/pole measurement.

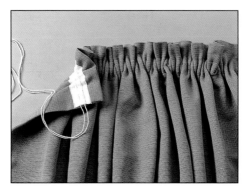

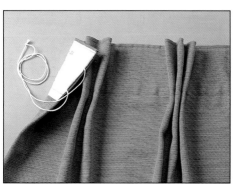

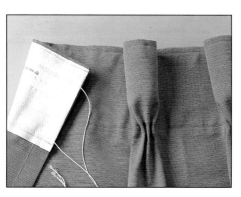

4 Net/voile pleat: A translucent heading tape for use with sheer voile fabrics or nets. In addition to the pockets in the tape to take curtain hooks, there are loops in the tape enabling the curtain to be suspended from a rod or wire. Fabric fullness required: 2 times track/pole measurement.

5 Triple pinch pleat: By pulling the two draw cords, the curtain fabric is gathered into evenly spaced elegant pinch pleats. Ensure the pleating positions match on both curtains. It is available in various depths and in a lightweight version. Fabric fullness required: 2 times track/pole measurement.

6 Goblet pleat: The top cord draws the fabric into rounded pleats across the width, while the lower cord gathers the base of each to form goblet shapes. These shapes can be further enhanced by stuffing with tissue paper, which holds the shape. Fabric fullness required: 2½ times track/pole measurement.

MEASURING A WINDOW

Take two basic measurements to estimate the amount of fabric needed for curtains or blinds (drapes or shades). For curtains: calculate the width by measuring the width of the track or pole. The length is a matter of personal choice: measure from the top of the track or pole, and decide whether the curtains are to fall to the floor, the windowsill or, for example, just clear the top of a radiator.

For blinds: measure the width of the window or recess in which the blind is to fit. For the length, measure the length of the window or recess.

RIGHT Simple lined curtains can have a lovely classic look to them. A plain or striped fabric with a firm weave is easiest to manage if it is your first attempt at making curtains. The starting point to all curtain making is calculating how much fabric is required and then cutting it out correctly. Be sure you are happy with your measurements before you cut any fabric.

MAKING LINED CURTAINS AND DRAPES

Curtains and drapes are the largest items of soft furnishing to make and, although they may appear difficult, they in fact require only the minimum of sewing skills. The secret of successful curtain-making lies in accurate measuring, estimating and cutting out. There is a wide range of ready-made curtain-heading tapes available, which will create different effects ranging from a narrow ruched band (standard tape) to an intricately pleated border (smocked tape). Stitch the tape along the top of the fabric, following the manufacturer's instructions, then gather or pleat the fabric by simply pulling up the cords in the tape. A series of pockets suspends the curtain from rings or hooks attached to the curtain (drapery) track or pole.

Lined curtains are suitable for most windows, but you may prefer unlined ones for the kitchen and bathroom, as these are easier to launder. To make unlined curtains, simply omit the lining steps shown below and turn and stitch a narrow double hem along the side edges before attaching the heading tape.

RIGHT Lined curtains and drapes hang well and the lining also acts as a barrier to sunlight, preventing fabric colours from fading.

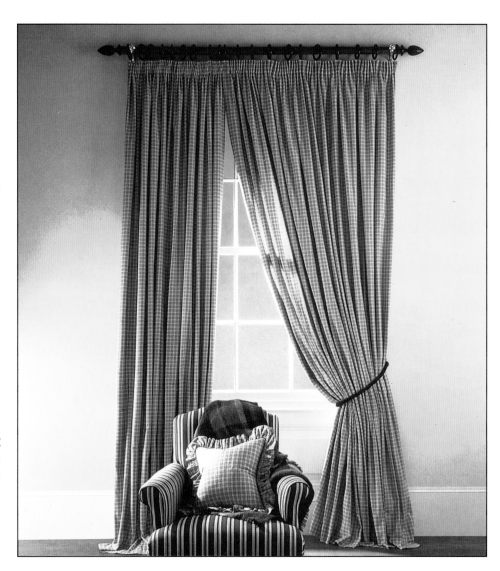

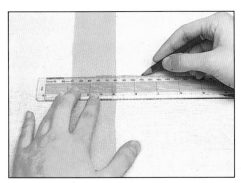

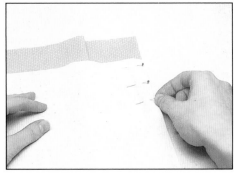

1 Place the lining on the fabric that you have chosen for the curtain (drape) with the right sides together and the lower raw edges aligning. Mark the centre point of the curtain on both the fabric and the lining, using a dressmaker's pencil.

2 With the right sides of the fabric and lining still facing, pin them together along the side edges, taking care that the lower edges of both the fabric and lining are still aligned. At the top, the lining should be 4 cm/1½ in shorter than the fabric.

3 Mark the finished length of the curtain and the sewing line for the hem on the lining with a dressmaker's pencil, taking into account the 15 cm/6 in hem allowance. Stitch along the side edges 12 mm/½ in from the raw edge, stitching from the top of the lining to about 10 cm/4 in from the hem sewing line.

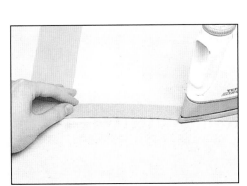

4 Turn to the right side. Press the side edges, making sure that the fabric pulls over to the wrong side by about 2.5 cm/1 in. Matching the marked points at the top of both fabric and lining, fold 4 cm/1½ in of fabric over on to the wrong side and press.

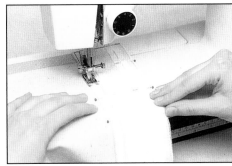

5 Tucking under the raw edges, pin the heading tape in position just below the top of the fabric. Following the manufacturer's instructions, machine stitch the tape to the curtain, taking care to stitch each long side in the same direction to avoid puckering.

CURTAIN AND DRAPE STYLES

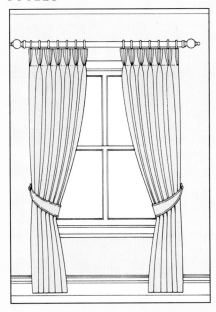

Floor-length curtains can add the illusion of height to square windows. Accentuate the effect by holding the curtains back at window-sill level, using a pair of tie-backs.

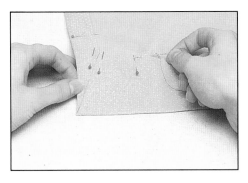

6 Fold over a double 7.5 cm/3 in hem along the lower edge of the fabric and press in place. If you are using heavyweight fabric, fold the corners over to form a mitre and then carefully trim away the surplus cloth. Tack (baste) along the hem.

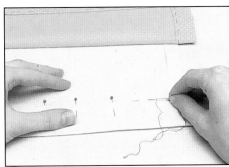

7 Turn up and pin a double hem along the lower edge of the lining so that the hem edge will hang about 20 mm/¾ in above the finished fabric hem. Trim away any surplus lining and then tack along the hem to hold it in place.

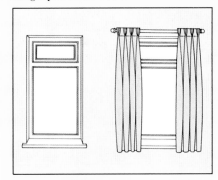

With a narrow window, extend the curtain (drapery) track or pole at each side so that, when open, the curtains do not obscure the window.

8 Pulling from the centre of the heading tape, pull up the cords until the curtain is the correct width. Knot the cords loosely at the centre of the curtain. Hang the curtain for a few days to allow the fabric to settle, then slip stitch both the cloth and lining hems. Finally, slip stitch the lining to the fabric down the remainder of the side.

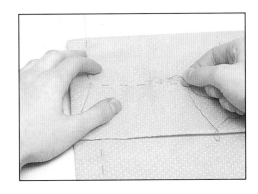

CALCULATING FABRIC REQUIREMENTS

To calculate the width of fabric, multiply the width of the curtain (drapery) track or pole by the amount of fullness needed for the chosen heading tape (usually between 1½ and 2½ times the width of the window), and allow 3.5 cm/1⅜ in for each side hem. Divide the curtain width required by the width of the fabric, rounding up as necessary. Allow 3 cm/1¼ in for each join that is needed.

To calculate the length, measure downwards from the track or pole to the required curtain length, then add on 4 cm/1½ in to accommodate the heading tape and 15 cm/6 in for the bottom hem.

To calculate the total amount of fabric, multiply the length by the number of widths required.

If you are making lined rather than unlined curtains, you will need almost the same amount of lining as curtain fabric, with just 5 cm/2 in less in the width and 4 cm/1½ in less in the length.

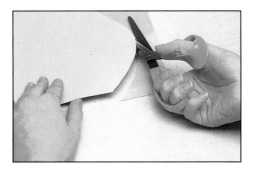

MAKING A PELMET (VALANCE) AND TIE-BACKS

The pelmet (valance) was originally used as a means of keeping curtains and drapes free from dust, and is now very popular simply as a decorative feature. Tie-backs are both attractive and practical, holding back curtains to let in the maximum light.

A fabric-covered pelmet is quick and simple to make with a special PVC (vinyl) material that is self-adhesive on one side and lined with velour on the other. The adhesive is covered with backing paper, which is printed with ready-to-cut pelmet patterns to suit most styles of decoration. Attach the finished pelmet to a batten (furring strip), with the returns secured to the wall above the curtain (drapery) track with angle irons. The batten should be 5 cm/2 in longer than the curtain track at each side of the window.

Plain-shaped tie-backs are easily made with the help of buckram shapes coated with iron-on adhesive. The buckram is available in kit form, pre-cut in several sizes to suit the curtain width. Attach the tie-backs to the wall with rings and hooks. Experiment with the position of the hooks, before fixing, to assess the most pleasing effect.

LEFT A fabric-covered pelmet (valance) provides the perfect finishing touch to this window treatment and echoes the shape of the wallpaper border.

MAKING A PELMET (VALANCE)

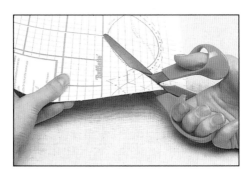 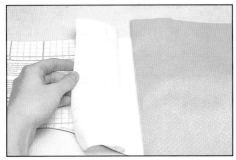 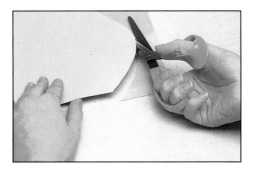

1 Measure the batten (furring strip) and the returns. Cut out the PVC (vinyl) pelmet material to this length, taking care to centre the chosen pattern. Cut out the shaped edge of the pelmet material along the correct line for the required shape. Cut out a piece of fabric about 3 cm/1¼ in larger all around than the pelmet material.

2 Lift the backing paper at the centre of the pelmet material, cut across it and peel back a small amount on either side. Matching the centre of the fabric with the centre of the pelmet material, press the fabric on to the exposed adhesive. Keeping the fabric taut, peel away the backing and smooth the fabric on to the adhesive.

3 Turn the pelmet material so that the velour backing is facing upwards. Using a sharp pair of scissors, carefully cut away the surplus fabric around the edge of the pelmet material.

PELMET (VALANCE) STYLES

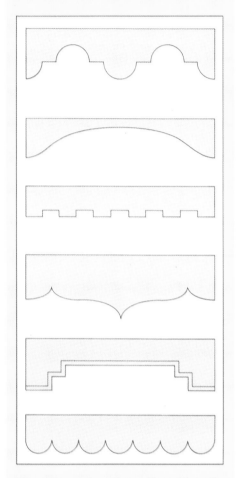

Pelmet styles can be plain or fancy, scalloped or stepped. Choose a style to suit your chosen fabric and the general décor of the room.

MAKING A SHAPED TIE-BACK

1 To make the back of the tie-back, pin the buckram shape on to the fabric and cut out around the edge of the shape. Lay this on the wrong side of the fabric to make the front, and, using a dressmaker's pencil, mark a line on the fabric 12 mm/½ in all around the outside of the buckram shape. Cut out the larger front piece.

2 With the wrong sides together, sandwich the buckram between the front and back pieces. Press with a hot, dry iron to fuse all the layers together, taking care not to scorch the fabric.

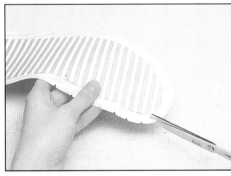

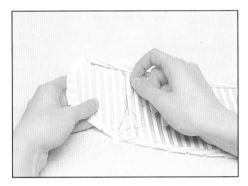

3 Snip into the edge of the surplus fabric all around the tie-back. This will help the fabric to lie neatly without puckering when you turn it over to the wrong side.

4 Fold the surplus fabric over to the wrong side of the tie-back and turn under the raw snipped edge. Using matching sewing thread, stitch the folded edge neatly in place, taking care that the stitches do not go through to the right side. Stitch a brass ring on to each end of the tie-back.

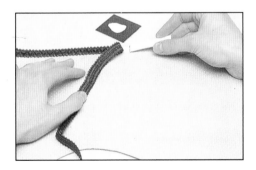

4 For a neat finish, glue a length of braid around the edge of the pelmet using a suitable craft adhesive. Attach strips of touch-and-close fastener to the batten with staples or tacks – use the hooked part only, as the velour backing of the pelmet material acts as the looped part of the fastener. Press the pelmet in position on the batten.

TIE-BACK VARIATIONS

It is easy to vary the look of plain tie-backs by adding narrow frills or by binding the edges with bias strips of contrasting fabric.

A strip of wide, ornate ribbon or braid makes an unusual tie-back – simply apply iron-on interfacing on the wrong side to stiffen the ribbon and cover the back with a strip of lining fabric in a toning colour. Turn under the raw edges, and slip stitch together around the edge.

RIGHT **Position tie-backs about two-thirds of the way down a short curtain for maximum effect, but do experiment with the positioning before making the final fixing.**

MAKING BLINDS AND SHADES

Blinds are becoming a very popular alternative window-dressing to a pair of curtains (drapes). The styles of blind described here, although made using very similar techniques, create very different effects – choose the softly ruched Austrian blind for a pretty, feminine window treatment and the smartly pleated Roman blind for a room with a modern décor.

Use a light- or medium-weight fabric to make an Austrian blind – anything from lightweight voile or sheer to standard cotton curtain fabric will be suitable. Avoid heavy brocades and handwoven cottons, as these are too thick to drape well. You will need a special type of track to hang and mount the blind; this is known as Austrian-blind track, and is widely available.

A Roman blind, on the other hand, will benefit from being made in a reasonably substantial fabric. You can line this type of blind if you wish, to add body to the pleats and also to retain the warmth of a room. You will need a batten (furring strip) and angle irons to mount the blind. Use strips of touch-and-close fastener to hold the blind in place on the batten.

MAKING A ROMAN BLIND (SHADE)

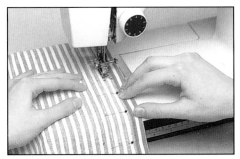

1 Cut out the fabric. Turn, pin and stitch double 12 mm/½ in side hems. Turn, pin and then machine stitch a double 2.5 cm/1 in hem along the top of the fabric. Press all the hems.

2 Pin and stitch a strip of Roman-blind tape close to the side edge, turning under 9 mm/⅜ in at the top. Stitch another strip along the remaining edge, then attach further strips at intervals across the blind, 25–30 cm/10–12 in apart.

3 At the bottom of the blind, turn over 9 mm/⅜ in and press, then turn over a further 5 cm/2 in to enclose the ends of the tape. Pin and stitch the hem close to the inner fold, leaving the sides open.

4 Stitch narrow tucks across the width of the blind to correspond with alternate rows of loops or rings on the tape. Make the first tuck level with the second row of loops or rings from the bottom of the blind. To make the tucks, fold the fabric with the wrong sides facing, and stitch 3 mm/⅛ in from the fold.

LEFT A tailored Roman blind (shade) is the perfect answer for a window or décor that demands a simple treatment.

MAKING AN AUSTRIAN BLIND (SHADE)

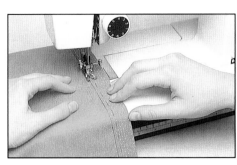

1 Cut out the fabric. Turn, pin, tack (baste) and stitch double 20 mm/¾ in side hems. Turn, pin, tack and stitch a double 20 mm/¾ in hem along the bottom of the fabric. Press all the hems.

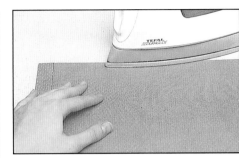

2 Fold the fabric, with the right sides together, vertically like a concertina at approximately 60 cm/24 in evenly spaced intervals and press. The resulting folds mark the positions of the vertical tapes.

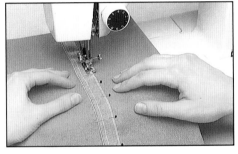

3 Pin and stitch a strip of Austrian-blind tape close to one of the side hems, turning under 12 mm/½ in at the bottom to neaten. Stitch another strip along the remaining side hem, then attach further strips vertically at regular intervals across the blind, aligning one edge of the tape with the pressed folds.

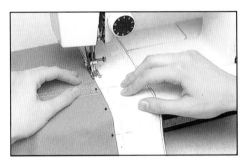

4 Turn over 20 mm/¾ in at the top of the blind and press. Pin the heading tape in position, folding under the raw edges, and stitch in place.

MOUNTING A ROMAN BLIND (SHADE)

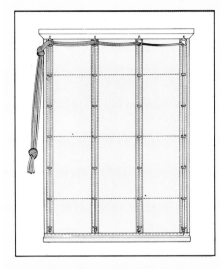

Attach the blind to the top of the batten with strips of touch-and-close fastener. Cut each length of cord to twice the length of the blind plus the distance of the right-hand edge. Thread each cord through the loops in the tape. Knot each length securely on the bottom loop and thread the other end through the corresponding screw eyes on the batten, ending with all the cord ends on the right-hand side of the blind. Knot the cords at the top, cut the ends off level and knot them again.

Austrian blinds are mounted in much the same way, with the cords threaded through rings attached to the track.

CALCULATING FABRIC REQUIREMENTS

Austrian blind (shade)

To calculate the length, measure the window drop and add 11 cm/2¼ in for hem allowances.

For the width, measure the width of the window and multiply by 2 to 2½ depending on the type of heading tape used. Add 8 cm/3 in for side hems.

You will need enough heading tape to extend across the width of the fabric, plus extra for turnings. You will also need sufficient strips of Austrian-blind tape to position at 60 cm/24 in intervals across the width of the blind. Each strip should be the length of the blind plus 12 mm/½ in; make sure there is a loop or ring 12 mm/½ in up from the bottom of each strip so that they will line up across the blind.

Roman blind (shade)

To calculate the length, measure the window drop, add 14 cm/4½ in for hem allowances and a little extra for the horizontal tucks.

For the width, measure the window and add 6 cm/2 in for side hems.

You will need sufficient strips of Roman-blind tape to position at 25–30 cm/10–12 in intervals across the width of the blind. Each strip should be the length of the blind plus 12 mm/½ in; make sure there is a loop or ring 12 mm/½ in up from the bottom of each strip so that they will match across the blind.

ABOVE **An Austrian blind makes a feminine, very decorative window treatment.**

USING CUSHIONS

Cushions are the quickest and least expensive way of changing the mood and style of a room, so it is surprising that we don't all have cupboards (closets) bursting with alternative covers awaiting their chance to be the main feature in response to our prevailing mood. It is difficult to imagine having too many cushions because each one adds to the atmosphere of comfort and relaxation, which is a priority in any living space.

Use the colour, texture, shape and size of cushions to add interest to a room. The same room with a plain sofa, carpet and neutral wall colour can be transformed by an arrangement of Chinese embroidered and tasselled satin cushions, rough homespun earthy-coloured bolsters or frilled red gingham squares mixed with patchworks and cotton lace. The mood each time will be entirely different. Just a few other options to consider are Provençal prints, Indian hand-blocked cottons, rich brocades, velvets and satins, or tactile velvets.

Cushions with borders (Oxford, pleated or gathered), edges adorned with colourful piping or braids, appliquéd patterns and pictures created from embroidery or fabric paint and patchwork covers: the ways that cushions can be adorned are limitless. Mix similar patterns but with different colours, or similar colours but a variety of patterns. Look at the many textured fabrics that add a tactile pleasure to the visual: slubby cottons, suede, leather, velvet, silk, wool; each has a place in the sitting room.

Large, square cushions mixed with smaller, rectangular or round ones can be piled very successfully one on top of the other. Bolsters, too, can be used as the base for a luxurious mix of cushions. The secret is to use them to fill the angle between a sofa seat and back or bed mattress and head. Then pile other cushions on top to make a

LEFT This square cushion made of dark wool is simply embroidered with three rows of running stitch around the edge. The white cord trim and toggle fastenings add to its old-fashioned homespun appeal.

BELOW Fabric remnants and odd bits of trimmings are just the materials to make a sumptuous patchwork cushion that will look lovely gracing a sofa or chair.

ABOVE Blue and white stripes and rope are two classic nautical themes. The rope idea would work just as well on a square cushion.

gentle slope at the perfect angle for an afternoon cup of tea or a long and absorbing book. Wrap a bolster in a lace-edged tablecloth, tying up the ends with ribbon, Christmas-cracker style, so that they spill out over the edge of the sofa, or use velvet-edged ribbons, fancy cords and tassels for a flamboyant Renaissance look.

A comfortable cross between a bolster and loose cushions can be made by stitching together a row of same-sized cushions. Use cushions covered in the same fabric or choose a mixture of plain covers and co-ordinating prints. Using a strong thread, sew one edge of each cushion together to make a single long, jointed cushion that is the same width as the sofa or bed.

Look out for fabric-remnant bins because they usually contain a wealth of short lengths that are ideal for cushion covers. It is also worth looking in haberdashery (notions) departments for dressmaker's trimmings such as fringing, lace, braids, ribbons and beadwork borders. These are not as hardwearing as upholsterer's trimmings but cost a fraction of the price and are perfectly adequate for cushions. Don't

RIGHT Few things immediately suggest luxury and comfort as easily as white linen cushions do, and they are well worth the investment.

despair if you don't like sewing as covers can be made just as effectively using iron-on hemming tape, double-sided carpet tape or pins and knots.

If you have always thought that cushions just belonged in the living room and pillows were only for sleeping on, then perhaps it is time to consider giving cushions a bit of bed space too. A cushion can be merely decorative and it can be highly pleasing to dress up your bed during the day, particularly if it is going to be on show, then removed at night. This sort of bed dressing is fun when decorating, because there will be periods when the room stands empty but still needs to look welcoming.

In addition to the essential equipment needed for creating any form of soft furnishing, there are specific items to help make cushions:

Corner turner: this tool is useful for turning points and corners of cushions.
Embroidery hoop: this consists of two hoops that fit snugly inside each other. Made of wood or plastic, with a spring closure, it is used for both hand and machine embroidery.
Fabric dyes: hot and cold dyes are available. Fabrics with natural fibres, such as cotton and linen, can be dyed most successfully.
Fabric paints: there is a wide range of easy-to-use products. Choose water-based paints that can be fixed (set) with an iron. The paints can be mixed and applied with a brush to create an unlimited number of colours.
Pair of compasses: use these for drawing circles. If you do not have your own compasses, draw around cups for small circles; to draw larger circles use plates or bowls.

MAKING CUSHION COVERS

Cushions add comfort and a stylish touch to most rooms. Newly covered cushions are also a relatively inexpensive way of enlivening a monotone colour scheme, as they require little fabric compared with curtains (drapes) or blinds (shades). Simple shapes such as squares and circles show off strong colours and patterns to the best advantage, and both shapes can be decorated with frills, piping or both combined.

Both types of cushion shown here have a zip (zipper) inserted in the back seam – a neater method than making the opening in a side seam. A zip is the most convenient method of fastening a cushion cover, making it easy to remove for laundering. If you prefer, however, you can close the opening with a row of slip stitches, which you will need to remove and then replace whenever you launder the cover.

MAKING A SQUARE CUSHION COVER

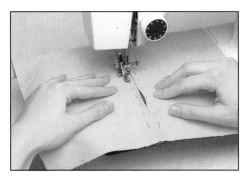

1 Measure the cushion pad, and add 12 mm/½ in all around for ease plus 12 mm/½ in for seam allowances. Do not forget to allow an extra 3 cm/1 in for the centre-back seam. Cut out the front and two back pieces. Pin and stitch the centre-back seam 12 mm/½ in from the raw edges, making sure to leave an opening large enough to accommodate the zip (zipper). Press open the seam.

BELOW Frills and piping in matching or contrasting fabric add interest and a nice finishing touch to round and square cushion covers.

2 Pin and tack (baste) the zip in position along the opening, allowing the fabric to meet centrally over the zip teeth. Using a zip foot on the machine, carefully machine stitch the zip in place.

3 Press the seam allowances around the zip. Open the zip, making sure that the fabric does not catch in the teeth and that the ends are stitched securely. With the zip still open, place the front and back pieces together so that the right sides are facing.

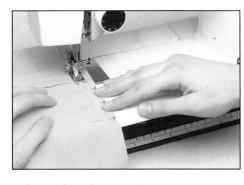

4 Pin and machine stitch twice around the edge, about 12mm/½ in from the raw edges. Carefully clip away the surplus fabric close to the stitching at the corners, in order to reduce the bulk. Press the seams and turn the cover to the right side through the zipped opening. Press the seams, insert the cushion pad and close the zip.

MAKING A FRILL

For this you will need a piece of fabric that is twice the depth of the finished frill plus 3 cm/1¼ in, and between 1½ and 2 times the outside measurement of the cover (you may have to join several strips together).

1 Join the ends of the strips together with a flat seam. Fold the strip in half lengthways with the wrong sides facing. Make one or two rows of running stitches along the raw edges of the strip, taking the stitches through both layers and leaving a long end of thread at one end of each row.

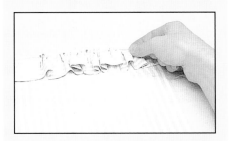

2 Gather the frill by pulling up the long threads until the frill is the correct size to fit around the cushion front. Wind the long threads around a pin to secure them and then even out the gather with your fingers.
 To add a frill to either a square or round cushion, align the raw edge of the frill with the raw edge of the front cover, right sides together. Tack (baste) and sew the frill in place, then make up the cover in the usual way.

PIPING

1 Fold a piece of fabric in half diagonally and press the fold. Open out the fabric and mark out strips parallel to the fold about 4–5 cm/1½–2 in apart. Cut out the strips. Join the strips with a flat seam to make the required length. Place the piping cord along the centre of the strip, fold it over and pin. Tack (baste) and stitch close to the cord.

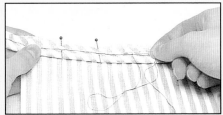

2 Lay the covered cord on the right side of the fabric, with raw edges aligning, and tack in place. Cover with a second piece of fabric, right-side downwards and with the raw edges matching. Stitch the layers together along the seamline using a zip (zipper) foot on the machine. Remove the tacking stitches. Make up the cover in the usual way.

MAKING A ROUND CUSHION COVER

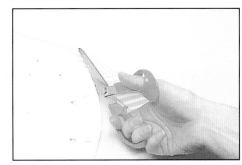

1 Measure the diameter of the cushion pad, and add 12 mm/½ in all around for ease plus 12 mm/½ in for seam allowances. Make a paper pattern to this size using dressmaker's pattern paper. Pin this on to the fabric and cut out one piece for the front of the cover.

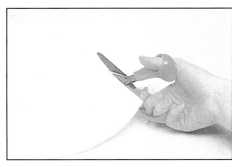

2 Rule a line across the paper pattern to mark the position of the back seam. The line should measure approximately 12.5 cm/5 in longer than the zip (zipper). Cut the paper pattern in 2 along this line.

3 Pin both pattern pieces on to the fabric and cut them out, remembering to allow an extra 12 mm/½ in for the seam allowance on the straight edge of each piece.

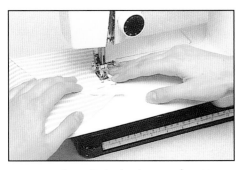

4 Pin and stitch the back seam, leaving an opening long enough to accommodate the zip. Finish off the cover in the same way as the square cover (see opposite page).

RIGHT **Choose sumptuous fabrics for cushion covers to complement curtains and wall coverings for a harmonious decorating scheme.**

BOX AND BOLSTER CUSHIONS

Box-cushion covers are often made to fit a particular chair or window seat as they can accommodate a thick cushion pad or piece of foam block. The covers should look neatly tailored and are best made in a crisp, cotton furnishing fabric. The seams can be enhanced with piping made from matching or contrasting fabric – plain piping looks particularly effective with patterned cushion fabric. Always pre-shrink cotton piping cord by washing it in hot water before use.

Circular bolster cushions look attractive on most types of furniture and make a good visual contrast against the more usual rectangular cushions. This shape of cushion works particularly well with striped, check and tartan cloth, especially when a contrasting tassel, ribbon bow or pompom is used as a trim.

FRENCH SEAMS

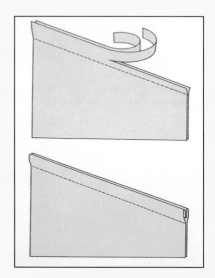

A French seam encloses the raw edges of fabric and prevents them from fraying. It is worked in two stages: first stitch with the wrong sides facing (top). Trim the raw edges close to the first row of stitching. Then stitch with the right sides facing (above).

BOX CUSHION

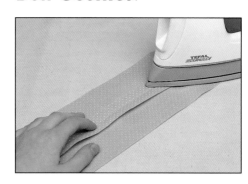

1 Cut out the fabric. Cut the back gusset in half lengthways and place together with the right sides facing. Pin and stitch the seam 12 mm/½ in from the raw edges, leaving an opening for the zip (zipper). Press the seam open.

2 Pin and tack (baste) the zip in position along the opening, as shown, allowing the fabric to meet centrally over the zip teeth. Stitch the zip in place using a zip foot on the machine.

3 With the right sides facing, join the four gusset pieces together along the short ends, taking a 12 mm/½ in seam allowance and leaving 12 mm/½ in unstitched at each end of the seams. Press the seams open.

4 With the right sides facing, pin and stitch the top edge of one gusset section to one edge of the top cover piece, taking a 12 mm/½ in seam allowance. At the gusset seam, leave the needle in the fabric, raise the machine foot and pivot the fabric so the next section of gusset aligns with the next side of the top cover piece. Continue pinning and stitching each section around the top in this way. Open the zip, then repeat the procedure to attach the bottom cover piece to the remaining side of the gusset. Trim away the surplus cloth at the corners and then turn the cover right side out.

BELOW A box cushion adds comfort and style to a sofa. This cushion has been made by tie-dyeing individual patches of contrasting fabric then sewing them together.

BOLSTER CUSHION

 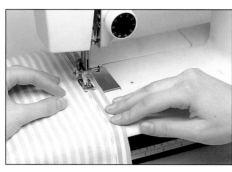 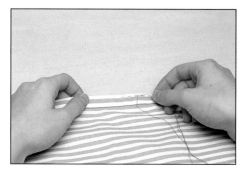

1 Cut out the fabric. Pin and stitch the length of the bolster cover with a French seam. Turn right side out and press. Turn under a double 12 mm/½ in hem at each end of the tube. Pin and tack (baste) the hem in place using a contrasting thread.

2 Stitch along the hems, keeping the stitching close to the inner folds. Remove the tacking (basting) stitches and press thoroughly.

3 Using double thread run a row of gathering stitches along each end of the tube, close to the outer fold of the hem, leaving a long thread end. Insert the bolster pad in the tube, then tighten the gathering threads to close the cover. Secure the thread ends, then cover the small hole left at each end by attaching a furnishing tassel, ribbon bow or a button.

MAKING TASSELS

There are a great variety of tassels available in shops to be attached to the corners of cushions or on the ends of a bolster. The colours, shapes, sizes and designs are infinitesimal, but if you want something a bit more tailor-made, create your own.

Cut out two pieces of cardboard to the length of your finished tassel and 10 cm/ 4 in wide. Place them together. Put 30 cm/12 in of your yarn to one side and then wind as much of the rest around the card from top to bottom until there is sufficient for the type of tassel you are making. The more you wind on, the fuller will be the result.

Thread the set-aside yarn through a needle and then pass the needle through the top of the wound yarn and tie at the top. Repeat several times so that you are left with a strong loop at the top of the tassel – it will attached later to the item you are dressing up.

Holding the yarn firmly in one hand, cut through the yarn at the bottom between the two pieces of card. Release the card and then bind the tassel as near as possible to the top to ensure that the head remains firm. To neaten, comb out the yarn using your fingertips and then give the whole tassel a good trim.

CALCULATING FABRIC

Box cushion: Measure the length and width of the top of the pad and then add 12 mm/½ in all around for seam allowances. Two pieces of fabric this size are needed, one for the top and one for the bottom of the cover. The gusset is made from four pieces of fabric joined together. Measure the depth and width of the pad and add 12 mm/½ in all around for seam allowances. Cut out three pieces of fabric to this size. Add an extra 2.5 cm/1 in to the depth of the fourth piece for the zip (zipper) seam in the gusset.

Bolster cushion: Measure the bolster from the centre point of one end, along its length and around to the centre point of the opposite end, adding a total of 5 cm/2 in for hem allowances. To calculate the width, measure the circumference of the pad and add an extra 2.5 cm/1 in for seam allowances. Cut one large piece to fit these dimensions.

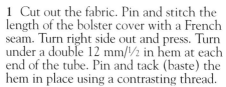

LEFT A luxurious velvet bolster looks good on a window seat or adorning a chaise-longue. Trim the ends or add tassels if you prefer.

EASY CUSHION EMBELLISHMENTS

APPLIQUE USING FUSIBLE BONDING WEB

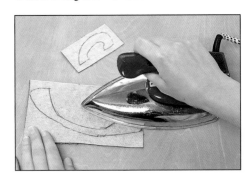

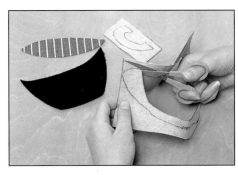

1 Trace your design on to the backing paper of the fusible web. Place the sticky (fusible) side face down on the wrong side of the appliqué fabric. Fuse in place with a hot iron.

2 Cut out the motif around the marked line and peel away the backing paper.

3 Place the motif, sticky side down, on the main fabric and press with a hot iron.

INSERTING EYELETS

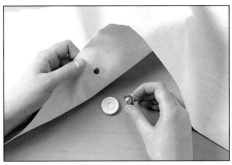

1 First mark the eyelet positions with a pencil, spacing them evenly. Place the plastic disc underneath the fabric at the first mark, then place the cutting part of an eyelet tool over the mark and strike with a hammer to punch the hole.

2 Turn the disc over and place the eyelet on it. Bring the fabric down so that the punched hole fits over the eyelet.

3 Place a washer over the eyelet. Place the flanging part of the tool over the washer and hammer to finish the eyelet.

MITRING RIBBON

CLIPPING CURVES AND CORNERS

To allow a curved seam or a hem to lie flat, it is helpful to snip the seam allowances. Cut out small triangular shapes along the edge, taking care not to snip through the stitching.

To clip corners, cut carefully straight across the corner, as near to the stitching as possible.

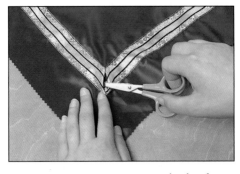

1 Starting at one corner, pin both edges of the ribbon parallel to the hem, making folds in the corner. Machine stitch all around to attach the ribbon to the fabric, and tuck the excess ribbon under at the corners to form a neat diagonal seam.

2 Next, ladder stitch the seam together. This is done by simply making horizontal stitches between the folds and running the needle through the fold.

BASIC MATERIALS

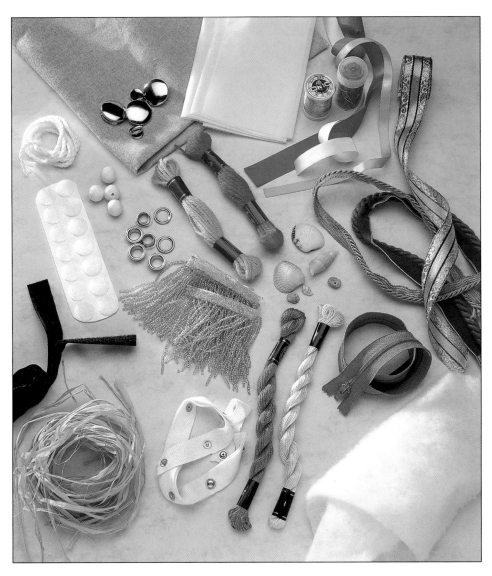

CLOCKWISE FROM TOP LEFT Piping cord, self-cover buttons, fusible bonding web, machine-embroidery thread, beads, ribbons, braid, shells, zip (zipper) fasteners, wadding, embroidery thread, press fastener tape, raffia, fringing, press-and-close fastening, eyelets and cotton balls.

Fusible bonding web: this is used to bond appliqué motifs to fabric prior to stitching; or to bond woven ribbons to a backing fabric.

Machine-embroidery thread: this thread is more lustrous than regular sewing thread. It is also available in metallic shades.

Piping cord: this plain cotton cord can be covered with bias binding and inserted in seams. Ready-made piping is available, though only in a limited range of colours.

Press-and-close fastening: this easy-to-use fastener simply presses together and is a good alternative to zips (zippers). It can be bought in strips or as small pads.

Press fasteners: these metallic fasteners are used for closing light-weight fabric cushions. Press-fastener tape is also available, and has the advantage of being quicker to apply than individual fasteners.

Ribbon: ribbon is available in a vast range of colours, widths and textures. Build up a collection of small pieces and leftovers of ribbon handy for trimming cushions.

Self-cover buttons: available in kit form and in a range of sizes, these may be used as decorative features – such as flower centres – or as closures.

Tapestry wools: hand sew wool to the edges of cushions to add definition.

Wadding: this synthetic padding can be used for filling piping or for making cushion pads.

Zip (zipper) fasteners: available in many weights, lengths and colours, zip fasteners come with either plastic or metal teeth.

Materials

As well as the fabric for your cushion, you will need to choose thread, a type of fastening and trimmings or other decorations. Experiment with dressing up cushion covers with the many fastenings, threads and trimmings available to ensure that the result is unique to you and your home.

Bias binding: buy this ready-made or make your own. Cut on the bias (or cross) to give stretch, these narrow strips may be used to make piping and rouleau loops.

Braid: this woven ribbon is used for trimming and is available in many colours, weights and widths.

Buttons: available in many colours and weights, buttons can be used both decoratively, as part of a design, and to close a cushion.

Cotton balls: available from specialist craft shops, these are used to shape fabric tassels.

Embroidery thread: available as perle, soft-cotton and stranded, use this for embroidery and for making tassels.

Eyelets: purchased in kit form along with a special fixing tool, eyelets can be used on their own or threaded with cord, ribbon or rope.

Fringing: an edging made from cut threads, fringing is an effective and easy way to trim cushions.

DECORATING WITH TABLECLOTHS

Both square and round tablecloths are quick to make. For practical uses choose a washable fabric, either plain or patterned, in a shade which matches or co-ordinates with the general colour scheme of the room as well as any favourite tableware.

Cotton and synthetic blends are easy to sew, require practically no ironing and so make a good choice for everyday table cloths in the kitchen or dining room. Plain, heavy cotton and linen look better for more formal occasions, but they require more hard work to keep them looking good over the years. Always treat stains on table linen immediately and launder as soon afterwards as possible.

BELOW Choose a pretty printed fabric to make a covering for a rectangular kitchen table.

SQUARE TABLECLOTH

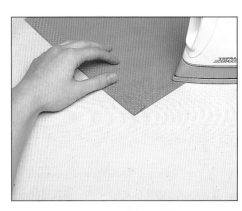

1 Measure the sides of the table top, adding twice the required drop from the edge of the table and 25 mm/1 in all around for hem allowances. Cut out the fabric. Turn and press a 12 mm/½ in hem around the sides.

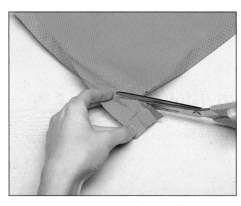

2 Unfold both hems and carefully cut across each corner diagonally, as shown, within 6 mm/¼ in of the corner point at the inner fold.

3 Pin the diagonal edges together, with the right sides facing, and stitch a narrow seam 6 mm/¼ in from the raw edge. Stitch from the inner corner point and make the seam 12 mm/½ in long. Press and turn the corners out to the right side.

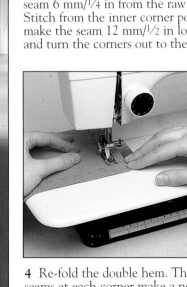

4 Re-fold the double hem. The diagonal seams at each corner make a neat mitre. Stitch around the edge of the table cloth, close to the inner fold. Press the hem.

RIGHT Cover a round occasional table with a floor-length plain undercloth, then top it with a small square cloth made of co-ordinating fabric.

JOINING FABRIC

When joining fabric to make either a square or round table cloth, avoid making a seam down the centre as this can look rather unsightly. Instead, cut out two pieces of fabric to the correct width and use one as the central panel. Cut the second piece in half lengthways and join to either side of the panel, matching the pattern if necessary. Use an ordinary flat seam and neaten the raw edges.

ROUND TABLE CLOTH

1 Measure the diameter of the table top and add twice the depth of the drop plus 25 mm/1 in for hem allowances. Make a pattern from dressmaker's pattern paper using a pencil tied to a piece of string measuring half your final measurement. Hold one end of the string and draw a quarter circle on the paper. Cut out.

2 Fold the fabric into four and pin on the quarter circle pattern, aligning the folded edges of the fabric with the straight edges of the paper. Cut out using sharp scissors.

3 Stitch around the outside of the fabric 12 mm/½ in from the raw edge. This line of stitching marks the hem. Press the edge over on the wrong side of the fabric along the line, without stretching the fabric.

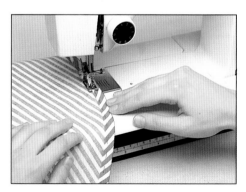

4 Carefully turn under the raw edge to make a double hem, then pin and tack (baste) the hem in place. Stitch around the edge of the table cloth close to the inner fold of the hem. Press the hem well.

TABLEMATS AND NAPKINS

Tablemats and napkins make the perfect table setting for an informal meal. They are simple to make and can be a good way of using offcuts and remnants of fabric.

Tablemats can be made from plain or patterned fabric and are most effective when machine quilted with a layer of wadding (batting) sandwiched between the top and bottom pieces of fabric. The layers help to protect the table surface beneath the plates. Bind the edges with matching or contrasting fabric or ready-made bias binding. Alternatively, choose ready-quilted fabric and follow the instructions for binding given here to finish the edges.

Napkins are simply a hemmed piece of fabric, usually square and made in a cloth which co-ordinates with the tablemats or a tablecloth. Give some thought to the practical purpose of napkins and always make them from fabric which is washable. Polyester and cotton blends are a popular choice for informal napkins, but nothing beats the look of pure, crisp linen for a formal occasion.

MAKING TABLEMATS

1 Decide on the size of the tablemat and cut out two pieces of fabric. Along the short edge of one piece, mark evenly spaced points 25 mm/1 in apart using a ruler and a sharp pencil. Join the points to make lines running across the fabric.

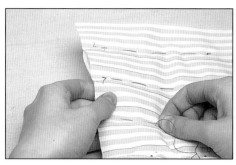

2 Cut a piece of wadding (batting) to the same size as the fabric and sandwich it between the two fabric pieces, with the wrong sides together and the marked piece on top. Pin together then tack (baste) between alternate pencil lines.

3 Lengthen the stitch on the sewing machine, then work parallel rows over the pencil lines using a matching or contrasting thread. Round off the corners by drawing around a cup or small plate, then trim away the surplus fabric.

4 Cut out and join the bias strips until it is long enough to go around the tablemat. Fold the strip so that the raw edges meet in the middle and press. Open out one folded edge of the binding and pin it around the tablemat with the right sides facing and raw edges aligning. Fold back the raw edges where the binding meets.

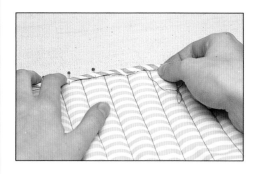

5 Fold over the binding to the wrong side of the tablemat. Pin and stitch the binding in place by hand as shown. Turn the tablemat to the right side and strengthen the edge by working one row of machine stitching around the edge close to the inside fold of the binding.

SIZES AND FABRIC REQUIREMENTS

Tablemats
To decide on a suitable size for tablemats, first arrange a place setting with two sizes of plate plus cutlery (flatware) and measure the area these cover. The side plate and glass can be placed on the table at the edge of the mat, if preferred.

Traditionally, rectangular tablemats measure approximately 20 x 30 cm/8 x 12 in but they can be larger – up to 30 x 45 cm/12 x 18 in. Having decided on the finished size of the tablemats, allow at least 5 cm/2 in extra all around for

working the quilting. Always trim the surplus fabric away after completing the machine quilting but before beginning to bind the edges.

Napkins
Napkins are usually square and vary in size from small napkins of 30 cm/12 in square for tea or coffee parties to large ones measuring 60 cm/24 in for formal occasions. However, the most practical, all-purpose size for napkins is 40 cm/16 in square.

SEWING NAPKINS

Cut out the fabric to the required size. Fold and press a double 6 mm/^{1}/4 in hem all around the edge, taking care to fold the corners over neatly. Pin, tack (baste) and stitch the hem close to the inner fold.

BIAS STRIPS

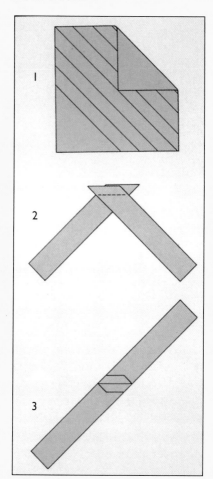

To make bias strips, mark out parallel lines the required distance apart on the cross of the fabric (1). Cut out along the lines, then join the strips together with narrow seams until you have the required length (2). Press the seams open (3).

ABOVE Make a feature of a linen napkin by adding a bow of narrow ribbon and a dainty fresh flowerhead.

BED DRESSING

If your budget were unlimited, you could change your bed linen to suit your mood, the way we change our clothes. What a luxury to slide between luxurious silk sheets one night and crisp white cotton the next, followed by country florals, fleecy tartans, faded stripes and fresh, bright ginghams on each succeeding day. However, practicality rules, and generally we dress our beds to match the room decor and can sometimes end up with the same designs for years on end.

Layering many different prints and textures is a style of bed dressing that is popular and it is both sophisticated and relaxed. The different fabrics can be combined successfully despite, or perhaps because of, their diversity. Frilled prairie prints can be teamed with cotton lace. Cosy tartans and faded patchworks create an attractive and comfortable style.

Use bed linen to set a mood of create an atmosphere. If you want the room to look light and airy, go for white cotton sheets, pillow cases and duvet covers. Dress up the look with hand-crocheted lace borders and cushion covers, mixing old and new together. Or for a touch of country freshness, add a gingham or floral bedcover or a patchwork quilt, or for something more Victorian, use a satin eiderdown. A mixture of plain sheets, duvet cover and pillow cases in different colours creates a modernist style that looks stunning with a black-framed bed.

You can also choose from the huge array of imported textiles now on the market. Layer and drape hot-coloured silks, batiks, ikats and hand-blocked prints to re-create the atmosphere of another continent. Cover pillows with silk scarves and drape saris from a four-poster, then dye your sheets strong earthy yellows, red and browns for a rich layered look.

It is important to consider the feel of fabrics as well as the look. There is nothing to compare with the luxury of Egyptian cotton sheeting, especially after years of laundering, so never say no to hand-me-down pure cottons – even though they need ironing, unlike mixed polycotton sheets. Woollen blankets are wonderfully warm, but very itchy against the skin, so turn back a wide border of top sheet to cover the blanket. Velvet bed throws feel very luxurious and can be made from old velvet curtains. Edge and join panels with a rich-coloured velvet braid for a medieval look.

If you have a four-poster bed, drape it with anything from chintz curtains to strings of beads, or perhaps floaty layers of net and muslin. But you don't need a four-poster to have drapes, and there are all sorts of ways in which fabric can be gathered or hung to give a variety of different effects. A half-tester is a

LEFT This stylish Japanese-inspired bed uses wooden pallets for the bed base and a cream decorator's dustsheet for the cotton bedcover.

ABOVE A draped canopy is a great way to define a sleeping area without completely enclosing it. Here, muslin is draped over a wooden support.

wooden box that is wall-mounted above the bed, with the fabric hung from the inside in two sections, to drape on either side of the bed. The effect can be solid and grand, or light and romantic, depending on the fabrics used. Alternatively, fit a simple semi-circular shelf to the wall above the bed from which to drape a length of muslin. A staple gun is the ideal tool for this type of draping because it allows you to pleat the fabric as you attach it to the shelf. Another advantage is that it is very quick – you can drape a bed in this way in just an hour or two.

A mosquito net is a ready-made bed drape that simply needs a ceiling hook for installation. For a fun look, evoke the African savannah by adding a few potted palms and fake animal-print rugs, or create an air of mystery with a deep colour on the walls to highlight the light drifts of net.

The most important thing to remember when draping a bed is that you will always need more fabric than you imagine. The success of the draped effect relies upon a generous amount of fabric to spill out on to the floor around the bed to add to the sense of luxurious splendour.

Basic tools

The three most invaluable tools for dressing beds are a cordless (hand-held) electric drill; a glue gun and a staple gun. Staples are used for most upholstery work these days and a medium-sized staple gun is ideal for drapes, pleats and upholstery. A cordless drill allows you the freedom of dashing up and down ladders and drilling in awkward places where there is no plug socket available. If you have never used a glue gun before, you will be delighted – they can be used for gluing almost any two surfaces together and provide an instant bond that makes life a lot easier.

BEDHEADS

Beds without headboards create a very utilitarian and temporary impression. A headboard can make the simplest of beds into an item of furniture with definite style, and the possibilities really are endless.

Revamp existing headboards to give a totally different character using paint, rope, upholstery, drapes or fabric wraps. An old padded headboard, for instance, may be very comfortable but quite unpleasant to look at. All you need is a length of fabric and a staple gun to give it a completely new appearance, such as the padded headboard made from chintz curtains, above. A leopard-skin-printed velvet; a rich chocolate brocaded stain; a woven Mexican striped blanket or a black and white hounds-tooth check all have strong designs to give instant attitude to a padded headboard.

You may prefer something a little more subtle. Rub down a new turned-pine bedhead with sandpaper, and then paint it with two coats of matt paint. The first should be a bright colour and the second a lot darker. When the paint has dried, rub it back with fine-grade sandpaper or wire (steel) wool to reveal flashes of the brighter colour beneath. Paint initials or a marriage date along the top rail to transform a mass-produced bed into a family heirloom.

MAKING BED LINEN

Be imaginative when choosing colour schemes and pattern combinations for bed linen. A matching duvet cover and valance looks stylish, particularly when the fabric co-ordinates with the curtains or drapes and other bedroom furnishings. Sheeting is extra-wide fabric sold for making bed linen, and is available in a good range of both plain colours and patterns.

The duvet cover is simply a large bag made from 2 pieces of fabric joined together around the four sides, with an opening left in the bottom edge to allow the duvet to be inserted. Close the opening with a strip of either touch-and-close fastener or press-stud tape. A valance is ideal for covering up an unattractive bed base. It fits over the base, underneath the mattress, and has a frill around 3 of the sides, reaching right down to floor level.

RIGHT **A matching gathered valance finishes off this arrangement perfectly. Lace edging sewn around the pillow cases and duvet cover adds a feminine touch.**

MAKING A DUVET COVER

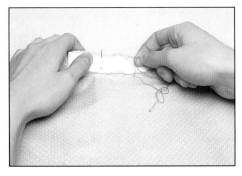

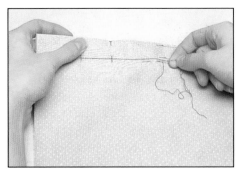

1 Measure the length of the duvet – usually 200 cm/78 in – and add 7 cm/2¾ in for hem and seam allowances. Measure the width and add 4 cm/1½ in for seam allowances. Cut out two pieces of fabric. Turn and stitch a double 2.5 cm/1 in hem along the bottom of each piece. Cut a length of touch-and-close fastener 3 cm/1¼ in longer than the desired opening, separate the strips and pin 1 to the right side of the hem on each piece. Machine stitch around the edge of each strip.

2 Place the 2 fabric pieces with the right sides together so that the fastener strips close. Tack (baste) along the bottom hem from 3 cm/1¼ in inside the strip of fastener and up to each corner.

3 Machine stitch through both layers at right-angles to the hem and 3 cm/1¼ in inside the fastener strip, to enclose the raw edges. Pivot the fabric and continue stitching along the tacked line to the edge of the fabric. Repeat at the other corner.

MAKING A VALANCE

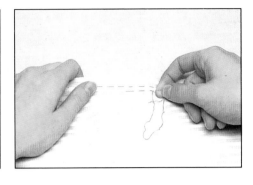

1 Measure the mattress top and add 3.5 cm/1½ in to the length and 3 cm/1¼ in to the width. Cut out 1 piece of fabric to this size for the panel. Round off the 2 bottom corners of the panel by drawing around a large plate and then cutting around the curves.

2 For the frill, you will need sufficient pieces of fabric wide enough to reach from the top of the bed base to the floor, plus 6.5 cm/2½ in, to make a long strip 4 times the mattress length plus twice its width. Join the strips with French seams (see Making a Duvet Cover, step 4) and press. Turn a double 2.5 cm/1 in hem along the lower edge. Pin, tack (baste) and stitch.

3 Divide the frill into 6 equal sections and mark with pins along the top edge. Work 2 rows of gathering stitches between the pins, leaving long thread ends.

CHOOSING FABRIC FOR BED LINEN

The best choice for bed linen is specially woven sheeting, either in pure cotton or a polyester-and-cotton blend. Although pure cotton is cooler in the summer, synthetic blends do have the advantage of needing little or no ironing. Sheeting is very wide, so joins are not necessary, and it is available in a large range of pastel and strong colours.

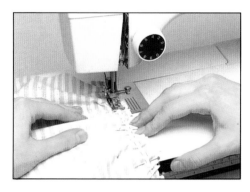

4 Divide the sides and bottom edge of the panel into 6 equal sections and mark with pins. Pull up the gathering stitches in each frill section until it fits the corresponding panel section. Pin each section in place with the right sides facing. Stitch the frill in place 12mm/½ in from the raw edge. Stitch again close to the first line of stitching and neaten the raw edges with machine zigzag. Press the seam allowance towards the panel. Turn a double 12 mm/½ in hem along the remaining raw edges of the frill and panel. Pin and stitch.

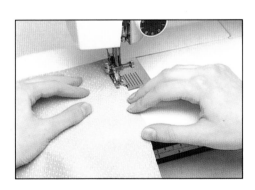

4 Turn so that the wrong sides are facing. Make a French seam around the remaining three sides, as follows. Pin and stitch 6 mm/¼ in from the raw edge. Trim the seam close to the stitching, then open the fastener and turn the cover so that the right sides are facing. Stitch around the three sides again to enclose the raw edges and complete the seam. Turn the cover to the right side and press.

LEFT **A crisply checked duvet cover and pillow cases accentuate the light and airy feel of a country bedroom.**

DECORATIVE EFFECTS – TECHNIQUES

You may not have the budget or the energy to give your house a complete make-over, but any one of the ideas contained within this chapter is certain to lift a tired piece of furniture or create a focal point in an uninspiring corner. Whether you want a quick fix with splashes of colour, or to make the most of natural textures, there are many ways to quickly and easily transform a room or object from the dull to the dramatic. You won't need specialist techniques to adorn a plain sofa cover with lengths of raffia or rope or suspend collections of shells from curtain rails and tie-backs.

With the recent developments in water-based paints, it is now easier than ever to use decorative paint techniques in your home. Whether you want to colourwash your walls or add graining or distressed patterns to your furniture, with a few emulsion (latex) and acrylic paints and water-based varnish to finish-off the surface, these effects are simple and quick to create. Of course, some paint techniques require more sophisticated materials, but start with the simpler ones and once you are comfortable with those techniques move on to gilding and marbling once you feel more confident.

In this section, there is technical advice given on, among other paint effects, stencilling, stamping, decoupage, antiquing, stippling and rag-rolling. The basic materials and equipment needed each time are listed together with the most important aspects of each technique. Read the relevant pages and then armed with a paintbrush or two, you can go ahead and do the real thing.

There is one very important point to remember with decorative effects and embellishments, however: don't overdo it. A room that has colourwashed walls, a stencilled frieze, gilded picture frames and a marbled chest might be too much of a good thing. Instead, concentrate your energies on one or perhaps two techniques for each room. In this way, the colours and artistry will make much more of a statement for you and your visitors to enjoy.

OPPOSITE There is virtually no limit to the versatility of modern wall coverings. This complementary match of broken colour and simple stripes is linked by a striking multicoloured border at dado (chair) rail level.

STENCILLING: BASIC MATERIALS AND EQUIPMENT

Materials

A variety of materials can be used for stencilling, from special stencilling paints and sticks to acrylics and latex. Each has its own properties and will create different effects.

Acrylic stencil paint: acrylic stencil paint is quick-drying, reducing the possibility of the paint running and seeping behind the stencil. Acrylic stencil paints are available in a wide range of colours, and can be mixed for more subtle shades.

Acrylic varnish: this is useful for sealing finished projects.

Emulsion (latex) paint: ordinary household vinyl emulsion can also be used for stencilling. It is best to avoid the cheaper varieties, as these contain a lot of water and will seep through the stencil.

Fabric paint: this is used in the same way as acrylic stencil paint, and comes in an equally wide range of colours. Set with an iron according to the manufacturer's instructions, it will withstand washing and everyday use. As with ordinary stencil paint, do not overload the brush with colour, as it will seep into the fabric. Always back the fabric you are stencilling with scrap paper or newspaper to prevent the paint from marking the work surface.

Gold leaf and gold size: these can be used to great effect. The actual design is stencilled with gold size. The size is then left to become tacky, and the gold leaf is rubbed over the design.

Metallic creams: these are available in many different metallic finishes, from gold to copper, bronze and silver. Apply as highlights on a painted base, or use for the entire design. Creams can be applied with cloths or your fingertip.

Oil-based stencil sticks and creams: the sticks can be used in the same way as a wax crayon, while the creams can be applied with a brush or your fingertip. With either one, there is no danger of overloading the colour, and they won't run. The disadvantage is their long drying time (overnight in some cases); also, the colours can become muddy when mixed. Sticks and creams are also available for fabrics.

Equipment

Stencilling does not require a great deal of special equipment; many of the items used are commonly found in most households. A few tools, however, will make the job easier.

Brushes: it is worth investing in a set of good stencil brushes. The ends of the brushes should be flat and the bristles firm, to let you control the application of paint. A medium-size brush (4 cm/ 1½ in diameter) is a useful, all-purpose size, but you may want to buy one size smaller and one size larger as well. You will need a selection of household paintbrushes for applying large areas of background colour, and small artist's paintbrushes for adding fine details.

Craft knife: use for cutting out stencils from cardboard.

CLOCKWISE FROM BOTTOM LEFT Acrylic stencil paint, oil-based cream and metallic creams, fabric paint, oil-based stencil sticks, emulsion paint, gold leaf, acrylic varnish and gold size.

Cutting mat: this provides a firm surface to cut into and will help prevent the craft knife from slipping.

Masking tape: as the stencil may need to be repositioned, it is advisable to hold it in place with masking tape, which can be removed fairly easily from most surfaces.

Paint-mixing container: this may be necessary for mixing paints and washes.

Pencils: keep a selection of soft and hard artist's pencils to transfer the stencil design on to cardboard. Use an ordinary pencil to mark on your object the positions of the stencils before applying.

Stencil card (cardboard): the material used to make the stencil is a matter of preference. Speciality stencil card is available waxed from specialist art stores, which means that it will last longer, but ordinary cardboard or heavy paper can also be used. It is worth purchasing a sheet of clear acetate if you wish to keep your stencil design, to re-use time and again.

CLOCKWISE FROM TOP LEFT Rulers, tape measure, stencil brushes, household paintbrush, cutting mat, stencil card (cardboard), tracing paper, pencil, craft knife, paint-mixing container, masking tape.

Tape measure and rulers: some patterns may require accuracy. Measuring and planning the positions of your stencils before you begin will aid the result.

Tracing paper: use to trace and transfer your stencil design on to stencil card.

BASIC TECHNIQUES

PAINTING TECHNIQUES

Stencilling is not difficult to master, and you can create some wonderful 3-dimensional designs but it is worth practising first to get used to handling the brush and to become accustomed to the properties of the paints you use. The tips and techniques suggested below will make the task easier.

CUTTING A STENCIL

1 Place the stencil on a cutting mat or piece of thick cardboard and tape in place. Use a craft knife for cutting.

2 It is safer to move the cutting mat towards you and the knife when working around awkward shapes. Continue, moving the mat.

TRANSFERING TEMPLATES

1 To transfer a template on to a piece of stencil card (cardboard), place some tracing paper over the design, and draw over it with a hard pencil.

2 Turn over the tracing paper and, on the back of the design, rub over the lines you have drawn with a soft pencil. Turn the tracing paper back to the right side and place on top of a sheet of stencil card. Draw over the original lines with a hard pencil.

1 Block stencilling: Use for filling in large areas in a single, solid colour. As in all stencilling, remember not to apply the paint too heavily – less is more. Always blot the paint on to a piece of cardboard before you begin.

2 Block stencilling with second colour stippled: When applying two colours, always apply the lighter shade first, then the darker. Do not cover the entire surface with the first colour; leave a gap for the second shade, then blend later. Use a separate, clean brush for each colour.

3 Dry-brushing, rotating from edge: Using big circular strokes, work from the outside of the whole stencil, moving inward. This should leave you with more paint on the outside, as there will be less on your brush as you move inward.

4 Two-colour blocking: When you apply the first colour, do not fully block out the petals; instead, outline them with the first colour and leave the centres bare. Use the second colour to fill. Take care not to apply your paint too heavily.

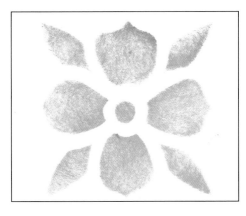

5 Stippling: This method uses more paint and less pressure than rotating or flicking. Taking a reasonable amount of paint on the bristles of your brush, simply place it down lightly. This gives a rougher look. Do not go over it too many times, as this spoils the effect.

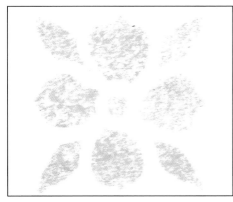

6 Dry-brush stippling: This is similar to stippling, except that it is essential to dab most of the paint off the bristles before you start. This gives a softer effect.

7 Rotating and shading: Using a very dry brush with a tiny amount of paint, place your brush on one side of the stencil and rotate the brush in circles. Repeat, using a slightly darker colour on the edges for soft shading.

8 Flicking: For the flicking effect on the leaves, use slightly more paint on the brush. Working from the centre, flick the paint outward once or twice. Be careful not to overdo.

9 Flicking upwards: Using a reasonable amount of paint (not too wet or too dry) on your brush, flick upwards only. This creates a line at the top of the petals and leaves.

10 Dry-brushing and rotating: Apply a tiny amount of paint by rotating the bristles from the centre and from the outside tips, to give more paint in these areas. Work along the line, using less pressure than on the centre and the tips. This gives a soft shade in between.

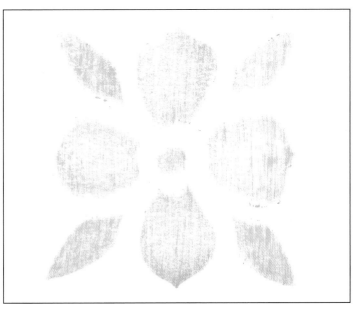

11 Brushing up and down: Using slightly more paint on your brush than you would for rotating, brush up and down only, taking care to keep your lines vertical.

STAMPING: BASIC MATERIALS AND EQUIPMENT

CLOCKWISE FROM TOP LEFT Dutch metal leaf and gold size, coloured inks, low-density sponge), precut stamp, high-density sponge, medium-density sponges, interior filler (spackle), emulsion (latex) paint, varnish, wallpaper paste.

Materials

When you are stamping, you will discover that different paints and stamps will produce very different results. Here are some of the best materials to experiment with.

Dutch metal leaf and gold size: metal leaf is a cheap, easy-to-use alternative to real gold leaf. Use a sponge stamp to apply gold size in a repeating pattern. When the size is tacky, carefully apply the gold leaf.

Inks: water-based inks are too runny to use on their own but can be added to wallpaper paste or varnish to make a mixture thick enough to adhere to the stamp. Use them for paper or card, but not for walls. If you are using rubber stamps, inkpads suitable for them are commercially available in a wide range of colours.

Interior filler (spackle): add filler, in its dry powdered state to emulsion (latex) paint to give it body without diluting the colour.

Paint: water-based paints such as emulsion and artist's acrylics dry quickly to a permanent finish. Use emulsion paint straight from the can or dilute it with wallpaper paste or varnish. For wall treatments, emulsion paint can be thinned with a little water and sponged or brushed over the wall as a colourwash.

Precut stamps: rubber stamps are widely available in thousands of designs, usually mounted on wooden blocks. Finely detailed motifs are best suited to small-scale projects, while bolder shapes are more effective when used for walls and furniture. Make your own from foam or sponge.

Sponge or foam: different types of sponge are characterized by their density and are easy to make yourself. High-density sponge is best for detailed shapes and will give a smooth, sharp print. Medium-density sponge or low-density sponge will absorb more paint and give a more textured result and is better for larger projects.

Varnish: use water-based, acrylic varnish (sold as quick-drying) for stamping projects. The varnish can be mixed with emulsion paint or ink to thicken the texture and create a range of different sheens.

Wallpaper paste: wallpaper paste allows you to thin emulsion paint without making it too runny to adhere to the stamp. Mix up the paste with the required amount of water first, then add the emulsion.

DECORATIVE EFFECTS – TECHNIQUES

Equipment

Stamping is a quick and effective way of repeating a design on a wide variety of surfaces, using many different mixtures of paints and inks. It does not require a great deal of specialist equipment; many of the items used are found in most households.

Craft knife: a sharp-bladed craft knife is essential for cutting your own stamps out of thick sponge or foam. Use a cutting mat to protect your work surface, and always direct the blade away from your fingers.

Lino blocks: linoleum blocks are available from art and craft shops and can be cut to make stamps which recreate the look of a wood block. You will need special lino-cutting tools, which are also easily available, to accurately scoop out the areas around the design. Hold the lino with your spare hand behind your cutting hand for safety. Always cut away from you.

Masking tape: use for masking off areas of walls and furniture when painting.

Natural sponge: available in various sizes, use for applying colourwashes to walls before stamping.

Paintbrushes: a range of decorator's brushes is needed for painting furniture and walls before stamping. Use a broad brush to apply colourwashes to walls. Stiff brushes can be used for stippling paint on to stamps for textured effects, while finer brushes are used to pick out details or to apply paint to the stamp.

Pencils, pens and crayons: use a soft pencil to trace templates for stamps, and for making easily removable guidelines on walls. Draw motifs freehand using a marker pen on medium- and low-density sponge. Always use a white crayon on black upholstery foam.

Rags: keep a stock of clean rags and cloths for cleaning stamps and preparing surfaces.

Ruler and tape measure: use these to plan your design.

Scissors: use sharp scissors to cut out medium- and low-density sponge shapes, and are especially useful for cutting out the basic shapes. Also handy for cutting out templates.

Sponge rollers: use to apply the paint evenly over the whole stamp. Small paint rollers can be used to load your stamps, though you will need several if you are stamping in different colours. Use a brush to apply a second colour to act as a highlight or shadow, or to pick out details of the design.

BASIC TECHNIQUES

Stamping is a quick and effective method of repeating a design on a wide variety of surfaces, using many different mixtures of paint and inks.

APPLYING PAINT

There are several efficient ways of applying paint to a stamp. If you are using a roller, pour a little paint on to the side of a flat plate, then use the sponge roller to pick up a small amount and roll it out over the rest of the plate until you have an even covering. Roll the paint on to the stamp.

Alternatively, use a fairly stiff brush and apply the paint with a dabbing or stippling motion. This technique enables more than one colour to be applied and for detail to be picked out. Be careful not to overload the stamp, as this may cause it to slip when stamping.

If you want to use a sponge, spread the paint on a plate and use a natural sponge to pick up the paint and dab it on to the stamp. This method allows you to put a light, even covering of paint on to the stamp. For a dry look, use an inkstamp pad. Press the stamp on to the inkpad several times to ensure a good covering.

MAKING STAMPS

1 Use high-density sponge for sharply defined and detailed designs. Trace your chosen motif on to the sponge using a soft pencil for dark, clear lines.

2 Roughly cut around the design, then spray the tracing paper with adhesive to hold it in place on the sponge while you are cutting it out.

3 Cut along the outline using a sharp blade, then, pinching the background sections, cut them away holding the blade away from your fingers.

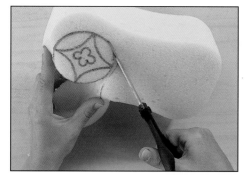

4 Sharp scissors, rather than a blade, can be used with medium-to-low density sponge and are especially useful for cutting out the basic shapes.

PLANNING A DESIGN

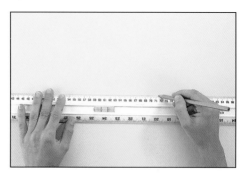

1 With the aid of a spirit level (carpenter's level), draw a faint pencil line to use as a guide when stamping. Once the stamping is finished and the paint is dry, this guideline can be removed using a cloth wrung out in soapy water and rubbed along the line.

2 Stamp the motif several times on scrap paper and cut out the prints. Tape them to the wall so that you can judge how your design will look.

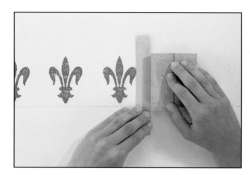

3 When using a stamp mounted on a block, draw a straight line on the back to help with positioning. Align the block with the pencil guideline on the wall. A piece of cardboard held between the previous print and the stamp will ensure consistent spacing between motifs.

Stamp Effects

Although stamping is sometimes thought of as another form of stencilling it is essentially a form of printing. You can achieve many different effects with stamps, depending on the paint mixture you use and the way it is applied. The same stamp, cut from high-density sponge, was used to make all these prints.

1 Half-shade: Roll the first, paler colour over the stamp, then roll a second, darker shade over one half only, to create a three-dimensional shadowed effect.

2 Sponge print: Applying the paint with a sponge gives variable, individual prints.

3 Two-tone: Using a dry roller, load the stamp with the first colour, then apply the second to the top and bottom edges only.

4 Stippled: This stippled effect gives the print lots of surface interest: apply the paint with a stiff brush and a dabbing, stippling motion.

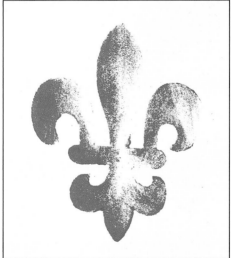

5 Light shadow: The paint has been applied with a roller, covering each element of the motif more heavily on one side to create a delicate shadow effect.

6 Contrasting detail: Pick out details of the design in a contrasting colour: apply the first colour with a roller, then use a brush to apply the second colour in the areas you want.

DECOUPAGE: BASIC MATERIALS AND EQUIPMENT

DECORATIVE EFFECTS – TECHNIQUES

SPIRALLING FROM TOP LEFT Traditional paints, wallpaper paste, masking tape, shellac, cuttings, paper glue, wood glue, white spirit (paint thinner), oil-based varnish, emulsion paint and PVA (white) glue.

Materials

The materials needed for decoupage are inexpensive and readily available from arts and crafts stores. The basic items are listed here.

Acrylic paint: comes in a range of colours. Ideal for applying colour highlights, acrylic paint can be used full strength or diluted with water or an acrylic medium. Mixing with an acrylic medium gives a strong colour.

Cuttings: images for decoupage can be gleaned from many sources such as wrapping paper, prints, newspaper, greetings cards and catalogues. They can be photocopied in black and white and colourwashed in your own choice of colours, or colour copied to make endless duplicates for a frieze or set of mats. Start a collection of decoupage images, motifs and pictures that catch your eye so you will always have a store of cuttings from which to choose.

Emulsion (latex) paint: this comes in a wide variety of colours and dries quickly. Ranges of traditional paints are manufactured in subtle colours that dry to a chalky finish similar to the old-fashioned casein or milk paints. They need sealing with a coat of acrylic varnish before the next coat is applied.

Glues: paper glue is a golden-coloured liquid glue that comes in a bottle. It is ideal for paper projects, although it may be slower to dry than other glues. PVA glue is a white glue that dries quickly to a clear finish. It can be used full strength or diluted as required. It can also be diluted to use as a sealer on finished decoupage projects.

Wood glue may be required for some projects involving woodwork. It is a stronger form of PVA glue.

Wallpaper paste is easy to mix up and use for larger projects, but it is not as strong as PVA glue. It contains fungicide, which prevents mould. It has a slippery feel, ideal for moving detailed motifs into position.

Masking tape: used for screening areas before painting and also for temporarily fixing the motifs while arranging them.

Spray adhesive: gives a light, even application of glue. Always work in a well-ventilated area when using this type of glue.

Varnishes: these are available as oil-based polyurethane or water-based acrylic varnishes. Both types are available in gloss, satin (mid-sheen) or matt finishes. Acrylic varnish has the advantage of not yellowing with age. Shellac dries to a transparent finish. It is less hardwearing than varnish and tends to be used between layers rather than as a finishing sealer.

White spirit (paint thinner): a clear solvent used for diluting oil-based paints, washing brushes and cleaning objects to be decoupaged.

Wood filler: necessary for filling any holes in furniture or other wooden items before applying the decoupage motifs. Sand down the dried filler to ensure a smooth surface.

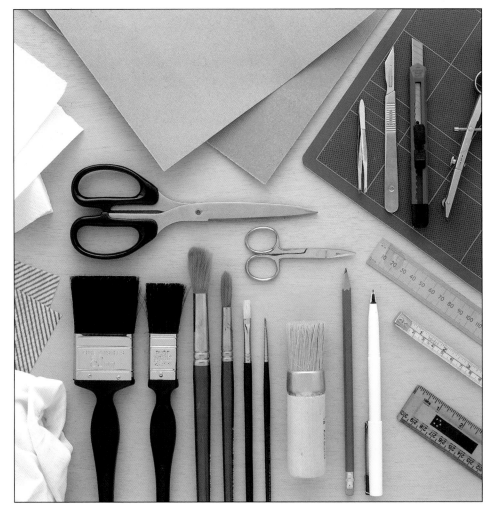

CLOCKWISE FROM TOP LEFT Cutting mat, tweezers, scalpel, craft knife, pair of compasses, metal ruler, tape measure, plastic ruler, felt-tipped pen, pencil, stencil brush, artist's paintbrushes, household paintbrushes, soft cloth, dish cloth, kitchen paper, medium-grade and fine-grade sandpaper, large scissors and small, sharp scissors.

Equipment

Apart from a pair of small, sharp scissors and a selection of paintbrushes in different sizes, there are very few pieces of equipment that are needed for decoupage projects, which makes it the ideal craft for beginners.

Artist's paintbrushes: used for hand-tinting prints and adding intricate decoration to a project.

Craft knife: some people prefer to use this instead of a pair of scissors and it is particularly good for cutting out intricate patterns. The blades are extremely sharp; they should always be used with a cutting mat so that the knife does not slip or damage your work surface. Replace the blade regularly so that it remains sharp and gives you a good, clean outline.

Household paintbrushes: used for painting basecoats and applying varnishes. You can buy specialist varnishing brushes, although household ones are perfectly adequate. Always ensure a different brush is used for the varnish and the paintwork, otherwise the varnish will have flecks of paint in it. Also, buy the best-quality paintbrush you can or the work may be spoilt by loose hairs caught in the varnish. Clean brushes immediately after use; clean them in water if the paint or varnish is water-based or in white spirit if the paint or varnish is oil-based.

Metal rulers (straightedges): essential if you are cutting along a straight edge with a scalpel (craft knife) because the blade will make nicks in a plastic ruler and then the line will not be straight. Metal rulers are also useful for cutting paper when you want a softer edge than can be made by scissors. A metal or plastic ruler can be used for measuring and designing projects.

Pair of compasses: sometimes needed for designing projects.

Pencil and paper: needed for planning designs and marking the positions of cut-outs.

Photocopier: access is also very useful because you may need to make large numbers of copies.

Sandpaper: comes in various grades from fine to coarse. Use a fine-grade paper for rubbing down between coats of paint and use a coarser paper for preparing surfaces before beginning your decoupage.

Scissors: a small, sharp pair is needed to cut around intricate motifs and a pair of larger ones for cutting out templates and larger pieces of paper and card (cardboard).

Shellac: this dries to a transparent finish. It is less hardwearing than varnish and tends to be used between layers rather than as a finishing sealer.

Soft cloths: useful for rubbing down images and removing excess glue from the surface. Kitchen paper and soft cloths are as good.

Stencil paintbrushes: used when a decoupage project also involves using stencilled images.

Tweezers: useful for picking up very delicate cut-outs, which may get damaged in your fingers.

BASIC TECHNIQUES

The craft of decoupage is a delightfully quick way of decorating all kinds of objects in the home. The techniques of decoupage are very simple and are quickly learned. The most important skill is that of carefully cutting out and handling the paper cutting. These pages describe all the basic processes involved in decoupage.

PREPARING SURFACES

For older and worn wooden items, it is essential to wipe the surface with white spirit (paint thinner), then fill any nicks with wood filler, following the manufacturer's instructions. Sand down the object with sandpaper until smooth and seal with shellac.

Then wipe away any dust with white spirit so that you have a clean surface. Finally, prime the object with two coats of white emulsion (latex) paint. An additional colour can then be painted on top before applying your decoupage.

LEFT This delicately-patterned screen adds a gentle feel to an otherwise bare corner of a room. The decoupaged leaves are complemented by vase of flowers.

SEALING AND CUTTING

1 Seal the image with a coat of shellac painted on to the paper. The images may be wrapping paper, colour or black-and-white photocopies or one-off pictures. Shellac also stiffens delicate images, making them easier to cut out and preventing discoloration.

2 Cut roughly around the image with a pair of large scissors. Then cut around the edge of the image with a smaller pair of scissors. For delicate images, hold the paper in your hand and rotate it as you cut the curves. Always use a ruler to tear straight edges.

3 To cut out internal unwanted paper, use a craft knife and cutting mat. Always take care when using a craft knife.

STICKING

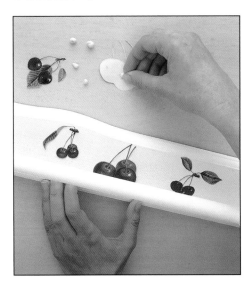  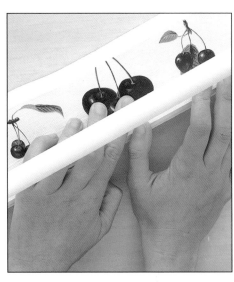

1 Hold and arrange your cut-out images on the painted surface with blobs of low-tack reusable adhesive. This allows you to try different arrangements without damaging and wasting your images.

2 When you are happy with the positioning, glue the motifs on to the background using PVA (white) glue diluted with a little water.

3 Use a pair of tweezers to pick up delicate images. Place in position, press down and rub over with your fingers or a soft cloth to get rid of any air bubbles or excess glue. Wipe off any excess glue with a damp cloth. Allow to dry.

VARNISHING

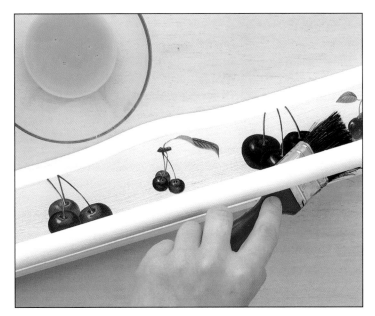 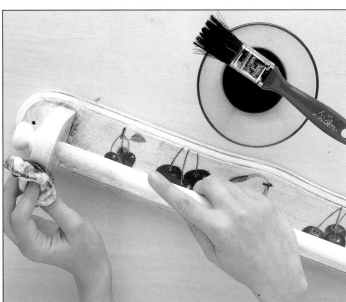

1 Varnishing is the final protection. Acrylic varnish is faster-drying and less toxic than oil-based varnish. Seal your finished design with up to twelve coats of clear varnish, giving it a light sanding between coats. The object must be left to dry in a dust-free atmosphere so that it does not pick up any dust particles.

2 Finally, to age an object and to blend the colours, paint on a stained varnish such as antique pine or oak. To get rid of any brushstrokes, rub off the excess stain with a clean cloth, lightly dabbed all over. You can then use a wax polish to give a deep satin feel to the finished piece.

GILDING: BASIC MATERIALS AND EQUIPMENT

LEFT The gilder's tools of the trade, including sizes, gesso, gold leaf and powders.

Materials

The materials needed for gilding are varied but they are readily available from craft shops due to the increasing popularity of this time-honoured decorative technique.

Bronze, aluminium and silver powders: can be mixed with varnish or blown or brushed on to size. They can be used to colour design work, or on small objects with fine detail.

Gesso: this fine chalk powder is the key ingredient of gesso solution. White or coloured ready-made acrylic gessos are also now available.

Gold leaf: gold leaf is available as loose- or transfer leaf. Both types come in books of 25 leaves. Gold leaf is available in many tones, weights and thicknesses and is classed in carats.

Gold and silver paints: these are made in the same way as liquid leaf but from cheaper materials. They are useful for decorative painting.

Liquid leaf: this mixture of metallic powder and deep red primer can be used to cover a wide variety of surfaces. It comes in many shades.

Methylated spirit (paint thinner): this spirit is used to clean brushes after using polishes and some oil-based primers. It is also used to dilute gilding water and for distressing gilded surfaces.

Oil paints: there are many different types of oil paints. The more expensive they are, the more intense and fast the colours.

Rabbit skin glue: this comes in granule form and constitutes part of the mix for gesso and gilding water.

Red oxide metal primer: this primer is the ideal base coat for metal before applying paint or substitute leaf. It prevents rust and allows paint to take to the surface.

Dutch metal leaf: this looks like gold leaf but is much cheaper and is made from a copper and zinc alloy. It is available in 15 cm/6 in square sheets.

Shellac and polishes: used to seal and protect gold but be aware that they will affect the colour.

Silver, copper and aluminium leaf: 15 cm/6 in square. Buy in books of 25 to 500 loose or transfer leaves.

Spray paints: oil- and water-based, these come in a vast range of colours including tones of gold, silver and metallic copper.

Talc: used in a pounce bag to make sure that the area is clean and that the leaf will adhere only to the sized areas.

Water-based size: a fast-drying synthetic size that sets tacky after 15 to 20 minutes. It can be used for oil gilding and with bronze powders and substitute leaf.

Waxes: clear and coloured waxes are available and are used as sealants or to protect gilded objects. Use coloured waxes to subtly change the tone of a gilded object.

LEFT A selection of brushes for gilding, plus other essentials, such as a craft knife and gloves for small decorating jobs.

Equipment

Some of the equipment needed for gilding is specialized but once you have bought it, it will last for a long time as long as it is looked after properly.

Agate burnishers: these are made from a small piece of agate mounted in brass on a wooden handle and are available in various sizes and shapes.

Bain marie (double boiler): use for melting beeswax pellets, ready-made gessos and sizes. You could improvise your own by placing a saucepan over another one containing plenty of boiling water.

Brushes: different brushes are needed for different purposes. Before you start a project, ensure you have the following: badger brushes for softening glazes and varnishes; bristle and decorator's brushes in varying widths for applying paints and varnishes; gilder's tips to pick up real gold leaf before applying it to a surface; sable brushes for detailed painting, and stippling brushes for taking dust off glazes.

Cloths: cotton rags are the best type of cloths for use in gilding and producing other decorative finishes. Small cotton dusters are ideal for gently burnishing delicate surfaces.

Cotton balls: use these for pressing real gold leaf into place and for small cleaning jobs.

Gilder's knife: used to cut loose-leaf.

Gilder's pad: a soft pad surrounded by a screen of parchment or a similar paper screen to shield delicate gold leaf from drafts.

Gloves: use disposable gloves for smaller decorative gilding jobs.

Glues: epoxy resin glue, rubber-based glue and white glue are all useful in decorative work.

Mask: always wear a face mask when working with bronze powders, sprays and some oil-based glazes.

Measuring tools, pens and pencils: these are necessary for positioning and measuring when stencilling and doing decorative painting.

Natural sponge: used to produce a variety of decorative finishes.

Paint kettles: available in metal or plastic for mixing paints and glazes. Oil-based paints and glazes should not be stored in plastic.

Sandpaper: comes in different grades for smoothing as well as producing an adhesive key for finishes. Wet-and-dry sandpaper is the best type for use on furniture and other items to be gilded.

Scalpels and craft knives: collect various types for decorative work.

Stencil card: this specialist card made from manilla coated in boiled oil is used for making your own stencils.

Wire (steel) wool: comes in different grades for smoothing and providing a key for finishes. It is also used for distressing gilded surfaces.

BASIC TECHNIQUES

Gilding is one of the most ancient and beautiful arts dating back thousands of years and simple, yet professional results are within the reach of everyone. The technique of water gilding is difficult to master, but the results are magnificent, especially on small areas. The secret to successful results lies in the preparation of the surface prior to gilding.

WATER GILDING

1 Make sure the surface you are gilding is clean and dry. Melt rabbit skin glue granules in a bain marie (double boiler). This will take 5 to 10 minutes. When the granules are dissolved, the size will be the consistency of runny caramel. Sift just enough gesso power into the melted granules to colour the liquid. Heat until the liquid is translucent. Paint on to the surface so that it takes into the grain and leave the object to dry overnight.

2 Melt two parts rabbit skin glue to one part water. Take off the heat and sift in enough gesso powder to come above the liquid. Put back over the heat and stir well to dissolve all the lumps. While still warm, apply the liquid to the surface. Apply up to 12 coats. Try to complete this stage on the same day and leave the final coat to dry overnight. Alternatively, apply up to 12 coats of ready-made gesso in white or your chosen colour.

3 To make the gilding water, half-fill a jar with water. Slowly add methylated spirit (paint thinner) until the water is lightly coloured. Add a teaspoon of melted rabbit skin glue. Stir well until the solution is thoroughly mixed. Paint a small amount on to the area you wish to gild first. It will enable the leaf to adhere to the surface.

4 Gently place loose gold leaf on to the dampened surface and press down lightly with cotton balls. Continue painting on the gilding water and applying the gold leaf until the whole area is covered. Any small bare patches can be covered using a sable brush and small pieces of leaf. Leave to dry for 1 hour.

5 When the surface is dry, burnish with an agate burnisher, going over the surface several times until a deep shine begins to appear. Do not press too hard, since this will soften the gesso.

6 To distress the surface to give an aged effect, gently rub the surface with wire (steel) wool. Do not rub too hard and take care to distress only the areas that would receive wear naturally. When satisfied, seal the whole surface with clear wax. Leave to dry, and then polish with a soft cloth to improve the lustre.

ALTERNATIVE GILDING METHODS

LIQUID LEAF

1 Apply an oil- or water-based primer to the surface to be gilded and leave to dry. Paint on a base coat in the desired colour and leave to dry.

2 Shake the bottle of liquid leaf and brush on to the surface with a bristle or gilding brush. Leave to dry for approximately 20 minutes. Seal with a poly-urethane varnish or shellac.

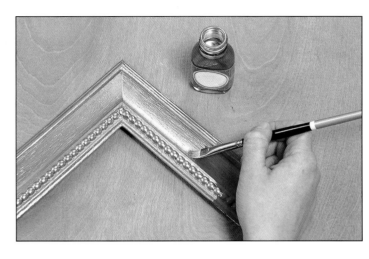

PASTES

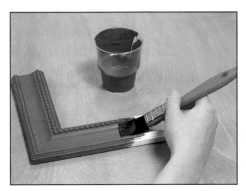

1 Apply an oil- or water-based primer to the surface and leave to dry. Paint on a base coat in the desired colour and also allow that to dry.

2 Apply the paste to the surface using a cloth or brush. Rub it in well, paying particular attention to any areas of detail. Leave to dry.

3 Rub the surface with a soft cloth, then seal with a wax or polish and polishing rubber if required.

POWDERS

1 Apply an oil- or water-based primer to the surface and leave to dry. Paint on a base coat in the desired colour and leave to dry. Apply oil- or water-based size and leave to become tacky.

2 Place a little powder at a time on a saucer and dip a brush into the powder, tapping off any excess, and brush on to the size. Always work in a well-ventilated area and a good distance from the powder.

3 Seal with a polishing rubber or a coat of French enamel varnish. The colour of the varnish adds a lovely jewel-like finish to the gold.

CREATING AN ANTIQUE LOOK

Through ageing and antiquing wooden furniture it is possible to make a new and shiny table or chair look as though it has been sitting around for a long time developing the patina of old age. Some techniques are more dramatic than others and some are more suitable for painted surfaces than bare wood while others make use of the two effects together to achieve a successful finish. Practise on an area that is not normally visible before starting the whole piece. In this way you can hone your skills for the best finished effect.

The materials and equipment that you need for this type of paint effect are much the same as for other general techniques: a variety of paints, paintbrushes and varnishes. However, in addition you may need a hot air stripper for more heavy-duty antiquing and some wire (steel) wool for rubbing back paint layers.

RESIST TECHNIQUES

1 Petroleum jelly: On a dried coat of emulsion (latex) brush on blobs of petroleum jelly, working inwards from the edges of the furniture. Then paint with a second colour of emulsion but don't worry about completely covering the surface. Leave to dry and then wipe with a cloth and soapy water. The paint over the petroleum jelly will peel away to reveal the paint beneath.

2 Candle wax: Use this technique alone or follow on from the petroleum jelly described above, as here. Once the paint has dried again, rub over the surface with candle wax, concentrating on the edges. Apply a third colour of emulsion and when dry rub over the surface with sandpaper. The top coat of paint will come off where there was wax. Finish with two coats of varnish.

ANTIQUING

1 Tinted varnishes: Are available in different colours so choose one to suit your furniture. Antique pine is used here and is applied with broad brush strokes. While wet, wipe away the excess; the more that is removed, the less old is the finish.

2 Button polish: For a more subtle finish, use button polish. Rub on with a soft cloth and then remove the excess while the polish is still wet.

3 Artist's oil colour: This time mix a little burnt umber with white spirit (paint thinner) in a paint kettle (mixing cap) to a very thin wash and apply with a paintbrush. While wet, wipe off the excess for a slightly stained finish. Varnish when dry to protect the surface.

Aging

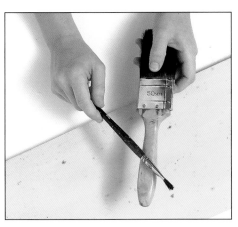

1 Age spots: Mix a little burnt umber with white spirit (paint thinner) until it is a thin wash. Splatter on with a brush to slightly dot the surface. While wet, take a dry brush and brush in one direction.

2 Heavy aged look: Paint a base coat in emulsion (latex), leave to dry and then apply a darker colour. When this is dry, remove random strips of paint with a hot air stripper and a knife. Finish off by smoothing and further ageing the surface with wire (steel) wool.

3 Lighter chipped look: Apply two coats of paint as for the heavy aged look. When dry, run a paint scraper across the surface. This will remove small chunks of paint which can be softened with sandpaper. Concentrate on the edges for a more authentic finish. Varnish when dry to protect the surface.

Distressed Floorboards

1 Using wood stains on wooden floors allows you to achieve quickly the subtle variations in colour that occur naturally with age. Before starting, remove old paint spills using a sander and knock in any protruding nails. Brush the boards with a wire brush along the direction of the grain, with the occasional cross stroke to give a distressed effect.

2 Experiment with a few different wood stains of the same make, mixing colours together – a little should go a long way. Use scrap wood, to test the effect before you commit yourself.

3 With either a lint-free cloth or a brush, apply the stain. This will stain anything porous, so wear rubber gloves and old clothes. Start by applying a generous quantity of stain but rub most of the surplus off. Don't stop till you've finished with the floor or there will be a definite line; keep the joins between areas random and avoid overlapping bands of stain.

4 It's better to do one thin coat all over, then go back to apply further coats, perhaps working the stain into knots or grooves, for a weathered look.

5 While this is still wet, brush on a wash of diluted white or cream paint, about one part emulsion to four parts water.

6 Using a dry cloth, rub off surplus or apply more until you have the effect you want. Apply two coats of clear varnish, sanding very slightly between coats.

SPECIAL PAINT EFFECTS

Many paint effects are based on a few simple techniques. These can be used on their own or combined to produce an infinite variety of paint effects. The techniques shown here all use ultramarine blue emulsion (latex) paint mixed with acrylic scumble glaze and/or water to be able to compare the different effects possible. Two coats of silk finish white emulsion paint were rolled on as a base. Before you start a project practise these techniques first.

COLOURWASHING

Dilute the paint with water and brush on randomly with cross-hatched brushstrokes, using a large decorator's brush. A damp sponge will give a similar effect.

DRAGGING

Mix paint with scumble glaze and brush on with cross-hatched brushstrokes. Drag a flat decorator's brush through the glaze. The soft effect is achieved by going over the glaze again to break up the lines.

SPONGING

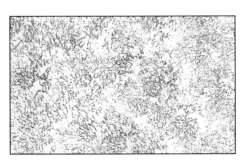

Dilute a little paint with a some water in a paint tray or saucer. Dip a damp, natural sponge into the paint and wipe off the excess on kitchen paper (paper towels). Dab the sponge on to the surface in different directions.

FROTTAGE

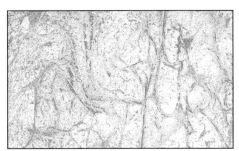

Dilute the paint with water or scumble. Apply paint with cross-hatched brushstrokes, then press a piece of tissue paper over the wet surface and peel it off.

COMBING

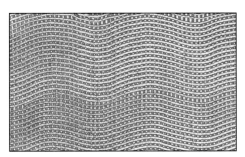

Mix paint with acrylic scumble and brush on with cross-hatched brushstrokes. Run a metal or rubber graining comb through the wet glaze.

CRACKLE GLAZE

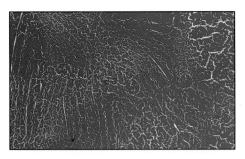

Brush on a coat of water-based crackle glaze and leave to dry. Using a well-laden brush, apply paint carefully on top so that you lay, rather than brush, it over the surface. Work quickly and do not overbrush an area already painted. If you have missed an area, touch it in when the paint has dried. Seal with acrylic varnish.

STONE WALL EFFECT

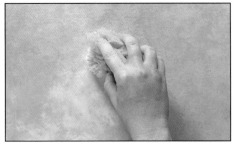

1 Paint the wall with cream emulsion (latex). Leave to dry and then mix a glaze of 1 part raw umber acrylic paint to 6 parts scumble. Stipple this on to the wall. Leave to dry. Mix a glaze with the white acrylic paint in the same way. Dampen a sponge and apply the glaze over the stippling, varying your hand position.

2 Using a softening brush, skim gently over the white glaze while it is still wet. Now mix a glaze with the yellow ochre paint as in step 1, but this time rub it into the wall with a cloth. Leave some areas of white glaze showing. Using another dampened cloth, rub some areas to disperse the paint. Leave to dry.

DECORATIVE EFFECTS – TECHNIQUES

BRUSHED OUT COLOUR GLAZE

This soft, patchy wall finish is pure country. It is traditionally achieved using either a very runny colourwash or an oil-based glaze tinted with oil colour, over eggshell paint. The technique below gives the same effect but is easier to achieve. Wallpaper paste adds a translucency to the colour and PVA (white) glue seals the surface when dry.

1 Paint the wall with a plain, light emulsion (latex) colour. Mix the glaze, using 1 part PVA (white) glue, 5 parts water and 1 part wallpaper paste. Tint it with three 20 cm/8 in squirts from an acrylic or gouache tube, or about 15 ml/ 1 tbsp of powder paint. Vary the intensity of colour to your own taste. Get the feel of the glaze and brush, and adjust the colour at this stage if necessary.

2 Begin applying the glaze in an area of the room that will be hidden by furniture or pictures; as your technique improves you will be painting the more obvious areas. Start near the top of the wall, dabbing glaze on with the brush and then sweeping it over the surface with random strokes.

3 The effect will be streaky and the brushstrokes will show. So after about 5 minutes, brush the surface lightly with your brush but don't use any glaze. The brush will pick up any surplus glaze on the surface and leave a softer, less streaky effect. When working on edges and corners, apply the glaze and then brush it away from the corner or edge.

'POWDERY' PAINT FINISH

This paint finish imitates the opaque, soft colour and powdery bloom of distemper, the wall finish most used before the invention of emulsion paint. The joy of decorating with this 'powdery finish' paint is that is can be used directly on concrete, plaster or plasterboard – indeed, most surfaces – without lining paper or undercoats.

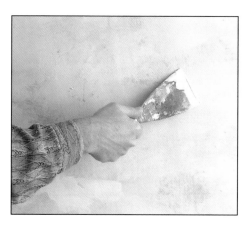

1 Prepare the walls by stripping off any wallpaper down to the bare plaster. Spread filler irregularly with a spatula to simulate the uneven texture of old plaster. Use thin layers and apply randomly from different directions. Don't worry about overdoing the effect; you can always rub it back with sandpaper when it's dry, after an hour.

2 Blend the dried filler into the original wall surface using rough-grade sandpaper, leaving rougher areas for a more obvious distressed effect. Mix water-based paint with water in the ratio 2 parts water to 1 part paint. Stir the paint well: it should have the consistency of single cream.

3 Begin painting at ceiling height. The paint is likely to splash a bit, so protect any surfaces. Use the paintbrush randomly rather than in straight lines, and expect a patchy effect – it will fade as the paint dries. The second coat needs to be stronger, so use less water in the mixture. Apply the second coat in the same way, working the brush into any cracks or rough plaster areas. Two hours later, the 'bloom' of the powdery finish will appear.

SPECIAL PAINT
EFFECTS (continued)

Stippling

For an attractive mottled appearance, try stippling; apart from being used as a decorative finish in its own right it can also be used to obliterate brushmarks in the base coat beneath other broken-colour effects. The only item of specialist equipment that you will need to create this effect is a stippling brush.

1 Brush on the glaze over the base coat, applying a generous layer. Do not worry about leaving brushmarks; the stippling will obliterate them.

2 Hold the stippling brush with the bristle tips parallel with the surface, and simply hit the paint film. Clean paint from the brush regularly by wiping it with a dry cloth.

Rag-rolling

Another simple 2-colour effect, rag-rolling involves brushing a diluted second colour over the base coat and then using a rolled-up 'sausage' of cloth to remove some of the second colour before it starts to dry.

The technique works best with a base coat of eggshell paint and a top coat of eggshell paint diluted with white spirit (paint thinner). Use lint-free cotton or linen rags and change them frequently before they become soaked with paint.

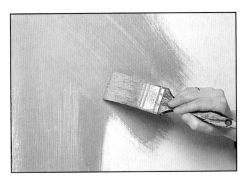

1 Once the base coat is completely dry, lightly brush on the second diluted paint colour in bands across the surface. As you do this, aim to leave a random pattern of brushstrokes that allows the base colour to show through.

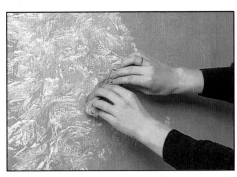

2 Roll the rag sausage across the surface in a continuous motion. Vary the direction for a random effect and touch in small areas by just dabbing with the cloth. Replace the rag at regular intervals.

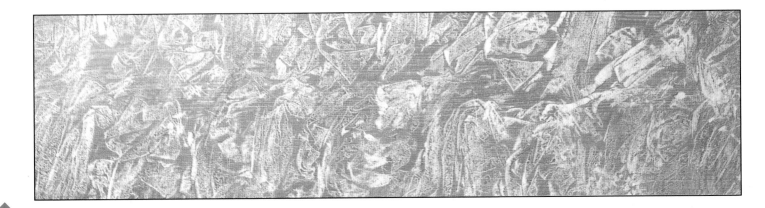

Marbling

As its name implies, marbling copies the appearance of marble. It is a relatively difficult technique to master, but the results can be quite spectacular. For a first attempt, choose a piece of real marble to copy. For best results, work with a solvent-based (oil) glaze, applied over an eggshell base coat. Add the veining details with artist's oils.

1 Either brush out the glaze or apply it with a pad of lint-free cloth. Only a relatively thin coat is needed.

2 Use a dusting brush (as here) or a special stippling brush to stipple the surface of the wet glaze. Add more colour to the glaze mixture, apply it selectively to some areas in order to create contrast and then stipple the glaze again.

VARNISHING SPECIAL PAINT EFFECTS

Some special paint effects, especially graining and marbling, should be sealed with a coat of clear varnish for protection once the effect has dried completely. Use satin varnish rather than gloss unless you require a particularly polished effect – such as on a wooden trim or similar surface, for example. When this has dried, burnish the surface with a soft cloth and add a little wax polish to create a sheen, if you wish.

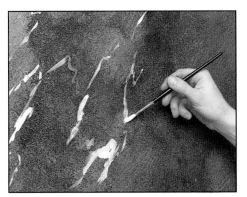

3 Working on the wet glaze, draw in the main areas of veining with an artist's paintbrush and a mixture of glaze and artist's oils. Use different weights of line to create a natural-looking effect.

4 Use the softening brush again to soften the outlines of the veining and to blend it into the background. Wipe the brush regularly to avoid smudges.

5 Highlight some areas of the veining by adding more colour or a second colour. Soften the effect once again, as in step 4.

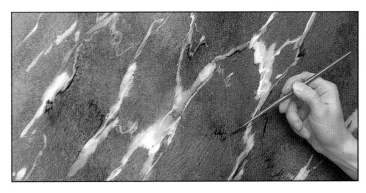

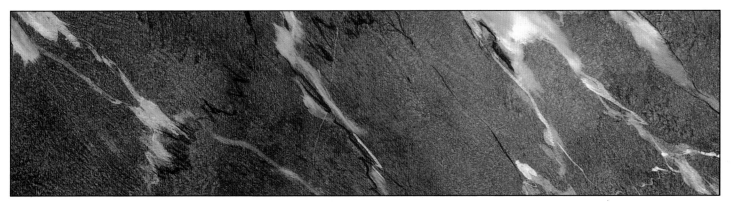

IDEAS FOR EASY EMBELLISHMENTS

Leading a frantically busy life should not stop you from enjoying some hands-on homemaking. You don't always need a lot of time for this and once you have given it a go, you are bound to find that it is worth the effort. Creativity is as much about your state of mind as actually sitting down and making something – an original idea is a creation in itself. The best way to add originality to your home is not to fit it out in one go, but rather to let it evolve. If you pass a second-hand shop and can spare five minutes, then go inside and see what you can find. You never know, you might just be in the right place at the right time to find something wonderful to start you off on a project.

The other good places to visit are haberdashers (notions departments), garden centres and the occasional boating store. In any of these shops you will find trimmings and other bits and pieces that are bound to spark your imagination. Trimmings can completely change the look and personality of everyday objects, such as lampshades and bases, simple tablecloths and curtains. They need not be expensive and many can be created using everyday things from around the home. Search cupboards (cabinets) and drawers for balls of string and lengths of twine.

Some colourful feathers to stitch down the edge of a voile curtain; handfuls of glass beads for the rim of a cheap and not so cheerful lampshade that you bought last year; lengths of rope to glue to the bottom edge of a pelmet (valance); or just some exotic remnants to use for appliqué will all dramatically change a room or object. Look to the many fabric paints that are on the market, too. Not only are there a great number of colours for stencilling and stamping with, but there are also metallic and luminous paints for a bright finishing touch.

As in so many things, simplicity is the key word. Where possible, use natural materials, such as cotton, linen and hessian (burlap); they all have a wonderful, tactile quality and look good in any situation.

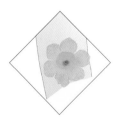

OPPOSITE Create a mosaic-effect border with a Moroccan flavour for a kitchen tablecloth using one simple stencil and a subtle blue and green colour combination.

WOOD EMBELLISHMENTS

Even the most minimal of design schemes includes a piece of wooden furniture. The variety of design possibilities and the practicality and indispensability of chairs, tables and doors mean that spending time, money and energy on them is very worthwhile. Junk-shop finds, sometimes bought for next to nothing, can become individual masterpieces of your own devising, giving your home a wonderful sense of personality and your own style.

Paint effects

A lick of paint is the quickest way to transform a piece of wooden furniture from a derelict shell to an object of baroque opulence or nonchalant charm. While painting, you can opt either for a decorative pattern or for a complete, all-over paint effect such as marbling. Sometimes, as in the case of the garden chair, rather than making something that is already old look as

good as new, you want a new piece to have a more weathered appearance. There is a particular charm in garden furniture that looks as though it has stood in its place for many years.

Modern technology means that the colour range available today is virtually unlimited, so painting allows you unrivalled opportunities for playing with colour. When selecting your colours, remember that complementary colours (red and green, violet and yellow) used together have tremendous impact. For the most subtle effects, use different shades of the same colour. If new to painting, you can buy kits for different paint techniques from good paint or craft shops.

Fabric effects for chairs

There is generally a distinction drawn between fabrics that are intended for upholstery and those that are destined for the world of high fashion and the couture house. However, there is no

reason why you can't use fabrics for something different from their original purpose, and there are many fashion fabrics that will give a magical richness to any upholstery. For example, a stunning effect can be created by using velvet instead of a dust cover for a buttoned chair. Wrap a chair in a large velvet tablecloth and then add buttons in the same or a contrasting colour. You can fold scraps of fabric over self-covering buttons and attach them to the back. With this in mind, always keep your eyes peeled for large pieces of material, such as old curtains that are no longer being used for their original purpose, because they can always be used as a chair throw. Second-hand shops are good hunting grounds for bargains and ideas.

To keep things simple, avoid using fussy buttonholes or zips on your covers, tie fastenings can look far more stylish as well as being extremely practical. Glue guns and staple guns are invaluable, as they give quick results. If you are at all nervous about sewing or do not have a sewing machine, take full advantage of both these and the many non-fraying fabrics available that do not need hemming.

RIGHT Using a dust cover as a throw is a simple and effective way of giving a new lease on life to an old chair. The large buttons are a neat finishing touch.

RIGHT Few things are as immediately effective as gold, and these gold tassels add a touch of luxury to everyday chairs.

OPPOSITE This table has been decorated with a stamped Egyptian motif, transforming it from the ordinary to something quite fun and individual.

- Stamp classic Egyptian figures around a freshly antiqued table top.
- Tassels are available in a wide range of colours, sizes and materials, from bright pink plastic and simple muslin to luxurious-looking soft silken yarns. On a wooden chair, hang them from the back struts, or for a soft armchair, sew them on to the front of the arms.
- Matching trimmings and braids are a quick and simple way of drawing attention away from worn patches in chairs and for covering blemishes.
- Go to craft stores and garden centres for more unusual materials to fire your imagination: rope, garden twine, raffia, even chains and electrician's wire could all be used.
- Use water-gilding techniques to add gold and silver to furniture.
- Glue flat pearly buttons in a straight line up the back struts and around the seat edge. This looks particularly effective on a dark wooden chair.

Instant embellishments

Great effects can often be achieved by simple techniques. It's worth attempting an easy, very fun look on a spare piece of furniture, which can then be a lasting centrepiece in a dull corner of the hall, cloakroom or bathroom. Here are some ideas, though don't be afraid to experiment:

- Colourwash the doors of kitchen units and stamp a simple floral pattern around the edges.

STARFISH BATHROOM CHAIR

1 Sand or strip the chair, then apply a coat of white emulsion (latex). Mix a thin wash of about five parts water to one part yellow-ochre emulsion. Use a dry brush to drag a little glaze at a time in the direction of the grain. Keep drying the brush as you work, to ensure you do not apply too much glaze.

2 Spread some light grey paint on to a plate and run a roller through it until it is evenly coated. Ink the starfish stamp and print around the edge of the chair seat so that the design overlaps on to the sides.

3 Fill in the seat area with starfish stamps, rotating the stamp to a different angle after each print. Space the stamps quite close together to make a dense pattern. Leave to dry before applying a coat of varnish to protect the surface.

WOOD EMBELLISHMENTS (continued)

PAINTED DRESSER

1 Apply a coat of shellac to seal the bare wood. When dry, paint the dresser dusky blue emulsion (latex), following the direction of the grain. Allow to dry.

2 If desired, rub candle wax along the edges of the dresser before painting with a second colour. The wax will prevent this coat from adhering completely, and will create a distressed effect. Add the second colour, if using.

3 Paint the backing boards cream, again following the direction of the grain. When dried, use medium-grade sandpaper and wire (steel) wool to rub down to bare wood along the edges, to simulate wear and tear. Finally, apply a coat of antique pine varnish to the whole dresser to protect the surface.

GRAINED DOOR

1 Sand the door and then paint with a coat of blue emulsion (latex). Leave to dry. Mix four parts blue emulsion to one part wall filler. Paint on to the door, working on one small section at a time. While still wet, comb in lines using a rubber comb and following the grain. Leave to dry.

2 Paint the door with a thin coat of lime green emulsion, applying in the same direction as the combing. Leave to dry and then sand, revealing lines of blue paint beneath the lime green coat. Seal with two coats of acrylic varnish to protect the surface.

CRACKLE GLAZED DECOUPAGE TRAY

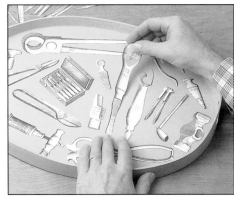

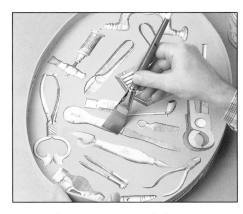

1   Prepare a large wooden tray by painting it with corn yellow emulsion (latex). When dry, gently rub the surface with fine-grade sandpaper.

2   Carefully cut out your paper shapes. Turn them over and paste the backs with wallpaper paste, right up to all the edges and then glue them in position on the tray. Use a soft cloth to smooth out any bubbles and leave to dry overnight.

3   Apply a sparing coat of clear satin varnish to the whole surface of the tray. When dry, rub lightly with fine-grade sandpaper and repeat this process as many times as possible.

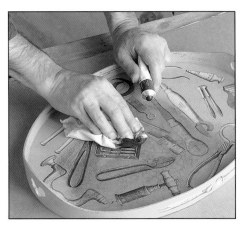

4   For the crackle glaze, first apply the base varnish on to the tray. Leave to dry (about 20 minutes). Then apply an even coat of the crackle glaze and again leave to dry for 20 minutes. Rub a small amount of artist's oil paint into the cracks, using a cotton cloth. Raw umber was used here, which gives a naturally aged effect, but any colour can be used.

5   When the cracks have been coloured, gently rub the excess paint from the surface, using a soft cloth. Finally, give the tray at least two more coats of clear satin varnish, though more are desirable as these will give it a better finish.

ABOVE A good tray will be strong enough to carry mugs and plates, and handsome enough to hang up as a decoration when not in use. This one has been decoupaged with a selection of old engraving tools, but you could follow the method using any design you choose.

EMBELLISHING LAMPSHADES

A plain lampshade is like a blank canvas, just waiting for the artist's creative touch. The best type for decorating is a simple shape made of plain smooth fabric or thick paper. If you are experimenting, it is best to use the least expensive type because you will feel less restricted knowing that

failure won't cost a fortune. A fabulous result can always be repeated on a better quality shade.

Stencils, stamps or freehand brushstrokes can be used to paint colourful motifs and patterns. The simplest are often the most effective and it is worth trying a light behind the shade to see how the pattern will show up at night. Try a pattern of dots, zigzags and stripes in earthy colours on a cream background to give an African look, or use black silhouettes on a terracotta-coloured shade for a classical Greek effect. Sky-blue stripes on a white shade look really fresh and burnt-orange patterns on a yellow shade seem like instant sunshine. Before you embark on the whole shade, first paint a small area to check the effect on the fabric or paper.

Photocopy a black and white image, then make copies to cut out for a decoupaged shade. Use wallpaper paste to stick the photocopied cut-outs in place on a paper shade, then apply clear varnish to give a smooth finish and prevent any curling at the edges. Another good alternative is to use your lampshade as an unusual photograph album. Stick old photographs all around the outside. They will fade with age, creating a nostalgic feel.

INSTANT EMBELLISHMENTS

Armed with a glue gun and a plain shade you can really go to town. Almost anything can be stuck on to the surface or dangled from the edge. The range of trimmings available today is very extensive and you can buy fringes, ribbons, beads and baubles to suit every style.

● Large shades look particularly striking dressed up with upholstery fringing and matching tassels glued around the bottom edge.

● Add beautiful ribbons in shot taffeta and silk tied into swags and bows. Or use milliner's velvet finished off with fake flowers or fruit.

● Dress smaller shades with finer decorations such as borders of beadwork or fine fringing.

● A border of bold buttons looks good in primary colours against a plain background and wooden or leather buttons have a solid country feel.

● Alter the hard-edged shape of a shade by covering it with another material, such as coloured net (tulle) or draped butter muslin, both of which allow plenty of light through. It is best to use lightweight fabrics otherwise the softening effect will be lost when the bulb is lit.

ABOVE Mix colourful hand-painted stripes with pieces of velvet ribbon to an old lampshade to give a rich variety of texture and colour.

RIGHT This lampshade has been enhanced by an Elizabethan border design, applied using a combination of sponge and stencil techniques. The pattern would also look sumptuous using a deep blue or red with gold.

TRIMMED SHADE EDGE

1 Measure the length of trimming needed to go around the shade plus a small seam allowance at each end. Stitch the seams flat to prevent the raw edges from fraying.

2 Heat a glue gun and apply some glue to the surface of the shade. Attach the trimming immediately. You will get an instant bond as the hot glue cools on contact. If you are working with very fine trimmings it may be neater to stitch the trimming on to the shade.

LACED LAMPSHADE

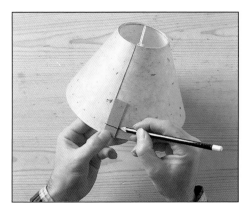

1 Carefully cut a strip of card to use as a spacer to accurately mark the position of the holes around the top and bottom edges of the lampshade.

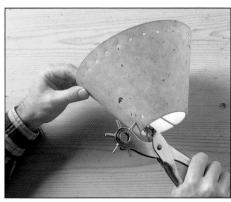

2 Set the punch to the required hole size and make a hole at each dotted mark.

3 Attach one end of the string to the inside of the shade using the glue gun or a dab of all-purpose glue.

4 Lace thick string in and out of the punched holes. Cut the string when you reach the end and secure it at the back with glue. Repeat with the other line.

ABOVE These delicate-looking shades, made from Japanese hand-made paper and photocopies of real leaves and flowers, match the soft glow of candlelight. They have been treated with fire-proofing spray for safety.

DECORATING GLASS

Etching and painting glass are the two most straightforward ways of embellishing glass. Once armed with these techniques you can create the most striking of finishes ranging from fantastically colourful glass vases to handsome panes of glass to install in interior and exterior doors. However, before embarking on these decorative ventures, you will need some specific materials and equipment. The results, however, make this effort worthwhile.

Materials

Contour paste: creates raised lines on glass, giving the look of leaded windows. Acts as a barrier for paints.
Cotton rags: needed for drying glass.
Etching paste: an acid paste that eats into glass to leave a matt 'frosted' finish. Use for decorating clear and pale coloured glass.
Eye goggles: vital for eye protection.
Fid: used for pressing down self-adhesive lead.

ABOVE The pretty stained-glass effect on this vase is created with glass paints and the stick-on lead is added afterwards.

LEFT The etched-glass panels add a light touch to what is otherwise quite a plain door.

Glass paints: translucent and give a vibrant colours. Be aware that these paints are not washable.
Masking tape: ideal for making straight lines for etching and painting.
Paintbrushes: a selection of sizes are essential for applying different paints and etching paste.
Rubber gloves: vital to protect your hands from etching paste.
Ruler: essential for measuring.
Scissors: small and large ones are useful for many cutting tasks.
Self-adhesive lead: this is easy to use and looks like real lead to given an authentic stained glass window effect when combined with coloured glass or glass paints.
Self-adhesive vinyl: useful for masking-off large areas when painting and etching glass.
Sponges: natural or foam, cut into pieces, these are ideal for applying paint over a large area of glass.
White spirit (paint thinner): used as a solvent to clean off most paints.

ETCHING GLASS

1 Self-adhesive vinyl makes a good mask when etching. Cut out shapes from self-adhesive vinyl. Decide where you want to position them on the glass, remove the backing paper and stick down.

2 Wearing rubber gloves, paint the etching paste evenly over the vase with a paintbrush. Make sure you do not spread it too thinly or you will find the effect quite faint. Leave to dry for 3 minutes.

3 Still wearing the rubber gloves, wash the paste off under a running tap. Then wipe off any residue and rinse. Peel off the shapes, wash again. Dry the glass with a clean cotton rag.

PAINTING GLASS

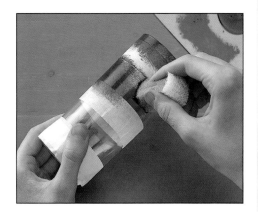

1 Glass paints should be used with white spirit (paint thinner). Use masking tape for large areas to define the edges. Pour a small drop of paint on to a tile or saucer, take a small piece of sponge and dab it into the paint and then on to the glass.

2 Take a small paintbrush and paint freestyle on to the glass. Clean your brush immediately you have finished with one colour so that it does not go hard.

ABOVE Lines of etched and coloured glass bring this carafe to life. Strips of masking tape quickly screen off the areas of the carafe ready for painting with etching paste. Fill the decorated carafe with lemonade and plenty of ice.

DECORATING CHINA

Until recently, to have individually designed china in your home usually meant paying a lot of money for hand-painted pieces from well known craftspeople. With the introduction of specialist china paints however, everything has changed: you can now paint on whatever you like and be sure that your designs will last. A quick and easy decorative technique, with the added advantage of the large amount of inexpensive white china available, this is a wonderful way of adding a splash of colour to everyday items. There are three different types of paint that you can use for decorating china. Not all of these are non-toxic so if you are making pieces to give away, remember to mark them accordingly.

Enamel paints are not made exclusively for china and ceramics, they are available in a range of colours and dry to an extremely hard finish. These paints contain lead and should only be used for decorative purposes.

Solvent-based ceramic paints come in a huge range of colours and lend themselves well to varied painting styles such as wash effects. White spirit

ABOVE A set of plain-glazed earthenware mugs can be made more interesting by adding some contrasting decoration. Use paints that match the original colours for a harmonious scheme.

(paint thinner) can be used to dilute the paint and to clean brushes after use. Protect the finish with varnish.

Water-based ceramic paints are specially made for painting glazed ceramics. They produce a strong, opaque, flat colour and can be diluted with water. Do not attempt to bake them until they are completely dry or the colour may bubble. Baking the painted item will make the colour durable enough to wash in a dishwasher. It is a good idea to do a test first as over-firing can turn the colour slightly brown.

BASIC EQUIPMENT

Low-tack adhesive tape: use to hold templates or stencils in place on the china if masking tape is not available.

Masking fluid: watercolour art masking fluid is used to mask off areas of the design while colour is applied to the surrounding area.

Masking tape: useful for holding stencils in place or to mask off areas when painting straight lines. Can be removed easily without damaging the painted surface.

Paintbrushes: choose sable watercolour paintbrushes in a range of sizes, including a fine brush for painting lines and details, and a broad soft brush for covering larger areas. Good synthetic brushes are adequate and affordable.

Pencils and pens: a hard lead pencil such as a 2H is good for transferring designs with carbon paper. For marking the ceramic surface directly, a softer 2B lead pencil or a fine felt-tipped pen would be more suitable.

Ruler: a good-quality metal or plastic ruler makes measuring and cutting easier and more accurate.

Scalpel or craft knife: scalpels with disposable blades are the most accurate cutting tools, especially for cutting stencils. Craft knives are a good alternative.

Sponges: use to produce interesting effects. Natural or synthetic sponges can be used.

DECORATIVE TECHNIQUES

Sponging: Load a sponge with paint and test the print on a scrap piece of paper first. The first print or two will be too saturated with paint to achieve a pleasing effect, so it is best to make a few.

Printing blocks: When using printing blocks, roll the block lightly on to the surface to ensure you get a good even print. Test the print on scrap paper before printing on the china.

Sponging variations: A stencilled design can be made more interesting by varying the density of the sponging within the image or by adding more than one colour. Allowing the first coat of paint to dry partially before applying the second will mean that there is more contrast and less blending of the two colours.

Using masking fluid: Add a drop of water-based paint to masking fluid before use when working on china that is completely white. This will help you to see where the masking fluid has been applied, enabling you to wipe it off easily when you are ready to do so.

White lines: If you want to leave thin lines of china showing through areas of colour, paint them first with masking fluid. This can be gently peeled off when the paint is dry to reveal the white china beneath. Use a sharp-pointed instrument such as a craft knife or compass point to lift off the dried masking fluid.

Watery effects: You can achieve subtle watery effects in oil-based colours by diluting paints with white spirit (paint thinner). Water-based paints are diluted by adding water.

HINTS AND TIPS

Before painting any white china, always clean it thoroughly to remove any invisible traces of dirt of grease. The most effective cleaning agents are cleaning fluid, methylated spirit (denatured alcohol), white spirit (paint thinner) or lighter fuel. Make sure there are no naked flames around when using these materials.

To ensure that there is no possibility of any paint being swallowed when drinking from a mug or glass, adapt designs so that any colour you paint is at least 3 cm/1¼ in below the rim of drinking vessels. Otherwise the piece should be fired in a kiln.

Always test out a technique that you have not tried before. Apply the new technique to a spare piece of china, which can be cleaned up easily, rather than a piece you are already in the process of decorating.

Use tracing paper and a soft pencil to transfer designs directly on to the surface of china. First trace the template or the design you wish to use, then fix the tracing paper to the china with masking tape. Gently rub over the traced design with a soft pencil to transfer.

Pencil or pen guide marks on the china can be easily wiped off once the paint is completely dry or has been baked. Use a damp cloth and take care not to rub the paint too hard.

FINISHING TOUCHES

Embellishing soft furnishings

Trimmings can completely change the look and personality of soft furnishings such as simple table cloths, napkins and fine muslin curtains. They need not be expensive and many can be created using everyday things from around the home. Search cabinets and drawers for balls of string and lengths of twine; make use of shells and pebbles; take a fresh look at a skein of raffia: it could look marvellous tied into a tassel to hold a napkin. Where possible, use natural materials, such as cotton, linen, silk and hessian (burlap); they have a wonderful tactile quality and look good in any situation.

ABOVE The simplicity of the plain muslin cheesecloth curtain and bamboo poles has been complemented by the natural tassel. The effect is understated yet very eye-catching.

LEFT Have fun with a classic white linen tablecloth by adding seashells, pretty stones and sticks, tied with natural string, to its edges.

The corners and edges of throws and cushions (pillows) are good places for embellishments, especially when the covering fabric is plain. These details maintain and enhance the style of the cushions, particularly if they are made from natural materials in a range of neutral colours. Make detailed decorations with traditional sewing and embroidery techniques, too, but interpret them in contemporary materials. The result is fully in keeping with today's fashion for interior-design schemes based on natural materials.

Ribbons and tassels

Ribbons come in a wonderful variety of colours, textures and widths. By tying a simple loop or bow, you can give a new contrasting or complementary accent to soft furnishings. Soft, floppy, translucent organza ribbons create a frothy cloud when gathered in folds and bows, but look simple and elegant

LEFT Ribbons play such a big part in trimming that it is worth searching out the most unusual ones possible.

RIGHT Stitch white cords to off-white, rough linen cushions, creating graceful loops at the corners.

RIGHT Try garden centres for twine and raffia, and art stores for canvas and hessian (burlap).

hung against the light of a window, where they lend an element of privacy and shield the eye from an unwelcome view without blocking the light at all. Rich silken and velvety ribbons, or rough linen and burlap, have completely different qualities.

Tassels, too, are flourishes: they bring a jaunty, nonchalant air to whatever they embellish. They come in a wide variety of materials and colours. The simplest can be homemade from household materials such as string, which is perfectly in keeping with decorated old terracotta pots. Made from natural materials, they bring a touch of style to design schemes based on neutral colours and natural fabrics; in rich colours and silken threads they can be opulent or restrained, depending on how they are combined. Rich red combined with a natural linen table napkin is a sunburst of bright colour that brightens but doesn't disrupt the neutral scheme. A traditional white tassel combined with a brick-red throw quilted in a simple, modern style is a graphic and modern interpretation of a classic upholstery trimming.

Instant embellishments

You can use just about any material that catches your eye for trimmings. Although notions and interiors shops were always the traditional suppliers of trimmings such as tassels and ribbons, look beyond the expected sources for rich pickings. From garden centers to boating supply stores, the only rule in using materials for trimmings is to collect what appeals to you and let your imagination take over.

HOME ENTERTAINING

Sharing food is the universal expression of friendship and hospitality, and much of the enjoyment of inviting friends and family to join in a meal is the pleasure of preparing it, making the table look inviting as well as the food delicious. A beautifully laid table provides an inviting ambience that both welcomes the guests and complements the meal. The basic elements of linen, crockery, glass and cutlery are always there, but even the same pieces can be set off in different ways to suit different occasions.

Home entertaining can be as formal or informal as you please. The set rules for dinner parties and suppers – whether sit-down or buffet – are far less stringent these days and so should be less stressful for the host and/or hostess. Make the evening something that you will enjoy and then everyone else will too. Careful planning in advance will help ensure this.

This section leads you through each element from making your initial decisions as to what sort of entertaining you would like to do, to preparing all those finishing touches. Choosing and making the food is the hardest work, of course, but here you will find hints and tips on how to make it as easy as possible for yourself. When it comes to laying the dining table, though, a great deal of fun can be had creating something that is as sophisticated or jolly as you choose. From table cloths and mats to flowers and cleverly folded napkins, the range of styles is enormous. The china, cutlery (flatware) and glasses add to the style, too, and here there are pages devoted to these areas. Round off the whole with decorative candles, both large and small, and you can rest assured that your home entertaining will be a successful and happy affair.

Look to an all-white table setting for a cool, restrained background, or go for a more eclectic mix of blues, greens and yellows, combining checked cloths and napkins with a china collection that you have built-up over the years. Whatever you favour, there is plenty of advice on making the most of it in this section.

OPPOSITE Painted glasses and organdie sachets
filled with pot-pourri perfectly complement
pure white and pewter.

PLANNING A PARTY

Many parties celebrate an event such as an annual feast, birthday, wedding, christening or anniversary; they can also take place for no special purpose at all other than to see friends. Whatever the occasion, it is most important to have a clear outline of the form of entertaining before you begin to work on any of the preparations – planning is the cornerstone of success.

Annual festivities, such as Thanksgiving, Christmas, New Year and Easter, often follow a traditional structure, but this does not mean that there is no need to plan ahead; it simply means that there will be fewer decisions to make and that they will all fall into an existing framework. For all other occasions, a decision on the type and size of celebration is the starting point, and the usual pre-arranging has to follow. Begin by considering your budget, then outline what sort of party you are planning within your financial restrictions. Work through all of the following points to establish a structure for planning all the details.

Degree of formality

If you decide on a formal party, this will provide you with a set of clear-cut rules to follow. You may opt for complete informality, in which case you need to work out your own pattern of rules. However, many occasions tend to fall somewhere between these extremes.

ABOVE Planning ahead will leave you time to add finishing touches such as flower arrangements.

The important thing is to decide exactly how you want to entertain, let everyone know what to expect and to stick to your decision by planning accordingly. Think in terms of dress, how you expect guests to participate and the type of refreshments, and pass all this information on to your guests.

The style of celebration will also dictate whether you need outside help. Caterers, waiting staff and bar staff may be hired for formal occasions, such as weddings, and may also be employed for any large party or even for formal dinner parties. These aspects of any party should always be planned at the outset, not as afterthoughts.

The guests

Bringing people together for small parties such as dinner parties is not always easy, and deciding on the group of people to invite to larger gatherings can also be difficult. Nevertheless, this is an essential and important first step in good planning. If you organize a dinner party for people who are strangers to one another, it is important to mix individuals who are likely to get on well together, or at least to express an interest in one another. When inviting friends to larger gatherings, always ensure that there are groups who will know or can relate to one another.

Think back over your own social experiences, and you will probably recall occasions when certain guests in the minority have obviously lingered on the fringe of a gathering, awaiting the first polite opportunity to take their leave. Having made the point, it is equally important to stress that there are exceptions – outstanding social successes do sometimes occur with the most unlikely groups of people.

Numbers

Although it may seem an obvious point, it is vital to make sure that you can cope with the numbers for the type of party that you are planning. This is

RIGHT A buffet can work as well as a more formal sit-down arrangement – perhaps in a marquee (closed-sided party tent) in the garden if numbers are too large for the house.

BELOW A traditional British cream tea provides an ideal opportunity for entertaining friends informally at home.

largely a matter of space. For example, it is not practical to arrange a formal dinner party for 8 guests if you can only sit 7 around the table: the eighth person who is perched on a stool at the corner of the table will make everyone else feel thoroughly uncomfortable. The same applies to a barbecue for 50 when you have one small grill; a cosy kitchen brunch for 10 in an area that is cramped with 6 people; or a children's party for 25 in a house that is overfilled when half-a-dozen children are invited and where there is only a small garden. Remember, however, that the equation can work the other way, and that, for some types of gatherings, success depends on having the party area fairly tightly packed with people.

Food and drink

Whether the gathering is small or large, it is important to decide on the level of refreshments – snacks, finger food, some form of buffet or a proper sit-down meal – and to make sure that the food and drink you provide are suited to the occasion. You need to think about this in relation to the time of day, numbers invited and your budget. Do not be afraid to make an unusual decision about the form of food, but do make sure that it is adequate and that you can cope with the preparation, or that caterers, if you are using them, do not need facilities that are not available.

Invitations

Whether printed, handwritten or extended by word of mouth, invitations should convey certain important information clearly to the recipients. They should state the names of those invited, your own name(s), the occasion and the reason for it, the place, the time and an address to which replies should be sent. Written invitations often include the formula 'RSVP' in one corner, which stands for the French '*Répondez, s'il vous plaît*' ('Please reply'), to remind guests that an answer is required. You should give details of any special form of dress on the bottom of the invitation.

Ready-made cards on which you write in the details yourself are available in styles ranging from formal to fun. You can also have cards printed for a special occasion.

HOME ENTERTAINING

GIVING A DINNER PARTY

A proper dinner party can be fun, as well as formal, especially if you know your guests well. This is an opportunity to lay the table with your best table linen and chinaware, to make your home look beautiful with flowers and other decorations, and to prepare dishes that are special and out of the ordinary. Plan to have all the cooking calmly under control and to allow yourself a period of all-important relaxation before your guests arrive, so that you can enjoy the occasion too.

To ensure that everything goes smoothly on the night of the party, draw up a checklist of things that you need to do, starting with jobs that you can easily complete a few days before the event, such as the shopping and cleaning. Try to prepare as much as possible in advance: make and freeze suitable dishes or, with dishes that cannot be frozen, make them the day before if possible and store them in the refrigerator. Leave only the finishing touches to be done on the day, to avoid a last-minute rush.

ABOVE A bouquet of fresh flowers completes an elegant dinner-party table.

MENU REMINDERS

Menus for dinner parties are best kept simple, and cook-ahead dishes are ideal, as most will not spoil if your guests linger over pre-dinner drinks.

Simple first courses often make the most memorable appetizers – opt for prime-quality ingredients and serve them attractively. You might try avocadoes and chopped walnuts with an oil-and-vinegar dressing, melon with Parma ham (prosciutto), fresh figs served with a twist of freshly ground black pepper, or perhaps something hot, such as Scallops Wrapped in Parma Ham (prosciutto).

Classic casseroles such as Coq au Vin or Boeuf Bourguignon make practical and versatile dinner-party fare, as do simple but delicious meat dishes such as Boned Pork Loin with Apple-cream

Sauce, or Pot-roast Chicken with Sausage Stuffing. For the latter, you can prepare the stuffing the day before, making the dish very simple to put together and cook on the day of the party. Lightly spiced curries, such as a Simple Chicken Curry served with rice and popadums, are also acceptable and often benefit from being cooked a day ahead so that the flavours mingle.

Even if you plan an elaborate dessert, it is a good idea to offer a simple alternative. Do not dismiss fresh fruit – pineapple and different types of melon, as well as other fruits, can be presented in eye-catching ways. There are many exotic fruits now available that make eye-catching displays. Fruit ices and sorbets are also wonderfully refreshing at the end of a meal.

A formal dinner party
Serving a meal of many courses can be an excellent way of entertaining, particularly when guests appreciate the nuances of different foods and subtle flavours. As lighter eating has become the norm, the most acceptable way of serving such a feast is to present small portions throughout the meal. Serve good-quality bought or home-made appetizers with drinks before dinner. The meal itself may consist of 4 or 5 courses, or more. Supper dishes and single-pot dishes are usually avoided on very formal occasions in favour of carefully sauced dishes with separate vegetables or side salads.

The simplest of formal dinner-party menus should include soup or a first

MAKING PLACE CARDS

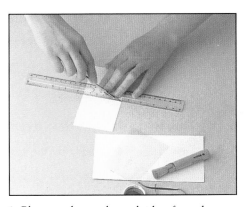

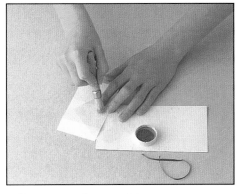

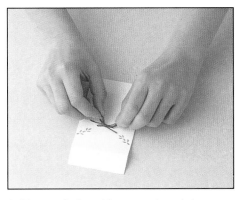

1 Place cards are always laid at formal or large dinners. Simple, elegant cards are best for such occasions. First cut a strip of card (cardboard) measuring 15 × 7.5 cm/6 × 3 in. Mark a fold across the centre and a 2.5 cm/1 in fold at each end of the strip. Using a craft knife, lightly score the folds.

2 Draw a simple stencil design on to a sheet of acetate using a waterproof felt-tip pen, and cut it out using a craft knife. Lightly load a stencil brush with gold paint. Hold the stencil firmly in position on the card (cardboard) and dab the paint through it, keeping the brush vertical.

3 To attach the ribbon, mark and then cut 2 small slits in the card. Thread the ribbon through and tie it into a bow. Trim the ends of the ribbon if necessary.

course, a main course and dessert. In Europe it is also usual to serve a cheese course towards the end of the meal. A fish course or light appetizer may be served after the soup or a refreshing sorbet may be served between the first and main courses, and a savoury dish may be served instead of cheese.

An informal dinner party

Although the style of an informal party will differ from that of a more formal occasion, your aim should still be to provide well-prepared and beautifully presented food. 3 or 4 courses are usually served at a party of this kind. The opening course may be a starter

4 Lay the finished cards in suitable positions on the table, such as on side plates or with the napkins.

(appetizer), salad or soup, and the main course will be followed by either dessert or cheese, or both. An informal dinner party can feature a more extensive menu, if you wish, even though the general approach to the evening is very casual. If the informal nature of the evening refers more to dress than to food, you may wish to offer 4 or more courses of less 'classic' food, with supper-style dishes (such as pasta or risotto), perhaps with a national theme, included on the menu.

PERFECT *PETITS FOURS*

Individual servings of *petits fours*, attractively arranged, will round off any meal. Arrange the *petits fours* in small fluted paper or foil cases. Try the following ideas:
- Dip the ends of brandysnaps in melted white and plain chocolate.
- Use a standard meringue mixture to pipe button-sized meringues, and dry them out in the coolest possible oven. Sandwich them in pairs by dipping their bases in melted plain chocolate.
- Stuff fresh dates with marzipan (almond paste) and roll in caster (superfine) sugar.
- Sandwich pecan or walnut halves in pairs with marzipan.

PREPARING FOR A BUFFET PARTY

Preparing a buffet is the practical and fun answer to most types of home entertaining when more than about 8 people are invited. A buffet can, of course, be just as impressive as a sit-down menu, if you give some thought both to the presentation and display of the food. A buffet table also provides the perfect excuse for impressive settings, perhaps with swags of flowers or greenery (see opposite page) as well as a large main decoration. All the food should be decorative, too, and it must be arranged for ease of access when guests serve themselves.

Depending on the size and shape of your room, you could either place the buffet against a wall so that guests move along in front of the table and serve themselves, or situate it in the middle of a room (or with space all around) so that guests move around the table. Whichever system you use, there should be an obvious starting point for serving, indicated by a pile of plates.

If you decide to set the buffet against a wall, the main decoration should be at the rear of the table and positioned centrally. If guests walk all around the table, place the decoration in the centre for maximum effect.

Make sure that all the dishes are easy to reach and that there are serving spoons nearby. If there is a ham or other food to be carved, set it in a

ABOVE Streamers and brightly coloured napkins and tableware enliven an informal buffet table.

ABOVE China plates add style to a buffet table, but plastic plates make a good alternative.

position to one side of the table so that guests do not obstruct access to other dishes while they carve. It should be someone's task to check the availability of foods, topping up dishes and tidying the buffet occasionally.

Set napkins and cutlery (flatware) separately on a side table. Large paper napkins are usually used for informal buffets. If you use disposable plates, they should be sturdy and of good quality, as thin plates sag miserably and make eating difficult. Buffet-style plates are now available which include a holder for a wine glass. Alternatively, keep a large number of good-quality, large plastic plates, which are ideal for entertaining in large numbers. They are easier to rinse, stack and wash than china plates, and are ideal for outdoor parties as well as for informal buffets.

Be sure to site the buffet in a cool, well-ventilated place, away from radiators, and cover the table with a protective cloth before adding the decorative linen as there are always spills when guests serve themselves. The buffet should be set with savoury food for the main part of the meal. If you are serving a starter (appetizer), you can bring it to the buffet at the beginning of the meal, and assist the guests with it.

Serve desserts and cheese from the buffet once you have removed the main dishes. If, at a large gathering, you set out the desserts and cheese before clearing the main course, prepare a side table for them.

Always make sensible arrangements for receiving the used dishes and cutlery (flatware) when preparing a buffet. At a large gathering some guests may not feel inclined to bring their dishes out to the kitchen, so it is a good idea to set up a trolley (cart) where these may be placed out of the way.

MAKING A GREENERY CHAIN

1 Join lengths of foliage together with plastic-covered or florist's wire cut into manageable strips.

2 Wire sprigs of herbs such as bay leaves, rosemary and thyme, and stitch them to the chain using a needle and thread.

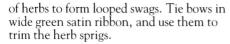

3 Pin 1 end of the chain to a corner of the table. Work along the length of the chain, pinning it to the table at each of the sprigs

of herbs to form looped swags. Tie bows in wide green satin ribbon, and use them to trim the herb sprigs.

ABOVE A selection of cheeses for the buffet table is always welcome, as is plenty of fresh fruit.

AVOIDING BUFFET PITFALLS

● Have dishes which are easy to serve – otherwise guests may feel inhibited about helping themselves.

● Avoid offering foods which really must be cut with a knife for easy eating.

● Avoid putting a first course on the buffet with all the main dishes so that everyone advances on all the food at once: if you want to keep a dish as a first course, make sure that you serve it yourself, otherwise guests will pile on the salads and other food, too.

● Arrange savoury and sweet foods on dishes at different levels, rather than in flat dishes, and 2 or 3 rows deep on the table. Use cake stands and stemmed dishes to full advantage so that the food creates a splendid display.

● Serve salad dressing separately for guests to help themselves, to avoid being left with a lot of dressed salad which has to be thrown out.

HOME ENTERTAINING

ORGANIZING A LARGER PARTY

Whatever the scale of the party you decide to give, the same principle applies, in that meticulous planning is essential. Decide first on the type of party you wish to give and think carefully about the date, then issue your invitations as soon as possible – this is particularly important at busy social times of year such as Christmas.

Make an inventory of your glasses, cutlery (flatware) and china, and the cooking and serving dishes that you have, so that you are alerted well in advance to any shortfall. If you only need a few extra items, you could probably borrow from friends, otherwise you would be best advised to use an outside supplier. Some wine merchants will lend glasses for a party, and some also offer a sale-or-return service. If your stock of tableware is inadequate for the numbers involved, you could consider good-quality disposable plates as an alternative to hiring (renting).

RIGHT Push back sofas and chairs to the edges of the room and cover them if necessary to avoid damage from spillages. A table left in the centre for people to put down food and drinks may be a good idea, but a plant left in this position would almost certainly be knocked over and should be removed to a safe place.

PARTY TIPS

- Clear the floor in the largest room to allow space for dancing. Set chairs aside but make sure that there are some comfortable areas where less-lively guests can congregate and talk.
- Subdued lighting always casts a flattering glow, so arrange table lamps around the room. The food and drinks tables should be well-illuminated.
- Lay a thick cloth on the drinks table for protection and pile plenty of clean towels and rolls of absorbent paper towels nearby in case of spillages. Place waste bags under the table.
- If you are short of chilling space, particularly for beer, use a clean dustbin

(trash can) and tip a large bag of ice into it. Pour in a couple of buckets of cold water. Stand the dustbin conveniently outside the back door and place all the unopened bottles and cans in it. Knot a few towels on the dustbin handles for wiping off chilled bottles and cans.
- Be sure to supply plenty of alcohol-free drinks: mineral water, soda water, lemonade, tonic, fruit juices, alcohol-free beer and low-alcohol wine.
- Make large chunks of ice for chilling punches: they do not melt as quickly as small cubes, so they dilute the punch more slowly. Use margarine tubs or similar containers for this.

- Make colourful ice cubes for mixed drinks and cocktails by freezing cherries and pieces of orange, lemon or lime in water in ice-cube trays.

RIGHT A platter of crudités and a dip makes quick-and-easy party food.

BELOW Hang paper streamers from the ceiling and scatter them around tables to establish the party mood.

ESTIMATING DRINKS

This is a general guide to the numbers you can expect to serve, giving a standard measure, from a standard bottle:

Drink	Glasses per bottle or carton
Table wine, 70–75 cl	6–8
Champagne and other sparkling wines, 75 cl	6–7
Gin, whisky, vodka and other spirits served as cocktails, or with 'mixers', 70–75 cl	30
Tonic water, ginger ale or dry ginger, soda water and other 'mixers', 500 ml/18 fl oz	4–5
Vermouth, 70 cl	12–14
Liqueurs, 70 cl	30
Tomato juice, 1 l/1¾ pts	10–12
Orange, pineapple and other fruit juices, 1 l/1¾ pts	8–10
Fruit cordials (add 3.5 l/6 pts water to each bottle)	16–18

Calculate the quantities of food that you will need, and check that your pantry is stocked with all the long-lasting items that you are likely to use for cooking, to save time on shopping later. Then make a shopping list of the fresh foods that you will need to buy nearer the time, and the flowers and foliage to compose any decorations.

If necessary, clean and de-frost your refrigerator days in advance and clear space for the party food, soft drinks and wines. Make quantities of ice cubes and fancy ice shapes, and store them in plastic bags in the freezer.

If it is to be a large gathering and your 'reception-room' space is limited, pack away any valuable ornaments to avoid damage and, on the day of the party, re-arrange or move back the furniture to make easy 'traffic' routes. Set out the drinks at one end of the room and organize a table with the food at the other end, or in a separate room.

How much food you make is up to you, but there should be sufficient refreshments to balance the alcohol intake. Preparing canapés, hors d'oeuvres and snacks for a party is deceptively time-consuming, so a better

option may be to make a large potful of something wholesome and to serve it accompanied by a great bowl of rice or a stack of baked potatoes. As most guests will find themselves a seat on the floor if the party atmosphere is informal enough, presenting food that needs to be eaten with the assistance of a knife is rarely a problem.

With your plans made in advance and put into operation smoothly, remember to build in enough time to get ready, as it is your welcoming and relaxed smile that will put your guests immediately at their ease.

DINING ETIQUETTE

No matter how easy-going you might consider yourself to be, or how old-fashioned etiquette appears, everyone conforms to an etiquette within their social circle. Etiquette is really another word for manners, which are simply a

GLASS SHAPES AND SIZES

Glasses for different drinks are usually of different sizes. They go up in this order: liqueur, port, sherry, white wine, red wine, water. Champagne should be sipped from tall, slender glasses, not wide, shallow ones. Water can be served in a tumbler. It is normal nowadays to provide glasses for water and a jug of water at every meal.

set of rules developed so that everyone instinctively knows what to do in certain situations and can therefore be comfortable within the group. Manners are constantly changing, however, and certainly social etiquette is no longer as rigid as it used to be. The overriding point of good manners is to be considerate to others and to make them feel at ease, and this is no less true at the table.

Before you lay the table (see the box, right), decide on whether or not you would like to include mats with your table setting. If you have a table with a fine polished surface, you may well want to show it off by using table mats, and that is acceptable. It is also perfectly correct to put a cloth on a table for a formal dinner. Traditionally,

this is white, although nowadays coloured cloths are also used.

When it comes to a seating plan, if equal numbers of men and women are present, they should be seated

ABOVE Lend interest to empty plates by laying cutlery tied with a flamboyant bow in the centre. This gold metal-shot ribbon teams perfectly with the metals of brass plate and silver knife and fork set.

LEFT Cutlery (flatware) is placed on either side of the plates in order of courses from the outside in, so that guests automatically know which implements to use for which dish.

LAYING THE TABLE

Formal tables are laid according to traditional etiquette, the purpose behind the ordered positions of all the items being the smooth running of the meal. More informal meals certainly do not have to adhere rigidly to the rules: indeed, many restaurants 'break the rules' to create more imaginative settings. However, the correct way to lay a formal table is outlined here.

Cutlery (flatware) should be laid on either side of the plates so that implements for the first course are on the outside, with those for subsequent courses arranged so that diners can work in towards the plates as each course arrives. Forks go on the left side and knives on the right. If the first course needs just a fork, this will be put on the outside at the left, despite the fact that most guests will use it in their right hand. Butter knives may be put on side plates, and dessert spoons and forks may be placed on either side of the table mat or above it.

When just one glass is used, place it above the knife or knives. Where more than one is used, these can be arranged in order from left to right or from right to left, or in a triangular pattern above the knife. It is correct to set all the glasses on the table before the meal begins. However, if there is not enough space, port and liqueur glasses can be brought to the table when they are needed at the end of the meal and the table has been cleared of everything that was needed for the main course.

Place the bread-and-butter plate to the left of the place setting. Warm plates are brought to the table as they are needed. If the starter is cold, it can be placed on the table before the guests are invited to be seated.

Finally, place salt and pepper containers on the table at regular intervals so that they are within easy reach of everyone. If not placing in the actual serving dish, servers should be laid within easy reach of them.

alternately in a way that the host and hostess feel will make for the best conversation. Place cards can be used if desired or needed. For very formal dinners, the whole name of the guest, including the title, should be used: Dr, Mrs, Miss, Ms, Mr. On less formal occasions, using just the first name is equally correct.

Serve each guest from the left. Although a formal dinner will probably be attended by a number of waiters and waitresses, this is not viable for most people, so pass the dishes around from the left, instead. This leaves the right hand of each of the guests free to do the helping. Then, once the main course is over, clear the table of everything to do with it – including condiments – before serving dessert.

ABOVE Look for pieces with elegant flowing lines. Good shape enhances all china, regardless of colour or pattern.

BELOW An unsophisticated glass plate is set on skeletonized magnolia leaves laid on a frosted glass underplate for a very pretty overall effect.

TABLE SETTINGS

China, glass, cutlery (flatware) and linens together make up the overall look of any setting. On to that framework can be added candles and their holders plus the table decorations, which are the icing on the cake. These are obviously areas where you can add personal touches that may be quite different from anyone else's, and not even very different each time you entertain. But with imagination and flair, you can be creative with all the elements that go into laying a table.

Your existing tableware will have the greatest influence on the table settings you create. You will probably instinctively choose designs that suit the style of your home, whether it is elegantly modern, traditional or has a more relaxed country look. Given this starting point, however, there is no reason why your table has to look the same each time you set it. Of course, you may have a favourite look, and you may always want to re-create it. But there will be occasions, such as Christmas, Easter or at special celebrations, when you wish to make your table look more special than usual. The other main reasons for wanting to adapt the look of your table settings are that, as time goes by, fashions in home style change and personal tastes develop. You may want to reflect these changes in your table settings.

China

The art of successful table setting is to be clever with the crockery, so mix, match, adapt and adorn your dinner service to suit the mood and the occasion. The effective way to mix pieces from different sets is to link them by colour. So by collecting all white or all cream, for example, you can create a wonderful overall effect from pieces that were not necessarily designed to match. Another way is to collect two different but harmonious colours, black and white for example.

Underplates, too, provide a lot of scope. Buy brass to lend sparkle at Christmas or other celebrations, or coloured glass to add a new look on any occasion. Alternatively, you could put clear glass plates on top of those from the main set, with something decorative between, such as leaves, fabric or flowers that will show through and can be changed to suit the mood.

LEFT Whatever style of cutlery (flatware) you choose, a collection that complements the overall setting will enhance the look of the table.

BELOW Highlight the gold rim of elegant porcelain soup cups by contrasting it with brass. Even if your dinner service is plain, it will look richer if set on metal. Add a gold tassel and wrap party favours in gold organza for very special occasions.

Cutlery (flatware)

Knives, forks and spoons can have a wonderful sculptural quality to them, which may be used in many ways in a table setting. The formal and obvious way is to lay them, in accordance with etiquette, soldier-like on either side of each plate. But try adorning the cutlery, tying it in pairs or threes with ribbon, raffia or string. You could also tie in a place card, or tuck in a flower, leaf or, if you wish, a chandelier crystal, a tassel or a shell for extra decoration.

Glass

Glass is so beautiful that it needs little decoration, but it is lovely to make something special of, say, a pre-dinner cocktail. Frosting the rim with egg white and caster (superfine) sugar is

DECORATIVE IDEAS

Create a table decoration that is as simple as a few seasonal flowers in a vase or as elaborate as a formal urn arrangement. But the real creativity comes when you add your own flair, perhaps transcending the obvious. Wrap vases in almost anything from brown paper to string to give myriad new looks. Place flowers in vases, ready-tied to give them natural-looking support; if the container is glass, the securing string will add to the decoration. Gild flowers, foliage and berries, and add fruits or vegetables to a floral arrangement. Stand flowers with straight, sturdy stalks, on plates or in shallow bowls, tied to keep them in an upright position.

Fruits and vegetables make wonderful organic table arrangements. As well as the more obvious grapes, pears, figs and pomegranates, use pumpkins and marrows (squashes), perhaps decoratively carved and internally lit with a night-light. Gilding fruits and vegetables, or tying them up with string or raffia, adds the extra touch to make them different.

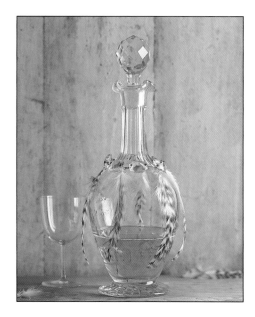

a traditional idea, and one that always delights. Tassels, ribbons, cords and beads can be tied decoratively around the stems of glasses, or golden wire wound around them in graceful imitation of Italian wine bottles.

LEFT A witty reference to silver chain decanter labels can be made with a necklace. There is something sensuous about this one, made of chandelier crystals and feathers.

Linen

It is not difficult to be innovative with linens. Napkins can very easily be equipped with unusual 'rings', embroidered or embellished with beads. Nor do table cloths necessarily have to have been purpose-made. Any suitable length of fabric – bedspreads, saris, sheeting or curtain lining – will do. When a fabric is not too expensive, you can embellish it with stamps, stencils or fabric paint; choose to appliqué or embroider it, or stitch on less obvious trimmings, such as buttons and shells, pebbles and even twigs.

BELOW Evocative of American Indian dress, a leather thong bound round and round natural linen, then trimmed with a few game feathers, looks fabulous.

HOME ENTERTAINING

DECORATING WITH CANDLES

An elegant array of candles adds the finishing touch to any table setting, creating an atmosphere that cannot be equalled by any other form of lighting. Their use does not stop at tables, however – candles can be used in all areas of the home and in all kinds of containers, to marvellous effect.

At Christmas time, for instance, you may like to incorporate candles into a large, deep swag filling a wide window sill or mantelpiece, using thick, stubby candles raised on flowerpots concealed among the greenery. Position tall candles to taper from a forest of twigs and pine-cones, or trim plain altar candles, beautiful in their simplicity, with evergreens, berries and bows to stand as a sign of welcome in a window.

At other times of the year, flowerpots make practical if somewhat rustic holders for candles of all kinds – from the highly-textured beeswax candles to those in traditional colours. Select the most earthy and weatherbeaten flowerpots you have, and plant the candles in heavy holding material such as gravel chippings concealed under (for safety reasons) damp moss or hay. A garland of ivy trailing around the top of the flowerpot, held in place with unobtrusive blobs of clay, will add to the pastoral look, while a large green and white gingham bow will add a touch more elegance.

A variety of household items, including pottery mugs and tumblers, casseroles and glass dishes, are ideal for holding candles of all shapes and sizes. Bargain-shop candlesticks can also be transformed with a simple verdigris look-alike technique using acrylic paints. You can even use hollowed-out vegetables – pumpkin-shaped gourds have a wonderful shape and colour – as bases for candles. Arrange these in a cluster on a dining table, a sideboard or in the kitchen, or use them as party decorations. Remember never to leave lit candles unattended.

PAINTING A CANDLESTICK

1 Paint the candlestick with a base coat of bronze acrylic paint, using criss-crossing brushstrokes for an uneven, textured finish. Allow the paint to dry.

2 Daub the bronze-coloured surface with green acrylic paint. If you prefer a more transparent finish, thin the paint with turpentine (methylated spirits) first. Leave to dry for 10 minutes, then daub on gold acrylic paint in uneven patches.

3 A verdigris-style candlestick makes an elegant flower stand. Fix a small foam-holder and a piece of soaked stem-holding foam to the top of the candlestick with florist's tape, and arrange a colourful combination of flowers and foliage.

CHRISTMAS CANDLES

1 Cut short lengths of evergreens and holly and bind them into bunches using silver wire. Place a few stems against a candle and bind them on with silver wire. Add more bunches, binding them on all around the candle, and secure the wire. Hook on false berries, if you wish. Tie ribbon around the stems to conceal the wire. Trim the other candles in a similar way.

2 Place the candles in appropriate holders and arrange them in the centre of a dining table or on a window sill among cuttings of mixed evergreens.

VEGETABLE CANDLE HOLDERS

1 To make gourd candle holders, first break off the stalks. If the gourds are soft enough, gouge out a shallow hole from each one that is wide enough to hold a candle, using a sharp knife. If the gourds are too hard to do this – and dried ones may well be – fix the candles securely in the indentations using a little florist's adhesive clay.

2 Arrange the gourds to make an attractive group. Here, trailing stems of Chinese lanterns (winter cherry) wind through the gourds, an element that could be repeated in neighbouring flower arrangements.

DISH OF CANDLES

1 Fill a shallow dish two-thirds full of clean sand, and place a tall candle in the middle. Position shorter candles around it.

2 Arrange a variety of pretty shells around the candles, pressing them into the sand.

3 Check that all the candles are securely positioned before lighting them.

TABLE DECORATING WITH FLOWERS

A garland is a lovely way to decorate a table – indoors or out – for a special occasion such as a wedding or christening reception, a birthday, or any other celebration. You can make the garland to loop across the front of the table, to encircle the rim, or to drape on all four sides of a free-standing table. Long, leafy stems work extremely well for this type of decoration – smilax (*Asparagus asparagoides*) has been used here. With its pliable stem and mass of bright green leaves, this forms a natural garland, and makes an attractive instant decoration, even without the addition of flowers.

Smilax is usually sold to order in bundles of 5 stems. Keep the stem ends in water until just before you assemble the garland, and the foliage should stay fresh for several days. Mimosa, gypsophila and spray chrysanthemums all make a good accompaniment for a bright, summery look.

GARLAND TIPS

Floral and foliage garlands are very simple to make and as they are almost invariably composed of short-stemmed plant materials, they can utilize clippings from larger designs. Side shoots of delphinium cut from stems arranged in a pedestal design; individual spray-chrysanthemum flowers that formed too dense a cluster; florets and leaflets that would come below the water level in a vase – you can form them all into posies and bind them on to a garland using silver wire.

Garlands can be composed on a central core. According to the weight of the plant materials, this may vary from tightly coiled paper ribbon, thin string, twine or wire, to thick rope or even a roll made of wire-mesh netting filled with offcuts of absorbent stem-holding foam. This latter core has the advantage of providing fresh flowers in a garland with a source of moisture.

1 Gather together your chosen flowers and foliage, and the other materials you will need: a roll of florist's silver wire, florist's scissors, 2.5 cm/1 in wide ribbon and pins for fixing the ribbon in place on the cloth.

2 It will save time just before the event if you make up the posies in advance. Choose materials that will contrast well with the bright foliage of the garland. Cut the flower stems short, using 5 or 6 pieces of gypsophila, 2 small snippings of mimosa, and either 1 or 2 spray chrysanthemums, according to their size. Gather the stems together and bind them with silver wire.

3 You can space the posies as close together or as wide apart on the garland as you wish, so make up as many as you will need. As a general rule, the smaller the table, the smaller the gap should be between the flowers. Once you have assembled the posies, place them in a shallow bowl of water before attaching them to the garland.

4 Measure the length of garland needed for the side drapes and mark the centre. With the stems of the first posy towards the end of one of the lengths of foliage, bind the posy to the main stem with silver wire. Bind on more posies in the same way, reversing the direction of the stems when you reach the centre of the draped garland. Repeat the decoration with the remaining lengths of garland, but without reversing the direction of the flowers of the side trails.

5 Pin the garland to the cloth, adjusting the fall of the drape so that it is equal on all sides, and pin on the side trails. Check that the garland hangs well. Sometimes the weight of the posies will cause it to twist, with the flowers facing inwards. If this happens, pin the garland to the cloth at intervals. Pin lengths of ribbon to the corners, and tie more lengths into bows and attach to the centres of the drapes.

RIGHT A garland of dried flowers, wired on to paper ribbon and finished off with an extravagant bow, makes a beautiful table decoration. The garland will retain its crisp and colourful appearance throughout the day, and can be carefully packed away and used another time.

MAKING A WREATH

Through the centuries, wreaths have been regarded as symbols of protection, love, friendship and welcome. Most are composed of a central core, although you can twist and weave supple stems of foliage such as clematis or hops into wreaths that are decorative in their own right, or construct a simple wreath base from supple grass or other stems and then decorate it with flowers.

With the revival of interest in decorative rings, it is now possible to buy a wide variety of wreath bases from florists and department stores. Dried-stem rings, vine wreath forms and twisted willow rings can all be adorned with posies of fresh flowers and foliage, or with dried plant material for long-term display. Pre-formed rings of absorbent stem-holding foam encased in a plastic base provide fresh flowers with a moisture source and can be used throughout the year for wall hangings or table decorations. They are, however, unattractive to look at, so you must plan your decoration to include an all-concealing cover – a handful of ivy leaves or other foliage would be ideal.

MAKING A FRESH-FLOWER WREATH

1 Gather up your materials: a pre-formed foam ring of 25 cm/10 in diameter, a selection of flowers such as sweet peas, roses, spray carnations, Peruvian lilies and gypsophila, evergreen foliage such as ivy, and florist's scissors. Arrange a ring of ivy leaves around the inside and outside of the ring form to frame the flowers. Cut each sweet-pea flower on a short stem and arrange at intervals around the ring.

2 Complete the ring of sweet peas and arrange more ivy leaves between the flowers, to give the design a natural and 'countrified' look.

3 Cut individual roses, Peruvian lilies and spray carnations and arrange them between the sweet peas. Insert short sprays of gypsophila around the ring.

4 Use the floral circlet to decorate a table top, a low shelf or a buffet table, where it would make an unusual centrepiece.

IDEAS FOR FOAM RINGS

Outline a foam ring with periwinkle leaves, fill it with some short-stemmed daffodils, tulips and pansies, and then embellish it with a cluster of lighted tapers for an Easter table decoration; cover a small ring with lady's mantle and cornflowers, and then stud it with strawberries pierced with cocktail sticks (toothpicks) for a midsummer party piece; or define a large ring with ivy leaves, fill in with sweet peas, Peruvian lilies and roses, and cover it with delicate gypsophila.

MAKING A POT-POURRI WREATH

1 Gather up the materials you will need: a dried-stem ring of 20 cm/8 in diameter, about 115 g/4 oz pot pourri, a hot-glue gun, dried flowers such as rosebuds and sea lavender, a roll of florist's silver wire, half a stub wire (floral pin), satin ribbon and a pair of scissors.

2 Spurt the glue on to the ring a little at a time, and press the pot pourri on to it. Take care not to burn your fingers when using hot glue. Allow to cool for a few seconds before pressing on the petals.

3 Work all around the ring, gluing and pressing on the petals until you have covered the form on top, both inside and outside. If there are any gaps, spurt on a little more glue and add more petals. Glue some of the most colourful petals on top to give the ring a bright appearance.

4 Arrange the dried flowers to make a small posy. Cut short the stems and bind them with silver wire. Bend the stub wire in half to make a U-shape, loop it over the stems and press the ends of the wire into the ring to secure the posy.

5 Tie the ribbon around the ring form, bringing the ends over the top, where they will cover the posy stems and binding wire. Tie the ribbon into a bow and then trim off the ends neatly.

NAPKIN FOLDING

Crisp, freshly laundered napkins are an essential feature of every well-set table. You can simply press them in large, plain squares and lay one at each place setting with the minimum of fuss. Alternatively, you can fold napkins in a variety of ways to complement the food, the table layout and the occasion.

Regardless of the simplicity of the meal, fabric napkins must be spotlessly clean and well-pressed. Plain white linen napkins are generally best folded very simply for an elegant effect. If they have a monogram or other decorative embroidery, fold them to display this. Press embroidered napkins on the wrong side to make the pattern stand out attractively.

Decorative napkins, trimmed with embroidery or lace or with a prominent self-pattern, should also be folded very simply; plain fabric napkins or those with a small decorative border are more suitable for elaborate folding.

If you are preparing a meal for a comparatively small number – that is, under about 15 guests – it is a good idea to use fabric napkins if possible. The fabrics do not have to be the same, and you can in fact make a virtue of their differences by combining contrasting colours or patterns to create an attractive arrangement. It is a nice idea to allow 2 or 3 different-coloured napkins for each place setting, perhaps fanned out simply, as shown on the opposite page.

For a larger gathering, especially when you are serving finger foods, or

ABOVE Neatly pressed and folded napkins add elegance to a dinner table when accompanied by sparkling cutlery (flatware) and glasses.

BELOW A tartan bow holds a neatly rolled napkin and spoon for a dessert course.

when there are a lot of children around, it is an advantage to use disposable paper napkins.

Elaborate folding methods are not used for buffet presentation as the emphasis is mainly on the practicalities of carrying a plate, napkin and cutlery (flatware). There are a number of standard options for placing napkins, all of which are practical for a buffet: roll a knife and fork in each napkin (do not roll cutlery for dessert in the napkin – you should offer this separately); stack a napkin on each plate; fold the napkins diagonally to make triangles and overlap these on one side of the buffet table; roll the napkins and stand them in a wide-necked jug; or arrange them in a rustic basket.

Tips for successful folding

For folding purposes, heavy linen is best, as it becomes firm and crisp when starched. Plain dinner napkins measuring 45–50 cm/18–20 in square, or more, are best, and are essential for many complicated folding techniques. The napkins must be cut square and the fabric must be cut straight on the weave so that the napkins will not pull out of shape easily.

HOME ENTERTAINING

Starch linen napkins after washing, using traditional starch, which you mix with boiling water (follow the manufacturer's instructions for this). You should use this method if at all possible, as spray starch will not give a really good, crisp finish. Iron the napkins while still damp, and dampen napkins which have already dried before ironing. When ironing, gently pull the napkins back into shape if necessary to ensure that they are perfectly square again. It is best to iron napkins on a large surface; an ironing-board can be too narrow when pressing large napkins. Protect the surface with a folded thick towel covered with a piece of plain white cotton.

Simple presentation
To form a neat square, press the napkin, making sure that all the corners are perfectly square. Fold the napkin into quarters, pressing each fold carefully. Lay a large quarter-folded napkin squarely between the cutlery (flatware) at each place setting, or turn it by 90 degrees.

To make a simple triangle, fold the square in half diagonally and press the resulting triangle neatly. Lay the folded napkin on a side plate, with the long side nearest the place setting. The triangle may also be laid on top of a plate in the middle of the setting.

For a simple rectangle, fold a square napkin in half again. This is an ideal way of displaying a decorative corner on the napkin. Plain napkins may be folded and pressed into quarters, then the sides folded underneath and pressed to make an oblong shape. Lay the hemmed edge on the short side at the bottom of the place setting.

Keep rolled napkins in place with napkin rings, or tie them with ribbon or cord. Alternatively, if you roll the napkins carefully and lay them with the ends underneath, they will usually sit quite neatly.

SPREADING FAN

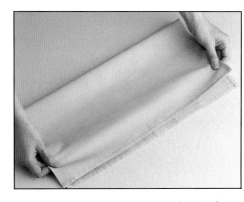

1 This is an elegant yet simple design that would be suitable for any occasion. To begin, fold up the napkin edge nearest to you to meet the top edge.

2 Rotate the napkin so that the folded edge is on your right, then make equal-sized 'accordion' pleats all the way up to the top of the napkin.

3 Insert the end of the napkin into a ring, or tie it with ribbon or cord.

4 Spread out the pleats neatly to make the fan shape, and lay the napkin on a plate. Here, 2 small napkins of different colours have been folded together to match the colours of the setting perfectly.

NAPKIN FOLDING (continued)

HOME ENTERTAINING

FOLDED WINGS

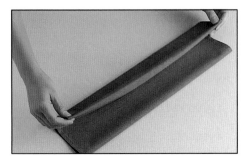

1 This design works best with a stiff cotton napkin. Fold the bottom and top edges of the open napkin into the centre. Bring the bottom fold up to the top.

2 Fold in the left side of the napkin by exactly one-third.

3 Fold this side back on itself to align with the outside edge again.

4 Repeat with the right side. Lift the top layers on both sides and curl them back under into their folds to form the wings.

IRIS IN A GLASS

1 This design creates a very striking display if folded with a large, colourful napkin. Starting with the corners of the open napkin top and bottom in the form of a diamond, bring the point nearest to you up to the top point to form a triangle.

2 With a finger at the centre of the fold line, fold up the 2 corners nearest to you so that they are level with the centre-top point and slightly to each side of it.

3 Fold the newly formed bottom point part-way up towards the top point.

4 Make accordion pleats across the napkin from left to right. Position the napkin in the glass and fan out the petals of the iris.

ELF'S BOOT

1 Use a fabric napkin for this fun design. Fold the top and bottom edges to meet in the middle. Bring the bottom edge to meet the top edge, folding the rectangle in half.

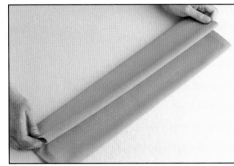

2 With a finger at the centre bottom, fold up both sides away from you so that the edges meet in the middle.

3 Fold the right and left sides closest to you into the centre to form a sharper point.

4 Fold the left side of the napkin over on to the right side.

5 Move the napkin round so that the bottom point now faces to your right. Fold the top-left tail down towards you.

6 Fold the bottom edge of the other left tail upwards, and tuck the tail securely into the pocket of the tail on the right.

ENTERTAINING AT CHRISTMAS

The celebration of Christmas is deeply woven into the fabric of home and family life. Much of the activity is centred on the kitchen which, as the culinary preparations get under way in the run-up to Christmas, more than ever becomes the heart of the home. The smooth running of the Christmas catering programme calls for a fair amount of advance planning and, nearer the day, meticulous timing, particularly if you have guests staying.

Entertaining over the Christmas period is a special pleasure, but there is no denying that it involves extra work and responsibility, as you will want to ensure that guests not only enjoy the highlights of their stay, but the quiet moments too.

For your own busy schedule and peace of mind, prepare guest bedrooms well in advance. Check that there are plenty of basic requirements such as fluffy towels, tissues, cotton wool (absorbent cotton) and guests' soap.

If you have the facilities, it is a good idea to take a leaf from the hoteliers' book and provide coffee- and tea-making equipment, something that is especially welcomed by those who wake up at unsociably early hours. Arrange a tray with an electric kettle, a small

ABOVE A bright wreath of evergreens, holly and berries gives a traditional sign of welcome.

cafetière and a jar of ground coffee (or just supply instant coffee, if it is easier), a teapot and a choice of two tea blends. Add wrapped sugar and a decorative tin of biscuits (cookies), with milk and fresh fruit to be replenished daily.

Make a small selection of books and magazines for friends who like to travel light. Check that there are bulbs in the reading lamps, and provide an electric torch (flashlight) or plug in extra nightlights to help with night-time navigation to the bathroom.

Flowers help to make a room more welcoming. If there are plenty of Christmas decorations in the other rooms, flowers can bring a breath of spring or summer to the guest rooms. Dried-flower arrangements are a pretty option that also have the advantage of being long-lasting, preventing the need for last-minute preparation.

When your guests arrive, be sure to show them such essentials as where the light switches and sockets (receptacles) are to be found, and which cupboard (closet) space is available. Such extra thoughtfulness has an advantage for you too, as it will give you a chance to get

on with household tasks while guests enjoy the warmth of your hospitality.

Sugared flowers and fruits
Sparkling under a light dusting of sugar as though tinged with frost or snow, sugared sweetmeats are a Christmas delicacy that add a lovely touch when displayed in bowls in guest bedrooms or in a living or dining room. You can prepare them several days ahead of the festivities and, once they are dry, store them in an airtight tin.

Not all flowers are edible, although many are – consult a reliable source if you are in any doubt. Marigolds, nasturtiums and pansies were all favourites in Victorian times, and offer an attractive variety of colour and shapes. Sugared fruits also look beautiful. Use small fruits, such as cherries, cranberries, strawberries and raspberries, whole. Peel and segment larger fruits such as oranges and tangerines, halve or quarter figs, according to their size, and halve and stone (pit) plums and apricots. You can also use sugared leaves with fruit and flowers, if you wish, to add contrast.

OPPOSITE Spoil your guests with breakfast in bed. Although the preparation is simple (coffee, orange juice and croissants warmed in the oven) the presentation is cheerful and welcoming – bright blue china is offset by flowers in complementary yellow.

RIGHT A plate is fitted with absorbent stem-holding foam for this pretty arrangement. Be careful to use freesias only in moderation in arrangements intended for bedrooms – their heavy scent, although lovely, may be oppressive to some guests.

SUGARING FLOWERS AND FRUITS

1 Hold fruits or flowers from a stem if possible, or pierce with a cocktail stick (toothpick), and dip into a bowl of lightly beaten egg white.

2 Lightly dust each petal, flower, fruit or leaf with caster (superfine) sugar to cover the whole surface.

3 Place on a wire rack covered with a sheet of greaseproof (waxed) paper, and leave to dry thoroughly.

ENTERTAINING AT CHRISTMAS (continued)

For a truly traditional Christmas, hark back to an era before the invention of tinsel and baubles when natural, organic materials provided the decoration, the textures and the evocative scents. Draw inspiration form the Elizabethans, who created a festive ambience rich with the aromas of oranges and bay, and of heady spices such as cinnamon and cloves. These ingredients can be the starting point of an elegant colour scheme, substituting russets and oranges for the more usual reds. Supplement the rich mood by looking for exotic fruits and vegetables like pomegranates, Chinese lanterns and artichokes, and highlight them with voluptuous bunches of black grapes. Use rusty metal vases, such as brass or amber glass plates, then add a hint of gold for the Midas touch. Here are just a few suggestions for creating a truly individual Christmas affair.

FLORAL URN ARRANGEMENT

1 Soak a florist's foam brick in water. Cut it to fit a metal urn and place inside. Trim a bunch of tree ivy to length and gild the berries using picture framer's gilt wax. Use the ivy to make a full base arrangement.

2 Trim five calla lilies to length and place them in the arrangement. Repeat with five russet roses to complete, making sure they are all at slightly different angles.

BROCADE PARTY FAVOURS

1 Cut two pieces of brocade, each measuring 15 x 30 cm/6 x 12 in. Fold down a 5 cm/2 in hem at the top edge of each piece and stitch the hem.

2 With right sides facing, stitch a seam around three sides, leaving the hemmed edges at the top open. Turn to the right side, fill with a small gift and tie a 20 cm/ 8 in silk cord around the bag.

ABOVE A charming brocade bag tied up with silken cord is a gift enough already; it can also contain a small present for each guest and be decoratively placed next to each setting. A single rosebud adds a final delicate touch.

ADVENT CANDLE CENTREPIECE

1 Soak a florist's foam brick in water and set it on a plate. Carefully push four church or beeswax candles into the foam.

2 Cut the stems of a bunch of tree ivy to size and push them into the florist's foam. Carefully gild the berries with picture framer's gilt wax.

3 Pass a wire through the base of each of the Chinese lanterns (winter cherries) and then twist the ends together. Firmly push the twisted wire ends into the florist's foam base to fix the Chinese lanterns in position.

SEASONAL GARLAND

1 First make the base. Roll a piece of chicken wire measuring the desired length of the finished piece and three times the width into a long sausage filled with florist's foam. Soak in water and then form into a circle. Push tree ivy sprigs into the foam to make a full base.

2 Pass a florist's wire through the base of an artichoke and two dried oranges, then fix these in position around the garland. Gild the ivy berries, the dried oranges and the tips of the artichoke leaves using picture framer's gilt wax.

3 Tie cinnamon sticks into bunches of two or three using gold cord. Fix a wire through the cord and then fix this into the garland.

DECORATIONS FOR OTHER OCCASIONS

EASTER EGG TREE

1 Cut six branches of pussy willow to length (even if no length needs taking off, trim the end of each branch). Place in a vase of water. Then blow seven eggs. If they are brown, paint them with white matt emulsion and allow to dry. Use royal icing to fix assorted small cake decorations, such as sugar flowers and mimosa balls, to the eggs.

2 Cut a piece of florist's wire 15 cm/6 in long and make a loop at one end. Thread the wire through the egg and bend the loop flat against the bottom of the egg. Thread the wire through a ribbon bow. Use the rest of the wire to make a hook for hanging the egg on the tree.

ABOVE Any seasonal branches about to burst into bloom can be used for an Easter tree, which is hung with decorated eggs.

WHITE CHOCOLATE HEARTS

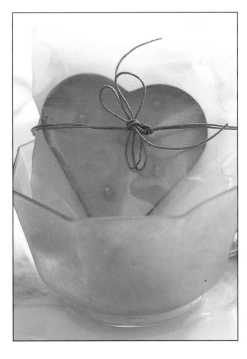

1 Break up 100 g/3½ oz good-quality white chocolate per heart and melt it in a bowl set over a pan of boiling water, stirring with a wooden spoon. Remove the bowl from the heat. Line a baking tin with aluminium foil, and place 10 cm/4 in heart-shaped metal cutters on the foil.

2 Using a metal tablespoon, drop the melted chocolate into the cutters. Decorate with gold or silver balls and leave to set. Wrap the whole heart, with the cutter, in glassine paper and tie with some fine linen string.

ABOVE Gift-wrap a pair of mouthwatering chocolate hearts for each place setting as romantic party favours. The glassine paper used to wrap the hearts creates a 'misty' effect.

BIRTHDAY PARTY NAME CARDS

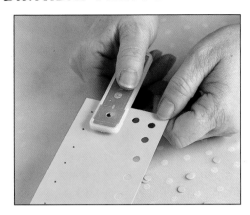

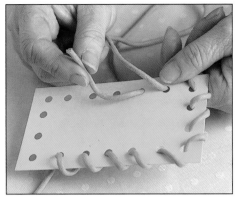

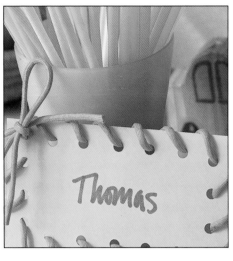

1 For each name card cut out coloured card (cardboard), 12 x 8 cm/5 x 3 in. Then mark out hole positions around the card, 2 cm/¾ in apart. Make the holes with a hole punch.

2 Lace a 1 m/1 yd cord through the holes, finishing with a bow at one corner. Write the child's name in the centre.

ABOVE: Let the children help you make these decorative name cards – even a youngster will want to assist with this fun task.

HOME-MADE COOKIES

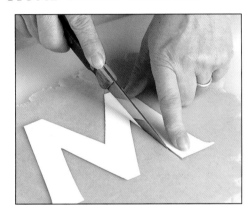

1 Draw large letters on a piece of paper and cut out. Following the instructions on a packet of ready-mixed biscuit dough, mix and roll out the dough. Place a letter on the dough and cut around it using a knife. Repeat for the other initials.

2 Cook on a greased baking tray according to the packet's instructions. Turn on to a wire rack to cool, then tie on ribbon bows.

ABOVE: Cut your favourite biscuit dough into the shape of each child's initial, and add candy-stripped bows once they are ready. They make exciting treats for the children to take home.

POTPOURRI SACHETS

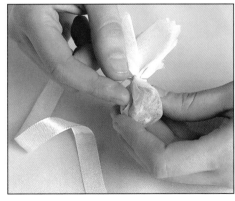

1 Cut a circle of organdie, and then fill the center with potpourri. Draw the organdie together around the filling.

2 Wind fine wire around the sachet to secure it. Tie on a length of ribbon and glue on some diamanté stones.

ABOVE: These sachets will scent the air during the meal and make party favours to take home.

FLOWER ARRANGING

Flowers are infinitely versatile. Available in every tint and hue, with masses of blowsy petals or elegantly simple forms, curiously textured or sweetly scented, the possibilities for creating memorable displays appear endless. For centuries, people have decorated their homes with greenery and flowers, both to celebrate nature and to soften the hard edges of what was often a hostile environment.

Fresh-cut flowers and foliage will always be the cheapest and quickest facelift a room can have. Whether you place a few daisies in a jam jar or fill a crystal vase with show-stopping blooms such as lilies or parrot tulips, flowers take centre stage in any décor. Look to the pages on fresh flowers in this section, and you will learn how to make the most of your flowers, from what to pick and how to treat them to arranging them in the most colourful and attractive of arrays. Consider too, the accompanying foliage – from rich, dark, waxy vine leaves and spiky blue-green grasses to gnarled tree bark and soft, damp moss: these form the perfect backdrop for stunning designs.

Flowers look great when dried, too. Dried flowers are rich in form and texture and can be made into striking table set pieces, contemporary arrangements or just simply gathered into a bunch. In fact, preserving summer flowers is a delightful occupation, requiring neither special equipment nor expertise. A visit to a florist supplier's warehouse for inspiration is recommended, and many speciality suppliers are happy to sell to the public. At these places you will find sensibly sized reels of florist's wire, florist's scissors to cut through wire as well as stems, packs of dried fruit slices, tiny terracotta pots, and florist's tape in every conceivable colour. The list is endless, but read the relevant pages in this section first so that you can make sure you have everything covered. As soon as you have a collection of dried flowers – using one or perhaps several of the methods described here – you can go ahead and create handsome centrepieces, a swag or two for a mantelpiece, and some wreaths for walls and doors. Your home will never before have looked so colourful.

OPPOSITE The mantlepiece offers a prominent position for a floral display. The challenge is to create not just a visual balance, but a physical one too. Ensure stability by keeping the weight of the flowers at the back and near the bottom.

CHOOSING FLOWERS

The chief thing to remember when choosing flowers for any type of flowercraft, from a single bloom in a jam jar for the kitchen table to a more labour-intensive arrangement on a grand scale for a big celebration, is to enjoy the whole experience. Choose flowers for their fragrance, their colour, their shape but, above all, let your decision be an emotional one. Choose flowers because you love them, because the soaring blue of delphiniums gladdens your heart, or the smell of an old-fashioned damask rose sets your head reeling. Do not discard flowers simply because they are not perfect – a single, rain-damaged rose, sprinkled with gold and taupe spots, is in itself a thing of great beauty. Placed in a Russian tea glass with a gilded rim and translucent painted decoration, it becomes a work of art.

Balance

Achieving a visual balance in a flower arrangement involves scale, proportion and colour as well as creating a focal point in the display. The focal point is an area to which the eye is naturally drawn and from which all display materials appear to flow. While the position of the focal point will vary according to the type of display, generally speaking it will be towards its centre. This is where the boldest colours and shapes should be concentrated, with paler colours around the outside.

Always think of the display in three dimensions, never forgetting that as well as a front, it will have sides and a back. This is not difficult to remember for a bouquet or a free-standing, pedestal-mounted display, but can be forgotten if a display is set against a wall. Even a flat-backed arrangement needs depth and shape if is to have the greatest impact. Recessing materials around the focal point will help give it depth and weight.

ABOVE These tulips create a wonderful domed effect which can be viewed from any side.

LEFT The classic combination of flowers and candlelight is usually associated with romantic dinners for two. However, this candelabra table decoration would be suitable for a variety of special dining occasions.

Scale and proportion

Scale is also a very important consideration when planning a floral display. To create an arrangement which is pleasing to the eye, the sizes of the various flower types used in the same display should not be radically different. For example, it would be hard to make amaryllis look in scale with lily-of-the-valley.

The type of foliage used should be in scale with the flowers, too, and the display itself must be in scale with its container, and the whole arrangement and its container must be in scale with its surroundings. A display in a large space in a public building must itself be appropriately large enough to make a statement, conversely a bedside table would require no more than an arrangement in a bud vase.

Proportion is the relationship of width, height and depth within a floral display and in this respect there are some rule-of-thumb guidelines worth bearing in mind.

● A vase with long-stemmed flowers such as lilies, should be around one-third the height of the flowers.
● The focal point of a corsage is about one-third the overall height up from the bottom.

- In a tied bouquet, the length of the stems below the binding point should be approximately one-third of the bouquet's overall height.
- In a trailing wedding bouquet, the focal point of the display will probably be about one-third of the overall length up from its lowest point.
- For a pedestal arrangement, the focal point will be approximately two-thirds of the overall height down from its topmost point.

Colour

The way in which colour is used can be vital to the success or failure of a display and there are several factors to bear in mind when deciding on a colour palette.

Though most people have an eye for colour, an understanding of the theory of colour is useful. Red, blue and yellow are the basic hues from which all other colours stem. Red, orange and yellow are warm colours, which tend to create an exciting visual effect, while green, blue and violet are cooler and visually calmer.

Generally speaking, the lighter, brighter and hotter a colour, the more it will dominate an arrangement. White (which technically is the absence of colour) is also prominent in a display of flowers. On the other hand, the darker and cooler the colour, the more it will visually recede into a display. It is important to bear this in mind when creating large displays to be viewed from a distance. In such circumstances, soft shades of blue and violet, in particular, can become lost in an arrangement. Usually a good visual balance is achieved if the stronger, bolder coloured flowers are positioned towards the centre of the display with the paler, more subtle colours around the outside.

Now, armed with some basic knowledge of colour theory, you can be braver in your choice of palette. 'Safe' colour combinations such as creams with whites, or pinks with mauves have their place, but experiment with oranges and violets, yellows and blues, even pinks and yellows and you will add a vibrant dimension to your flower arranging.

BELOW This feast of red flowers and coloured foliage is bursting with exotic vibrance.

FLOWER ARRANGING

MAKING THE MOST OF COLOUR

Your choice of flowers for the home will generally take into account the furnishings of a room, the background against which the arrangement will be seen, and the effect that you wish to create – subtle and restful, or bold and eye-catching. When 2 colours that oppose each other on the colour wheel, such as mauve and yellow, are arranged together, the result can be dazzling.

Add to the impact of the design by using a scooped-out melon, with its deeply ridged texture, as an unusual container. Watermelons, pumpkins and marrows (squash), or oranges and lemons also make interesting short-term flower holders. You can dry the shells in an oven at a low temperature for a longer-lasting display.

Choose flowers that contrast dramatically with each other in size, shape and texture for this arrangement, such as huge, glossy yellow lilies and tiny, fluffy mimosa flowers, as well as yellow roses, mauve Singapore orchids and carnations. Eucalyptus foliage makes an attractive accompaniment.

OTHER CONTAINER IDEAS

You can use all kinds of baskets, pots, jugs, teapots and even decorated food cans as unusual holders for flowers. Rustic baskets always look attractive, either left plain or painted to harmonize with a particular colour scheme. If you are using soaked absorbent stem-holding foam in a basket, line the basket with a sheet of plastic, or fit a plastic container inside.

1 Gather together the materials you will need: a scooped-out melon or other container, a knife, a dessertspoon, a plastic foam-holding saucer, a cylinder of absorbent stem-holding foam, pre-soaked in water, narrow florist's adhesive tape, scissors and florist's scissors.

2 Cut a thin slice from the top of the melon, and a sliver from the base so that it will stand steadily. Using the spoon, scoop out the melon seeds into a bowl. Scoop out the melon flesh into a second bowl, taking care not to pierce and damage the shell.

3 Press the plastic saucer over the top of the melon and press the soaked foam into the indent. Criss-cross 2 lengths of adhesive tape over the foam and saucer and down on to the melon shell. Arrange stems of mimosa to make an irregular shape.

4 Arrange the orchids to make a triangular outline, the tallest one in the centre and 2 slightly shorter stems at the sides. Position the carnations to give weight to the design at the top and sides. Cut the lily stems and position them at the heart of the design, where the fully opened flowers will be seen head-on.

5 Add the cream roses, positioning some at the back so that they will be viewed through the more prominent flowers, and one low at the right. Complete the design with light sprays of foliage, placing some on the left of the arrangement to balance the rose. Keep the foam permanently moist, adding water at least once a day.

FIXING A SAUCER OF STEM-HOLDING FOAM

Preparing a container in this way allows you to use a tall vase, carafe or jug as a pedestal, positioning flower and foliage stems to slant both downwards and horizontally, or in any direction you choose. You will need a tall container, a strip of florist's adhesive clay, a plastic foam-holding saucer, a cylinder of stem-holding foam (either absorbent or dry according to the materials to be arranged), narrow florist's adhesive tape and scissors.

1 Cut small lengths of adhesive clay and press them on to the underside of the plastic saucer, where they will come into contact with the top of the container. Press the saucer firmly in place to hold it securely.

2 Soak the foam if it is to hold fresh flowers and foliage. Press the foam cylinder into the indent in the saucer. Cut 2 lengths of adhesive tape long enough to go over the foam, across the saucer and down on to the container rim. Stick them in place, criss-crossing them on top of the foam.

FLOWER ARRANGING

DECORATING WITH FRESH FLOWERS

Materials and equipment

For many arrangements, little is needed beyond a good pair of sharp, strong scissors and some florist's wire, but elaborate displays on special occasions may need more support.

Canes: thin canes can be used to support hollow and top-heavy stems.

Carpet moss (sheet moss): this moss is useful for covering the surface of arrangements to conceal individual containers, creating the illusion that the flowers are growing in the basket or container.

Cellophane: use for wrapping bouquets, as a waterproof lining for porous containers and scrunched up as an invisible support for stems in a vase.

Floating candles: a bowl of these surrounded by beautiful fragrant flowers makes a stunning table centrepiece, especially at night.

Florist's adhesive tapes: waterproof tape is useful for sticking plastic or cellophane to the inside of containers. Strong adhesive double-sided tape provides a removable surface on which to stick decorative materials such as moss or vegetation to the sides of vases and containers.

Florist's foam: as well as the brick shape, spheres and rings are available in various sizes. Rings have a built-in plastic drip tray to make table centre-pieces without the worry of flooding.

Florist's scissors: the most important piece of equipment that no flower arranger can afford to be without is a pair of strong and very sharp scissors. There are numerous designs for both left- and right-handed flower arrangers.

Florist's wires: useful for making false stems to fix cones and nuts to fresh flower designs.

Flower food: the correct amount of flower food should be used in every vase. This harmless preparation of mild disinfectant and sugar inhibits growth of bacteria in the water and encourages buds to mature and open.

Gilt cream paint: gives a sheen to nuts, cones and fruits as well as containers. It is available in gold, silver and bronze.

Glass stones: widely available from gift shops and garden centres. The transparent ones are most versatile as they resemble precious crystals in the bottom of a glass vase or bowl.

Glue gun and glue sticks: the glue gun is a dream machine for instantly attaching fresh flowers to containers, wreaths and garlands. The liquid glue is extremely hot and potentially dangerous if left unattended and should be kept out of reach of children.

Nuts and cones: walnuts, hazelnuts, acorns and all types of cones can be combined with fresh flowers.

Pebbles and shells: these make a decorative mulch and an attractive support for flower stems in glass vases.

Raffia: natural raffia is ideal for tying flowers together as it is strong but does not bite into the stems. Coloured raffia is perfect for making lush trailing bows.

Secateurs (pruners): these are more practical than scissors for cutting wires and tough branches.

PREPARING FLOWERS

If you are picking your own flowers, gather them in the morning, when the sun has caused the dew to evaporate but before there is a danger of wilting. Ideally, have a container of water with you to hold your harvest. Once back in the house, re-cut the stems, remove all foliage that will be below the waterline, then plunge the stems into a bucket of deep water to allow them to have a good, long drink. Stand the bucket in a cool, draught-free room, in the dark if you wish to slow the development of the blooms, or in indirect light to accelerate blossoming. During the conditioning time, which should be a minimum of 6 hours, check that the flowers are taking in water. Drooping foliage and limp heads indicate an airlock – roses are particularly susceptible to this problem.

All stems must be cut again before the flowers are placed in the display container. Research has shown that a single, diagonal cut provides the best uptake of water. Fill the hollow stems of flowers such as delphiniums with water and plug the ends with cotton.

Containers

The type, size and colour of container you choose should complement the flowers you are arranging. Here are some simple ideas.

Baskets: shallow baskets lined with plastic and filled with florist's foam concealed with moss provide a support for flowers, and deeper baskets can hide several containers within it filled with fresh blooms.

Glass tanks: very versatile and are effective used singly or in a group of varying heights. They can be used to contain a mass of flowers of just a few stems supported with coloured glass pebbles or stones.

Glasses and jars: simple, straight-sided drinking glasses are cheap and perfect for small posies and table centrepieces.

Terracotta pots: natural coloured terracotta pots complement country-style arrangements, and with a simple wash of diluted emulsion paint they can be gently coloured in minutes to suit any number of styles. Terracotta is porous, so use an inner container or line them with plastic.

Metal containers: some metals react with water and can cause flowers to die prematurely and obviously shouldn't be used. But galvanized metal is safe and rustproof. A tall metal bucket is ideal for supporting the height of long stems or large branches of foliage. Buckets in bold colours provide instant cheer.

CLOCKWISE FROM TOP LEFT Raffia, carpet moss (sheet moss), cellophane, floating candles, glue gun, adhesive tapes, nuts and cones, canes and florist's wire, florist's scissors, flower food, secateurs (pruners), pebbles and shells, glass stones, gilt cream.

FLORAL DISPLAYS FOR THE HOME

Just as each room in the home serves a different function, so different floral displays in appropriate styles will enhance their environment.

The dining room has a high profile in flower-arranging terms, as it becomes the centre stage whenever the family gathers for a leisurely meal – at Sunday lunchtime, perhaps – or when entertaining friends. If you have more than one arrangement in the room, it is a good idea to compose them with a linking theme. You could choose similar flowers, but in different colours: deep-pink Peruvian lilies, for example, in one case and the palest of pinks in another. A tall pitcher of white iris on the sideboard could be interpreted by floating similar flowers in a glass bowl on the dining table, by placing a single flower in a specimen vase at each place setting, or by blending white iris in an arrangement with anemones or roses.

In the living room, the well of the fireplace forms a dramatic arch for a flamboyant arrangement of seasonal plant materials chosen according to the colour and texture of the fireplace surround: a large earthenware jug of horse-chestnut buds in spring, a cool blend of blues and greens in summer, and the fiery hues of red, orange and yellow as winter approaches.

In summer, fresh flowers – especially if placed on a sunny window sill – are vulnerable and will fade quickly. In these circumstances, achieve the best of both worlds and choose the brightest and boldest of containers to display sun-bleached seedheads; fill a large white jug with a burst of fresh or dried gypsophila and strawflowers; pack a basket full of wild oats and decorative grasses, and wrap it with a brightly coloured paper-ribbon bow; or arrange some arching stems of translucent, dramatically back-lit foliage.

Flower arrangements for a bedroom or guest room are unashamed tokens of indulgence, and should be both

ABOVE The vertical outline of irises combined with hosta (plantain lily) leaves makes an elegantly proportioned window-sill decoration.

RIGHT Spring flowers are complemented perfectly by a rustic basket in this simple arrangement.

romantic and restful. Try filling a pretty jug with a handful of fully opened roses or a nosegay of roses, lilies and larkspur in muted colours. Arrange a posy for a dressing table with spray carnations and daisy chrysanthemums in apricot and

FAR LEFT Bright tulips, daffodils, irises and hyacinths create a wonderfully colourful corner in a traditional-style kitchen.

LEFT Arranged in glorious profusion, dried flowers are a sophisticated and long-lasting choice for a dining-room centrepiece.

peach tints, or compose a miniature group of moody blues with forget-me-nots and cornflowers tumbling over the side of a blue-glass pitcher.

In a bathroom, take account of the likely temperature and humidity changes, and select the sturdiest and most long-lasting of blooms. These include chrysanthemums of all kinds, marigolds, carnations, spray carnations, lilies and tulips.

For a dried-flower bathroom arrangement, choose, again, from the most good-tempered examples, which include all the everlastings – strawflowers, rhodanthe, and acroclinium – statice, honesty, Chinese lanterns (winter cherry), and other seedheads. Or protect more delicate flowers under glass: an arrangement composed in dry foam on a board and covered with a glass dome – a modern cheese dish or an upturned container for preserves – satisfies both aesthetic and practical considerations.

The kitchen is another room that is subject to rapid temperature changes, so many of the same ground rules apply as for the bathroom. A jug of marigolds on the kitchen table signals a cheery early-morning greeting; a pot of herbs on the window sill has both decorative and culinary properties; and a hanging basket of foliage plants, or grains and grasses, lifts floral décor to a high level.

BELOW Well-chosen colours provide a seasonal feel, as in this side-table arrangement of flowers, foliage, fruit and nuts.

FLOWER ARRANGING

CREATING A CENTREPIECE

A design that is destined to be seen from all angles, as it would be in the centre of a dining table or occasional table, for example, must be an all-round attraction. It should also look as good when seen from above – dome shapes, low pyramids and both regular and irregular all-round shapes, as here, are all effective. Turn the arrangement round one-quarter of a circle as you compose it, and give it a final check to make sure that it looks well-balanced from all viewpoints.

In order to create a lush and luxurious look for this semi-formal centrepiece, a colour scheme in the rich, warm colours of velvet has been used; choose the flowers for your arrangement from a selection such as anemones, roses, *Euphorbia fulgens* and flowering shrub, and foliage such as eucalyptus. Here, a wide-necked, bulbous pot was painted to give a feeling of nineteenth-century opulence, but a brass, copper or pewter pot, or any container in black, dark red, deep blue, purple or forest green would be equally suitable. A surface of polished wood makes the perfect complement to this jewel-bright arrangement.

1 Gather together the flowers and foliage, pot and all the materials that you will need: a piece of plastic-covered florist's wire-mesh netting, narrow florist's adhesive tape, scissors and florist's scissors.

2 Crumple the wire-mesh netting into a neat ball and press it into the top of the container. Secure it in place by threading 2 strips of florist's adhesive tape through the wire, criss-crossing them in the centre and sticking them to the top of the pot (see the box on the opposite page), where the ends will be concealed by the overhanging plant materials. Arrange the foliage to make a full shape all around the pot. Turn the container to check that the leaves are distributed evenly on all sides.

3 Work on one-quarter of the arrangement at a time. Place short stems of euphorbia to arch over the side of the container at different levels. Next, position the anemones all around the centre, alternating their colours to heighten the interest, and the spray carnations fairly close to the container rim. Position the fully opened roses at the heart of the design.

4 Compose the opposite side in a similar way, and fill in the gaps with short sprays of variegated foliage to separate the rich, deep colours of the flowers.

5 Turn the container around and repeat the design on the reverse, matching the first side in essence if not in detail. When you feel that the arrangement is complete, give it a final inspection and make any minor adjustments as necessary.

FIXING FLORIST'S WIRE-MESH NETTING

Preparing a container in this way helps to anchor stems of fresh or dried flowers in a casual and informal design.

1 Gather your materials: a container with a large aperture, plastic-covered florist's wire-mesh netting, wire-cutters, narrow florist's adhesive tape and scissors.

2 Crumple the wire netting into a ball and place it in the neck of the container. If you wish to position some of the stems to slant at a low angle, ease the wire so that it forms a mound extending slightly above the level of the container rim. Remember that you will have to position the lowest of the plant materials so that they conceal this holding material from view.

3 Cut 2 lengths of tape slightly longer than the diameter of the container's opening. Thread the first strip under the wire in 2 places, take it across the container, and stick it to the rim on each side. Cross the second strip at right-angles to the first and fix it in the same way. Threading the tape under the wire will ensure that the ball of wire does not slip down into the container.

FLOWERS FOR A SPECIAL OCCASION

A basket of roses and Peruvian lilies makes a beautiful gift – perhaps for a special birthday, anniversary or Mother's Day. It would also add a lovely touch of colour and interest to a window sill, a fireplace or an otherwise dull corner that you feel needs cheering up. The basket, painted to tone with the flowers, would be ideal to use afterwards as a container for yarns, sewing materials or bath preparations.

1 Gather together your materials: a shallow basket with a handle, a waterproof liner such as a plastic box, a block of absorbent stem-holding foam (soaked beforehand), narrow florist's adhesive tape, scissors, long-lasting foliage such as eucalyptus and flowering shrub, flowers such as roses and Peruvian lilies, florist's scissors, secateurs (pruning shears), paper ribbon and a stub wire (floral pin). Prepare the basket to co-ordinate with the flowers that you are using, if you wish; the one shown here was painted in stripes of pink gloss paint, to add a touch of sparkle to the arrangement.

2 Put the liner in the basket and place the block of foam in it. Cut 2 strips of adhesive tape and criss-cross them over the foam and down on to the sides of the basket, to hold the foam firmly in place. Arrange the tallest stems of foliage to make a fan shape at the back of the basket. Cut progressively shorter stems for the centre and front, positioning them so that they droop and trail over the rim.

3 Arrange the roses to make a gently rounded shape in the basket, alternating the colours (pink and pale yellow were used here) so that each complements the other to create an attractive effect.

4 Add the Peruvian lilies, cutting some individual flowers on short stems and positioning them close against the foam. Fill in the gaps with short sprays of flowering shrub.

5 Unfurl the twisted paper ribbon by pulling it out gently from one end. You need about 1 m/1 yd to make a full, generous bow.

6 Cut the length of ribbon required and tie it into a bow. Gently ease the loop until it looks neat, and trim the ribbon ends by cutting them at a slant. Thread the stub wire through the back of the loop, and twist and insert the 2 ends into the foam at the front of the basket. Spray the flowers with a fine mist of cool water, and keep the foam moist by adding a little water to it at least once a day.

MATERIALS AND EQUIPMENT FOR DRIED FLOWERS

You will find it easier to create successful displays with dried materials if you use the appropriate equipment. You should be able to obtain the following basic items from good florist's shops or suppliers:

Adhesive clay: this may be used to set trunks in pots for topiary displays or to hold down baskets so that they do not overbalance under the weight of a large display.

Candleholders: these plastic fittings are available in a range of sizes. They have a star-shaped base, which is easily pushed into dry foam to hold a candle.

Canes: if you are creating a very large display, you need to extend the length of a stem by taping it to a cane. Canes can also be used to create a square or triangular frame for a garland, or to fix terracotta pots in a display.

Chicken wire: this is a useful base for some displays (moss balls, for instance) and can also be used to hold flowers in large containers.

Copper or steel rings: these, in fact, comprise two thin wire rings, which are used as the base for garlands. They are particularly useful if you plan to build a garland with heavy items.

Florist's adhesive tape: this is excellent for binding blocks of dry florist's foam together. It can also be used to hold foam firmly in a container.

Florist's clear sealer: a type of fixative, like a clear lacquer or very light varnish, which is specifically for use on dried materials. When sprayed on to a display, it holds loose material in place and will also help to keep it clean.

Florist's foam: this is usually grey or brown and available in rectangular blocks, spheres and cones. It is best to avoid foam that is intended for fresh flowers, because it tends to crumble if it is used with dried materials.

Florist's wire: these are available in different lengths and gauges; it is best to use wires that are as thick as you can comfortably work with and to buy long wire which you can cut to length as

BELOW Whenever possible, use the specified tools and materials – it always makes a display much easier to create.

required. The heavier the material, the thicker the wire you will need to hold it in place.

Glue gun: this is extremely useful as it dramatically reduces the time needed to make a display (it is much faster to use glue than to wire materials). As with many things, better quality guns are more expensive. A gun with a trigger feed for the glue is easiest to use. Take care not to burn yourself.

Gutta percha tape: use for wrapping around false wire stems.

Mossing (floral) pins: these are ready-made pins that are used to hold materials in place.

Pliers: use these to secure and twist florist's wire, chicken wire and so on.

Raffia: traditionally used by gardeners, this makes an attractive binding material, particularly if you are wanting to achieve a rustic look.

Reel (spool) wire: this comes in a range of gauges and is essential for making swags and garlands. Experiment with different thicknesses until you find one with which you like working.

Scissors: sharp dressmaker's scissors are best for cutting fabric and ribbons. Resist using scissors to cut stems or the blades will quickly become blunt.

Secateurs (pruners): a strong pair of these will cope with most material. Always use a pair that feels comfortable to work with.

Sharp knife: invaluable for cutting dried florist's foam to size as well as for cutting woody stems of natural materials. Keep knives in good condition and cut away from yourself to avoid injury.

String: if you prefer, you can often substitute reel (spool) wire with string. The type used for gardening tends to be most suitable and comes in a range of brown and green colours that blend well with dried materials.

Twine: Strong sring or twine is essential when tying spiralled bunches, making garlands or attaching foliage to gates and posts.

Wire cutters: use to cut medium- and heavy-gauge wire.

Wire mesh: use to strengthen plastic foam and stop it crumbling when large numbers of stems are pushed into it.

ABOVE The advantage with ready-made cane rings is that they are fairly inexpensive, readily available and simple to use.

LEFT Any type of container can be used to hold a display. However, if you plan to use something made of glass, place a piece of dry foam in the centre of the container, and then pack potpourri, quantities of moss or even coloured glass stones, around the foam so that none of the working will be visible.

FLOWER ARRANGING

DRYING YOUR OWN FLOWERS

The key to drying flowers is to remember that you need to remove the moisture from the flower or other plant material as quickly as possible. The simplest form of flower preservation is air-drying as it requires no special materials or expertise. It is excellent for beginners. Moisture is removed from the petals by the circulation of air, using no preservative. Flowers will dry, if there is no residual moisture from rain or dew. Choose perfect specimens only. Remove any large leaves as they become shrivelled and unattractive when dried; smaller leaves can be removed by rubbing them off after drying if you wish.

Gather the stems into small bunches – not too large or they will rot. Fasten each bunch with elastic bands, which will contract as the stems dry and shrink. Hang the bunches heads down in a dry, dark, airy place. Some plants are best dried upright, so their pendulous nature is preserved. Simply prepare them as normal and place in a completely dry container.

Other ways of drying flowers are preserving foliage in glycerine and using desiccants, both of which are covered alongside.

FLOWERS THAT DRY EASILY

Artichoke and cardoon (*Cynara*)
Bells of Ireland (*Mollucella*)
Cape honey flower (*Protea*)
Chinese lanterns or winter cherry
  (*Physalis*)
Cornflower (*Centaurea cyanus*)
Eucalyptus
Flowers from the onion family (*Allium*)
Globe thistle (*Echinops*)
Helichrysum
Hydrangea
Kangaroo paw (*Anigozanthos*)
Love-in-a-mist (*Nigella*)
Statice (*Phsylliostachys*)
Yarrow (*Achillea*)

PRESERVING FOLIAGE IN GLYCERINE

1 Choose a container large enough to take the foliage and add the glycerine.

2 Top up with 2 parts hot water to 1 part glycerine to a depth of no more than 8 cm/3 in. Mix well.

3 For wood-stemmed foliage, cut and split the stem ends, then place in the glycerine mixture immediately. For calyces, seed heads, herbaceous foliage and soft-stemmed leaves, allow the mixture to cool first. Stand the container in a warm, dry, dark place.

4 Check the container every day and top up with fresh glycerine mixture if necessary. You will notice the foliage changing colour as the glycerine is gradually absorbed. Wipe the stems dry after removing from the mixture.

5 If the leaves have absorbed too much glycerine they will look oily and be prone to mildew. If this occurs, immerse the foliage in warm water with a drop of washing-up liquid, rinse, shake off excess water and stand in a warm place to dry.

ABOVE More dried materials are available to buy than ever before, but many plants can be dried successfully at home. Make up arrangements using a combination of home-dried plants and other, more exotic bought ones, such as the large *Banksia cookinea* used in this lovely dried arrangement.

DRYING WITH DESICCANT

1 Spoon a layer of silica gel or borax into a container to a depth of 1 cm/½ in. For silica gel, use a clean airtight container. Preserve one layer of flowers per container to avoid damaging them.

2 Continue sprinkling the material so the crystals gradually cover the flower. Continue until there is a 1 cm/½ in layer on top of the flowers.

3 If using silica gel, cover the container with a lid or with kitchen foil sealed with tape to make it airtight. Label with the plant name and date. If using borax, do not seal the container, but leave in a warm place with a constant temperature, such as an airing cupboard. As a rough guide, miniature flowers may take 3-4 days to dry, roses 7-10 days and fleshy flowers, such as orchids, 2-3 weeks. To test the flowers, gently scrape back the desiccant and remove a single flower. If it looks dry, flick it gently with your finger. If it makes a crisp, papery sound it is dry. Pour off the desiccant, catching each flower as you do.

ABOVE A rewarding aspect of dried-flower arranging is drying and preserving the plant material yourself, such as bunches of lavender.

RIGHT Do not allow dried flowers to become damp and be particularly aware of condensation in bathrooms and on window ledges.

ARRANGING DRIED FLOWERS

Most of the equipment and techniques used for fresh-flower arrangements can be applied to dried-flower designs as well. You can fit a jug or vase with a block of stem-holding foam and hold it in place with florist's adhesive tape, or use a purpose-made saucer if you wish, so that the stems may be angled in any direction. Alternatively, you can bind stems with florist's silver wire, as shown in this arrangement.

A hanging bunch of dried flowers, the interior-design version of a posy, makes a charming wall decoration for any room in the home, especially when complemented by a pretty floral paper ribbon. This design was created for a girl's bedroom, where it is displayed with a collection of Greek pottery.

1 Collect up dried flowers such as larkspur, lady's mantle, marjoram, sea lavender, strawflowers, rosebuds and hydrangea, and some dried grasses, in colours to blend with the proposed site for the decoration. Those to be placed at the back of the bunch will need long stems. Collect the other materials that you will need: a roll of florist's silver wire, florist's scissors, paper ribbon and scissors.

2 Compose the flower bunch on a table. Place the longest stems (the grasses) so that they will fan out at the back. Cover them with blue larkspur, the tips widely spaced and the stems close together.

3 Arrange stems of pink larkspur over the blue ones. Position marjoram stems in the centre and shorter sprays of lady's mantle from side to side. Place pink roses in the centre, and then strawflowers at varying heights. Place short stems of sea lavender so that they will fan out at the sides.

4 Bind the stems with silver wire. Before pulling the wire tight, re-arrange the stems until the shape is pleasing. Tuck in a few short stems of hydrangea.

DRYING IN WATER

Although it seems a contradiction in terms, some delicate plant materials such as hydrangea, as well as cornflowers and statice (used in the project overleaf) may be air-dried with their stems standing in a little water. The principle is that the water gradually evaporates as it is absorbed by the stems and, over a week or 10 days, the plant material dries naturally. Other flowers in this category include gypsophila and mimosa.

5 Unfurl the length of paper ribbon from each end but leave the centre section tightly furled. Wrap the centre section tightly around the stems and tie in a knot. Tie the ends into a bow, adjusting the ribbon to make a full, rounded shape, and then cut the ends at a slant.

WIRING DRIED FLOWERS

1 To bind flowers that have a reasonable length of stem, such as the air-dried rose and the delphinium shown above, place a stub wire (floral pin) close against the stem and then bind the 2 together securely using a length of silver wire.

2 To wire a dried flower that has a very short stem, such as the ranunculus shown above, place a stub wire close against the short stem length and then bind it and the stem together securely with silver wire. Bind the false wire stem with a length of gutta-percha (floral) tape (available from most good florists).

3 To wire a dried flower that has no stem – strawflowers are a frequent example – push a stub wire through the flower from the base. Bend a short hook in the top of the wire and pull it down so that the hook is concealed within the flower centre. Bind the false wire stem securely with a length of gutta-percha tape.

DRIED FLOWERS FOR A BATHROOM

A dried-flower arrangement may seem paradoxical in a hot and steamy bathroom, breaking all the rules about displaying dried flowers in a dry, airy environment. If the flowers are under permanent protection, however, as with this arrangement, they will stay beautiful indefinitely. The design, a modern version of a Victorian flower dome, is created on the pine base of a cheese dish and covered with the glass lid. Select dried flowers in sharply contrasting colours so that they do not blend into an unidentifiable mass.

1 Collect together the materials you will need: a glass-covered dish, florist's adhesive clay, scissors, a plastic prong, a cylinder of dry stem-holding foam, a knife, a selection of dried flowers such as helichrysum, statice, lady's mantle, cornflowers and rosebuds, and florist's scissors.

2 Press a small strip of adhesive clay to the base of the plastic prong and press it on to the centre of the base. Cut the foam to the size and shape required and press it on to the prong. Arrange a ring of white statice around the base, positioning the stems horizontally in the foam. Make a dome shape with yellow rosebuds. Put on the glass cover to check that the stems are not too tall to fit inside, then remove the cover again. If the stems are too long, carefully extract them from the foam and trim the ends as necessary, using the florist's scissors. Replace the stems as before.

KITCHEN COVER-UP

You need not confine this type of flower decoration to a bathroom. The frequently changing and sometimes steamy environment of a kitchen would be another area in which a covered arrangement would be ideal – perhaps on a dresser or in the centre of the table. The glass cover will not only shield the flowers from changes in temperature, but will also provide excellent protection from dust and dirt. Many kinds of dried flowers are suitable for displaying in this way, although small flowerheads look the most effective.

3 Arrange short stems of blue and yellow statice between the rosebuds and, to soften the effect, add some short sprays of helichrysum and lady's mantle.

4 Position cornflowers evenly throughout the design. Turn the base around slowly and check that it is equally well-covered and attractive from every angle.

5 Once the cover is in place, the dried flowers will be well-protected from any steam. To make a complete seal, press a narrow strip of modelling clay such as Plasticine all around the rim of the base, and scatter a few highly absorbent silica-gel crystals among the dried flowers. These crystals, which are available from some chemists (drugstores), florist's shops and camera retailers, are very effective in drawing away any moisture from the surrounding air. Press the cover on to the clay to complete the seal.

HOME COOKING

Good home cooking has to be one of the most important ingredients of family life. Not only does cooking at home ensure that the meals put on the table are to everyone's taste, but it is just about the only way of ensuring that the family is eating healthy, nourishing food, using ingredients that you are sure of. Whether your are a complete novice, an experienced cook or an occasional dabbler, there are times when everyone longs for basic techniques and methods to be laid out clearly and simply. This chapter does just that. In addition there are lots of recipes and ideas, too, so you can try out the skills you are learning.

KITCHEN BASICS

A well organized and stocked kitchen simplifies meal preparation, making it easier and quicker to manage and therefore more pleasurable. They key to this is planning. First of all the kitchen itself has to be organized to make working in it efficient and safe, with consideration being given to lighting working stations and adequate storage. Identifying what equipment you need and then ensuring it is always accessible will make the daily round of food preparation less of a cumbersome chore.

You also need to consider how you wish to feed your family. You need to know what ingredients are healthy and tasty and which can be used to produce wholesome, balanced meals. It is a good idea to plan menus for the following few days or the week ahead, then make a shopping list that includes fresh foods as well as frequently used storecupboard (pantry) foods that are running low. Allow yourself to be a little flexible, though. When shopping, take advantage of fresh seasonal foods and special offers. Once your shopping is at home, it needs to be quickly and correctly stored to keep it in peak condition until it is used.

Ensuring that all the elements of a meal are ready on time can be tricky. To make meal preparation a smooth operation, it can sometimes be a good idea to plan each meal, working out start times for food preparation and cooking. This is particularly useful if less confident in the kitchen, or if you are cooking for a large number. Often a great part of the preparation can be undertaken in advance. Sauces, stocks and soups, for example, can be made well in advance and kept in the refrigerator or freezer, ready for use at any time.

As well as preparing healthy, balanced meals, trying out new ingredients and recipes can be, and should be, highly enjoyable. This section covers all the principal techniques called for when cooking, which will allow you to experiment with many new dishes.

OPPOSITE It is essential to choose the right balance of foods. While most of us are aware of the benefits of following a balanced diet, in reality diets and eating habits are frequently far from ideal. With a little awareness and effort, however, it is possible to ensure healthy, delicious meals on a regular basis.

A WELL-ORDERED KITCHEN

Successful meal preparation is as much dependent on a good working environment and organization as on culinary skills. It is worth spending some time ensuring your kitchen is arranged and equipped for convenient and safe movement and access between all the key areas. Once it is arranged to your satisfaction, you will be able to undertake the daily tasks of planning and cooking in the minimum of time.

Decide how the various contents of your kitchen can be grouped and where they should be stored in relation to how you use them. Roasting and cake tins (pans), saucepans, cooking utensils, china and glassware, cutlery, fresh and packaged food all need to be sited nearest to where they will be used.

Make sure that equipment is always stored in its allotted place so that it is easily found whenever required. In cupboards (cabinets), plan shelving so that everything is accessible; don't put items that are in daily use in difficult to reach corners. You may prefer to keep items that are used everyday readily accessible, either on racks, open shelves or standing in large pots. But remember they will be on display and so may create cluttered look or get in the way. Where open shelving is used to display items such as jars and pots decoratively, it will attract dust and grease so increasing your cleaning load.

Work surfaces need to be kept as clear of clutter as possible so that you can work on them at any time without having to make space first. Wash utensils immediately after use and put them away. Clear and wipe work surfaces down after every activity to keep them spotless and ready for use.

Site large appliances such as the cooker (stove) and refrigerator in relation to the sink area and work surfaces to minimize time-consuming travel in the kitchen. Keep appliances clean and in good working order, wiping them down or washing them after each use and before storing them away.

Always read and follow the manufacturer's instructions for any kitchen appliance; misusing an appliance may lead to damage and may nullify any guarantees. Keep instruction booklets together with the phone numbers or addresses of service agents.

Lighting

Good lighting is essential in any working environment and the kitchen, where sharp knives and scalding hot pans are handled, is no different. Shadow-free general lighting needs to be supplemented by focused lighting for areas of more intense activity , that is the sink, the cooker (stove), the refrigerator and all preparation surfaces.

Avoid a central fluorescent strip as it can be harsh and gives poor colour rendering (when preparing food it is important to be able to see that your ingredients are fresh). However, consider fixing concealed fluorescent strips on top of wall-mounted units (cabinets), against the wall at the back; these will cast light upwards which, if reflected by a white ceiling, can create a pleasing glow. Strip lights can also be fixed to the underside of a unit, behind a baffle, deflecting the light, to cast an even light on the work surface below.

Spotlights or downlighters can be used to create pools of general light. Downlighters are a useful solution to kitchen lighting because, being recessed they attract less dirt and grease and so require less cleaning. they can be placed to shed light in specific areas. Wall-mounted adjustable spotlights can be angled to shine light wherever you want.

LEFT **A well lit kitchen is essential. Natural lighting is always best, but wall mounted units can provide focused lighting in work areas.**

LEFT Clean,
uncluttered work
surfaces not only are
more hygienic, they
are also pleasing
to the eye.

Safety

Kitchen safety is paramount. Not only for the cook, but for anyone else visiting the kitchen, especially children and even pets, both of which should probably be discouraged from being there. Being closer to the ground, both could trip you up when you are carrying a pan of hot water or a knife.

The oven door gets hot when the oven is on and so can burn the unwary. Pan handles protruding over the edge of the hob (burner) can tempt small hands with disastrous results. Adults, too, can knock into them, so always get into the habit of turning handles inwards.

Install a fire blanket, available in neat packs and designed for kitchen use, next to the hob (burner). In case of a fat fire, this can be released and thrown over the flames to put them out. A kitchen fire extinguisher is also a good idea.

Kitchen knives need to be kept sharp if they are to be of any use in the kitchen, so store them carefully. This will help to preserve their edges and to avoid the risk of getting cut. Either keep them in a knife block or use a magnetic holder; never leave them loose in a drawer.

Hygiene

A regular programme of cleaning and disinfecting will ensure that all the work surfaces and sink are kept clear of germs. Wash up as soon as you have used items; not only do piles of dirty dishes look unsightly but the warm atmosphere of a kitchen encourages germs to breed.

The refrigerator is probably one of the most overlooked areas when it comes to kitchen hygiene. Check all the contents regularly so that you can discard food that is past its best and before it starts to rot or go mouldy. Wipe down all the surfaces, with a clean cloth. If you disinfect, wipe the surfaces with clean water to remove the smell. For more information on how to store fresh foods in the refrigerator, see Getting the Most From Fresh Ingredients.

Planning a meal

Successful meal preparation is as much dependent on organization as on culinary skills. Try and include a good range of flavours, colours and textures, as well as a balance in protein, fat, fibre and other healthy considerations. Consider what you can prepare ahead, and what remains to be done at the last minute so that all is ready together.

The first step is to read all the recipes before making a final choice. The main dish, with simple accompaniments such as a salad and bread, is a good starting point. Serve that with a cold starter (if there is to be one) and a cold dessert that can be made ahead of time. This way you can concentrate your efforts.

If you do choose two or more hot dishes, consider their cooking times and oven temperatures. If you have only one oven, and the temperatures required for the two dishes are different, this will present difficulties.

Next, make a shopping list and check that you have all the equipment you require. Read each recipe through again so you know what lies ahead, and try to estimate how long each preparation stage will take. Review techniques in the preparation that are unfamiliar. Set the time you want to serve the meal, and work back from there so you know when to start the preparation.

If you are serving a starter, you'll need to plan what can be cooked unattended while you are at the table. If your chosen dessert is frozen, it may need some time out of the freezer before serving, so decide when to do that.

Remember to allow time for the final draining of vegetables, or carving of meat, or seasoning of a sauce. It is usually the case that all of these need to be done at the same time – but you only have one pair of hands. So decide what can wait and what will keep hot.

If any recipe requires the oven to be preheated or tins to be prepared, do this first. Pots of boiling salted water for cooking vegetables or pasta can be brought to the boil while you are doing the chopping and slicing. Set out all the ingredients required and prepare them as specified in the recipe. If more than one dish calls for the same ingredients, say chopped onion, you can prepare the total amount at the same time.

THE WELL-EQUIPPED KITCHEN

To be able to cook efficiently, and with pleasure, you need good equipment in your kitchen. That is not to say that you should invest in an extensive and expensive collection of pots, pans, tools and gadgets, but a basic range is essential.

Buy the best equipment you can afford, adding more as your budget allows. Well made equipment lasts and is a sound investment; inexpensive pans and tins are likely to dent, break or develop 'hot spots' where food will stick and burn so will need replacing. Flimsy tools will make food preparation more time consuming and frustrating.

The following lists the basic essentials for a well-run kitchen. Depending on your preferences, you will no doubt wish to add other utensils to this list. You may also wish to add an electric mixer, a blender and/or a food processor to speed up various processes, but hand tools all do a fine job.

Essential utensils

Baking sheet: For cookies, biscuits and meringues. Shiny, sideless ones lightly brown.

Cake, bun and loaf tins (pans): To ensure even heat distribution, shiny metal (aluminium, tin or stainless steel) is the best material. Try to equip yourself with: 2 round cake tins (pans); 20 cm/8 in or 23 cm/9 in round and square cake tins; a large baking tin (33 x 23 cm/13 x 9 in); a deep bun tin; a 23 cm/9 in springform cake tin; a Swiss(jelly) roll tin; 2 baking sheets. Additional cake tins, round and square tins, springform tins and tartlet tins in alternative sizes are also useful.

Casseroles: A least 1 heavy bottomed casserole (round and oval are available) with a lid is essential for roasting, stewing baking and browning. Casseroles can be made of enameled cast iron, earthenware or ovenproof glass-ceramic. Buy a flameproof one if you want to start cooking on the hob then transfer to the oven.

Chopping boards: Use different boards for different uses, and keep separate boards for vegetables and raw and cooked meat and fish. In addition to wood, boards are often made in modern, dishwasher-proof materials, and often include anti-bacterial agents. A good quality board will last for years.

Colander: For draining food.

Double boiler: In two parts, which can also be used independently, a double boiler will be useful for heating any tender ingredients that should not be exposed to direct heat.

Flour sifter: For sifting and adding air to flour.

Food mill: Useful for puréeing food without destroying the texture. Will also mash and grind. Buy one that clamps over a saucepan or mixing bowl.

Frying pans: You need at least one small and one large frying pan, preferably with lids. Useful extras would be an omelette pan, a pancake pan and/or a sauté pan. Frying pans should

BELOW Choose frying pans and saucepans with good, strong bases, in a variety of sizes.

CLOCKWISE FROM TOP
LEFT A variety of
utensils for successful
baking: electric whisk,
mixing bowls, non-
stick baking paper,
brown paper, scissors,
ring mould, wire rack,
measuring jug, deep
round cake tin, muffin
tin, Swiss roll tin,
measuring spoons,
nylon sieve, nutmeg
grater, wire sieve,
juicer, box grater,
knives, balloon whisk,
wooden and large
metal spoon, baking
sheet, square and
rectangular cake tins,
cake tester, vegetable
knife, pastry brush,
honey twirl, pastry
cutters.

have a good, thick base, to allow the heat to spread evenly and maintain a constant temperature, but whether you choose non-stick ones or not is a matter of personal preference. They make life easier for some recipes, such as egg-based dishes, as they are less likely to stick. However, it is harder to get good browning on foods as non-stick pans cannot withstand a high heat. If your pans come with instructions to season before use, do so, as seasoning helps to prolong the life of the pan.

Grater: For grating and slicing various vegetables and cheese. One that stands upright with several sizes of teeth and a slicer is most useful.

Kitchen scales: Essential for weighing larger amounts of ingredients. Balance scales give the most accurate readings.

Kitchen scissors and shears: You will be surprised how often a pair of sturdy kitchen scissors are needed, whilst poultry shears are a useful extra for all types of kitchen cutting. Make sure the handles are sturdy and comfortable.

Knives: A good set of knives is most important in food preparation. Flimsy, dull or nicked knives can turn even the chopping of onions into an arduous task. Carbon steel knives can be given the sharpest edge, but they rust and discolour easily so must be washed and dried immediately after use. High-carbon stainless steel knives will take a sharp edge and resist discoloration, but are more expensive. Ordinary stainless steel knives are very difficult to sharpen efficiently.

Always use the right-sized knife for the job: a 18–20 cm/7–8 in-bladed knife is essential for chopping vegetables, meats and herbs; a small-bladed paring knife, about 7.5 cm/3 in, will do for trimming and peeling fruits and vegetables; and a flexible vegetable knife with serrated edge and pointed tip is good for slicing. A chef's knife with 25 cm/10 in blade is also useful. You may also want: a filleting knife with a thin, flexible 18 cm/7 in blade and sharp point; a boning knife with

a thin 15 cm/6 in blade; a 15 cm/ 6 in-bladed utility knife; a grapefruit knife with curved serrated blade; and a carving knife and fork. Store knives in a knife block or a magnetized bar and keep them sharp; more accidents occur with blunt knives than sharp ones.

Measuring jug (pitcher), spoons and cups: It is important to measure ingredients carefully when following a recipe, and good measuring equipment makes this easier. Buy a standard set of spoons ($1/4$ tsp, $1/2$ tsp, 1 tsp and 1 tbsp) for measuring small amounts of liquid and dry ingredients. Measuring cups are also available for recipes using cup sizes; glass is useful for liquids and metal for dry ingredients.

Meat grinder: A sturdy metal grinder that clamps to the table can be used for grinding meat, nuts and vegetables.

Metal spoons: Very useful, keep several in various sizes for general mixing, stirring and blending.

Mixing bowls: A graduated set of stainless steel, glass or glazed earthenware bowls will be adequate for most mixing jobs; an unlined copper bowl helps egg whites to expand.

Palette knives (spatula) and slices: A palette knife with a flexible 25 cm/10 in blade and a fish slice are probably the most useful to buy.

Pastry board: Formica and marble are excellent materials for rolling and kneading pastry, but a hardwood board will also do.

Pastry brush: A medium-sized brush with sturdy bristles for applying liquids (fat, milk, water) to surfaces.

Pestle and mortar: When using fresh spices, crush small amounts with a pestle and mortar.

Pie and flan tins (pans): These should be made of dull metal, glass or ceramic. Include a 23 cm/9 in pie tin, an oval or round pie dish and a 23 cm/ 9 in flan tin with removable bottom, or a flan ring in your collection. Additional pie and flan tins in alternative sizes will also be useful. Ring moulds are ideal for angel cakes.

Roasting tins (pans): These can be made of any material but they must be sturdy and supplied with racks. Use a size in which the ingredients fit comfortably: if a tin is too full, the ingredients will take longer to cook; if it is too empty, they may burn.

Rolling pin: A heavy one is best, buy one about 35–40 cm/14–16 in long.

Rubber spatula: For folding foods, but also useful for other jobs.

Saucepans: Buy heavy-bottomed pans with sturdy insulated handles and knobs and tight-fitting lids. Bear in mind how much the pan will weigh when full (a large pot for pasta or stock must not be too heavy for you to lift when full). Copper conducts heat best, but is hard to care for. Aluminium is good as is cast iron, although the latter needs scrupulous care to prevent rust. A vitreous enamel coating is a good compromise. Stainless steel is lightweight and durable but it conducts heat unevenly. One containing another metal can improve heat conduction.

You need a set of pans of varying sizes with at least 3 saucepans. It is especially important to have the right-sized pan when cooking soups, stews and pot-roasts; ingredients packed in a pan that is too small may overflow or increase the cooking time whilst liquid in a pan that is too big will evaporate, causing the dish to dry out. A large stockpot or casserole dish with lid is also handy.

Sieves: 1 metal and 1 nylon for general sifting and straining.

Thermometers: An oven thermometer is useful for gauging the degree and evenness of heat in your oven. Use a meat thermometer for measuring the internal heat of meat and poultry by inserting the spiked end into the thickest part of the meat without touching bone or resting in fat.

Wire racks: For cooling cakes, buns and bread.

BELOW For those who love cooking, good equipment or specialized items, such as a pasta machine, make wonderful gifts.

Wire whisk: One about 20–25 cm/ 8–10 in for beating egg whites and whipping cream, stirring gravies and smoothing sauces, and perhaps a large balloon-shaped one specifically for egg whites (it adds more air and increases the volume).

Wok: Essential if you enjoy stir-fried food and Asian dishes. Make sure you buy the right wok for your type of cooker (stove); if you cook on electric rings, you'll need one with a flat base so that it comes into contact with the heat source. Consider also steamers for cooking vegetables.

Wooden spoons and spatulas: For creaming, beating and stirring.

Miscellaneous utensils

Everybody has their own preferences when it comes to extra tools and gadgets, but the following are probably on everyone's list of kitchen-drawer essentials: can openers (wall-mounted and a bottle/beer can type, slotted spoon, potato masher or ricer, colander, sieve, bulb baster, metal tongs, juicer, corkscrew, vegetable peeler and kitchen timer. In addition you may want to include a meat mallet, citrus zester, cannelle knife, apple corer, melon baller, pastry blender, pastry scraper, trussing needle, cherry stoner (pitter), pasta machine, salad spinner.

ABOVE This stainless steel spice container is ideal for storing dried spices. The individual pots are sealed when the inner lid is closed: a second lid ensures that no light or moisture gets in.

Measuring techniques

Cooks with years of experience may not need to measure ingredients, but if you are a beginner or are trying a new recipe for the first time, it is best to follow instructions carefully.

Both metric and imperial measurements are given in this book. When preparing a recipe, use all metric or all imperial measures. Eggs are size 3 (medium) unless specified otherwise and recipes have been tested using a conventional not fan-assisted oven.

● *For liquids measured in ml or litres (pints or cups):* Use a glass or plastic measuring jug. Put it on a flat surface and pour in the liquid. Check that the liquid is level with the marking on the jug, as specified in the recipe.

● *For liquids measured in spoons:* Pour the liquid into the measuring spoon, to the brim, and then pour it into the mixing bowl. Do not hold the spoon over the bowl when measuring because liquid may overflow.

● *For measuring butter:* Cut with a sharp knife and weigh, or cut off the specified amount following the markings on the wrapping paper.

● *For measuring dry ingredients by weight:* Surprisingly useful in the kitchen, scoop or pour on to the scales, watching the dial or reading carefully. Balance scales give more accurate readings than spring scales.

● *For measuring dry ingredients in a spoon:* Fill the spoon, scooping up the ingredients. Level the surface even with the rim of the spoon, using the straight edge of a knife.

● *For measuring syrups:* Set the mixing bowl on the scales and turn the gauge to zero, or make a note of the weight. Pour in the required weight of syrup.

USEFUL CONVERSIONS

Metric	Imperial
Liquids	
2.5ml	$^1/_2$ tsp
5 ml	I tsp
15 ml	3 tsp = I tbsp
150 ml	$^1/_4$ pint/$^2/_3$ cup
300 ml	$^1/_2$ pint/I $^1/_4$ cups
450 ml	$^3/_4$ pint/scant 2 cups
600 ml	I pint/2$^1/_2$ cups
900 ml	I $^1/_2$ pints/3$^3/_4$ cups
1.2 litres	2 pints/5 cups
1.5 litres	2$^1/_2$ pints/6$^1/_4$ cups
Weights	
25 g	I oz
50 g	2 oz
75 g	3 oz
115 g	4 oz/$^1/_4$ lb
225 g	8 oz/$^1/_2$ lb
340 g	12 oz/$^3/_4$ lb
450 g	16 oz/I lb
500 g	I $^1/_8$ lb
I kg	2$^1/_4$ lb
2 kg	4$^1/_2$ lb
Centigrade	**Farenheit**
110°C	225°F/Gas $^1/_4$
120°C	250°F/Gas $^1/_2$
140°C	275°F/Gas I
150°C	300°F/Gas 2
160°C	325°F/Gas 3
180°C	350°F/Gas 4
190°C	375°F/Gas 5
200°C	400°F/Gas 6
220°C	425°F/Gas 7
230°C	450°F/Gas 8
240°C	475°F/Gas 9

A HEALTHY DIET

A healthy diet provides the body with all the nutrients it needs to be able to grow and repair itself, as well as to protect against the development of serious diseases such as heart disease, bowel disorders, cancers and obesity.

It is recommended that we should eat plenty of fruit, vegetables (at least five portions a day, not including potatoes); plenty of high-fibre cereals, pasta, rice and potatoes; moderate amounts of meat, fish, poultry and dairy products; and only small amounts of food containing fat or sugar. By choosing a good balance of food from these five main food groups every day, you can ensure that you are supplying your body, and everyone else in the family, with all the essential nutrients they need for optimum health.

A low-fat diet
Choose lower fat alternatives wherever possible, but don't cut out fats altogether. Fat is a valuable source of energy and our bodies need small amounts for general health and well-being. It also helps to make foods more palatable.

There are two main types of fat: saturated and unsaturated. The unsaturated group contains polyunsaturated and monounsaturated fats. In any food there is always a combination of saturated and both types of unsaturated fats, but the ratios vary greatly from one food to another. Saturated fats should be avoided because they are thought to increase the level of cholesterol in the blood, which can increase the risk of

developing heart disease. They are mostly found in animal products such as meat, butter and lard, but they also exist in coconut and palm oils and in some margarines and oils labelled as 'hydrogenated vegetable oil'.

Small quantities of polyunsaturated fats are essential for good health and are thought to reduce the level of cholesterol in the blood. They are derived from plants (omega 6), especially sunflowers, or oily fish (omega 3) and are usually liquid at room temperature.

Monounsaturated oils are also thought to reduce blood cholesterol

BELOW Eating plenty of fruit and vegetables is not only good for you, but with the great range available today, a chance to explore different textures and tastes from around the world.

LEFT Bread has been an important part of the diet in many countries for thousands of years and continues today to contribute to a healthy, balanced diet. A good source of carbohydrate as well as being low in fat, choose wholemeal (whole wheat) breads and bakes, such as scones and muffins, for added fibre.

BELOW Some oils, such as olive and rapeseed are thought to help lower blood cholesterol.

level. They are found in foods such as olive and rapeseed oil, some nuts, oily fish and avocados.

Aim to limit your family's daily intake of fats to no more than 30 per cent of total calories. This means that for an average daily intake of 2,000 calories per day, 30 per cent of energy would come from 600 calories. Since each gram of fat provides 9 calories, a total daily intake should be no more than 66.6 grams of fat, of which the total intake of saturated fats (see below) should be no more than 10 per cent of the total calories.

About one quarter of the fat we eat comes from meat and meat products, one-fifth from dairy products and margarine and the rest from cakes, biscuits, pastries and other foods. It is easy to cut down on obvious sources of fat in the diet, such as butter, oils, margarine, cream, whole milk and full fat cheese, but we also need to watch out for 'hidden' fats. Hidden fats can be found in food such as cakes, biscuits and many nuts. Even lean, trimmed red meats may contain as much as 10 per cent fat.

Cooking for vitality

Eat as much raw food as possible. Vitamins B and C are particularly unstable and are easily destroyed by heat, so include plenty of salads in your diet. Use really fresh produce and prepare it just before eating. Keep a well-stocked fruit bowl for between-meal nibbles.

Cook vegetables in the minimum amount of water or steam them. Reserve any cooking water, which will contain leached nutrients, to add to soups, stews and sauces.

Trim all visible fat from meat and remove skin from poultry. If the skin is required to keep the flesh succulent, remove it after cooking.

Choose low-fat cooking methods, such as grilling, stir-frying, steaming, poaching, casseroling, baking and microwaving, wherever possible.

Use the minimum amount of oil for cooking and choose a type that is low in saturated fats, like olive oil or sunflower oil.

Substitute low-fat yogurt, fromage frais or half-fat crème fraîche for cream and use reduced-fat cheeses. Parmesan and other strong-tasting cheeses are useful because you only need to use a little for a lot of flavour.

Even if you are not a vegetarian, aim to have a vegetarian meal once or twice a week. Alternatively, use less meat in dishes and make up the quantity with pulses and vegetables.

The five main food groups
- Fruit and vegetables
- Rice, potatoes, bread, pasta and other cereals
- Meat, poultry, fish and alternative proteins
- Milk and other dairy foods
- Foods which contain fat and foods which contain sugar

GETTING THE MOST FROM FRESH INGREDIENTS

Fresh ingredients are essential to a healthy, balanced diet, and we are now encouraged to eat at least five portions of fresh fruit and vegetables a day. Vitamin C is found almost exlusively in fruit and vegetables and because it cannot be stored by the body, levels need to be topped up continually.

Fruit and vegetables are also extremely rich in fibre, particularly when eaten with the skin on. High-protein foods such as meat, game, poultry and eggs contain many other essential nutrients. Use frozen produce when fresh is not available; it is perfectly acceptable from a nutritional point of view.

Fresh ingredients

Fresh fruit: Fruits are very versatile and can be enjoyed raw or cooked, on their own or as part of a recipe. They are also good sources of vitamins and minerals, particularly vitamin C. A piece of fresh fruit makes a quick and easy, nutritious snack at any time of the day. Try topping wholewheat breakfast cereals with some fruit such as raspberries for a tasty and nutritious start to the day.

Fresh Vegetables: Vegetables are nutritious and are valuable sources of vitamins and minerals, some being especially rich in vitamins A, C and E. Vegetables also contain some dietary fibre and those that are particularly good sources include broccoli, brussels sprouts, cabbage, carrots, fennel, okra, parsnips, spinach, spring greens (collard) and sweetcorn.

Vegetables are also very versatile and many can be eaten either raw or cooked. Add vegetables to dishes such as soups, stews, casseroles, stir-fries and salads, or simply serve them on their own, raw or lightly cooked and tossed in a little lemon juice.

RIGHT **A piece of fresh fruit makes a quick and easy, nutritious snack at any time of the day.**

Potatoes: Potatoes are one of the most commonly eaten vegetables in the world and are valuable in terms of nutrition. They are high in carbohydrate, low in fat and contain some Vitamin C and dietary fibre. Wash old and new potatoes thoroughly and cook them with their skins on – for example baked, boiled and roasted. The flavour will be just as delicious and you will be getting extra fibre.

Potatoes are very versatile and are used in many dishes. Mashed potatoes (with their skins left on, of course) make an ideal topping for pies and bakes. For roast potatoes use a minimum amount of oil, and if you like to make chips, leave the skins on and cut the chips thickly using a knife. With baked and mashed potatoes avoid adding high fat butter, soured cream or cheese and instead use skimmed milk, reduced-fat hard cheese and herbs to add flavour.

Fresh beans and other pulses: There are many varieties of fresh beans and pulses available, either fresh or canned, including peas, broad (fava) beans and runner beans, and more unusual ones such as fresh flageolet beans, black-eyed (peas) beans and butter (wax) beans. Fresh corn on the cob and sweetcorn are also popular.

All are good sources of dietary fibre and contain other nutrients including vitamins and minerals. Beans and pulses are very versatile and can be used in many dishes including hot and cold salads, stir-fries, casseroles, pasta sauces, soups and curries. Some varieties, such as sugar-snap peas and mangetouts (snow peas) can be eaten either raw or lightly cooked.

Eggs: Virtually a complete food and extremely versatile, eggs provide protein, iron, zinc and vitamins A, B-group and E.

Fish: Increasingly research points to the great benefits gained from a diet high in fish. All fish is rich in protein, B vitamins and minerals. White fish is very low in fat. Oily fish, such as sardines, mackerel, herring, tuna, trout and salmon, also provide vitamins A and D and Omega 3 fatty acids, which are believed to be beneficial in helping to prevent coronary heart disease.

Poultry: A good source of quality protein, B vitamins and some iron, poultry is also low in fat, particularly if the skin is removed.

Meat and game: Although the general health advice is to moderate your intake of red meat, thus reducing the amount of saturated fat in your diet, red meat is still the best source of readily absorbed iron, zinc and B vitamins. Meat today is much leaner than it used to be, and it fits the profile for a healthy diet if it is cooked with low-fat cooking methods.

Storing

Because nutrients in fresh foods, especially valuable vitamins, deteriorate as food ages it is important to always buy the freshest and best quality available. Storing the food correctly at home will also ensure that the minimum of nutrients are lost before they are eaten. Whilst some fruit and vegetables can be kept at room temperature, they will not last for long in a hot kitchen and should be stored in a cooler environment. Quickly perishable foods such as meat, poultry, fish and dairy products should be stored in a refrigerator.

A freezer is useful for keeping many fresh foods longer term. You can buy them when they are plentiful and cheap for the freezer, using them when they become out of season or more expensive in the shops. Follow the freezer manufacturer's instructions for storing and blanch fruit and vegetables as required.

Storing fresh fruits: Those fruits that can be kept at room temperature while still unripe include apricots, kiwi fruits. mangoes, nectarines, papayas, peaches, pears, pineapples and plums. Once ripe, refrigerate and eat within 2–3 days.

Fruits that can be stored at cool room temperature include apples (although they will be crisper if refrigerated), bananas, dates, grapefruit and oranges. Apples can be kept at room temperature for a few days, dates for several weeks, and grapefruit and oranges for up to a week.

Unless you intend to eat them on the day of purchase, refrigerate fully ripe and perishable fresh fruits. These include berries, cherries, figs, grapes, lemons, limes, melons, pomegranates and tangerines. They can be kept refrigerated for 2–3 days.

Storing fresh vegetables: Like fruits, there are some vegetables that can stored at room temperature. A dark, cool place (about 10°C/50°F) with good ventilation is ideal, however. Suitable vegetables are garlic, onions, potatoes and sweet potatoes, swede and pumpkin. All can be kept for about 2 months. Store tomatoes at room temperature until they are ripe. After that, refrigerate.

Perishable vegetables should be refrigerated. Some, such as peas or sweetcorn, should be used quickly, while others, like carrots or cabbage, can be kept for a longer period. In most cases, do not wash the vegetable until just before using. Celery, frisée, escarole, spring greens (collard), herbs, lettuce, spinach and watercress should be washed before storage.

Cold storage: All foods kept in the refrigerator or freezer should be well wrapped or stored in sealed containers. This preserves flavour and moisture, and prevents the flavours and odours of other, stronger foods being transferred. It is essential to keep raw meat and poultry well wrapped as their drippings can transfer bacteria to other foods.

Perishable fresh foods, such as meats, poultry, fish and seafood, eggs, cheese and other dairy products, and many fruits and vegetables must be kept refrigerated at a temperature of 1–5°C/35–40°F. For longer storage, many can also be frozen at –18°C/0°F or lower. Cooked leftovers must also be refrigerated or frozen. Use a special thermometer to check temperatures; integral thermostats often give false readings over time. If temperatures are too high, food will spoil rapidly.

KITCHEN BASICS

USING DRY INGREDIENTS

No matter how much fresh food you use in your cooking, you will always rely on a well-stocked store cupboard (pantry) for a ready supply of dry and canned ingredients. In addition to the staples of flour, sugar, jams and pickles, a stock of nutritious ingredients such as pulses and wholegrains will ensure you always have sufficient resources with which to produce wholesome dishes.

Storing canned and dry foods

Full cupboard shelves are a boon for a busy cook, but canned and dry foods can deteriorate if not stored properly or if left too long on the shelf. Kitchen cupboards should be cool (no more than 18°C/65°F) and dry. Staples such as flour, salt, sugar, pasta and grains are best stored in moisture-proof containers. If necessary, remove them from their wrappings and decant them into canisters or jars. Whole-grain products (wholemeal flour and pasta, brown rice, etc.) cannot be kept as long as refined ones.

Breakfast cereals: Wholewheat or whole grain are the best choice for fibre – preferably those that are also low in fat and sugar. Try using wholewheat cereals when making home-made bakes and breads; for crumble toppings and cheesecake bases; for coating foods; in meatloaves or burgers.

Brown rice: There are many varieties of brown rice available including long grain, basmati, jasmine and risotto, as well as canned brown rice and boil-in-the bag brown rice for convenience.

The flavour of brown rice is quite nutty and because the rice undergoes only minor milling, the bran layer is retained, making it higher in fibre, vitamins and minerals than white rice. Rice is also low in fat. Cooking time for brown rice is 35 minutes, during which time it expands by up to three times the volume. Allow at least 50 g/2 oz/⅓ cup uncooked rice per person.

Beans and other pulses: These are good sources of protein, starch carbohydrates, fibre, B vitamins and minerals and are low in fat. When buying dried pulses choose ones that are plump, bright and clear in colour and avoid broken, shrivelled or dusty beans. Pulses should be stored in a cool, dry place in an airtight container and used within one year.

Many dried pulses need soaking in water before cooking and to be boiled for a period, until tender. The older the beans are, the longer they will take to cook, and salt should be added at the end of the cooking time. Some beans, such as red kidney beans, contain a harmful, toxic substance known as haemaglutinin which can lead to acute gastroenteritis if it is not destroyed by adequate cooking. These beans need to be boiled vigorously for at least 10 minutes to destroy the haemaglutinin, then simmered until they are tender.

ABOVE High-fibre foods include, clockwise from left, split peas, green and red lentils, wholegrain rice, pinto beans, red kidney beans and nuts.

If you haven't got time to soak dried pulses, canned varieties are just as good. Add beans and pulses to soups, stews and salads, and experiment with dishes based on beans, lentils and tofu (soya bean curd). Try recipes from around the world for authentic traditional ways with beans and pulses.

Dried fruit: A good selection of dried fruit and ready-to-eat dried fruit is available including apples, apricots, bananas, currants, figs, kiwi fruit, lychees, mangoes, papayas, peaches, pears, pineapple, prunes, raisins and sultanas (golden raisins). They are very versatile and can be used in both sweet and savoury dishes. Dried fruit is low in fat, So it makes a delicious healthy snack. Add dried fruit to your breakfast cereals, muesli or porridge and use it in cake, scone, biscuit, dessert and wholemeal muffin recipes.

RIGHT It is worth trying out some of the many grains and pulses readily available – they are ideal for quick and easy, healthy meals.

Nuts: Nuts have many uses in a wide selection of sweet and savoury dishes. They also make a tasty snack, but as they are high in fat and calories, eat them only in small quantities. Add nuts to salads, cakes and bakes, biscuits, desserts, stuffings, coatings and stir-fries.

Oats and oatmeal: Oats and oatmeal are valuable sources of soluble fibre which is absorbed into the body and is thought to help reduce high levels of blood cholesterol. Oats and oatmeal come in a variety of types including porridge oats, quick-cook oats, jumbo oats, fine and medium oatmeal. Use them in muesli, oatcakes, mixed with flour for breads and rolls, cakes and bakes such as gingerbread and flapjacks, and crumble toppings. Fine oatmeal also makes a good thickener for soups and sauces.

Seeds: Very versatile, seeds, such as sesame, sunflower and pumpkin can be eaten on their own as a snack or added to recipes such as salads, stir-fries, stuffings, cakes and bakes, coatings, muesli, biscuits and crackers. Seeds also contain vitamins and minerals but are high in fat and calories, so should be eaten in small quantities.

Sugars and honey: There is no calorific difference between white (refined) and brown (unrefined) sugar but the flavours do vary.

Honey can be used in sweet and savoury dishes. It is a little sweeter than sugar so often a smaller amount is needed in a recipe.

Wheat bran: Natural wheat bran is the hard outer layer or casing that surrounds the wheat grain and it is therefore high in fibre. It is a useful ingredient and can be added to many recipes to enrich breads, muffins, cakes, puddings, bakes and cereals.

Wholemeal (whole wheat) biscuits and crackers: Whole wheat or wholemeal biscuits and high fibre crackers make good storecupboard

standbys for a healthy, high fibre snack. When crushed, sweet wholemeal biscuits are good for cheesecake bases and crunchy toppings for fruity desserts.

Wholemeal (whole wheat) flour: 'Whole' means that the grain has not had the bran, vitamins and minerals refined out, so it contains all the nutrients. Wholemeal flour is coarser than white flour and is available in several types including plain, self-raising and strong.

It can be used in many dishes that traditionally specify white flour, including cakes, bakes, breads, pastry and biscuits. It makes a good thickener

for sauces and can be used to coat foods. A mixture of half wholemeal and half white flour can be used for a lighter mix.

Wholewheat pasta: Dried wholewheat or wholemeal pasta is a good source of dietary fibre, is low in fat and contains some B vitamins. It can be used in many dishes including salads, pasta bakes and filled pasta which can be topped with low fat sauces. Allow 115–225 g/4–8 oz/1–2 cups pasta per serving for a main course and 50–115 g/2–4 oz/1/2–1 cup per person for a starter. Dried wholewheat pasta takes about 12 minutes to cook.

HERBS AND SPICES

The judicious use of a herb or spice, or both, can transform a dish. It's fun to experiment, once you know what you like and which seasonings go well with what foods.

Herbs

In cookery, herbs are used mainly for their flavouring and seasoning properties, as well as for adding colour and texture. They have a great deal to offer and by simply adding a single herb or a combination of herbs to foods, everyday dishes can be transformed into delicious meals.

Whenever possible, use fresh herbs, for their wonderful flavour, scent and colour. They're widely available in supermarkets and are also easy to grow, even in pots on a windowsill. Fresh herbs impart their flavour very quickly, so chop just before using and add to

ABOVE Fresh or dried herbs can be used singly or combined to bring flavour to savoury dishes.

PREPARING GARLIC WITH A GARLIC PRESS

Using a garlic press, leave the clove unpeeled and cut off the root end. Place the clove cut end down in the press.

Crush the clove into a bowl. The garlic skin can be removed in one piece, making the press easier to clean.

If you don't own a garlic press: peel the outer papery layer off the garlic bulb. Cut the ends off the cloves. Using the side of a knife blade, crush the cloves flat to extract all of the juices. Then chop finely.

hot dishes towards the end of cooking. If fresh herbs are not available, you can, of course, substitute dried. Use them in a ratio of 1 teaspoon dried to 1 tablespoon fresh.

Garlic

The health benefits of garlic are well known and include helping to increase overall strength and vitality and reduce lethargy. Use it fresh or cooked, in salads, dressings and main dishes.

Spices

Essential in any storecupboard, many spices can be used in both sweet and savoury dishes. These age-old flavourings from all over the world are available in a variety of forms – whole, ground or blended – in a vast range of different types. Each spice has its own unique flavour and aroma and with a single spice, or a simple blend of spices, everyday dishes can be transformed.

GRATING WHOLE NUTMEG AND FRESH GINGER

To get a fine powder of nutmeg, use a specialized nutmeg grater. Place the grater on a board, then simply rub the whole nutmeg against the grater.

To grate ginger, thinly peel or scrape off the skin from the root, then grate it on the fine blade of a stainless steel grater until you have the amount you require. Take care not to graze your fingers! Peeled ginger can be ground to a paste with garlic, other spices and a little oil to make a smoother mixture.

Most spices, both whole and ground, need time to impart their aroma and flavour to a dish. Some are pungent and spicy-hot, others are sweet and fragrant. If you can, grind spices freshly, using a spice mill, nutmeg grater or mortar and pestle. The difference in flavour and aroma between pre-ground and freshly ground is amazing. Fresh roots, such as ginger, galangal and fresh lemon grass have an entirely different flavour than their dried versions.

Dried spices should be kept in airtight, tinted glass containers and stored in a cool, dark cupboard.

Ground spices should be used within 6 months and whole spices within a year and so it is better to buy them in small quantities. Freshly ground spices provide the best flavour and aroma so it is well worth investing in a small pestle and mortar so that you can grind your own spices.

Spices are often ground, crushed, pounded or puréed to create powders and pastes. Smooth china pestles and mortars come in many sizes and are useful for grinding small amounts of dry spices. An electric coffee grinder is excellent for grinding dry spices. If you are going to do a lot of spice cooking, it is worth keeping a separate grinder purely for this purpose. For making large quantities of spice pastes, an electric food processor is invaluable.

Unless you are going to use fresh spices on the day they are bought, they should be chilled rather than stored at room temperature. To keep them longer, fresh spices can be pounded to a paste, then put in sealed containers and frozen for up to 6 months.

BELOW Nuts and seeds not only provide essential B vitamins, minerals and protein, they also make a tasty treat.

MAKING STOCKS

A good home-made poultry stock is invaluable. It is simple to make, and you can store it in the freezer for up to 6 months. Add the giblets if available, but not the livers, as these make stock bitter. Fish stock is very quick to make. Ask your fishmonger for heads, bones and trimmings from white fish. The most delicious meat soups, stews, casseroles, gravies and sauces rely on a good home-made meat stock for success. Once made, you can keep meat stock in the refrigerator for 4–5 days, or freeze it for longer storage (up to 6 months). Vegetable stock is also easy to make. Refrigerate, covered, for up to 5 days, or freeze for up to 1 month.

MAKING POULTRY STOCK

MAKES ABOUT 2.5 LITRES/4 PINTS

1.12–1.35 kg/2½–3 lb poultry wings, backs and necks (chicken, turkey, etc.)

2 unpeeled onions, quartered

4 litres/6½ pints cold water

2 carrots, roughly chopped

2 celery stalks, with leaves if possible, roughly chopped

a small handful of fresh parsley

a few fresh thyme sprigs or 5 ml/1 tsp dried thyme

1 or 2 bay leaves

10 black peppercorns, lightly crushed

1 Combine the poultry wings, backs and necks and the onions in a stockpot. Cook over a moderate heat, stirring occasionally, until the poultry and onion pieces are lightly browned.

2 Add the water and stir well to mix in the sediment on the bottom of the pot. Bring to a boil and skim off the impurities as they rise to the surface.

3 Add the remaining ingredients. Partly cover the pot and gently simmer for 3 hours. Strain the stock into a bowl and leave to cool, then refrigerate.

4 When cold, remove the layer of fat that will have set on the surface.

MAKING FISH STOCK

MAKES ABOUT 1 LITRE/2 PINTS

700 g/1½ lb heads, bones and trimmings from white fish

1 onion, sliced

2 celery stalks with leaves, chopped

1 carrot, sliced

1 bay leaf

a few fresh parsley sprigs

6 black peppercorns

1.35 litres/2¼ pints water

150 ml/¼ pint/⅔ cup dry white wine

1 Rinse the fish heads, bones and trimmings well. Put in a stockpot with the vegetables, herbs, peppercorns, water and wine. Bring to a boil, skimming the surface frequently, then reduce the heat and simmer for about 25 minutes. Strain the stock, without pressing down on the ingredients in the sieve. If you do not intend to use the stock immediately, leave it to cool and then refrigerate. Use fish stock within 2 days, or freeze it for up to 3 months.

MAKING MEAT STOCK

MAKES ABOUT 2 LITRES/3½ PINTS

1.8 kg/4 lb beef bones, such as shin, leg, neck and clod, or veal or lamb bones, cut into 6 cm/2½ in pieces

2 unpeeled onions, quartered

2 carrots, roughly chopped

2 celery stalks, roughly chopped

2 tomatoes, coarsely chopped

4.5 litres/7½ pints cold water

a handful of parsley stalks

a few fresh thyme sprigs or 5 ml/1 tsp dried thyme

2 bay leaves

10 black peppercorns, lightly crushed

1 Preheat a 230°C/450°F/Gas 8 oven. Put the bones in a roasting tin (pan) or flameproof casserole and roast, turning occasionally, for 30 minutes or until they start to brown.

2 Add the onions, carrots, celery and tomatoes and baste with the fat in the tin. Roast for a further 20–30 minutes or until the bones are well-browned. Stir and baste occasionally.

3 Transfer the bones and vegetables to a stockpot. Spoon off the fat from the roasting tin. Add a little of the water to the roasting tin or casserole and bring to a boil on top of the stove, stirring well. Pour this liquid into the stockpot.

4 Add the remaining water. Bring to a boil, skimming to remove foam from the surface. Add the parsley, thyme, bay leaves and peppercorns. Cover and simmer for 4–6 hours, topping up with water from time to time.

5 Strain the stock through a sieve. Skim as much fat as possible from the surface. The best way to do this is to cool the stock and then refrigerate it; the fat will then rise to the top and set in a layer that you can remove easily.

MAKING VEGETABLE STOCK

MAKES ABOUT 2.5 LITRES/4 PINTS

2 large onions, coarsely chopped

2 leeks, sliced

3 garlic cloves, crushed

3 carrots, coarsely chopped

4 celery stalks, coarsely chopped

a large strip of lemon zest

a handful of parsley stalks (about 12)

a few fresh thyme sprigs

2 bay leaves

2.5 litres/4 pints water

1 Put the vegetables, lemon zest, herbs and water in a stockpot and bring to a boil. Skim off the foam that rises to the surface from time to time.

2 Reduce the heat and then simmer, uncovered, for 30 minutes. Strain the stock and leave it to cool.

MAKING SAUCES

Some chefs consider flour-thickened sauces old-fashioned and replace them with butter sauces, vegetable purées or reduced cream. A basic white sauce is, however, an essential ingredient in many dishes, and lends itself to many flavourings. The recipe given here makes a medium-thick sauce.

Tomato sauce is a very useful standby to have on hand in the refrigerator or freezer. When tomatoes are in season, make a large batch and freeze it. At other times of the year, use canned whole Italian plum tomatoes (drain, cut in half, scrape out the seeds and chop).

MAKING WHITE SAUCE

MAKES ABOUT 600 ML/1 PINT/ 2½ CUPS

45 g/1½ oz/3 tbsp butter

45 g/1½ oz/6 tbsp plain (all-purpose) flour

600 ml/1 pint/2½ cups milk

a good pinch of grated nutmeg

salt and pepper

SAUCE-MAKING TIP

A whisk will blend the mixture more thoroughly than a spoon and will help to prevent lumps from forming.

1 Melt the butter in a heavy saucepan over a low heat. Remove the pan from the heat and stir in the flour to make a smooth, soft paste (known as a 'roux').

2 Add about one-quarter of the milk and mix it in well, using a whisk. When smooth, mix in the remaining milk.

3 Set the pan over a moderately high heat and bring gradually to a boil, whisking constantly.

4 When the sauce bubbles and starts to thicken, reduce the heat to very low and simmer the sauce gently for 5–10 minutes, whisking well from time to time. Add the grated nutmeg and season the sauce to taste with salt and pepper. Serve the sauce hot.

WHITE-SAUCE VARIATIONS

- For *Thin White Sauce* to serve with meat or to use as a base for cream soups: use 30 g/1 oz/2 tbsp butter and 30 g/1 oz/ 4 tbsp plain (all-purpose) flour.
- For *Thick White Sauce* to use as a soufflé base: use 55 g/2 oz/4 tbsp butter and 55 g/2 oz/½ cup flour.
- For *Blond Sauce*: add the flour to the melted butter and cook, stirring constantly, for 1–2 minutes or until the roux is a pale beige colour. Heat the liquid and then add it to the roux, off the heat. Bring to a boil, whisking, and simmer for 3–5 minutes.
- For *Velouté Sauce*: cook the roux as for a blond sauce until it is lightly browned and smells nutty. Use hot chicken or fish stock, or a mixture of stock and wine, instead of milk.
- For *Béchamel Sauce*: heat the milk with a slice of onion, 1 bay leaf and a few black peppercorns. Remove from the heat, cover and infuse for 20 minutes. Strain before adding to the roux, made as for a blond sauce.
- For *Cream Sauce*: substitute cream for some of the milk.
- For *Cheese Sauce*: stir 115–225 g/ 4–8 oz grated cheese and 5–10 ml/ 1–2 tsp spicy brown mustard into white, blond or béchamel sauce; add a pinch of cayenne pepper instead of nutmeg. Use a flavourful cheese that melts easily.
- For *Mustard Sauce*: stir 15 ml/1 tbsp Dijon mustard and 2.5 ml/½ tsp sugar into white, blond or béchamel sauce.
- For *Mushroom Sauce*: cook 225 g/8 oz sliced mushrooms in about 20 g/⅔ oz/ 1½ tbsp butter until soft; continue cooking until the excess liquid has evaporated. Add to white, blond, béchamel, velouté or cream sauce.

MAKING TOMATO SAUCE

**MAKES ABOUT 600 ML/1 PINT/
2½ CUPS**

30 g/1 oz/2 tbsp butter

900 g/2 lb tomatoes, skinned, seeded and
  finely chopped

1.25–2.5 ml/¼–½ tsp sugar

salt and pepper

COOK'S TIP

Skinning and seeding the tomatoes will
improve the texture of the sauce.

1 Melt the butter in a heavy-based
saucepan over a low heat. Add the
tomatoes and stir to mix with the
butter. Cover and cook for 5 minutes.

2 Uncover and stir in the sugar. Partly
cover the pan and simmer gently,
stirring occasionally, for 30 minutes or
until the tomatoes have softened and
the sauce is thick.

3 Season the sauce to taste with salt
and pepper. Use immediately, or cool
and then refrigerate or freeze.

EGGS BAKED IN TOMATO SAUCE

For each serving, put 20 ml/1½ tbsp
of tomato sauce in a lightly buttered
ramekin. Break an egg into the
ramekin and sprinkle with pepper to
taste and 15 ml/1 tbsp of freshly grated
Parmesan or Cheddar cheese. Make as
many servings as needed, then put the
ramekins in a roasting tin (pan) and
add cold water to come halfway up the
sides. Bring to a boil on top of the
stove, then transfer to a 200°C/400°F/
Gas 6 oven and bake for 5–7 minutes.
Serve immediately.

TOMATO-SAUCE VARIATIONS

- For *Rich Tomato Sauce*: stir another
20 g/⅔ oz/1½ tbsp butter into the sauce
before serving.
- For *Smooth Tomato Sauce*: purée the
sauce in a blender or food processor to
achieve a smooth texture.
- For *Tomato-garlic Sauce*: use 15 ml/
1 tbsp olive oil instead of butter. In a
separate small pan, cook 1–2 finely
chopped garlic cloves in the olive oil
for approximately 1 minute. Add the
garlic to the tomato sauce for the last 5
minutes of cooking.
- For *Tomato-herb Sauce*: stir in about
60 ml/4 tbsp chopped fresh herbs
(parsley, basil, chives, thyme, oregano,
marjoram – either singly or in a
mixture of 2 or 3 different herbs at the
most) before serving.
- For *Italian Tomato Sauce*: finely chop
1 onion, 1 small carrot and 1 celery
stalk. Cook gently in 30 ml/2 tbsp olive
oil until soft. Add 1–2 finely chopped
garlic cloves and cook for a further
minute. Add the tomatoes with 1 bay
leaf and 1 large sprig of fresh rosemary
or 2.5 ml/½ tsp crumbled dried
rosemary. Continue cooking as for
ordinary tomato sauce. Discard the
herbs before serving.
- For *Tomato-wine Sauce*: finely chop
3 shallots or ½ onion and cook in
30 g/1 oz/2 tbsp butter or 30 ml/2 tbsp
olive oil until soft. Add 1 finely
chopped garlic clove and cook for a
further minute. Stir in 120 ml/4 fl oz/
½ cup dry white wine, bring to a boil
and boil until almost completely
evaporated. Add the tomatoes and
continue cooking as for tomato sauce.
For a smooth sauce, purée in a blender
or food processor.
- For *Tomato-mushroom Sauce*: fry
225 g/8 oz thinly sliced mushrooms in
30 g/1 oz/2 tbsp butter for about 5–7
minutes until they are soft and lightly
browned. Add the tomatoes and cook
as for the basic tomato sauce.

COOKING WITH MEAT, POULTRY AND FISH

Many people like to eat meat, poultry or fish at least once a day with their main meal but find that their knowledge of different cuts, preparation and basic techniques limits what is possible. Cooking with meat, poultry and fish requires only a few basic skills, which once learnt will ensure delicious dishes. Depending on the cut, meat can be roasted, pot-roasted, stewed, sautéed, pan- or stir-fried, grilled or barbecued. Understanding how these techniques affect meat gives the home cook the confidence to successfully cook any meat and get the best flavour out of it, whether or not they are following a recipe.

Knowing how to prepare meat prior to cooking is also important; trimming, removing the chine bone (backbone) in a joint, wrapping a joint in fat or bacon to keep it moist during cooking and tying up a boned joint to keep it in shape, are all skills that may be required from time to time, and although the butcher will always do it for you if you ask, it is worth trying to bone a joint at home.

Poultry is particularly good roasted, sautéed or fried and can also be grilled with good results. Jointing a whole chicken at home has the benefits of allowing you to cut it into four or eight portions according to your requirements, leaving you with a carcass for making delicious stock and saving money on buying ready-jointed portions.

Although a good fishmonger will always prepare fish for you, it is useful to know how to prepare and cut or fillet fish at home, especially if you are lucky enough to be able to buy fresh fish directly from the quayside or market place. Fish is also an extremely versatile ingredient, with a wide range of textures and flavours. It can be poached, steamed, grilled and fried, each method producing quite different results. Knowing which fish are best suited to which cooking methods will guarantee excellent results.

In addition to explaining how best to prepare and cook meat, poultry and fish, the following pages also contain some simple recipes to try.

OPPOSITE Cooking with meat, fish and poultry need not be limited to simply frying or grilling. Learning a few simple techniques and knowing more about the wonderful variety available, can transform everyday meals.

PREPARING MEAT FOR COOKING

You can buy meat ready for cooking from butchers and supermarkets. However, some cuts need further preparation depending on how they are to be cooked. Also you may prefer to bone a joint at home.

For large joints of meat that contain rib bones, such as pork loin and best end of lamb, it is a good idea to cut the chine bone (backbone) where it is joined to the rib bones, to loosen it or to remove it completely before cooking.

If a very lean piece of meat is to be roasted without a protective crust (a spice mixture, oil and crumbs or pastry, for example), use foil to keep it moist.

Joints that have been boned should be tied into a neat shape for roasting or pot roasting. The butcher will do this, but if you want to add a stuffing or seasoning, you will need to retie the joint yourself.

A boned leg of lamb is much easier to carve than a joint with the bone in. By removing the bones, you can also stuff the pocket left before tying the joint into a neat shape with string.

Boning lamb and leaving the meat opened up flat (called 'butterflying' it) shortens the cooking time by about a third. A butterflied leg can be roasted, grilled or barbecued over charcoal.

Before boning, carefully trim off all fat from the surface of the leg. The pelvic bone comprises the hip bone and the aitchbone.

HOW MUCH TO BUY

As a general guide, when buying boneless meat that has little or no fat, allow 145–200 g/5–7 oz per serving. For meat with bone that has a little fat at the edge, you will need to allow for about 225 g/8 oz per serving. Very bony cuts such as spareribs have proportionally little meat so you will need up to 450 g/1 lb per serving.

PREPARING MEAT

1 To trim: Use a sharp knife to trim skin or rind and fat from the surface. Leave a little fat on steaks to be grilled, and slash this fat at regular intervals to prevent the steak curling up during cooking. Joints to be roasted should retain a thin layer of fat about 3–5 mm/⅛–¼ in. Cut away the sinews and tough connective tissue. Cover the bone ends with foil to prevent charring.

2 To chine a joint: Without the chine bone, the joint will be easy to carve. Cut the bone where rib bones are attached to it then remove it using a meat saw and sharp knife. Alternatively, ask your butcher to do it.

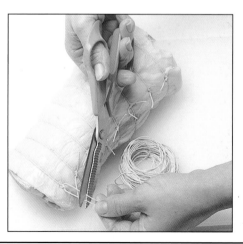

3 To bard a joint: Wrap thin slices of beef fat, pork fat or blanched bacon around the joint and tie them in place with string. Discard the fat before serving but keep the bacon, if liked.

4 To tie a boned joint: After boning and stuffing, a roast will need to be tied. Reshape it into a neat roll that is even in circumference. Use butcher's string to make ties around the circumference of the joint at 2.5 cm/1 in intervals.

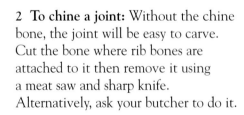

BONING A LEG OF LAMB

1 Set the leg pelvic bone upwards. Working from the fillet end, cut around the ball and socket joint between the hip bone and the main leg bone to free it. Remove the pelvic bone.

2 Cut through the meat straight down the length of the leg bone, from the hip to the knee.

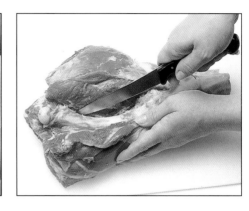

3 Using short strokes, cut and scrape the meat away from the bone all around. Cut off the white chip of bone (the knee cap) if it is there.

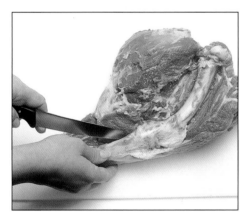

4 Continue cutting down the length of the leg bone below the knee (the shank end). Cut and scrape the meat away from the bone as before to free the bone.

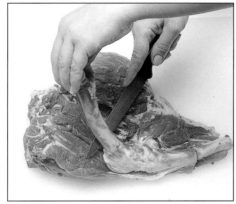

5 Lift the fillet end of the leg bone and cut around the knee to detach it from the meat. To avoid tough meat, cut out the tendons from the meat at the shank end.

6 To butterfly: Lay the boned leg out flat. Trim off all visible fat, then slash the thick portions of meat and open them so that the whole leg is reasonably even in thickness.

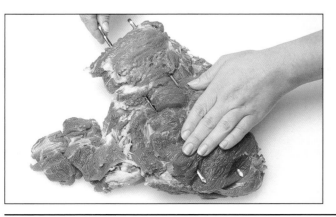

7 Thread 2 skewers crosswise through the meat at its widest part. These will keep the butterflied leg flat during cooking.

ROASTING MEAT

The dry heat of oven roasting is best suited to tender cuts of meat. If they do not have a natural marbling of fat, bard them by covering with strips of bacon to prevent the meat from drying out. Alternatively, marinate the meat or baste it frequently with the roasting juices during cooking.

Meat should be at room temperature for roasting. Roast on a rack in a tin (pan) as, without a rack, the base of the joint will stew and not become crisp. There are 2 methods of roasting meat: searing the joint at a high temperature and then reducing the heat for the rest of the cooking time; or roasting at a constant temperature throughout. Both methods produce good results – it is prolonged cooking, not the method, that affects juiciness and shrinkage – so use whichever method you prefer.

1 According to the recipe, rub the joint with oil or butter and season. If you wish, for extra flavour, make little slits in the meat all over the surface, using the tip of a sharp knife. Insert flavourings such as herbs, slivers of garlic, olive slices, shards of fresh ginger and so on.

2 Insert a meat thermometer into the thickest part, not touching a bone. (An instant-read thermometer is sometimes inserted towards the end of roasting.) Roast for the suggested time (see below left), basting if necessary.

SUGGESTED ROASTING TIMES

Using the second roasting method, in a 180°C/350°F/Gas 4 oven, approximate timings in minutes per 450g/1 lb are as follows:

    Beef, rare, 20 + 20 extra*
          medium, 25 + 25 extra
          well done, 30 + 30 extra
    Veal, 25 + 25 extra
    Lamb, 25 + 25 extra
    Pork, 35 + 35 extra
(*Prime cuts such as rib of beef and tenderloin need less time.)

3 Transfer the cooked meat to a carving board. Leave it to 'rest' for 10–15 minutes before carving so that the flesh can re-absorb the juices. During this time, make gravy with the roasting juices, if you like.

ROAST LEG OF LAMB

Trim a 2.25–2.7 kg/5–6 lb leg of lamb, removing almost all the fat. Cut 2–3 garlic cloves into very thin slices. Pull the leaves from 3 sprigs of fresh rosemary. Insert the garlic slices and rosemary leaves into slits in the lamb. Rub the lamb with olive oil and season with salt and pepper. Roast until cooked to your taste. *Serves 8.*

MEAT-THERMOMETER READINGS

Beef		Lamb	
rare	52–54°C/125–130°F	rare	54–57°C/130–135°F
medium-rare	57°C/135°F	medium	60–63°C/140–145°F
medium	60–63°C/140–145°F	well-done	71°C/160°F
well-done	71°C/160°F		
		Pork	
Veal		medium	66°C/150°F
well-done	71°C/160°F	well-done	71–74°C/160–165°F

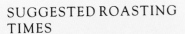

BROWNING OR SEARING MEAT

Large joints and pieces of meat to be roasted or pot-roasted are sometimes seared as the first step in their cooking. This may be done either by roasting briefly at a high temperature and then reducing the heat or by frying. The result is a browned crust that adds delicious flavour.

POT-ROASTING

This method of cooking tenderizes even the toughest cuts of meat. Prime cuts can also be pot-roasted, but cooking times are usually cut short – just long enough to reach the degree of cooking you like.

Depending on the desired result, meat to be pot-roasted may or may not have an initial searing.

1 To sear by frying: Dry the meat well with paper towels. Heat a little oil in a frying pan, flameproof casserole or roasting tin (pan) until it is very hot. Put in the meat and fry over high heat until it is well browned on all surfaces. Turn the meat using two spatulas or spoons. (Piercing with a fork would let the juices escape, which would then be boiled away.)

2 If roasting, transfer the meat, in its roasting tin, to the oven. If pot-roasting, add a small amount of liquor and cover the pot tightly. If a frying pan has been used for searing, be sure to deglaze it: add some of the liquid called for in the recipe and bring to the boil, scraping up the browned bits from the bottom. Add this flavourful mixture to the pot.

MAKING GRAVY

Gravy made from the roasting juices is rich in flavour and colour. Alongside the vegetables, it is the traditional accompaniment for roast meat.

For a thinner sauce, an alternative method to that explained here is de-glazing, where liquid is added to skimmed pan juices and boiled to reduce to the desired consistency.

RESTING A JOINT BEFORE CARVING

Once a joint is removed from the oven or pot, it should be left in a warm place to 'rest' for 10–15 minutes. During this time, the temperature of the joint evens out, and the flesh re-absorbs most of the juices. Thus, the juices won't leak during carving.

1 Spoon off most of the fat from the roasting tin. Set the tin over moderately high heat on top of the stove. When the roasting juices begin to sizzle, add flour and stir to combine.

2 Cook, scraping the tin well, and mix in all the browned bits from the bottom, until the mixture forms a smooth brown paste. Add stock or another liquid as specified in the recipe and bring to the boil, stirring and whisking constantly. Simmer until the gravy has the right consistency, then season to taste.

COOKING WITH MEAT, POULTRY AND FISH

PAN-FRYING, SAUTÉING AND STIR-FRYING MEAT

Tender cuts of meat, such as steaks and chops, slices of calf's liver and hamburgers, are ideal for cooking quickly in a heavy frying pan. Before pan-frying and sautéing, trim excess fat from steaks, chops, escalopes, etc., then dry them very thoroughly with paper towels. For cooking, choose a fat that can be heated to a high temperature. If using butter, an equal amount of vegetable oil will help prevent burning, or you could use clarified butter if you prefer.

After pan-frying or sautéing, you can make a simple yet delicious sauce in the pan; the same method is ideal for making gravy to accompany roast meats. It is also a good way to maximize flavour in stews and casseroles. Before de-glazing, remove the meat and keep it warm. Pour or spoon off all the fat from the pan, unless a recipe calls for shallots, garlic, etc., to be softened. In that case, leave 5–10 ml/1–2 tsp of fat and cook the vegetables in it.

For stir-frying, a wok is excellent because its high sides let you stir and toss the ingredients briskly so that they cook quickly and evenly. Use long cooking chopsticks or a wooden spatula to keep the ingredients moving.

CUTS FOR PAN-FRYING

Beef: fillet steak (tournedos), sirloin steak (porterhouse), rump steak, T-bone steak, hamburgers.
Lamb: cutlets, noisettes (boned cutlets), loin chops, chump chops, leg steaks, fillet.
Pork: loin chops, spare-rib chops, cubes or slices of fillet (tenderloin).

CUTS FOR STIR-FRYING

Beef: strips of rump and other steaks.
Lamb: strips of shoulder fillet, leg.
Pork: cubes of fillet (tenderloin).

PAN-FRYING OR SAUTÉING MEAT

1 Heat the fat in the pan over a high heat until very hot but not browning. Put in the meat, in one layer. Do not crowd the pan.

2 Fry until browned on both sides and done to your taste. If pan-frying pork or veal chops, reduce the heat to moderate once they are in the pan.

PAN-FRIED TERIYAKI STEAK

Combine 45 ml/3 tbsp vegetable oil, 15 ml/1 tbsp each soy sauce, honey, red-wine vinegar and finely chopped onion, 1 crushed garlic clove and 2.5 ml/½ tsp ground ginger in a plastic bag. Add 4 rump or sirloin steaks and turn to coat well. Put the bag in a dish and marinate for 2 hours. Drain the steaks and pat dry, then pan-fry until cooked to your taste. The steaks can also be grilled (broiled). *Serves 4.*

DE-GLAZING FOR A PAN SAUCE

1 Pour in the liquid called for in the recipe (wine, stock, vinegar, etc.). Bring to a boil, stirring well to scrape up the browned bits from the bottom of the pan and dissolve them in the liquid.

2 Boil over a high heat for 1–2 minutes or until the liquid is almost syrupy. If the recipe instructs, enrich the sauce with cream or butter. Season to taste with salt and pepper and serve.

TESTING STEAK

A reliable way to test steak is by pressing it with your finger. When raw, it is soft and can be squashed. When cooked rare, it will be only slightly springy. When medium-cooked, it will offer more resistance and drops of red juice will appear on the surface. When well-done, it will be firm to the touch.

STIR-FRYING MEAT

1 Prepare all the stir-fry ingredients in uniformly sized pieces, following recipe instructions if you wish.

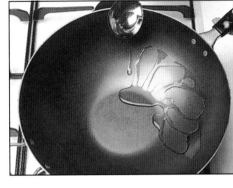

2 Heat a wok or large, deep frying pan over a moderately high heat. Dribble in the oil down the sides.

STIR-FRIED BEEF WITH MANGE-TOUT (SNOW PEAS)

Cut 450 g/1 lb lean, boneless, tender beef into very thin strips. Combine 45 ml/3 tbsp soy sauce, 30 ml/2 tbsp dry sherry, 15 ml/1 tbsp brown sugar and 2.5 ml/½ tsp cornflour (cornstarch) in a bowl. Heat 15 ml/1 tbsp vegetable oil in the hot wok. Add 15 ml/1 tbsp each finely chopped fresh ginger and garlic and stir-fry for 30 seconds. Add the beef and stir-fry for 2 minutes or until well browned. Add 225 g/8 oz mange-tout (snow peas); stir-fry for 3 minutes. Stir the soy sauce mixture until smooth, then add to the wok. Bring to a boil, stirring and tossing, and simmer just until it is thickened and smooth. Serve immediately, accompanied by freshly boiled rice. *Serves 4.*

3 When the oil is hot (a piece of vegetable should sizzle on contact), add the ingredients in the order specified in the recipe. (Those that take longer to cook should be added first.) Do not add too much to the wok at a time, or the ingredients will start to produce steam rather than frying properly.

4 Fry, stirring and tossing constantly with chopsticks or a spatula, until the ingredients are just cooked: vegetables should be crisp-tender and meat and poultry tender and juicy.

5 Push the ingredients to the side of the wok or remove them. Pour liquid or sauce as specified in the recipe into the bottom. Cook and stir, then mix in the ingredients from the side of the wok. Serve immediately.

COOKING WITH MEAT, POULTRY AND FISH

GRILLING, BARBECUING AND STEWING

Grilling and barbecuing are dry-heat methods of cooking which are most suitable for naturally tender cuts of meat or those that have been tenderized. In grilling, meat is cooked under direct heat either electric or gas powered; in barbecuing, meat is cooked over hot charcoal. The cooking time is determined by the heat and the distance the meat is from the heat source – normally 7.5 cm/3 in below the grill or 10–15 cm/4–6 in above the coals.

Fry-start stews have a wonderful rich flavour, due greatly to the initial searing of the meat and vegetables. The long cooking period, in a seasoned liquid, produces a very tender result. Be sure to use a heavy-based pan or casserole.

In stews where you want to emphasize the natural flavours of the ingredients rather than the flavours that result from browning, the initial searing stage is omitted.

Sweat-start stewing is a combination of two stewing methods. It doesn't use any oil or fat, relying on the fat naturally present in the meat.

STEWING WITH A FRY START

1 Cut the meat into equal-sized cubes and dry it with paper towels. Coat it lightly with flour, if necessary.

2 Heat a little oil in a frying pan or flameproof casserole until it is very hot. Add a few cubes of meat – just enough to cover the bottom of the pan without touching each other. If the temperature drops too much, a crisp brown crust will not form.

3 Fry over moderately high heat until well browned on all sides. Remove them as they are done.

4 Add the vegetables and cook, stirring occasionally, until they are well browned. Discard excess oil.

5 Return the meat to the pan. If flour is added now, sprinkle it over the meat and vegetables and cook until it is well combined.

6 Add liquid barely to cover and stir to mix. Add any flavourings and bring the liquid to the boil. Reduce the heat to a gentle simmer and complete the cooking as specified.

7 The liquid may be thickened at the end of cooking. One method is adding 'beurre manié', butter and flour paste, stirred in gradually. Alternatively, thicken with cornflour (starch) mixed with water. Or remove the meat and vegetables and boil the liquid to reduce it and to concentrate the flavour.

TESTING FOR WHEN MEAT IS COOKED

The cooking times given in a recipe are intended to be a guideline. The shape of a cut can affect how long it takes to cook, and people have different preferences for how well cooked they like meat to be. Ovens can also vary, so testing is essential.

NATURAL LAW OF ROASTING

A joint will continue to cook in its own retained heat for 5–10 minutes after being removed from an oven or pot, so it is a good idea to take it out when it is just below the required thermometer reading.

1 Test roasted or pot-roasted joints with a metal skewer. Insert the skewer into the thickest part and leave it for 30 seconds. Withdraw the skewer and feel it: if it is warm, the meat is rare; if it is hot, the meat is well cooked.

2 The most reliable test is with the use of a meat thermometer, inserted in the centre of the joint, away from bones. Some instant-read thermometers are inserted at the end of cooking. Follow the manufacturer's instructions.

COOKING METHODS AND CHOICE OF CUTS

Roasting
- *Beef:* rib (fore), wing or prime rib, middle rib, fillet, sirloin, topside, aitchbone.
- *Veal:* shoulder (oyster), best end of neck, loin, fillet, breast, leg, topside (cushion).
- *Lamb:* shoulder, best end of neck (crown roast), saddle, loin, breast, leg (whole or divided into fillet and knuckle).
- *Pork:* shoulder (spare rib), hand and spring, blade, loin, fillet (tenderloin), leg (whole or divided into fillet and knuckle), fresh belly, spareribs. Also gammon joints and bacon collar and hock.

Pot-roasting and braising
- *Beef:* brisket, silverside, top ribs, sirloin, topside, aitchbone, chuck, flank, rump (thick flank), braising steak.
- *Pork:* shoulder (spare rib), loin, fillet (tenderloin). Also gammon joints and bacon collar and hock.

- *Veal:* shoulder, best end of neck, middle neck cutlets, breast.
- *Lamb:* shoulder, middle neck cutlets, breast, loin, leg.

Stewing
- *Beef:* neck (clod or sticking), blade, chuck, shin, flank, leg, skirt.
- *Veal:* neck, shoulder, scrag, breast, knuckle (osso buco), stewing veal or pie veal.
- *Lamb:* middle neck, shoulder, breast, scrag end, chump chops
- *Pork:* spare rib, fillet (tenderloin), loin.

Pan-frying
- *Beef:* fillet steak (tournedos), sirloin steak (porterhouse), rump steak, T-bone steak, entrecote, chateaubriand, hamburgers.
- *Veal:* cutlets, loin chops, chump chops, escalopes, fillet steaks.
- *Lamb:* cutlets, noisettes (boned cutlets), loin chops, chump chops, leg steaks, fillet.

- *Pork:* loin chops, spare rib chops, cubes or slices of fillet (tenderloin). Also bacon rashers, gammon steaks, chops and rashers.

Grilling
- *Beef:* fillet steak (tournedos), sirloin steak (porterhouse), rump steak, T-bone steak, hamburgers
- *Veal:* cutlets, loin chops, chump chops, fillet steaks.
- *Lamb:* cutlets, noisettes (boned cutlets), loin chops, chump chops, leg steaks, cubes of fillet.
- *Pork:* loin chops, spare rib chops, cubes or slices of fillet (tenderloin). Also streaky and back bacon rashers, gammon rashers, steaks and chops.

Stir-frying
- *Beef:* strips or cubes of rump steak and other steaks.
- *Veal:* strips of escalope.
- *Lamb:* strips or cubes of shoulder fillet, leg.
- *Pork:* strips or cubes of fillet.

JOINTING POULTRY

Although chickens and other poultry are sold already jointed into halves, quarters, breasts, thighs and drumsticks, sometimes it makes sense to buy a whole bird and to do the job yourself. That way you can prepare either 4 larger pieces or 8 smaller ones, depending on the recipe, and you can cut the pieces so that the backbone and other bony bits (which you can save for stock) are not included. In addition, a whole bird is cheaper to buy than pieces. A sharp knife and sturdy kitchen scissors or poultry shears make the job of jointing poultry very easy.

SAFE HANDLING OF RAW POULTRY

Raw poultry may harbour potentially harmful organisms, such as salmonella bacteria, so it is vital to take care in its preparation. Always wash your hands, the chopping board and all cutting tools in hot soapy water before and after handling the poultry. It is a good idea to use a chopping board that can be washed at high temperature in a dishwasher and, if possible, to keep the chopping board just for the preparation of raw poultry. Thaw frozen poultry thoroughly in a refrigerator – never at room temperature, as this can breed salmonella – before cooking.

1 Using a sharp knife, cut through the skin on 1 side of the body down to the point at which the thigh joins the body. Holding the leg between your thumb and fingers, bend it out away from the body and twist it to break the ball-and-socket joint.

3 To separate the breast from the back, cut through the flap of skin just below the rib cage, cutting towards the neck. Pull the breast and back apart and then cut through the joints that connect them on each side. Reserve the back for making stock.

5 Cut the breast in half lengthwise, cutting through the wishbone. You will now have 2 breasts with wings attached and 2 leg portions.

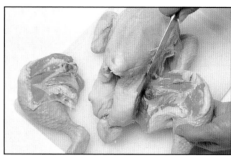

2 Hold the leg out away from the body and cut through the ball-and-socket joint, taking the 'oyster meat' from the backbone with the leg. Repeat the procedure on the other side.

4 Turn the whole breast over, so that it is skin-side down. Take one side of the breast in each hand and bend it back firmly so that the breastbone pops free. Loosen the bone on both sides with your fingers and, with the help of the knife, remove it.

6 For 8 pieces, cut each breast in half at an angle so that some breast meat is included with a wing portion. Trim off any protruding bones.

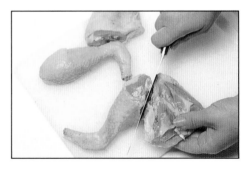

7 Finally, cut each leg portion through the ball-and-socket joint to separate the thigh and drumstick.

SIMPLE CHICKEN CURRY

SERVES 4

30 ml/2 tbsp vegetable oil
1 onion, chopped
1 green or red pepper, seeded and diced
1 garlic clove, finely chopped
20 ml/1½ tbsp curry powder
2.5 ml/½ tsp dried thyme
450 g/1 lb tomatoes, skinned, seeded and chopped, or canned chopped tomatoes
30 ml/2 tbsp lemon juice
120 ml/4 fl oz/½ cup water
55 g/2 oz/⅓ cup currants or raisins
salt and pepper
1 × 1.5 kg/3½ lb chicken, cut into 8 pieces and the pieces skinned
boiled rice, to serve

1 Preheat a 180°C/350°F/Gas 4 oven.

2 Heat the oil in a wide, deep frying pan that has an ovenproof handle, or in a flameproof casserole. Add the onion, diced pepper and garlic. Cook, stirring occasionally, until the vegetables are soft but not browned.

3 Stir in the curry powder and dried thyme, then add the tomatoes, lemon juice and water. Gradually bring the sauce to a boil, stirring frequently. Stir in the currants or raisins. Season to taste with salt and pepper.

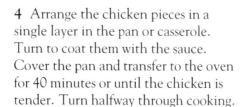

4 Arrange the chicken pieces in a single layer in the pan or casserole. Turn to coat them with the sauce. Cover the pan and transfer to the oven for 40 minutes or until the chicken is tender. Turn halfway through cooking.

5 Remove the chicken and sauce to a warmed serving platter. Serve with freshly boiled rice.

VARIATION

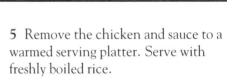

For Curried Chicken Casserole, omit the diced pepper and cook 20 ml/ 1½ tbsp finely chopped fresh ginger and 1 green chilli, seeded and finely chopped, with the onion and garlic in a flameproof casserole. In step 3, stir in the curry powder with 450 ml/¾ pint/ ⅞ cup plain yogurt; omit the tomatoes, lemon juice and water. Add the chicken pieces, cover tightly and cook in a 170°C/325°F/Gas 3 oven for between 1–1¼ hours.

ROASTING POULTRY

Where would family gatherings be without the time-honoured roast bird? Beyond the favourite chicken, all types of poultry can be roasted – from small poussins to large turkeys – although older, tougher birds are better pot-roasted (see opposite page).

PROTECT AND FLAVOUR

Before roasting, loosen the skin on the breast by gently easing it away from the flesh with your fingers. Press in softened butter – mixed with herbs or garlic for extra flavour – and smooth back the skin.

POUSSINS WALDORF

Preheat a 180°C/350°F/Gas 4 oven. For the stuffing, melt 30 g/1 oz/2 tbsp butter and fry 1 finely chopped onion until soft. Tip into a bowl and add 300 g/10 oz/2¼ cups cooked rice, 2 finely chopped celery stalks, 2 cored and finely diced red apples, 55 g/2 oz/ ½ cup chopped walnuts, 75 ml/5 tbsp cream sherry or apple juice and 30 ml/ 2 tbsp lemon juice. Season and mix well.

Divide the stuffing among 6 poussins, each weighing about 575 g/ 1¼ lb, stuffing the body cavities. Truss and arrange in a roasting tin (pan). Sprinkle with salt and pepper and drizzle over 55 g/2 oz/4 tbsp melted butter. Roast for 1¼–1½ hours. Untruss before serving.

1 Wipe the bird inside and out, using damp paper towels. Stuff the bird if you wish and truss it. Spread the breast of a chicken with butter or oil; bard (cover with strips of bacon) a lean game bird; prick the skin of a duck or goose.

2 Set the bird breast-up on a rack in a small roasting tin (pan) or shallow baking dish. If you are roasting a game bird which has very little fat, set the bird in the tin breast-down.

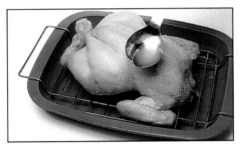

3 Roast the bird, basting it every 10 minutes after the first ½ hour with the accumulated juices and fat in the tin. If the skin is browning too quickly, cover the bird loosely with tin foil.

4 Transfer the bird to a carving board and leave to rest for at least 15 minutes before serving. During that time, make a simple sauce or gravy with the juices in the tin if you wish.

ROASTING TIMES FOR POULTRY

Note: Cooking times given here are for unstuffed birds. For stuffed birds, add 20 minutes to the total roasting time.

Poussin	450–700 g/1–1½ lb	1–1¼ hours at 180°C/350°F/Gas 4
Chicken	1.12–1.35 kg/2½–3 lb	1–1¼ hours at 190°C/375°F/Gas 5
	1.5–1.8 kg/3½–4 lb	1¼–1¾ hours at 190°C/375°F/Gas 5
	2–2.25 kg/4½–5 lb	1½–2 hours at 190°C/375°F/Gas 5
	2.25–2.7 kg/5–6 lb	1¾–2½ hours at 190°C/375°F/Gas 5
Capon	2.25–3 kg/5–7 lb	1¾–2 hours at 170°C/325°F/Gas 3
Duck	1.35–2.25 kg/3–5 lb	1¾–2¼ hours at 200°C/400°F/Gas 6
Goose	3.6–4.5 kg/8–10 lb	2½–3 hours at 180°C/350°F/Gas 4
	4.5–5.4 kg/10–12 lb	3–3½ hours at 180°C/350°F/Gas 4
Turkey (whole bird)	2.7–3.6 kg/6–8 lb	3–3½ hours at 170°C/325°F/Gas 3
	3.6–5.4 kg/8–12 lb	3–4 hours at 170°C/325°F/Gas 3
	5.4–7.2 kg/12–16 lb	4–5 hours at 170°C/325°F/Gas 3
Turkey (whole breast)	1.8–2.7 kg/4–6 lb	1½–2¼ hours at 170°C/325°F/Gas 3
	2.7–3.6 kg/6–8 lb	2¼–3¼ hours at 170°C/325°F/Gas 3

POT-ROAST CHICKEN WITH SAUSAGE STUFFING

SERVES 6

2 × 1.12 kg/2½ lb chickens
30 ml/2 tbsp vegetable oil
360 ml/12 fl oz chicken stock, or half wine and half stock
1 bay leaf
FOR THE STUFFING
450 g/1 lb pork sausagemeat (ground sausage)
1 small onion, chopped
1–2 garlic cloves, finely chopped
5 ml/1 tsp hot paprika
2.5 ml/½ tsp hot pepper flakes (optional)
2.5 ml/½ tsp dried thyme
1.25 ml/¼ tsp ground allspice
45 g/1½ oz/¾ cup coarse breadcrumbs
1 egg, beaten to mix
salt and pepper

1 Preheat a 180°C/350°F/Gas 4 oven.

2 For the stuffing, put the sausagemeat (ground sausage), onion and garlic in a frying pan and fry over a moderate heat until the meat is lightly browned and crumbly, stirring and turning so that it cooks evenly. Remove from the heat and mix in the remaining ingredients with salt and pepper to taste.

3 Divide the stuffing between the chickens, packing it into the body cavities (or, if you prefer, stuff the neck end and bake the left-over stuffing separately). Truss the birds.

4 Heat the oil in a flameproof casserole just big enough to hold the chickens. Brown the birds all over.

VARIATION

For Pot-roast Guinea Fowl, substitute 2 guinea fowl for the chickens.

5 Add the stock and bay leaf and season. Cover and bring to a boil, then transfer to the oven. Pot-roast for 1¼ hours or until the birds are cooked (the juices will run clear).

6 Untruss the chickens and spoon the stuffing on to a serving platter. Arrange the birds and serve with the strained cooking liquid.

SAUTÉING AND FRYING POULTRY

A sauté combines frying and braising, producing particularly succulent results. It is a method suitable for pieces of poultry as well as for small whole birds such as quails and poussins. Be sure to dry the poultry thoroughly with paper towels before cooking to ensure that it browns quickly and evenly.

Fried chicken is justifiably popular – crisp and brown on the outside and tender and juicy within. It is a quick and easy cooking method that can also be applied to pieces of rabbit and hare, and small turkey joints. Dry the pieces thoroughly with paper towels before frying. If they are at all wet, they will not brown properly. If the recipe directs, lightly coat the pieces with egg and crumbs or with a batter.

COUNTRY-CHICKEN SAUTÉ

Cook 175 g/6 oz chopped bacon in 10 ml/2 tsp oil over a moderately high heat until lightly coloured. Remove and reserve. Dredge a 1.5 kg/3½ lb chicken, cut into 8 pieces, in seasoned flour. Fry in the bacon fat until evenly browned. Add 45 ml/3 tbsp dry white wine and 240 ml/8 fl oz/1 cup poultry stock. Bring to a boil and add 225 g/8 oz quartered mushrooms sautéed in 15 g/ ½ oz/1 tbsp butter and the reserved bacon. Cover and cook over low heat for 20–25 minutes, or until the chicken is tender. *Serves 4.*

MAKING POULTRY SAUTÉS

1 Heat a little oil, a mixture of oil and butter, or clarified butter in a heavy-based frying pan or sauté pan.

2 Add the poultry and fry it over a moderately high heat until it is golden brown, turning to colour evenly.

3 Add any liquid and flavourings called for in the recipe. Bring to a boil, cover and reduce the heat. Cook gently until the pieces or birds are done, turning once or twice.

4 If the recipe instructs, remove the poultry from the pan while finishing the sauce. This can be as simple as boiling the cooking juices to reduce them, or adding cream for a richer result.

THICKENING COOKING JUICES

1 Thicken with equal weights of butter and flour mashed together, called 'beurre manié'. Use 30 g/1 oz/2 tbsp of this paste to 240 ml/8 fl oz/1 cup liquid. Whisk small pieces gradually into the boiling sauce until smooth and silky.

2 Another method of thickening cooking juices is to add 10 ml/2 tsp cornflour (cornstarch) blended with 15 ml/1 tbsp water to 240 ml/8 fl oz/1 cup liquid. Boil for 2–3 minutes, whisking constantly, until the sauce is syrupy.

PAN-FRYING POULTRY

1 Heat oil, a mixture of oil and butter, or clarified butter in a large, heavy-based frying pan over a moderate heat. When the oil is very hot, carefully put in the poultry pieces, skin-side down. Do not crowd them or they will not brown; cook in batches if necessary.

2 Fry until deep golden brown all over, turning the pieces so that they colour evenly. Fry until all the pieces are thoroughly cooked. Remove pieces of breast before drumsticks and thighs (dark meat takes longer to cook than white meat). Drain on paper towels.

DEEP-FRYING POULTRY

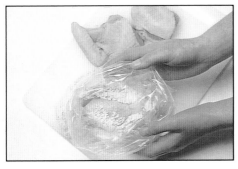

1 Dip the pieces into a mixture of milk and beaten egg, then coat lightly with seasoned flour; leave to 'set' for 20 minutes before frying. Alternatively, coat with a batter before frying.

2 Half-fill a deep pan with vegetable oil. Heat it to 185°C/365°F. You can test the temperature with a cube of bread: if it takes 50 seconds to brown, the oil is at the correct temperature.

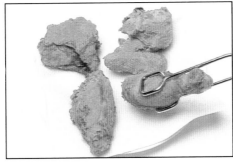

3 Using a fish slice (spatula) or tongs, lower the poultry pieces into the oil, a few at a time, without crowding them. Deep-fry until they are golden brown all over and cooked. Turn them so that they colour evenly.

4 Drain on paper towels and serve hot. If you want to keep a batch of fried poultry hot while you fry the rest, put it into a low oven, but don't cover it or it will become soggy.

SUCCULENT FRIED CHICKEN

Mix 240 ml/8 fl oz/1 cup milk with 1 beaten egg in a shallow dish. On a sheet of greaseproof (waxed) paper, combine 145 g/5 oz/1¼ cups plain (all-purpose) flour, 5 ml/1 tsp paprika, and some salt and pepper. One at a time, dip 8 chicken pieces in the egg mixture and turn them to coat all over. Then dip in the seasoned flour and shake off any excess. Deep-fry for 25–30 minutes, turning the pieces so they brown and cook evenly. Drain on paper towels and serve very hot. *Serves 4.*

GRILLING (BROILING) POULTRY

If you prefer to cook poultry without using oil or butter, grilling (broiling) is a good alternative. Small birds can be 'spatchcocked' by removing the backbone, flattening out the bird and securing it with skewers. Cook whole birds or large pieces 10–15 cm (4–6 in) from the heat, or thinner pieces nearer the heat. If the poultry browns too quickly, turn the heat down slightly.

PREPARING FISH FOR COOKING

Most fish have scales, and you should remove these before cooking unless you are going to fillet the fish or remove the skin before serving. Fish sold by fishmongers will normally be scaled as well as cleaned (eviscerated or gutted), but you can do this yourself, if necessary. Trimming the tail gives a whole fish a neat appearance.

Round fish and large flat fish such as halibut are often cut into steaks and cutlets for cooking. Steaks are cut from the tail end of the fish, while cutlets are cut from the centre. They are usually cut about 2.5–4 cm/1–1½ in thick.

Fillets are boneless pieces of fish, and for this reason are very popular. A sharp filleting knife, with its thin, flexible blade, is the tool to use for removing the fillets. Be sure to keep all the bones and trimmings for making stock. Round fish are easy to fillet and they produce a boneless piece from each side. Large flat fish are filleted slightly differently from round fish and yield 4 narrow fillets – 2 from each side.

Before cooking, dark or tough skin is usually removed from fish fillets. If you salt your fingers, you will get a better grip on the tail end so that you can hold the skin taut as you cut. If you are going to grill (broil) fish fillets, however, do not remove the skin as it will help to keep the shape.

All fish preparation is best done in or near the sink, with cool water running.

PREPARING WHOLE FISH

1 To scale: Grasp the tail firmly and scrape off the scales using a special fish scaler or a knife, working from the tail towards the head. Rinse the fish well. Repeat on the other side.

2 To trim: For flat fish to be cooked whole, use kitchen scissors to trim off the outer half of the small fin bones all round the fish.

3 For round fish, cut the flesh on both sides of the anal and dorsal (back) fins and pull them out; the small bones attached will come out too. Trim off the other fins. If you intend to cook the fish whole, leave the fins on, or just trim them, because they will help to keep the shape of the fish.

4 To trim the tail: If you are leaving the tail on, cut a neat V-shape in the centre with scissors. The fish is now ready for cooking.

CUTTING FISH STEAKS AND CUTLETS

1 Using a large, sharp knife, slice the fish across, at a right-angle to the backbone, into slices of the desired thickness.

2 If necessary, cut through the backbone using kitchen scissors or a knife with a serrated blade.

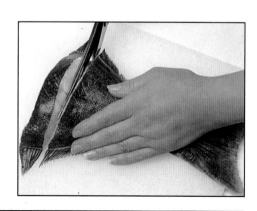

CUTTING FISH FILLETS

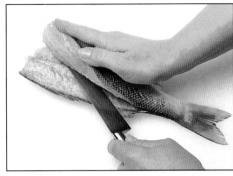

1 To fillet a round fish: Lay the fish flat, on its side. First cut off the head. Using the tip of a filleting knife, cut through the skin all along the length of the backbone.

2 Working from head to tail and holding the knife almost parallel to the fish, use short strokes to cut 1 fillet off the rib bones. Follow the slit cut along the backbone. At the tail, cut across to release the fillet. Repeat on the other side to remove the second fillet.

FILLETING SMALL FLAT FISH

You can take 2 fillets from smaller flat fish (1 from each side). To do this, cut behind the head and down the sides of the fish as described for filleting flat fish, but do not make the central cut. Starting from the head end on one side and working down the fish, cut the flesh away from the rib bones until you reach the centre (the backbone). Rotate the fish and repeat on the other side to cut away the whole fillet. Turn the fish over and repeat.

3 Run your fingers over the flesh side of each fillet to locate any stray bones. Use a pair of tweezers to pull them out.

4 To fillet a flat fish: Lay the fish flat and make a curved cut behind the head, cutting down to but not through the backbone. Using the tip of the knife, slit the skin down both sides of the fish where the fin bones meet the rib bones, 'outlining' the fillets, and slit across the tail.

5 Slit straight down the centre line of the fish, from head to tail, cutting down to the backbone. Working from the centre at the head end, cut 1 fillet neatly away from the rib bones on 1 side. Hold the knife blade almost parallel to the fish as you do this and use short strokes.

6 Rotate the fish and cut away the second fillet. Turn the fish over and repeat to remove the 2 fillets on the other side. Pull out any stray bones using a pair of tweezers.

SKINNING FISH FILLETS

1 Lay the fillet flat, skin-side down, with the tail end towards you. Make a small crosswise cut through the flesh down to the skin at the tail end.

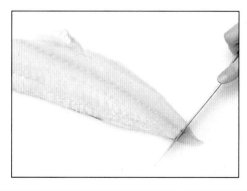

2 Grip the skin and insert the knife blade so that it is almost parallel to it, then cut away the fillet. Use a gentle sawing motion and make a continuous cut.

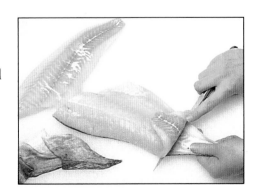

POACHING FISH

Whole fish, large and small, as well as fillets, cutlets and steaks, are excellent poached because the gentle cooking gives succulent results. Poached fish can be served hot or cold, with a wide variety of sauces. The poaching liquid may be used as the basis for the sauce.

POACHING CONTAINERS

A long, rectangular fish kettle with a perforated rack will enable you to lift the fish out of the liquid after cooking. You could also use a large wire rack set in a deep tin (pan).

1 To oven-poach small whole fish, fillets, cutlets or steaks: Place the fish in a buttered flameproof dish large enough to hold the pieces comfortably. Pour in enough liquid to come two-thirds of the way up the side of the fish.

2 Add any flavourings called for in the recipe. Press a piece of buttered greaseproof (waxed) paper on top to keep in the moisture without sticking to the fish.

3 Set the dish over a moderate heat and bring the liquid just to a boil. Transfer the dish to a 180°C/350°F/Gas 4 oven and poach until the fish is just cooked. To test this, make a small cut into the thickest part of the fish using the tip of a sharp knife: the flesh should be slightly translucent.

4 To poach whole fish, fillets, cutlets or steaks on top of the stove: Put large whole fish on the rack in a fish kettle, or set on muslin (cheesecloth) used like a hammock. Poach small whole fish, fillets, cutlets and steaks in a fish kettle on a rack, or set them directly in a wide saucepan or frying pan.

5 Prepare the poaching liquid (salted water, milk, wine or stock) in the fish kettle or in a large casserole, or in a wide saucepan or frying pan for fillets, cutlets and steaks. Set the rack in the kettle, or the muslin hammock in the casserole. Add more liquid, if necessary, so that it covers the fish.

6 Cover the kettle or casserole and bring the liquid just to a boil. Reduce the heat and simmer very gently until the fish is cooked.

POACHED SOLE FILLETS

Oven-poach 8 skinless sole fillets, about 700 g/1½ lb, each 1.5 cm/½ in thick. Use 300 ml/½ pint/1¼ cups dry white wine or fish stock with 4–6 chopped spring onions (scallions), 4–6 lemon slices and a few allspice berries for flavouring. Simmer for 3–5 minutes, then remove the fish. Boil the cooking liquid until reduced to 60 ml/4 tbsp, then strain it. Season with salt and pepper. *Serves 4.*

STEAMING AND BAKING FISH

The simple, moist-heat method of steaming is ideal for fish and shellfish. If you don't have a steamer, it is easy to improvise.

Most fish are suitable for baking – whole or in fillets, cutlets or steaks. Lean fish, in particular, benefit from some protection to prevent them from drying out: choose recipes that include a stuffing or coating or bake them in a little liquid or sauce, which can also be served with the fish. All of these add extra flavour to the fish too.

Cooking in foil or paper parcels is suitable for many fish, both small whole ones and pieces (fillets, cutlets or steaks). This seals in moisture, so the effect is similar to steaming.

One rule of thumb when calculating cooking time for fish is 10 minutes in a 220°C/425°F/Gas 7 oven for each 2.5 cm/1 in, measured at the thickest part.

STEAMED SALMON WITH HERBS

Line a heatproof plate with fresh herb sprigs (dill, parsley, chives etc). Set 2 portions of seasoned salmon fillet, each 2.5 cm/1 in thick, on top. Steam Chinese-style for about 10 minutes. If liked, top with a flavoured butter or serve with Hollandaise. *Serves 2.*

STEAMING FISH

1 Using a steamer: Arrange the fish on the rack in the steamer and set over boiling water. Cover and steam.

2 Chinese-style steaming: Arrange the fish on a heatproof plate that will fit inside a bamboo steamer or wok. Set over boiling water; cover and steam until done.

3 Steaming larger fish and fillets: Arrange the fish on a rack or on a plate in a roasting tin of boiling water. Cover tightly with foil and steam until done.

4 Steaming in foil: Seal the fish and seasonings in foil, and set on a rack in the steamer or in a roasting tin of boiling water. Steam until done.

BAKING FISH

1 To bake fish with liquid, pour over a small amount of stock, wine, water or other liquid as specified in the recipe, then add seasonings.

2 To bake fish in foil or paper, wrap tightly with seasonings and flavourings as specified and place the parcel on a baking sheet.

GRILLING FISH

The intense dry heat of this method of cooking is best used for fish with a lot of natural oil, such as salmon, mackerel and tuna. However, leaner fish can also be grilled, as long as you baste them frequently to keep them moist or cook them in a little liquid.

Always preheat the grill. If liked, line the grill pan with foil to save on washing up.

Fish can also be very successfully grilled over charcoal. Choose full-flavoured fish that will not be overwhelmed by the smoky taste. Thin pieces are easier to handle if placed in a hinged wire fish basket. Be sure to baste well during cooking to prevent the fish from drying out.

FISH KEBABS WITH LEMON BUTTER

Combine 2 tbsp each of melted butter and lemon juice with 1 tsp of mustard powder and 1 finely chopped garlic clove. Cut 700 g/1½ lb halibut, monkfish or sea bass steaks into 2.5 cm/1 in cubes. Thread these on to skewers with pieces of red pepper. Brush with the butter mixture and grill, basting frequently and turning to cook evenly, until done. *Serves 4.*

1 To grill oilier fish: For small whole fish, boned and butterflied fish, fillets, cutlets and steaks that are at least 1.5 cm/½ in thick, or cubes of fish for skewers, rinse the fish and pat it dry with paper towels. Marinate the fish if the recipe instructs.

3 Set the fish pieces under the grill, 7.5–10 cm/3–4 in from the heat (thin pieces should be closer to the heat for a shorter time than thicker ones). Grill, basting once or twice and turning if the recipe specifies, until the fish is done.

2 Preheat the grill with the grill pan in place. When hot, lightly brush the hot pan with oil. If using foil, line it before preheating and then brush with oil when hot. Arrange the fish in the pan, in one layer, skin side down. Brush with butter, oil or a basting mixture, according to the recipe instructions.

4 To grill leaner fish: For small whole fish, and fish steaks, cutlets and fillets that are at least 1.5 cm/½ in thick and prepared for cooking as above, arrange in a buttered flameproof dish. Add a little liquid (wine, stock, etc.) just to cover the bottom of the dish. Brush the fish with butter, oil or a basting mixture, according to the recipe instructions. Grill as above, without turning the fish.

COATING AND FRYING FISH

Fish to be fried is often coated with egg and crumbs, or with a batter. The coating makes a crisp crust to protect the fish and keep it moist. Many other foods – boneless chicken breasts, veal escalopes and vegetables, for example – are also egg-and-crumbed.

DEEP-FRIED CATFISH

Egg-and-crumb 8 catfish (or trout) fillets, using seasoned flour, egg and cornmeal. Deep-fry and serve with tartare sauce. *Serves 4*.

1 Lightly beat an egg in a shallow dish. Spread flour on a plate or sheet of greaseproof paper and season to taste. Spread breadcrumbs on another.

3 Next dip the floured fish in the egg, turning to moisten both sides.

2 **To egg-and-crumb large pieces of fish**: Dip the fish first in the seasoned flour, turning to coat both sides lightly and evenly. Shake off excess flour.

4 Dip the fish in the crumbs, turning to coat evenly. Press to help the crumbs adhere. Shake off excess crumbs. Chill for 20 minutes to set the coating.

5 **To egg-and-crumb small pieces of fish (strips of fish fillet or goujons, prawns/shrimp etc.)**: Put the crumbs in a plastic bag. After dipping the fish in seasoned flour and egg, toss a few pieces at a time in the bag of crumbs.

6 **To pan-fry**: Heat oil or a mixture of oil and butter in a frying pan (enough fat to coat the bottom of the pan in a thin layer or as recipe instructs). When it is very hot, put the fish in the pan, in one layer. Fry until golden brown on both sides and the fish is done. Drain.

7 **To deep-fry**: Half fill a deep pan with oil and heat it to 190°C/375°F. Gently lower the coated pieces of fish into hot oil. Fry until golden brown, turning them occasionally so that they cook evenly. Remove and drain on paper towels before serving.

PREPARING PRAWNS (SHRIMP)

Prawns (shrimp) can be cooked in their shells, and are often presented in this way as an appetizer or garnish for a salad. More often, however, they are peeled first (the shells can be used to make an aromatic stock). The black intestinal vein that runs down the back is removed from large prawns mainly because of its appearance, although the vein may also contain grit which makes it unpleasant to eat.

Prawns in shells are sold with their heads still on. These are easily pulled away from the bodies, and can be used to enhance the flavour of stock made with the discarded shells.

1 Holding the prawn (shrimp) firmly in 1 hand, pull off the legs with the fingers of your other hand. Pull off the head above the legs.

2 Peel the shell away from the body. When you reach the tail, hold the body and pull away the tail; the shell will come off with it. Alternatively, you can leave the tail on the prawn and just remove the body shell.

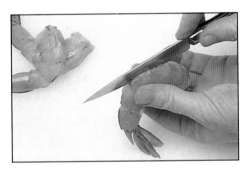

3 Make a shallow cut down the centre of the curved back of the prawn. Pull out the black vein, using a cocktail stick (toothpick) or your fingers.

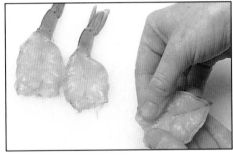

4 To butterfly prawns: Cut along the de-veining slit to split open the prawn, without cutting all the way through. Open up the prawn flat.

5 To de-vein prawns in the shell: Insert a cocktail stick crosswise in several places along the back where the shell overlaps, and lift out the vein.

SPICY BUTTERFLIED TIGER PRAWNS (SHRIMP)

SERVES 4–6

90 ml/6 tbsp olive oil
75 ml/5 tbsp orange juice
60 ml/4 tbsp lime juice
1 large garlic clove, finely chopped
5 ml/1 tsp allspice berries, crushed
1.25 ml/¼ tsp hot chilli flakes
salt and pepper
900 g/2 lb raw tiger or king prawns (shrimp), peeled, de-veined and butterflied
lime wedges, to serve

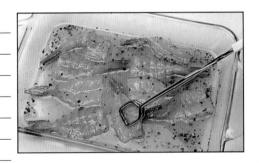

1 Combine the oil, fruit juices, garlic, allspice, chilli flakes and seasoning in a large, shallow baking dish. Add the prawns (shrimp) and turn to coat completely with the spiced oil.

2 Cover the dish and leave to marinate for 1 hour at room temperature, or for at least 2 hours in the refrigerator.

3 Preheat a grill (broiler).

4 Spread out the prawns in one layer in the baking dish, arranging them cut-side up as much as possible. Grill (broil) about 10 cm/4 in from the heat for 6–8 minutes or until the flesh becomes opaque. There is no need to turn them.

5 Serve hot, with lime wedges.

A SELECTION OF FISH VARIETIES

Choose the freshest fish you can find. If necessary, substitute another variety with similar qualities and use this guide to experiment with varieties you are unsure of.

LEAN FISH

Bream
- round fish, saltwater
- firm, moist texture; delicate, sweet flavour
- fry, grill, bake, steam
- substitute red mullet, John Dory

Brill
- flat fish, saltwater
- fine texture; delicate flavour
- fry, grill, bake, steam, poach
- substitute other flat fish

Cod
- round fish, saltwater
- flaky texture; mild flavour
- grill, bake, steam, poach
- substitute haddock, halibut

Haddock
- round fish, saltwater
- soft, moist texture; mild flavour
- grill, bake, steam, poach
- substitute cod, halibut

Hake
- round fish, saltwater
- white flesh with good flavour
- grill, bake, steam, poach
- substitute cod, haddock

Halibut
- flat fish, saltwater
- firm, moist texture; mild, sweet flavour
- grill, bake, steam, poach
- substitute plaice, sole

John Dory
- flat fish, saltwater
- flaky texture; nutty sweet flavour
- poach, bake, grill, steam
- substitute brill, halibut

Plaice
- flat fish, saltwater
- fine texture; delicate flavour
- fry, grill, bake, steam
- substitute sole, other flat fish

Sea bass
- round fish, saltwater
- flaky or firm flesh; mild flavour
- grill, fry, bake,
- substitute salmon, grey mullet, John Dory

Skate
- flattened body with large fins (wings), saltwater
- flaky, well-flavoured flesh
- fry, grill, poach, steam

Sole (Dover and lemon)
- flat fish, saltwater
- fine texture; delicate flavour
- fry, grill, bake, poach
- substitute plaice

Turbot
- flat fish, saltwater
- succulent; firm yet tender; superb flavour
- bake, grill, poach, steam
- substitute brill, John Dory

MODERATELY LEAN FISH

Grey mullet
- round fish, saltwater
- delicate, easily digested flesh
- fry, grill, poach, bake

Monkfish
- round, saltwater
- firm texture; sweet, similar to lobster
- fry, grill, bake, poach, stew
- substitute cod, halibut

Red mullet
- round fish, saltwater
- delicate texture with excellent flavour
- grill, bake, fry
- substitute trout

Swordfish
- thick central bone, saltwater
- firm, meaty texture; mild flavour
- grill, bake, steam, poach
- substitute dogfish/rock salmon, tuna

Trout
- round fish, freshwater
- tender, flaky texture; delicate flavour
- fry, grill, bake
- substitute sea trout, small salmon

Tuna
- thick central bone, saltwater
- some varieties more oily
- firm, meaty texture; strong flavour
- bake, steam, poach, grill
- substitute swordfish, rock salmon

OILY FISH

Carp
- round fish, freshwater
- soft, flaky texture; mild flavour
- bake, grill, fry, steam
- substitute cod, haddock

Herring
- round fish, saltwater
- moist and tender; rich flavour
- grill, bake, fry
- substitute mackerel

Mackerel
- round fish, saltwater
- moist and tender or firm texture; rich, distinctive flavour
- grill, bake, fry
- substitute herring

Salmon
- round fish, freshwater/saltwater
- flaky, tender texture; rich flavour
- bake, grill, steam, poach
- substitute large sea trout

Sea trout/salmon trout
- round fish, saltwater
- moist, flaky texture; mild flavour
- grill, bake, fry
- substitute salmon, rainbow trout

COOKING WITH VEGETABLES, FRUIT AND EGGS

Vegetables, fruit and eggs are extremely versatile and nutritious foods, which should be regularly included in any diet; vegetable and fruit on a daily basis, eggs perhaps less often. Whether served either on their own or as accompaniments to meat, poultry or fish, they should always be appetizing.

Knowing how to prepare and present vegetables can make all the difference to how they are received by the diner. What might often appear as boring extras accompanying more 'important' food, always deserve to be presented in their best guise, tempting diners to enjoy them for their own sakes. For flavour and goodness, vegetables should always be selected as fresh as possible, and generally younger rather than older. They should always be simply prepared and cooked, in the manner that produces the best result for the vegetable concerned. Knowing whether a vegetable should be peeled or scrubbed, how to successfully remove grit, and even how to cut or chop it are all just as important to its eventual success at the table as knowing whether it would be best boiled, baked, fried or braised.

Fruit is often overlooked as a healthy dessert, with a sugary confection often winning out over the less tantalizing prospect of a peeled orange or bunch of grapes. The answer is to prepare fresh fruit, particularly when in season, so that it becomes a tempting dessert in its own right. Melons and pineapples can be transformed into attractive vessels for delicious fruit salads, ice creams or sorbets. And refreshing fruit ices and sorbets, which do not require the addition of cream, are easy to make.

Eggs are an extremely nutritious food that can be prepared in numerous ways to create a wide range of savoury or sweet dishes. Cooking methods such as boiling, poaching and scrambling are simple, but do need to be done in just the right way to ensure perfection. Omelettes and souffles require only marginally more skill and, with the addition of various other ingredients, any cook can produce endless variety. Mixing eggs with flour and liquid produces batters which can be used to make savoury puddings or pancakes (crêpes). The latter can be turned into savoury treats or sweet desserts.

OPPOSITE Whether served as an accompaniment or on their own, vegetables, fruit and eggs are always versatile, nutritious and delicious.

PREPARING AND COOKING VEGETABLES

To enjoy their full flavour, fresh vegetables are often best prepared and served in simple ways. These guidelines for vegetable preparation and cooking will help you to make the most of seasonal bounty.

Serving ideas include suggested amounts of raw prepared vegetable to serve per person. Season all dishes according to taste.

ROOTS AND BULBS
Carrots
Preparation: If carrots are young, just trim the ends and scrub well; peel larger carrots. Leave whole or cut as specified in the recipe.

Cooking: *To boil*, drop into boiling salted water and simmer until just tender: 8–10 minutes for whole baby carrots, 10–20 minutes for larger whole carrots, 4–10 minutes for sliced or grated carrots. *To steam*, cook whole baby carrots, covered, over boiling water for about 10 minutes. *To braise*, cook whole baby carrots or thinly sliced carrots with 45 ml/3 tbsp stock or water and 30 g/1 oz/2 tbsp butter per 450 g/1 lb, tightly covered, for about 5 minutes. Boil, uncovered, to evaporate excess liquid before serving.

Serving ideas (115 g/4 oz each)
- Dress hot carrots with butter and chopped fresh herbs.
- Add a little sugar or honey and a squeeze of lemon or orange juice when braising; or try spices such as nutmeg, ginger or curry powder.
- Serve raw carrot sticks with a dip.

Parsnips
Preparation: Trim and peel. Leave small parsnips whole; cut up large ones.

Cooking: *To roast*, blanch in boiling salted water, then put in a roasting tin (pan) with butter or oil and cook in a 200°C/400°F/Gas 6 oven for about 40 minutes. Baste occasionally. *To boil*, simmer in salted water for 5–10 minutes. *To fry*, blanch in boiling water for 1–2 minutes and drain. Fry in butter for 10–12 minutes.

Serving ideas (145 g/5 oz each)
- Sauté sliced parsnips with sliced carrots; sprinkle with chopped herbs.
- Bake 600 g/1¼ lb parsnips with 150 ml/¼ pint/⅔ cup orange juice and 45 g/1½ oz/3 tbsp butter, covered, in a 180°C/350°F/Gas 4 oven for 1 hour.

Swede (Rutabaga)
Preparation: Peel, removing all tough skin and roots. Cut as recipe specifies.

Cooking: *To boil*, simmer chunks or slices in salted water for 15 minutes or until tender. *To braise*, cook with 30 g/1 oz/2 tbsp butter and 75 ml/5 tbsp stock or water per 450 g/1 lb, covered, for 5–7 minutes. *To roast*, put chunks around meat and coat with fat. Roast at 200°C/400°F/Gas 6 for 45 minutes.

Serving ideas (145 g/5 oz each)
- Braise 600 g/1¼ lb grated swede (rutabaga) seasoned with 15 ml/1 tbsp brown sugar and 5 ml/1 tsp soy sauce.
- Mash 600 g/1¼ lb boiled swede; beat in 2 eggs, 60 ml/4 tbsp cream, 30 ml/2 tbsp flour and 1.25 ml/¼ tsp nutmeg. Bake in a buttered dish in a 180°C/350°F/Gas 4 oven for 30 minutes.

Potatoes
Preparation: If the potato skins will be eaten, scrub them well. Otherwise, peel potatoes.

Cooking: *To bake*, prick skins and bake in a 200°C/400°F/Gas 6 oven: 1–1½ hours or 30–40 minutes for sweet potatoes. *To boil*, put into cold salted water, bring to a boil, and simmer for 10–20 minutes. *To roast*, blanch for 1–2 minutes and drain. Put around meat in a roasting tin (pan) and roast for 1–1½ hours. *To sauté*, boil until partly cooked, then fry slices in butter until crisp. *To deep-fry* (chips), cut into sticks, soak in cold water for 30 minutes and drain. Fry in oil heated to 190°C/375°F until beginning to colour: 3–7 minutes. Drain, then fry again for 3 minutes until golden.

Serving ideas (170 g/6 oz each)
- Dress boiled new potatoes with butter and chopped parsley and mint.
- Mash boiled or baked sweet potatoes. Add butter to taste, orange juice to moisten and ground cinnamon.

Onions

Preparation: Peel off the papery skin, then slice, chop, etc. as the recipe specifies. For spring onions (scallions), trim the root end and cut off any wilted or discoloured green leaves. Cut as specified, using just the white bulbs or both white and green parts.

Cooking: *To fry*, cook chopped or sliced onions, uncovered, in butter and/or oil over moderate heat, stirring occasionally, for about 5 minutes or until soft and translucent. If directed, continue cooking until the onions are golden brown. *To slow-cook*, cook sliced or chopped onions, covered, in butter and/or oil over low heat, stirring occasionally, for about 30 minutes or until very soft and golden. *To boil* small onions, drop into a pan of boiling salted water and simmer for about 15–20 minutes or until tender.

Serving ideas
● Top hamburgers or steaks with slow-cooked sliced onions.
● Combine 450 g/1 lb boiled button (pearl) onions with 45 g/1½ oz/3 tbsp butter and 70 g/2½ oz/5 tbsp soft light brown sugar; cook over a low heat, stirring, for about 10 minutes or until the sugar has caramelized.
● Trim all but 5 cm/2 in of green from spring onions (scallions). Stir-fry in hot oil and sprinkle with soy sauce.
● Use thin slices of sweet red onions raw in salads.

Leeks

Preparation: Trim the root end and the dark green leaves, leaving just the pale green and white. (Save the dark green leaves for the stockpot.) Unless you are going to cook the leeks whole, slit them open lengthwise, to the centre. Put them in cold water and soak for about 20 minutes, then drain well. If slicing or chopping leeks, do this before rinsing them thoroughly under cold water.

Cooking: *To braise*, cook with 30 g/1 oz/2 tbsp butter and 75 ml/5 tbsp stock or water per 450 g/1 lb, tightly covered, until just tender. *To boil*, drop into boiling salted water or stock and simmer for 10–15 minutes or until tender. *To steam*, cook in a covered steamer over boiling water, allowing approximately 5–7 minutes for sliced or whole baby leeks.

Serving ideas (170 g/6 oz each)
● Boil whole leeks, then cool slightly. Marinate in a vinaigrette dressing; serve the leeks cool, not cold.
● Toss hot sliced leeks with butter and fresh herbs such as sage, tarragon, thyme or parsley.

FRUITING VEGETABLES

Aubergines (Eggplant)

Preparation: Trim off the stalk end. Leave whole or cut according to the recipe instructions.

Cooking: *To grill (broil)*, brush cut surfaces with oil. Grill, 7.5–10 cm/3–4 in from the heat, for 10 minutes or until tender and well-browned; turn once and brush with oil. *To fry*, coat slices or thick sticks with flour if recipe specifies, then fry in hot oil or butter for 5 minutes on each side or until golden. *To braise*, brown slices or wedges in a little hot oil, add 60 ml/4 tbsp stock or water per 450 g/1 lb, cover and cook for 12 minutes or until tender. *To bake*, prick whole aubergines all over with a fork. Bake in a 200°C/400°F/Gas 6 oven for about 20 minutes or until soft.

Serving ideas (145 g/5 oz each)
● Baste grilled aubergines (broiled eggplant) with garlic- and herb-flavoured olive oil.
● When braising aubergines, after browning add skinned, seeded and chopped tomatoes and basil.

Courgettes (Zucchini)

Preparation: Trim the ends from courgettes (zucchini). Cut as specified.

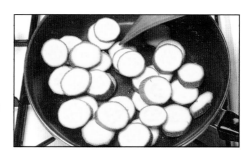

Cooking: *To fry*, cook sliced courgettes in butter or oil for 5–10 minutes or until tender and golden brown. *To boil*, drop into boiling salted water and simmer until tender: 10–12 minutes for whole courgettes, 3–8 minutes for slices. *To steam*, cook in a covered steamer over boiling water until tender. *To braise*, cook sliced courgettes in a covered pan, with 30 g/1 oz/2 tbsp butter and 75 ml/5 tbsp stock or water per 450 g/1 lb, for 4–5 minutes or until tender.

Serving ideas (115–145 g/4–5 oz each)
● Sauté sliced courgettes (zucchini) with finely chopped garlic and chopped fresh parsley and oregano.
● Cut small courgettes in half lengthwise and spread the cut surfaces with wholegrain mustard. Grill (broil) 10 cm/4 in from the heat for about 5 minutes or until tender but still firm.

PREPARING AND COOKING VEGETABLES (continued)

COOKING WITH VEGETABLES, FRUIT AND EGGS

LEAFY, GREEN AND OTHER VEGETABLES

Spinach

Preparation: Spinach can hide a lot of grit, so it needs careful rinsing. Immerse in cold water, swish round and soak for 3–4 minutes. Lift out the spinach and immerse in fresh cold water, repeat, then drain. Pull off tough stalks.

Cooking: *To steam-boil*, put into a large pan with no extra water. Cook for 5–7 minutes, stirring occasionally to help evaporate the liquid. Drain well and press the spinach between two plates or squeeze it in your fist. *To braise*, cook, covered, with a large knob of butter until wilted. Uncover and boil to evaporate excess liquid. *To stir-fry*, cook small or shredded leaves in hot oil for 3–5 minutes or until wilted.

Serving ideas (145–175 g/5–6 oz each)
● Add 30–45 ml/3–4 tbsp double (heavy) or whipping cream and mix a generous pinch of grated nutmeg into braised spinach.
● Steam-boil spinach leaves; chop finely after draining. Fry in olive oil with chopped garlic, stirring, until the garlic just starts to turn golden.
● Combine equal parts of chopped cooked spinach and cooked rice with butter and seasoning to taste.

Green beans

Preparation: Top and tail using scissors or a knife. For older beans with strings, snap off the ends, pulling the strings from the sides as you do so. Cut large beans diagonally or into slivers.

Cooking: *To boil*, drop into boiling salted water and simmer until just tender but still crisp and bright green: 3–15 minutes, according to size. *To steam*, cook in a covered steamer over boiling water until tender. *To braise*, cook tightly covered, with about 75 ml/ 5 tbsp stock or water and 30 g/1 oz/2 tbsp butter per 450 g/1 lb, until tender. *To stir-fry*, blanch in boiling water for 2 minutes; drain, refresh and dry. Stir-fry in hot oil for 2–3 minutes.

Serving ideas (115 g/4 oz each)
● Dress boiled or steamed beans with melted butter, chopped herbs and a squeeze of lemon juice.
● Add 90 ml/6 tbsp cream to 450 g/1 lb braised beans. Cook uncovered, stirring, until the liquid has reduced and the beans are glazed.

Peas

Preparation: If green peas are in the pod, split the pods open and pop out the peas. Top and tail mange-tout (snow peas) and sugar-snap peas, and pull any tough strings from the sides.

Cooking: *To steam*, cook in a covered steamer over boiling water until tender. *To boil*, drop into boiling salted water

and simmer until tender: 5–10 minutes for peas, 1–2 minutes for mange-tout. *To braise*, cook covered, with 30 g/1 oz/ 2 tbsp butter and 60 ml/4 tbsp stock or water per 450 g/1 lb, until tender: 5–10 minutes for green peas, 2 minutes for mange-tout and sugar-snap peas.

Serving ideas (115 g/4 oz each)
● Add sliced spring onions (scallions), shredded lettuce and a little sugar when braising green peas.
● Stir-fry mange-tout (snow peas) with sliced onions and mushrooms.
● Add 60 ml/4 tbsp whipping cream to 450 g/1 lb braised sugar-snap peas and cook uncovered, stirring, until almost all the liquid has evaporated.

Broccoli

Preparation: Trim off the end of the stalk. According to recipe instructions, leave the head whole or cut off the florets, taking a little stalk with each one. Cut the remainder of the peeled stalk across into thin slices.

Cooking: *To steam*, cook in a covered steamer over boiling water until tender. *To boil*, drop into boiling salted water and simmer until just tender: 7–12 minutes for whole, 4–6 minutes for florets and stalks. *To braise*, cook covered, with 75 ml/5 tbsp stock or water and 30 g/1 oz/2 tbsp butter per 450 g/1 lb, until tender.

Serving ideas (145 g/5 oz each)
● Toss hot broccoli with butter mixed with chopped fresh herbs.
● Cover hot broccoli with a cheese

sauce, sprinkle with grated Parmesan and brown under a grill (broiler).

● Blanch small broccoli florets for 1 minute; drain and refresh. Serve cold dressed with vinaigrette and sprinkled with toasted nuts.

Cauliflower

Preparation: Cut away the large green leaves. Trim the stalk level with the head. Cut out the core. Leave the head whole, or break into florets before or after cooking.

Cooking: *To steam,* cook florets in a covered steamer over boiling water for 12–15 minutes. *To steam-boil,* place core-down in a pan with 2.5 cm/1 in boiling salted water and a bay leaf. Cover and cook until just tender: 15–30 minutes for whole heads, 5–9 minutes for florets. Drain well. *To braise,* cook florets covered, with 30 g/1 oz/2 tbsp butter and 75 ml/5 tbsp stock or water per 450 g/1 lb, for 5–7 minutes.

Serving ideas (145 g/5 oz each)
● Dress hot cauliflower with butter; sprinkle with chopped fresh chives, toasted flaked almonds or chopped pecan nuts, or paprika.
● Coat florets in egg and crumbs, then deep-fry and serve with mayonnaise flavoured with garlic or a little Worcestershire sauce and a dash of Tabasco sauce.

Cabbage

Preparation: Discard any wilted or discoloured outer leaves. Cut the heads into small wedges or halve long, loose heads. Cut out the stalk from the wedges before cooking, or quarter heads and shred them. Leave loose heads whole and cut across the leaves to shred.

Cooking: *To braise,* quickly blanch chopped or shredded green, Savoy or red cabbage. (There is no need to blanch Chinese leaves.) Cook tightly covered, with about 75 ml/5 tbsp stock or water and 30 g/1 oz/2 tbsp butter per 450 g/1 lb, allowing 3–4 minutes for green, Savoy and Chinese leaves and 30 minutes for red cabbage (use more liquid). *To boil,* drop into boiling salted water and simmer until just tender: 6–8 minutes for wedges and 3–5 minutes for shredded green, Savoy or Chinese leaves. *To steam,* cook in a covered steamer over boiling water until tender.

Serving ideas (115 g/4 oz each)
● Blanch larger outer leaves of green or Savoy cabbage, then roll them up around a minced-meat stuffing and simmer in a rich tomato sauce.
● Add sliced apples, cooked diced bacon and spices (cinnamon, nutmeg) when braising red cabbage.
● Use shredded Chinese leaves raw in tossed salads.

Brussels sprouts

Preparation: Remove any discoloured leaves. Cut an 'X' in the base of the stalk so that it will cook in the same time as the rest.

Cooking: *To braise,* put in a pan, with 75 ml/5 tbsp stock or water and 30 g/ 1 oz/2 tbsp butter per 450 g/1 lb. Cover tightly for cooking. *To boil,* drop into boiling salted water and simmer for 7–10 minutes or until just tender but not soft. *To steam,* cook in a covered steamer over boiling water for about 10–12 minutes.

Serving ideas (115–145 g/4–5 oz each)
● Toss with butter and orange zest and serve immediately.
● Toss with toasted nuts, braised or poached chestnuts or some canned water chestnuts.
● Shred and blanch for 2–3 minutes; drain and refresh in cold water. Add chopped onion and celery and toss with a vinaigrette dressing.
● Cut the heads in half lengthwise and blanch in boiling water for about 2–3 minutes, then drain and refresh in cold water. Stir-fry in hot oil with a little finely chopped ginger and garlic for about 2–3 minutes or until tender and lightly browned.

CAULIFLOWER CHEESE

Cut a large cauliflower into florets and steam until just tender. Spread in a buttered gratin dish and scatter over 85g/3 oz sliced, fried mushrooms. Pour 600ml/1 pint cheese sauce evenly over the top and sprinkle with a mixture of grated Cheddar and fine breadcrumbs. Brown quickly under a hot grill (broiler) until golden. *Serves 4.*

CHOPPING AND SHREDDING VEGETABLES

In countless recipes, vegetables are required to be chopped or shredded to varying degrees of fineness. Rough chopping requires no skill, but when a vegetable plays a starring role in a dish, it can be cut into neat shapes such as cubes or dice or matchstick shapes known as 'julienne'; this also promotes even cooking. For most cutting, a large, sharp chef's knife should be used. You can also use a food processor, but take care not to over-process the vegetables to a pulp (this can happen very quickly with juicy kinds like onions, leeks, celery and peppers).

TIP

Vegetable preparation is easy, and much safer, with a sharp knife. Hone the knife's cutting edge regularly with a sharpening steel.

SHREDDING LEAVES

Individual leaves of vegetables such as cabbage, lettuce, spinach and some herbs can be cut into neat shreds. Stack 6–8 leaves and roll up tightly, parallel with the central rib; if the leaves are very large, roll them up individually. Slice across the roll into shreds of the required thickness, guiding the knife with your knuckles. Make sure the knife is very sharp and cut straight down through the roll.

CUBING AND DICING

Cubes are 1.5 cm/½ in square, and dice are generally 3–6 mm/⅛–¼ in square. Cut a long vegetable, like a carrot or celery, into 7.5cm/3 in pieces and shave off any curved sides. Lay each piece flat and cut it lengthwise into uniform slices of the required thickness. Then stack the slices and cut lengthwise into uniform strips. Gather the strips together and cut across to make cubes or dice.

CHOPPING

1 **To chop an onion:** Peel it, leaving on the root, then cut in half through the root. Holding one onion half steady at the root end, make horizontal cuts to the root but without cutting through it. Make vertical lengthwise cuts in the onion half, again not cutting the root. Cut across the onion to chop it, guiding the side of the knife with your knuckles.

2 **To chop fresh herbs:** Hold the leaves or sprigs together in a bunch and chop coarsely. Then chop finely: holding the tip of the knife on the board, raise and lower the handle with your other hand, moving the blade back and forth over the herb. You can also use this method for fine-chopping vegetables and root ginger. For garlic, alternate the chopping with crushing, using the flat side of the blade, until it is almost a paste.

CUTTING MATCHSTICKS

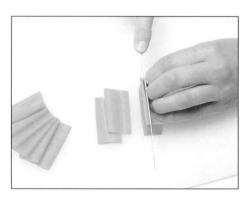

For vegetable matchsticks or 'julienne', cut across the peeled vegetable into pieces about 5 cm/2 in long. Lay each piece flat and cut it lengthwise into 3 mm/⅛ in thick slices. Stack the slices and cut them lengthwise into strips about 3 mm/⅛ in thick or less.

BLANCHING AND SWEATING VEGETABLES

Vegetables are often blanched, that is placed briefly in boiling water, as an initial cooking process prior to stir-frying or roasting or if they are to be briefly re-heated in butter before serving. Some are also blanched to be used in a salad. The process can also help to loosen the skins before skinning (tomatoes, peaches and nuts), to set colour and flavour (before freezing) or to reduce bitterness. After blanching, most foods are 'refreshed' stop them cooking any further.

Sweating is another common preliminary step in vegetable cooking, particularly for onions and leeks. This process, essentially a form of steaming, draws out the juices and develops the vegetable's flavour. Use a pan with a heavy base that will conduct the heat evenly, so the vegetables don't stick or burn, and make sure that the lid is tight fitting to keep in moisture.

BLANCHING AND REFRESHING

1 **To blanch:** Immerse the food in a large pan of boiling water (ideally use a wire basket or sieve so the vegetable can be lifted out easily). Bring the water back to the boil for the time specified, usually 1–2 minutes. Remove the vegetable from the water.

2 **To refresh:** Quickly immerse the vegetable in iced water or hold under cold running water. If the recipe specifies, leave until it has cooled completely. Drain well.

SKINNING TOMATOES

Cut a small cross in the skin at the base of each tomato. Immerse, 3 or 4 at a time, in boiling water. Once the cut skin begins to roll back, in about 10 seconds, lift the tomatoes out and immerse in iced water. Drain and peel.

SWEATING

1 Heat fat (usually butter) in a heavy saucepan or frying pan over a low heat. Add the vegetable and stir to coat with the melted fat.

2 Cover the pan tightly and cook gently until the vegetable is softened but not brown; onions will be translucent. This can take 10–15 minutes or longer. Stir occasionally during the cooking.

PREPARING ASPARAGUS

When asparagus is young and tender, you need do nothing more than trim off the ends of the stalks before cooking. However, larger spears, with stalk ends that are tough and woody, require some further preparation.

COOKING UPRIGHT

Asparagus spears can be cooked loose and flat in simmering water (as described below) or they can be tied into bundles and cooked standing upright in a tall pot. With the latter method, the tips are kept above the water so they cook gently in the steam.

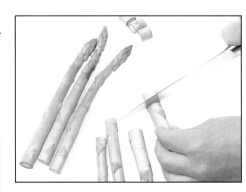

1 Cut off the tough, woody ends. Cut the spears so that they are all roughly the same length.

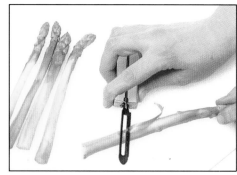

2 If you like, remove the skin. To do this, hold a spear just below the tip. Using a vegetable peeler, shave off the skin, working lengthwise to the end of the stalk. Roll the spear so that you can remove the skin from all sides.

ASPARAGUS WITH HAM

SERVES 4

700–900 g/1 ½–2 lb medium-sized
  asparagus spears, prepared for cooking

180 ml/6 fl oz/¾ cup clarified butter (see
  below right)

10 ml/2 tsp lemon juice

30 ml/2 tbsp chopped spring onions
  (scallions)

15 ml/1 tbsp chopped parsley

salt and pepper

4 slices Parma ham (prosciutto)

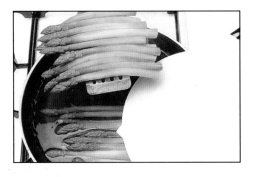

1 Half-fill a frying pan with salted water. Bring to a boil. Simmer asparagus spears for 4–5 minutes or until they are just tender. (Pierce the stalk to test.) Remove and drain well.

2 Combine the butter, lemon juice, spring onions (scallions) and parsley in a small saucepan. Season with salt and pepper to taste. Gently heat the mixture until it is lukewarm.

3 Divide the asparagus among 4 warm plates. Drape a slice of ham over each portion. Spoon over the herb butter and serve.

CLARIFIED BUTTER

Put the butter in a heavy saucepan over a low heat. Melt gently. Skim off all the froth from the surface. You will then see a clear yellow layer on top of a milky layer. Carefully pour the clear fat into a bowl. Discard the milky residue.

GREEN SALAD WITH ORANGES AND AVOCADO

SERVES 4

1 round lettuce

1 small bunch of watercress

a few leaves of frisée lettuce

1 small bunch of rocket (arugula)

1 red onion, thinly sliced into rings

2 seedless oranges, peeled and segmented

1 ripe avocado, peeled, stoned (pitted) and cubed

55 g/2 oz/½ cup walnut pieces, toasted

FOR THE DRESSING

90 ml/6 tbsp olive oil

15 ml/1 tbsp walnut oil

45 ml/3 tbsp lemon juice

30 ml/2 tbsp orange juice

5 ml/1 tsp grated orange zest

5 ml/1 tsp Dijon mustard

pinch of caster (superfine) sugar

salt and pepper

1 Combine all the dressing ingredients in a bowl or screw-top jar. Whisk or shake together well.

VARIATION

For Green Salad with Tuna and Peppers, omit the oranges and walnut pieces. Add 1 × 200 g/7 oz can drained, flaked tuna and 1 roasted red pepper, peeled and sliced.

2 Put the rinsed and crisped salad greens in a bowl and add the onion, orange segments and avocado.

3 Add the dressing and toss the salad to combine well. Scatter the walnuts on top and serve immediately.

PREPARING FRESH FRUIT

Fresh fruit presented in unusual ways can make a table look very attractive, and will be a real talking point at a party. The ideas shown here take very little time to carry out.

Pineapples, for example, can be prepared in many decorative ways in addition to rings, spears and cubes.

Melons make attractive containers for salads, both sweet and savoury. Small melons can be used for individual servings, while large watermelons will hold salads to serve a crowd. Special tools, including melon cutters and melon-ball scoops, make decorative preparation easier.

Sorbets and fruit ices are most refreshing desserts. A fruit ice is made by freezing a sweetened fruit purée, whereas a sorbet is made from fruit juice or purée mixed with a sugar syrup. In addition, there are sorbets based on wine or liqueur. The Italian 'granita' uses the same mixture as a sorbet, but it is stirred during freezing to give it its characteristic coarse texture.

MAKING PINEAPPLE BOATS

1 Trim off any browned ends from the green leaves of the crown. Trim the stalk end if necessary. Using a long, sharp knife, cut the pineapple in half lengthwise, through the crown. Cut a thin slice from the base of each half so that it has a flat, stable surface and will not rock about.

2 Using a small, sharp knife, cut straight across the top and bottom of the central core in each half, then cut lengthwise at a slant on either side of the core. Remove the core.

3 Using a curved, serrated grapefruit knife, cut out the flesh from each half. The boats are now ready for filling with a salad, a dessert, or with ice cream, fruit ice or sorbet.

WATERMELON BASKET

Cut a watermelon basket as directed on the right, but leave a strip for the 'handle'. Scoop out the flesh using a melon-ball scoop and nick out the pips. Mix the melon balls with balls of charentais and honeydew melon, blueberries and strawberries. Pile the fruit into the basket.

PREPARING MELON

1 Cut a line around the circumference of the melon and insert a sharp knife on the line at an angle. Make a cut 1.5–5 cm/½–2 in long, according to the size of the melon, right into the centre. Insert the knife again at the top of the angled cut, and cut back to the line at a right-angle, forming a V-shape.

2 Continue in this way all round the melon, then lift the 2 halves apart. Remove the seeds and scoop out the flesh.

MAKING A FRUIT ICE

1 Prepare the fruit, removing peel, stones (pits), hulls, stalks, etc. Purée the fruit with sugar and liquid in a blender or food processor until very smooth. Be sure that the sugar has dissolved completely.

2 Add additional flavourings as directed in the recipe (alcohol or herbs, for example). If using berries with seeds (raspberries, blackberries, etc.), press the purée through a fine-mesh nylon sieve. Chill the purée well. Transfer to an ice-cream machine and freeze following the maker's instructions.

MAKING A SORBET

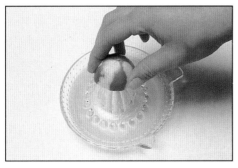

1 If you are using citrus fruit, peel off strips of zest. Squeeze the juice from the fruit. Alternatively, purée fruit in a blender or food processor (cooking it first if necessary).

2 Put the strips of zest (or other flavouring such as a vanilla pod or spices) in a saucepan with sugar and water and bring to a boil, stirring to dissolve the sugar. Leave to cool.

3 Stir in the fruit juice or purée. Strain the mixture into a bowl, if necessary, and chill well. Transfer the mixture to an ice-cream machine and freeze following the maker's instructions.

STILL-FREEZING FRUIT ICE

If you do not have an ice-cream machine, you can 'still-freeze' the fruit ice or sorbet in the freezer. Pour it into a metal tin (pan) or tray, cover and freeze until set round the edge. Turn it into a bowl and break it into small pieces. Beat with an electric mixer or in a food processor until slushy. Return to the tin and freeze again until set round the edge. Repeat the beating twice more, then freeze until firm.

STRAWBERRY ICE

Purée 500 g/1 lb 2 oz strawberries with 100 g/3½ oz caster (superfine) sugar and 120 ml/4 fl oz/½ cup orange juice. Be sure the sugar has dissolved completely. Add 15 ml/1 tbsp lemon juice. Taste the mixture and add more sugar or orange or lemon juice if required. (The mixture should be highly flavoured.) Chill well, then transfer to an ice-cream machine and freeze until firm. *Makes about 600 ml/1 pint.*

VARIATIONS

● Use raspberries or blackberries instead of strawberries, or, as another idea, 700 g/1½ lb peeled and sliced peaches or nectarines.
● Add 15–30 ml/1–2 tbsp of fruit liqueur (to match the fruit used).

BOILING, POACHING AND SCRAMBLING EGGS

The derisive expression, 'can't boil an egg', indicates the importance of this basic cooking skill, although, to be accurate, eggs are in fact simmered rather than boiled.

For many people, a boiled egg with toast is an everyday breakfast. But the soft-boiled egg and its cousin the coddled egg have many delicious applications. If you are going to peel them for serving, cook them for the longest time suggested below. The salt in the cooking water aids in peeling. Hard-boiled eggs can be used to make classic salads and sandwich fillings, as well as cold first course and buffet dishes and hot main dishes.

The perfect poached egg has a neat oval shape, a tender white and a soft yolk. It is unbeatable on a slice of hot buttered toast, or it can be partnered with vegetables (artichoke hearts, asparagus), seafood (crab, smoked salmon) or meat (ham, bacon, steak) and dressed with a rich sauce. Use the freshest eggs possible because they will be the easiest to poach.

Tender, creamy scrambled eggs are perfect for breakfast or brunch, but you can also add flavourings for a more unusual snack or supper dish.

IDEAS FOR SOFT-BOILED AND CODDLED EGGS

● For *Caviar-crowned Eggs*: cut the top 20 mm/¾ in from each egg, in its shell. Put a spoonful of soured (sour) cream on top, followed by a little caviar, for an exotic taste.
● For *Smoked-salmon Eggs*: prepare as above and top each egg with a spoonful each of soured cream and diced smoked salmon.
● Put a hot peeled egg in the centre of a bowl of cream-of-spinach or watercress soup to give it extra richness and flavour.

BOILING EGGS

1 To hard-boil eggs: Bring a pan of well-salted water to a boil. Using a slotted spoon, lower each egg into the water. Reduce the heat so that the water is just simmering. Cook for 10 minutes. Immediately plunge the eggs into a bowl of iced water to cool.

3 To coddle eggs: Lower them into a pan of boiling salted water. Cover the pan and remove it from the heat. Leave for 6–8 minutes or until the eggs are done to your taste. Lift out each egg, place in an egg cup and cut off the top of the shell for serving. Alternatively, to peel, plunge the eggs into a bowl of cold water. When they are cool enough to handle, peel carefully.

EGG MAYONNAISE

Chop several hard-boiled eggs. Mix with chopped spring onions (scallions) and chopped parsley to taste. Bind with mayonnaise. Season with mustard.

2 When the eggs are cool enough to handle, peel them. If you do not intend to use them immediately, keep the peeled eggs in a bowl of cold, salted water. Alternatively, store the eggs, still in their shells, in the refrigerator; they will keep for up to a week.

4 To soft-boil eggs: Bring a pan of well-salted water to a boil. Using a slotted spoon, lower in each egg. Reduce the heat so that the water just simmers. Cook for 3–5 minutes or until the eggs are done to your taste (depending on how firm you like the white; the yolk will be runny).

HARD-BOILED-EGG TIPS

● Always cool hard-boiled eggs in iced water. The abrupt temperature change helps to prevent a grey layer from forming round the yolk.
● To peel hard-boiled eggs, tap them on a hard surface to crack the shell. Peel under cold running water.

EGG, POTATO AND BEAN SALAD

Bring a pot of salted water to a boil. Add 450 g/1 lb small, unpeeled new potatoes. Bring back to a boil and simmer for 10 minutes. Add 225 g/8 oz green beans and simmer for 4–5 minutes or until the potatoes and beans are just tender. Drain well in a colander and refresh under cold running water. Turn the vegetables into a large bowl. Sprinkle 60 ml/4 tbsp olive oil and 30 ml/2 tbsp balsamic vinegar over them. Season with salt and pepper to taste and toss well. Scatter 2 grated hard-boiled eggs and 45 ml/3 tbsp coarsely shredded mixed fresh mint and basil over the top. Serve the salad warm or at room temperature. *Serves 4–6.*

SCRAMBLING EGGS

1 Put the eggs in a bowl and add a little salt and pepper. Beat the eggs with a fork until they are well blended. Melt butter in a frying pan over a moderately low heat (there should be enough to cover the bottom of the pan fairly generously). Pour in the beaten eggs.

2 Cook, scraping up and turning the eggs over, for 3–5 minutes or until they are softly set and still moist. The eggs will continue to cook after being removed from the heat, so undercook them slightly even if you prefer a firmer end result.

POACHING EGGS

1 Bring a large, deep pan of water to a gentle boil. Break each egg and slip into the water. Reduce the heat to low so that the water just simmers. Poach for 3–4 minutes or until the eggs are cooked to your liking.

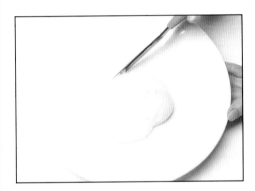

2 Using a slotted spoon, lift out each egg and press it gently; the white should feel just firm to the touch but the yolk should still be soft.

3 If there are any strings of cooked egg white, trim them off with a knife or kitchen scissors. Drain briefly on paper towels. Serve immediately, if wished, or warm the eggs in a bowl of hot water for serving. If the eggs will be served cold, immerse them in a bowl of iced water until ready to serve. Drain and gently blot dry before serving.

THE CLOTTING FACTOR

If your eggs are not really fresh, adding white-wine vinegar to the poaching water will help the egg white to coagulate, although it will flavour the egg slightly. Use 30 ml/2 tbsp vinegar to 1 litre/2 pints water.

IDEAS FOR ENLIVENING SCRAMBLED EGGS

- Add chopped fresh herbs (chives, tarragon) to the eggs.
- Cook diced vegetables (onions, mushrooms, peppers) or ham in butter before adding the eggs.
- Stir in a little grated cheese or bits of full-fat soft cheese just before the eggs are ready.
- Fold some peeled, cooked prawns (shrimp) into scrambled eggs.

MAKING ROLLED OMELETTES AND SOUFFLES

The versatile rolled or folded omelette can be served plain or filled with a range of ingredients. There are also flat omelettes and soufflé omelettes. At its simplest, an omelette is made with 2 or 3 eggs, 5–10 ml/1–2 tsp water, and salt and pepper.

Despite their reputation as tricky, soufflés are not difficult to make. The base for a soufflé is simply a thick sauce (sweet or savoury) or a purée. Into this, stiffly whisked egg whites are folded, and the whole is baked until it has risen and is lightly set. Proper preparation of the dish, enabling the soufflé to 'climb' up the sides, will encourage good rising. Generously butter or oil the dish, including the top edge. If the recipe specifies, coat the bottom and sides with a thin layer of fine crumbs, sugar, etc., before adding the mixture. Serve the soufflé as soon as it is cooked.

IDEAS FOR OMELETTES

● Add 15 ml/1 tbsp chopped fresh herbs (a mixture of parsley, chives and tarragon, for example) to the beaten-egg mixture.
● Scatter 30–45 ml/2–3 tbsp grated cheese (Gruyère, Cheddar) over the omelette before folding it.
● Sauté skinned, seeded and chopped tomatoes in butter for 1–2 minutes. Season and stir in a little chopped fresh basil. Use to fill the omelette.
● Fill the omelette with strips of cooked ham or Parma ham (prosciutto), roasted vegetables, sautéed sliced mushrooms, sautéed potatoes, buttered asparagus tips or slow-cooked onions.
● Warm left-over pasta (buttered or in sauce); if the shape is long, such as spaghetti, cut it into short pieces. If using buttered pasta, add strips of canned pimiento, sliced black olives, capers, etc. Use to fill the omelette, fold and sprinkle with a little grated Parmesan or other cheese.

MAKING A ROLLED OMELETTE

1 Break the eggs into a bowl, and add the water and some salt and pepper. Beat with a fork until just blended but not frothy.

2 In a 20 cm/8 in omelette or frying pan, melt 30 ml/2 tbsp butter over a moderate heat. Rotate the pan to coat the bottom and sides with butter.

3 When the butter is foaming and just beginning to turn golden, pour in the egg mixture. Tilt and rotate the pan to spread the eggs in an even layer over the bottom.

4 Cook for 5–10 seconds or until the omelette starts to set. Using a palette knife (spatula), lift the cooked base and tilt the pan so that the uncooked egg mixture runs underneath. Continue in this way until most of the omelette is set but the top is still creamy.

5 Using the palette knife, loosen the edge of the omelette on one side and tilt the pan so that one-third of the omelette folds over on to itself.

6 Continue loosening the omelette from its folded edge, holding the pan over a warmed plate. As the omelette slides out, use the edge of the pan to guide it so that the omelette folds over again on itself into thirds.

MAKING A SOUFFLÉ

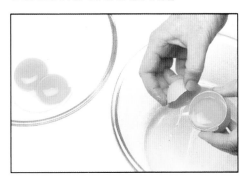

1 Separate the eggs, taking care that there is no trace of egg yolk in the whites. (It is best to separate 1 egg at a time and to check each white before adding to the rest.)

2 For a savoury soufflé, make a thick white sauce. Beat in the yolks and the soufflé flavouring. For a sweet soufflé, make a thick custard using the yolks; mix in the flavouring.

3 In a large, scrupulously clean bowl, whisk the egg whites until they hold stiff peaks. (Any grease on the bowl or beaters will prevent maximum volume.) If not using a copper bowl, add a pinch of cream of tartar once the whites are frothy. For a sweet soufflé, add sugar once the whites hold soft peaks (the tips flop over), then continue whisking.

4 Add one-quarter of the egg whites to the sauce base. Using a large metal spoon or a rubber spatula, stir in the whites to lighten the base. Add the remaining whites and fold them in as lightly as possible by cutting down with the spatula to the bottom of the bowl and then turning over the mixture.

5 Spoon the mixture into the prepared dish. Bake in a preheated oven until the soufflé has risen about 5 cm/2 in above the rim of the dish and is lightly browned. Serve the soufflé immediately because it will only hold its puff for a few minutes, once out of the oven, before it begins to deflate.

SEPARATING EGGS

It is easier to separate the yolks and whites if eggs are cold, so take the eggs straight from the refrigerator. Tap the egg once or twice against the rim of a small bowl to crack the shell. Break open the shell and hold half in each hand. Carefully transfer the unbroken yolk from one half shell to the other several times, letting the egg white dribble into the bowl. Put the yolk in a second bowl.

CHEESE SOUFFLÉ

Butter a 1.5 litre/2½ pint soufflé dish and coat it with a layer of breadcrumbs. Make 300 ml/½ pint/1¼ cups thick white sauce (see sauces). Add 4 egg yolks and 115 g/4 oz grated cheese such as Gruyère, mature (sharp) Cheddar, blue, or a mixture of Parmesan and Gruyère. If you like, season the mixture with 10 ml/2 tsp Dijon mustard. Whisk 6 egg whites until stiff, then fold into the sauce base. Bake in a 200°C/400°F/Gas 6 oven for about 20–25 minutes until well-risen and golden brown on the top. Never open the oven door while a soufflé is cooking, as this will cause it to sink dramatically. *Serves 4.*

MAKING BATTER AND PANCAKES (CRÊPES)

Batter consists mainly of flour, eggs and liquid. It may be thick in consistency – for making fritters or coating food to be fried – or thin and pourable, for Yorkshire pudding, or other batter puddings, and pancakes. For a very light result, you can separate the eggs, whisk the whites and fold them in.

Thin, lacy pancakes, or crêpes, are wonderfully versatile. They can be served very simply with just lemon juice and sugar, or turned into more elaborate dishes: folded and warmed in a sauce, rolled round a savoury or sweet filling, or layered with a filling.

PORK AND APPLE BATTER PUDDINGS

Make the batter with 115 g/4 oz/1 cup plain (all-purpose) flour, a pinch of salt, 1 egg and 300 ml/½ pint/1¼ cups mixed milk and water. Mix together 450 g/1 lb pork sausagemeat (ground sausage), 115 g/4 oz/¾ cup finely chopped or coarsely grated cooking apple, 1 small grated onion, 15 ml/ 1 tbsp chopped fresh parsley, and salt and pepper. Form into 16 balls. Oil 4 600 ml/½ pint baking dishes and heat in a 220°C/425°F/Gas 7 oven. Divide the balls among the dishes and bake for 10 minutes. Pour over the batter and bake for 35–40 minutes or until risen and golden. Serve hot. *Serves 4.*

MAKING BATTER

1 Sift plain (all-purpose) flour into a bowl with other dry ingredients such as sugar, baking powder or bicarbonate of soda (baking soda), salt, ground spices, etc., as directed in the recipe.

2 Make a well in the centre of the dry ingredients and add the eggs or egg yolks and some of the liquid.

3 Using a wooden spoon, beat the eggs and liquid in the well just to mix them.

4 Gradually draw in some of the flour from the sides, stirring vigorously.

5 When the mixture is smooth, stir in the remaining liquid. Stir just until the ingredients are combined – the trick is not to overmix.

6 If the recipe specifies, whisk egg whites to a soft peak and fold them into the batter (made with yolks). Do this just before using the batter.

MAKING PANCAKES (CRÊPES)

MAKES ABOUT 12

170 g/6 oz/1½ cups plain (all-purpose) flour

10 ml/2 tsp caster (superfine) sugar (for sweet pancakes)

2 size 3 (medium) eggs

450 ml/¾ pint/scant 2 cups milk

about 30 g/1 oz/2 tbsp melted butter

1 Make the pancake batter and leave to stand for 20 minutes. Heat a 20 cm/8 in pancake (crêpe) or frying pan over a moderate heat. The pan is ready when a few drops of water sprinkled on the surface jump and sizzle immediately. Grease the pan lightly with a little melted butter. Pour 45–60 ml/3–4 tbsp batter into the pan. Quickly tilt and rotate the pan so that the batter spreads out to cover the bottom thinly and evenly; pour out any excess batter.

2 Cook for 30–45 seconds or until the pancake is set and small holes have appeared. If the cooking seems to be taking too long, increase the heat slightly. Lift the edge of the pancake, using a palette knife (spatula); the base of the pancake should be lightly brown. Shake the pan vigorously back and forth to loosen the pancake completely, then turn or flip it over. Cook the other side for about 30 seconds. Serve or leave to cool.

RICOTTA AND PEACH PANCAKES (CRÊPES)

Combine 450 g/1 lb ricotta cheese, 30 g/1 oz/4 tbsp icing (confectioners') sugar, 5 ml/1 tsp vanilla essence (extract) and 30 ml/2 tbsp brandy in a bowl. Mix well. Add 4 large, ripe peaches, peeled and diced, and fold in gently. Divide the ricotta and peach mixture among 12 pancakes (crêpes) and spread it evenly over them. Fold each pancake in half and then in half again, into quarters. Arrange the pancakes in a buttered large oval baking dish, slightly overlapping them. Brush with 30 g/1 oz/2 tbsp melted butter and sprinkle generously with icing sugar. Bake in a 190°C/375°F/Gas 5 oven for about 10 minutes. Serve hot. *Serves 6.*

3 To fill pancakes: For folded pancakes, spread 45–60 ml/3–4 tbsp of filling evenly over each pancake. Fold in half then in half again, into quarters. For rolled pancakes, put 45–60 ml/3–4 tbsp of filling near one edge of each pancake and roll up from that side. For pancake parcels, spoon 45–60 ml/3–4 tbsp of filling into the centre of each pancake. Fold in two opposite sides, over the filling, then fold in the other two sides. Turn the parcel over for serving. Filled pancakes are usually baked before serving, to re-heat them.

PANCAKE- (CRÊPE-) MAKING TIPS

- Pancake (crêpe) batter should be the consistency of whipping cream. If the batter is at all lumpy, strain it. If it does not flow smoothly to make a thin pancake, add a little more liquid.
- Like most batters, pancake batter can be made in a blender or food processor. Leave to stand before using.
- Your first pancake may well be unsuccessful because it will test the consistency of the batter and the temperature of the pan, both of which may need adjusting.
- If more convenient, pancakes can be made ahead of time. Cool, then stack them, interleaved with greaseproof (waxed) paper, and wrap in tin foil. They can be refrigerated for up to 3 days or frozen for 1 month.
- A pancake pan has a flat bottom and straight sides; these give the pancake a well-defined edge.

GRAINS, BREADS AND BAKING

Grains are an important staple food; they provide carbohydrate for energy and many vitamins essential to health. They can be used whole, with or without their bran, or they can be ground and processed to produce ingredients such as polenta (made from semolina) and couscous (made from sweetcorn).

Pasta, which is made from ground wheat, is available in dozens of shapes and in a variety of colours. It can be bought either fresh or dried and both types are straightforward to cook.

Rice is used as an intact grain, although white rice has had the bran removed. There are thousands of varieties of rice grown all over the world, with differing flavours and aromas. But for the cook, the choice of which rice to use in a dish is based mainly on the length of the grain. Long-grain rice has grains that are four to five times as long as they are wide. It is dry and fluffy after cooking with the grains remaining separate and is excellent steamed or baked, in pilafs or salads. Examples are Basmati, which is aromatic and much used in Indian cooking; brown long-grain has the nutritious bran layer left intact which gives it a nutty flavour

and chewy consistency; and white or polished long-grain rice has a milder flavour. Short-grain rice, with a round shape, is very starchy and tends to cling together after cooking; different varieties are used for puddings, risotto, croquettes, sushi, stir-fried rice and moulded rice dishes. Medium-grain rice is more tender than long-grain but less moist than short-grain. It is fluffy and separate if served hot, but clumps as it cools.

Flour, of course, is ground grain, usually wheat, and used to make bread and pastry. Bread can be made in endless variety using different additional ingredients as flavourings and to affect texture. One of the most popular breads today is pizza and although bases are readily available in shops, the dough is easy to make at home to which you can add your own toppings.

Freshly made pies and tarts are other favourites that every home cook can make once they have mastered the art of pastry-making. The secret lies in simply knowing how to do it, rather than requiring any great expertise. And with a little decorating know-how the results will be good-looking as well.

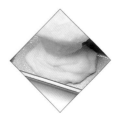

OPPOSITE One of the delights of home cooking is learning how to bake truly satisfying breads and bakes. Essential to a good diet, the results can also be irresistible.

COOKING RICE AND PASTA

There are many different ways to cook rice, and each has its adherents. The simplest is to cook rice in a large quantity of boiling water, then drain. However, valuable nutrients will be discarded in the water. The ways given here retain the rice's nutrients. Timings are for long-grain white rice (one part rice to two parts water).

Both fresh and dried pasta are cooked in the same way. The golden rules for success are: use plenty of water and keep checking the pasta to be sure it does not overcook.

Fresh pasta will cook much more quickly than dried – in 1–4 minutes as opposed to 5 minutes or more depending on the packet instructions. To test pasta to see if it is done, cut a piece in half. There should be no sign of opaque, uncooked pasta in the centre. Alternatively, bite it – it should be tender but still firm. In Italian, this is when it is 'al dente', or to the tooth.

If you are going to cook the pasta further, by baking it in a lasagne for example, undercook it slightly at this first stage. Pasta for a salad should also be a little under-cooked, so that it will not become soggy when it is mixed with the dressing.

COOKING PASTA

1 Bring a large pot of salted water to the boil. Use 4 litres/6 pints of water and 10 ml/2 tsp salt to 450 g/1 lb of pasta. Drop in the pasta all at once and stir to separate the shapes or strands.

2 If you are cooking spaghetti, allow the ends in the water to soften slightly and then gently push in the rest as soon as you can.

3 Bring the water back to the boil, then reduce the heat slightly and boil until the pasta is just done. To test, lift a piece of pasta out on a wooden fork or slotted spoon.

4 Drain the pasta well in a colander, shaking it vigorously to remove all excess water. Serve immediately because the pasta will continue to cook from its own heat.

COOKING RICE

1 To steam rice: Put the measured quantity of salted water in a saucepan. Bring it to the boil. Add the rice and stir. Bring back to the boil, cover and steam until tender. Remove from the heat and leave for 5 minutes.

2 To sauté and steam rice (pilaf): Heat oil or butter in a saucepan over moderate heat. Add the rice and stir to coat the grains. Sauté for 2–3 minutes. Add boiling water. Bring back to the boil, then cover and steam until tender.

3 To bake rice: Put the rice in a baking dish and add the measured quantity of boiling water. Cover with foil and bake in a preheated 180°C/ 350°F/Gas 4 oven until the water has been absorbed and the rice is tender.

PREPARING COUSCOUS AND POLENTA

A staple in North-African cooking, couscous is a type of tiny pasta made from semolina (which is ground from durum wheat). Its mild taste makes it the perfect accompaniment for spicy dishes, in particular the Moroccan and Tunisian stews also called couscous. It is delicious in stuffings for roasts and baked casseroles and even as a breakfast cereal.

Polenta is a coarse ground cornmeal, derived from sweetcorn, much used in Italian cooking. It may be served plain or mixed with butter and cheese, to take the place of rice or potatoes, or it can be cooled until firm, sliced and then fried or toasted.

COOKING POLENTA

Use four parts water to one part cornmeal. Bring the liquid just to the boil in a saucepan. Gradually add the polenta in a steady stream, stirring constantly. Do not add the polenta all at once or it will form lumps. Reduce the heat to low and simmer, uncovered, for 10–20 minutes or until thick and pulling away from the sides of the pan. Stir constantly. The polenta is now ready to be served or moulded.

If to be cooled and then later fried or toasted, put the polenta into an oiled or buttered pan or dish and leave it to cool completely.

Cut the set polenta into shapes or slices, about 1.5 cm/½ in thick.

COOKING COUSCOUS

1 To prepare regular couscous: Put the couscous in a sieve and rinse under cold running water until the water runs clear. Put the couscous in a bowl, cover with plenty of fresh cold water and soak for at least 30 minutes. Drain well in a sieve.

2 Rub the couscous in your fingers to be sure there are no lumps, then put it in a muslin-lined colander. Set over a pan of boiling water (or over the pot containing the spicy stew) and steam, uncovered, for 30 minutes or until soft and heated through.

3 To prepare quick-cooking couscous with water: Put the couscous in a bowl, cover with boiling water and soak for 20–30 minutes or until plump. Drain well. Use for salads.

4 To prepare quick-cooking couscous with stock: Put the stock in a saucepan, with 30 g/1 oz butter if liked, and bring to the boil. Off the heat, gradually add the couscous and stir. Return to the boil, cover the pan, remove from the heat and leave for 5–10 minutes. Fluff the couscous with a fork. Serve hot as an accompaniment, with seasonings, or use as a stuffing for vegetables or poultry.

MAKING YEAST AND PIZZA DOUGH

Making bread is an extremely enjoyable culinary experience. With no other preparation do you have such 'hands-on' contact, and from the kneading to the shaping of the risen dough, you are working with a living organism, yeast, not a chemical raising agent. You can use either fresh or dried yeast, which is also available in an easy-blend variety.

Although you can buy pizza bases, it is very easy to make your own at home, and takes much less time than you would expect. The range of toppings for pizzas is virtually limitless.

EVERYDAY WHITE BREAD

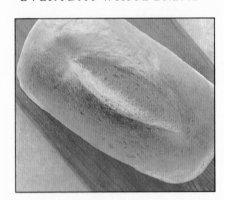

Sift 700 g/1½ lb strong plain (all-purpose) flour into a large bowl with 7.5 ml/1½ tsp salt and 15 ml/1 tbsp caster (superfine) sugar. Stir in 10 ml/ 2 tsp easy-blend dried yeast. Make a well in the centre and add 450 ml/ ¾ pint/scant 2 cups mixed warm water and milk and 30 g/1 oz/2 tbsp melted and cooled butter. Mix to a soft dough, adding more flour or liquid if necessary, then knead until smooth and elastic. Leave to rise until doubled in bulk. Knock back the dough to deflate. Divide it in half and shape each piece into a loaf, tucking the ends under. Put in 2 greased 21 × 11 cm/8½ × 4½ in loaf tins (pans). Leave in a warm place to rise for 30–45 minutes. Glaze the tops of the loaves with 1 egg beaten with 15 ml/1 tbsp milk. Bake in a 230°C/450°F/Gas 8 oven for 30–35 minutes. *Makes 2 loaves.*

MAKING YEAST DOUGH

1 If using ordinary dried yeast, put it in a bowl, add some of the warm liquid called for in the recipe and mix until dissolved. Add sugar if specified. Sift the flour into a warm bowl with other dry ingredients. Make a well and add the yeast plus any other liquid ingredients.

2 Using a spoon, gradually draw the flour into the liquids. Mix until all the flour is incorporated and the dough pulls away from the sides of the bowl. If the dough feels too soft and wet, work in a little more flour. If it fails to come together, add a little more liquid.

3 Turn the dough on to a floured surface. Fold the dough over towards you and then press it down away from you. Continue kneading until the dough looks satiny and feels elastic.

4 Put the dough in a lightly greased bowl and turn to grease all over. Cover with a towel or cling film (plastic wrap). Leave to rise in a warm place until doubled in bulk, 1–1½ hours.

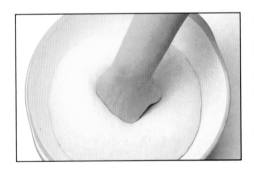

5 Gently punch the centre of the dough with your fist to deflate it and fold the edges to the centre. Turn the dough on to a lightly floured surface and knead it again for 2–3 minutes.

6 Put into prepared tins (pans) or on to baking sheets. Cover and leave for 1 hour. Bake until golden brown. To test, tip the loaf out of the tin and tap the base – it should sound hollow.

MAKING PIZZA DOUGH

MAKES A 35 CM/14 IN PIZZA BASE

10 ml/2 tsp dried yeast
180 ml/6 fl oz/¾ cup warm water
315 g/11½ oz/scant 3 cups strong plain (all-purpose) flour
5 ml/1 tsp salt
20 ml/1½ tbsp olive oil

TOMATO AND MOZZARELLA PIZZA

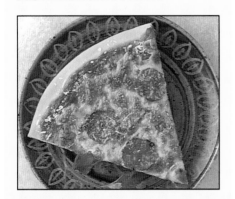

Spread 300 ml/½ pint/1¼ cups tomato purée (paste) over the pizza base, not quite to the edges. Scatter 115 g/4 oz grated Mozzarella cheese evenly over the sauce (plus thinly sliced pepperoni or salami if liked). Sprinkle over freshly grated Parmesan cheese and then add a drizzle of olive oil. Bake in a 240°C/475°F/Gas 9 oven for 15–20 minutes.

FOOD-PROCESSOR PIZZA DOUGH

Combine the yeast, flour, salt, olive oil and half of the warm water in the processor container. Process briefly, then add the rest of the water. Work until the dough forms a ball. Process for 3–4 minutes to knead the dough, then knead it by hand for 2–3 minutes.

1 Put the yeast in a small bowl, add 60 ml/4 tbsp of the water and leave to soak for 1 minute. Whisk lightly with a fork until the yeast has dissolved.

3 Using your fingers, gradually draw the flour into the liquids. Continue mixing in this way until all the flour is incorporated and the dough will just hold together.

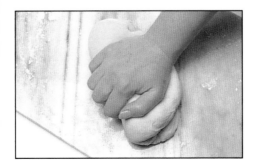

5 Cover the bowl with cling film (plastic wrap). Set aside in a warm place to rise for about 1 hour until doubled in bulk. Turn the dough on to the lightly floured surface again. Gently knock back to deflate it, then knead lightly until smooth.

2 Sift the flour and salt into a large, warm bowl. Make a well in the centre and add the yeast mixture, olive oil and remaining warm water.

4 Turn the dough on to a lightly floured surface. Knead it until it is smooth and silky, about 5 minutes. Shape the dough into a ball. Put it in an oiled bowl and rotate to coat the surface evenly with oil.

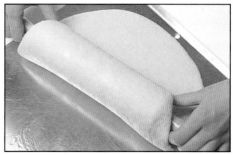

6 Roll out the dough into a round or square about 5 mm/¼ in thick. Transfer it to a lightly oiled metal pizza tin (pan) or baking sheet. Add the topping as specified in the recipe, then bake until the pizza crust is puffy and well browned at the edges. Serve hot.

SESAME-SEED BREAD

MAKES 1 LOAF

10 ml/2 tsp active dry yeast
300 ml/½ pint/1¼ cups lukewarm water
200 g/7 oz/1¾ cups plain (all-purpose) flour
200 g/7 oz/1¾ cups wholewheat flour
10 ml/2 tsp salt
70 g/2½ oz/5 tbsp toasted sesame seeds
milk, for glazing
30 ml/2 tbsp sesame seeds, for sprinkling

1 Combine the yeast and 75 ml/5 tbsp of the water and then leave to dissolve. Mix the flours and salt in a large bowl. Make a well in the centre and pour in the yeast and water.

4 Grease a 23 cm/9 in cake tin (pan). Punch down the dough and knead in the sesame seeds. Divide the dough into 16 balls and place in the tin. Cover with cling film (plastic wrap) and leave in a warm place until risen above the rim of the tin.

5 Preheat a 220°C/425°F/Gas 7 oven. Brush the loaf with milk and sprinkle with the sesame seeds. Bake for 15 minutes. Lower the heat to 190°C/375°F/Gas 5 and bake until the bottom sounds hollow when tapped, about 30 minutes more. Cool on a wire rack.

2 Using a wooden spoon, stir from the centre, incorporating flour with each turn, to obtain a rough dough.

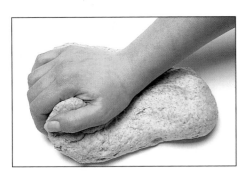

3 Transfer to a floured surface. To knead, push the dough away from you, then fold it towards you and push away again. Repeat until smooth and elastic, then return to the bowl and cover. Leave in a warm place until doubled in volume, 1½–2 hours.

DRIED-FRUIT LOAF

MAKES 1 LOAF

450 g/1 lb mixed dried fruit, such as currants, raisins, and chopped ready-to-eat dried apricots and cherries

300 ml/¹/₂ pint/1 ¹/₄ cups cold strong tea

200 g/7 oz/scant 1 cup dark brown sugar

grated rind and juice of 1 small orange

grated rind and juice of 1 lemon

1 egg, lightly beaten

200 g/7 oz/1 ³/₄ cups plain (all-purpose) flour

15 ml/1 tbsp baking powder

0.75 ml/¹/₈ tsp salt

1 In a bowl, mix the dried fruit with the tea and soak overnight.

2 Preheat a 180°C/350°F/Gas 4 oven. Line a 23 × 13 cm/9 × 5 in loaf tin (pan) with greaseproof (waxed) paper and grease the paper.

3 Strain the fruit, reserving the liquid. In a bowl, combine the sugar, orange and lemon rind, and fruit.

4 Pour the juice from the orange and lemon into a measuring jug (cup); if the quantity is less than 250 ml/8 fl oz/1 cup, top it up with the soaking liquid.

5 Stir the citrus juices and egg into the dried fruit mixture.

6 In another bowl, sift together the flour, baking powder and salt. Stir into the fruit mixture until blended.

7 Transfer to the prepared tin and bake until a skewer inserted in the centre comes out clean, about 1 ¹/₄ hours. Leave the loaf to stand in the tin for about 10 minutes before turning out. Cool on a wire rack.

MAKING SHORTCRUST PASTRY

A meltingly short, crumbly pastry sets off any filling to perfection, whether sweet or savoury. The pastry dough can be made with half butter or margarine and half white vegetable fat, or with all one kind of fat, depending on your personal preference.

Baked-custard and cream fillings can make pastry soggy, so the cases for these flans and tarts are often given an initial baking before the filling is added and the final baking is done. The technique is also used for pastry cases that are to be filled with an uncooked or pre-cooked mixture. Such pre-baking is referred to as baking 'blind'. The

purpose of using weights during the baking process is to prevent the bottom of the pastry case from rising too much and becoming distorted, thus losing its neat, flat shape.

FOR A 23 CM/9 IN PASTRY CASE

225 g/8 oz/2 cups plain
    (all-purpose) flour

1.25 ml/¼ tsp salt

115 g/4 oz/½ cup fat, chilled
    and diced

approximately 45–60 ml/3–4 tbsp
    iced water

1 Sift the flour and salt into a bowl. Add the fat. Rub it into the flour with your fingertips until the mixture resembles coarse crumbs.

PASTRY-MAKING TIPS

● It helps if the fat is cold and firm, particularly if you are making the dough in a food processor. This is because cold fat has less chance of warming and softening too much when it is being rubbed into the flour, resulting in an oily pastry. Use block margarine rather than the soft type.
● When rubbing the fat into the flour, if it begins to soften and feel oily, put the bowl in the refrigerator to chill for 20–30 minutes. Then continue making the dough.
● Liquids used for making pastry should be ice-cold so that they will not soften or melt the fat.
● Take care when adding the water: start with the smaller amount (added all at once, not in a dribble), and add more only if the mixture will not come together into a dough. Too much water will result in tough pastry.
● When gathering the mixture together into a ball of dough, handle it as little as possible: overworked pastry will be tough.
● To avoid shrinkage, refrigerate the dough before rolling out and baking. This 'resting period' will allow any elasticity developed during the mixing process to relax.

2 Sprinkle 45 ml/3 tbsp water over the mixture. Using a fork, toss gently to mix and moisten it.

4 Wrap up the ball of dough with a piece of cling film (plastic wrap) or greaseproof (waxed) paper, or place it in a plastic bag. Refrigerate the dough for at least 30 minutes to allow the elasticity to relax.

3 Press the dough into a ball. If it is still too dry to form a dough, add the remaining water.

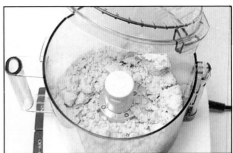

5 **To make pastry in a food processor:** Combine the flour, salt and cubed fat in the work bowl. Process, turning the machine on and off, just until the mixture is crumbly. Add the iced water and process again briefly – just until the dough starts to pull away from the sides. Remove the dough and gather it into a ball. Wrap and refrigerate.

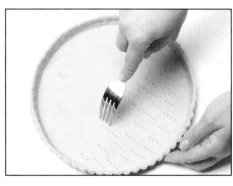

BAKING BLIND

SHORTCRUST-PASTRY VARIATIONS

- For *Nut Shortcrust*: Add 30 g/1 oz/ 2 tbsp finely chopped walnuts or pecan nuts to the flour mixture.
- For *Rich Shortcrust*: Use 225 g/8 oz/ 2 cups flour and 170 g/6 oz/¾ cup fat (preferably all butter), plus 15 ml/1 tbsp caster (superfine) sugar if making a sweet pie. Bind with 1 egg yolk and 30–45 ml/2–3 tbsp water.
- For a *2-crust Pie*, increase the proportions by 50%, so the amounts needed for basic shortcrust pastry are: 340 g/12 oz/3 cups flour, 2.5 ml/½ tsp salt, 170 g/6 oz/¾ cup fat, 75–90 ml/ 5–6 tbsp water. For Nut Shortcrust, as above with 55 g/2 oz/4 tbsp nuts. For Rich Shortcrust, as above but using 260 g/9 oz/1¼ cups fat, 1 egg yolk and 60–75 ml/4–5 tbsp water.

1 Set the pie or flan tin (pan), or flan ring, on a sheet of greaseproof (waxed) paper or tin foil. Draw or mark around its base. Cut out a circle about 7.5 cm/ 3 in larger all round than the drawn or marked one.

2 Roll out the pastry dough and use it to line the tin or ring set on a baking sheet. Using a fork, prick the bottom of the pastry case (pie crust) all over.

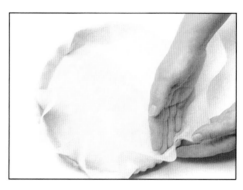

3 Lay the circle of greaseproof paper or foil in the bottom of the pastry case and press it smoothly over the base and up around the side.

4 Put enough dried beans or baking beans in the pastry case to cover the bottom thickly.

ROLLING-OUT AND LINING TIPS

- Lift up the dough and give it a quarter turn from time to time during the rolling. This will prevent the dough from sticking, and will help to keep the thickness even.
- When rolling out and lining the pie or tart tin (pan), do not stretch the dough. It will only shrink back during baking, spoiling the shape.
- A pastry scraper will help to lift the dough from the work surface, to wrap it around the rolling pin.
- When finishing the edge, be sure to hook the dough over the rim all round or to press the dough firmly to the rim. This will prevent the dough from pulling away should it start to shrink.

5 For partially baked pastry: Bake the case in a 200°C/400°F/Gas 6 oven for 15–20 minutes or until it is slightly dry and set. Remove the paper or foil and beans. The pastry is now ready to be filled and baked further.

6 For fully baked pastry: After baking for 15 minutes, remove the paper or foil and beans. Prick the bottom again with a fork. Return to the oven and bake for 5–10 minutes or until golden. Leave to cool before adding the filling.

USING SHORTCRUST PASTRY

Succulent layers of pastry enveloping a sweet filling – what could be nicer? Use the same method for making small pies, such as mince pies.

A neat pastry case that does not distort or shrink during baking is the desired result. The key to success is handling the dough gently. Remove the chilled dough from the refrigerator and allow it to soften slightly at room temperature. Unwrap and put it on the lightly floured surface to roll.

A woven pastry lattice also makes a very attractive finish for a pie. Prepare shortcrust for a 2-crust pie, then roll out half the pastry dough and line the pie tin (pan). Trim the dough to leave a 12 mm/½ in overhang all round. Put in the filling. Roll out the second piece of dough into a circle that is about 5 cm/ 2 in larger all round than the pie tin.

AMERICAN-STYLE APPLE PIE

Combine 900 g/2 lb peeled, cored and thinly sliced green eating apples, 15 ml/1 tbsp plain (all-purpose) flour, 100 g/3½ oz/scant ½ cup caster (superfine) sugar and 3.75 ml/¾ tsp mixed spice (allspice). Toss to coat the fruit evenly with the sugar and flour. Use to fill the two-crust pie. Bake in a 190°C/375°F/Gas 5 oven for about 45 minutes or until the pastry is golden brown and the fruit is tender (test with a skewer through a slit in the top crust). Cool on a wire rack.

MAKING A 2-CRUST PIE

1 Roll out half the pastry dough on a floured surface and line a pie tin (pan) that is about 5 cm/2 in deep. Trim the dough even with the rim.

2 Put in the filling. Brush the edge of the pastry case evenly with water to moisten it.

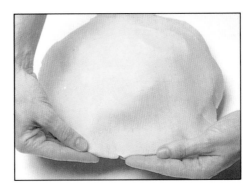

3 Roll out a second piece of dough to a circle 2.5 cm/1 in larger than the tin. Roll it up around the rolling pin and unroll over the pie. Press the edges together. Trim to leave a 12 mm/½ in overhang and cut steam vents.

4 Fold the overhang of the lid under the edge of the case. Press the pastry together gently and evenly to seal. Finish the edge as wished.

5 Brush the top of the pie with milk or cream for a shiny finish, or brush with 1 egg yolk mixed with 5 ml/1 tsp water for a glazed golden-brown finish.

6 If you like, cut out decorative shapes from the trimmings. Moisten these with water and press them on to the top. Glaze the decorations before baking.

MAKING A LATTICE TOP

1 With the help of a ruler, cut neat, straight strips of dough, each about 12 mm/½ in wide, using a knife or fluted pastry wheel.

2 **For a square woven lattice**: Lay half the strips across the pie filling, keeping them neatly parallel and spacing them at equal intervals.

3 Fold back every other strip from the centre. Lay another strip across the centre, on the flat strips, at right-angles to them. Lay the folded strips flat again.

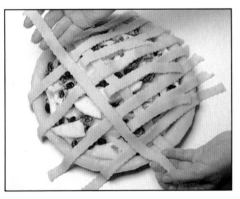

4 Fold back those strips that were not folded the first time. Lay another strip across those that are now lying flat, spacing this new strip an even distance from the centre strip.

5 Continue folding the strips in this way until you have completed half the lattice. Repeat the procedure to cover the other half of the pie.

APRICOT LATTICE PIE

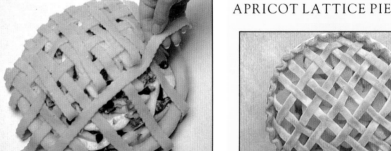

Toss together 1 kg/2¼ lb peeled, stoned (pitted) and thinly sliced apricots, 30 ml/2 tbsp plain (all-purpose) flour and 100 g/3½ oz/scant ½ cup sugar. Fill the pastry case and make a lattice top. Glaze with milk and bake in a 190°C/ 375°F/Gas 5 oven for about 45 minutes or until the pastry is golden and the filling is bubbling. Leave to cool completely on a wire rack.

6 Trim the ends of the strips even with the rim of the pie tin (pan). Moisten the edge of the pastry case with a little water and press the strips gently to it to seal. Finish the edge.

7 **For a diamond lattice**: Weave as above, laying the strips diagonally instead of at right-angles. Alternatively, lay half the strips over the filling and the remaining strips on top.

COOK'S TIP

A simple cut-out lattice top can also make a pie look very attractive. To do this, roll out the dough for the top into a circle. Using a small pastry cutter, cut out shapes in a pattern, spacing them evenly and not too close together.

BASIC SPONGE RECIPES

The quick-mix sponge cake is a no-fuss, all-in-one cake, where the ingredients are quickly mixed together. The following quantities and instructions are for a deep 20 cm/8 in round cake tin (pan) or a 20 cm/8 in ring mould.

Swiss (jelly) rolls are traditionally made without fat, so they do not keep as long as most other cakes. However, they have a deliciously light texture and provide an ideal basis for all sorts of delicious fillings and tasty toppings.

MAKING A QUICK-MIX SPONGE CAKE

INGREDIENTS

115 g/4 oz/1 cup self-raising (-rising) flour
5 ml/1 tsp baking powder
115 g/4 oz/½ cup soft margarine
115 g/4 oz/½ cup caster (superfine) sugar
2 size 3 (medium) eggs

1 Preheat a 160°C/325°F/Gas 3 oven. Grease the round cake tin (pan), line the base with greaseproof (waxed) paper and grease the paper, or grease and flour the ring mould.

2 Sift the flour and baking powder into a bowl. Add the margarine, sugar and both of the eggs.

3 Beat with a wooden spoon for 2–3 minutes. The mixture should be pale in colour and slightly glossy.

4 Spoon the mixture into the prepared tin or mould and bake for 20–30 minutes. To test if cooked, press the cake in the centre. If firm, it is done; if it is still soft, cook for a little longer. Alternatively, insert a skewer into the centre. If it comes out clean, the cake is ready. Turn out on to a wire rack, remove the paper and leave to cool.

STORING

The cake can be wrapped in cling film (plastic wrap) and stored in an airtight container for up to 2 days.

FLAVOURINGS

The following amounts are intended for use in a 2-egg cake, as for the recipe given here. Increase the amounts proportionally in order to make larger-sized cakes.

To make a chocolate cake: fold 15 ml/ 1 tbsp cocoa powder blended with about 15 ml/1 tbsp boiling water into the cake mixture.

For a citrus flavouring: fold 10 ml/2 tsp finely grated lemon, orange or lime zest into the cake mixture. (You can add a little more than this if you wish, but too much will destroy the delicate 'tang'.)

MAKING A SWISS (JELLY) ROLL

INGREDIENTS

4 size 3 (medium) eggs, separated

115 g/4 oz/½ cup caster (superfine) sugar

115 g/4 oz/1 cup plain (all-purpose) flour

5 ml/1 tsp baking powder

1 Preheat a 180°C/350°F/Gas 4 oven. Grease a 33 × 23 cm/13 × 9 in Swiss-roll tin (jelly-roll pan), line with greaseproof (waxed) paper and grease the paper.

2 Whisk the egg whites in a clean, dry bowl until stiff. Beat in about 30 ml/ 2 tbsp of the sugar.

3 Place the egg yolks, remaining sugar and 15 ml/1 tbsp water in a bowl and beat for about 2 minutes until the mixture is pale and leaves a thick trail when you lift the beaters.

4 Using a large metal spoon, carefully fold the beaten egg yolks into the egg-white mixture.

5 Sift together the flour and baking powder. Using a large metal spoon, carefully fold the flour mixture into the egg mixture.

6 Pour the cake mixture into the prepared tin and then smooth the surface, being careful not to press out any air as you do so.

7 Bake in the centre of the oven for 12–15 minutes. To test if cooked, press lightly in the centre. If the cake springs back, it is done. It will also start to come away from the edges of the tin.

8 Turn out the cake on to a piece of greaseproof paper lightly sprinkled with caster (superfine) sugar. Peel off the lining paper and cut off any crisp edges of the cake. Spread with jam and roll up, using the greaseproof paper as a guide. Leave to cool on a wire rack.

VARIATION

Vary the flavour of a Swiss (jelly) roll by adding a little grated orange, lime or lemon zest to the basic mixture.

MAKING FRUIT CAKES

A rich fruit cake is the traditional choice for many special occasions such as weddings, Christmas, anniversaries and christenings. Make the cake a few weeks before icing, keep it wrapped and stored in an airtight container and it should mature beautifully. Because of all the rich ingredients that it contains, this fruit cake will keep moist and fresh for several months.

If you prefer a lighter fruit cake, you can make a less-rich version that is still ideal for marzipanning and covering with either sugarpaste or royal icing.

MAKING A RICH FRUIT CAKE

MAKES A 23 CM/9 IN ROUND OR A 20 CM/8 IN SQUARE CAKE

450 g/1 lb/3 cups currants

300 g/11 oz/1¾ cups sultanas

175 g/6 oz/1 cup raisins

115 g/4 oz/½ cup glacé cherries, halved

115 g/4 oz/1 cup almonds, chopped

100 g/3½ oz/⅔ cup mixed (citrus) peel

grated rind of 2 lemons

45 ml/3 tbsp brandy

300 g/11 oz/2¾ cups plain (all-purpose) flour

7.5 ml/1½ tsp ground mixed spice (allspice)

5 ml/1 tsp ground nutmeg

75 g/3 oz/1 cup ground almonds

250 g/9 oz/scant 1¼ cups soft margarine or butter

275 g/10 oz/1⅓ cups soft brown sugar

20 ml/1½ tbsp black treacle or molasses

6 size 3 (medium) eggs

1 Preheat a 140°C/275°F/Gas 1 oven. Grease a deep cake tin (pan), line with a double thickness of greaseproof (waxed) paper and grease the paper.

2 Place all the ingredients in a large mixing bowl.

3 Stir to combine and then beat thoroughly with a wooden spoon for 3–6 minutes, until well-mixed.

4 Spoon the mixture into the tin and smooth the surface with the back of a wet metal spoon. Make an impression in the centre to help prevent doming.

5 Bake in the centre of the oven for 3¼–3¾ hours. Test the cake about 30 minutes before the end of the baking time. If it is browning too quickly, cover the top loosely with a piece of tin foil. To test if baked, press lightly in the centre. If the cake feels firm and when a skewer inserted in the centre comes out clean, it is done. Test again at short intervals if necessary.

6 Leave the cake to cool in the tin, then turn out when it is completely cool. The lining paper can be left on to help keep the cake moist.

MAKING A LIGHT FRUIT CAKE

MAKES A 23 CM/9 IN ROUND OR A 20 CM/8 IN SQUARE CAKE

275 g/10 oz/1⅓ cups soft margarine or butter

275 g/10 oz/1⅓ cups caster (superfine) sugar

grated rind of 1 orange

6 size 3 (medium) eggs, beaten

400 g/14 oz/3½ cups plain (all-purpose) flour

5 ml/1 tsp baking powder

12.5 ml/2½ tsp ground mixed spice (allspice)

225 g/8 oz/1½ cups currants

225 g/8 oz/1⅓ cups sultanas

225 g/8 oz/1⅓ cups raisins

75 g/3 oz/21 ready-to-eat dried apricots, chopped

150 g/5 oz/1 cup mixed (citrus) peel

1 Preheat a 150°C/300°F/Gas 2 oven. Grease a deep cake tin (pan), line the base and sides with a double thickness of greaseproof (waxed) paper and grease the paper.

2 Place all the ingredients in a large mixing bowl. Stir to combine, then beat thoroughly with a wooden spoon for 3–4 minutes, depending on the size of the cake, until well-mixed.

3 Spoon the mixture into the prepared cake tin and then smooth the surface with the back of a wet metal spoon. Make a slight impression in the centre in order to help prevent the cake from doming as it begins to rise during the cooking process.

4 Bake in the centre of the oven for 3¼–3¾ hours. Test the cake about 15 minutes before the end of the baking time. If it is browning too quickly, cover the top loosely with tin foil. To test if baked, press in the centre. If the cake feels firm, and when a skewer inserted in the centre comes out clean, it is done. Test again at intervals if necessary. Leave the cake to cool in the tin, then turn out. The lining paper can be left on to help keep the cake moist.

STORING

Wrapped and in an airtight container, a fruit cake will keep for several months.

MAKING BASIC ICINGS

The creamy, rich flavour and silky smoothness of butter icing are popular with both children and adults. The icing can be varied in colour and flavour and makes a decorative filling and coating for sponge cakes or Swiss (jelly) rolls. Simply swirled, or more elaborately piped, butter icing gives a delicious and attractive finish. The quantity given here makes enough to fill and coat the sides and top of a 20 cm/8 in round sponge cake.

Glacé icing can be made in just a few minutes and can be varied by adding a few drops of either food colouring or flavouring. The quantity specified in the recipe makes sufficient icing to cover the top and decorate a 20 cm/8 in round sponge cake.

Rich, delicious fudge frosting can transform a simple sponge cake. Spread the frosting smoothly over the cake, or swirl or pipe it – it is very versatile. The amount given in the recipe will fill and coat the top and sides of a 20 cm/8 in round sponge cake.

As shiny and smooth as silk, dark satin-chocolate icing can be poured over a sponge cake. A few fresh flowers, pieces of fresh fruit, simple chocolate shapes or white-chocolate piping add the finishing touch. The recipe given here makes sufficient to cover a 20 cm/ 8 in square or a 23 cm/9 in round cake.

MAKING GLACÉ ICING

MAKES 225 G/8 OZ

225 g/8 oz/2 cups icing (confectioners')
sugar

30–45 ml/2–3 tbsp warm water or
fruit juice

food colouring (optional)

1 Sift the icing (confectioners') sugar into a large mixing bowl to eliminate any lumps.

2 Using a wooden spoon, gradually stir in enough water to make an icing with the consistency of thick cream. Beat until the icing is completely smooth. It should be thick enough to coat the back of the spoon. If it is too runny, beat in a little more sifted icing sugar to thicken it slightly.

3 To colour the icing, beat in a few drops of food colouring. Use the icing immediately for coating or piping, before it begins to set.

MAKING BUTTER ICING

MAKES 350 G/12 OZ

75 g/3 oz/6 tbsp butter, softened, or
soft margarine

225 g/8 oz/2 cups icing (confectioners')
sugar, sifted

5 ml/1 tsp vanilla essence (extract)

10–15 ml/2–3 tsp milk

FLAVOURINGS

These amounts are for a single quantity of butter icing. Increase or decrease the amounts proportionally as needed.
Chocolate: blend 15 ml/1 tbsp cocoa powder with 15 ml/1 tbsp hot water. Cool before beating into the icing.
Coffee: blend 10 ml/2 tsp instant-coffee powder or granules with 15 ml/1 tbsp boiling water. Allow to cool before beating into the icing.
Lemon, orange or lime: substitute the vanilla essence (extract) and milk for lemon, orange or lime juice and 10 ml/ 2 tsp finely grated citrus zest. Omit the zest if using the icing for piping. Lightly colour with the appropriate shade of food colouring, if you wish.

1 Put the butter or margarine, icing (confectioners') sugar, vanilla essence (extract) and 5 ml/1 tsp milk in a bowl.

2 Beat with a wooden spoon, adding sufficient extra milk to give a light, smooth and fluffy consistency.

MAKING FUDGE FROSTING

MAKES 350 G/12 OZ

50 g/2 oz/2 squares plain chocolate

225 g/8 oz/2 cups icing (confectioners') sugar, sifted

50 g/2 oz/4 tbsp butter or margarine

45 ml/3 tbsp milk or single (light) cream

5 ml/1 tsp vanilla essence (extract)

1 Break or chop the chocolate into small pieces. Put the chocolate, icing (confectioners') sugar, butter or margarine, milk and vanilla essence (extract) in a saucepan. Stir over a very low heat until the chocolate and butter or margarine melt. Remove from the heat and stir until blended.

2 Beat the icing frequently as it cools until it thickens sufficiently to use for spreading or piping. Use immediately and work quickly once it has reached the correct consistency.

MAKING SATIN-CHOCOLATE ICING

MAKES 225 G/8 OZ

175 g/6 oz/6 squares plain chocolate

150 ml/¼ pint/⅔ cup single (light) cream

2.5 ml/½ tsp instant-coffee powder

1 Break or chop the chocolate into small pieces. Put the chocolate, cream and coffee in a heavy-based saucepan. Place the cake on a wire rack.

2 Stir over a very low heat until the chocolate melts and the mixture is smooth and evenly blended.

3 Remove from the heat and pour the icing over the cake, letting it run down the sides to coat it completely. Spread the icing with a palette knife (spatula) as necessary, working quickly before the icing has time to thicken.

DECORATING IDEAS

Generous swirls of butter icing give a mouth-watering effect to a cake.

Drizzled or spread, glacé icing can quickly turn a plain cake into something special.

Thick, glossy swirls of fudge frosting almost make a decoration in themselves.

Satin-chocolate icing brings a real touch of sophistication to the most humble of cakes.

THE HOME GARDENER

Gardening is a therapeutic and rewarding pastime, and can make a real difference to the overall comfort and beauty of the home. For those who simply haven't the time or energy to devote a portion of every week to maintenance, however, it can appear a daunting task. This chapter contains hints and tips on how to achieve an outdoor environment that best suits your individual needs and at the same time restricting upkeep to a minimum.

CREATING A BEAUTIFUL OUTDOORS

There is something very special and satisfying about having your own outdoor space, however small it may be. And as part of your home, there is no reason why you shouldn't plan and decorate it with as much care and thought as you would give the rooms inside.

To achieve a good result requires careful consideration of many factors other than the plants, that will all come together to create the garden you want. First of all you need to think about how you want to use your garden, and what you want to include in it: seating areas, play areas, beds and borders, shrubs, vegetable plots, sheds etc. You also need to decide on a style, so that the garden has an identity. You can also create impact using paint and stain on different surfaces such as fences, walls, furniture or pots to complement the planting.

You will need to put your ideas down on paper to see how they work out. It is sensible to work out a scale plan of your design, so that you can see how your ideas work in your existing garden.

Be prepared to make some adjustments to suit the actual situation, although there is much that can be done to alter or even move existing features, depending on how determined you are.

The major part of your garden is probably devoted to flat surfaces, such as lawns, paths and paved areas. When deciding what proportions of hard and soft surfaces you want, consider different types of paving, gravel and alternatives to grass. It is very important, too, to bear in mind the amount of time you want to spend maintaining your garden.

Finally, once a garden is in place, there are finishing touches to add. Ornaments, arches and pergolas can all be used to perfect vistas and aspects within the garden. And adding seating and lighting will extend your use and therefore enjoyment of your outdoor room.

The following pages contain helpful suggestions, hints and tips to give you all the inspiration and information needed to create an exquisite, personalized outdoor room of your own.

OPPOSITE Use paint and well-placed furniture to bring add splashes of colour and a sense of fun to your garden.

ASSESSING OUTDOOR AREAS

The most comfortable and visually pleasing garden rooms are usually the result of careful planning. You will need to consider how best to use the available space, the vista, and the ambience before you prepare the 'canvas' for the decorative touches.

You will probably want somewhere to sit and, perhaps, eat or even entertain. If you have children, you will want somewhere for them to play, and you will also need to allow for some kind of storage area for tools, pots, and other garden paraphernalia. All this is perfectly possible even in tiny gardens. An area 2 m/7 ft square is sufficient space in which to sit and eat. Children would be thrilled with a sandpit just 1 m/3 ft square and, if there is just a little more space, there will be room enough for a small playhouse.

Plan out in your mind the best place for each of these activities in much the same way as you might plan your kitchen, where you also need to provide space for working, eating, and leisure. Once these priorities are set, it will be much easier to work out the layout of the garden. This is important, even if you don't have the resources for new pavings and landscaping, at least for the foreseeable future. For example, there may be a neglected flower bed just where you feel it would be best to create a seating area. With the garden layout left as it is, you would continually have to bring furniture in and out when you need it. However, with a few little changes, like simply turfing over the flower bed, you can re-organize the garden so it is ready for relaxation any time you want.

Once the main areas are worked out, it is much easier to decide where you want to have planting areas, and within this framework, you will be able to transform the space into a decorative outdoor room that you will want to use and enjoy for more than just the few summer months.

ABOVE A small patio area and a collection of planted containers can be incorporated into most gardens, no matter what the size.

Planning for privacy

You will only be able to relax in the garden once you have organized the basic needs: privacy and shelter. If necessary, trellis can be fixed on top of walls and fences to create extra height. You can then grow decorative climbers to provide a natural wallpaper.

You could plant fast-growing conifers, such as thuja, though check their potential final height or you could end up deeply overshadowed.

Seating areas, in particular, need privacy. Even if you live in the middle of the country and have a huge garden, you will feel much more comfortable if you site these where, at least on one side, there is the protection of a wall of some sort. This could be the garden boundary wall, a hedge, or even a trellis screen to lend a more intimate feel. If you are closely overlooked, you may also want to create privacy from above. One of the most successful ways of doing this is to put up a pergola and let it become entwined with vines or other climbers.

RIGHT Secret places can be created in even the smallest of spaces. This pathway winds through plantings in a tiny 5m/15 ft plot.

Atmosphere and romance

Once the space is defined, you can begin to act the mood. Creating ambience relies on stimulating the senses: sight, sound, touch, taste, and

ABOVE Even on a tiny patio area, there is room to create levels. Here, raised beds are built in white-painted brick to match the garden walls.

smell, all of which are supplied free of charge by nature. To the sound of birds and buzzing insects, you can add the music of wind chimes or the evocative trickling of water in even the smallest plot. The outdoors also provides the most glorious fragrances, from sweet-smelling flowers such as roses, honeysuckle and jasmine to aromatics such as lavender and piquant herbs. Touch, too, can be stimulated. Plan for a variety of plants with interesting textures – there are many plants with leaves ranging from fleshy to frondy and feathery. Finally, eating out in the garden contributes taste to complete the sensory picture.

The most romantic gardens hint at intimacy. They could literally be enclosed outdoor rooms, such as courtyards, balconies, or roof gardens, which automatically offer intimacy. If your space is large, you can add romantic interest by creating hidden places. This isn't difficult, even in the smallest garden. You can put a door in the fence or wall to hint at another space, put up an archway to give the feeling of moving from one area to another, or, perhaps, add a trellis screen to section off an eating area. As well as creating intimacy, these dividing tactics also give the illusion of space. Adding an archway or screen means you are able to see beyond into another area, which lends perspective to the whole space, giving it structure and shape. However light the resulting screening is, it hints at secret places and romance just around the corner.

Finding the levels

Unless you have a very tiny space, or you have decided to have a particular and probably formal design, such as a knot garden, you will probably want to create some changes in level.

Even a single step up from one area to another can do the trick. But if you are not in a position to completely re-landscape for the sake of a few levels, there is still a lot you can do. You can add staging at one side, and use that to display potted plants. You can use a plant stand to lend a little height, and you can make a feature of garden buildings for higher-than-ground-level architectural interest. You can also use plants of various heights to create levels.

BELOW Part of the enjoyment of being outside is having a view to admire. This seating area on the patio next to the house overlooks an almost classical vista in an urban garden.

PLANTING FOR COLOUR

Herbaceous borders bring wonderful colour in summer but die down to next to nothing in the winter, so it is good to provide an evergreen structure of plants to get you through all the seasons. These can also contribute to the 'architecture' of the garden, creating levels, screens, and even sculpture. You can plan to have taller shrubs at the back of the borders, slowly graduating toward the front, or you can make more structured steps. You can arrange rows of small, lightly screening plants across the garden to create a living screen, and you can use specimen trees or neatly trimmed topiary as living sculpture.

The colour scheme can be planned against this basic structure. The decorative garden room is at its prettiest with plenty of colour. The structural shrubs and trees also can be chosen to make certain there is some colour all the year round – fruit trees for blossom in spring; shrub roses for summer colour and late-flowering clematis and wonderful berries, such as those of the pyracantha, in autumn, and of holly in winter. This display can he complemented by autumn-flowering bulbs such as colchicum, schizostylis, and cyclamen.

But the most variety of colours can be added with pots and containers. There is always a choice of seasonal colour at garden centres. By planting up in movable pots, you can easily put the colour where you want it and replant with new seasonal colour as the old blooms die.

BELOW Throw a blue-checked cloth over the garden table, add some seasonal potted arrangements, and you have the perfect setting for enjoying drinks outside on a spring day.

ABOVE Bright, bold Caribbean colours in pink and tangerine make for a lively look in a brightly coloured garden.

Colour creates much more impact if it is kept to a theme – of blues and pinks, perhaps, or oranges and yellows. This theme can be strengthened with the use of paint and stain on nearby fences, garden buildings, furniture, or even the pots themselves.

Adding decorative colour

In a decorative garden, colour is very important. Not only can the paint you choose suggest mood and ambience, just as it does indoors, it can emphasize the colour scheme of the planting.

The surfaces you paint may be the house walls, walls of outside buildings, or the garden walls. Maybe you have a hopscotch of fencing and trellis work, all of slightly different woods and ages, that has resulted in a visual muddle. Paint them all in the same decorative finish, and you will have a much more coherent look. Or you may have newly erected trellis work that has a year or more to wait for a verdant covering of creepers. Paint it, and you will have a reasonable finish while you wait.

Colour can also be used to highlight areas. You may pinpoint an area destined for a particular colour scheme or you may wish to highlight the planting. Burnt-orange fencing would

LEFT An enchanting little pond, complete with fountain and cherub, adds colour and interest to a shady corner of the garden.

provide a stunning background for marigolds, while yellow picket would highlight the nodding heads of pansies. Painted fences and surfaces also lend colour throughout the year. They are particularly valuable in winter when many plants have died down.

Ideas with paint

Whether you want to paint your garden wall or a house wall that makes up part of the garden, there is plenty of inspiration to be had. Experiment not only with colour but with technique.

As well as straight colour, you can create depth by layering the colour. Try trompe l'oeil effects such as marble, stone, slate, or moss or by stencilling on to a wall. The trick is to consider the scale of the garden.

These effects will have to be seen from much further away than they would be if used inside the house. Even a 10 m/30 ft garden is much larger than the average room, so everything has to be exaggerated a little.

ABOVE Although you may spend less time in the front garden, colourful plants growing by the door will create a welcoming impression.

Paint practicalities

Any outdoor paint job has to be able to withstand a lot of beating from the weather, such as frosts, strong winds, torrential rain and the summer sun. For this reason, it is best to use exterior-quality products. They are less likely to peel and flake, their colours are less likely to fade and they are specifically designed to protect the surface they are covering. Alternatively, when decorating items such as pots and containers, which are not crucial to the garden structure, you can achieve a reasonably hard-wearing finish using a wider variety of paints over a primer, finished with a varnish.

Whatever you plan to paint or stain, it is important to use primers and varnishes that are compatible with each other, otherwise they may react adversely. Remember too that, if you have the patience and time, several thin layers of paint always produce a more enduring and better-looking finish than one thick one.

PLANNING YOUR GARDEN

Simply moving a few plants is rarely enough to transform an uninspiring garden into something special. It is worth having a goal, a plan to work to, even if you have to compromise along the way. Bear in mind that you may be able to stagger the work and cost over several seasons, but having a well thought out design ensures the garden evolves in a structured way.

Use the checklist to clarify your needs, then decide in your own mind the style of garden you want. Make a note of mundane and practical considerations, like where to dry the clothes and put the refuse, plus objects that need to be screened, such as a compost area, or an unpleasant view.

Labour-saving tips

To minimize cost and labour, retain as many paths and areas of paving as possible, but only if they don't compromise the design.

If you want to enlarge an area of paving, or improve its appearance, it may be possible to pave over the top and thus avoid the arduous task of removing the original.

Modifying the shape of your lawn is easier than digging it up and relaying a new one.

Garden styles

The garden styles outlined here are not exhaustive, and probably none of them will be exactly right for your own garden, but they will help you to clarify your thoughts.

Formal

Parterres and knot gardens: Shaped beds and compartments originally designed to be viewed from above. Knot herb gardens, such as ones based on intricate Elizabethan designs, can be stunning but are expensive to create, slow to establish and labour intensive.

Formal herb gardens: Easier to create than knot gardens. Seek inspiration from illustrated herb garden books – both old and new. It is easier to create one if based on a theme.

Formal rose gardens: Easy to create and can look good in first season. For year-round interest underplant with spring bulbs and edge beds with seasonal flowers.

Paved gardens: Particularly suitable for small gardens. Plant in open areas left in paving, up walls and in raised beds and containers.

Courtyard gardens: Floor tiles and white walls (to reflect light), together with some lush green foliage, an 'architectural' tree or large shrub and the sound of running water will transform a backyard into a delightful courtyard garden.

BELOW A modern interpretation of an Elizabethan knot garden, with gravel and brick paving to keep weeding to a minimum.

Traditional designs: A small formal garden, with rectangular lawn, straight herbaceous border plus rose and flower beds is a popular choice for growing a variety of summer bedding and other favourites.

Informal

Cottage gardens: The juxtaposition of 'old-fashioned' plants and vegetables creates a casual but colourful look. Place brick paths or stepping stones through the beds.

Wildlife gardens: Even a tiny plot can attract small animals and insects. Planting must provide shelter and food, while a water feature will encourage aquatic wildlife.

Woodland gardens: Shrubs and small deciduous trees suit a long narrow garden and are effective for screening and dividing up the garden. Under-plant with naturalized bulbs, woodland spring flowers and ferns.

Meandering meadows: Where there is an attractive view, a sweep of grass between curved borders can merge with an unobstructed boundary. If the view is unappealing, curve the border round so that the lawn finishes beyond the point of view.

LEFT In most cities and urban environments, back gardens are small and shady, but these factors need not restrict the garden's potential, as these great splashes of colour show.

Bright beds and borders: If plants are more important than design, use sweeping beds and borders with lots of shrubs and herbaceous plants to give shape. Use focal points such as ornaments, garden seats or birdbaths to create a strong sense of design.

Distant influences

Japanese gardens: Raked sand and grouped stones translate well to a small space, making a confined area appear larger. Plants can be kept to a minimum.

Stone and gravel gardens: These materials can be used to create a dry-river bed feel. Minimal maintenance if you select drought-tolerant plants.

Choosing a style

The most comfortable and visually pleasing gardens are usually the result of careful planning, even those with an informal feel to them. Formal gardens appeal to those who delight in crisp, neat edges, straight lines and a sense of order. Many traditional suburban gardens are formal in outline, with rectangular lawns flanked by straight flower borders, and perhaps rectangular or circular flower beds cut into them. Such rigid designs are often dictated by the drive for the car and straight paths laid by the house builder.

The informality of the cottage garden and the 'wilderness' atmosphere of a wild garden are difficult to achieve in a small space, especially in a town. However, with fences well clothed with plants so that modern buildings do not intrude, an informal garden can work even here.

Professional garden designers are frequently influenced by classic styles from other countries, especially Japan, but amateurs are often nervous of trying such designs themselves. Provided you start with the clear premise that what pleases you is the only real criterion of whether something works, creating a particular 'foreign' style can be great fun. Adapt the chosen style to suit climate, landscape and the availability of suitable plants and materials.

CHOICES CHECKLIST

Before you draw up your design, make a list of requirements for your ideal garden. You will almost certainly have to abandon or defer some of them, but at least you will realize which features are most important to you.

Use this checklist of suggested features at the rough plan stage, when decisions have to be made… and it is easy to change your mind!

Decorative features
Barbecue
Beds
Borders, for herbaceous
Borders, for shrubs
Borders, mixed
Birdbath
Changes of level
Conservatory
Fruit garden
Gravelled area
Greenhouse

Herb garden
Lawn (mainly for decoration)
Lawn (mainly for recreation)
Ornaments
Patio/terrace
Pergola
Pond
Raised beds
Summer house
Sundial
Vegetable plot

Functional features
Compost area
Garage
Toolshed

Necessities
Children's play area
Climbing frame
Clothes drying area
Dustbin (trash can) area
Sandpit
Swing

CREATING THE DESIGN

Having decided on the style of garden that you want, and the features that you need to incorporate, tackle the much more difficult task of applying them to your own garden. The chances are that your garden will be the wrong size or shape, or the situation or outlook is inappropriate to the style of garden that you want. The way around this is to not try to recreate a particular style too closely.

If you can't visualize the whole of your front garden as, say, a stone or Japanese garden, it may be possible to include the feature as an element within a more general design.

Basic patterns

Most successful garden designs fall into one of the three basic patterns described below, though clever planting and variations on the themes almost always result in individual designs.

Circular theme: Circular themes are very effective at disguising the predictable shape of a rectangular garden. Circular lawns, circular patios, and circular beds are all options, and you only need to overlap and interlock a few circles to create a stylish garden. Plants fill the gaps between the curved areas and the straight edges.

Using a compass, try various combinations of circles to see whether you can create an attractive pattern. Be prepared to vary the radii and to overlap the circles if necessary.

Diagonal theme: This device creates a sense of space by taking the eye along and across the garden. Start by drawing grid lines at 45° to the house or main fence. Then draw in the design, using the grid as a guide.

Rectangular theme: Most people designing a garden use a rectangular theme based on a grid – even though they may not make a conscious effort to do so. The device is effective if you want to create a formal look, or wish to divide a long, narrow garden up into smaller sections.

How to make a scale drawing

To make a scale drawing, choose a scale that enables you to fit the garden on a single large sheet of graph paper. For most small gardens, a scale of 1:50 (2 cm to 1 m or ¼ in to 1 ft) is about right. If your garden is large, try a scale of 1:100. Draw your base line (a long straight edge such as a fence) in first, then transfer the scale measurements. When the right-angle measurements have been transferred, draw in the relevant outlines.

Drawing the garden plan

Whether designing a garden from scratch or simply modifying what you already have you need to draw a plan of the garden as it is. A drawn plan will enable you to see the overall design clearly and to experiment with different ideas.

Stage 1: the basic grid: Make a rough sketch of your existing garden, add accurate measurements, then make a scale drawing from this. Transfer the measurements to graph paper to create a scale plan of your garden, showing any permanent structures and features that you want to retain.

Now superimpose on to this grid the type of design you have in mind – one based on circles, rectangles or diagonals, for example. You can draw these directly onto your plan in a second colour, but if you think you might change your mind, draw the grid on a transparent overlay. Use grid lines 1.8–2.4 m/6–8 ft apart for small areas.

Using an overlay, or a photocopy of your plan complete with grid, mark on the new features that you would like to include, in their positions. You might find it helpful to cut out pieces of scrap paper to an appropriate size and shape so that you can move them around.

CIRCULAR THEME

DIAGONAL THEME

RECTANGULAR THEME

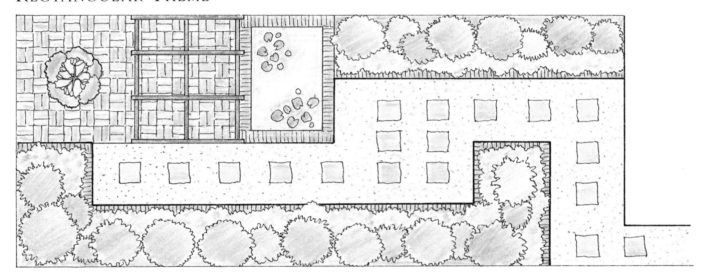

Stage 2: the rough: Using an overlay or a photocopy, start sketching in your plan. If you can visualize an overall design, sketch this in first in as detailed a fashion as possible, then move around your features to fit into it. If you have not reached this stage, start by sketching in the features you have provisionally positioned though you may have to adjust them later.

You will need to make many attempts. Don't be satisfied with the first one – it may be the best, but you won't know this unless you explore a few other options first. Don't worry too much about planting details at this stage, except perhaps for a few important focal plants.

Stage 3: the detailed drawing: Details such as the type of paving should be decided now – not only because it will help you to see the final effect, but also because you need to work to areas that use multiples of full blocks, slabs or bricks if possible. Draw in key plants, especially large trees and shrubs, but omit the more detailed planting plans at this stage.

Trying it out

Before ordering materials or starting construction, mark out as much of the design as possible in the garden. Use string and pegs to indicate the areas, then walk around them. If possible take a look from an upstairs

window. This will give a much better idea of the overall design and whether paths and sitting areas are large enough.

Use tall canes to indicate the positions of important plants and new trees. This will show how much screening they are likely to offer, and whether they may become a problem in time. By observing the shadow cast at various parts of the day, you'll also know whether shade could be a potential problem – for other plants or for a sitting-out area. If your design includes irregularly shaped beds, use a length of garden hose or thick rope, adjusting the curves to roughly mark out the shape.

LOW-MAINTENANCE GARDENING

Low maintenance does not mean low impact. It means choosing surfaces and ground covers that do not require regular attention, and plants that remain within their allotted space and look good without regular pruning or hacking back. Plants are chosen that do not demand frequent feeding or require spraying almost as a matter of routine to control pests and diseases.

A low-maintenance garden is one in which you never feel that keeping the garden shipshape is a chore. If you love pottering around with plants but hate mowing the grass, the simple expediency of replacing grass with gravel or paving might be all that is necessary. If you quite enjoy the exercise involved in mowing the lawn but find the battle against pests and the need to prune or replant frequently tedious, then placing the emphasis on easy-care, no-fuss plants will probably be the best solution.

BELOW Paving stones surrounded by ground-cover plants form a practical and decorative surface for a garden path.

Cut the mowing time

There's a lot you can do to keep mowing time to a minimum. It may be necessary to buy a new and better mower, but just cutting out fussy beds and curved edges might simplify and speed things up by allowing you to mow up and down in straight lines.

Another way to cut down on the mowing for a large lawn is to create a 'sculptured' effect. Keep the broad 'pathways' cut regularly, cut other areas with the blade set higher, and mow only every second or third time. Leave some uncut except for a couple of times a season. However, do remember that very long grass can't easily be cut with a mower; you need to get out your nylon line trimmer.

Watering aids

You can avoid watering altogether if you choose drought-resistant plants, abandon containers, and don't mind a brown lawn in a dry summer. However, if you want lush, green grass and lots of colourful containers without the sometimes twice-daily chore of watering, some kind of automatic watering system is essential in the low-maintenance garden. There are several different kinds of hoses, sprinklers and timing devices available. Look at garden centres and in magazine advertisements to see which appear to be the most appropriate for your needs.

Labour-saving tools

Appropriate tools can save you time and effort, and will make the difference between a job being a pleasure or a chore. Good tools and equipment, especially power tools, take up a lot of space, so decide which ones are really essential and spend as much as you can afford on a few good quality tools that will last, rather than purchase a lot of gimmicky tools that you'll seldom use.

MAKING A MOWING EDGE

If you have a mowing edge like this, edge-trimming will be required much less often. If the edging is set level with the grass, the mower, which is run onto the edging, will trim off the long grass at the edge. You may still have to trim any spreading grass stems that grow over the paving, but this will only be necessary occasionally.

1 Lay the paving slabs on the grass for positioning, and use a half-moon edger (edging iron) to cut a new edge.

2 Slice off the grass with a spade, and remove enough soil for a couple of centimetres (inches) of sand and gravel mix, mortar, and the slabs. Consolidate the sub-base.

3 Use blobs of mortar on which to bed the slab, and tap the paving level, using a mallet or the handle of a club hammer.

4 Make sure the slabs are flush with the lawn, and use a spirit level to check that the slabs are laid evenly. Mortar the joints for a neat finish, otherwise weeds will grow in them.

LEFT Scalloped shells cajoled from a fish store make a delightful edging in soft coral shades that co-ordinate well with terracotta pavings.

THE GARDEN FLOOR

The garden floor – lawn, paving, paths, even areas of gravel or ground cover plants – can make or mar your garden. These surfaces are likely to account for more area than the beds and borders. Although they recede in importance when the garden is in full bloom, for much of the year they probably hold centre stage.

Removing existing paths and paved areas presents a practical problem. Provided these areas do not compromise your design too much, it is much easier to leave as many as you can in position. Consider paving over the top with a more sympathetic material. It should be relatively easy to extend the area if you want to.

Lawns are more easily modified than paths and paved areas. At worst you can dig them up and re-sow or relay them. If you simply want to change the shape, you can trim off surplus grass or lift and relay just part of the lawn.

There are useful alternatives to grass for areas that are not used for recreation or are seldom trodden on. Ground cover plants not only suppress weeds in flower beds, but can replace a lawn where the surface does not have to take the wear and tear of trampling feet. Inset stepping-stones to protect the plants. Where the garden is very small, low-growing ground cover may be much more practical than a lawn that is almost too tiny to cut with a

mower. Other alternatives to grass are lawns of thyme, chamomile or clover, or gravelled areas.

Timber decking is very popular in some countries, seldom used in others. Much depends on the price of timber locally, and to some extent the climate, but decking should always be on your list of options.

Ground cover with plants

If you want to cover an area of ground with a living carpet simply for texture, but you don't expect to walk on the area, suitable ground cover plants are the answer.

To use ground cover plants like this, rather than simply as a means to suppress weeds in a flower bed, they must be evergreen, compact, and grow to a low, even height. Some of the best plants for the job are *Armeria maritima*, bergenias, *Cotoneaster dammeri*, *Euonymus fortunei* varieties, *Hypericum calycinum*, and *Pachysandra terminalis*. If you want a pretty spread of flowers as the main feature, heathers are an excellent choice.

Lawns

The lawn is often the centrepiece of a garden, the canvas against which the rest of the garden is painted. For many gardeners this makes it worth all the mowing, feeding and grooming that a good lawn demands.

If your lawn has to serve as a play area too, be realistic and sow tough grasses, and settle for a hard-wearing lawn rather than a showpiece. It can still look green and lush – the important consideration from a design viewpoint. Instead of aiming for a bowling-green finish, the shape of the lawn or a striking edging could be its strong visual message.

LEFT **A sweeping lawn or one with curves can help to create a sense of perspective and also add interest to a garden.**

Keeping a trim edge

Circular lawns must be edged properly. Nothing looks worse than a circle that isn't circular, and of course constant trimming back will eat into the lawn over the years. To avoid this, incorporate a firm edging, such as bricks placed on end and mortared into position, when you make the lawn.

Where the edges are straight use proprietary lawn edging strips.

Naturalizing bulbs in grass

Naturalizing spring-flowering bulbs in a lawn of any size gives you the justification for leaving the grass uncut until late spring or early summer, when the leaves have died down. Choose bulbs that will multiply and flower freely, such as crocuses, daffodils, snowdrops, small fritillaries, and winter aconites. There are many different kinds of crocuses and daffodils, so you'll have plenty of choice even if you limit yourself to these particularly reliable bulbs and corms.

Timber decking

Timber decking creates a distinctive effect, and will make a refreshing change from ordinary paving for the patio area. As with paving, the material used should be in proportion to the size of the garden, so the width of the planks is important. Wide planks look best in a large garden, but in a small, enclosed area narrower planks are usually preferable.

All timber used for decking must be thoroughly treated with a wood preservative. Some preservatives and wood stains are available in a range of colours, and this provides the opportunity for a little creativity.

Different designs can be achieved by using planks of different widths and fixing them in different directions, but on the whole it is best to keep any pattern fairly simple. Leave small gaps between each plank.

ABOVE The loose feel of this garden is held in check by using bricks, placed on their sides as edging.

PATTERNS OF TIMBER DECKING

SUCCESSFUL PAVING

Most small gardens have a patio or at least a paved area close to the house. Often it is the main feature around which the remainder of the back garden is arranged. It can be the link that integrates home and garden. At its worst, paving can be boring and off-putting; at its best it really adds to the overall impact of the garden.

Choosing the material is only part of the secret of successful paving – how you use it, alone or combined with other materials, is just as important, and is what can make an area of paving mundane or something special.

Colour combinations
Your liking for bright and brash paving colour combinations will depend on the effect you want to create. Be wary of bright colours though – they can detract from the plants, although they will mellow with age.

Sizing up the problem
In a small garden, large-sized paving units can destroy the sense of scale. For a small area, try small-sized paving slabs (which are also easier to handle), or go for bricks, pavers, or cobbles.

Mix and match materials
Paving often looks a more integrated part of the garden if you combine it with raised beds or low walls made from the same or matching materials – but always check that bricks used for walls are suitable for paths as well.

Using the same or matching paving for paths and patios is another way of giving the entire garden area a more integrated look.

If the area is large, try mixing materials. Using two or three different types usually works well, but more than three is likely to look confused. Try bricks or clay pavers with timber, or railway sleepers, or natural or artificial paving slabs. You could perhaps leave out some areas of paving and fill them with gravel or pebbles.

Paving patterns
You can go for a completely random pattern – crazy-paving is a perfect example – but most paving is laid to a pre-planned pattern using rectangular paving slabs or bricks. Look at the brochures for paving slabs. These usually suggest a variety of ways in which the slabs can be laid.

Although a large area laid with slabs of the same size can look boring, avoid too many different sizes, or complex patterns in a small space. Simplicity is often more effective.

Bricks and clay pavers are often the best choice for a small area, because their small size is more likely to be in harmony with the scale of the garden. Choose carefully, as the way they are laid can make a real visual difference.

The simple design of stretcher bond is usually most effective for a small area, and for paths. The herringbone pattern is suitable for both large and small areas, but the basket weave needs a reasonably large expanse for the pattern to be properly appreciated.

Clay pavers
These cannot be bedded on mortar like paving slabs and bricks. Clay pavers are usually designed to interlock without mortar joints and are intended for bedding on sand.

Concrete paving blocks
Cheaper than natural stone blocks, neutral colours are best, offset by lavish plants, spilling over onto the paving.

PAVING PATTERNS

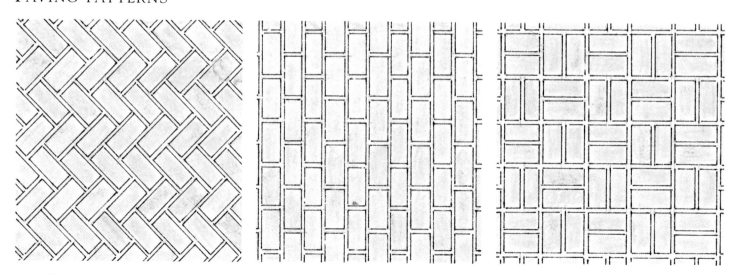

ABOVE **Herringbone.**   ABOVE **Stretcher board.**   ABOVE **Basket weave.**

LAYING PAVING

1 Always lay paving on a firm base. Excavate the area to a depth that allows for hardcore, mortar, and paving. Firm the ground, then add 5–10 cm/2–4 in of hardcore for foot traffic, about 15 cm/6 in if vehicles will use it.

2 Compact the ground thoroughly. Bed the slabs on five blobs of mortar, using five parts of sharp sand to one part cement.

3 Alternatively, you can lay the slabs with a solid bed of mortar, although this will make it more difficult to adjust them.

4 Start at a known straight edge, then position each slab in turn. The best way is to lower the slab down from one side, then slide it if adjustments are necessary.

5 Tap the slab level with a mallet or the handle of a club hammer, using a long spirit level that spans adjoining slabs. If a large area of paving is being laid, it may be necessary to lay it on a slight slope to drain rainwater, in which case you must allow for this.

6 Unless the slabs are designed to be butt-joined, use spacers to ensure a gap of consistent width. You can make these from scraps of wood. A few days after the slabs have been laid, point with mortar.

ALTERNATIVES TO GRASS

If you like a green lawn, but don't enjoy the regular grass cutting, why not try a grass substitute? None of those suggested here will stand up to the hard wear of a children's play area like grass, but just for occasional foot traffic and as a feature that is for admiration only, there are some practical alternatives that don't need regular mowing.

Some common alternatives
Thyme: Thyme is aromatic when crushed, and makes a good grass substitute, but don't use the culinary thyme (*Thymus vulgaris*), which is too tall. Choose a carpeter like *T. pseudolanuginosus* or *T. serpyllum*.

Chamomile: Highly aromatic, chamomile (*Chamaemelum nobile*, syn. *Anthemis nobilis*) also looks good. Look for the variety 'Treneague', which is compact and does not normally flower.

Clover: If clover is a problem in your lawn, it may make a good grass substitute. Once established it will keep green for most of the year, and will tolerate dry soils. It tolerates walking on and can look quite attractive in summer, and is probably greener than grass in dry weather. You'll only have to mow a couple of times a year, after the flowers appear, to keep it looking smart. White clover (*Trifolium repens*) is a good one to use for lawns, though you will need to mail-order the seeds from a company that sells wild or agricultural seeds.

Cutting costs
Pot-grown plants from a garden centre can be expensive if you need a great number. You can cut the cost by buying just some plants and using these for cuttings. Grow them on for a year before planting in the garden. Some thymes are easily raised from seed, but start them off in seed trays then grow on in pots.

PLANTING A THYME LAWN

You must prepare the ground thoroughly and eliminate as many weeds as possible otherwise weeding will become a tiresome chore if left unchecked. Time spent now will be time saved later.

1 Prepare the ground thoroughly by digging over the area and levelling it at least a month before planting. This will allow the soil to settle and weed seedlings to germinate. Then dig out any deep-rooted perennial weeds that appear. Hoe out seedlings. Rake level again.

2 Water all the plants in their pots first, then set them out about 20 cm/8 in apart, in staggered rows as shown (a little closer for quicker cover, a little further apart for economy but slower cover).

3 Knock a plant from its pot and carefully tease out a few of the roots if they are running tightly around the edge of the pot.

4 Plant at its original depth, and firm the soil around the roots before planting the next one. Finally, water the ground thoroughly and keep well watered for the first season.

GRAVEL GARDENS

Gravel is an inexpensive and flexible alternative to paving or a lawn, although it is not suitable for a patio. It blends beautifully with plants, needs little maintenance, and can be used in both formal and informal designs. It is also a useful 'filler' material to use among other hard surfaces, or in irregularly shaped areas where paving will not easily fit and a lawn would be difficult to mow.

Types of gravel

Gravel comes in many different shapes, sizes and colours. Some types are angular, others rounded, some are white, others assorted shades of green or red. All of them will look different in sun or shade, when wet or dry. The subtle change of colour and mood is one of the appeals of gravel. The gravels available will depend on where you live, and which ones can be transported economically from further afield. Shop around first going to garden centres and builders merchants to see what is available in your area before making your choice.

Many garden centres and stone merchants sell, or can obtain, a wide range of gravels in different sizes and colours. You will find the appearance changes according to the light and whether the stones are wet or dry.

Gravel gardens can be a formal or informal shape, but an edging of some kind is required otherwise the gravel will become scattered into surrounding garden beds.

Gravel paths

Gravel is often used for drives, but it is also a good choice for informal paths within the garden. It conforms to any shape so is useful for paths that meander. However, it is not a good choice for paths where you will have to wheel the mower. Fine gravel is an ideal ground covering for a Japanese-style garden design.

MAKING A GRAVEL GARDEN

1 Excavate the area to a depth of about 10 cm/4 in, with a slight slope to avoid waterlogging after heavy rain. If the gravel garden is low-lying or in a hollow, provide a sump for excess water to drain into.

2 Make sure the surface is reasonably smooth, then lay thick plastic sheeting over the area (to suppress weed growth). Overlap the joints.

3 Tip the gravel over the plastic sheet, and rake it level. It can be difficult to judge how deeply or evenly the gravel is being spread once the plastic sheet has been covered, so if necessary carefully scrape back the gravel occasionally to check progress.

4 If you want to plant through the gravel, scoop back the gravel to expose the plastic sheet. Then make cross-slits through the plastic with a knife.

5 Make the planting hole with a trowel, enrich the soil with garden compost and fertilizer and plant normally. Fold back the sheet, and replace the gravel without covering the crown if it's a small plant.

FINISHING TOUCHES

Many of the focal point techniques used in large gardens can be scaled down and applied on a small scale, and even in a small space the garden can express the owner's sense of fun and personality in the little extras that are grafted on to the basic design.

In a small garden, every corner can be exploited with devices if not plants, and a degree of flexibility can be built in that makes variety a real possibility.

In a large garden most ornaments, furniture and fixtures like garden lights are a static part of the design. In a small garden a slight rearrangement of the furniture, the changed position of a light, or the simple exchange of one ornament for another according to mood and season means that the garden need never be predictable despite limitations of size.

Well chosen ornaments in particular can set a tone for the garden: serious or frivolous, classic or modern. They suggest the owner's taste… and even sense of humour.

Garden lighting can be practical and even a useful security measure, but it also offers scope for artistic interpretation. Experiment with spotlights in various positions and discover the dramatically different effects created by the use of light and shadows from different angles.

Arches and pergolas are a more permanent element of the garden's design, but they don't have to be planned in at the design stage and are easily added to an existing garden.

Using ornaments

Ornaments can be used around the garden in much the same way as around the house. Choose them simply because you like them, because they will look good in a particular position, or as a device for attracting attention and admiration.

In a small garden their use as a focal point is paramount. Large focal points

ABOVE This kind of ornament needs careful placing in a small garden – always take time to consider position.

are impractical or can only ever be few in number, but small ornaments, birdbaths, sundials, and attractive urns can be used liberally. The only 'rule' is not to have more than a couple in view at once, as they will then compete for attention rather than taking centre stage. There is no limit to the number you can use in a small garden provided they form part of a journey of discovery. Use them among plants that you only discover from a particular viewpoint, or around a corner that is not visible from where you viewed the previous focal point.

Never let ornaments detract from major focal points that form part of the basic design, and don't allow the garden to look cluttered. Aim for simplicity with surprises.

Sculptures: The classic garden decoration is sculpture. For centuries, stone statues, busts, and fountains have graced formal and informal gardens, though the use of sculptures and

artistic objects demands confidence. Few people react adversely to a sundial or birdbath, but sculptures or artistic ornaments that generate admiration in one person can be abhorrent to another. This should never deter anyone from using ornaments, but they are bound to be somewhat more difficult to place in a small garden.

Human figures: Busts can look great in an alcove or on a plinth in a dull corner. Let ivy tendrils grown up and around figures to soften the statue.

Animal figures: Animal figures are always a safe bet, especially if set among the plants, or even on the lawn.

Abstract ornaments: At times difficult to blend into the overall scheme, abstract ornaments should be used with restraint.

Wall masks, plaques and gargoyles: These are great for relieving a dull wall, but are almost always best set amid the leaves of a climber such as ivy.

Gnomes: You probably love them or hate them, and that is the problem with using gnomes. One or two little people cleverly used with restraint can be very effective and add a sense of fun, but usually either they are banished from the garden or there is a whole army of them. The problem with the latter approach is that the garden will simply appear as no more than the setting for a gnome collection.

Plinths and pedestals: Plinths are essential for raising a sundial, birdbath or bust to an appropriate height, but they can look stark in a small garden. Make more of a feature of a plinth by planting some low-growing plants around the base, and then use a few tall ground cover plants that can gradually stretch up around the base.

A plinth can look severe on a lawn and mowing around it can be difficult. Try setting one in a gravel bed with alpines around the base, or leave the bed as soil and plant thymes or other low-growing aromatic herbs.

PERGOLAS AND ARCHES

A sense of height is important even in a small garden. Small trees, wall shrubs and climbers can provide the necessary verticals, but if these are in short supply an arch or pergola may be the answer. Alternatively, if a pergola or arch seems inappropriate, similar construction techniques can be used to create a welcoming, intimate arbour.

Traditionally, and especially in cottage gardens, pergolas and arches have been made from rustic poles, but where they adjoin the house or link the home with patio, timber is better.

Their visual effect is to take the eye to further down the garden and rustic arches and pergolas look particularly attractive covered with roses or other climbers. You can be creative with the designs, but the same few basic joints shown here are all that you will need.

How to Join Rustic Poles

1 To fix horizontal poles to vertical ones, saw a notch of a suitable size for the horizontal piece to fit snugly.

2 If you have to join two horizontal pieces, saw two opposing and matching notches so that one sits over the other, and secure them.

3 To fix cross-pieces to horizontals or uprights, remove a V-shaped notch using a chisel if necessary to achieve a snug fit, then nail into place with rust-proof nails.

4 Use halving joints where two pieces cross. Make two saw cuts half way through the pole, then remove the waste timber with a chisel. Secure the joint with a nail. For extra strength, paint the joint with woodworking adhesive first.

5 Bird's mouth joints are useful for connecting horizontal or diagonal pieces to uprights. Cut out a V-shaped notch about 3 cm/1 in deep, and saw the other piece to match. Use a chisel to achieve a good fit.

6 Try out the assembly on the ground, then insert the uprights in prepared holes and make sure these are secure before adding any horizontal or top pieces. Most pieces can be nailed together, but screw any sections subject to stress.

GARDEN LIGHTING

Garden lights not only make your garden look more dramatic as dusk falls, they also extend the hours during which you can enjoy it. If you like entertaining in the garden on summer evenings or just want to sit and relax, lights will add another dimension to the space. When illuminating your garden you are not attempting to fill the entire garden with floodlights, but rather to use spotlights to pick out a particular tree, highlight a semi-hidden ornament, or bring to life the droplets of a cascade or fountain.

You don't even need elaborate mains lighting. Low-voltage lighting supplied from a transformer indoors is perfectly adequate for most lighting jobs in a small garden. Low-voltage lighting is designed for DIY installation, but mains voltage requires a professional.

Lighting beds

Summer bedding looks good with pools of light thrown downwards onto the beds. If you find the lights obtrusive during the day, choose a low-voltage type that is easy to move around. Simply push the spiked supports into the bed when you want to use the garden in the evening.

LEFT Ordinary terracotta pots, gilded and filled with candle wax, offer the most enchanting outdoor lighting.

Picking out plants

Use a spotlight to pick out one or two striking plants that will form focal points in the evening. The white bark of a birch tree, perhaps underplanted with white impatiens, the tall ramrod spikes of red hot pokers (kniphofias), or a spiky yucca, make excellent focal points picked out in a spotlight. Tall feathery plants, such as fennel, also illuminate well.

Spotlighting ornaments

Ornaments and containers full of plants also make striking features to pick out in a spotlight and are easy ways of creating a dramatic impact.

Before highlighting an ornament, try moving the beam around. Quite different effects can be achieved by directing it upwards or downwards, and side lighting creates a very different effect to straight-on illumination.

Illuminating water

Underwater lighting is popular and you can buy special sealed lamps designed to be submerged or to float, but the effect can be disappointing if the water is murky or if algae grows thickly on the lenses. A simple white spotlight is often the most effective.

Thinking of the neighbours

When using garden lights in a small garden, you have to consider neighbours. It is unsociable to fix a spot where the beam not only illuminates your favourite tree but also falls on the windows of your neighbour's house. If you direct beams downwards rather than upwards, the pools should not obtrude. If using candles, flares or underwater lighting, never leave it unattended and should be kept out of the reach of children and animals.

BELOW A lantern is suspended from a bracket normally used for a hanging basket. The soft light will enhance nearby foliage after sunset.

LEFT This eclectic collection of lamps, candles and lit tapers creates a wonderful outdoor effect.

FURNISHING THE GARDEN

A few seats and a table make the garden an inviting place to eat, or to sit and relax. Where space is at a premium choose and place each item with care. Built-in seats, and especially tree seats, are a good choice for a small garden.

Portable furniture

Furniture that can be moved is particularly useful if there are children or pets and helps to prevent the garden becoming predictable.

Built-in

Built-in furniture saves space and helps prevent a small garden looking cluttered. The best place for built-in seating is the patio, where it can often be designed along with the rest of the structure. White-painted planks look smart, and can quickly be transformed with cushions to look elegant.

Built-round

A tree seat makes an eye-catching garden feature, and this is one occasion when the advice not to have a seat beneath a tree can be ignored! White paint will help the seat to stand out in the shade of its branches.

Wrought and cast iron

Genuine cast and wrought iron furniture is expensive and very heavy, but alloy imitations are available with all the charm of the original but at a more manageable price and weight. White is again a popular colour, but it will soon become dirty and cleaning the intricate patterns isn't easy. Colours such as dark green look smart yet don't show the dirt.

Use cushions to add patches of colour, and to make the chairs less uncomfortable to sit on!

ABOVE An arbour is one of the easiest ways to introduce architectural structure to a garden, and it is no more difficult to make one than it is to put up a fence. This arbor is made up of trellis panels, then painted with a decorative outdoor stain to blend with the bench. The result is an enchanting, original bower.

Wooden seats and benches

Timber seats can be left in natural wood colour to blend with the background or painted so that they become a focal point. White is popular, but green and even red can look very smart. Be adventurous with colour; bright colours can be very effective. Yacht paint is weather-resistant.

Plastic

Don't dismiss plastic. Certainly there are plenty of cheap and nasty pieces of garden furniture made from this material, but the better pieces can look very stylish for a patio in the setting of a modern garden.

LEFT This leafy corner is just the place for a table and chairs and secluded arbour.

GROWING PLANTS

Not all of us have the luxury of big, spacious outdoor areas, but that need not mean giving up entirely on the garden. Beautiful hanging baskets and over-filled window boxes feature in many small city gardens, to wonderful effect.

In order to achieve a beautiful, healthy outdoor garden area, or to use plants effectively indoors, it is necessary to know something about which plants will best suit your climate and situation, what plant combinations are best, and general information about care and maintenance.

Gardening in urban spaces presents the gardener with particular challenges; space is usually at a premium, sites may be less than ideal and specific characteristics, such as pollution or shade, may need to be accommodated if plants are to thrive. Even in larger spaces, basic knowledge about plants' needs will be necessary to keep them in the best of health from one season to the next.

Plants can create an interior style of their own or can be used to enhance existing decorations in your home. Flowering plants add a further dimension by either complementing or contrasting with interior colour schemes. There is now a wide variety of houseplants available for the indoor gardener, but making the most of them, and helping them to thrive, is not always easy.

This section provides a helpful start to selecting the best housplants for you and your home, and a practical guide to caring for and displaying them to the best advantage. There is information on which kinds of foliage and flowering plants are available as houseplants, where to shop for them and how to choose the best specimen for your home. Success with houseplants depends a great deal on placing and grouping them properly and this section offers a wealth of advice on display in containers and pots.

For indoor and outdoor plants there is information on taking cuttings, weeding and feeding, mulching and watering, pruning and propagation. Beautiful colour photographs give novice gardeners the confidence to plant and maintain an indoor or outdoor garden that will flourish, whatever the condition.

OPPOSITE It is often possible to accommodate a water feature in the smallest garden. This will add an extra dimension to your overall planting scheme, that is easily maintained.

CHOOSING PLANTS FOR THE HOME

By using houseplants as ornaments, focal points and as integrated decorations in the home, you will derive even more pleasure from your plants than you would by regarding them merely as botanical specimens. Although plants are constantly changing – they grow, die, or simply alter their shape – this very lack of stability can be turned to your advantage. Unlike any other decorative element that you can place and forget, and eventually even take for granted, plants have a dynamic existence. You have to move them, re-arrange them, even re-pot them into different containers, all of which gives them an extra dimension and vitality that other kinds of ornaments lack.

Many evergreens are tough enough for the more difficult positions around the home, such as a draughty hallway. They will be far more robust than plants with thin or papery leaves, feathery and frondy ferns, or even those with hairy leaves. You need these other leaf textures, as well as flowering plants, to add variety of shape and form, and a touch of colour, but it makes sense to use the toughest evergreens as the basis of your houseplant displays. Ivies are ideal if you need a tough climber or trailer, and there are lots of varieties to choose from, with a wide choice of leaf shape, size and colour.

Palms are the epitome of elegance and will add a touch of sophistication to your home. Many are slow-growing, and, consequently, large specimens are often expensive. But do not be deterred from trying palms; if you provide the right conditions, even small plants will gradually become very impressive specimens. The most common mistake is to regard all palms as lovers of hot sunshine and desert-dry air. They often have to cope with both in countries where they grow outdoors, but as

LEFT A mixed array of foliage and flowering plants on a sunny window sill creates an attractive focal point in a room.

BELOW The evergreen *Monstera deliciosa* is easy to care for and makes a very striking specimen plant. Here, the clever positioning of a mirror reflects the bold leaves.

OPPOSITE A tall, elegant plant such as this palm is best positioned in a large, open area such as a conservatory to show it off to best effect.

RIGHT The fern *Nephrolepis exaltata* is one of the best ferns for a pedestal or table-top display. It needs frequent misting with water to keep it in peak condition.

GERBERA

Although it will flower less profusely than when planted out in the garden, a gerbera can be grown successfully in a pot and makes a delightful houseplant. Ideally, place a gerbera in a sunny position, although, if you plan to discard it after flowering, you can use it to brighten up dull spots too.

houseplants you want them to remain in good condition with unblemished leaves. Brown leaf tips are usually caused by over-dry air, and yellowing leaves by underwatering.

Ferns are grown mainly for the grace and beauty of their fronds. The majority of ferns will thrive in shade or partial shade, conditions that are easily provided in any home. Unfortunately they also require a lot of moisture and high humidity, both of which are in short supply in the average living room. Although most of the ferns sold as houseplants come from tropical regions, central heating spells death to many of them unless you counteract the dry air by taking measures to increase the humidity. The ideal place for ferns is in a conservatory, porch or garden room where it is easier to establish a moist atmosphere. If you wish to grow the delicate types with feathery fronds, try planting them in a bottle garden, where they will happily thrive.

Although generally short-lived in the home, flowering houseplants will bring a wonderful splash of colour and vibrancy. They also add an element of seasonal variation that ordinary foliage houseplants lack. The most rewarding

ABOVE A year-round chrysanthemum makes an excellent short-term houseplant, and will flower for several weeks.

flowering houseplants are those that grow bigger and better each year, with each subsequent blooming crowning another year of good cultivation and care. Flowers that you should be able to keep growing in the home from year to year include beloperones, bougainvillaeas, *Campanula isophylla*, clivias, gardenias, hoyas, *Jasminum polyanthum*, *Nerium oleander*, pelargoniums, saintpaulias, spathiphyllums and streptocarpus.

Many flowering pot plants are difficult to keep permanently in the home and are best discarded when flowering has finished (or placed in a greenhouse if you have one). You should therefore really regard them as long-lasting cut flowers. A lot of them are annuals (in other words, they live for only 1 year) and can, therefore, be inexpensively raised from seed. Try browallias, calceolarias, cinerarias and exacums, which all make bright and cheerful plants for the home.

DESIGN IDEAS FOR THE INTERIOR GARDEN

Displaying plants indoors

Plants can create an interior style of their own or can be used to enhance existing decorations in your home. Flowering plants add a further dimension by either complementing or contrasting with interior colour schemes.

The architectural style of your apartment, its proportions and the way it is decorated will affect the choice of plants you display there. Traditional interiors tend to suit small plants that complement fabrics, wallpapers and other furnishings. Starkly decorated modern rooms can take a bolder statement in the form of larger, more sculptural plants. The other main considerations to take into account when selecting plants for your home are the size of the plants in relation to the room area, the way that they grow and their shape and colour.

Plants and scale

If plants are to make a positive addition to an interior, they must be compatible with the space in terms of both size and shape. A large specimen, for example, needs a spacious, high-ceilinged room in order to spread its elegant, arching branches and to make a suitably dramatic impact. These large indoor plants generally grow very slowly, and are cultivated in a wide range of heights, so if the room requires a 2 m/ 6 ft palm, select one at that height or slightly smaller – you could wait a long time for a 1 m/3 ft specimen to fill the space you have allowed for it.

If you want height and a compact shape, select a climbing plant that can be trained to grow up a mossed pole or bamboo stake. Ivies will naturally wrap themselves around poles and stakes and with a little pruning can be trained into the desired shape very easily. Several ivy plants grown together in a large container soon make a tower of green or variegated foliage.

Tiered displays

Shelving is another useful way to gain height, with the added advantage that you can display a range of plants in one self-contained unit. A multi-tiered étagère is a specially designed piece of plant furniture, consisting of an upright from which stem six or seven small square or circular shelves. It is often made from wrought iron, and was particularly popular in Victorian times. Originals are much sought after, but authentic reproductions are now available thanks to the revived popularity of conservatories.

As a variation, you could create a striped sandwich effect by interspersing green plants with seasonal colours.

The advantage of fixed shelving is that it can be used to combine both display areas for plants and storage for other items. Fitting triangular shelves in the corner of a room is an economical way of providing a permanent plant-display area. Painted the colour of the walls or the wallpaper, the shelves simply merge into the background, making the plants the focus.

Higher shelves and those above shoulder level should be filled with cascading varieties to avoid only the container being seen, with lower shelves devoted to upward-growing types of plants.

RIGHT The lush, bushy shapes of *Soleirolia soleirolii* make an ideal choice for a low coffee table. These plants can tolerate bright, indirect light or semi-shady conditions.

LEFT This wrought-iron candle sconce has been designed to incorporate a small plant such as this ivy. Be careful not to let the candle burn too low and scorch the leaves of the plant.

RIGHT This moth orchid provides a graceful organic touch to a collection of wall-mounted stone-coloured vases.

Colour

Colour is another important consideration when it comes to choosing plants for your home. A delicate paint effect or softly toned wallpaper can be swamped by heavy, dark green foliage. However, the pale fronds of fragile ferns or pastel and white flowering plants will enhance a gentle colour scheme rather than dominate it. Pale plain-coloured walls will complement most plants, but introducing foliage or flowering plants into a scheme with floral or patterned wallpaper and furnishings needs more thought. Take a piece of the fabric or wallpaper with you to the garden centre or plant specialist and use this to help you select an appropriate shade of green.

With the huge selection of seasonal flowering plants available, it is quite feasible to create a continuity of colour with different varieties throughout.

With this in mind, consider widening a window sill to provide a deeper platform for plants. A recessed window fitted with narrow glass or solid shelves provides the ideal support for a display of small bushy or trailing plants; while light-loving climbers will quickly provide a green curtain right to the top of the window if the plants are given a series of thin wires to clamber up. Climbers can also be encouraged to act as a frame. A climbing plant trained to scramble around a large

picture hanging above a mantelpiece, for instance, looks stunning.

If siting plants at the window, it is essential to select ones that can tolerate hot summer rays or at the very least strong, bright light.

A light, bright room may be partially separated by using a group of tall plants to create a room divider, usually partitioning, say, a dining space from a sitting area. As an alternative, fill an open shelving unit in the centre of a similar well-lit room with plants that are viewed from both sides. If the light levels on the lower shelves prohibit living plants, use them for storing books or displaying other inanimate objects instead.

Grouping plants

Metal wall sconces designed to hold candles are easily adapted for trailing plants. Decorative wire wall containers for bathroom and kitchen accessories also make excellent pot holders. A group of these arranged closely together creates a considerable impact. Table-top displays are the other obvious choice for many rooms, but most plants hate being moved around, so it is important that they can be left in peace. Narrow console tables require little space and are ideal for the purpose. If the space around the table is restricted, limit the display to upright plants. Bushy or trailing plants can be introduced if they will not be regularly brushed against. Combined with several treasured objects and planted in carefully chosen containers, these create an attractive still life that needs only a lamp to highlight the collection at night.

A group of low-level plants arranged together in one shallow basket or ceramic bowl, is perfect on a coffee table where it will be viewed from above. Put all the plants in one container making it more convenient if they need to be moved temporarily. A central display table needs plants that

are attractive from all sides. Several small pots of miniature roses, *Exacum affine* (Persian violet) or primulas grouped together when the table is not in use can then be split up to form a pretty line of colour for a dinner or lunch party. Because these plants will be viewed at very close proximity, they need to be in perfect condition and may remain so only for a couple of weeks.

Plants seen at a distance are better able to carry imperfections, especially if they are arranged in a tight group. With a sensitive selection of colours and shapes, considerable impact can be made using relatively small, inexpensive plants. Choose a colour theme of, say, white and green where a *Dieffenbachia compacta* sets the height of the arrangement for a range of smaller, bushier plants such as *Tolmiea menziesii* (piggyback plant), *Syngonium* and *Fittonia*.

A trailing tradescantia will add a further dimension to the overall shape of the display, and a brilliant white azalea, *Argyranthemum frutescens* (marguerite) or scented gardenia will provide seasonal interest and variation. The success of these loose, informal groupings relies on establishing a strong central theme. While they offer numerous possibilities of choice and presentation, it is important to remember that the permanent plants must share the same light and temperature requirements.

GROWING PLANTS

WATERING AND HYDROCULTURE

No plant can survive without water, yet more plants probably die from overwatering than from underwatering. Getting to grips with this apparently simple procedure is one of the essentials of good plant care in the home.

There are no fixed 'rules' about watering. How much a plant needs, and how often, depends not only on the plant but also the kind of pot (clay pots need watering more often than plastic ones), the compost (potting soil), (peat-based composts retain more water than loam-based), and the temperature and humidity of the environment.

When you water, fill the pot to the brim – dribbles are not sufficient. If the root-ball has completely dried out, water may run straight through, down the inside of the pot, in which case stand the pot in a bucket of water until the air bubbles stop rising. After watering, always check whether surplus water is sitting in the saucer or cache-pot. This will not matter if there are pebbles or marbles to keep the bottom of the pot out of contact with the moisture, but otherwise you must tip out the extra water. Failure to tip out standing water is the most common cause of problems. With just a few exceptions, if you leave most ordinary houseplants standing in water for a long period, they will probably die.

Examine the pots daily if possible – appearance alone can be a guide. Loam-based composts look paler when dry than when moist. A dry surface does not mean that the compost is dry lower down, but, if it looks damp, you will know that you do not need to water.

The touch test is useful for a peat-based compost. Press a finger into the surface – you will know immediately if it feels very dry or very wet. The bell test is useful for clay pots. Push a cotton reel on to a garden cane and tap the pot: a dull thud indicates moist compost; a clear ring suggests dry compost.

Tap water is far from ideal for watering, but most houseplants will tolerate it. If the water is hard (has a high calcium or magnesium content), however, you need to make special arrangements for plants that react badly to alkaline soil or compost. These include aphelandras, azaleas, hydrangeas, orchids, rhododendrons and saintpaulias. Rain water is usually recommended for these plants, but a good supply is not always available. If your tap water is only slightly hard, simply filling the watering cans and allowing the water to stand overnight may be sufficient. For harder water, try boiling it: part of the hardness will be deposited in the form of scale, and you can use the water once it has cooled.

HOLIDAY-CARE TIPS

● Porous wicks are sold for insertion into the base of a plant pot, which is then stood above a reservoir of water. You can make your own porous wicks by cutting a piece of capillary matting (available at all good garden centres) into strips, as shown above. Make sure that the wicks and compost (potting soil) are moist before you go on holiday, and that the wick is pushed well into the compost.

● If it is summer, stand as many plants as possible outdoors. Choose a shady, sheltered position, and plunge the pots up to their rims in the soil. Apply a thick mulch of chipped bark or peat over the pots to keep them cool and to conserve moisture. Provided that you water them well before you leave, most plants will survive a week like this.

● Move plants that are too delicate to go outdoors into a few large groups in a cool position out of direct sunlight.

For easy and convenient watering, choose a watering can that is well-balanced to hold and has a long, narrow spout that makes it easy to direct the water to the compost (potting soil) rather than over the plant.

Just a few plants tolerate standing with their roots in water, like this cyperus. With these you can add water to the saucer or outer container, but never do this unless you know the plant grows naturally in marshy places.

If you find watering a chore, self-watering pots may be the answer. The moisture is drawn up into the compost (potting soil) through wicks from a reservoir below, and you will need to water much less frequently.

STARTING OFF A NEW PLANT

Hydroculture

Watering correctly is an acquired skill, but, with practice, you will come to learn exactly how much or how little water your plants need. If you do find watering difficult or time-consuming, however, other alternatives would be to use self-watering containers, or to try the technique of hydroculture (also known as hydroponics) which will enable you to grow plants successfully with the minimum of attention. Hydroculture is a method of growing plants without soil or compost (potting soil). Watering is normally only necessary every fortnight, and feeding is only a twice-yearly task.

You can buy plants that are already growing hydroponically, but, once you realize how easy hydroculture plants are to look after, you will probably want to start off your own plants from scratch. Not all plants respond well to hydroculture, so you may need to experiment, but the range of suitable plants is surprisingly wide, and includes amaryllis, aspidistra, some begonias, ficus, saintpaulia and yucca, as well as cacti and succulents.

Routine care is very simple. Wait until the water indicator (see step 3) registers minimum, but do not water immediately. Allow an interval of 2 or 3 days before filling again. Always use tap water because the special ion-exchange fertilizer used for hydroculture (available from garden centres) depends on the chemicals in tap water to function effectively. The water must be at room temperature. As there is no compost (potting soil), cold water has an immediate chilling effect on the plant – a common cause of failure with hydroculture. Make a note of when you replace the fertilizer, and renew it every six months. Some systems use the fertilizer in a 'battery' fitted within the special hydroculture pot, but otherwise you can just sprinkle it on to be washed in with a little water.

1 Choose a young plant and wash the roots free of all traces of compost (potting soil). Place the plant in a suitable-sized container with slatted or mesh sides.

2 Pack expanded clay granules around the roots, being careful to damage the roots as little as possible.

3 Insert the inner pot into a larger, watertight container, first placing a layer of clay granules on the base to raise the inner pot to a level of about 12 mm/½ in below the rim. Insert a water-level tube (available from garden centres). If you cannot find one specially designed to indicate the actual water level, use one that indicates how moist the roots are.

4 Pack with more clay granules to secure the inner pot and water indicator. Sprinkle special hydroculture fertilizer (available from garden centres) over the granules.

5 Wash the fertilizer down as you water to the maximum level on the indicator. If the indicator does not show an actual level, add a volume of water equal to one-quarter of the capacity of the container – and only water again when the indicator shows dry.

6 A few months on and the houseplant is flourishing.

DEALING WITH HOUSEPLANT PROBLEMS

Not all plant disorders are caused by pests and diseases. Sometimes physiological problems such as chills and cold draughts, or nutritional deficiencies, can be the cause. Tracking down a physiological problem calls for a bit of detective work. The following descriptions of some common problems will help to pinpoint some potential causes, but be prepared to look for anything that has disturbed the usual routine – has the plant been moved, watered more or less heavily, has the weather become much colder, or have you turned the central heating on but not increased humidity or ventilation? By piecing together the various clues you can often deduce probable causes, and thereby work out what you can do to avoid a repetition.

Temperature

Most houseplants will tolerate cool but frost-free temperatures if they have to. It is sudden changes of temperature or icy draughts in a warm room that cause most problems. If leaves drop, it may be due to low temperature. This often happens with newly bought plants that have been on display outdoors or chilled on the way home. Leaves that look shrivelled and slightly translucent may have been touched by frost.

Hardy plants such as *Euonymus japonicus* may drop their leaves if kept too warm in winter, and berries are also likely to fall prematurely.

Light and sun

Light is usually beneficial, but direct sunlight, intensified through glass, will often scorch leaves – the effect will be brown, papery areas on the leaf. Plants that need a high light intensity in order to grow properly will become elongated and drawn if the illumination is poor, and leaves and flower stalks will be drawn towards the window. Lopsided growth is another indication of inadequate light.

ABOVE This plant is clearly showing signs of neglect and lack of nutrients. It may be best to discard a plant in this state.

ABOVE RIGHT Yellowing lower leaves are often a sign of overwatering, but may also be due to a chill. This is a *Fatshedera lizei* beginning to show signs of overwatering.

RIGHT Plants that are not adapted to grow in very strong light are easily scorched by strong sunlight intensified by a glass window. This dieffenbachia is suffering from scorch.

Humidity

Dry air can cause leaf tips to turn brown and papery on vulnerable plants.

Feeding

Pale leaves and short, stunted growth may be due to lack of fertilizer in the compost (potting soil). Try liquid feeding for a quick boost.

Bud drop

Bud drop is often caused by dry compost (potting soil) or dry air. Some plants also resent having to re-orientate their buds to light from a different direction if they are moved.

Wilting and collapse

Plants usually wilt for the following reasons: too much water; too little water; or insects or a disease affecting the roots. The first of the problems will usually be obvious, but, if the compost seems neither overwatered nor underwatered, check the base of the plant. If the stem looks black or rotten, a fungal disease is the likely cause and the plant is best discarded.

If none of the above symptoms is present, remove the plant from its pot. If many of the roots are soft or black and decaying, a root disease is likely to be the problem. It will be very difficult to revive a plant with a severe root rot, but you can try drenching the compost (potting soil) with a fungicide, then after a couple of hours letting it dry out

FIRST AID FOR A DRY PLANT

1 If the leaves of a plant have started to wilt like this, the compost (potting soil) is probably too dry. Feel it first – overwatering also causes wilting.

2 Stand the pot in a bowl or bucket of water and leave it until the air bubbles have ceased to rise. It will take some hours for the water to revive the plant. In the meantime, help it further by misting the leaves with water from time to time.

3 Once the plant has revived, remove it from the bowl and stand it in a cool place out of direct sunlight for at least a day.

FIRST AID FOR A WET PLANT

1 Knock the plant out of its pot. If it does not come out easily, invert the plant while holding the compost (potting soil) in with one hand, and knock the rim of the pot on a hard surface.

2 Wrap the root-ball in several layers of absorbent paper.

3 Stand the plant in a warm place, out of direct sunlight, with more absorbent paper wrapped around the root-ball. Change the paper periodically if it is still drawing moisture from the compost. Re-pot and water very cautiously for the next week.

on absorbent paper. If the root system is badly damaged, re-pot the plant in sterilized compost before treating it.

Some soil pests, such as root aphids, can be controlled if drenched with an insecticide. Wine weevil grubs and other serious soil pests are not so easy to control. Try shaking the old soil off the roots, dusting them with an insecticidal powder, then re-potting in fresh, sterilized compost. The plant may survive once it makes new growth.

OTHER POSSIBLE CAUSES OF COLLAPSE

Plants may collapse for one of the following physiological reasons:
- Cold air at night may cause plants to collapse, especially if they have been warm during the day.
- Strong, hot sunshine through glass will make many plants wilt. They will usually recover when given cooler, shadier conditions.

- Hot, dry air will have a similar effect on some plants, such as the more delicate ferns.
- Poor light will eventually cause a plant to exhaust itself. This is likely to be a gradual process, however – much less rapid than the collapse caused by watering problems or by soil pests such as root aphids.

CREATING INDOOR PLANT DISPLAYS

Small plants can be displayed more creatively than just in individual pots. Plant them in groups in planters or baskets, or in a shallow container on a pedestal. You can even create a miniature garden in a large bottle. An advantage of grouping plants is that you can get away with less-than-perfect specimens: a plant with lopsided growth, or one that is bare at the base, can be arranged so that its defects are hidden by other plants.

Grouped plants also benefit from the microclimate created when plants are grown together. The local humidity is likely to be a little higher as the leaves tend to protect each other from drying air and cold draughts, and it is easier to keep the compost (potting soil) evenly moist in a large container than a small one. Groupings are ideal for self-watering containers and for plants grown hydroponically, and simply ensuring a steady and even supply of moisture produces better growth.

Pedestals make good bases for plant displays. If you have an attractive pedestal, use short trailers that will cascade over the pot but will not completely hide the pedestal under a curtain of leaves. Plants with an arching rather than a cascading habit are also ideal for a pedestal where you want to show off both pot and pedestal.

Another display idea is a *pot-et-fleur* arrangement. This makes an ideal centrepiece, and gives plenty of scope for artistic presentation.

The still, protected and humid environment of a sealed bottle garden, with moisture re-circulating as it condenses and runs down the glass, makes it possible to grow many small jungle and rainforest-type plants that would soon die in a normal room environment. Yet, if you leave the top off and water very carefully, a bottle garden can also be a pretty way to display those plants that enjoy less-humid conditions.

PLANTING A PEDESTAL ARRANGEMENT

1 Fill a wide, shallow, stable container with a layer of compost (potting soil). Choose a mixture of flowering and foliage plants for a spectacular display. Try them for position while still in their pots, until you are happy with the arrangement.

2 Remove the plants from their pots for final planting. Set those at the edge at an angle so that they tumble over the side.

3 Water, then sit the container in a saucer and position it on the pedestal.

CREATING A *POT-ET-FLEUR* WITH FOAM

1 If you are using a basket, line it with plastic to ensure that it is waterproof.

2 Position your foliage plants first, preferably in shallow pots.

3 Cut a block of absorbent stem-holding foam (this should be soaked overnight in water first) into pieces of the size required. Pack the pieces of foam between the pots to fill up all the gaps and hold the pots securely in position.

4 Insert your flowers (and some additional cut foliage if you wish) into the moist foam. Stand back from the arrangement and view it from a distance to see whether you are happy with the result, and add more flowers and foliage if necessary.

5 Place the arrangement in a fairly cool position, and replace the flowers and cut foliage as necessary (adding water to the foam will help to preserve them). If any of the foliage plants deteriorate in time, simply replace them with fresh ones.

PLANTING A BOTTLE GARDEN

1 Place a layer of charcoal and gravel or expanded clay granules in the bottom of a thoroughly clean, fairly deep bottle. Add compost (potting soil), using a funnel or cone made from a sheet of thick paper or thin cardboard as a guide.

2 If necessary, remove a little of the compost from the plants to make insertion easier. Unless the neck of the bottle is very narrow, you should be able to insert the plants without difficulty. If you cannot get your hand into the bottle, use implements such as those shown to lower the plants into position. Add another layer of charcoal and gravel or expanded clay granules around the bases of the plants.

3 After tamping the compost around the roots (use a cotton reel on the end of a cane if necessary), mist the plants and compost. If necessary, direct the spray to remove compost adhering to the sides of the bottle. This type of open-topped bottle will require careful watering. Place it in good light, but away from direct sun as the plants may easily be scorched through the glass.

GROWING PLANTS

CHOOSING OUTDOOR PLANTS

Before making the journey to select plants for your garden make sure you have a clear idea of where you are going to plant them, the type of soil and the aspect of your garden. Read the label and examine each plant before you buy it to make sure it is right for the spot you have in mind. Buying the wrong plant could waste a whole growing season.

Always check the plant's label for information about final height and spread – and how many years it will take to grow to full size – and ask for help if the label doesn't tell you. Then consider the situation you have in mind for the plant and whether the fully grown specimen will be in scale and in keeping with its surroundings.

Be sure to check when the main season of interest is, or whether the plant has the added bonus of a second one. The plant has not yet been discovered which can be interesting in all four seasons of the year, but many evergreen variegated plants, such as *Elaeagnus* x *ebbingei* 'Gilt Edge', do come close to it. This shrub has bright golden-yellow markings on leaves which are retained on the plant throughout the year and do not easily succumb to weather damage. *Cotinus coggygria* 'Royal Purple' is a tall, handsome shrub that, though leafless during the winter, has fluffy pink flowers in summer and rich plum-purple leaves throughout the spring and summer, which turn a dazzling red colour in autumn before they fall. The small, upright flowering cherry tree, *Prunus* 'Amanogawa', produces masses of soft pink flowers in spring and a spectacular show of colour in autumn, as the leaves turn to fiery reds, oranges and yellows, making the tree resemble a bright flame.

Any plant should earn its keep and rewards you for your efforts, but nowhere more so than in a smaller garden, where space is at a premium.

RIGHT **Before making the journey to select plants for your garden make sure you have a clear idea of where you are going to plant them, the type of soil and the aspect of your garden. Dwarf conifers are a good choice in a small garden as they will mature without becoming a danger to nearby buildings.**

Site preferences

Every plant has a preference for the ideal conditions it needs in order to grow well, whether it is hot or shady, acid or alkaline, dry or damp, and most will have the greatest of difficulty growing in the wrong position.

Many conditions can be modified, at least to some extent, to extend the range of plants which can be grown. Improve the drainage of a localized wet spot, for example, by incorporating sharp sand or gravel into the soil, and by adding organic matter, such as well-rotted farmyard manure, to encourage worm activity. Dry areas will also benefit from the addition of organic matter, which will hold moisture during the vital summer months. The use of a mulch will also reduce the amount of moisture lost by evaporation and reduce competition from weeds.

Acidic conditions can be modified by the addition of ground limestone or chalk, to raise the pH. It is difficult to lower the pH if the soil is alkaline, however. Flowers of sulphur will have some effect on alkalinity but the difference is only very slight and you will have to repeat the treatment every year. On the whole, it is better to choose plants that will thrive in your soil rather than labouring to change its pH, which may involve a lot of effort for little reward; indeed a great range of plants will not mind a slight alkalinity. If your soil is alkaline, you would be best to stick with growing acid-lovers in containers, and this can be very successful and suitable for many of them. Many fascinating and attractive plants also enjoy growing in acidic conditions, so choose wisely and watch your plants thrive.

BUYING PLANTS

Once you have established what plants will thrive in the conditions in your garden, you can prepare to make your selection with confidence. Plants are living, perishable things, and supplies often fluctuate widely according to season and what the commercial growers decide to market. The condition of the plants is also never certain, though there are certain signs to look out for to ensure you are choosing a healthy specimen.

Plants are sold in different places, from supermarkets to nurseries, and they will have received different levels of care. Those sold on the same site where they were raised are likely to be younger and healthier than those which had to endure a journey to their destination. As they are transported, plants may undergo a period of drought, which will affect their growth.

Conditions at the point of sale also affect the health of plants: the longer they remain unsold, the more they will begin to suffer as the reserve of slow-release fertilizer in their pot runs out.

Nurseries are a good choice for specialized and more unusual plants, and expert advice on choosing and caring for them. The selection in garden centres is improving and they stock a wide range of plants.

Plant health

Before buying a plant inspect it for signs of pests, disease or damage. Leaves should be free from holes, bitten edges, wiggly patterns across the middle, yellow patches (unless it is variegated) or brown spots, and they should feel firm and should not be floppy. Stems should also feel firm, with no signs of being eaten, and no small, oval, brown bumps (scale insects) on them. Look for signs of fungal attack, particularly the tiny coral-coloured spots of *Nectria cinnabarina*, a fungus that will attack both live and dead wood and can easily kill a young plant.

If the compost (soil mix) is covered with weed seedlings, moss or liverwort, the plant has most likely spent some time in the same place and is likely to be under-nourished.

The plant may also be pot-bound, a condition in which the roots circle round and round inside the pot. The plant may find it hard to break this habit, leading to a poorly anchored plant that will be susceptible to being blown over in a high wind. The roots of a healthy plant will be fat and swollen, and white, yellow or chestnut-brown, but they should not be shrivelled or dark brown. Don't be afraid to knock the plant out of its pot to inspect the roots.

Often, newly potted plants are on sale alongside ones from previous deliveries that have not sold; younger ones will establish much more quickly, even if they are slightly smaller to start with. Don't be fooled – biggest is not best in the world of plants!

ABOVE Aphids are the best-known plant pests. Greenfly and blackfly are the most common ones, but there are many species, some affecting the roots of plants rather than the leaves.

RIGHT Some commercial growers supply plants by mail order. These fuchsias have been dispatched in lightweight but highly protective packages, and the quality of the plants is high.

PREPARING THE SOIL

The key to any successful gardening is good soil preparation. Inadequate attention to preparation at the outset is difficult to remedy once the plant has put down its roots and become established.

First of all, it is extremely important to clear the soil of perennial weeds. If only one piece of many of these remains, it will soon re-grow and, if the roots become entwined in those of the climber, could become impossible to eradicate. Once the planting area is completely cleared, however, it is not such a difficult task to remove weed seedlings and keep the bed and the plants clear from then on.

Digging is important, too, as it breaks up the soil, allowing moisture and air to enter, both being vital to the well-being of the plant. The process also allows the gardener to keep an eye out for any soil pests. Dig the soil some time before you intend to plant the bed; digging in autumn and planting in early spring, after checking for any emerging weeds, is ideal.

As you dig the soil, incorporate well-rotted organic material. Not only does it provide food for the plants but it also helps to improve the structure of the soil. The fibrous material helps to break down the soil to a crumbly consistency, which allows free drainage of excess water and, at the same time, acts as a reservoir to hold sufficient water for the plants without water-logging them.

The final breaking down of the soil with a rake is more for aesthetic appeal than usefulness; the planting area will look more attractive if it has a smooth tilth than if it is left rough.

If possible, prepare an area of at least 1–1.2 m/3–4 ft in diameter, so that the roots can spread out into good soil as they grow.

Soil conditioners

Most gardens have patches where, for whatever reason, there is less moisture than elsewhere. If you improve the soil and select plants that are able to thrive in dry conditions, however, this need not be a problem.

Chipped or composted bark has little nutritional value, but makes a good mulch when spread on the surface, by reducing water evaporation and discouraging weeds. It will break down in time. Farmyard manure is rich in nutrients but often contains weed seed; it is a good conditioner. Garden compost (soil mix) is also very good as a conditioner and has good nutrient value. Leaf mould, made from composted leaves, also has good nutritional value and is an excellent conditioner and mulch. Peat is not very suitable as it breaks down too quickly and has little nutritional value.

LEFT Chipped bark makes a good mulch when spread on the surface of the soil and also looks attractive.

TENDING TO THE SOIL

1 Using a chemical spray is the only way to be sure of completely eradicating perennial weeds. Use a non-persistent herbicide, which breaks down when it comes into contact with the soil. It is vital always to follow the instructions on the pack exactly, not only for the obvious safety reasons but also to ensure you use the correct dose to kill all the weeds in the area first time.

2 If the turf to be removed does not include perennial weeds, or the soil is friable enough for the weed's roots to be removed by hand, it is safer to remove the turf by slicing it off with a spade. Stack the turves in a heap, grass-side down, and use them as compost (soil mix) when they have broken down.

3 Dig over the soil and, as you dig, remove any weed roots and large stones. Double dig, if the subsoil needs to be broken up. Add as much well-rotted organic material as you can to the soil before it is planted, in order to improve its condition.

4 Add the compost (soil mix) or manure to the soil as you dig, or spread it over the top after all weed roots have been removed, and fork it in.

5 If you dig in the autumn, leave the soil for the winter weather to break down; at any other time, break the soil down by hand into a reasonably fine tilth. Use a rake or hoe to break down the larger lumps of soil, until the bed has an even appearance.

GROWING PLANTS

FEEDING AND WATERING

Feeding really does pay dividends. If you see a garden with particularly lush and healthy-looking plants, the chances are they have been well fed and supplied with sufficient water. Giving plants sufficient nutrients will ensure strong growth, abundant flowering and fruit production, and make them healthy enough to withstand pests and diseases.

Types of fertilizer
There are two groups of fertilizer: organic and inorganic. The organic ones are derived from natural ingredients, such as other plants (seaweed or nettles), blood, fish or bone, and generally last longer, although they tend to become available to the plant only slowly after application. Inorganic fertilizers are mineral-based and break down more quickly after application.

Feeding used to be a job that had to be tackled several times during the course of a season, and some enthusiasts still feed their plants once a week or even more frequently with liquid feeds. If you use modern slow-release and controlled-release fertilizers, however, feeding is something you can do just a couple of times a year.

Slow- and controlled release fertilizers both allow the nutrients to seep out into the soil over a period of months, but the latter are affected by soil temperature. Nutrients are only released when the soil is warm enough for growth in most plants.

Liquid feeds are more instant in effect and still have a use, being invaluable when plants need a quick pick-me-up. This is especially true of foliar feeds, which are applied directly to the leaves rather than the soil around the roots, and are absorbed straight into the plant's system. These can have an effect within 3–4 days, compared with up to 21 days for a general granular fertilizer applied around the roots.

Applying fertilizer
In an established garden, you can apply fertilizer in granular form as a dressing around the plants early in the season, or in soluble form as the plants are watered during the spring. For a new plant, mix fertilizer with the soil as it is replaced in the planting hole around the rootball. Lawns will benefit from dressings of mixed weed-killer and fertilizer in the spring and autumn,

keeping the grass healthy, and helping fight the effects of any dry periods in summer and cold spells in winter.

Watering
Lack of attention when plants are first planted can easily kill them if there has not been much rain recently.

The best water to use is rain water. If possible, use water butts or tanks connected to the down-water pipe to collect water that falls on the roof of the house, garage or any other building. Tap water can be used but it is best poured first into a barrel and left to breathe before you use it. This allows time for any chlorine used in the treatment of the water to be given off.

Beware hard water that comes from chalky (alkaline) areas. Although your soil may be acidic, the water from your tap may be collected, where the soil is alkaline. Hard water should not be used on ericaceous (lime-hating) plants.

The most important aspect of watering is to always be certain to give the plants a good soaking. A sprinkle on the surface is not enough. If in doubt, dig well into the soil and see how far the moisture has penetrated through the surface.

FEEDING BEDS AND BORDERS

1 Most established plants, benefit from annual feeding. Apply a slow- or controlled-release fertilizer in spring or early summer, sprinkling it around the bushes. Sprinkle it out further where most of the active root growth is.

2 Hoe it into the surface so that it penetrates the root area more quickly.

3 Unless rain is expected, water it in. This will make the fertilizer active more quickly in dry conditions.

There are several methods of watering, but a can is probably best for a small number of plants. Alternatively, a garden hose with a spray attachment can be used. For a large number of plants use a sprinkler or dribble hose.

Feeding containers

Container plants require supplementary nutrients to keep them in good health.

A controlled- or slow-release fertilizer added to the potting soil at planting time will keep most containers blooming well all summer. Follow the instructions for application rates.

The N:P:K ratio

On the back of the pack of fertilizer, there should be some information about the nutrient it contains, the three most important elements being nitrogen (N), phosphorus (P) and potassium (K). Nitrogen promotes healthy growth of leaves and shoots, phosphorus is needed for healthy root development and potassium improves flowering and fruit production. The ratio is given on the pack because certain plants need some elements in a greater quantity than others.

FEEDING THE LAWN

1 The quickest way to feed your lawn is with a wheeled spreader and you can usually adjust the delivery rate. Test the rate on a measured area of path first, then sweep up the fertilizer and weigh it to make sure the application rate is correct.

2 An easy way to give your lawn a liquid boost is to use a sprinkler system into which you can introduce special fertilizer pellets. It will feed the lawn as it waters.

3 A hose-ended sprayer like this is a good way to apply a soluble fertilizer for a quick response. You can use this type of hose-ended sprayer for beds and borders as well as for the lawn.

WATERING PLANTS

1 Give the plant a good soaking, covering the whole area around the plant where the roots will be. A watering can is ideal for a small area, such as around a newly planted plant that is still getting established.

2 If you need to water a large number of plants, a sprinkler is a good method of providing water. To make certain that you provide sufficient water, place a jam jar or other container within the sprayed area, to give a rough idea of how much water has been delivered. It should be at least 2.5 cm/1 in full if the watering is to do any good.

3 A dribble or seep hose is an efficient method of supplying water to exactly where it is needed. It is snaked around those plants that need to be watered and left permanently in position. It can be covered with a bark mulch, to hide it. When connected, it provides a slow dribble of water.

WEEDING AND MULCHING

Controlling weeds

The only place where weeds are acceptable is in a wildlife corner, although some people find daisies in the lawn a very attractive feature. Generally, however, weeds have to be controlled.

Any perennials that arise from small pieces of root left in the soil should be dug out, as should any suckers, and any seedlings should be hoed off.

It is inevitable that there will be some annual weeds appearing from time to time around plants, such as climbers, but, if these are removed before they set their seed, their numbers will gradually drop as the reserve of seed in the soil is used up.

There are two main weapons if you want to cut down on weeding: mulching, which uses no chemicals, and herbicides.

Killing weeds in beds and borders

Although there are herbicides that will kill some problem grasses growing among broad-leaved plants, generally you can't use selective weedkillers in beds and borders. Most herbicides will kill or damage whatever they come into contact with, but there are ways in which you can use herbicides around ornamental plants to minimize the amount of hand weeding necessary.

You may be able to treat areas in a shrub border with a watered-on weedkiller simply by shielding the cultivated plants. If deep-rooted perennials are not a problem you can use a contact weedkiller that will act rather like a chemical hoe (a real hoe may be an easier alternative to mixing and applying a weedkiller if the area is small enough).

Deep-rooted perennial 'problem' weeds, such as bindweed, are best treated by painting on a translocated weedkiller such as one based on glyphosate. Ordinary contact weedkillers may not kill all the roots, but this chemical is moved by the plant to all parts. Even so, you may have to treat really difficult weeds a number of times for long term eradication. Use a gel formulation to paint on where watering on the weedkillers may cause damage to adjacent ornamentals.

Mulching

Once the soil is clean, applying a mulch will do a great deal to help to keep weeds under control. It will not prevent perennial weeds that are already established from coming up but it will prevent any further germination from the seed in the soil. It will also reduce the amount of moisture lost to evaporation. A wide variety of materials can be used.

The main advantages of loose organic mulches are that they look attractive, can often be home-made (and are therefore inexpensive), and are gradually incorporated into the soil by the activity of worms, adding to the organic-matter content. It is important to top them up every year if they are to remain effective.

Inorganic mulches, such as black plastic and woven membranes, are less pleasing to the eye but provide a much

WEEDING BY HAND

1 The advantage of hand-weeding is that you can thoroughly check which weeds are present and can take more rigorous action if perennials are spotted. At the same time, it also enables you to spot any seedlings produced by plants that you may want to transplant or pot up.

2 Hoeing is quicker than handweeding and allows you to get round more frequently. It is very effective against annual weeds but chopping the top off a perennial does not kill it and it will soon re-emerge. Do not dig too deeply with the hoe or you may disturb the plant's roots.

USING A LOOSE MULCH

First, prepare the ground thoroughly, digging it over and working in plenty of organic material such as rotted manure or garden compost if the soil is impoverished. Dig up deep-rooted perennial weeds, otherwise they could grow through. Then water the ground thoroughly. Do not apply a mulch to dry ground. Finally, spread the mulch, such as the bark mulch shown here, thickly over the ground.

more effective barrier against weeds. They are most useful in shrub beds that can be left undisturbed for some years, and are best used when the bed or border is newly planted. When using inorganic mulches, always prepare the ground as thoroughly as you would if not using a mulching sheet.

It is possible to use a combination of both types of mulch. Lay the artificial material, then cover it with an even layer of bark or gravel. This creates the best of both worlds, providing good protection against weeds and a pleasing appearance in the garden.

Weeds in lawns are best controlled by a selective hormone weedkiller, ideally applied in mid- or late spring. These are usually applied as a liquid,

using a dribble bar attached to a watering-can. To ensure even application you should mark out lines with string, spacing them the width of the dribble bar apart.

Always mix and apply the weedkiller as recommended by the manufacturer. There are a number of different plant hormones used in those products, some killing certain weeds better than others, so always check that it is recommended for the weeds you most want to control. If your lawn also needs feeding, you can save time by using a combined weed and feed. The most efficient way to apply these – which are likely to be granular rather than liquid – is with a fertilizer spreader. Check with your local nursery, if unsure.

If you have just a few troublesome weeds in a small area, it is a waste of time and money treating the whole lawn. For this job a spot weeder that you dab or wipe onto the offending weed will work well.

Mulching with grass cuttings
Grass cuttings are readily available in most gardens. They are not the most attractive form of mulch but can be used effectively at the back of borders, where they are not easily seen. Do not heap them on thicker than 5 cm/2 in or they may heat up too much as they decompose, harming the plant. Do not use cuttings from lawns that have recently been treated with a lawn herbicide which might harm the plant.

INSTALLING A SHEET MULCH

1 Make a slit around the edge of the bed with a spade, and push the sheet into this. For a vegetable plot you can use special plastic pegs, but these are too conspicuous for an ornamental position.

2 Make cross-shaped planting slits in the sheet with a knife or scissors. If planting a shrub you will probably have to make slits large enough to take a spade for planting. This won't matter as the sheet can be folded back into place.

3 Small plants can be planted with a trowel, but for shrubs you will need to use a spade. Provided the ground has been well prepared before the sheet was laid, it should be easy to dig out the planting hole.

4 Although most of the sheet mulch will be hidden as the plants grow, it will be very conspicuous initially. A layer of a decorative mulch such as chipped bark or gravel will make it much more acceptable.

GENERAL CARE AND MAINTENANCE

In addition to feeding, watering, mulching and weeding as already described, plants may require other forms of maintenance. Shrubs for example, may need regular pruning, depending on the species and how you want them to look.

Climbers need to have stray stems regularly tied to the main supports or other stems. Stems that grow away from the wall will probably need to be cut off, in which case trim them off neatly back to a bud or a branch.

Although many perennials will support their flower stems without any extra staking or supports, some – like large-flowered peonies with heavy buds and full flowers – will flop onto other plants, especially during a spring shower, others may blow over in wind. Ideally, stakes or supports should be put in place when you are planting the border; the foliage will grow to cover the frame. Failing this, you will need to check regularly that susceptible plants are upright and insert supports wherever you can when necessary.

You will need to go through the border regularly, removing flowers as they fade. This will stimulate many species of plants to produce another crop of flowers, so keeping the border in bloom over as long a period as possible.

Perennials need to be lifted and divided every few years to keep them youthful. Work through the border in autumn, looking for plants that are beginning to die in the middle as their roots become congested.

In winter it may be necessary to protect tender shrubs or climbers from the weather. Draping hessian (burlap) over the plant will give temporary protection against frost, but for more prolonged periods, protect with straw first then cover with hessian. Many marginally hardy plants benefit from a bulky, dry, winter mulch of leafmould, straw or dry fern closely packed over their roots.

PESTS AND DISEASES

ABOVE **Aphid damage.**

ABOVE **Blackspot.**

ABOVE **Mealy bug insect.**

Routine inspection of plants for attack by pests or diseases, will allow you to deal with a problem before it becomes serious. Learn how to identify the various signs so that you can identify what the cause is.

Diseases
Fungal diseases affect the leaves of many plants, and often they are difficult to control. Where possible grow varieties that have a disease resistance, and always spray or remove affected leaves at the first sign of trouble.

Most root diseases are a minor inconvenience that occur from time to time, but club-root is a serious problem that will restrict the types of plants that you can grow successfully.

Insects
Sap-sucking insects are particularly unpleasant pests because they transmit virus diseases by injecting infected sap from one plant into another. They also cause distorted growth if they attack developing buds, and generally weaken the plants that they feed on. Always deal with aphids promptly.

Leaf-eating pests can soon devastate a plant. If the culprits are caterpillars you will easily identify the cause, but many leaf-eaters move on, so tracking them down may call for a little deduction. Again, regular inspection is the best preventative action to take.

Root pests often go unnoticed until the plants collapse, but many of them can be controlled successfully if you are vigilant.

OTHER FACTORS

Some problems that at first appear to be caused by pests or diseases have physiological causes (like wind chill or sun scorch). Others are caused by accidents with weedkillers, or even by nutritional deficiencies in the soil.

STAKING BORDER PLANTS

1 Proprietary supports are very efficient at supporting border plants that are not very tall but have a mass of tallish floppy or fragile flowering stems.

2 Twiggy sticks pushed into the ground around the plants can be very effective. They may look unsightly initially, but will blend in with the surroundings more easily than artificial supports.

3 Short canes can be used to support plants such as carnations. If you use a stout cane, loop string or twine around it and the plant. Use thinner split canes to keep individual flower stems upright.

TYING IN STEMS ON CLIMBERS

Regularly tie in any stray stems to the main supports. In some cases, it will be easier to attach them to other stems, rather than the supports. Always consider the overall shape of the climber and how you want to encourage it to grow in the future.

PRUNING

Whether it is to improve the shape of a plant, to make it produce more flowers or fruit, or to correct some damage, pruning is an important part of the procedure for maintaining the health of many plants.

On some plants, pruning is an annual procedure, carried out to keep the plant to a suitable size or to encourage it to produce larger flowers, more fruit or better coloured stems. On others, it is an operation carried out occasionally, perhaps as a result of damage, to prevent the open wound becoming infected and harming the plant. As a matter of routine, every plant should be checked regularly for signs of the "three Ds" – disease, damage and death. If a diseased branch is caught early, and pruned back to uninfected wood, there is less chance of the problem infecting the rest of the plant. Areas of damage expose the tissue underneath the bark, and are ideal sites for fungal spores and diseases to enter the plant. Dead branches can also act as hosts to fungi and diseases, some of which can easily travel into the living tissue and damage it. Any suspect shoots should be pruned back to clean, healthy tissue as soon as possible, using clean equipment.

Types of pruning

The main types of pruning are:

● Formative pruning, when the plant is young, to encourage the early development of a strong framework of branches.

● Containment pruning, where, as the plant ages, it is regularly pruned in order to keep its size and shape within the constraints of the garden.

● Remedial pruning, when the "three Ds" rule is put into operation, to maintain the health of the plant. Remedial pruning is also used to eliminate any crossing or congested branches and, on variegated shrubs, to remove any shoots which have reverted

to plain green (variegated shoots are weaker than green ones, as they contain slightly less chlorophyll, so that if the green ones are left in place, the whole plant will revert).

Timing

Timing the pruning operation correctly is critical to the performance of the plant; if you prune at the wrong time, you may cut off all the flower buds for the season. Not all plants can be pruned for the year in early spring; in fact, the best time to prune many, especially flowering shrubs, is right after they have flowered, so that they have the maximum time to develop their buds for the following season.

Making a good cut

One way of gaining confidence when pruning your climbers is to learn how to make the correct cuts. Always use

sharp secateurs (pruners) or a sharp saw if you are cutting larger branches. Pruning cuts should always be clean; try not to bruise or tear the wood by using worn or blunt secateurs.

Cuts to remove main stems or thick stems branching off the main stems should be made close to their origin, making certain that there is no "snag" or stump left. On the other hand the break should not be so tight that it cuts into the parent wood. Thinner stems should be cut back to a bud, leaf joint or the previous junction.

Pruning winter damage

Some plants, such as shrubs of borderline hardiness, may be damaged but not killed by a cold winter. In spring cut out cold-damaged shoots. Remove the affected tip only. This will greatly improve the appearance and new growth will soon hide the gaps.

MAKING A GOOD CUT

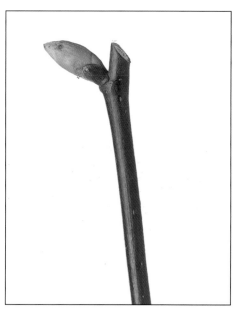

1 Make the cut just above a bud. This bud should usually be an outward-facing one, so that future growth is away from rather than towards the centre of the plant. The cut should be angled slightly away from the bud.

2 If the leaves are in pairs on the stem, one opposite the other, make the cut straight across, rather than sloping. The position should be the same, just above an outward-facing bud.

Pruning a new hedge

If you buy plants sold specifically for hedging they are likely to be young plants with probably a straight single stem. These keep the cost down, but formative pruning is particularly important to ensure that they make bushy plants later on.

New shoots will be produced if you cut back the main (leading) shoot to about 15 cm/6 in after planting. Trim these back by about half in early or midsummer. If you buy bushy hedging plants, shorten the height of these plants by one-third. Do not remove the main (leading) shoot of a conifer,

large-leaved evergreens such as aucuba or laurel, beech or hornbeam. Trim that off only when the hedge is approaching the desired height. If you like, shorten other shoots on these plants by between one-quarter and one-third, to stimulate instead bushy outward growth.

FORMATIVE PRUNING FOR SHRUBS

1 The best time to prune shrubs is as soon as possible after the flowers have faded. Shorten the growth from the last summer by half. It will be paler and more supple than older wood.

2 Avoid cutting into dark, older wood as new shoots are seldom produced from this.

3 From a distance the difference after pruning will not be obvious but it should be neater and more compact. The real benefit will be cumulative. Remember to start pruning while the plant is still young.

CONTAINMENT PRUNING FOR SHRUBS

1 Simply cut back all the previous summer's growth to within about 5 cm/ 2 in of last year's stem. Do not worry if this seems drastic. The plant will soon produce vigorous new shoots and replace the ones you are cutting out.

2 Cut back to just above a bud. Keep to outward-facing buds as much as possible to give a bushier effect. Most of the shoots should be cut back to within about 5 cm/ 2 in of the base of last year's growth, but if the bush is very old, cut out one or two stems close to ground level. This will prevent stems rubbing against each other, and improve air circulation.

3 This is what a plant that has been cut back to a low framework of old stems looks like. Try to keep the height after pruning about 90 cm/3 ft or less.

GROWING PLANTS

THE KITCHEN GARDEN

For most of us living in developed countries, producing our own food has become a pleasant pastime and an opportunity for healthy exercise, rather than a matter of survival. While we are fortunate that we can take a fairly relaxed attitude towards vegetable production, there is nothing quite like eating home-grown food, such as fruit, vegetables and herbs, and there is also pleasure to be had in the rituals and requirements of the orchard and vegetable plot.

If you have a reasonably sized garden – large enough to divide off a section for a kitchen garden – growing vegetables in the ground is the most practical way to yield them, and much of the fruit. But for those with less space, it is still possible to enjoy freshly grown home produce.

LEFT Rosemary may be grown in pots or as an informal hedge. There are cultivars available with flowers in various shades of blue, white and pink.

Vegetables that are hungry for space such as potatoes and cabbages may lose out to flowers. But if you are content with smaller vegetables such as lettuces, carrots, beetroot and dwarf beans, and have room to be able to relegate tall climbing beans and expansive plants like globe artichokes to the mixed or herbaceous border at the back of the garden, it is quite practical to grow a range of vegetables even where space is restricted.

BELOW Even in the tiniest spaces you can plant up a wooden box with a selection of different herbs, providing ample variety for cooking throughout the summer months.

PLANTING UP A HERB BOX

1 Cover the base of a wooden box with a layer of broken pots or coarse gravel to improve drainage, followed by a covering of compost (soil mix).

2 Arrange the herb plants inside the trough and place a small amount of compost around the base of each plant, to hold them in position.

3 Fill the trough with compost until it is level with the rim. Firm it gently around the plants. Water the trough, to settle the compost and remove any air-pockets around the plants' roots. Cover the surface of the compost with a layer of coarse gravel to act as a mulch.

Making your selection

Grow a whole range of vegetables, from lettuces to peas, in containers like windowboxes and growing bags. Even potatoes can be harvested from pots and growing bags and tomatoes of all types have been grown with great success in growing bags. This kind of small-scale vegetable gardening is, unfortunately, demanding, and the yields always very modest for the effort involved, but if the idea of harvesting your own fresh vegetables just before you pop them into the pot appeals, you may find it worth the effort.

Fruit trees and bushes are often ornamental and can be happily and easily integrated into the flower garden. Trained fruit trees like espalier and fan apples look attractive even with bare branches in winter.

Herbs are much more easily accommodated than vegetables. Many are highly ornamental and lots of them make good container plants. Others look perfectly in place in a border. To ensure your herbs are made a feature of, include it in the original garden design.

There are dwarf versions of all the most popular varieties and some grow well in pots. Recently, some of the soft fruits have become available as standards and look wonderful.

Herbs are a particularly good choice for the area close to the house, such as a patio or courtyard, for a number of reasons. Most herbs are used in the kitchen during cooking, so it makes sense to have them close by for easy collection, even in the rain. Placing herbs near the house also means that their wonderful fragrance can be

appreciated to the full as it wafts in through the open windows, so the patio or courtyard is the ideal place.

Many of the most popular herbs have their origins in the countries of the Mediterranean region, and need a warm, dry position in which to flourish. If the garden does not have these conditions, the answer is to grow them in containers, handily placed near the kitchen door, where the drainage is good and they can be moved around to make the most of the available light. Herbs are a boon for the area where you plan to be sitting and eating al fresco, because some of them have excellent properties as insect repellents: pennyroyal (*Mentha pulegium*) keeps ants away, basil discourages flies and scented plants such as lavender and rosemary deter mosquitoes.

CONTAINER GARDENING

Whether containers are used indoors or outside for growing plants, the key to their success is understanding their special needs. Container plants need careful watering. Outdoor containers and baskets will probably need daily watering during summer months, even in overcast weather, as they dry out very quickly. Check the compost (potting soil) regularly as it can be difficult to wet once it has dried out. Adding water-retaining granules or gels to the compost before planting will help reduce the frequency of watering. For indoor plants, too much water can be as bad as too little, however.

Most potting composts contain only sufficient foods for six weeks of plant growth, after which the plants will slowly starve unless other food is introduced into the container. Slow-release plant food granules, added to the compost when planting will ensure that the plants receive adequate nutrients throughout the growing season. Other plant foods, such as liquid feeds, need to be applied fortnightly. While standard potting compost is suitable for all purposes, container compost, which is especially formulated for containers and hanging baskets, contains extra fertilizer and

moisture-retaining granules. Lime-hating plants, such as heathers and camellias, must be grown in compost which contains no added lime.

Container plants are readily available, but if you want to use a lot of them in your displays, they can be expensive. One way of having a plentiful but cheap supply is to grow the easier ones yourself from seed. Sooner or later young seedlings will need repotting as they don't thrive in large pots. Divide the plants, if necessary, and plant them in pots the same size as the ones they were previously grown in.

LINING BASKETS

1 Traditionally, hanging baskets are lined with sphagnum moss. This looks very attractive and plants can be introduced at any point in the side of the basket. As sphagnum moss does tend to dry out rather faster than other liners, it is advisable to use a compost (soil mix) containing water-retaining gel.

2 Coir fibre liners are a practical substitute for moss. Although not as good to look at, the coir will soon be hidden as the plants grow. The slits allow for planting in the side of the basket.

ABOVE A pretty Victorian wire plant stand brings flashes of white high up in the middle of a largely green planting area.

PLANTER STYLES

Part of the fun of container gardening is experimenting with the different planters available. Garden centres stock an increasing variety of styles and junk shops, car boot sales and flea markets are also worth a visit.

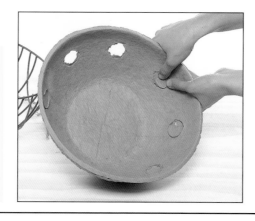

3 Cardboard liners are clean and easy to use. They are made in various sizes to fit most hanging baskets. Press out the marked circles on the cardboard liner if you wish to plant into the side of it.

PLANTING IN POTS

1 Cover the base of the container with a layer of coarse gravel or polystyrene (plastic foam), to help the drainage.

2 Cover the drainage material with a layer of compost (soil mix) until the container is about half full.

3 Arrange the plant inside the container and place compost around it to hold it in position. Add compost to the container until it is level with the rim, then firm it around the plant.

4 Cover the surface with more compost if necessary, then water the container and remove any air-pockets around the plant's roots. Add a top layer of coarse grit, to act as a mulch.

RIGHT Container-grown plants can be enhanced by the choice of pot used. Remember this is not a low-maintenance option as the plants will not be able to draw as much nourishment or water from surrounding soil.

SEED SOWING

Some plants are very easy to sow from seed – sunflowers rarely disappoint, even if you are a complete beginner. Whether sowing large or small seeds, water the pot from above using a fine hose on a watering can, or by standing the pot in a saucer of water until the surface of the compost is moist. Cover the pot with a black plastic bag as most seeds germinate best in a warm dark place. Check daily and bring into the light when the seedlings are showing.

1 Fill the pot with seed compost (soil mix). Gently firm and level the surface by pressing down on the compost using a pot of the same size.

2 When sowing large seeds, such as sunflowers, use a dibber, cane or pencil to make holes for each seed. Plant the seeds and then firmly tap the side of the pot using the flat of your hand to fill the holes with compost.

3 When sowing small seeds they should be thinly scattered on the surface of the compost and then covered with just enough sieved compost to conceal them. Firm the surface using another pot and then treat in the same way as large seeds.

POTTING-ON

Sooner or later plants need repotting. Young seedlings, shown here, don't thrive in large pots. Divide the plants, if necessary, and plant them in pots the same size as the one they were previously grown in.

1 Seedlings will probably be ready to move into larger pots when the roots start to emerge through the holes in the base of the pot. To check, gently remove the rootball from the pot and if there are plenty of roots showing, you will know the plants are ready for a move.

2 If there is more than one seedling in the pot, gently break each seedling away with a good rootball. (Some plants hate to have their roots disturbed. The information on the seed packet will tell you this. These seeds are best sown individually in peat pots.)

3 Lower the rootball of the plant into the pot and gently pour compost around it, lightly pressing the compost around the roots and stem. It doesn't matter if the stem of the seedling is buried deeper than it was previously as long as the leaves are well clear of the soil. Water using a can with a fine hose.

MULCHES FOR CONTAINERS

A mulch is a layer of protective material placed over the soil. It helps to retain moisture, conserve warmth and prevent soil splash on foliage and flowers. There are a variety of mulches to choose from, principally:

Clay granules
Clay granules are widely used for hydroculture, but can also be used to mulch houseplants. When placing a plant in a cachepot, fill all around the pot with granules. When watered, the granules absorb moisture, which is then released slowly to create a moist microclimate for the plant.

Gravel
Gravel makes a decorative mulch for container plants and also provides the correct environment for plants such as Alpines. It is available in a variety of sizes and colours which can be matched to the scale and colours of the plants used.

Stones
Smooth stones can be used as decorative mulch for large container-grown plants. You can save stones dug out of the garden or buy stones from garden centres. Cat owners will also find they keep cats from using the soil surrounding large houseplants as a litter tray.

PRICKING OUT

When seedlings have grown to a manageable size, such as these cacti seedlings shown here, prick them out using tweezers, taking care to avoid root damage. Some seedlings will be uniform in size, if not, sort by size into individual pots for the larger ones, in rows in a seed tray for the smaller ones.

SAUCERS AND FEET

Saucers act as water reservoirs for the plants, and are used under houseplants to protect the surface they are standing on. Clay saucers must be fully glazed if they are used indoors or they will leave marks. Plastic saucers can be used to line containers which are not waterproof, such as this wooden apple basket, pictured. Clay feet are available for terracotta pots.

PLANT SUPPORTS

Climbing plants need support even in containers. Support can be provided by using canes which can be pushed into the pot, or a trellis which is fastened to a wall or a free standing frame.

GROWING PLANTS

POTTING PLANTS

Never be in too much of a hurry to pot on a plant into a larger container. Plants do not appreciate having their roots disturbed, and any damage to them will result in some check to growth. Some types of houseplants also prefer to be in small pots.

Re-potting should never simply be an annual routine. It is a job to be thought about annually, but should not actually be done unless a plant needs it. Young plants require potting on much more frequently than older ones. Once a large specimen is in a big pot, it may be better to keep it growing by re-potting into another pot of the same size, by top-dressing (see below right), or simply by additional feeding.

When re-potting is necessary

The sight of roots growing through the base of the pot is not in itself a sign that re-potting is immediately necessary. If you have been watering the plants through a capillary mat, or have placed the pot in a cache-pot, some roots will inevitably have grown through the base to seek the water.

If you are in doubt, knock the plant out of its pot. To remove the root-ball easily, invert the pot and knock the rim on a hard surface while supporting the plant and compost (potting soil) with your hand. It is normal for a few roots to run around the inside of the pot, but if there is also a solid mass of roots it is time to pot on. There are several ways to re-pot a plant, but the 2 methods described here are among the best.

WHEN TO RE-POT

A mass of thick roots growing through the bottom of the pot (top) is an indication that it is time to move the plant into a larger one. Equally, a mass of roots curled around the edge of the pot (above) is a sign that it is time for a larger container.

The vast majority of plants on sale are grown in plastic pots, which are inexpensive, light and remain largely free of algae. Plastic pots do become brittle with age, however, and even a slight knock can break them, whereas a clay pot will not break unless you actually drop it on a hard surface.

POT-IN-POT METHOD

1 Prepare the new pot as in step 1 of the Traditional Method if you are using a clay pot. However, if you are using a plastic pot and you intend to use a capillary watering mat, do not cover the drainage hole at all.

TOP-DRESSING

Once plants are in large pots, perhaps 25–30 cm (10–12 in) in diameter, continual potting on into a larger pot may not be practical. Try removing the top few centimetres (inches) of compost (potting soil), loosening it first with a small hand fork. Replace this with fresh potting compost of the same type. This, plus regular feeding, will enable most plants to be grown in the same pot for many years.

2 Put in a little dampened compost (potting soil). Insert the existing pot (or an empty one of the same size), ensuring that the soil level will be 12 mm/½ in below the top of the new pot when filled.

3 Pack more compost firmly between the inner and outer pots, pressing it down gently with your fingers. This will create a mould when you remove the inner pot.

4 Remove the inner pot, then take the plant from its original container and place it in the hole formed in the centre of the new compost. Gently firm the compost around the root-ball, and water thoroughly.

TRADITIONAL METHOD

1 Prepare a pot that is either 1 or 2 sizes larger than the original and, if the pot is a clay one, cover the drainage hole with pieces of broken pot or a few pieces of chipped bark.

2 Water the plant to be re-potted, and leave it for a few minutes. Remove the root-ball from the old pot, either by pulling gently on the plant, or by inverting the pot and tapping the rim on a hard surface.

3 Place a little compost (potting soil) in the base of the new pot, then position the root-ball so that it is at the correct height. If it sits too low or too high, adjust the amount of compost in the base.

4 Trickle more compost around the sides, turning the pot as you work. It is a good idea to use the same kind of compost – peat- (peat-moss) or loam-based – as used in the original pot.

5 Gently firm the compost with your fingers. Make sure that there is a gap of about 12 mm–2.5 cm (½–1 in) between the top of the compost and the rim of the pot, to allow for watering. Water thoroughly.

POTTING ON, POTTING UP, RE-POTTING

Potting up is what happens the first time a seedling or cutting is given its own individual pot.

Potting on is the action of re-planting the root-ball in a larger pot.

Re-potting is sometimes taken to mean replacing the plant in a pot of the same size, but with the bulk of the compost replaced, if the plant cannot be moved into a larger pot.

TAKING STEM AND LEAF CUTTINGS

Many plants, for the garden and indoors, can be raised from stem and leaf cuttings. The techniques are easy, and you will gain even more pleasure from your plants by seeing them grow from the start.

Taking stem cuttings

Most houseplants can be propagated from softwood cuttings taken in spring, and many of the shrubby plants root from semi-ripe cuttings taken later in the year. The method of taking softwood cuttings is similar to that of semi-ripe cuttings (see right), but choose the ends of new shoots. Take softwood cuttings after the first flush of spring but before the shoots have become hard, and follow the same procedure as for semi-ripe cuttings. Geranium (pelargonium) softwood cuttings root readily, and are therefore good to try if you are a beginner.

Softwood cuttings – especially easy ones such as coleus and impatiens – can often be rooted in water. Fill a jam-jar almost to the top with water and fold a piece of wire-netting (chicken wire) over the top. Take the cuttings in the normal way but, instead of inserting them into compost (potting soil), rest them on the netting, with the ends of the stems in water. Top up the water as necessary. When roots have formed, pot up the cuttings into individual pots.

Taking leaf cuttings

Some of the most popular houseplants, such as saintpaulias, foliage begonias, streptocarpus and sansevierias, can be raised from leaf cuttings, using a variety of methods. For leaf-petiole cuttings, you need to remove the leaves with a length of stalk attached. For square-leaf cuttings, instead of placing a whole leaf on the compost (medium), cut it into squares and insert these individually. With leaf-midrib cuttings, slice the long, narrow leaves of plants such as streptocarpus into sections and treat them as for square-leaf cuttings.

TAKING SEMI-RIPE STEM CUTTINGS

1 Make the cuttings 10–15 cm/4–6 in long, choosing the current season's growth after the first flush of growth but before the whole shoot has become hard. Fill a pot with a cuttings compost (medium) or use a seed compost, and firm it to remove any large pockets of air.

2 Trim the cutting just below a leaf joint, using a sharp knife, and remove the lower leaves to produce a clear stem to insert into the compost.

3 Dip the cut end of the cutting into a rooting hormone. If using a powder, moisten the end in water first so that it adheres. Make a hole in the compost with a small dibber or a pencil, and insert the cutting so that the bottom leaves are just above the compost. Firm the compost gently around the stem to remove large air pockets. You can usually insert several cuttings around the edge of a pot.

4 Water the cuttings, then label and place in a propagator, or cover the pot with a clear plastic bag, making sure that it does not touch the leaves. Keep in a light place, but out of direct sunlight. If a lot of condensation forms, reverse the bag or ventilate the propagator until excess condensation ceases to form. Do not allow the compost to dry out. Pot up the cuttings once they have formed a good root system.

USING ROOTING HORMONES

Some plants, such as impatiens and some tradescantias, root readily even without help from a rooting hormone. Others, and especially semi-ripe cuttings, will benefit from the use of a rooting hormone. Rooting hormones are available as powders or liquids, and their use usually results in more rapid rooting and, in the case of the trickier kinds of plants, a higher success rate.

TAKING LEAF-PETIOLE CUTTINGS

1 Use only healthy leaves that are mature but not old. Remove the leaf with about 5 cm/2 in of stalk, using a sharp knife or razor blade. Fill a tray or pot with a suitable rooting compost (medium), then make a hole with a dibber or pencil.

2 Insert the stalk into the hole, angling the cutting slightly, then press the compost gently around the stalk to firm it in. The base of the blade of the leaf should sit on the surface of the compost. You should be able to accommodate a number of cuttings in a seed tray or large pot. Water well, preferably with the addition of a suitable fungicide, and then allow any surplus moisture to drain away.

3 Place the cuttings in a propagator, or cover with a clear plastic bag. Make sure that the leaves do not touch the glass or plastic, and remove condensation periodically. Keep the cuttings warm and moist, in a light place out of direct sunlight. Young plants usually develop within a month or so and can then be potted up individually, but leave them until they are large enough to be handled easily.

TAKING SQUARE-LEAF CUTTINGS

1 First cut the leaf into strips about 3 cm/ 1¼ in wide, in the general direction of the main veins, using a sharp knife or razor blade (be sure to handle the latter very carefully). Cut across the strips to form small, even-sized squares of leaf.

2 Fill a tray with a rooting compost (medium), then insert the squares on edge, with the edge that was nearest to the leaf stalk facing downwards. Once the young plants are well-established, after a month or so, pot them up individually.

PLANTS TO GROW FROM LEAF CUTTINGS

Leaf-blade cuttings
Begonia rex
Leaf-petiole cuttings
Begonias (other than *B. rex*)
Peperomia caperata
Peperomia metallica
Saintpaulia
Leaf-midrib cuttings
Gesneria
Sansevieria
Sinningia speciosa (gloxinia)
Streptocarpus

TAKING LEAF-MIDRIB CUTTINGS

1 Remove a healthy, undamaged leaf from the parent plant – ideally one that has only recently fully expanded.

2 Place the leaf face-down on a firm, clean surface, such as a sheet of glass or piece of wood. Cut the leaf into strips no wider than 5 cm/2 in.

3 Fill a pot or tray with a rooting compost (medium), and insert the cuttings 2.5 cm/ 1 in apart, with the end that was nearest the stalk downwards. Pot up the plants when they are large enough to handle.

GROWING PLANTS

OUTDOOR SAFETY

One in six domestic accidents actually happens outside the house. Most are the result of falls or collisions, but injuries are also caused by garden tools, especially powered ones, and by garden furniture (especially things that fold up), by insect and animal bites, foreign objects in the eyes and accidents with garden chemicals. Ponds, paddling pools and swimming pools sadly take their toll too, especially among children. Many of these accidents are easily preventable, and one encouraging statistic proves the point: electric shocks and electrocution in the garden are now much less common than they were, thanks to the now widespread use of residual current devices (RCDs) when working with mains-powered (power) tools and equipment out of doors.

Avoiding falls

There are several simple precautions you can take to minimise the risk of a fall in the garden (yard). Keep all hard surfaces such as paths and steps in good condition, so there are no potholes or raised edges to trip over. Fit railings or other guarding round raised patios and balconies, and also alongside any flights of steps with more than four treads. Keep unnecessary obstacles in the garden (yard) to a minimum, always putting away garden tools at the end of the day and coiling up hoses and extension leads as soon as you have finished working with them.

RIGHT Make sure you are at the correct height and distance to use powered tools comfortably and safely.

BELOW Always wear protective headgear in case of flying wood or other hard pieces.

Avoiding injuries from tools and equipment

Common sense is the best approach when working outdoors, but there are a few rules worth remembering. Always let the moving blades of a power tool such as a lawnmower, hedgetrimmer or shredder come to a complete stop before attempting to clear a blockage. To be on the safe side, unplug electrical tools and immobilise petrol-driven (gas-driven) ones (by disconnecting the spark plug) before doing any work on them. If you need to use one with an extension lead with a power tool, use white or orange flex (cord) rather than black so it is visible at all times.

Check that bladed power tools are well clear of the flex before switching them on. Never use mains-powered tools in wet conditions.

With hand tools, mind your feet when using a fork, spade or lawn edger. Cut away from your body when using knives and other sharp bladed tools, and watch where your other hand is when using secateurs (pruners).

Avoiding collisions

Many outdoor accidents involve bumping into low tree branches and thoughtlessly-positioned hanging baskets, and falling over unseen planters, bird baths and other low-level garden ornaments. If possible, remove the offending article. Children are mainly at risk from collisions with garden (yard) play equipment, especially swing seats. Make sure these have padded edges. Minimize the risk of injuries from falls round play equipment such as swings and slides by excavating the area round them and putting down bark chippings to provide a softer landing.

Avoiding injuries from furniture

Folding outdoor furniture causes a surprisingly high number of injuries each year. They are caused mainly by equipment collapsing because it was not set up or adjusted properly, and by hands getting caught in the mechanism. Always check that the furniture is fully extended, braced and locked in its folded-out position before using it. Never try to adjust such furniture when sitting or lying on it. Lastly, check the condition of all garden (yard) furniture at the beginning and end of each season, looking for splits or weak areas in fabrics and loose components in joints. Repair or replace any faulty items before they can cause injury.

Avoiding accidents with water

If you have a pond in your garden (yard) or your children use a paddling pool, remember that a small child can quickly drown in just 7.5 cm/3 in of water. Fence round your pond unless you can guarantee constant supervision, and always keep an eye on children. Empty a paddling pool onto the garden (yard) when playtime is over. Fit a fence with a secure gate round the swimming area.

Avoiding accidents with chemicals

Lots of garden chemicals are potentially harmful. Always read the instructions before using them, even if you think you know what to do with them. Water chemicals on rather than spraying them if possible, to lessen the risk of inhaling droplets or getting them in your eyes. Wash out equipment after use, and store bottles and packets securely out of the reach of children and pets. Never transfer chemicals to unmarked bottles or cans.

Avoiding accidents with fire

Beware bonfires and fireworks. Always site a bonfire (if you are allowed to have one) well away from trees, shrubs, sheds and fences. Burn only dry material, using a proper incinerator. Never use petrol (gas) or other solvents to start the fire, supervise it once it is burning and keep a bucket of water or the hose on standby. Lastly, follow the firework code on bonfire night.

LEFT Swimming pools should be a source for complete relaxation, and are so, if care is taken when children are around.

STORAGE

Gardening brings with it an extraordinary amount of practical paraphernalia. Tools, pots, and planters, potting compost, raffia, string, seeds, and baskets are but a few of the bulky and space-consuming examples. For tools and equipment, garden sheds are the classic solution that most gardens can accommodate, though smaller gardens may be restricted to a mini-shed or tool shed, which can be as small as 30 cm/12 in deep and so can be tucked into a corner. However, sheds can become an attractive part of the garden architecture if decorated.

Another solution is to put your goods on show. Garden pots can be very visual and, displayed on weatherproof shelves, can become part of the decorative appeal of the garden. This is an excellent solution for very small gardens and patios, which still need space for the practicals. Instead of buying ready-made garden shelving, you could build your own from timber and treat it with exterior-quality paint. Metal shelves can be given a new life using car spray paint or specially manufactured metal paint, which can even be sprayed straight over old rust.

ABOVE A pretty little wire shelving unit, intertwined with clematis, makes a delightful garden detail that serves a practical purpose too, providing storage for pots, string, pruning shears and wire.

All shelves should be attached firmly to the garden wall – avoid attaching to the house wall since this could lead to water damage. Once fitted, use the shelves for displays, to store tools, or for bringing on young seedlings, which can look delightful planted in ranks of terracotta pots.

Means of disguise

In an ideal world, garbage bins and recycling containers would be beautiful in themselves, but unfortunately, in reality they are seldom an attractive sight. They are necessary, however, and they do need to be accessible.

You can spend a little effort painting them, using a screen of plants to hide them or camouflaging them with a trellis with plants growing up it. Trellises have the advantage of being compact, long-lasting and attractive.

LEFT Old clay pots make a decorative corner display in a blue-painted plant stand.

THE POTTING SHED

In spite of its utilitarian name, the potting shed is far more than a useful storage area and behind-the-scenes workroom for the gardener's al fresco performance. For many gardeners, it is a rustic refuge from everyday concerns, a quiet and solitary place for contemplation and gentle activity, which may or may not be of a horticultural nature.

Potting sheds are seldom shared. In households of more than one individual, one person will generally claim territorial rights and others will trespass at their peril, for here the gardener's true nature may flourish without interference. Tidiness is optional. Some people will hang meticulously cleaned tools in serried ranks, while others fling rusting relics in heaps on the floor. Pots may be carefully cleaned and sorted ready for use or left where last discarded, according to inclination. Compost (soil

mix) is neatly sacked and stacked or thrown with abandon over every surface. Most of us come somewhere between the two extremes, for while we admire orderliness, a natural

impatience engenders a tendency towards disorder, and in this one area of our lives, we feel completely free to be occasionally tidy and well organized, but rather more often not.

ABOVE String, pots and other favourite pieces of paraphernalia find a welcome home in the potting shed.

LEFT Romantic or utilitarian, the potting shed is the starting point for the gardener's dreams.

MAKING A GARAGE STORAGE WALL

The garage is a favourite place to store all manner of things, including tools and materials for do-it-yourself, gardening and car maintenance. Unless these are kept under control, they will spill over until there is no room for the car. The solution is to build a shallow full-height storage unit along either the side or the end wall of the garage, tailor-made to suit whatever will be stored there.

The design concept of the storage wall is quite simple, and is based around creating bays offering different storage facilities. One can have floor-to-ceiling shelves, another a drawer system using plastic washing-up bowls (washbowls) sliding on wooden support strips. The next bay can offer full-height open storage for stepladders and scaffold boards, and another wider one provides space to store sheet materials neatly on edge beneath a wall-mounted rack for hanging up things such as a portable workbench or a set of car ramps. Simply select whatever types of bay are needed, and arrange them in any order.

The structure is based on ladder frames fixed to the wall to support shelves, drawers and whatever else is required. The frame is made mainly from 50 mm/2 in square sawn softwood, with 75 x 25 mm/3 x 1 in wood for the shelves and the slatted hanging rack. The hinged section drops down to allow sheets of plywood and the like to be placed on edge behind it, and is held shut with a simple hasp and staple at each side. The wall-mounted rack allows heavy items to be hung safely out of the way yet readily to hand on metal S-hooks.

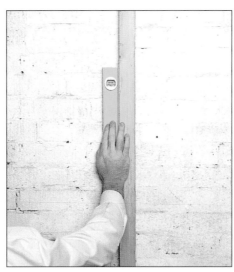

1 Start by securing the uprights to the garage wall to form the various bays. Check that each is vertical before fixing it in place.

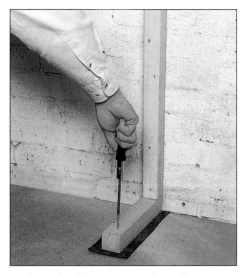

2 Set sole plates on something damp-proof (here sheet vinyl flooring), and screw them down into wall plugs in holes drilled in the garage floor.

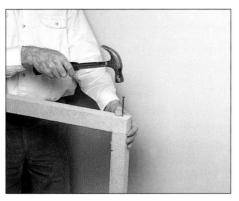

3 Simply nail components together as required to form the frames making up each bay. Add horizontals to support shelves or plastic bowl drawers.

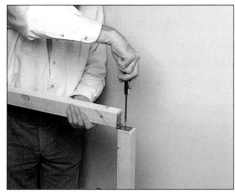

4 To make up the drop-down flap for the sheet materials storage bay, hinge the two front uprights to their baseplates and add a cross rail.

5 To make up the wall rack, nail on the slats, using an offcut as a spacer. Make the shelves in the same way, nailing the slats to 50 x 25 mm/2 x 1 in bearers.

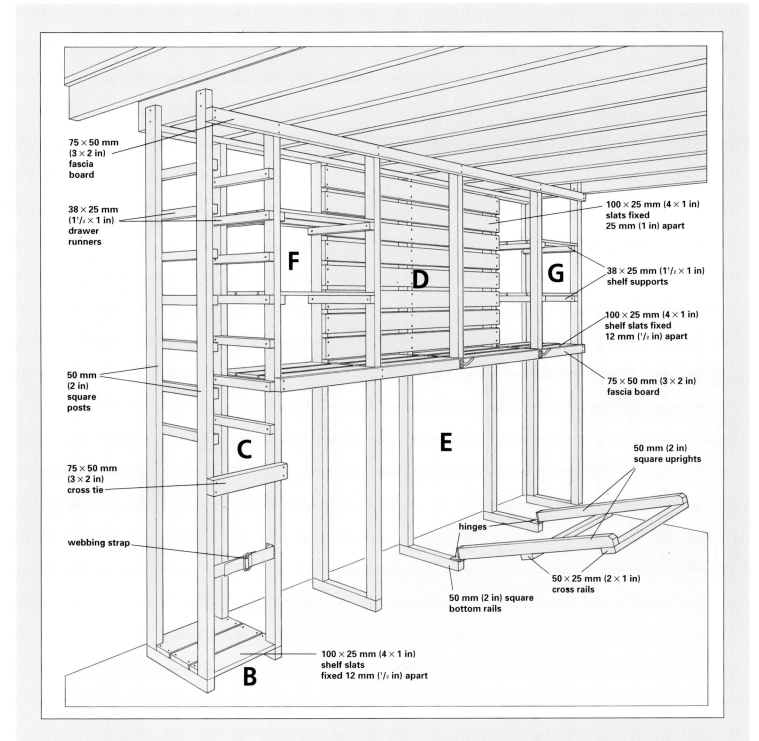

75 × 50 mm
(3 × 2 in)
fascia
board

38 × 25 mm
(1¹/₂ × 1 in)
drawer
runners

50 mm
(2 in)
square
posts

75 × 50 mm
(3 × 2 in)
cross tie

webbing strap

F

D

C

B

E

G

100 × 25 mm (4 × 1 in)
slats fixed
25 mm (1 in) apart

38 × 25 mm (1¹/₂ × 1 in)
shelf supports

100 × 25 mm (4 × 1 in)
shelf slats fixed
12 mm (¹/₂ in) apart

75 × 50 mm (3 × 2 in)
fascia board

50 mm (2 in)
square uprights

hinges

50 × 25 mm (2 × 1 in)
cross rails

50 mm (2 in) square
bottom rails

100 × 25 mm (4 × 1 in)
shelf slats
fixed 12 mm (¹/₂ in) apart

The garage storage wall offers a variety of options. Bay A is a full-height space ideal for storing stepladders and lengths of wood and mouldings, copper or plastic pipe and the like.

Bay B provides a raised platform for sacks of cement or garden fertilizer, which must be kept clear of the floor in case of damp; a sturdy webbing strap keeps them in place.

Bay C, above the platform, has a series of parallel runners supporting plastic baskets, which slide in and out like drawers and provide storage for a host of small and easily lost items.

Bay D has a slatted back on which large items such as car ramps or a portable workbench can be hung on wire hooks.

Bay E provides a wide compartment designed for storing sheet materials – boards, plastic laminates, etc. – on edge and clear of the damp floor. A simple fold-down front frame prevents the sheets from falling forward and can be quickly released when necessary.

Bays F and G complete the structure, offering full-depth shelf storage space for items like paint, garden chemicals and car lubricants.

GLOSSARY

Most of the manufacturers listed here supply their products to good independent retailers, major stores and do-it-yourself multiples. Try your local outlets first; they will usually be able to help you and can be found in the area business directory.

If you have difficulties in obtaining specific items, contact the relevant head office for more information.

UK

Amtigo Company Ltd
1177 St George Street
London
W1R 9DE
tel: 0171 629 6258

Crown Paints
PO Box 37
Crown House
Hollins Road
Darwen
Lancashire
BB3 0BG

Harlequin Wallcoverings Ltd
Crossington Road
Sileby
Nr Loughborough
Leicestershire
LE12 7RU
tel: 01509 816 575

Laura Ashley Ltd
150 Bath Road
Maidenhead
Berkshire SL6 4YS
tel: 01628 770345

Lesley Hart Dried Flowers
37 Smith Street
Warwick
CV3 4JA
tel: 01926 490356

MFI
Southon House
333 The Hyde
Edgware Road
Collingdale, London
NW9 6TD
tel: 0181 200 0202
Storage, features and fittings

Mosley Stone
Wellington Road
Leeds
LS12 1DU
tel: 0113 251 1450
Painting and decorating tools

Paint Magic
79 Shepperton Road
Islington
London
N1 3DF

Phillips Lighting
PO Box 298
City House
420/430 London Road
Croydon, Surrey
CR9 3QR
tel: 0181 665 6655

Plasplugs
Wetmore Road
Burton-on-Trent
Staffordshire
DE14 1SD
tel: 01283 530 303

The Stanley Works Limited
Stanley Tools Division
Woodside, Sheffield
S3 9PD
tel: 0114 276 8888

Traditional Garden
  Supply Company
Mail Order Catalogue
Unit 12
Hewitts Industrial Estate
Elmbridge Road
Cranleigh, Surrey
GU6 8LW
tel: 01483 273 366

Westco Ltd
Penarth Road
Cardiff
South Glamorgan
CF1 7YN
tel: 01222 233 926
*Vinyl cork and wood-block
  floor tiles*

USA

Arnie's Arts and Crafts
3741 W. Houghton Lake Dr.
Houghton Lake
MI 48629
tel: (800) 563 2356
fax: (517) 366 5931
E-mail: info@arnies.com

Aubuchon Hardware
Ames Plaza
14 Boulevard Avenue
Catskill, NY 12414
tel: (518) 943 0338

Bulb Store, Inc.
1111 West El Camino Real
Sunnyvale
CA 94087
tel: (800) 737 7301
fax: (408) 739 5067
E-mail: info@bulbstoreinc.com

Cactus Flower Florists
10822 N. Scottsdale Rd
Scottsdale, AZ 85254
tel: (800) 922 2887

Carpet 'N Things
8740 Cherry Ln.
Laurel, MD 20707
tel: (301) 206 2200
fax: (301) 206 2285
E-mail: CarpetNT@aol.com

Carpet Outlet Store
842 N. Sheridan Road
Tulsa, OK
tel: (918) 836 6676

Cole Hardware
956 Cole Street
San Francisco, CA 94117
tel: (888) 301 2648
fax: (415) 753 0957

Fabric Bonanza, Inc.
72 Newton Road
Danbury, CT 06811
tel: (203) 792 0417
fax: (203) 743 7604

Factory Paint
505 Pond Street
S. Weymouth, MA 02190
tel: (781) 331 1200

Distinctive Treasures
200 N. W. Railroad Ave.
Hebron, MD 21830
tel: (410) 749 9221

Hancock Fabrics
5520 Military Parkway
Dallas, TX 75227
tel: (214) 381 5656

Hardware Distribution
  Warehouse, Inc.
6900 Woolworth Road
P.O. Box 3945
Shreveport, LA 71133 3945
tel: (800) 256 8527
fax: (318) 686 8550
E-mail: hdw@hdwinc.com

Highland Hardware
1045 N. Highland Ave., NE
Atlanta
GA 30306
tel: (800) 241 6748
fax: (404) 876 1941
E-mail: custservice@highland-
hardware.com

Jo-Ann Fabrics and Crafts
Riverfront Plaza
2647 N. Elston Ave.
Chicago
IL 60647
tel: (773) 645 9075

Linder's Greenhouse
270 W. Larpenteur Ave.
St. Paul, MN 55113
tel: (651) 488 1927
fax: (651) 488 9508
E-mail: rob@linders.com
Louiseville Tile Distributors,
   Inc.
4520 Bishop Lane
Louisville, KY 40218
tel: (502) 452 2037

Mark's Paint Store
4830 Vineland Avenue
North Hollywood, CA 91601
tel: (818) 766 3949

Master Nursery Garden Center
2211 Olympic Blvd.
Walnut Creek
CA 94595
E-mail:
   info@masternursery.com

Mazer's Discount Home
   Centers Inc.
41st Street S,
Birmingham
Alabama 35222
tel: (205) 591 6565

Summitville Tiles Inc.
Box 73
Summitville
Ohio 43962
tel: (216) 223 1511

Wilson W A & Sons Inc.
Industrial Park Drive
Wheeling
WV 26003
tel: (304) 232 2200

Woodhaven Wallpaper & Paint
43 Howard Street
Watertown, MA
tel: (617) 926 0630

Australia

Brickmart
380 Pittwater Rd
Brookvale 2100 NSW
tel: (02) 9907 110

Bristol – in all states
289 Victoria Ave
Chatswood 2067 NSW
tel: (02) 9419 2480

Cordon Bleu Australia Pty Ltd
169 Parramatta Rd
Annandale
2038 NSW
tel: (02) 9569 5444

The Garden Light Company
23 Carrington Rd
Nedlands
6009 WA
tel: (08) 9389 7060
fax: (08) 9389 7050

Greenbank Tertech Pty Ltd
Hereford Street
Berkely Vale
2259 NSW
tel: (043) 88 4522

Hardwarehouse – in all states
256 Ferntree Gully Rd
Notting Hill 3168 VIC
tel: (03) 9545 5822

Ikea – in all states
Moore Park 2021 NSW
Ph: (02) 9313 6400
*Furnishings, storage solutions,
   floor coverings*

International Paints
Birmingham Avenue
Villawood 2163 NSW
tel: (02) 9728 7577

Kitchen Kapers
63 Wilson St
Burnie 7320 TAS
tel: (03) 6431 4734

Mitre 10 – in all states
319 George St
Sydney 2000 NSW
tel: (02) 9262 1435

Nichimen Australia Ltd
3rd Floor
60-70 Elizabeth Street
Sydney
2000 NSW
tel: (02) 9223 7122

The Restoration Centre
267 Cleveland St
Redfern
2016 NSW
tel: (02) 9698 5511
fax: (02) 9319 5878
Email: restore@bigpond.com.au

The St Johns Ambulance
   Brigade
90 Australia St
Camperdown
2050 NSW
tel: (02) 9516 1581
First Aid courses

Sikkens (Tenaru Pty Ltd)
PO Box 768
Darlinghurst Sydney
2010 NSW
tel: (02) 9357 4500

New Zealand

The following are all
nationwide stores; for local
details please consult your
business directory, or if you
have difficulties, contact the
head office.

Guthrie Bowron
Paint, wallpaper

ICI
Hutt Park Road
PO Box 30749
Lower Hutt

Mitre 10
*Hardware, paint, garden supplies,
building supplies*

Placemakers
Hardware, paint, garden supplies

Nees Hardware Ltd
11–15 Pretoria Street
Lower Hutt

Stanley Tools (NZ) Ltd
PO Box 12–582
Penrose, Auckland

Stevens Home and Giving
Kitchen utensils, kitchen gifts

Taubmans (New Zealand) Ltd
10 Portsmouth Road
PO Box 14064
Kilbirnie, Wellington
tel: (0800) 735 551

INDEX

INDEX

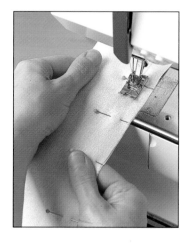

Acknowledgements

Some of the material in this book
has been previously published in
*The Illustrated Hints, Tips and
Household Skills, The Complete
Decorating and Home Improvement
Book,* and *The Cook's Kitchen Bible.*

The following people have
contributed to this book:
Authors: Deena Beverley,
Richard Bird, Valerie Bradley,
Victoria Brown, Sacha Cohen,
Anna Crutchley, Stephanie
Donaldson, Sarah Edmonds, Kathy
Ellis, Tessa Evelegh, Mary Fellows,
Shirley Gill, Manisha Kanani,
Mike Lawrence, Gilly Love, Peter
McHoy, Terence Moore, Ercole
Moroni, Maggie Pannell, Maggie

Philo, Gabriella Rossi, Deborah
Schreebeli-Morrell, Anne Sheasby,
Judy Smith, Andrea Spencer,
Isabel Stanley, Liz Trigg,
Catherine Tully, Liz Wagstaff,
Stewart and Sally Walton,
Pamela Westland and
Josephine Whitfield

Photographers: Karl Adamson,
William Adams-Lingwood,
Jonathon Buckley, Andrew
Cameron, James Duncan, John
Freeman, Michelle Garrett, Nelson
Hargreaves, Tim Imrie, David
Jordan, Thomas Odulate, Marie

O'Hara, Lizzie Orme, Debbie
Patterson, Spike Powell, Steve
Tanner, Adrian Taylor, Mark
Wood and Polly Wreford

The publishers would like to thank
the following companies for their
kind permission to reproduce the
following pictures in this book:
t = top; b = bottom; c = centre;
l = left; r = right.

A–Z Botanical Garden Collection:
p453 tr.
Houses and Interiors: p2, p11tr,
p12tr, p13tl, p19tr, p77tr, p119tr,
p226bl, p227tl, p360bl.
Image Bank: p13bl, p18bl, p227br,
p361tl.
Images Colour Library: p6–7,
p10bl, p12bl, p176, p214br, p216tl.